GREEK AND ROMAN OARED WARSHIPS

GREEK AND ROMAN OARED WARSHIPS

BY

J. S. MORRISON

WITH CONTRIBUTIONS BY

J. F. COATES

OXBOW BOOKS 1996

First published in the United Kingdom in 1996. Reprinted in 2016 by
OXBOW BOOKS
10 Hythe Bridge Street, Oxford OX1 2EW

and in the United States by
OXBOW BOOKS
1950 Lawrence Road, Havertown, PA 19083

Paperback Edition: ISBN 978-1-78570-401-7
Digital Edition: ISBN 978-1-78570-432-1 (ePub)

A CIP record for this book is available from the British Library

For a complete list of Oxbow titles, please contact:

UNITED KINGDOM
Oxbow Books
Telephone (01865) 241249, Fax (01865) 794449
Email: oxbow@oxbowbooks.com
www.oxbowbooks.com

UNITED STATES OF AMERICA
Oxbow Books
Telephone (800) 791-9354, Fax (610) 853-9146
Email: queries@casemateacademic.com
www.casemateacademic.com/oxbow

Oxbow Books is part of the Casemate Group

Front cover illustration by Rebecca Forwood

CONTENTS

ABBREVIATIONS

AE	L'Année Epigraphique
AJA	American Journal of Archaeology
ANS	American Numismatic Society
APhS	American Philosophical Society
AT	Morrison and Coates (1986 and 1995)
B	Basch (1987)
BAR	British Archaeological Reports
BCH	Bulletin de Correspondance Hellénique
BGU	Berliner griechische Urkunden
bn	born
BSA	Annual of the British School of Archaeology at Athens
BOA	Breadth overall
BIW	Blade in water
BWL	Breadth on waterline
CA	Classical Archaeology
CAH	Cambridge Ancient History
CIL	Corpus Inscriptionum Latinarum
CPL	Corpus papyrorum latinorum
CQ	Classical Quarterly
CR	Classical Review
CVA	Corpus Vasorum Antiquorum
D	Deck at side
d	died
dr	drachma. drachmae
Ephem. Epigr.	Epheméris Epigraphica
frg.	fragment
G	Centre of gravity
GOS	Morrison and Williams (1968 and 1996)
HMND	Tarn (1930 and 1984)
HSCP	Harvard Studies in Classical Philology
IJNA	International Journal of Nautical Archaeology
Jal.-Mout.	Jalabert et Mouterde: Paris (1929-)
JdI	Jahresbericht der deutsches Institut (in Rome)
JKD	Jahresbericht der Kreuzschule zu Dresden
JHS	Journal of Hellenic Studies
JRS	Journal of Roman Studies

JFC	John F. Coates
JSM	John S. Morrison
K	under side of keel
LF	Lepper and Frere (1988)
LOA	Length overall
LSRS	Morrison (1980)
LWL	Length on waterline
M	Metacentre
MB	Münchener Beiträge
MIMA	Basch (1987)
MIT	Massachusetts Institute of Technology
MM	Mariner's Mirror
NBA	Nürnberger Blätter zur Archäologie
NS	Numismatic Studies
NZ	Numismatische Zeitschrift
OLP	Orientalia Lovaniensia Periodica
RA	Révue Archéologique
REG	Révue des études grecques
Riv.Fil.	Rivista di Filologia e istituzione classica
RE	Pauly-Wissowa-Mittelhaus-Kroll *Real Encyclopedie der Altertumswissenschaft*
SNG	*Sylloge Nummorum Graecorum* I-V
SSAW	(Casson 1971 and 1986)
TAPS	Transactions of the American Philosophical Society
W	Waterline

LIST OF MAPS

LIST OF PLANS

LIST OF ILLUSTRATIONS

PREFACE

THIS BOOK IS A STUDY of the new types of warship evolved in the navies of the Mediterranean in the fourth and third centuries BC and of their later employment culminating in the battle of Aktion. Since the ships were in some cases invented, built and manned not only by Greeks and Romans but by Phoenicians, Egyptians, Italians and Carthaginians, the title *Greek and Roman Oared Warships* seems a bad fit.

Our defence is partly that a title must be short and partly that in the Hellenistic centuries there was a Greek and Macedonian, and a Phoenician and Roman design of oared warships.

The Greek historian Arrian, who was a citizen of both Rome and Athens and governor of the Roman province of Cappadocia (AD 132–7) and then archon of Athens (AD 148–49), records (*Anabasis* 7.16.1: p. 19) that in 323 BC Alexander sent a party to the Caspian sea 'to build long ships' i.e. warships 'both aphract and cataphract in the Hellenic mode (*ἐς τὸν κόσμον Ἑλληνικόν*)'. Since Alexander at this time (p. 11) was building a great harbour at Babylon for the contemporary warship types, threes, fours and fives, some brought overland from Phoenicia, and planning a great fleet of sevens, possibly tens as well, it is reasonable to recognise that at any rate some of the warships in common use were 'of the Hellenic mode' and some were not.

Aristotle knew that fours were of Carthaginian design (Frg. 600); and one of the more startling results of our investigation has been the recognition that the five which played so large a part in the naval history of Rome was not the Greek five invented by Dionysius of Syracuse but a five the design of which was derived by Rome from Carthage. It also seems likely that the Carthaginian design of the five came from her mother city Tyre and can be traced in the Phoenician iconography of the last half of the 4th century BC. Nevertheless this ship of Phoenician design and ancestry has her place in history as the warship in which Rome achieved her command of the Mediterranean. *Greek and Roman Oared Warships* is accordingly a not inappropriate title for a book which relates the steps of that achievement and ventures to challenge Theodore Mommsen's *dictum* that 'the marine always remained the weak side of Roman warlike organisation'.

Our purpose is to present, as the result of the better understanding of the *τριήρης*, now achieved by the construction and sea trials of *Olympias*, a better account of the later ships than currently given and accepted. They, like the *τριήρης*, played a central role in their time, during which sea-power determined a great part of the course of history.

For convenience sake we shall call warships twos, threes, fours, fives and so on according to the number of files of oarsmen rowing on each side of the ship. We shall also follow Lionel Casson's good example and use the miscegenic but convenient term polyreme to mean all warships with more than one man to an oar, the innovation which sparked off the developments in naval architecture of the 4th and 3rd centuries BC.

Since the book will concentrate on the new types, an account of the activities of the Greek and Macedonian fleets of threes in the early part of the 4th century (399–334 BC) will be omitted, since it is described in our previous book *The Athenian Trireme* (1986: 1996). Representations of threes belonging to the fourth, fifth and earlier centuries will however be shown in the iconography (chapter 5) to provide a background for and comparison with the later representations of oared warships.

The design of the reconstructed three was based on the prolific and eminently reliable historical and literary sources of the age, and the inventories of the naval dockyards of Athens, some of which have been preserved, fragmentarily, in stone and provide a great deal of sound information about the Athenian navy in the last third of the 4th century. A reasonably secure design could accordingly be made and a ship reconstructed which exemplifies in its general characteristics at least, the Athenian three of the 5th and 4th centuries BC.

The evidence for the many new types developed in the 4th and 3rd centuries BC is nothing like as good as that available for the three, much less in quantity and, for some periods, in quality. References (see the Index of Citations p. 386ff) in historical writers, in particular those in Polybios, Livy and Caesar, are useful and reliable, but in areas not covered by them the later historians, Diodoros, Appian, Arrian and Dio Cassius, though often useful and relaying valuable information, are only reliable where their sources can be guessed and on occasion identified. References to the new types in Vergil, Lucan and even Silius Italicus are unexpectedly useful, and reliable, we believe, beyond the usual estimate.

There is a good number of representations of warships in reliefs and on coins of the period, but they are difficult to recognise as showing any particular type of the several employed at the time, because the invention of the marine catapult and the use of hand missiles led to the boxing-in of the hull and the resulting concealment of the oarsmen. Yet in spite of these difficulties, an amount of information may be gleaned, enough, we think, to justify some secure new conclusions about most of the warships in question.

Pliny the Elder, who was in command of the Roman fleet at Misenum and lost his life at the eruption of Vesuvius in AD 79, in his *Natural History* gives an almost too succinct list of longship development, of the developers and the authorities for them. (7.207) The first sentence is concerned with mythology beginning with Philostephanos's claim that Jason was the first to put to sea (navigasse) in a longship: *'Biremem Erythraeos Damastes [auctor est] fecisse, triremem Thucydides Ameinoclem Corinthium, quadriremem Aristotles Carthaginienses, quinqueremem Mnesigeiton Salaminios, [navem] sex ordinum Xenagoras [auctor est fecisse] Syracosios. Ab ea [nave naves] ad decemremem Mnesigeiton Alexandrum Magnum, ad XII ordines Philostephanos [auctor est fecisse] Ptolomaeum Soterem, [naves] ad quindecim [ordines] Demetrium Antigoni filium, [naves] ad triginta [ordines] Ptolomaeum Philadelphum, [navem] ad XL [ordines] Ptolomaeum Philopatorem qui Tryphon cognominatus est'.*

'Damastes is authority that the Erythraeans [first] built the two, Thukydides that Ameinokles of Corinth [first built] the three, Aristotle that the Carthaginians [first built] the four, Mnesigeiton that the Salaminians [first built] a five, Xenagoras that the Syracusans [first built] a ship of six files. From that ship Mnesigeiton is authority that Alexander the Great built [ships] up to the ten, Philostephanos that Ptolemy Soter built [ships] up to twelve files, that Demetrios son of Antigonos built [ships] up to fifteen [files], that Ptolemy Philadelphos [built ships] up to thirty [files], and that Ptolemy Philopator who was given the cognomen of Tryphon [built ships] up to forty files'.

The most important contribution made by Pliny's list is the clear demonstration of the principle on which the name series of ancient oared warships was built from the two to the forty, that is to say the number of files (*ordines*) of oarmen on each side of the ship (p. 90). The first in the series, the 'one', which went by default, was of course the *Argo* and the Homeric longship, which had one file of oarsmen on each side. The historical value of the list begins with the recorded testimony of Damastes of Sigeion who was a contemporary of Herodotos, that the two was first built by the Erythraeans (presumably of Ionia). It is interesting also to see that Pliny interpreted Thukydides (1.13.3: p. 2) to mean that Ameinokles was the inventor of a three (and built them for the Samians). His statement that Aristotle attributed the invention of the four, present in Peiraieus in his lifetime (*Constitution of Athens* 46), is generally accepted (Frg.600 Rose). Mnesigeiton is an unknown possibly Hellenistic historian and his attribution of the invention of the five to the Salaminians is uncorroborated, but not so Alexander's building of bigger ships shortly before his death (p.13). Xenagoras is a reputable historian probably of the third century BC and his attribution of the invention of the six to Syracuse is otherwise acceptable (p. 3). There is no other evidence that Ptolemy Soter built warships bigger than fives. But it is not unlikely that he emulated

Demetrios his rival on the sea; and Philostephanos is a reputable Alexandrian writer of a book entitled *Περὶ εὑρημάτων* *'Inventions'*. The further attributions of ships up to the fifteen to Demetrios, ships up to the thirty to Ptolemy Philadelphos and the forty to Ptolemy Philopator are all well attested.

The first four chapters will pursue certain historical themes selected for their relevance to the new types and where the available accounts seem reliable and the resultant information useful. The first of these themes (Chapter 1) will be the age of naval innovation expressed in the persons of Dionysios I of Syracuse and Alexander of Macedon, in the naval ambitions of Athens on Alexander's death, the naval competition between Antigonos I and his son Demetrios on the one hand and Ptolemy I on the other, and the Grand Fleet of Ptolemy II. The second historical theme (Chapters 2 and 3) follows the naval aspects of the wars of the Roman Republic with Carthage, with Philip V of Macedon and his son Perseus, with Antiochos III of Syria and with Mithridates, also finally Julius Caesar's campaign at sea against the Veneti leading to the invasions of Britain. The final theme (Chapter 4) will be the Roman civil wars as fought at sea after Caesar's murder and culminating in the battle of Aktion.

Since a number of ship portraits shown derives from the early empire, two Appendices to the fourth chapter will present the evidence for the fleets of that period given (A) by Tacitus and (B) by inscriptions.

Chapter 5, after an attempt to fill in the background of earlier warship development, will set out the iconography of the polyremes from the 4th century BC to the 1st century AD, describe and as far as possible interpret it.

In Chapter 6 the construction of a typology will be attempted, bringing together the information collected in Chapters 1–4 and the iconography, as interpreted, of Chapter 5. In Chapter 7 Dr Coates will make the buildings with the bricks that have been supplied and reduce the information and the conclusions, in the case of the historically more important of the new types, to designs and drawings which will give a reality, hitherto lacking, to the fleets of the period in their movements and engagements. Chapter 8 will assemble such information as is available about crews, ships and battle tactics, Dr Coates adding a section on the third topic from the point of view of the ship constructor and designer. D. J. Blackman provides an Appendix to Chapter 1, a report on recent excavation of shipsheds in Kition, a maritime city of Cyprus.

Writing about Venetian ships and shipbuilding (1934: p.2) Lane said:

> A history of merchant shipping which attempted a complete explanation of the creation and abandonment of the various types would become the history of maritime commerce; and a similar study of warships would include the history of naval warfare.

We have found this to be true in the case of the creation of the new types of warships in the 4th and succeeding centuries. The history of naval warfare of the period has proved to be a quite indispensable prelude to the interpretation of the iconography and the resultant characterisation of the new types, and to their design and reconstruction.

These studies, based on the evidence at present available, have thrown a clearer but by no means definitive light upon ancient navies, naval warfare and the exercise of sea power. We have all too little idea of the knowledge, skills and personal qualities needed in the officers and men afloat, in the dockyard tradesmen and in the naval administrators of the time, the main factors setting the culture of navies. There is also much yet to be understood about how oared warships were used both strategically and tactically, in maintaining the use of the sea or in denying it to the enemy, about their effective ranges and the speed of fleet deployment to theatres of operations, about their operational capabilities and limitations, about their building, logistics and maintenance and, not least, about the recruitment, training and terms of service of personnel. Our present understanding of naval affairs during the major wars at sea fought out in the period ending with the *pax Romana* is patchy and contrasts sharply with what is known about contemporary military matters, despite the evident but sometimes reluctantly recognised importance of sea power to all who have contended for influence and domination around the Mediterranean.

The undoubted patchiness of present understanding, and reluctance to recognise the importance, of sea power has been largely caused, in contrast with land power, by a sometimes total lack of evidence about the units and still more about the logistics of warfare at sea. Such evidence as is provided for the Athenian navy by the inventories of the dockyards in Peiraieus, and for the navy of Venice by extensive records, is totally lacking for the Macedonian, Carthaginian and Roman, and almost totally for the Egyptian navies of the period.

In this book we use such evidence as appears to us to exist in an attempt to realise, certainly inadequately, the aims set out above, primarily, as a beginning, in relation to the ships themselves. We trust that this attempt may stimulate an interest which may lead to the discovery of more evidence than we have been able to find and use; and bring to greater life and realism than can be achieved with the means available at present the history of a period in which sea power played so great a part.

Acknowledgements

THE PLAN OF THIS BOOK was laid some eleven years ago with the encouragement, which we gratefully acknowledge, of Dr Basil Greenhill, then Director of the Maritime Museum Greenwich. Work on it was interrupted when the energies of the present authors were diverted to writing *The Athenian Trireme* and those of John Coates to preparing also the working drawings and to supervising the building in Peiraieus of the reconstructed trireme, duly commissioned in July 1987 as a training ship of the Hellenic Navy with the name *Olympias*.

Five years later, after the experience of building and operating *Olympias* had taught both authors much that proved relevant to the later Mediterranean oared warships, a draft of the greater part of the text had been completed and was submitted to David Brown of Oxbow Books. He had published the Trireme Trust's reports on the sea trials of *Olympias* in 1988, 1990, and 1992, the report on the first trials (1987) having appeared as one of the volumes in the series *British Archaeological Reports*.

We express our gratitude to David Brown, in the first place for the encouragement he gave us in accepting the original text, and for accepting one with an incomplete iconography (chapter 5) and lacking both the numerous necessary maps and John Coates's chapter 7 containing the reconstructions. We are grateful, in the second place, for the patience with which he has watched the original text being altered and added to as the completion of the iconography and recognition of the reconstructions of chapter 7 led to numerous revisions; also for the efficient and long-suffering care of the text and its various *adminicula* by Gabriela Canseco. Our second expression of gratitude is to Roddi Williams, collaborator with JSM in *Greek Oared Ships* (Cambridge UP: 1968; Oxbow Books 1995) in producing the archaeological catalogue. At the early stage of this book, before the Trireme diversion, he did much valuable work on the iconography chapter, in particular on the numismatics, and when serious work on it was resumed most generously handed it over to JSM. The latter, who is no numismatist, is deeply indebted to him and also in the later stages to Martin Price of the Medals and Coins Department of the British Museum and Kevin Butcher of the Medals and Coins Department of the Fitzwilliam Museum for much expert help generously and patiently given. For any mistakes and inadequacies in this field, as in the rest of the iconography, JSM is solely responsible.

Among the books listed in the Bibliography which helped JSM in the preparation of chapter 5 two deserve special gratitude. Lucien Basch in *Musée imaginaire de la marine antique* (Athens 1987) has collected an unsurpassed range of representations of ancient ships of all kinds and types which is of the greatest value to the student (when he has made his own index), although he may not always agree with the interpretations. The second is Michael Crawford's *Roman Republican Coinage*, providing a comprehensive and reliable guide to evidence which, rather unexpectedly, has proved of great value in reconstructing ships of the period when Rome 'first took to the sea'. JSM wishes also to express his thanks to Dr Stronk of Amsterdam for his unexpected, unsolicited and quite invaluable gift of a copy of Dr Grach's article in Ukrainian in which the Nymphaion fresco (**13**) was published.

In chapter 7 we are grateful to René Burlet for making his ergonomic studies of the working of multi-manned oars in the French XVIIth century galleys available to us, for contributing **(62)**, **(68)** and **(75)** and for analysing and commenting on a number of the reconstructions. We are also grateful to Timothy Shaw for kindly contributing Appendix B and thus bringing his analysis of power and pace to bear on these studies; and to Garth Denning for contributing (**65**) and (**66**) which help to bring one of the reconstructions to life.

All who have tried to answer questions raised by the scanty evidence for the oarsystems and employment of ancient oared warships recognise the debt they owe to the pioneers, in particular Augustin Cartault, Ernst Assmann and Cecil Torr in the last century and R. C. Anderson and Lionel Casson in this. Their wide reading, methodical assembly of the literary and iconographical, and in Casson's case also of the papyrological, evidence, and good sense in its interpretation, have pointed the way, and laid the foundation on which present and future work must necessarily be based.

Much as we have tried to follow their good examples we would be foolish to think that any of them would have accepted, or in the case of the last-named will accept, more than a few of our conclusions. Pyrrhos said, when leaving Sicily before the 1st Punic War, 'My friends, what a wrestling school (*παλαίστρα*) for the Carthaginians and Romans we are leaving behind us!' Now we have completed this book we hand over the problems of Greek and Roman warships to those who will continue to wrestle with them. Of that hard and demanding school we may claim at most to have revised the curriculum: mathematics and physics are now compulsory for would-be wrestlers.

1

THE AGE OF INNOVATION

IN THE 4TH CENTURY BC four new types of oared warships were developed, the four, the five, the six and the one-and-a-half-er (*ἡμιολία*); and Alexander is said to have invented sevens and tens. Later, types of still higher denomination were built in the Hellenistic centuries, no ship higher than a ten being used in battle. A reasonable conclusion from these higher denominations has been that the numerical element in the type names did not refer to the levels of oars. In the case of the three which had three levels of oars such reference was possible, but since more than three levels of oars is a physical impossibility the numerical element must have referred, as it did in the case of the galleys of Renaissance Italy, to the number of fore-and-aft files of oarsmen on each side of the ship, increased by manning the oars with more than one oarsman.

In the *ἡμιολια* (**73**) there was, on each side, one complete fore-and-aft file of oarsmen; and also, taking advantage of the ship's greater breadth amidships, an additional half file on each side of the medial gangway. The *ἡμιολία* accordingly either had the half of its oars that were amidships double-manned or the oarsmen in each of the two files amidships rowed single-manned oars in pairs *alla sensile*. In either case there were one and a half files of oarsmen a side and the ship was properly named *ἡμιολία*. The first three new types exemplify the same innovation and the *ἡμιολία* may do so, i.e. the use of oars manned by two oarsmen at one, two and three levels; the seven involves triple- and double-manning at three levels and the nine quintuple manning at one level and quadruple manning at the other of two levels of oars.

1. DIONYSIOS I'S NAVAL PROGRAMME

Under the year 406 BC Diodoros relates (13.91.3–96.4) the rise of Dionysios to autocratic power in Syracuse in the face of the Carthaginian threat to the Greek cities of Sicily which he is depicted as turning to his own advantage. In 404 (14.7.3) he speaks of Dionysios, when he had made peace with the Carthaginians, turning to strengthen his rule in Syracuse by building on the island a fortified acropolis and including within its wall the naval installations of the small harbour of Lakkion, which were able to accommodate sixty threes and had a restricted opening through which only one three was able to pass at a time. Later (14.18) Diodoros describes his determination, now that his position was firmly established, eventually to make war on Carthage, and of his preparations involving the fortification of Epipolai which overlooked the city. By 399 (14.41.2) Dionysios judged that the occasion for war was favourable; and started to acquire the necessary armaments for a struggle which 'would be great and lengthy since he was proposing to engage the most powerful people in Europe'.

(4.41.3) 'Accordingly he began at once to assemble by decree craftsmen from the cities under his control, and attracted them with high wages from Italy and even from territory controlled by Carthage. He planned to manufacture a great quantity of arms and missiles of all kinds; and, in addition to them, threes and fives (*ναῦς τε τριήρεις καὶ πεντήρεις*), although a ship with the latter oar system had at that time not yet been built.' Aristotle (Frg. 600: Preface xii) says that the four was invented in Carthage and Dionysios would certainly have known about it from the shipwrights from Carthaginian territory if her invention had occurred before this date. But either the four had not been yet been invented or he decided to build the more powerful five in preference.

Diodoros goes on to describe the public enthusiasm for the work at Syracuse and Dionysios's part in it (14.42.1–3): 'In fact the catapult was invented at this moment in Syracuse, when the best craftsmen had been brought together from everywhere to one place. The high wages, of course, and the number of bonuses offered for those who were adjudged the best, stimulated their enthusiasm. Quite apart from that, Dionysios every day going about among the work force spoke friendly words to them, rewarding the keenest with presents and inviting them to take food with him. As a result the craftsmen brought a spirit of competition to their work that was unsurpassable, and invented many new missiles and original devices of great potential usefulness. Dionysios began also to build threes and ships of the five kind (*ναυπηγεῖσθαι <ναῦς> τε τριήρεις καὶ πεντηρικὰ σκάφη*), being the first to devise this latter type of warship. The fact was that Dionysios was aware that a three had been built first in Corinth and was keen to increase the size of warships built in the city which had been colonised from Corinth.'

Thukydides' statement (1.13.2) that 'threes were built first in Greece at Corinth' has been taken to imply that they had *previously* been built elsewhere. His words certainly imply that threes were built elsewhere, but not that their building was previous to Corinth's. That may be the case; but it is clear from Diodoros's text, which derives from a fourth century source, that this latter implication was not drawn then and that Corinth was recognised as the inventor of at any rate a type of three. She also devised towards the end of the Peloponnesian war, as Thukydides also describes (7.34.5), the tactical and structural answer to Athenian battle tactics (*AT* p. 167) which played an important part in the defeat of the Athenian fleet in the Great Harbour of Syracuse in 414 BC. Dionysios could justly claim a place for Syracuse in the Corinthian tradition of naval innovation.

Dionysios also arranged for the importation of timber, *ἐλάτη*: 'oar-tree' and *πεύκη* (*AT* Ch. 10), and when he had collected a sufficient supply of wood (D.14.42.5): 'he began to build simultaneously more than 200 ships, and refit the 110 ships he already had. He was constructing also expensive shipsheds around the so-called Great Harbour, 160 in number, the majority accommodating two ships, and he repaired the existing sheds, which numbered 150'.

The euphoric tone of this account, its favourable attitude to Dionysios in general and in particular its repetitious emphasis on his invention of the five, is in strong contrast to the previous story of Dionysios' rise to power. The Dionysios portrayed is no ruthless unapproachable tyrant, but a friendly, dynamic leader, a man of the people. The source is accordingly not Timaios, but may well be Dionysios's faithful supporter and naval commander, Philistos, directly or indirectly. The passages quoted may be excerpts, incorporated by Diodoros in his *Bibliotheca* from Philistos's biography of Dionysios I.

It has seemed illogical (and caused in the last century unnecessary emendations in the text of Diodoros and Aelian) that the five should have been invented before the four.[1] There is no illogicality. The four with two levels of double-manned oars was a very natural development of the two-level single-manned pentecontor or *λέμβος*. The five, with three levels of oars, two of them double-manned, and five fore-and-aft files of oarsmen on each side of the ship, was a similarly strengthened three. The number of oarsmen in a five at the battle of Eknomos in 256 BC is given as 300 with 120 *ἐπιβάται*, here probably decksoldiers and *ὑπηρεσία*, a total complement of 420. This may be an exaggerated figure since, the Roman fleet at Eknomos being an invasion force, it is likely that the number of decksoldiers was greater than if it had been a fleet prepared solely for battle.

A Calenian dish (**18 I**: second half of the first century BC), shows heavy warships, probably Carthaginian, with oars at three levels. The oars emerge *en échelon* from a boxed-in *παρεξειρεσία*. It will be argued below that the ships represented are fives.

The naval forces deployed by Dionysios I in the years of his long reign following his early naval programme do not suggest that the plans so optimistically described in Diodoros were carried out at all rapidly or completely. One five at least seems to have been built. In 398 Dionysios sent the prototype to bring back from Lokroi to Syracuse the daughter of a distinguished Locrian to whom he had proposed a diplomatic marriage. Eight years later, in 390, Dionysios, in a five, which was his flagship in a fleet of 50 warships attacking Rhegion, is described as escaping shipwreck in a storm in which seven of his ships, probably threes, were lost. The greater power of a five would have been useful on a lee shore.

Nor are the numbers of his ships impressive in the earlier years. In 397 at the siege of Motya Diodoros says that he had 'a little less than 200 warships' (D.14.47.7). (The newly invented catapult is reported to have been used effectively there from the land against warships (D.14.50.4)). After the fall of Motya Dionysios sent his *ναύαρχος* Leptines with 120 ships to lie in wait for the expected Carthaginian invasion fleet (D.14.53.5), which, when it set out the following spring, deployed (D.14.54.5) four hundred warships. Dionysios at this time is said to have had 'a hundred and eighty ships of which a few were threes' (D.14.58.2). The text of this statement is suspect, and perhaps should read 'of which a few were' (fives and the rest) 'threes'; but it certainly does not suggest a fleet commensurate with Dionysios's reported plans; and in the fleets sent to sea by him in the next thirty years the numbers are no larger: a hundred in 393 (14.90.4), a hundred and twenty in 390 (D.14.100.2), forty in 389 (14.103.2), sixty threes in 384 (D.15.14.3), nine threes sent to help the Spartans in 374/3 (D.15.47.7). Suddenly at the very end of his reign Diodoros presents a different picture of Dionysios's military and naval power. He describes him in 368/7 (15.73.2) as 'getting ready an invasion force of 30,000 footsoldiers, 3,000 cavalry and three hundred threes with an appropriate supply fleet', and attacking the Carthaginian territory in Sicily. In the following winter Dionysios died. His son inherited his large fleet but not his interest in naval matters.

Aelian (*Var.Hist.* 6.12) speaks of Dionysios II having 'his rule well fortified by the possession of not less than 400 ships, sixes and fives'. It is of course impossible that the fleet of 400 ships Dionysios inherited from his father contained *only* sixes and fives. Dionysios is described as using a five as a flagship or as a suitable ship for him to use on a diplomatic mission; but it is most unlikely that he had more than a very few. It is not impossible that he also had a few sixes, which like the fives his son inherited. Xenagoras (Pref. xii) says that the six was invented in Syracuse, and Dionysios who invented the five might well have proceeded at the end of his reign to invent the *ἑξήρης* or six. Diodoros (21.16) credits Agathokles of Syracuse in 289 with sixes in the fleet which at his death he was assembling for the invasion of Libya.

Lucan describes Brutus's flagship at the battle of Massalia (p. 129) as standing higher than the other ships which included threes, fours and fives. She was however the only ship to be described as carrying towers. The six could have been a development of the four by triple manning oars at two levels but it seems more likely that Dionysios took the simpler step of double manning all the oars of a three-level ship.

We need not expel *ἑξήρεις* from Aelian's text, emending it, as Scheffer (1642) and Delts (Teubner 1974), to *τετρήρεις*. Nevertheless the reading *ἑξήρεις καὶ πεντήρεις* is nonsense as it stands, stating that the fleet consisted of nothing but fives and sixes. We must either accept it, supposing that Aelian, knowing that Dionysios had both sixes and fives in his fleet naively thought that he had nothing else; or find a lacuna, e.g. after *πεντήρεις* and fill it with such words as (*καὶ τριήρεις*) 'and threes', or before *ἑξήρης*, and fill it with the words (*ὧν ἐνίαι ἦσαν*) 'some of which were' as in the parallel passage, Diodoros 2.5.6. The text confirms, however, Pliny's attribution of the invention of the six to Syracuse.

2. ALEXANDER THE GREAT (*Map H, p. 74*)

In the early spring of 334 (Arrian 1.11.3) Alexander set out from Macedonia for the Hellespont, leaving Antipatros in charge of Greek and Macedonian affairs. Plutarch (*Moralia* 327 d) writes that Ptolemy, who was one of Alexander's generals and a historian, gave the size of his army as 30,000 infantry and 5,000 cavalry. He reached Sestos in twenty days and put Parmenion in charge of ferrying most of the infantry and the cavalry across the narrow strait to Abydos with 160 threes and a large number of round ships (*στρογγύλοι*). The threes would have towed the round ships (p. 30). Both Arrian (1.11.6 'according to the general story') and Diodoros (17.17.1) say that Alexander himself went on south to Elaios with 60 ships and made the longer (14.5 km) crossing from there to Sigeion, 'the harbour of the Achaeans', first to honour Protesilaos's tomb at Elaios and then to honour the tombs of the heroes at Troy. He must have taken the rest of the footsoldiers with him (as the Summary of Curtius Book 2 in fact says), probably the Macedonian élite. Some of the 60 ships at any rate would have been in the category of 'heavier *στρατιώτιδες*' (p. 21) of higher denomination than three. These ships were directly Macedonian (Hammond 1988 p. 25) as distinct from the 160 threes which when they were later taken south to Miletos by Nikanor are described as the Greek fleet, that is to say the fleet of the Hellenic League which its members were bound under treaty to provide (Curtius 3.1.20). At Miletos there is also reference in Arrian (1.19.4) to Macedonian threes as distinct from Nikanor's threes. The 60 ships seem to have been Alexander's personal squadron and 'the rest of the infantry' his bodyguard. There is reason to recognise specifically Macedonian ships again at the siege of Tyre (p. 6).

Shortly after the crossing Dareios was defeated at the Granikos river and Alexander moved southwards against first Ephesos which surrendered (A. 1.17.10) and then against Miletos, where the Rhodian Memnon, a Persian satrap, and other (mercenaries) survivors from the Granikos battle, organised resistance (D.17.22.1). The Persian fleet of about 400 (A.1.18.5), later described as made up of Cypriot and Phoenician ships with well-trained crews, was in the offing. Nikanor with his Greek fleet of 160 threes arrived at Miletos three days before the Persians and took up moorings on the island of Lade, to which Alexander was able to ferry on his ships the Thracians and about 4000 mercenaries in addition, from his land forces. It must be assumed that Alexander's squadron of 60 was already in the harbour of Miletos, in support of his land troops already besieging the city.

At this point (A.1.18.6) Arrian gives a debate between Alexander and Parmenion, the general who had served his father and was now his leading military adviser, analysing in an interesting way the strategic choices open to Alexander concerning power at sea. In spite of the gross disparity in numbers of ships (160 + 60 v. c.400) Parmenion advised Alexander to engage the Persian fleet, 'expecting that the Greeks would win, for other reasons and because of the omen'. If they won, he argued, it would be a great advantage for the whole campaign, while if they lost it would not be a great disaster, because in any case the Persians had command of the sea. Alexander replied that Parmenion was wrong both in his assessment and in his interpretation of the omen. It was quite unreasonable to fight with few ships against so many, and with an untrained fleet against the practised ships of the Cypriots and Phoenicians. He was also unwilling to expose the skill and courage of the Macedonians to the barbarians in a risky situation. If they were defeated, he added, the Greeks would revolt. Furthermore, the omen indicated that he would beat the Persians from the land.

The reference to 'the skill and courage of the Macedonians' may apply only to the Macedonian decksoldiers who are likely to have been on board Nikanor's threes, but if so it might have been more precise. If however, as it appears, the Macedonian squadron was present its imprecision may be the result of application to the skill of the seamen as well as to the courage of the soldiers.

(A.1.19.2) Brushing aside a Milesian offer of neutrality, Alexander proceeded to bring siege engines against the walls with good effect and threatened an assault the following day at dawn. At this point Nikanor's men, observing the attack of Alexander's men, moved along the coast under oar, and entered the Milesian harbour. At the place in its mouth where the channel was narrowest they moored with their prows facing outwards blocking it; and succeeded in denying entrance to the Persian fleet and Persian relief to the Milesians. Then the Milesians and the mercenaries, attacked on all sides by the Macedonian (land) forces, tried to escape, some on their inverted shields by swimming over to a little nameless island off the city. Others boarded small craft, and putting on all speed tried to steal ahead of (*ὑποφθάσαι*) the Macedonian threes but were caught by the threes at the mouth of the harbour.

What Arrian appears to be describing is a successful assault on the city by Alexander's land forces resulting in the inhabitants and mercenaries trying to escape by water, either swimming across to an island on their shields or attempting to get out to sea on small craft. The latter went as fast as they could to outstrip the Macedonian threes chasing them inside the harbour, but were caught by the Greek threes blocking the harbour mouth. This interpretation, which is not that given by Brunt (Loeb: 1976 I p. 81), makes sense of Greek which is not entirely clear. If accepted it puts beyond doubt the existence of a Macedonian squadron in Alexander's fleet which accompanied him at least in his move against Ephesos and Miletos. It is likely to have been a mixed squadron of heavier ships and threes, the latter being used, as the faster, to pursue the escaping light craft.

When Miletos fell, (A.1.20.1; D.17.22.5) Alexander decided to disband the fleet (*τὸ ναυτικόν*) except for a few ships, which he used for the transport of siege engines, including the twenty ships from Athens. Brunt suggests that the latter were hostages for Athens' good conduct. This may be partly true; but by 'the fleet' Arrian and Diodoros probably mean the Greek fleet which gives a reason for noting the exception. The Greek fleet subsequently reassembled by Hegelochos was of a similar number. Brunt rejects Diodoros' reason for the retention of a few ships to carry siege engines on the ground of their vulnerability; but Diodoros records (17.24.1) that at the siege of Halikarnassos shortly afterwards Alexander successfully brought up siege engines and provisions by sea, the Persian fleet having left the area. He brought up siege engines similarly for the siege of Gaza (p. 9).

'Alexander considered that since he now held Asia with his land forces he no longer needed a navy, and that his capture of the cities of the coastal region would lead to the disintegration of the Persian fleet since they would no longer have a source for the recruitment of naval personnel (*ὑπηρεσία*) and no bases in Asia'. 'Beating the Phoenician fleet from the land' well describes the strategy Alexander now followed. He next marched into Karia and brought over the cities between Miletos and Halikarnassos. The latter withstood a long siege. From Karia he moved into Lykia and Pamphylia, and brought over the important naval cities of Phaselis, Side, and Aspendos. He was taking a risk which was well illustrated by the brief but successful naval campaign in the Aegean which the resourceful Memnon of Rhodes, in command of the Phoenician fleet and satrap of lower Asia, then used the absence of naval opposition to carry out.

(D.17.29.1) Memnon's campaign was pursued at Dareios's instigation, who hoped thereby to turn the war from Asia to Macedon and Greece. He provided Memnon with money to man 300 ships and enlist mercenaries so as to retake Chios and the cities of Lesbos. Mitylene resisted and was besieged. The Kyklades began to approach him and mainland Greece was awaiting his arrival in Euboia, when he died of a sudden illness. Pharnabazos took over his command; and concluding the siege of Mitylene, attacked and took Tenedos in the approaches to the Hellespont.

Before news of Memnon's death had reached him (Curtius 3.1.19), Alexander put Amphoteros and Hegelochos in command of sea and land forces at the Hellespont with orders to liberate Lesbos, Chios and Kos. Later (A.2.2.3) he ordered Hegelochos to reassemble the Hellenic fleet, and Antipatros in Macedonia to collect from Euboia and the Peloponnese ships to 'protect the islands and mainland Greece'. Under Proteas 15 ships from Chalkis captured eight of a squadron of ten Phoenician ships at Siphnos. Immediately before the second defeat of Dareios, at Issos (333 BC), (A.2.13.4) Pharnabazos at Chios divided his fleet sending part to Kos and Halikarnassos and the rest (100 ships: Curtius 4.1.37) across the Aegean to Siphnos where he met Agis of Sparta at the moment when the news of Dareios's defeat at Issos came through, causing Pharnabazos to withdraw to Chios.

Although Alexander's naval resources had been and continued to be overstretched by the necessity of containing Persian initiatives in the Aegean, after the battle of Issos (A.2.17; D.17.40.2) Alexander seems to have felt free to turn his attention to Phoenicia with a view to the conquest of Egypt for which naval forces would undoubtedly be required. Arrian again makes his thinking plain. Gerostratos, king of Arados, was serving in the Persian fleet, like the other Phoenician and the Cypriot kings. His son, Straton, came to meet Alexander and surrendered his kingdom to him. Byblos and Sidon also surrendered (A.2.15.6).

Arrian represents Alexander, before moving against Tyre, addressing his allies as follows (2.17.1): 'We cannot march to Egypt in safety so long as the Persians command the sea, nor is it safe for us to pursue Dareios' (eastwards) 'leaving Tyre behind us with her allegiance doubtful and Egypt and Cyprus still in Persian hands, especially in view of the state of Greek affairs' (made plain by the recent moves of Memnon and of his successor Pharnabazos). 'The Persians might again get control of the coastal positions' (indeed they had gained control of some, e.g. Chios and Halikarnassos, already), 'when we will have advanced in full force against Babylon and Dareios; and with a larger expedition they might switch the war to Greece, where the Lacedaimonians are actually at war with us and the city of Athens is at present kept in check by fear rather than goodwill. Yet with Tyre destroyed the rest of Phoenicia will be in our hands; and it is to be expected that the Phoenician naval squadron, which is the most numerous and the most efficient contingent in the Persian fleet, will come over to us. For neither the Phoenician oarsmen nor the ἐπιβάται[2] will risk serving another power at sea while we hold their cities. Cyprus will then come over to us or be easily subdued by a seaborne invasion. And if we deploy a naval force of Macedonian and Phoenician ships, and Cyprus adheres to our cause, we would securely command the sea, and the Egyptian expedition would at the same time be easily carried out. When we have brought Egypt to our side, there remains no uncertainty about the position in Greece or at home, and we shall make the expedition to Babylon with the home front safe and with greater prestige, having effectively deprived the Persians of the whole maritime area, and territory this side of the Euphrates'.

Arrian shows Alexander setting out his strategic objections to his soldiers' caution with sound military logic. Tyre was a naval power based on a fortified island four stades (710 m) from the mainland (D.17.40.4), whose defeat would be no easy matter so long as Persia retained command of the sea. But her capture was the key to the whole plan to deprive Persia of naval superiority, not by a head-on confrontation at sea but by striking at its logistical roots outside Asia Minor: Phoenicia, Cyprus and Egypt. Alexander's aim to achieve command of the sea with a fleet of *Macedonian*, Phoenician and Cypriot ships indicates that the Macedonian squadron (but not of course the Greek fleet which would be deployed under Hegelochos in the Aegean) was regarded as an essential part of the fleet to accompany the Egyptian expedition. For a long time after the Salamis campaign Egypt had not contributed to Persian military strength. But she had been in the fifth century, and would be again, a considerable naval power.

The Siege of Tyre: 332 BC (Plan 1)

(A.2.18.–3) The siege presented a formidable task since 'the advantage by sea appeared to lie with the Tyrians in view of the Persian supremacy at sea and the large Tyrian fleet'. Diodoros (17.41.1) says that they had 80 threes, but Arrian speaks of Tyrian fours and fives.

Alexander began the attack on Tyre by building a mole, with towers and wooden structures at the far end, to connect the mainland to the city, which was an island. The Tyrians replied by using a cavalry transport as a fireship to destroy the towers. In the opening stages Alexander could not moor ships at Tyre but had to keep them at Sidon, some distance (35 km) away, and that was his naval base (A.2.19.6; Curtius 4.2.15, 4.4.2) until he was able to make his approach to the city with his full fleet.

His strategy was however beginning to pay off (A.2.20.1–3). The kings of Arados and Byblos and the Sidonian threes came over to him, 80 ships in all. Rhodes sent a contingent of ten ships, three came from Soloi (in Cyprus) and Mallos (in Kilikia), ten from Lykia and a pentecontor from Macedon bringing Proteas (who had captured the eight Phoenician ships at Siphnos). Then, 'soon after', the kings of Cyprus put in at Sidon with about 120 ships (Curtius 4.3.11); 'they had heard of the defeat of Dareios at Issos and it frightened them that all Phoenicia was now in Alexander's hands'. With 224 ships in addition to the Macedonian squadron Alexander had now swung the balance of naval power in his favour. Apart from the Sidonian threes and the Macedonian pentecontor the additional ships are as yet of unspecified type.

Alexander was now (A.2.20.4: 332 BC) able to challenge the Tyrian fleet and prepared to move his ships against the island, making preparation for a naval engagement if that proved necessary and also constructing siege engines. He made a ten-day sally into the interior of Phoenicia (Curtius 2.24 and 3.1) to stop the inhabitants interfering with the supply of timber. Then when all was ready (A.2.20.6) his fleet 'moved out of Sidon against Tyre in battle order, himself on the right (seaward) wing with the Cypriot kings except Pnytagoras' (king of Salamis) 'and all the Phoenicians'. Pnytagoras with the Macedonian Krateros commanded the left wing of the line.

If the c.120 ships of the three Cypriot kings (Salamis, Amathus and Kourieus p. 8) are to be divided equally between them, on the right wing there would have been 160 ships: those of two Cypriot kings (c.80) and the Phoenician ships (80). On the left wing there would be only the ships of Pnytagoras (c.40) who with Krateros commanded the wing, and the 24 remaining ships (Rhodes 10, Lykia 10, Soloi and Mallos 3 and the Macedonian pentecontor), sixty-four in all. This is a grossly unbalanced arrangement unless it is assumed that the Macedonian Krateros was leading the Macedo-

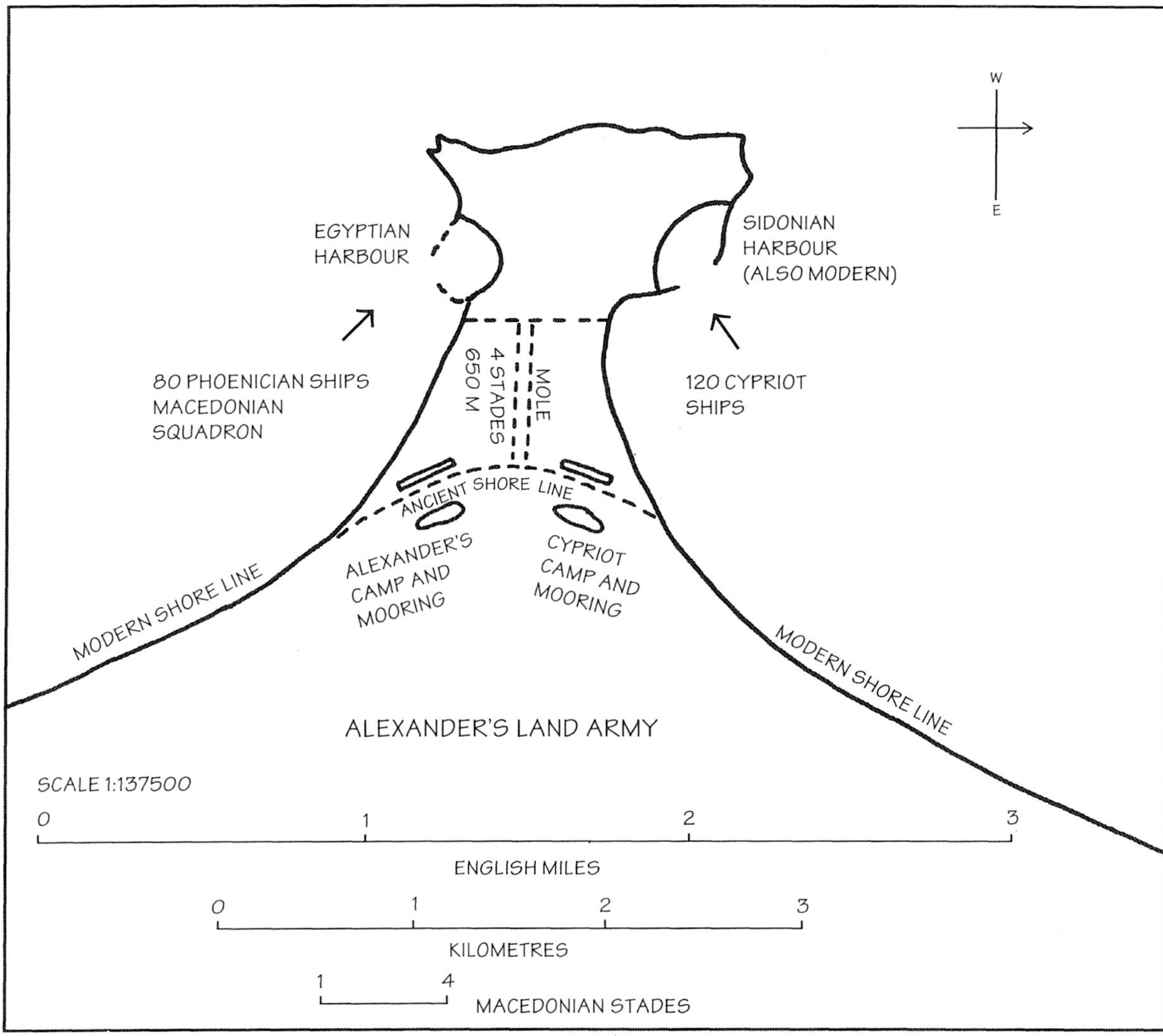

PLAN 1. *Alexander's siege of Tyre*

nian squadron of c.60 ships. Only if Pnytagoras is given half the ships of the Cypriot kings and the other half is divided among the others are the two wings brought into exact balance. The presence of the Macedonian squadron seems to be required. Later (2.21.1) Arrian speaks of Alexander bringing up horse transports and 'threes which were not fast from Sidon' to carry siege engines, and refers to them (2.21.4) as 'the horse transports belonging to the Macedonians'. There were then Macedonian auxiliaries as well as front-line ships.

It is possible that Alexander's ships were in line abreast (*μετοπηδόν*), a formation which it would not be easy to maintain on a voyage of about 35 km, more likely that squadrons (of ten or fifteen ships) were in line ahead (*ἐπὶ κέρας*), the normal formation for ships on passage, behind their commanders. Alexander himself would then have headed the leading squadron, the normal place for the fleet commander. This squadron on the signal to form line of battle (line abreast) would have formed line on his left, the other squadrons doing likewise. Curtius says (4.3.11) that Alexander was on board a 'royal five (*quinqueremis regia*)', i.e. one of the 'fives' belonging to the Cypriot kings, on the right wing. Krateros may have been on board Pnytagoras's 'royal five'.

The Tyrians, who had intended to come out and fight, were alarmed at the size of Alexander's fleet and contented themselves (A.2.20.8) 'with blocking entrance with as many threes as the mouths of their harbours would take and preventing the enemy fleet entering one of them to moor'. (A.2.20.10) 'On that day Alexander's squadron (*οἱ σὺν Ἀλεξάνδρῳ*) came to a mooring quite close to the artificial mole along the beach (of the mainland) where there appeared to be shelter from the winds (Curtius 4.2.7 speaks of a prevalent 'African wind'). On the following day Alexander gave orders to the Cyprians with their ships and Andromachos the Macedonian *ναύαρχος* to set up a blockade of the city at the harbour for ships coming from Sidon; and to the Phoenicians on the other side of the mole to do the same at the harbour facing Egypt, where in fact his tent was. The arrangements (Plan 1) are very neat. Alexander's ships are moored along the beach close to the base of the mole stretching out (Curtius 4.2.7: 4 stades: 710 m) to the island. On the north side the 120 Cypriot ships blockade the Sidonian harbour and on the south side the 80 Phoenician ships (together with Alexander's 60 ships, it will appear) blockade the Egyptian harbour. Alexander's tent is pitched at the focus of operations on the beach with his land forces behind and east of him. There can be no doubt of the presence of the Macedonian squadron here.

A passage throws some light on the bigger ships in the fleets on both sides. Arrian describes (2.22.2) a later surprise attack by a Tyrian force of three fives, three fours and seven threes, manned by the best-trained oarsmen and the best-equipped and most courageous decksoldiers. The attack was against the Cypriot ships detailed to block the north facing harbour, as they lay at their moorings (*ὁρμούσαις*) on the mainland beach. The 'five of king Pnytagoras', 'the (five) of Androkles of Amathus', and 'the (five) of Pasikrates of Kourieus' were (holed and) swamped and the rest (presumably threes) driven ashore and damaged. It seems that these fives were all flagships of the kings named. When Alexander, who was in his tent with the ships blockading the southern harbour, heard of the attack, he manned the ships there and left most of them under oar to prevent Tyrian ships coming out, while he 'took the fives he had with him and five threes, all hastily manned, and moved to the northern harbour against the Tyrian ships that had moved out...' A few of these 'managed to get back in time, but Alexander's ships ramming most of them put some out of action and a five and a four were captured at the entrance to the harbour'. (Arrian adds the note that there was no loss of life among the decksoldiers on these two ships since they swam away into the harbour without difficulty.) It appears then that Alexander 'had with him' a number of fives as well as threes. These then belonged to the Macedonian squadron. Hitherto only threes have been specified as belonging to it (p. 7).

In addition to these two references to fives in Curtius and Arrian there is a third, in Curtius (4.4.6–7 which will be discussed below). It is to a five which belonged to Alexander's Macedonian squadron 'which it chanced that he had ordered to be brought to the opposite side' i.e from the south side, where it was normally moored with the Phoenician ships, to the north side. 'She moved out from the Macedonian line, superior among the rest in speed'. They show that in Cyprus the five was an exceptional warship used by the kings as prestigious flagships, and that there were others in Alexander's fleet, some probably Phoenician, others belonging to the Macedonian squadron. They were chosen to lead an attack. In these ships speed, by which acceleration rather than speed may have been meant, was one of the qualities which were valued.

Nevertheless, Alexander as a true Macedonian relied on hand-to-hand fighting rather than agility of movement in his ships. Arrian says (2.20.6) that when his fleet first advanced on Tyre from Sidon in battle order 'he put on deck' i.e. as *ἐπιβάται* 'as many of the *ὑπασπισταί*' the equivalent of the Greek *ὁπλῖται* 'as he thought the occasion demanded in case the (expected) engagement turned out to be fought not by manoeuvres (*διέκπλοι*) but by hand-to-hand combat'.

In addition to the fives Arrian speaks only of threes and triacontors in Alexander's fleet. Some threes 'which were not fast', he says, were used, with the 'horse transports he had brought from Sidon' to carry siege engines (2.21.1 cf. 4). By implication there were also threes which were fast (*ταχυναυτοῦσαι*, a technical term). Curtius mentions 'fours' in Alexander's fleet, which were tied together in pairs to form an assault vessel (4.3.13–18). Their presence, if not mentioned, might have been inferred. They may have belonged to the ships of the Greek fleet, including the Athenian squadron (thus fours) retained, to carry siege engines and subsequently used at the siege of Gaza.

The Tyrian action against the Cypriot ships blockading the northern harbour marked the end of Tyrian naval activity. Alexander's ships were employed to carry siege engines and landing gangways, to land parties at strategic points and to carry bowmen and devices to shoot missiles at the defenders. The ships participated also in the final assault.

The Egyptian Expedition

As Alexander had forecast, the fall of Tyre opened the way for him to carry out his planned expedition to Egypt. (Curtius 4.5.10) He ordered Hephaestion to move south along the coast of Phoenicia and came with all his forces to Gaza. When the city refused to admit him he sent for the siege engines from Tyre to be dispatched by sea. (D.17.48.7) He took the city after a siege of two months and set out (332/1 BC) for Egypt, his ships moving alongside him (A.3.1.1). The fleet was moored at Pelousion when he arrived there. He garrisoned the city and ordered his ship-captains to move up the Nile to Memphis. He was welcomed as a liberator from Persian rule.

Hegelochos arrived in Egypt by sea (A.3.2.3) and reported that Tenedos and Chios had come over to Macedonia and that Aristonikos, the Persian-backed tyrant of Methymna, was captured at Chios when, thinking that the city was still in Persian hands, he had arrived in the harbour 'with five pirate *ἡμιολίαι*', a type of ship which appears first in the mid-fourth century (with a piratical reputation). Hegelochos also reported that he had reduced Mitylene with the rest of Lesbos and that he had sent Amphoteros, subsequently reinforced by 100 Cypriot and Phoenician ships, to take Kos and then to support the opponents of Sparta in the Peloponnese.

(A.3.6.1) Returning to Phoenicia where his fleet awaited him at Tyre, he heard of revolt against him in the Peloponnese and sent Amphoteros in support of loyal cities there. At the same time he ordered the Phoenicians and Cypriots to send 100 ships in addition to those Amphoteros already had.

By 330 BC the situation in the eastern Mediterranean had been sufficiently stabilised to allow Alexander to move east in pursuit of Dareios and for the march which was to take him four years later to the upper reaches of the Indus.

The Indus Flotilla

Book 6 of Arrian's *Anabasis of Alexander* begins with the sentence: 'Since there had been built for Alexander on the banks of the Hydaspes (a tributary of the Indus) many triacontors and *ἡμιολίαι* and many horse-transports and other vessels useful for transport of an army by river, Alexander decided to go down the Hydaspes as far as the Great Sea'.

After the defeat of Dareios at Gaugamela and his subsequent death, Alexander had taken his army eastwards to the Indus, crossed it on a bridge of boats made from local timber recognised to be suitable, transported the vessels by wagon in sections to the Hydaspes, put them together again, and then, when the powerful local ruler Poros had been defeated, they were lying ready to suggest no small adventure to a man who had already been seen to be both practical and adventurous, romantic and hardheaded. The voyage and march down river to the sea, followed by Nearchos's voyage and Alexander's march from the Indus mouth to Babylon, are by themselves theme for a book. Here only the voyage down river is relevant for the light it throws on the *ἡμιολία*, the oarsystem of which is a puzzle in itself and leads to a further puzzle, the oar-system of the *τριημιολία* (or *τριηρημιολία*) which will engage attention.

Alexander had used triacontors (thirty-oared ships) at Tyre (A.2.21.6). He boxed them in to protect the crew and placed them over and across the anchors of threes, placed near the walls of the city, to prevent the cables being cut. There then they appear as small, normally open, vessels rowed by fifteen men a side, probably at one level. On the Hydaspes the triacontors and *ἡμιολίαι* were similar low-hulled vessels on which a bridge could be laid, and small enough to be carried by wagon in sections. A little later (6.2.4) Arrian says: 'the ships (*αἱ νῆες*), (as Ptolemy, son of Lagos, says, whom I mostly follow), were altogether eighty triacontors, while all the auxiliaries (πλοῖα) including horse-transports, κέρκουροι etc ...were not short of two thousand'. The 80 ships at any rate include those which in the earlier passage and in a later one (6.18.3) are called triacontors and ἡμιολίαι, so that it is reasonable to infer that they are all thirty-oared ships but some have an oar-system which justifies the more specific name ἡμιολία. It will be seen that among the triacontors which were not ἡμιολίαι there were also two kinds.

At the confluence of the Hydaspes and Acesines (6.4.4) Arrian relates that the current was rapid because of the narrows. Alexander had been warned by the Indians and told his men: 'Yet when the flotilla drew near the confluence there was such a din that they stopped rowing, not at a word of command but because the boatswains (κελευσταί) were struck dumb with amazement', and accordingly were not giving the time (see A.6.3.3); and the oarsmen were holding their oars out of the water, because of the noise. (6.5.1) But when they were not far from the confluence the helmsmen gave orders to them to row as strongly as possible and get out of the narrows, so that the ships, getting into the whirlpools, would not be turned round by them, but should master the eddies of the water with their rowing.

'Those of the στρογγύλοι that were turned round by the current suffered no ill-effects of the turning, apart from the distress of the passengers, and were put on a straight course, righted by the current itself. The long ships however did not get off so lightly in the turning, not standing as high out of the seething swell, nor did those that were δίκροτοι, having their lower oars not very far above the water. Further, when they were broadside on to the eddies their oars clashed together, at any rate in the case of those oarsmen who were caught by the water because they did not get their oars clear in time' (i.e. caught a crab). 'The result was that many of the ships were damaged, and two which collided with each other were lost with many of those on board'.

In the category of longships triacontors are then of two kinds, those with oars at one level and those with oars at two. Since it is clear from their experience in the rapids that the second file of oars in some triacontors was inserted below the oars of the single file, triacontors of both kinds would have stood about the same height out of the water and thus have been equally suited to be units in a boat-bridge. These ἡμιολίαι (**73** p. 318) were light open oared ships with oars at one level.

The two-level pentecontor appears to have been so designed to reduce the size of the ship while retaining the same oar-power. The rowing area of the simple one-level ship would have been 6.666 m or 7.4 m according to the cubit used (.444 m or .495 m) while the rowing area of the two-level ship would similarly have been 3.5 or 3.96 m). The rowing area of the ἡμιολία, with half the oars double-manned would be the same as that of the two-level triacontor, but it would present, with the same oar-power, the advantages in terms of weight of both the one-level and the two-level triacontors, a short rowing area and one level of oars. It is not therefore surprising that when Alexander (A.6.18.3) chose the fastest ships in his fleet (τὰς μάλιστα τῶν νεῶν ταχυναυτούσας) for his reconnaissance of the western mouth of the Indus, the first in the list were the ἡμιολίαι, next 'all the triacontors' i.e. both kinds, and third the κέρκουροι (an oared auxiliary type).

Alexander's Naval Plans

The happy conclusion of Nearchos's voyage and Alexander's march from the Indus was a meeting of the two at Alexander's camp in Karmania (324 BC: A.6.28.5). From there Nearchos went back to his ships and continued his voyage to the mouth of the Tigris, while Alexander proceeded to Pasargadai and Persepolis (A.6.29). There, Arrian says (7.1–2) 'a longing seized him to go down the Euphrates and Tigris to the Persian sea, and to see for himself the mouths of the rivers entering the sea, like those of the Indus; and the sea itself in that region'.

The success of his naval operations on the Indus encouraged him thus far. But his further success in sending Nearchos's fleet on its coastal voyage seems to have led to still bolder plans. Arrian continues: 'Some have also written that Alexander was conceiving the idea of circumnavigating most of Arabia and the land of Ethiopia and of both the Libyans and the Nomads beyond Mt Atlas, to Gadeira (Cadiz) and into our sea, and that after subduing Libya and Carthage he would justly be called king of all Asia...'.

Plutarch (*Alexander* 68) directly connects these further plans with the Indian naval operations by saying that Alexander had them in mind when Nearchos went up to meet him from Harmozia: 'Alexander was so delighted to hear the details of his coastal voyage that he desired himself to go down the Euphrates with a large fleet, and then after circumnavigating Arabia and Africa to enter the inner sea through the Pillars of Herakles. And vessels of every sort were built for him at Thapsakos, and seamen and pilots were recruited from all parts'.

Before he died a year later Alexander took a variety of steps, reconnaissance missions and a naval building programme, which make clear the direction in which his mind was now turning.

On his journey down to Babylon, he was met by embassies from many countries, including Libya, Italy, Carthage, Spain and Ethiopia, and after his arrival others from Greece. (A.7.15.5) 'Both to himself and to his entourage Alexander appeared to be master of all the land and sea'. After the reception of the embassies, Alexander 'sent Herakleides son of Argaios to Hyrkania' at the southern end of the Caspian Sea, 'taking with him shipwrights, with orders to cut timber in the Hyrcanian mountains and build longships both aphract and cataphract on the Greek model (*ἐς τὸν κόσμον τὸν Ἑλληνικόν*). For he was seized with a longing to learn about the sea which is called Caspian and Hyrcanian, with what sea it is joined, whether it joins the Euxine Sea or whether on the eastern side towards India the great sea goes round and has continuous with it a gulf which is the Hyrcanian Sea, just as he had discovered the Persian Gulf, which is called the Red Sea. For the sources of the Caspian Sea had not yet been discovered...'. No more is heard of this project of Alexander's, but it is interesting as illustrating the effect the Indian expedition was having on his mind at this time, both in regard to the scope of future naval operations and of the calibre of the ships to be involved.

Aristoboulos (A.7.19.3) said that Alexander on his entry to Babylon found his fleet there, made up partly of Nearchos's squadron which had moved up from the Persian Gulf (Curtius 10.1.16), and partly of ships brought from Phoenicia. The latter consisted of two fives, three fours, 12 threes and 30 triacontors. These had been dismantled (in Phoenicia) and transported to the Euphrates at Thapsakos where they were reassembled and moved down to Babylon.[3] 'Other ships were being built for him from the cypresses he had felled in Babylon. Cypresses were the only trees which were in good supply in Assyria, the country being badly off for the other timber used in shipbuilding'.

Strabo (16.1.11) also quotes Aristoboulos to the same effect but with different detail, connecting the moves specifically with his intention of conquering Arabia: 'Alexander had built fleets (*στόλους*) and naval bases (*ὁρμητήρια*), having constructed some of his ships in Phoenicia and in Cyprus, such as could be taken to pieces (*διαλυτά*) and were fastened with tenons (*γομφωτά*). These were transported to Thapsakos in a journey of seven days and then taken down river to Babylon. The others were constructed in Babylon of the cypresses in the local woods and parks, since there was a shortage of wood there, while in the country of the Cossaeans and certain other peoples there was a fairly good supply'.

(A.7.19.4) 'As oarcrews for the ships and specialist crews as well there had come to him a large number of recruits – purple-shell divers and other people employed at sea from Phoenicia and other maritime areas. Aristoboulos says also that Alexander was constructing at Babylon an excavated harbour big enough to take a thousand longships as well as shipsheds at the harbour'. (A.7.19.5–6) Mikkalos of Klazomenai was also sent to Phoenicia and Syria with 500 talents to hire some, and buy (as slaves) others, who were seamen. Alexander's plan was to establish settlements on the sea coast along the Persian Gulf and on the islands there. It seemed to him that this region was on the way to becoming no less prosperous than Phoenicia. His naval programme was directed mainly at the Arabs, on the grounds that they alone of the non-Greeks in this region had sent no embassy; and no other courteous or honorific action had been taken by them towards him. Aristoboulos is reported by Strabo (6.1.11) as saying that Alexander's real reason for planning to attack the Arabs was his desire 'to be lord of all'. As Brunt observes (II p. 270 n. 4), Arrian adopts this opinion as his own by concluding: 'In my own opinion the truth is that Alexander was an inveterate acquisitor'.

(A.7.20.2) Alexander had been told that Arabia was a large and prosperous country, and that 'there were many islands off shore and harbours everywhere in the country to give mooring for his fleet and sites for cities which could be built and become prosperous'. (A.7.20.7) He had sent Archias in a triacontor to reconnoitre the further of two islands said to lie near the mouth of the Euphrates. Archias had reported that it was about a day and a night distant from the mouth 'for a ship running before the wind'.

Androsthenes was also sent with a triacontor 'and went along part of the Arabian peninsula; but of all those dispatched Hieron of Soloi, the Cypriot helmsman, who also was given a triacontor by Alexander, went the furthest. Yet, although he received instructions to go the whole way round the coast of Arabia as far as the Arabian gulf towards Heroonpolis adjoining Egypt, after going the greater part of the distance he turned back, reporting that 'the peninsula was amazingly big, not far short of India in size, and that a promontory ran far out into the great sea'.

These voyages of reconnaissance, exploring the islands adjacent to the mouth of the Euphrates and the coast of the Arabian peninsula, their nature and the conditions of navigation there, show that Alexander's plan for the conquest and colonisation of Arabia was one which he was taking seriously in the winter of 324/3, urged on probably by Onesikritos, whose wish to take Nearchos's fleet across to Arabia had been vetoed, an incident which Arrian recalls at this point (7.20.9–10).

Arrian reports (7.21.1), again probably on the authority of Aristoboulos (cf. Strabo 16.1.11), that while his threes were being built and the harbour of Babylon dug out, Alexander did some reconnaissance of his own, comparable to his exploration of the mouths of the Indus before Nearchos's voyage. He set out down the Euphrates to the so-called river Pallakopas, and 'down it to the lakes in the direction of Arabia. There having seen a good site he built and fortified a city and settled in it some of the Greek mercenaries, volunteers and men unfit for service through age or wounds'.

He also went (A.7.22.1–5: Aristoboulos), this time without relevance to the Arabian expedition, exploring the marshes on the Euphrates above Babylon in a three which, on one occasion at any rate, he was steering himself. On another occasion some of the flotilla without a pilot lost their way in the narrow channels until he sent them a pilot and brought them back into the main stream. The threes which were being built at this time must be the ships constructed at Babylon from the local cypress timber.

The fleet with which he intended to circumnavigate the greater part of Arabia and Africa was, at this stage, composed of two fives as flagships, three fours, and a number of threes, the 12 ships brought from Phoenicia and an unspecified number built in Babylon. There were also the 30 triacontors from Phoenicia as well as Nearchos's triacontors, some of which were *ἡμιολίαι*, for reconnaissance and, probably, communication within the fleet.

Alexander did not neglect training: (A.7.23.5) 'At this time', i.e. on his return to Babylon from the voyages just described, 'Alexander was frequently conducting trials of his fleet (*τοῦ ναυτικοῦ ἀπεπειρᾶτο*)' employing the time-honoured means of races between threes and between such fours as were on the river. There were also contests between oarsmen (i.e. between crews of ships of a single type) and between helmsmen (conducting manoeuvres competitively).

The information given about the ships of this fleet adds nothing to knowledge about their size, crew numbers or oarsystem. There is however a piece of information from an unexpected source about the dimensions of fives, the tomb of Hephaistion (p. 270–271).

Mention has already been made of Arrian's reference (7.1.2) to 'some writers' who had recorded Alexander's naval plans to send a fleet round 'most of Arabia' i.e. presumably to the entrance of the Red Sea and then 'Ethiopia, Libya and the Nomads beyond Mt Atlas, Gadeira and into our sea after subduing Libya and Carthage'. The first part of this plan at any rate is corroborated strongly by the reconnaissance voyages of Archias, Androsthenes and Hieron. The more ambitious second part is mentioned briefly by Plutarch (*Alexander* 68.1) saying that he planned 'after circumnavigating Arabia and Africa to enter the inner sea through the pillars of Herakles'.

Curtius (10.1.17–19) mentions the grand circumnavigation and goes into detail about the fleet involved: 'For this purpose Alexander gave orders to the satraps (*praetores*) of Mesopotamia to cut timber in the mountains of Lebanon and bring it down to the Syrian city of Thapsakos on the Euphrates, and then lay down the keels of 700 ships. They were all to be 'sevens' and to be taken down to Babylon. The Cypriot kings were instructed to supply copper, caulking material and sails'. Pliny (see above Preface xii) quotes the tradition which attributes to Alexander the first building of sevens to tens. The tradition may partially derive from this, probably latest, addition to Alexander's project. Justin's mention (13.5.7) of Alexander's orders to his allies 'to build 1000 ships for his war in the West (*quibus in occidente bellum gereret*)', when he heard of the revolt of Athens and Aitolia, may also derive from it. Its proximity to supplies of ship-timber in the Lebanon and to Phoenicia makes sense of the choice of Thapsakos. The building of 'sevens' is again not surprising, given Alexander's ambition, now turning to naval projects. As we have seen, 'sixes' were to be found in the Syracusan fleet earlier in the century, and before the end of it Demetrios Poliorketes had ten 'sixes' and seven Phoenician 'sevens' in his fleet at the battle of Cypriot Salamis (304 BC). Ten years earlier there were ten 'tens' and three 'nines' in the fleet which Antigonos assembled to challenge Ptolemy.

On Alexander's death (D.18.4.2–4) Perdikkas found in the memoranda (*ὑπομνήματα*) of Alexander 'the completion of the pyre of Hephaestion, which required a great deal of money, as well as many other great projects requiring enormous expense'. The first item in the list which Diodoros gives of 'the greatest and most memorable' projects is: 'to build a thousand long ships, larger than threes, in Phoenicia, Syria, Kilikia and Cyprus for the campaign against the Carthaginians and the others (non-Greeks) who live along the coast of Libya and Iberia and the adjoining coasts as far as Sicily; to make a road along the coast of Libya as far as the Pillars of Herakles; to build six costly temples each for 1500 talents; and, as was needed for such a large fleet, to construct harbours and port installations in suitable places'.

The western plan of the *Hypomnemata* has the same aims as the grand circumnavigation, but is clearly distinct from it, although it could be complementary. In the former the substantial fleet would accompany a Macedonian army as it marched by a newly constructed road against the Libyans and Carthage in the first place, and then return by way of 'Iberia and the adjoining coasts as far as Sicily' in the second. This plan and the whole account of the *Hypomnemata* in Diodoros is likely to have the good authority of Hieronymos behind it, and, like the grand circumnavigation, must be taken seriously.

Alexander's enthusiasm for discovery of unknown lands and his confidence in the effectiveness of sea power and sea communications visibly grew and were nurtured, though it would be too much to say that they derived, from the Indian adventure and the naval operations which it involved. The plan of the *Hypomnemata* could have been conceived after the conquest of Egypt, of which it is the logical continuation. The assembly and building of the fleet at Babylon, its training and the reconnaissances, are the logical continuation of the naval operations begun on the Indus. It is difficult to believe that Alexander's romantic imperialism and his vaulting ambition could contemplate both. All that can be said is that in 323 BC in the months before his death he appears to have been more interested in the grand circumnavigation, of the actual implications of which he was entirely ignorant.

The arguments for the rejection of Alexander's western plans as later inventions and absurd and impossible have been put forward by Tarn (1948 ii 379 f) and Hampl (1953). These arguments have been rebutted by F. Schachermeyr (1954 p. 118ff) and by Badian (1968 p. 183 ff). This rebuttal has been accepted by Brunt (1983 II Appendix xxiii 3–6) with whom there seems no reason to disagree.

If Alexander had died in Egypt and his plans for the conquest of India as far as the mouth of the Ganges (in fact only partly carried out) had been found among his papers, they would have been pronounced as no less absurd and impossible than the western plans which he died too soon to put in motion. Perdikkas presented the projects which were the subject of the *Hypomnemata* to the common assembly of the Macedonians (that is to say the Macedonians in the army); and it was decided not to go ahead with any of the major projects in Diodoros's list.

3. ATHENS' NAVAL AMBITIONS

On Alexander's death in June 323 BC and the distribution of the satrapies by Perdikkas the stage was set for the power struggle, and the competition for sea power, among Alexander's successors. As Tarn (1913 p. 72) observed, there were three fleets of importance in the Eastern Mediterranean in the latter part of the fourth century, the Persian, the Athenian and the Macedonian. The naval activities of Hegelochos and Amphoteros in the Aegean and the Asian coastal area, reported to Alexander in Egypt and continued no doubt in his absence, and Alexander's successful attraction to his flag of the Phoenician and Cypriot navies, had brought the Persian sea power to an end. The Athenian dockyards at Peiraieus still contained a substantial fleet of threes with a growing squadron of fours and a few fives; but to activate their sea power resources of money and men were required. The Macedonians had a core of Macedonian ships and great naval resources at their command from Egypt Phoenicia, and Cyprus. Their ships ranged from the 'heavier stratiotides' to threes and the smaller auxiliaries. These at any rate were the sources, together with the western and south-western maritime satrapies of Asia Minor including their Greek cities and offshore islands, as well as the Hellespontine area, constituting the prizes which the contestant for sea power must now aim to win. The first bid was made by Athens (see JSM: 1987).

Rumours of Alexander's death reaching the mainland of Greece led to a movement of revolt against the Macedonian hegemony fostered by Athens. The account of this movement in Diodoros by reason of its Macedonian bias is probably to be attributed to Hieronymos of Kardia (J. Hornblower: 1981). It is contained in a number of passages:

(i) D.18.9.4: 'When people from Babylon who had been eye-witnesses of the king's death arrived (in Athens), then the (Athenian) demos came out openly in favour of the war'.

(ii) D.18.10.1–3: 'While the propertied men were advising no action to be taken and the rabble-rousers were stirring up the people and calling on them to take up the war vigorously, far more numerous were those who chose war and were accustomed to make their living from service pay... Straightway then the rhetors gave expression to the popular intentions and drafted a decree to the following effect: the demos should take thought for the common freedom of the Greeks; they should on the one hand set about liberating the garrisoned cities, and on the other procure 40 threes and 200 fours, call up all Athenians under the age of forty, three tribes to guard Attika and seven to be ready for foreign service. They should send out also envoys to go round the Greek cities and carry the message that as in former times the demos, regarding all Greece as the common fatherland of the Greeks, had repelled at sea the barbarians who had come to enslave them, so at the present time the demos recognised it as their duty to risk their lives and treasure and ships in the cause of the common freedom of Greece'.

The decree's emphasis on naval action and 'the Salamis spirit' is to be noted; the 200 fours recall the 200 threes which repelled an earlier threat to Greece, as it may also have recalled the 200 ships Dionysios planned to build to repel the Carthaginians. Notable also is the critical tone of the reporter, as in what follows.

(iii) The doubts of the wiser heads among the Greeks are mentioned; but (18.10.5) 'Nevertheless, as the envoys went round the cities and roused them to war with their usual cleverness of speech, most of the Greeks joined the alliance, some on a national basis, some city by city'.

(iv) When Antipatros, who was in charge of affairs in Macedon, heard of the Greek revolt, (18.12.2) 'He set out from Macedon to Thessaly accompanied by the whole naval squadron which Alexander had sent to convoy a quantity of money from the king's treasury to Macedon, being in all 110 threes'.

(v) After a description of the Greek successes against Antipatros on land, there is a brief and condescendingly dismissive summary of the Athenian defeats at sea in the summer of 322, on which the outcome of the Greek challenge to Macedon ultimately turned. 18.15.8–9: 'The fortunes of the Greeks were thus enjoying fair weather. Since the Macedonians had naval superiority, the Athenians fitted out other ships in addition to those they already had (at sea), with the result that the total was 170. Kleitos was in command of the Macedonian fleet which numbered 240. He engaged the Athenian commander and defeated him in two naval battles, and (also) destroyed many of the enemy ships near the islands called Echinades'.

This account raises two matters which need elucidation: the Athenian naval forces mentioned in the decree and involved in the subsequent actions; and the naval actions themselves.

The Athenian Naval Forces 323/2 BC

In the passage (ii) above, line 8, the Greek word *παρασκευάσαι* translated 'procure' has universally been taken to mean 'to prepare for immediate service'. The Athenian Assembly has accordingly, with the text as it stands in the manuscripts, to be represented as ordering the launching (from the shipsheds in which they were kept when not in service) of 240 ships including 200 fours. This rendering leads to two difficulties.

In the first place, it seems impossible that Athens, whom the naval inventories show (*IG* 2^2 1629 805–12) to have had only 50 fours in 325/4 should contemplate launching 200 for immediate service. Wesseling accordingly transposed *τετρήρεις/τριήρεις* in the text of Diodoros and has been followed by subsequent editors (Fischer: 1906, Geer: 1962, Goukowski: 1978) in spite of the fact (recently pointed out by Ashton) that in the naval inventories, which like the decree are offical documents, threes are regularly listed before fours. It is therefore read in all modern texts that the Athenians proposed to launch from their shipsheds '40 fours and 200 threes'.

The second difficulty arises whether or not a transposition is accepted. If the Assembly took the decision to launch 240 ships they must have believed that they were capable of providing in a few months, largely at any rate from their own resources, in addition to the ships at sea, the ships, money, men and gear needed for this substantial force. It could hardly have been expected that the proposed diplomatic moves would produce results in time. Yet when the time came Athens could maintain her fleet at a strength of 170 ships and no more (see (v) above). This outcome is the more surprising if the decision was for *launching* 200 threes and 40 fours, since the inventories show that at the end of 325/4 she had 360 threes and 50 fours, and at the end of 323/2 315 threes and 50 fours, 49 of the latter at sea.

Ashton (1977) argues that 170 is not the overall total for the ships at sea, but 'a campaign total for a specific theatre of the naval war'. This view is hardly to be reconciled with (v) above which gives what is plainly a global statement of the naval position in relation to Macedon: 'In the face of Macedonian naval superiority the Athenians fitted out other ships in addition to those they already had (at sea) with the result that the total was 170. Kleitos was in command of the Macedonian fleet which numbered 240'. There was no other theatre of war for the Athenians, and if they had had any other naval forces at sea they would surely have employed them against Kleitos to reinforce Euetion's sorely outnumbered fleet.

The decree then, which the rhetors, expressing the popular feeling, proposed to the Assembly, must embody some comparatively long-term programme of expanding the number of ships which could be sent to sea by a newly organised Hellenic League, to form which diplomatic moves were being set on foot. The Athenian demos seems to have been persuaded that the death of Alexander offered an opportunity for Athens to rebuild and exercise on behalf of the Greeks a thalassocracy in the eastern Mediterranean such as Themistokles had secured with his 200 *τριήρεις* long ago. Knowledge, after the event, of the defeats of 322 prompts the question, what was the point of proposing measures at that moment which looked beyond the immediate threats by land and sea.

The land threat had in fact been contained when Antipatros was besieged in Lamia, and Leonnatos, who had succeeded in crossing the Hellespont, was defeated; and the prospect by sea may have seemed good enough. The Macedonians had 110 threes supporting Antipatros in the Malian Gulf; and there were 130 (probably for the most part heavier) ships probably in the area of the Hellespont to secure the crossing. The Athenian fleet in the dockyards, after some casualties, numbered 315 threes and 50 fours at the end of the archon year, and at the beginning may have had 392 or more. The number of these which were first-line ships and could be launched, manned and equipped may not have been realised in the heat of the argument, but the naval position could well have given ground for belief that Athens could hold her own at sea in the immediate future while she built up the number, and modernised the type, of her active naval units with the help of her allies. If each of the two Macedonian squadrons could be outnumbered and defeated separately, she had a chance; but it would be a different matter if they were able to join forces.

If, as Hieronymos in Diodoros makes clear, Athens contemplated challenging the Macedonians at sea for the command of the Aegean, but was not, as events showed, in a position to send to sea a fleet of more than 170 active units including about 50 fours, it is not surprising that she should decide to plan the provision and preparation, with the help of her allies, of a substantial fleet in the coming years. In that case the word *παρασκευάσαι* in the decree ((ii) above) must be given what Liddell-Scott-Jones regards as its 'proper meaning', i.e., to provide and prepare *what one has not*. The active verb in naval contexts has this 'proper meaning', which in fact covers two specific activities, acquiring ships by building or contribution from allies and fitting them out for sea. For the latter activity separately the word *κατασκευάζειν* is frequently used (e.g. (v) above) and LSJ gives it the proper meaning of 'to fit out and prepare *what one has*'.

For the composition of the fleet which Athens was then proposing to acquire the choice lies between two alternatives, either that shown in the manuscript tradition which is the one translated in (ii) above, 40 threes and 200 fours, or that given by transposition of Wesseling (1746: and now generally adopted), 40 fours and 200 threes.

The Macedonian ships in the Malian Gulf were threes, fast, probably Macedonian, ships (in view of their mission, to take bullion safely). Unfortunately there is no information about the ships in Kleitos's fleet. It is likely to have contained a good number of the newer sorts, fives and fours. Alexander had both, as has been seen, in his fleets at the siege of Tyre and at Babylon. It seems also that he had plans, frustrated by his death, for building a large fleet of ships larger than threes. Seven years later Antigonos had 90 fours among 113 ships larger than threes. At the battle of Cypriot Salamis in 307 Ptolemy's entire fleet of 140 warships were fives and fours, Demetrios had 57 ships larger than threes on one wing. It looks as if fours at that date, like the more expensive fives, were favoured as the ships of the future.

At Athens in the seven years before 323 there is a marked trend towards fours accompanied by a reduction in the number of threes (JSM: 1987 p. 91–92). The fact that her battle fleet of 322 contained all but one of her force of fours, but only a little more than a third of the threes at her disposal shows the value that was now placed on these warships. It looks as if the lighter but about equally powerful fours[4] were now preferred to the threes. There are two other qualities which may have recommended the four to the Athenians. Double-manned oars were more powerful but only one of each pair of oarsmen needed skill and experience, and a two-level ship was probably cheaper to build than the three-level three and five. The five is likely to have been an expensive ship to build and run. It is remarkable that although there are seven fives in the dockyard in 325/4 (*IG* 2^2 1629 808) there is no mention of them either at sea or in the dockyard in 323/2.

The conclusion reached is that Wesseling's transposition is unnecessary. The Athenian Assembly, emulating in contemporary terms Themistokles's building programme of 200 threes to defeat not this time the threat but the reality of Greek subjection, planned to assemble and prepare a large force of 200 fours, with 40 new threes.

The problem of accommodating such a large number of new ships under cover is not a serious one. Since new building was continuous, there must have been a regular procedure for scrapping the older ships, and making use of them to produce those that were not rated 'fast', the troop- and horse-carriers. They could have been stood in the open (*ὑπαίθριοι* in *IG* 2^2 1611.6 of 357/6) if there was no room for them under cover. In fact the number of shipsheds was always less than the number of ships. Although gear for fours was routinely so designated, there is nothing in the inventories to suggest that they needed special sheds, although there is some evidence of building new shipsheds in this period of naval expansion (see below p. 19).

The Naval Engagements of 322 BC *(Map B)*

The final decisive action of the naval campaign of 322 is generally recognized to have taken place near Amorgos in the Kyklades. It is recorded on the *Marmor Parium* (*FGrH* 239 B 9) as the sole naval battle of the archon year 323/2: 'From the war which broke out between the Athenians and Antipatros for Lamia and from the sea-battle which took place between the Macedonians and the Athenians near Amorgos and in which the Macedonians were victorious, (it is now) 59 years, when Kephisodoros was archon at Athens'.

The battle of Amorgos was clearly the best known, because for the Athenians it was the most decisive, action of the campaign. Plutarch refers to it twice, mentioning Kleitos on one occasion as the Macedonian commander. His evidence, however, gives some, perhaps slight, indication that the de-

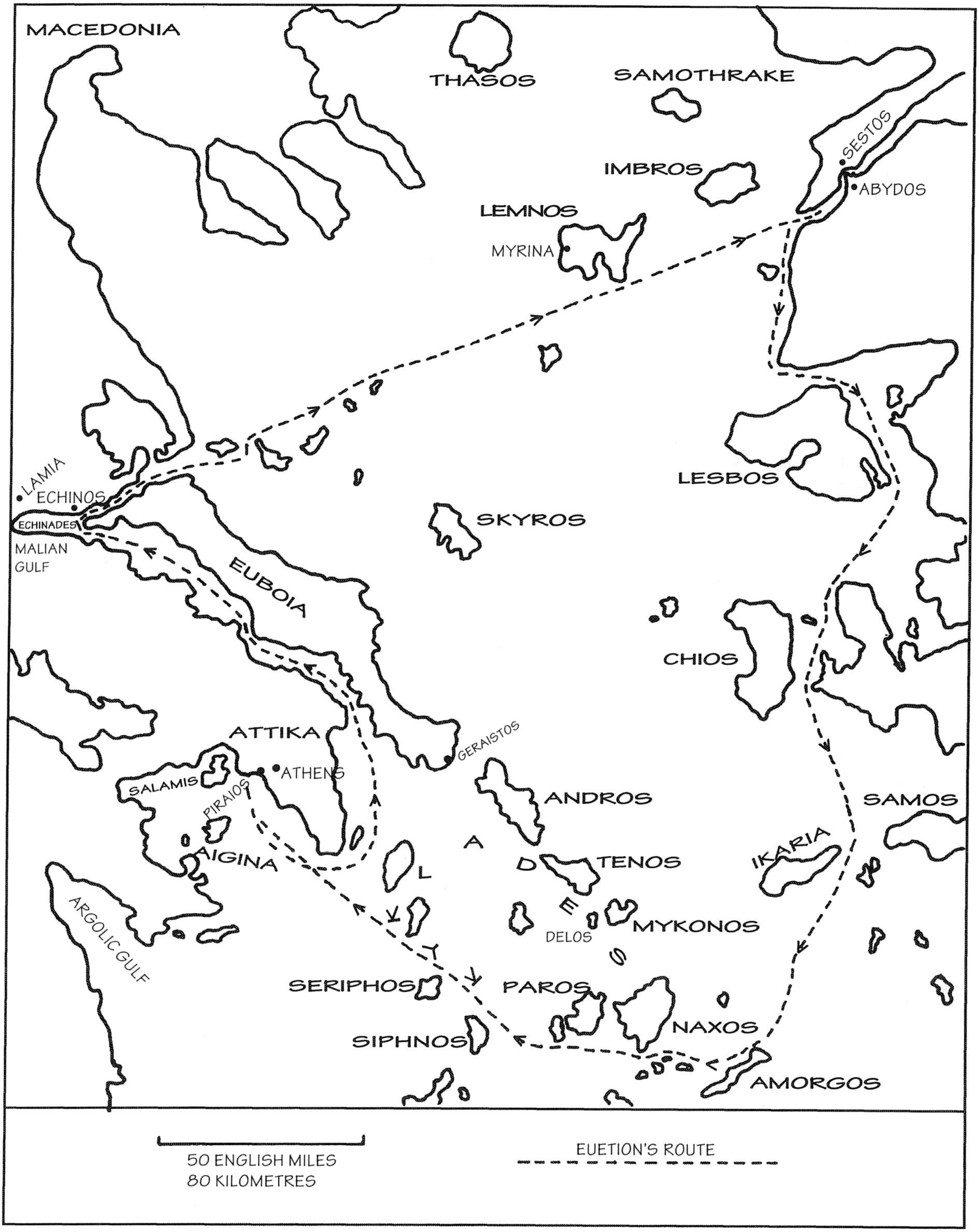

MAP B. *The Aegean Sea*

feat was not a rout and that the Athenian losses were not heavy. At *Demetrios* (11.3) he mentions that the wrecks from the battle were towed back to Peiraieus more than half-way across the Aegean, a distance of over 100 sm. A heavily defeated force usually had to surrender its wrecks to the enemy, for whom they were a mark of victory. In another passage (*Moralia* 338a) Plutarch speaks of Kleitos being hailed as the god Poseidon 'after capsizing (*ἀνατρεψας*) three or four Greek threes at Amorgos'. The battle was nevertheless decisive and it could hardly be other than the last in which Athens fought as an independent city.

Ashton and Goukowski give the evidence, which seems conclusive, that the other battle of the campaign took place at the Hellespont near Abydos. It consists of two inscriptions. The first (*IG* 2^2 398)is a fragment of an Athenian decree dated 320/19 honouring an anonymous person: 'And when the battle in the Hellespont took place he rescued many and after paying their ransoms sent them home, being responsible for their release'. The second (*IG* 2^2 493 19–21) is a fragment of another Athenian decree dated 303/2 in honour of Nikon of Abydos: 'And in the foregoing war he helped to rescue many (Athenian) citizens, gave them money for their journey and sent them back to Athens'.

An obvious strategical objective for Euetion's fleet was the prevention of Macedonian forces crossing the Straits into Europe and coming to raise the siege of Lamia. To this end command of the Hellespont was necessary. First Leonnatos and then Krateros made the crossing. It appears then from these facts taken together with the two inscriptions which imply a (necessarily naval) battle at the Hellespont that Euetion disputed the crossing with Kleitos and was defeated.

The second strategic objective for Euetion was the destruction of the squadron of threes which had accompanied Antipatros's march south; and when Antipatros was besieged in Lamia would naturally then have remained in the Malian Gulf, at the head of which Lamia stands.

The two *ναυμαχίαι* mentioned in Diodoros 18.15.9 (p. 14), that is to say, formal fleet engagements, are the battles at the Hellespont (early in 322) and at Amorgos later in the year. After mentioning these two *ναυμαχίαι* the passage in Diodoros continues: 'And he (Kleitos) destroyed many of the enemy ships in the neighbourhood of the Echinades islands'. It has been debated whether he is speaking of a third engagement, short of a formal *ναυμαχία*, or is adding a comment on one of those he has mentioned. The difficulty is that the only known Echinades islands are off the coast of Akarnania where no engagement relevant to this campaign could ever have taken place. The suggestion that *Ἐχινάδας* is a scribal error for *Σποράδας* and that the reference is accordingly to Amorgos is not philologically attractive. Against it there is also the admittedly slight evidence that Euetion did not lose many ships at Amorgos. More attractive is the possibility of a third engagement favoured by the introduction of the last sentence of the passage with *καὶ* 'and'.

Those who have adopted this interpretation regard *Ἐχινάδας* as an error for *Λιχάδας*, the name of a group of islands off the tip of Euboia, in the Malian Gulf (Map B). It is not necessary to suppose an error, scribal or otherwise, since north and west of the islands in question on the northern coast of the entrance to the Gulf there is a cape named in modern times Ekino and west of it a city Echinos (mod. Ekino) mentioned three times by Strabo (9.5.10, 5.13, 5.22). In ancient times these islands may also have borne the name Echinades, because of their association with, or proximity to, Echinos. If the mainland and Euboia were hostile to the Macedonians as the siege of Lamia attests, these islands would provide a convenient base for the Macedonian threes (as the Sybota islands did for the Corcyraean fleet in similar circumstances: Thuk. 1.50.3).

The most cogent argument for an engagement between Euetion's and Kleitos's fleets at the entrance to the Malian Gulf is the presence there of Antipatros's squadron of 110 threes, fair game for Euetion's more numerous ships at first launching. If Euetion could destroy them before Kleitos could link up with them, he would turn the balance of naval power in his favour. The fact that in Diodoros's text it is Kleitos who is said to have 'destroyed many of the Athenian ships near the Echinades islands 'shows that Euetion tried but did not succeed in achieving this objective. Kleitos got there first, and since there was no formal *ναυμαχία* it seems that Euetion's fleet was attacked, but declined a formal battle escaping with some losses. This then is likely to have been the first contest between the two fleets. Failing to achieve his first objective, Euetion would then have moved to prevent Krateros's army from crossing into Europe. Kleitos followed and defeated him again at the Hellespont, and later in the year for the third time at Amorgos as he made a circuitous return.[5]

There is a third inscription of great interest relating to the campaign as a whole (*IG* 2^2 505). It belongs to an Athenian decree of 302/1 in honour of two Athenian *μέτοικοι* (see Glossary), Nikandros and Polyzelos, who had been enthusiastic supporters of Athenian naval activities in the years before 323/2. After the usual preliminaries it proceeds as follows, before becoming defective and breaking off in a most tantalising manner: 'Since Nikandros son of Antiphanes of Ilion and Polyzelos son of Apollophanes of Ephesos have consistently supported the demos at every turn, and, being resident in Athens, have given assistance in many projects beneficial to the demos both in the building of the shipsheds and the gearstore, paying their contributions each year to the ten talents (Cf. *IG* 2^2 43.68) with admirable enthusiasm from the archonship of Themistokles to the archonship of Kephisodoros (347/6–323/2) and (in particular) at the time of the Greek war, in respect of the fleet setting forth with Euetion, with admirable public spirit shared the responsibility for seeing that it set out to its first (encounter) and when the expedition returned to port from the sea battle (*ναυμαχία*)...' (the case for the supplement (encounter) is put by JSM (1987)).

Like those considered above this decree dates from the years at the end of the 4th century when Athens felt free to honour those who had assisted her in her naval efforts leading up to the battle of Amorgos. It testifies to the expansionist naval policy of those years as shown by the building of the shipsheds and the gear store. It recalls the two metics' good service to Athens in a naval programme, which culminated in their activity in the 'Greek war', that is to say the war conducted by the new Hellenic League against Macedon, both in the dispatch of Euetion's fleet and on its return to port after the sea battle (of Amorgos).

The *ναυμαχία* from which the fleet returned to port must be Amorgos. For the purpose of the decree 20 years after the campaign, Amorgos had become the sea battle *par excellence*, as it had for the *Marmor Parium*. The phrase 'first encounter' (*σύστ)ασιν*) is well chosen if it refers to the skirmish in the Malian Gulf, which was Euetion's first contact with the enemy but was not a formal *ναυμαχία* as the two subsequent engagements were. The arguments for three engagements and for the supplement *(σύστ)ασιν* are independent of each other, but fit neatly together, making the inscription given above contain an informative reference to the whole campaign.

The decision of the Athenian Assembly, as recorded in Diodoros's text, to assemble 40 threes and 200 fours as a battle fleet to win command of the Aegean for the Greeks, fits well both the fashion of the time in naval shipbuilding and the mood of jingoism which the decree as a whole breathes, in spite of the unconcealed cynicism of its reporter Hieronymos. Yet if Athens was to match the hour and achieve the naval supremacy in which lay her only hope of resistance to Macedon, planning had to begin at once. Steps had to be taken before she had, as it were, passed the qualifying test which naval encounters in the spring and summer were to bring. A real change, needing explanation, in the balance of power at sea has been noticed between 323 and 322. The argument here has been that there was no real change, only a sharp contrast between the dream of 323 and the reality of 322. Athens failed the qualifying test.

4. ANTIGONOS I, DEMETRIOS AND PTOLEMY I, AGATHOKLES AND ANTIGONOS II

In the period 318–306 there are four occasions when large fleets of oared warships of different types are recorded and described, principally by Diodoros who is likely to be relying in these passages on his Macedonian source Hieronymos of Kardia. The first occasion is the assembly in 315/4 by Antigonos of a Grand Fleet. The second is the successful attempt by his son Demetrios in 307 to conquer Cyprus and thus complete Antigonos's possession of all the main east Mediterranean sources of shipbuilding material, ships and crews. The third was the invasion of Egypt by Antigonos and Demetrios in 306, and the fourth Demetrios's attack on Rhodes in the following year. The four are interesting in showing the increasing use of the larger types of oared warship, and in one case of the *τριημιολία*, the newer, and more economical, version of the three, and occasionally of their nature and method of employment.

The Fleet of Antigonos

Tarn remarked (1913 p. 72): 'It was the elder Antigonus who showed the firmest grasp of the meaning of sea power and the firmest resolution to win it'. For sea power the possession of Phoenicia, Koile-Syria, Cyprus and the maritime cities of southern Asia Minor, with their resources of timber, shipwrights, ships and skilled naval personnel, were, as Alexander had been aware, essential. In his way stood the royal fleet of Macedon, and Ptolemy to whom Egypt had been allocated and who had taken there the Phoenician contingent of the Macedonian fleet (Diodoros 19.58.2).

Control of the fleet had at first been in the hands of Perdikkas as guardian of the infant 'kings' of Macedon. He used it under the command of Attalos for the invasion of Egypt, where he was murdered by his own army in 321 BC. The fleet then moved to Tyre from where Attalos attacked Rhodes. Antipatros had succeeded Perdikkas as guardian. On his death in 319 his chosen successor Polyperchon at Phokis had the fleet at his disposal. Antipatros's son Kassandros, who rejected the new guardian, gained the naval support of Antigonos in Asia, and with 35 ships was welcomed into Peiraieus and Munychia by the Macedonian governor Nikanor.

To prevent forces reaching Kassandros from Asia the royal fleet under its former commander Kleitos was sent to the Hellespont, and Nikanor followed with the fleet, there joining forces with the rest of Antigonos's fleet making a total of more than 100 vessels. Kleitos defeated Antigonos in the naval battle that followed near Byzantion (318 BC) swamping 17 enemy ships and capturing 40 with their crews.

Antigonos refused to accept defeat: (D.18.72.5) 'At night he sent for auxiliary ships from Byzantion and used them in putting across the strait archers and slingers and an adequate number of light armed units. Before daybreak these attacked the men who had gone ashore from the enemy ships and were bivouacking. They threw Kleitos's men into panic. Soon they were all confused by the alarm and were leaping on board the ships, so that there was a great hubbub because of the surplus baggage and the crowd of prisoners. At this critical moment Antigonos, who had made his warships ready and put on deck many of his staunchest soldiers, sent them out (under Nikanor) with encouragement to attack the enemy with good heart since victory entirely depended on them'.

Nikanor put to sea at night and at first dawn his ships suddenly fell on the enemy still in a state of confusion because of the first attack. They put them to flight and tore some of the ships apart by ramming, brushed off the oars of others without risk, the crews surrendering. In the end, apart from Kleitos's flagship, they captured all the rest. Kleitos escaped to the shore and abandoning his ship tried to get away through Macedon, but fell in with some of Lysimachos's soldiers and was killed.

Meanwhile (319–318), Antigonos's other rival for sea power, Ptolemy, had seized the opportunity to invade Phoenicia and Koile-Syria (D.18.43.1–2): 'a natural springboard for the invasion of Egypt' and estabished garrisons and naval squadrons in the maritime cities.

(D.18.73.1) At this point (318 BC) Diodoros records Antigonos's resolve 'to gain command of the sea and place control of Asia beyond dispute'. However, in the following year, when Athens had come to terms with Kassandros, Nikanor brought the successful fleet back to Peiraieus ornamented with the spoils of victory; and Antigonos was left with no ships at all when Kassandros turned against him.

Antigonos's first step was to take Phoenicia, which in the meantime Eumenes had invaded in the Macedonian interest. (D.19.57.1): 'Antigonos set up shipyards in Tripolis, Byblos and Sidon, and gained the agreement of the Rhodians to make ships for him with imported timber'.

Tyre, still garrisoned by Ptolemy, resisted him; and while he was besieging it from a camp at Old Tyre, Seleukos I, expelled from Syria, and taking refuge with Ptolemy in Egypt, sailed past his camp with 100 ships decorated in royal style and moving at a good pace (D.19.58.5) on his way to Cyprus. The sight discouraged Antigonos's Phoenician allies, but he cheered them up with the promise that in the summer (of 315) he would be in a position to put to sea with 500 ships. At any rate (D.19.61.5) 'sending for the ships from Rhodes and fitting out most of those that had been built, he achieved local command of the sea and pressed on with the siege of Tyre' which surrendered to him in the following year (314). In face of Antigonos's growing power at sea Ptolemy had been able in 315 to send a force of 10,000 men and 100 ships to Cyprus under the command of his brother Menelaos, there joining up with Seleukos's 100 ships. Of this force Ptolemy also had the confidence to detach 50 ships under Polykleitos against Polyperchon in the Peloponnese.

At about this time (315/4), Diodoros says (19.62.7–8), 'there came to Antigonos from the Hellespont 40 ships under the command of Themison; and from the Hellespont and Rhodes his nephew Dioskorides brought in 80 ships'. (As Hauben (1977) p. 336 has shown, the Rhodian ships here were naval ships sent at Antigonos's request under the terms of the alliance). He already had equipped for service the first to be finished of the ships built in Phoenicia. These latter numbered, together with the ships captured at Tyre, 120, so that the sum total of the warships in service with him was 240. Of these 90 were fours, 10 were fives, 3 were nines and 10 were tens, while 30 were aphracts.

Since Diodoros says that all 240 ships were warships (*νῆες μακραί*), and gives the number of aphracts, it follows that the unspecified 97 were all cataphracts. The only type of cataphract which could at this time have reached that number is the three (as the Loeb translator suggests). This conclusion is so obvious that there is no need to suppose a lacuna in the text. Transports which are also unmentioned are again implied. The important feature of the list is the large number of fours in this new model fleet, nearly up to the number of threes, confirming the contemporary trend to fours, reversed later, which was noticed in the fleet Athens planned in 322.

The overall pattern of Demetrios's invasion fleet for Cyprus nine years later not surprisingly is the same as that of Antigonos's Grand Fleet, although different in detail. Two categories of warship are specified and the numbers given: 110 (+) fast threes (at least 78 of which subsequently in the battle line must have been cataphract) and 53 *στρατιώτιδες* heavier than the threes (p. 257). Transports *(πόρια)* are there mentioned.

The fleet which Antigonos assembled to assert his claim to power at sea greater than his rivals', after the detachment of 50 ships to the Peloponnese, presumably to balance the 50 ships Ptolemy had dispatched under Polykleitos to that area, was sent under Dioskorides on a cruise in the eastern Mediterranean to show the flag. Ptolemy's Peloponnesian squadron found nothing to do in Greece and returned to Asia. There Polykleitos intercepted Antigonos's commander Theodotos with the Rhodian ships off Kilikia, defeated him and captured the ships. He then returned to Egypt via Cyprus. Antigonos's Peloponnesian squadron of 50 ships reappears later under the command of Telesphoros. He defected later and was defeated by Antigonos's nephew Ptolomaios, who sold the ships (D.19.87.1).

Antigonos and Ptolemy's Naval Preparations
(Will: 1984 p. 53)

In the following eight years mainland Greece, Cyprus, Kilikia, Syria and Phoenicia were the scenes of naval movements by Ptolemy and Antigonos's son Demetrios, competing with each other as liberators of the Greeks from Macedon in the person of Antipatros's son Kassandros. In 314 Medios in command of a fleet of 150 ships based in Phoenicia was summoned by Antigonos to the south coast of Asia (D.19.69.3) where he fell in with 36 ships from Pydna (Macedon) and captured them with their crews. Medios was needed for Antigonos's campaign in the following year against Asandros the ruler of Karia, who had transferred his allegiance to Ptolemy and Seleukos (D.19.75.1–4). Miletos, Iasos and Kaunos, all important maritime cities, were captured by him.

In the same year Antigonos sent Medios's fleet across the Aegean to Euboia (D.19.75.6–7) 'to set the Greeks free' under a treaty of alliance with the Rhodians; and received 10 ships from them for the purpose. After Demetrios's defeat at Gaza in 312 Phoenicia was temporarily lost to Antigonos but regained on Ptolemy's return to Egypt. Two years later he lost some cities in Kilikia to Ptolemy, but shortly afterwards Demetrios regained them. In 309 Ptolemy made a concerted effort, invaded the south Asian coast taking Phaselis and Xanthos in Lykia and Kaunos in Karia, before moving his fleet the following year from Myndos across the Aegean, liberating Andros and taking Corinth and Sikyon. There he proclaimed his intention of 'freeing the Greek cities from Kassandros's garrisons'; but receiving little support in the Peloponnese he made peace with Kassandros (308) and withdrew to Egypt.

Antigonos now saw his opportunity. The fleet under Demetrios first relieved Halikarnassos which was under siege by Seleukos. Then (D.20.45.1) 'receiving from his father strong forces on land and sea', also an appropriate supply of missiles and other equipment suitable for carrying on a siege, Demetrios put out from Ephesos. He had orders to free all the cities throughout Greece, but first of all Athens which was held by a garrison of Kassandros. His fleet of 250 ships (Plutarch *Demetrios* 8.3) moved into Peiraieus unchallenged. He occupied Peiraieus, allowing Kassandros's governor to withdraw, and then Munychia. On the establishment of friendship and alliance with the Athenians (June 307) Antigonos gave them a supply of grain and timber for 100 ships, betraying by his last donation his interest in Athens as a source of the skilled manpower and shipbuilding potential he needed to support his naval programme. These measures, which he had adopted before with Rhodes, indicate a policy which the Persian kings had used earlier towards the maritime cities of Asia and Phoenicia for the development of naval power.

The Invasion of Cyprus: 306 BC (Map C)

Antigonos considered that his fleet was now sufficiently seasoned and his resources adequate for a major confrontation with Ptolemy, a challenge for possession of the island from which first Seleukos as Ptolemy's ally, then Ptolemy's brother Menelaos, and finally Ptolemy himself had sent naval forces against the mainland of Asia and from there to Greece. (D.20.46.5) He 'ordered Demetrios to proceed to Cyprus (from Athens) and finish the war with Ptolemy's generals as soon as he could'.

Demetrios's first move was to Karia, which earlier had supplied him with crews for the ships built for him at Rhodes. He again called on the Rhodians to send him ships, but they refused 'preferring to keep a common peace with all'. Moving from Karia by sea to Kilikia (D.20.47.1) he added ships and *στρατιῶται* (a word used of crewmen as well as soldiers) to his force, and made the crossing to Cyprus with 15,000 footsoldiers, 400 cavalry and a fleet composed of 'more than 110 fast threes, 53 of the heavier *στρατιώτιδες* and sufficient *πόρια*[6] for the great number (*πλῆθος*) of cavalry and footsoldiers (i.e excluding the regular decksoldiers of the threes and *στρατιώτιδες*). These *στρατιώτιδες*, i.e. warships of higher denomination than three, are distinguished from the lighter *στρατιώτιδες* which are threes, in Xenophon's words (*HG* 1.1.36) 'troopcarriers rather than fast'.

It is reasonable to suppose that his coasting journey from a landfall in Karia (? Myndos) to his unspecified port of departure in Kilikia was for the purpose of retaking the cities which had fallen into Ptolemy's hands in 309, Myndos and Kaunos and any others such as Miletos and Iasos which may have been lost in Karia, in Lykia Phaselis and Xanthos, and others in Kilikia, where Antigonos had first set up a shipyard for the construction of his Grand Fleet. All these must be numbered among the 'captured cities' from which he drew an important part of the men and units of his fleet.

The landfall of the invasion fleet was near the north-eastern tip of the island, where he 'constructed a camp and hauled his ships ashore'. The purpose of 'hauling ships ashore' (p. 355) is maintenance, often but not always carried out in winter, but the prospect of battle would have made it necessary to bring the warships up to peak performance after their voyage across the Aegean. The neighbouring cities of Ourania and Karpasia (which had a harbour: Strabo 14.6.3) were taken by storm; then, leaving a force to guard the ships, he moved across the island to Salamis 'where Ptolemy's brother was biding his time after drawing in his outposts'. In the ensuing land engagement Menelaos was defeated and both sides prepared for a siege, Demetrios constructing an elaborate siege-engine which Menelaos succeeded in setting on fire.

Ptolemy's Reply

Ptolemy took up Antigonos's challenge (D.20.49.1), and set out in person from Egypt with a considerable army and fleet. He landed at Paphos where he incorporated the ships of the Cypriot cities in his fleet and coasted along to Kition, modern Larnaka[7], 200 stades, Diodoros says, from Salamis. If a stade of 185 m is taken, the distance is 37 km, close to that by land (35 km) between the two cities. The distance by sea, round a promontory, is much greater.

'Ptolemy's total number of warships was 140, and of these the largest was a five and the smallest a four. Following these were more than 200

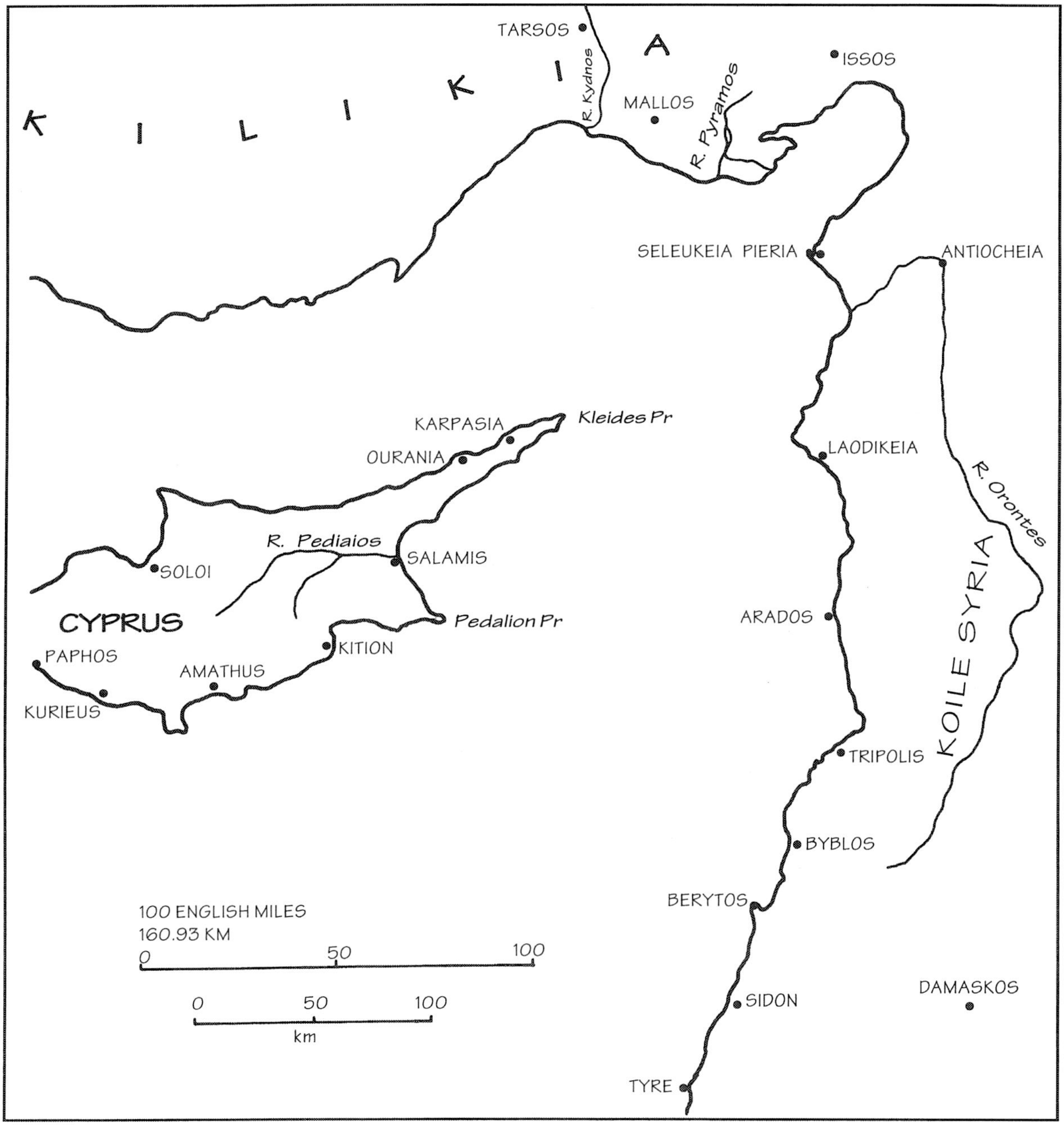

MAP C. *Cyprus, Kilikia, Phoenicia*

στρατιωτικὰ πόρια carrying not less than 10,000 soldiers' (50 soldiers in each). The sentence 'the largest was a five and the smallest a four' is rightly taken to mean that all Ptolemy's warships were either fours or fives[8]. It also has the interesting implication that the fours and the fives were built in different sizes. Such a difference within each type could only consist, since they must have all been cataphract, in the numbers in the fore-and-aft oar-files, so that some ships in each type were longer than others. There is no evidence of such a difference in the case of the three, but that is not to say that it did not exist.

Ptolemy's *στρατιωτικὰ πόρια* carried only 50 soldiers each, compared with the 150 soldiers (p. 123) in each of Julius Caesar's *onerariae* in the invasion of Britain and the slightly larger number of soldiers probable in the *πόρια* of Demetrios's invasion fleet. This needs some explanation. The clue lies in the description of Ptolemy's *πόρια* as 'following' (*ἐπηκολούθει*) the warships. To keep up with a column of warships the *πόρια* must have been oared, probably *κέρκουροι* (*SSAW* 163–166) oared cargo vessels common in Egypt, whereas Julius Caesar's troop-carrying *onerariae* relied on sail, and Demetrios's *πόρια* in the crossing from Kilikia to Cyprus would have been escorted by threes to take them under tow if the wind was not favourable (cf. p. 267). It is important at the outset to realise that Ptolemy's fleet, unlike Demetrios's but like Julius Caesar's, was an expeditionary force hoping at this stage to avoid a battle but having no certainty that he would. It was thus encumbered with non-fighting oared auxiliaries and therefore, although as a precaution cleared for action, not seeking battle if it could reach port first.

That all Ptolemy's fighting vessels were either fives or fours is an indication of how far the supersession of the three as a first line unit had gone by this date among the Phoenician cities from which a good number of his ships must have been drawn, and among the Cypriot cities from which he had just acquired more. Fours and fives have been noticed earlier in Phoenician and Cypriot fleets. It is interesting also that the cautious Ptolemy, unlike the Phoenicians and Cypriots and later the Carthaginians and the Romans, but quite unlike the later Ptolemies, did not share the Macedonian passion for ships larger than fives.

From Kition Ptolemy sent messengers to his brother Menelaos in Salamis asking him to send the 60 ships under his command, if possible, as speedily as he could. These 60 ships were the remainder of the 200 ships sent to Cyprus under Menelaos in 315, after the withdrawal of Seleukos's 100 and the dispatch of forty ships from Cyprus to the Peloponnese which had returned to Egypt. 'The fact was that Ptolemy expected that he would gain an easy victory at sea if he could add those to his fleet and enter the contest with 200 ships'. Since there is some difficulty in establishing the number of warships at Demetrios's disposal in the ensuing battle, it is to be noted that 200 ships, still only fives and fours, were regarded by Ptolemy as constituting clear naval superiority over his enemy.

Preliminaries to the Battle

When Demetrios's ships had been last mentioned they were hauled up and under guard at his base camp at Carpasia with its harbour on the north-facing shore of the island. At some point he must have hauled them down and launched them before bringing them round the Kleides promontory to his forward camp on the north side of Salamis. When Ptolemy's approach from Kition was expected early on the following day.

Demetrios guessed what was in Ptolemy's mind (D.20.49.4). Leaving part of his land force to press on with the siege, 'he manned all his ships with oarsmen and embarked the most effective of his soldiers. He put on board also missiles and stonethrowers, and set up catapults in the prows able to throw penetrating missiles of three spans (*ὀξυβελὴ τρισπίθαμα* i.e. 3 spith.= 1½ cubits @ .490 m = .735 m). After fitting out his fleet for battle without regard for expense he moved round the city (to the coast on the southeast side, between the city and the Pedalion promontory) and spent the night at anchor at the mouth of the harbour just out of catapult range', thus with one move preventing the ships from the city joining forces with the rest of Ptolemy's fleet, and at the same time keeping a look-out for the enemy's approach and standing ready for battle.

Fleets never spent the night at anchor if it could possibly be helped. But on this occasion the need was imperative if Ptolemy was to be prevented from entering the harbour by night or in the early morning and joining Menelaos, or Menelaos from coming out and joining Ptolemy.

'As Ptolemy moved towards Salamis with the auxiliary vessels (*ὑπηρετικὰ πλοῖα* = (presumably) *στρατιωτικὰ πόρια*) following at a distance, the fleet was a formidable sight to see by reason of its numbers (140 warships and 200 (+) auxiliaries)' (Plan 2, p. 28). Two points are to be made: the first has been mentioned: this is a fleet in transit, otherwise the auxiliaries would have been left behind at Kition. Ptolemy was gambling on the chance of Menelaos being able to give him superiority in numbers of warships by breaking out. In the second place if the oarcrews were at the end of a voyage of over 43.7 sm from Kition undertaken by night (20.50.5), the crew would have been in need of food and rest before going into action. It is possible that the Egyptian fleet bivouacked at a beach between Kition and Salamis, e.g. modern Famagusta which Strabo calls Arsinoe and is otherwise known as Ammochostos less than 25 km, 13.5 sm from Salamis. If so it is strange that no authority mentions such an important factor. After the battle Ptolemy put back to Kition (p. 30).

When Demetrios became aware of Ptolemy's approach, he left Antisthenes with ten fives (*δέκα τῶν πεντηρικῶν*) to prevent the ships coming out of the harbour to join in the battle, the exit from the harbour being narrow, and gave orders for his cavalry to patrol the beach, so that they would be able to give protection to men swimming ashore in the event of a ship being swamped. Demetrios himself went to meet the enemy with his ships deployed in line of battle. He had in all eight more than a hundred ships with (*σύν*) those that had been manned from the places he had captured. Of these (*τούτων*) the largest were sevens and the most numerous fives. The 108 are presumably the 110 (+) fast threes (of the invasion fleet) less two or more; and the latter the heavier *στρατιώτιδες* (of the invasion fleet) with some additions[9].

During the night all Demetrios's ships lay at anchor off the mouth of the harbour just out of catapult range. At daybreak his first moves were to detach ten of his fives to prevent Menelaos's sixty ships coming out, and to detail his 400 cavalry to patrol the beach and carry out the salvage-and-rescue duty normally performed by supporting land forces, where such were available, in a sea battle. With the rest of his warships he moved out into the path of Ptolemy's approaching fleet to join what has been described (Tarn: 1913 p. 81) as 'one of the decisive battles of antiquity'.

This description of Demetrios's fleet contains what are at this stage two apparent linked ambiguities. In the last sentence 'of these' (*τούτων*) could refer either to the whole fleet or to 'the ships that had been manned from the places that had been captured'. However, the former alternative must be ruled out since Demetrios is said to have brought over from Kilikia 110 (+) fast threes; and it is impossible that the fives should now be the most numerous (more than 110+) in a fleet which Ptolemy reckoned would be numerically inferior to his own if he could bring his own up to the strength of 200 (with Menelaos's ships). The second ambiguity lies in the words of the penultimate sentence: 'eight more than a hundred with (*σύν*) those that had been manned from the places he had captured'. The preposition *σύν* could mean either including or excluding (as at D.20.82.4). But if the 53 'heavier *στρατιώτιδες*' are rightly to be identified as warships of higher denomination than three, together with the 110+ fast threes of which the rest of his fleet was at that time made up, he can hardly have had only 108 ships at his disposal for the battle[10]. The meaning of these last two sentences must then be as follows (with the ambiguities resolved): 'Demetrios's whole fleet consisted of 108 ships and *in addition* (an unspecified number of) those ships which he had manned from the captured places. *Of these latter* the largest were sevens built in Phoenicia and manned (as Antigonos's Rhodian ships had been) as likely as not in Karia, and the most numerous fives. This conclusion underlines the importance, in naval terms, of the 'captured places' (D.20.47.1).

The description of the battle line then follows (D.20.50.3): The left (seaward) wing was held by seven Phoenician sevens and 30 Athenian fours with Medios in command. In support of these Demetrios placed ten sixes and an equal number of fives, having taken the decision to make that wing strong on which he himself intended to fight; in the centre of the line he placed 'the smallest ships' (*τα ἐλάχιστα*: possibly 'the fewest') under the command of Themison of Samos and Marsyas 'who wrote the history of Macedon'. The right (shoreward) wing was held by Hegesippos of Halikarnassos and Pleistias of Kos, who was the chief helmsman of the fleet.[11]

As far as the 57 ships on the left wing are concerned the account is specific and detailed, but thereafter it is less so as regards numbers and types. If however *τὰ ἐλάχιστα* means the smallest ships all the ships in the centre were threes. It may be inferred that the right wing would have roughly balanced the left in numbers if not in weight (cf. the Athenian battle order at Arginousai: Xenophon *HG* 1.6.29: *AT* p. 91).

For the overall number of warships in the line Demetrios's invasion fleet provides a starting point: 163 ships, 110 + fast threes and 53 *στρατιώτιδες* of the heavier sort. Since in the battle Demetrios had 57 of the ships larger than threes on the left wing and ten fives in the harbour guard it appears that the number of heavier ships has been increased by at least 14, so that if all the threes were put into the line the overall number would be 175. Plutarch (*Demetrios* 16.2) gives a total of 180 excluding, and Polyainos (4.7.7) a total of 170 including the 10 ships of the harbour guard. Following the line of argument so far the distribution could be:

Harbour Guard	*Left wing*	*Centre*	*Right Wing*
Antisthenes	Medios	Themison Marsyas	Hegesippos Pleistias
10 Fives	7 Sevens 30 Fours -- 10 Sixes 10 Fives	(50 Threes)	(58 Threes)

Comparison of this hypothetical arrangement of the 175 ships with the description of the battle fleet (excluding the Harbour Guard) which went into action as '108 ships together with the ships manned from the captured cities, of which the largest were sevens and the most numerous fives' leads to some necessary modifications. At first sight the comparison suggests that the category of the heavier *στρατιώτιδες* is coextensive with 'the ships manned from the captured cities'. But if the fives in the battle line are to be the most numerous of the heavier ships they must be more numerous than the 30 Athenian fours, say 33–35 in number. The only position for the additional 23–25 fives is on the right wing since they cannot belong to the smallest (or fewest) at the centre, and in any case some of the heavier ships would surely be on the right wing to give balance in face of Ptolemy's ubiquitous fours and fives in the new style of fighting at sea.

There is an upper limit to the overall number of ships in Demetrios's battle fleet, since it must be such that Ptolemy would think that he would have an easy victory if he could confront it with a fleet of 200 ships, if Menelaos's 60 ships could join him. Plutarch's total of 180 Macedonian ships is a maximum, and a lower number is perhaps more likely. Polyainos gives 160 for the battle fleet. If then 23–25 additional fives are to be added to it, the number of threes to be put into the battle line must be correspondingly reduced. The detailed account of the ships placed on Demetrios's left wing has already required the addition of 14 heavier ships to the number of them (53) reported in the invasion fleet. Now a further 23–25 fives must be added. In view of Demetrios's well-attested reliance on the heavier ships it is not surprising to find that he appears to have increased the weight of the fleet after arrival at Cyprus, standing down some of his threes whose most useful task was the escort and probably towing of troop-carrying *πόρια* at the crossing from the mainland. Either he obtained these additional fives with the extra margin of oarsmen from 'the captured places' on the island or they were later arrivals from 'captured places' on the mainland.

It is however difficult to believe that Demetrios would have left 32 of the fast threes out of the battle if they were available and were suitable. it is possible that after manning the bigger ships he had not the crews for the threes. Alternatively he may have left out of the battle fleet those threes that were aphract. In Antigonos's Grand Fleet there were 97 cataphract threes and 30 aphract warships some at least of which were probably threes. If the 32 or so threes Demetrios left out of his battle line were aphract, that would not have reduced their value as escort for towing the *πόρια;* it might have increased it. But it would have been good reason for their absence from a battle line facing fours and fives, all cataphract.

On the assumption then that the total of Demetrios's ships engaged was 170–172 it may be described either in the way used for the invasion fleet as 80 fast threes and 90–92 heavier ships, or in the way used for the battle line total as 52–54 'manned from the captured places' and 108 otherwise manned, with the ten fives of the Harbour Guard belonging to the latter category. These two modes of description, by type and by crew source, are perfectly compatible.

The conclusions are as follows (hypothetical figures in brackets):

1. Demetrios's Line of Battle (160 ships)

Left: 57 ships	Centre (46)	Right (57)
Cdr. Medios	Cdrs Themison Marsyas	Cdrs Hegesippos Pleistias
7 Phoenician Sevens	(46 Threes)	(25 Fives)
30 Athenian Fours	Both fewest and smallest	(32 Threes)
10 Sixes		
10 Fives		

2. The Harbour Guard: 10 fives

If these figures may be taken as a basis for assessment of Demetrios's naval building policy, a comparison may be drawn in terms of percentages of threes, fours and fives-tens between Antigonos's fleet nine years earlier and Demetrios's battle fleet at Salamis in 306 BC:

	Threes	Fours	Fives-tens
Antigonos	46%	43%	11%
Demetrios	45.8%	17.6%	36.4%

Whereas the percentage of threes has diminished very slightly, there is a 25% increase in fives-tens and a similar decrease in fours. The reason emerges in the accounts of the battle.

It has been argued that Ptolemy, who was a cautious man, would not have risked battle against a numerically superior fleet, 140 ships against 170. But Diodoros says that he reckoned on joining forces with Menelaos's sixty ships and that then with 200 ships against 170 he would have had an easy supremacy. Demetrios plainly caused Ptolemy's plan to miscarry by lying in wait for him in transit before he could bring his ships into harbour, and then, with his crews refreshed and the ships cleared for action, as well as substantially reinforced, come out to do battle. (D.20.50.5) 'At first, while it was still night, Ptolemy made for Salamis in haste, thinking to enter the harbour before the enemy could stop him; but as day broke, the enemy's fleet was in sight not far off in battle order'.

Demetrios clearly achieved surprise by deploying his ships during the night, at anchor off Salamis. He was thus able to fight the inevitable battle at sea on terms favourable to himself. He had numerical superiority so long as Menelaos's ships could be kept shut up in Salamis harbour; his ships were cleared for action fighting a fleet in transit; and his men, although they might have spent an uncomfortable night, were not as Ptolemy's men were, tired after hours at the oar. The hasty passage from Kition suggests that they did not stop on the way. By detaching only 10 fives to keep Menelaos's 60 ships (fours or fives) from coming out and taking a decisive part in the battle Demetrios was taking a calculated risk, but the 10 fives were able to hold them off long enough, and Ptolemy's ships were in flight before Menelaos eventually managed to break out (Polyainos and Plutarch).

The Battle of Cypriot Salamis (Plan 2)

When the morning light revealed Demetrios's line blocking his path to the harbour, Ptolemy had no option but to fight. Diodoros's account of the engagement follows:

(20.50.5) 'Ptolemy himself made preparations for the battle. Ordering the *πόρια* to follow at a distance, he placed the rest of the ships in an appropriate formation. He occupied the left (shoreward) wing, with the largest ships providing him support... When Demetrios was about three stades (533 m: about 13 ship's lengths) distant from the enemy, he raised the agreed signal for battle, a gilded shield. The signal was seen by all as it was relayed from ship to ship. Ptolemy's men doing the same, the distance between the fleets rapidly narrowed.

(20.51.2) When the trumpets gave the signal for close engagement and both sides raised the paean, all the ships moved to ram each other in a terrifying manner. First men using bows and stone-throwers and others with a shower of javelins struck down their victims. Then as the ships came close together and the impact of the ram was imminent, those on the deck sat down as one man, while the oarsmen urged on by the *κελευσταί* bent more intently on the task. Driven with power and force some of the ships swept away each other's oars, so as to become useless for flight or pursuit, and so that the men on deck eager to fight were prevented

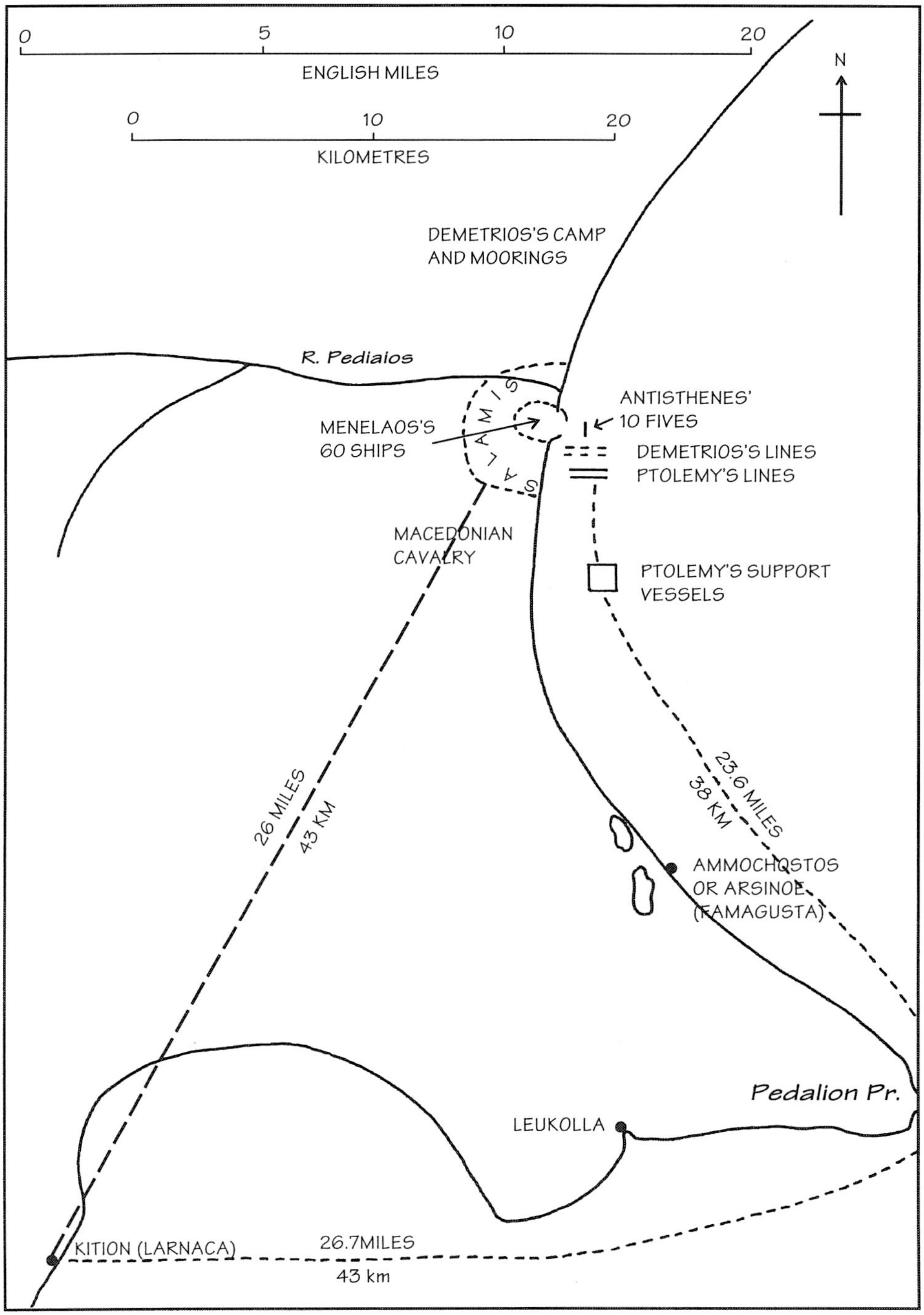

PLAN 2. *The Battle of Cypriot Salamis*

Note: This rough plan is based for distances on the Admiralty Chart (1:100,000). The site of Salamis Harbour and town is chosen at the mouth of the R. Pediaos, now dammed 7 km inland. By the Admiralty Chart the distance between Kition and Salamis (as here shown) is about 43 km, 26 miles as the crow flies, 81 km, 50 miles, 43.5 sm by sea.

from taking part in the battle. Other ships, smashing into each other with their rams prow to prow, tried to back off for another impact, and those on their decks struck each other down since each had a target at close range.

Some of the trierarchs scored a sideways hit, and the rams becoming hard to disengage, the men leapt on to enemy ships, receiving and giving many terrible wounds. Some, indeed, taking hold of the ships' sides as they approached and missing their footing, fell into the sea and were immediately dispatched by the men on deck with their hand missiles; others achieving their goal, killed some of their opponents, and driving others into the narrow part of the deck hurled them into the sea. In general the fighting was varied and surprising in its outcome. It often happened that the weaker were successful because of their ships' higher decks, while the stronger fighters were hard pressed because of their lower stance, and the unfairness of the outcome of such fighting. In combats on land courage is evident and succeeds in getting the upper hand, if no fortuitous circumstance intervenes. But in sea battles it turns out that those who by their valour justly deserve victory are unexpectedly defeated by many circumstances of various kinds which affect the outcome'.

The account of the engagement is unusually detailed. Demetrios's line was probably composed of 82 heavy ships (35–33 fives, 30 fours, seven sevens and ten sixes) and 78 threes. Ptolemy's fleet had only fives and fours in unspecified numbers but probably more fours than fives. Compared with other earlier and later detailed descriptions of naval battle that survive, this is notable for the absence of any suggestion of concerted attempts to effect an outflanking movement (*περίπλους*) or breakthrough (*διέκπλους*). The reason may be the predominance of the heavier *στρατιώτιδες* and the consequent (though temporary) return to what Thukydides (1.49.1) called 'the old-fashioned way of fighting at sea'. Instead the fleets moved towards each other apparently in line abreast with support astern, and maintained that formation.

When the lines met three kinds of ship-to-ship encounter are described:

i. Ships sweeping away each other's oars

Such a clash can hardly have been deliberate, since the damage inflicted is expressly said to be equally fatal to both sides. If deliberate, for the purpose of breaking through the line, the ship initiating it would have pulled in her oars and relied on momentum to carry her through. There is no mention of that.

ii. Ramming bow to bow

In earlier times this tactic was avoided if possible, or only adopted after special strengthening of the *ἐπωτίδες*. Here it may be a deliberate, but not very skilful, move of a heavier ship to damage a lighter one and get away. It provided, if disengagement was effected, a brief opportunity for exchange of missiles, otherwise, if it was not, an opportunity for boarding.

iii. Ramming a ship abeam or in the quarter

This manoeuvre is described as resulting, apparently normally and hence purposely, in the ramming ship becoming stuck fast into the ship rammed, which the decksoldiers accordingly board and clear.

Here the interesting observation is made about the difference in deck height between some ships and others, and the difficulties thus created which give an unfair advantage to weaker fighters at a higher level (at this date there is no mention of towers). All the ships involved are cataphract i.e. decked, and either threes, fours, fives, sixes or sevens. There is good evidence in Livy (p. 68: 30.25.2–9) that fours were significantly lower than fives, decksoldiers from fours being unable to leap aboard a five. Threes, fives, sixes and sevens all have three levels of oars (p. 269–272) with double, and in the case of the seven with triple manning of some oars (p. 272). Double and triple manning of oars would incur some but no significant additional height, so that it is reasonable to conclude that the significant difference in height between the sides in this battle was caused by the fours, of which Ptolemy had at least 70, probably a good many more, while Demetrios had only 30.

The complaint has been recognised (by Seibert) as the excuse put forward by an apologist in Ptolemy's camp for the Egyptian defeat. The factor was however something which affected the 30 Athenian fours on Demetrios's side as much as the more numerous fours on Ptolemy's. The point is as likely to be made by Hieronymos of Kardia as an impartial observer of an important aspect of the development of the new types. It is certainly the case that after the battle fours lost the first line status attested by their place in the Athenian naval programme before Amorgos, in Antigonos's Grand Fleet and lastly in Ptolemy's fleet at Salamis. The most remarkable aspect of the account is the prevalence of the Macedonian attitude and tactic, the emphasis on fighting either hand to hand on deck or with missiles of various kinds from deck as the decisive factors in a battle at sea, rather than on manoeuvre of ships and the use of the ram. Had Rhodian ships been present tactics might have been different.

Diodoros's narrative now turns to details of the battle (20.52.1). Standing in the stern of his seven, Demetrios fought with javelins and spears. His left wing routed Ptolemy's right wing as well as the ships of the adjoining centre. On the other wing Ptolemy with the largest of his ships, that is to say the fives, and the most powerful of his fighting men easily routed his opponents and swamped some ships while capturing others with their crews. But when he saw the defeat of his right wing and of part of the centre, he put back to Kition. Here again there is no hint of any tactical movements. Emphasis is not laid on speed or manoeuvre of ships but on their size and the power of the fighting men on deck.

'When the fighting was over Demetrios sent *τὰ στρατιωτικὰ τῶν πλοίων* with orders to go after Ptolemy and pick up any men swimming in the sea'. The ships sent were probably oared auxiliaries, which had not taken any part in the battle. He himself decorated his warships with enemy *ἀκροστόλια* (the fore and aft ornamental finials of a warship, and towed the captured ships to his own harbour (i.e the moorings north of Salamis). Diodoros adds that Menelaos's 60 ships did succeed in breaking out, forcing the harbour guard to the camp; but they arrived at the scene of action too late to affect the result.

As to losses, Diodoros says that more than 100 of Ptolemy's *πόρια* were captured, containing nearly 8000 soldiers (@80 each). 'Of the warships 40 were captured with their crews and about 80 were 'disabled' (*διεφθάρησαν*), which their captors brought to land full of water at the camp near (north of) the city. 20 of Demetrios's ships were 'disabled', but when they had received the necessary repairs all were able to return to service'.

The passage illustrates the meaning given to the words used in the description of sea battles in Diodoros. Ships which surrender with their crews are largely undamaged. Those which are 'disabled' are those put out of action by swamping after their hulls are breached by the ram. They can be towed away by the victor and may be repaired and sent back into service. This practice is attested earlier, the word 'sink' (*καταδύειν* in Thukydides and Xenophon being often used instead of 'disable' (*διαφθείρειν*). Both words if literally translated present a wrong picture to the reader. The fact that about 80 of Ptolemy's fives and fours were swamped by ramming suggests that such action probably by Demetrios's fast threes, unmentioned in Diodoros's description, played a not negligible part in the victory. It may have taken place in the pursuit, after the main battle.

Diodoros concludes: (20.53) Ptolemy surrendered Cyprus, Demetrios taking over all the cities and their garrisons. He quickly put on board his largest ship (probably the seven in which he fought) messengers to take news of his victory to Antigonos. It is typical of him that he should take the largest, which certainly would not have been the fastest, ship for the purpose. The conquest of Cyprus and its supplies of long timber enabled Demetrios to carry to extremes in the coming years his obsession with the building of ever larger oared warships (Plutarch *Demetrios* 20.1).

The Invasion of Egypt: 304–3 BC

The immediate result of the defeat of Ptolemy at Salamis and Demetrios's conquest of the island was the decision of Antigonos to invade Egypt by land accompanied at sea by a great fleet under Demetrios. The land force, assembled at Antigoneia in Bithynia, accordingly moved south through Syria to Gaza. It was made up of 80,000 footsoldiers, 8,000 horse and 83 elephants. The fleet consisted of 150 warships and 100 transports (*πόρια στρατιωτικά*) carrying (this time not soldiers but) a great number of missiles. At the outset the warships are not specified by type.

Antigonos's land army moved, with some difficulty, south through the desert to Pelousion, taking provisions for ten days and further supplies of grain and fodder loaded on camels. (D.20.73.3) 'Carrying his missiles on carts he went forward through the desert with difficulty since much of the region was marshy, particularly near the area called Barathra'. The distance is about 140 miles

(225 km). Since the coast between Gaza and Pelousion has no sheltered harbours or safe beaches, the army and the fleet made their way independently.

(D.20.74.1) 'Demetrios's force, setting out from Gaza about midnight, at first, since there had been calm weather for several days, put the transports under tow by the fast ships (*αἱ ταχυναυτοῦσαι νῆες*, i.e. threes. It is interesting to observe that all threes are here characterised as fast sailing in contrast to the fours and fives. Then 'when the Pleiad overtook them and a north wind set in, it came about that many of the fours were driven dangerously by the storm to make a landfall at Raphia, a city with difficult mooring facilities and beset by reefs. Of the ships' (under tow to the threes) 'carrying missiles some were swamped by the storm and lost (*συγκλυσθέντα διεφθάρη*) others returned to Gaza. The most powerful ships forced their way along the coast to Kasion, which is not far' (about 56 km or 30 sm) 'from the Nile, but is without a harbour and has no facility for beaching in stormy weather'.

'The ships were accordingly obliged to drop anchor and ride out the storm about 2 stades (255 m) from the land in a very perilous situation, since the seas were breaking violently and the ships were in danger of foundering with their crews. Since the land offered no beaching and was enemy territory, neither could the ships get inshore without danger nor could the men swim ashore. But the greatest danger lay in the fact that they had run out of drinking water and were reduced to such straits that if the storm had continued a single day more they would all have perished of thirst. But when morale was at its lowest and the men were facing death, the wind died down, and Antigonos's army made contact with them and pitched camp near the shore, so the crews were able to leave the ships and recuperate in camp, waiting for the ships that had been separated from them to come up. In this rough water three of the fives were flooded, but some of the men from them succeeded in swimming ashore. Then Antigonos took his army forward to the vicinity of the Nile and made camp two stades (255 m) from the river'.

This extraordinarily vivid narrative gives a clear picture of the difficulties attending the movement of a fleet of warships accompanied by supply transports in tow under a combination of difficult geographical and bad weather conditions.

Only 'the strongest of the ships' reached Kasion first and three of them, named as fives were swamped[12] there. It seems that Demetrios left his sixes and sevens behind. Seeing that a second naval confrontation with the Ptolemaic fleet of fives and fours was hardly to be expected, and possibly for other reasons to do with seaworthiness and manageability, they were not needed. The five had a reputation for strength as well as weight (p. 271, 64–65). Those used by the Romans 50 years later for the invasion of Libya are said by Polybios (1.26.7) to have had 300 oarsmen and to carry 120 men on deck. Some at this date may have had fewer oarsmen in the fore-and-aft files, but would still be 'the strongest'. All the fives then and those alone reached Kasion. 'Many of the fours' got as far as Raphia in the storm. Presumably the remaining fours did not get as far and turned back to Gaza. These fours (p. 268–269) were two-level oared warships probably with 44 double-manned oars a side. They are clearly less strong than the fives (and being rated among the heavier ships less fast than the threes). Some of the missile carrying transports (towed by the threes) were swamped and presumably lost, 'others returned to Gaza' presumably the rest under tow. When the storm was over they, under tow, would have joined the rest of the fleet at Kasion. It looks as if the fleet of 150 warships and 100 transports may have consisted at the outset of 50 fives and fours and 100 threes towing the 100 transports.

The reliance of oared warships on harbours or at any rate good beaches is well illustrated. Regular landings were needed to get rest, food and in particular fresh water. Lack of fresh water became a serious problem in the run of about 225 km, 121.5 sm between Gaza and the beach just short of Pelousion.

The width of the Nile, then at the height of its flood, made a crossing to attack Pelousion impossible. When the fleet had been brought up to strength by the stragglers from Raphia and Gaza (fours and threes with their *πόρια*), Antigonos used it in an attempt to land troops (under Demetrios) at a place called Pseudostomon (Falsemouth); but finding it strongly held by Ptolemy, Demetrios moved by night to another mouth of the river (Phatnitikon) attempting to achieve surprise. But in the darkness the ships lost contact with each other; and when the objective was reached he had to send out the fastest ships (threes) in the squadron to find those that had strayed. The delay gave Ptolemy's men time to organise a defence and Demetrios withdrew 'having failed to make this landing also and learning that the adjacent coast was impregnable by reason of swamps and marshes'. On his way back a north wind arose and three fours and some *πόρια στρατιωτικά* (carrying troops) were driven on to a lee shore where they were captured by Ptolemy. The vulnerability of the four on a lee shore, underpowered in contrast with threes and fives, is to be noted.

Running short of food and fodder Antigonos consulted the army on whether to remain in Egypt and continue the offensive or to return to Syria for the time being and make a second invasion later with more complete preparation and at a time when the Nile was lowest. The decision was to withdraw.

Antigonos's invasion of Egypt was a failure for the reasons given, hurried and inadequate preparation and the high Nile making an attack on Pelousion impossible. The fleet proved useless because the landing places on the Delta were few and easy to defend. Pausanias (1.6.6) speaks of Ptolemy using threes defensively against Antigonos's attack, but Diodoros makes no mention of Ptolemy using or indeed needing any ships. After his losses at Salamis it would have been foolish for him to risk a challenge to Antigonos by sea, and it proved in the end unnecessary. Antigonos was wise to cut his losses.

The Siege of Rhodes: 305/4 BC

(Berthold: 1975) Map D

In the year following the invasion of Egypt Demetrios launched an attack on the city of Rhodes which had declined to give him naval assistance in the conquest of Cyprus. Plutarch says that the reason for their refusal was an alliance with Ptolemy, but Diodoros is probably more strictly accurate when he says that they 'preferred a common peace with all' and that 'having made pacts of friendship with all the rulers they were most favourably disposed towards Ptolemy, because they derived the greater part of their revenues from merchants sailing to (and presumably from) Egypt, and in general imported their supplies of food from that kingdom'. Antigonos had in 317 obtained naval assistance from Rhodes, but on what looks like a commercial basis, Antigonos supplying the timber and enlisting crews from Karia. After their loss to Ptolemy in 315, he enlisted Rhodes as ally in the 'liberation of the Greeks' from Kassandros and obtained 10 ships from them completely fitted out (D.19.77. 2–3). He might then well regard Rhodes's refusal to assist him against Cyprus as a rebuff which required punishment.

At this time Rhodes was, as Diodoros observes (20.81.2), a considerable naval power. She had on her own account waged war on the pirates as the enemies of commerce, who infested the south coast of Asia Minor in particular Kilikia (cf. Vergil's Cilician pirate in *Georgic* IV 127). Diodoros says that Rhodes freed the seas of them, but in the siege pirates turn up as Demetrios's allies.

Antigonos's first move was to send a squadron of ships with orders to sieze and bring in Rhodian merchant ships sailing to Egypt, but the squadron was driven off. He then sent Demetrios with a land and sea force and siege equipment. The Rhodians agreed to participate in the war against Ptolemy; but they demurred when he also demanded 100 hostages and the right to enter their harbour, and prepared for war.

Demetrios assembled his force at Loryma about 30 km (19.5 sm) from Rhodes on the Kynossema promontory in Karia, and made his fleet ready. 'He had 200 warships of all sizes, and more than 170 fleet auxiliaries (*ὑπηρετικὰ πλοῖα*). These had on board nearly 40,000 soldiers as well as cavalry, and pirates who were his allies. He had also a large supply of missiles and of everything needful for a siege'. A few more details about the fleet are given when the expedition's approach to the city is described 'as if for a battle, to frighten the enemy'. The warships had on their bows catapults to throw bolts of about three spans *τοὺς τρισπιθάμους τῶν ὀξυβελῶν* (1½ cubits @0.490m = 0.735m) in length. They went in front and were followed by the ships carrying soldiers and cavalry towed by ships under oar, while behind them all were the *πόρια* of the traders and merchants. Later 'the towing ships' are mentioned as moving Demetrios's siege engines (D.20.86.3). Some of the large ships attack the three 'strongest' Rhodian ships (probably fives) which had been sent out to destroy the ship-borne siege engines.

Nowhere in Diodoros's narrative are any of

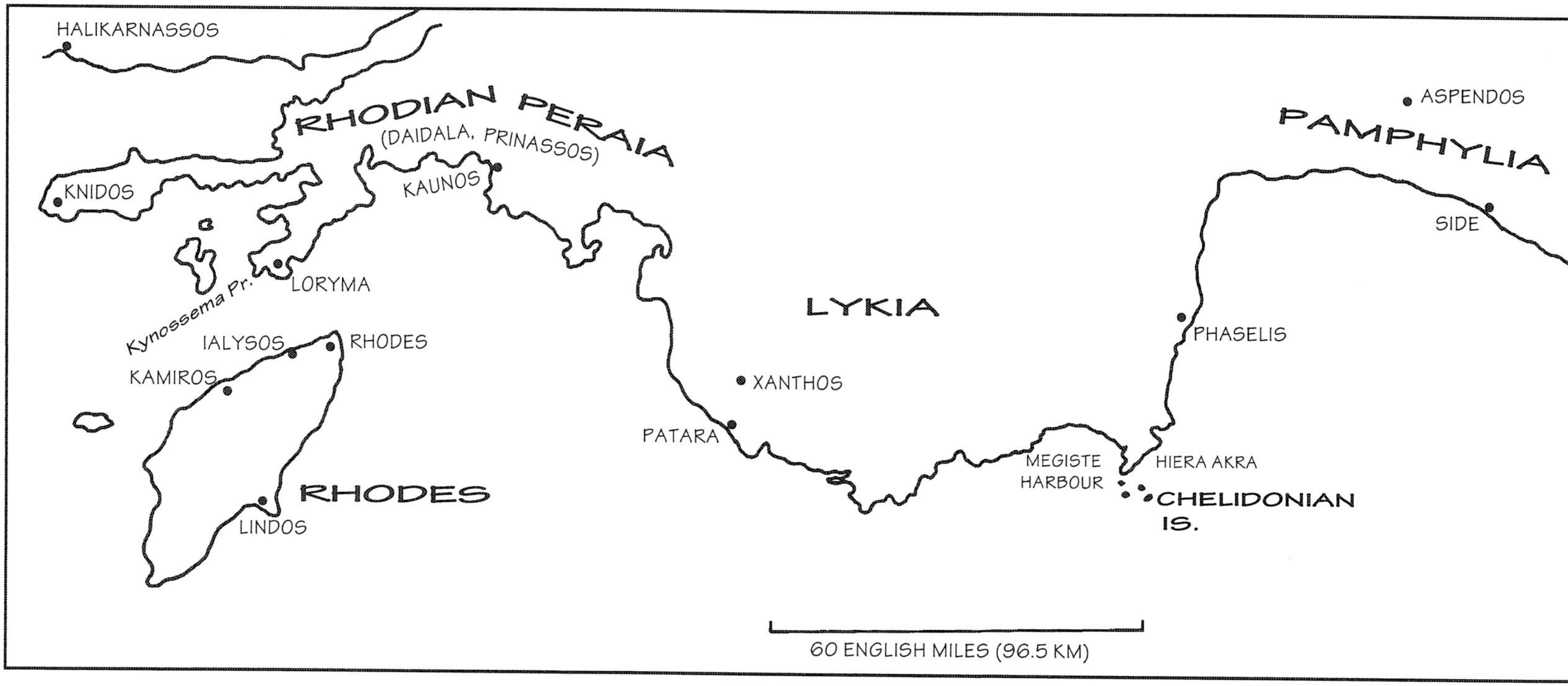

MAP D. *Rhodes, Lykia,Pamphylia*

Demetrios's ships specified on this occasion, but it is reasonable to assume that, since the object of the parade was to impress the Rhodians with his naval power, all the types used in the battle of Cypriot Salamis were deployed. Nor, with one important exception, are the Rhodian ships specified, but it is again reasonable to infer that their three 'strongest' were fives. In the 3rd and 2nd centuries there is much evidence of Rhodian fours, but it is unlikely (p. 269) that they were rated as strong.

The type specified is the *τριημιολία*, which is known from monuments and inscriptions (p. 266–267) to have been a particularly Rhodian type. It turns up, not surprisingly, in view of the strong connection of Rhodes with Egypt also in the fleet of Ptolemy II Philadelphos (p. 37), and for a similar reason also in the Athenian fleet.

(D.20.84.5) During the siege the Rhodians first sent out commerce-raiders; first 'three of their fastest ships', then (20.93.2) nine ships divided into three squadrons. 'Damophilos who had ships with the Rhodian name of 'guard or patrol ships' (*φυλακίδες*) went (south-west) to Karpathos where he found many of Demetrios's ships and swamped (*κατεπόντιζεν*) some, damaging them with his rams. Others he beached and burnt after selecting from their crews the most useful men. Quite a number of those that were bringing grain from Karpathos he brought back to Rhodes'. It looks as if all these ships were merchant ships. The grain-carriers certainly were and since the other two categories were at anchor rather than beached when Damophilos found them they are likely to have been the same.

The second squadron was under Menedemos and consisted of three *τριημιολίαι*. He went eastwards to Patara in Lykia, burnt a cargo ship which he found at anchor with her crew ashore, captured a number of cargo vessels carrying provisions to Demetrios's army and sent them to Rhodes. 'He also captured a four en route from Kilikia' containing Demetrios's wardrobe of purple robes 'fit for a king to wear' consigned to him by his wife Phila, which Menedemos sent to Egypt. The third squadron under Amyntas made for the islands (the Dodecanese: north west) where he found cargo vessels carrying war materials for the siege, some of which he sank and others he took back to Rhodes. On board 'he captured eleven men with reputations in missile and catapult technology'.

In Diodoros's account of Demetrios's preparations of various siege engines (20.85.3) he says that while they were being constructed he assembled the sturdiest of his *λέμβοι* and 'after boxing them in (*καταφράξας*) i.e. giving them decks (if they were undecked) and side-protection, and providing them with oarports which could be closed' he placed on them (on deck) long-range catapults and catapult crews, and Cretan archers, to harass the Rhodians who were heightening their walls.

The siege of Rhodes ended when the Rhodians came to terms with Demetrios after Athenian mediation. In 304 (Plutarch *Demetrios* 23) Demetrios moved his fleet of 330 ships (including transports) to Athens, from where he was summoned in 302 to help his father. Antigonos was faced by a serious challenge to his power in Asia where Seleukos, Lysimachos and Ptolemy had now succeeded in fielding a considerable land force against him. Kassandros's brother Pleistarchos was sent in a six to support Lysimachos (D.20.112.4) but his ship was swamped in a storm in the Black Sea. Pleistarchos was one of thirty-three survivors of a complement of 500.

In the following year Antigonos was defeated and killed at the battle of Ipsos, and Demetrios was left in possession of a considerable sea power, but no secure base in the eastern Mediterranean. Ptolemy seized the opportunity to occupy Phoenicia and its maritime cities.

The Competition in Naval Construction: 301–262 BC *(Will: 1984 p. 101 ff)*

During his narrative of the siege of Rhodes Diodoros observes (20.92.5) that it was after the siege and the death of his father that Demetrios launched the largest ships. His control of Cyprus and the resources of long timber there gave him the opportunity (Theophrastos *H.P* 5.8.1). Plutarch (*Demetrios* 31.1 cf. Pliny *NH* 16.203) speaks of a thirteen of his fleet which he left at Peiraieus before Ipsos; and he mentions (ibid. 20) an unidentified occasion a good deal later (p. 274) when his enemy Lysimachos stood on the shore admiring his fifteens and sixteens as they moved past.

After Antigonos's death Athens closed her gates to Demetrios, but she allowed him to take away his ships and his treasure. Leaving his brother-in-law Pyrrhos, ruler of Epeiros, in charge of his forces in

Greece, he moved his fleet to the Thracian Chersonese and ravaged Lysimachos's territory. Seleukos made overtures to him, entertaining him in his camp; and in turn Demetrios entertained Seleukos on board his flagship, the thirteen, ratifying the alliance by the marriage of his daughter Stratonike to Seleukos. Demetrios still controlled Cyprus and the Island League based on Delos which Antigonos had founded, and had regained Kilikia; but his power lay in his great fleet based on a few fortresses, Corinth, Ephesos, Tyre and Sidon. Through the mediation of Seleukos he made peace with Ptolemy and to mark the occasion dedicated two silver models of warships in the temple of Apollo at Delos. The reconciliation was however shortlived when Seleukos demanded cession of Kilikia and then Tyre and Sidon.

In 296 Demetrios returned to mainland Greece with his fleet (Plutarch *Demetrios* 33.1). He invaded Attika, off which most of his fleet was lost in a storm. Nevertheless he blockaded Athens. Ptolemy sent 150 ships to Aigina, but was frightened off when Demetrios was able to assemble 300 ships from the Peloponnese and Cyprus. The Athenians eventually admitted him on the flight of their ruler Lachares; and he placed garrisons in Peiraieus and Munychia, extending his power in the Peloponnese. Ptolemy then recaptured Cyprus from him, and Seleukos took Kilikia. Lysimachos occupied the Asian cities. Demetrios did however succeed in regaining Macedon, and subsequently Boiotia and Thessaly.

In the autumn of 289 BC Demetrios was in a position to put into effect plans (Plutarch *Demetrios* 43.2) 'to recover all the territory which had been subject to his father'.

'He had already assembled an army of 98,000 footsoldiers and 12,000 cavalry. At the same time he had laid down the keels of 500 ships, most of them in Peiraieus, some in Chalkis and some in Pella. He would pay personal visits to all these places, pointing out what was to be done and assisting in the planning, while all men wondered, not only at the great number but also at the size of the ships being constructed. Up to this time no one had seen a fifteen or sixteen. At a later time Ptolemy Philopator had built a forty (p. 274–277), which had a length of 280 cubits, 124 m, and a height, to the top of her stern, of 48 cubits, 21 m. She was manned by 400 crewmen apart from the oarsmen and by 4,000 oarsmen. Besides this she had room on her side gangways and decks for nearly 3000 soldiers. But she was merely a showpiece, not much different from a stationary building, made for exhibition not for a practical purpose, and was moved with great diffficulty and danger. In Demetrios's ships on the contrary, beauty of appearance was not at the expense of fighting qualities, nor were they denied usefulness by the opulence of their equipment; but speed and efficiency in them was more remarkable than size'.

Plutarch's testimony must be taken seriously. Its message is that the monstrosity of the forty must not diminish the status of Demetrios's thirteen, fifteen and sixteen as practical warships.

Demetrios's preparations produced an immediate reaction from Seleukos, Ptolemy and Lysimachos. They formed an alliance and invited Pyrrhos to attack Macedon, while in the spring of 287 Ptolemy was to move to Greece with his fleet. Athens declared herself independent. Pyrrhos and Lysimachos attacked Macedon from the west and east. Demetrios was forced to flee, appearing before Athens with a hastily collected army. He crossed to Asia and after many vicissitudes surrendered to Seleukos in 285.

Ptolemy was heir to Demetrios's sea power in the Aegean. Philokles, prince of Sidon, who had commanded the Phoenician contingent of Demetrios's fleet at Miletos, went over to Ptolemy, bringing Tyre and Sidon. The rest of the fleet had moved to Kaunos. In one of his many journey's before his death in captivity in 283, Demetrios tried to reach it. He failed, and it joined his son Antigonos Gonatas in Greece, while Kaunos fell to Philokles, with Cyprus already in Ptolemy's possession. The Island League and Delos transferred their allegiance to Ptolemy at the same time.

Agathokles of Syracuse

Diodoros gives some information about the naval forces assembled by Agathokles, the autocratic ruler of Syracuse, shortly before 289 BC for his second invasion of Carthaginian territory (21.16.1). They numbered 200 ships and included fours and sixes. He describes (22.8.5) also the fleet which Pyrrhos of Epeiros, who had married Agathokles' daughter, inherited eleven years later when he relieved Syracuse then under siege by Carthage. 'The ships he took over in Syracuse were 120 cataphracts and

20 aphracts. There was the royal nine and the whole fleet including the ships he had brought made up a total of more than 200'. This 'royal nine' was Pyrrhos's flagship. In naval construction, it seems, he was influenced by his brother-in-law Demetrios. Later, in 260, the commander of the Carthaginian fleet which was defeated by the Romans at Mylai is said to have been on board a seven which had previously belonged to Pyrrhos.

Antigonos Gonatas (*Tarn: 1916*)

Antigonos Gonatas had at his disposal in Greece an army of mercenaries, a few garrisoned cities and what was left of his father's fleet. He formed an alliance with Pyrrhos and helped him when Lysimachos invaded Pyrrhos's half of Macedonia, partitioned as the outcome of the alliance against Demetrios. Lysimachos, as well as founding Lysimacheia on the site of Kardia, had acquired also in 289 BC a naval base in Herakleia on the Black Sea coast of Asia Minor, and he had taken over the ships which Demetrios had laid down at Pella. In 284 Antigonos brought his fleet to Peiraieus and besieged it, eventually agreeing to a peace favourable to Athens but retaining Peiraieus. Lysimachos and Seleukos quarrelled, met in battle at Kouroupedion in 281 and Lysimachos was killed. Ptolemy Keraunos, who then became king of Macedon, had Seleukos assassinated and inherited part of Lysimachos's fleet including the remarkable eight built at Herakleia. This ship of original design, the *Leontophoros* (p.273), was said to have been responsible for Ptolemy Keraunos's defeat of Antigonos at sea in 280 when he was attempting an invasion of Macedon with the fleet, including thirteens, fifteens and sixteens, which he had taken over from his father.

In the subsequent general rising of the cities against the garrisons imposed upon them by the kings, Antigonos succeeded in retaining only Corinth, Euboia and Peiraieus, as well as the city of Demetrias which had been founded by his father on the gulf of Pagasai. Like his father he was now a king without a country, relying on a few garrisoned seaports and his fleet. On Ptolemy Keraunos's death and with the laurels of his defeat of the invading Celts in 277 at Lysimacheia, he was restored to Macedon. Ptolemy Philadelphos, who had succeeded Ptolemy Soter in 283, was now left in undisputed control of the eastern Mediterranean.

When Antigonos in 265 invaded Attika, Ptolemy sent the Egyptian fleet under his admiral Patroklos to support Sparta and the Peloponnesian League, but the Egyptian troops carried on board were unwilling to meet on land the Macedonian phalanx, and although the ships controlled the sea their aid was ineffective.

In the two decades before Antigonos Gonatas in 245 regained naval control of the Aegean and leadership of the Island League which his grandfather had founded, there appear to have been three battles at sea, off Kos, Ephesos and Andros, in which Ptolemaic fleets were defeated and Egyptian command of the sea gradually eroded. Antigonos defeated Ptolemy's admirals off Kos probably in 261 (Walbank: 1982 p. 239) and off Andros fifteen years later (ibid. p. 248–9). An Egyptian fleet was defeated by Rhodes off Ephesos 'in the 250s' (ibid. p. 233). Only in the last case are any details known (p. 55).

Athenaios (5.209e) speaks of 'the sacred *τριήρης* of Antigonos in which he defeated the *στρατηγοί* of Ptolemy off Leukollas in Kos, (sacred) since he dedicated it to Apollo (so before the battle)'.[13]

Twice in Plutarch's *Moralia* and once in the *Life of Pelopidas* Plutarch quotes the famous saying of Antigonos to his helmsman before a sea battle in which his fleet is outnumbered: 'Think how many ships I am worth'. In *Moralia* 545B Antigonos is called 'the Second' and the battle is 'off Kos'. In *Moralia* 183c-d the opponents are Ptolemy's *στρατηγοί*. But in *Pelopidas* (2.2) Antigonos is 'the old man' and (consistently) the battle is off Andros. The attribution of the same famous saying to different famous occasions is a common occurrence which does not diminish the historical status of either.

The text of Athenaios does not imply a dedication of Antigonos's flagship at Delos or anywhere else. This might however have occurred, but the identification (by Tarn: 1910) of his ship as the one at Delos mentioned enigmatically by Pausanias (1.29.1: *τὸ ἐν Δήλῳ καθῆκον εἰς ἐννέα ἐρέτας*) is hardly a description of a flagship, nor firm ground for the conclusion that Antigonos after Kos regained the Antigonids' earlier status at Delos. As Walbank says (1984 p. 242): 'As far as one can tell Ptolemy suffered a substantial defeat at Kos, but it has yet to be shown that he had been ousted from his general control of the Aegean'. An important factor must be the time when and the extent to which the Grand Fleet of Ptolemy II was operational.

Egypt at any rate seems to have continued to control Phoenicia, and she maintained her base at Samos even when in 245 she lost her control of the Island League.

5. THE FLEET OF PTOLEMY II PHILADELPHOS 283–246 BC

In a discussion of the wealth of kings Athenaios (5.203 c) says that of those of Egypt Philadelphos excelled many in wealth and was keenly ambitious in all matters of construction (*κατασκευάσματα*) with the result that he surpassed all kings in the number of his ships. At any rate the biggest of the ships in his dockyard (*παρ' αὐτῷ*) were: two thirties, one twenty, four thirteens, two twelves, 14 elevens, 30 nines, 36 sevens, five sixes and 17 fives, while the ships from four to *τριηρημιολία* were double these (2 × 111): whereas those which were dispatched to the islands and the other cities which he ruled, as well as Libya, were more than 4,000.

Ellen Rice (1983 p. 138–9) has put a convincing case for the acceptance of Athenaios (2nd-3rd cent. AD) as a reliable and painstaking compiler. In this case he does not quote his source; but he lived at Naukratis in the Delta and could have had access to the royal records (*βασιλικαὶ ἀναγραφαί*) of Ptolemy Philadelphos, to which Appian (AD 95–c.165), his older contemporary and a native of Alexandria, refers in paragraph 10 of the preface to his *Roman History*.

Appian describes 'the second king of Egypt after Alexander', in terms which recall Athenaios's description of Philadelphos, as 'the cleverest of the kings in raising money, the most splendid in spending, and the grandest in construction'. He goes on to give an account of the military and naval forces, and treasure, of the kings of Egypt. His list, however, of the naval units bears little resemblance to Athenaios's account of Philadelphos, except in one phrase. It goes as follows: '(the kings of Egypt) for naval service had 2000 barges propelled by poles and other smaller craft, 1500 *τριήρεις* (here = warships) from the *ἡμιολία* to the five and warship gear (*σκεύη τριηριτικά*) for twice that number; also 800 cabin vessels (*θαλαμηγοί*) with gilt sterns and rams for a naval review, on board which the kings went as they moved through the lines (of ships)'.

His general description of the Egyptian royal navy betrays an amateur with an eye for the picturesque, while Athenaios is more professional and concerned with the ships built by Ptolemy Philadelphos as instruments of naval power. There is no evidence that Ptolemy Soter had any ships bigger than fives, so that his successor in 283 must have begun an ambitious naval programme to bring Egypt into competition at sea with the programme on which Demetrios embarked soon after his father's death in 301.

The two phrases which resemble each other in the two accounts are: Athenaios's 'ships from four to *τριηρημιολία*' i.e. from bigger to smaller with the three in between, and Appian's '*τριήρεις* from the *ἡμιολία* to the five', i.e. from the smaller to the bigger with the *τριημιολία*, the three and the four in between.

Athenaios's main categories of warships make sense. They are both cataphract. The first is of strong ships down to and including the five, while the second is of ships regarded as less powerful by comparison, the four to the *τριημιολία*. The name *τριηρημιολία* is not found elsewhere, but it states more clearly than the commoner name *τριημιολία* that the word *τριημιολία* indicates a ship which has three files of oarsmen on each side with one file on each side being a half file.

Appian's phrase also makes sense as referring to the ships of Ptolemy II Soter so long as it is recognised (as Torr: 1894 p. 15 n. 41 did) that he uses '*τριήρης*' and '*τριηριτικά*' in a general sense to mean 'warship' and 'belonging to a warship'. His contemporary Aristeides (*Rhodiaka* 341) has the same usage. Appian starts with a lower rating of warship, the *ἡμιολία* or *ἡμιόλιος λέμβος* (p. 62) which features in Philip V's fleet at the battle of Chios and is accordingly likely to be cataphract. It may appear later in large numbers in the Roman invasion fleet of the third Punic war (p. 113), as a lighter version of the liburnian.

It appears then that the resemblance of the two phrases is not significant and that Appian who begins with the smaller craft and goes on to warships from *ἡμιολίαι* to fives, the types in between being *τριημιολία* and fours, is speaking of Ptolemy Soter's warships which at the battle of Salamis were in fact fours and fives. There is no reason to believe that the account is incorrect. He omits however the description of Ptolemy Philadelphos's warships, beginning with the largest, which Athenaios gives. Appian concludes: 'To such a state of preparedness for war (ἐς τοσοῦτο παρασκευῆς καὶ στρατίας, a hendiadys) does the second king of Egypt after Alexander appear from the royal records to have advanced his country, and left it' (therein, an anakolouthon). 'He was the cleverest etc'.

There is some ambiguity in the phrase 'the second king of Egypt after Alexander' since if Alexander is regarded as the first king Ptolemy I would be the second, and in that case the whole passage refers to him and there is no carelesness or omission on Appian's part. But it is difficult to believe that Appian could have said of Ptolemy Soter: 'He was...the grandest in construction', if he had known, as he must have known, about the magnificent fleet of his successor', yet omitted it from his text. The conclusion must be that 'the second king of Egypt after Alexander' does in fact refer to Philadelphos and that the list of his ships which appears in Athenaios and probably derives from the royal records was known to Appian but has somehow been omitted, either by his own carelessness or scribal error, from his text.

APPENDIX

by D. J. Blackman

The Shipsheds at Kition

Important remains of shipsheds are currently being excavated at Kition by the French mission, directed by Marguerite Yon of the university of Lyon.

The Phoenician character of the Kingdom of Kition gives particular interest to this site, which abuts the north side of the sanctuaries of Astarte and Melqart/Herakles (9th–3rd century BC) on the south side of a small harbour basin, filled in by the British authorities in 1879/80, at the foot of Bamboula hill. The harbour was originally connected with the sea by a canal, also filled in 1879/80, and was described by Strabo as 'closable'. The basin was probably used as a harbour from the 9th century, but the shipsheds belong to the later 5th and 4th centuries; they may then have completely lined the basin, but so far only the south side has been excavated.

Here excavations since 1988 have revealed partially or completely the remains of 7 shipsheds; three phases have been identified. The first phase seems to belong to the second half of the fifth century, and is the best preserved. Stone ramps almost 2 m wide, and 1.90 m high at the upper end, sloping towards the water with a gradient of 13°, have been uncovered over a length of 11 m only; the ramps are lined by low walls of plastered masonry, with a rubble inner fill, covered by a white coating still bearing traces of red paint. Rabbets along the side walls may have held longitudinal timbers, either to support cross-timbers laid on the ramps, or to serve as groundways for some sort of stern poppets or a stern cradle about which the ships would have hinged as the bow rose under its own buoyancy during launching. The excavators suggest that some of the cross-timbers may have been rollers (and new finds at Marseille would support this interpretation).

At the south (upper) end of each ramp a stone bracket projected from the back wall, presumably to support the overhanging stern of the ship when slipped; the excavators speak of supporting the ram, but the ships would have been slipped stern first. An east/west cross-passage, 1.20 m wide, provided communication between the tops of the slips, with three steps up to the walkways which ran down both sides of each ramp. Behind, to the south, stood a high retaining wall with buttresses, containing slots for cross-timbers to which the ships were made fast when slipped. Small basins at the foot of the wall between the buttresses have yet to be explained (perhaps for soaking timbers?); the excavators suggest that there may have been fixtures for capstans. They also suggest that ships' gear may have been stored beyond the back wall to the south. Alternating with the ramps, at 6 m intervals, longitudinal walls separated the shipsheds. They consisted of a series of stretches of wall, 3 m long and 0.80 m wide, serving as the bases for timbers supporting the roof. Many fragments of roof tile were found among the remains, and the excavators suggest that the roofing was a descending series of saddle roofs. The dividing walls also had apertures in their sides, which must have supported stays for the slipped ships.

The second phase, of the (first half of the?) fourth century, involved a major rearrangement, with materials of much poorer quality. The ramps were widened (to 3 m) and raised (to 2.50 m for the eastern slips and 3.20 m for the western), and were no doubt extended in length (so far the excavations have revealed 15 m). It is not yet clear whether the modifications were caused by changes in the ships' dimensions or by a rise in sea level.

A third phase, also of the fourth century (second half?), has only been defined at a high level on the westernmost slip.

The excavators stress the close similarities between these shipsheds and those discovered in Piraeus: similar date: similar interaxial width; similar alternation of ramps and dividing walls; similar solid back wall. The main difference is in length – so far a maximum of only 15 m has been established on the preserved parts of the slips at Kition. Further excavation will show whether the slips were intended for short ships, or supported only part of the ships' length, or whether the lower ends have been destroyed. Further excavation will also help to determine the chronology: provisionally Prof. Yon associates the first reconstruction with King Milkyaton (392–362); the second with his son Pumayyaton (362–332); and the end of use of the shipsheds with the conquest of Cyprus by Ptolemy I in 312 (though the reference in Strabo indicates that the harbour basin continued in use thereafter: 14.6.3 *ἔχει δὲ λιμένα κλειστόν*).

Note: This account is based on the annual reports in *BCH*; Yon, *Dossiers*; and Calvet, 1993; elucidated by a recent visit to the site, which enables me to correct several errors in the short description of Kition in my recent survey of ancient naval installations (Blackman, 1995, 229): the three steps run *upwards* from the cross-passage to the sides of the ramps; and in phase 2 the ramps were raised *to* 2.50 m and 3,20 m, not *by* 2.50–3.20 m. A full discussion of the site by Callot, 1994, is eagerly awaited: the advance abstract indicates that the ramps of phase 2 have now been traced for more than 25 m; and that phase 3 shows *three* westernmost ramps.

Endnotes

1. For a treatment of the textual problems the reader is referred to JSM (1990 i).
2 The word *ἐπιβάται* can have a precise or general meaning (p. 349). It can mean decksoldiers only. In that case the Phoenician decksoldiers would have been in addition to the normal Macedonian contingent. Alternatively it may refer to the *ὑπηρεσία* as men carried on deck.
3 JFC 'This could have been done by building them in sections, each made watertight by a bulkhead about 1 m high where they joined, and each weighing about two tonnes. Alternatively they could have simply been built with clenched or partially clenched plank-to-frame fastenings and with all timbers and planks marked to allow ready dismantling and reassembly.'
4 If, as will be argued p. 268–269 a four employed 88 double-manned oars at two levels, 44 on each side of the ship, and accordingly 176 oarsmen against 170 rowed at three levels in the three, she would have been broader than the three but shorter with a maximum of 22 as against 31 'rooms', and with no structure to accommodate a third level probably lighter while her power/weight ratio could have been better
5. There is no obvious reason why Amorgos was the scene of the final battle. After failing to prevent the Macedonian fleet from joining forces and then failing to prevent reinforcements for Antipatros from leaving Asia, Euetion's sole objective would be to bring his ships home without further losses. It may be that he tried unsuccessfully to achieve this aim by moving south before crossing the Aegean, possibly to a rendezvous with reinforcements.
6. 115 *πόρια* would have been needed if each of the 95 troop *πόρια* took 155–160 soldiers and 20 cavalry *πόρια* took 20 horses and cavalrymen each. These could have made the crossing under tow to the 110 (+) threes.
7. Strabo (14.6.3) describes the coast of Cyprus between Salamis and Kition. He does not mention a harbour at Salamis. He mentions two harbours as he passes from Salamis to the Pedalion promontory: *εἶτ' Ἀρσινόη πόλις καὶ λιμὴν· εἶτ' ἄλλος λιμὴν Δεύκολλα· εἶτ' ἄκρα Πηδάλιον ... εἶτα κολπώδης καὶ τραχὺς παράπλους ὁ πλείων εἰς Κιτιον· ἔχει δὲ λιμένα κλεῖστον. Arsinoe* (otherwise *Ammochostos* mod. Famagusta) has the best claim to be a stopping place if one was used. For Kition see D. J. Blackman's report (Appendix to Chapter 1) on the recent excavations of the shipsheds there.
8. Hauben (1975/6) and Seibert (1969) also infer that there were more fours than fives. The pattern of the Athenian fleets and of Antigonos's fleet makes this in any case virtually certain.
9. Hauben (1976) recognises that the 'heavier *στρατιώτιδες*' were warships with many soldiers on deck (see Cary: 1963 p. 385) and not troop-transports (*πόρια*)

which are mentioned next. Casson (*SSAW* 90 n. 65, 93 n. 83) followed by Seibert (1969 p. 190–206), took them to be the heavier threes. But in this age the boarding tactic favoured by the Macedonians had resulted in bigger ships designed to carry an increased number of decksoldiers and the replacement of the ram by the boarding potential as the principal naval weapon. The change in tactics resulted in a change in the meaning of the name *στρατιῶτις* which in the 5th cent at Athens had meant a second class three, not fast but built to transport soldiers on deck not for boarding at sea but for fighting on land. Now the phrase 'heavier *στρατιῶτις*' had come to mean a ship of size increased (at the expense of speed) to enable it to carry more decksoldiers for boarding (as Nietzold: 1905 p. 15 n. 16, Beloch: 1925–7 p. 154–5, and Cary: 1963 p. 385–6). The phrase for troop-transports was now *στρατιωτικά πόρια* or just *πόρια*. Hauben also says that the Athenian squadron of thirty fours which was later mentioned cannot form part of the 53 'heavier *στρατιώτιδες*' because 37 other heavy ships, fives and upwards, are also mentioned subsequently and this would make too high a total (67). But the 110 (+) fast threes and the 53 heavier *στρατιώτιδες* comprise the invasion fleet, whereas it is the eventual battle fleet which is said to be composed of 118 ships including seven sevens, ten sixes, ten fives (with a further ten 'heavy ships' as harbour guard) and 30 fours. Diodoros says that further ships had joined Demetrios's fleet 'from the places captured', thus accounting for the 14 additional heavier ships in the battle fleet.

10. Hauben says (1976 ii p. 2): 'Just before the battle (Demetrios) is stated to have 118 (108+10) ships (20.50.1–2) excluding or including – *σύν* is ambiguous – a number of craft from subjected Cypriot cities, (presumably Karpasia and Ourania). The fleet consisted of *ἑπτήρεις, πεντήρεις... τετρήρεις* and lighter vessels'. Here Hauben misrepresents Diodoros whose words are 'vessels which had been manned from the conquered places'. Diodoros does not say that the places were Cypriot or that the ships came from them, only the manning. He admits the ambiguity of *σύν* but not the equal ambiguity of *τούτων* which he takes as unambiguously referring to the whole fleet. Such reference is possible, but the reference is more natural to the last mentioned 'ships from the captured places'. Hauben is driven to the scholar's last refuge, the conclusion that, since 118, even if augmented by a few ships (as he supposes) from Karpasia and Ourania, is too small a number for Demetrios's fleet and 'an error has crept in to Diodoros's text. We should read 190 with Reckman or 180 with Schmitt (both in private communications).' With the benefit of this generous addition he concludes that '*σύν* has without any doubt inclusive force'.

11. Two other helmsmen are known by name. Xenophon *HG* 1.5.11 relates how Alkibiades in 409 BC left his fleet at Notion in charge of his pilot Antiochos who disobeyed orders and provoked a battle with Lysander in whiich the Athenians were defeated and according to Plutarch (*Alkibiades* 35) Antiochos killed. Plutarch also says (*Alkibiades* 10) that Antiochos was a tiresome and foolish fellow who won favour with Alkibiades by catching a quail which Alkibiades had let loose by mistake. The second is Phantias 'the foremost Greek helmsman of the time' (before 405 BC) whom Lysias (21.10) claims that he employed for the whole period of his trierarchy 'persuading him with money'.

12. JFC writes: The swamping of the three fives 'strongly suggests that they had oarports near the waterline – and some defective oarsleeves (*ἀσκώματα*). They could also have had some stores on board, reducing freeboard'.

13. Athenaios is using *τριήρης* in the late general sense of 'warship' as Appian and Aristides do. The Teubner text of Athenaios reads *ἐπεὶ δή* 'since', emended gratuitously to *ὅπου δή* 'on which occasion' by Meineke.

2

SEA POWER IN THE MEDITERRANEAN: 3RD CENTURY BC

1. PYRRHOS

The intervention of Pyrrhos, king of Epeiros and protegé of Demetrios, first in Italy against the Romans at the invitation of Tarentum (281 BC) and then in Sicily (278 BC) against the Carthaginians at the invitation of Akragas, Leontinoi and Syracuse, provides an instructive prelude to the Roman 'war about Sicily', the First Punic War. It throws light on the configuration of powers in the area. The death of Agathokles in 289 had left a power vacuum which in the years that followed first Pyrrhos attempted to fill and then Rome succeeded in filling.

Plutarch (*Pyrrhos* 15.1), relying on Dionysios of Halikarnassos and, more importantly, on Hieronymos of Kardia (e.g. 17.4), gives an account of Pyrrhos's crossing from Greece to Tarentum. The Tarentines sent 'many horse-transports, cataphracts and carriers of all kinds (πορθμεῖα παντοδαπά) to bring over Pyrrhos's army. He put on board 20 elephants, 3,000 horse, 20,000 foot and 500 slingers'.

The Crossing: May 280 BC

The fleet put to sea; and as it was crossing the Ionian strait was thrown into confusion and scattered by an unseasonably strong north wind.

'Some of the ships failed to reach Italy and were driven off course towards the Libyan and Sicilian sea. Others, failing to round the Iapygian promontory and overtaken by nightfall, were thrown by a heavy and violent sea on to the blind and harbourless shore and were destroyed. The king's ship was an exception. While the waves were those of the open sea [i.e. a long swell: reading the manuscripts' πελαγίου], she held her own and escaped the onslaught of the sea by dint of her size and power [under oar]. But when the wind backed and met her off the land, the ship was in danger of breaking up, meeting the thick surf [i.e. short, steep waves] head on; but it seemed more frightening than the present plight to let her drive [before the wind] committing her again to the mercy of the raging open sea and a wind which changed in all directions. Pyrrhos accordingly got up and dived into the sea, and his friends and bodyguards competed with each other to bring him assistance. Night and the waves with great noise and violent undertow made it difficult to help him, so that it was not until daylight when the wind dropped that he succeeded in getting ashore, quite exhausted in body but in courage and strength of spirit equal to his plight'.

Pyrrhos is then said to have been looked after by Messapians (who inhabited the Iapygian peninsula), and 'some of the ships that had escaped the storm' are said to have come up 'containing a few horsemen, less than two thousand footsoldiers and two elephants'. 'After the shipwreck', Appian says (*Samn.* 8), 'Pyrrhos arrived at Tarentum'.

The account of the crossing, made dangerous by a strong northerly (beam) wind (which usually blew in the late summer), is not as clear as it might be, and emendation of the text has made it worse. Reference to the advantage the flagship had from its power indicates that the crossing, for the cataphracts, was to some extent at least, made under oar, which is likely to have been the case if the ships were to keep together under difficult weather conditions (cf. Thukydides 6.33–4: *AT* p. 100–101). The course of the fleet was probably from the northern end of the Kerkyra channel due west across the sea (84 sm) to the Iapygian promontory, round it and then NW to Tarentum. Some ships were blown south off course (but not very far because they were able to get back when the wind dropped next morning). The others, including the king's flagship, kept on course, but arrived at nightfall off the Iapygian promontory which (owing to the north wind) they were unable to round (by taking a course NW). All these were wrecked because they could not see ahead and because there were no harbours ('blind and harbourless shore').

The king's flagship was able to keep out of danger while she was in the open sea, because she was a larger ship and more powerfully rowed than the others (and thus could be safe in a long swell. By implication the others could not); but when she came near the shore the wind backed to the NW and produced a short steep sea repeatedly hitting the ship's prow and putting her in danger. The alternative of going about and running for the open sea in a wind which was changeable was considered too dangerous. Pyrrhos accordingly decided to swim ashore, and succeeded. Nothing is said about the fate of the ship. Appian's reference to 'the shipwreck' could refer to the other ships which were lost.

Nearly twenty years later, as has been said, at the battle of Mylai (262 BC) early in the Ist Punic War the Carthaginian flagship (Polybios 1.23.4) was the seven which had previously belonged to Pyrrhos. Whether the royal flagship of the crossing in 281 was the same ship as the one at Mylai is perhaps immaterial. Certainly Pyrrhos, as a result of his connection with Demetrios, would have had at least a seven at the crossing, whose size and strength gave it safety in the long swell of the open sea, even if the short steep seas whipped up by a strong wind off shore put it in danger. This evidence about the sea-keeping qualities of the seven is interesting and may give one of the reasons for building the larger oared warships.

From Italy to Sicily: Autumn 278 BC

The austere military discipline of Pyrrhos, as imposed on the Tarentines, soon made him unpopular; and in spite of a number of 'Pyrrhic victories' in his engagements with the Romans he began to see that he would never conquer them. When therefore in 278 he was invited to Sicily by Akragas, Leontinoi and Syracuse to help them to drive out the Carthaginians, he saw this as a stepping stone to the conquest of Libya (Plutarch *Pyrrhos* 22.3 cf. 14.5) and accepted it after waging war in Italy, Diodoros says (22.8.1), for two years and four months.

Diodoros describes the state of affairs in Sicily (22.7). After Agathokles' death in 289, Hiketas had ruled Syracuse for nine years and had been succeeded by Thoinon and Sostratos. By 278 they were fighting each other, Thoinon in the island of Ortygia, Sostratos in the city. 'Both becoming exhausted with the war sent ambassadors to Pyrrhos'. Meanwhile the Carthaginians in treaty with Rome (Polybios 3.25), taking 500 legionaries on board their ships, were attacking Rhegion and were on the look-out there to prevent Pyrrhos crossing the strait. They were also besieging Syracuse and blockading the Great Harbour with 100 ships. Pyrrhos (D.22.8) 'embarked his men, his elephants and his war equipment on board his ships, moved from Tarentum and put in at Lokroi on the tenth day' (a slow voyage of about 170 sea miles).

From Lokroi he moved to the strait, crossed over to Sicily apparently without opposition and was welcomed by the ruler of Tauromenion and by the people of Katana. There he disembarked his army which marched on Syracuse accompanied at sea by the fleet. Thirty of the Carthaginian blockading ships had been dispatched elsewhere and the rest declined battle. He reconciled Thoinon and Sostratos and restored harmony in Syracuse, taking over there all the military equipment and 120 cataphract ships, 20 aphracts and the royal nine. His total naval force, including the ships he had brought with him, amounted to more than 200. The 'ships he brought with him' are likely to have included a seven (either his original flagship or its replacement). It appears then that he had left Tarentum with about 60 ships and that in view of the Roman-backed Carthaginian opposition consisting of an unspecified number of ships in the force attacking Rhegion and the 100 Carthaginian ships originally at Syracuse, Pyrrhos had taken some risk.

The nine which Pyrrhos took over in Syracuse would have belonged as flagship to the fleet of 200 fours and sixes (Diodoros 21.16.1) which Agathokles had assembled for the invasion of Libya just before his death.

In Sicily again, as in Italy, Pyrrhos had military success and with a force of 30,000 footsoldiers,

25,000 cavalry and 200 ships reduced the Carthaginian presence in Sicily to a mere foothold at Eryx. His recruitment of oarsmen and plans for the invasion of Libya alarmed the Siceliots and turned them against him. In 276 he returned to Italy remarking to his followers (Plutarch *Pyrrhos* 23.6) 'what a ring for a wrestling bout between Carthaginians and Romans we are leaving behind us!' From Italy he returned to his kingdom of Epeiros after six years in which he had unsuccessfully tried to emulate in the west his cousin Alexander the Great's conquest of the East.

2. THE FIRST PUNIC WAR 264–241 BC (*Map E*) (*Scullard: 1989 p. 537–566*)

The expansion of Roman power outside Italy began with the first Punic war, and the development, virtually from nothing, of the naval capability which, at any rate in the case of Sicily, Pyrrhos had shown to be necessary. The principal authority for this initial expansion is Polybios, whom Heitland (1909: vol. i p. 193) described as 'the most trustworthy of the ancient historians'. It is certainly a pleasant change to be able to rely on a historian rather than, as hitherto in the case of Diodoros, on a compiler whose evidence is as good as the source, not always identifiable, which at any one time he is incorporating in his narrative.

At the outset of the war, which Polybios calls 'the war about Sicily', the island was occupied by the Carthaginians, allied to Hiero of Syracuse, and long masters of the sea in that region (P.1.7.6, 1.20.5 and 1.20.12). Polybios regards a detailed treatment of this war as a necessary introduction to his history of Roman expansion (1.20.8) 'so that the reader will not be unaware of this starting point, that is, how, when and for what reason the Romans took to the sea'.

(P.1.20.13–14) A band of mercenaries called Mamertines had seized the city of Messana on the Sicilian side of the straits; and when attacked by the Carthaginians in alliance with Hiero they appealed to Rome. When the Romans decided to give them aid 'not only did Rome possess no cataphract ships but had no warships at all, not even a light craft (*λέμβος*)'. This statement is surprising in view of the ten cataphract ships, probably threes, with which the consul Cornelius went on a tour of Magna Graecia twenty years before. It is possible that they may have belonged to Rome's 'naval allies' (*socii navales*), as on this occasion when they borrowed fifty-oared ships and threes from the Greek maritime cities of Tarentum, Lokroi, Velia and Neapolis and sent their men across in these at great risk. The Carthaginians put to sea and attacked them. One of the Carthaginian cataphracts in hot pursuit ran aground and was captured by the Romans. They used it, Polybios adds, as a model, when later after the capture of Agrigentum (Gk. Akragas), the war dragging on, they saw that they must (1.20.7) 'like the Carthaginians, get on the sea', and for the first time took steps to build ships in the regular pattern of ships of the time and a smaller force of fast-reconnaissance ships, 100 fives and 20 threes. 'As their shipwrights were completely inexperienced in building fives, since at the time no one in Italy had required ships of this type they had difficulty', and used the captured cataphract as a model.

We shall argue from the iconography that the Carthaginian and Roman fives were of the same design and that this design which had some practical advantages was different from the Greek, based on the Greek three. This latter design admitted development to the six and to the whole range of larger ships while the Carthaginian-Roman design did not. Polybios whose knowledge of naval matters was good could hardly have been ignorant of this difference. The reason for the choice of the Carthaginian design certainly needed explanation but it cannot have been solely the chance capture of a Carthaginian cataphract. The Romans however were a hard-headed people and if they thought the Carthaginian design was better they would have gone for it. They never showed any interest in the larger ships in any case. To Polybios as a Greek this attitude needed an excuse and that is what rather obviously he gave. Had the Romans thought that the Greek design was better they could without much difficulty have hired Greeks, as they did in other matters, to give their craftsmen the necessary instruction.

The appearance of the Roman fives of the 3rd cent. BC may be given by a series of coins of that date (**12**) showing the bow section of warships in which the oarbox is deep and has a pair of horizontal slats on its lateral face which would provide three longitudinal openings through which three levels of oars could be worked. This is a slight variation of the deep oarbox with three rows of

MAP E. *Rome and Carthage*

oarports set quincunx fashion which appears a little later in the Calenian dishes (**18**) and is likely to be Carthaginian.

When the construction of the ships and the training of the crews (p. 353) was completed, and after short sea trials, the ships moved along the coast under Gnaeus Cornelius Scipio, one of the two consuls for 260 BC, who had been given the command of the fleet. He had ordered the ship captains to take the fleet to Messana as soon as it was ready, but he himself put to sea with 17 ships, fives as it later appears, eager to make the preparations urgently necessary for the reception of the fleet. In the harbour at Lipara he was caught and blockaded by a slightly superior Carthaginian force of 20 ships, and surrendered. A few days later the Carthaginian commander Hannibal rounding the Cape of Italy (*τὸ τῆς Ἰταλίας ἀκρωτήριον*) with 50 ships on reconnaissance, met the rest of the Roman fleet (83 fives) moving in fleet formation, and lost most of his ships, escaping himself (P.1.21.10–11). This engagement has been thought by some to be a version (by the historian Philinos of Akragas) of the coming battle of Mylai. There seems to be no good reason for this suggestion, since Polybios was usually critical of Philinos, and Walbank rejects it.

When the Roman fleet reached Sicily, Marcus Duilius, the other consul, was sent for. Learning that the Carthaginian fleet was not far off, he made preparations for an engagement.

The battle of Mylai which followed is interesting for a number of reasons, in particular because of the use made by the Romans of a boarding bridge, the *korax*. The Romans had no illusions about the quality of their ships which were 'ill constructed and difficult to manoeuvre'. They acccordingly devised a means of overcoming their disadvantage. The *korax* appears to have been a ramp kept stacked upright against a mast in the forepart of the ship. At the moment of impact on an enemy ship the ramp, which had a sharp spike under its upper extremity (hence the name *korax*, raven) was guided to fall and penetrate the enemy deck, preventing disengagement and giving access to it; Tarn regarded this device as practically impossible and the story an invention by Polybios, but Wallinga (1956) has given a satisfactory interpretation of Polybios's description (see *SSAW* pl. 111). The device is a blunt illustration of the Roman, as opposed to the classical Greek, concept of naval tactics.

The fleet of which Duilius had inherited command from his unfortunate colleague consisted of 83 fives (the 100 less 17 lost by Scipio), and 20 threes. The Carthaginians had 130 ships, probably all fives except the commander Hannibal's flagship, a seven, which, Polybios says, had belonged to Pyrrhos of Epeiros (brought over to Sicily in 278: p. 35). It will be recollected that Demetrios's flagship at the battle of Cypriot Salamis was a seven.

At first the Carthaginians, underestimating their opponents, adopted no special tactics (the *διέκπλους* or *περίπλους* which would have been normal where one fleet was faster and more agile than its opponents), but advanced bow to bow. The *korax* was brought into action as the ships engaged; 'and the action developed into something like a land battle', which was just what the Romans planned. The Carthaginians at this stage in the battle lost 30 ships including the seven, although Hannibal escaped in the ship's boat (*σκάφη*). Both the five and the seven are likely to have been ships with three levels of oars and about the same height. The larger size of the oar-gangs in the seven would have led to some additional height, but not such as to make the *korax* unusable.

After the surprise effect of the *korax* had worn off, the Carthaginians gave up ramming bow to bow, and used their superior speed hoping to make a ramming attack, some broadside and in the stern, (*ἐκπεριπλέοντες*) by moving out and round the enemy ships, but were still unable to avoid the *korax*, which swung round in all directions. They lost a further 20 ships.

Polybios's description of the battle underlines the normal tactics of a faster fleet, even in the day of the five, to move round an enemy line (if there was sea room) and attack ships abeam (if stationary) or in the stern. The Romans with their usual clear-sighted realism had recognised that they were inferior in the manoeuvrability of their ships but superior in the hand-to-hand fighting of their soldiers on deck. They had to accept that their ships would be rammed; but if, once rammed, they could prevent the enemy from disengaging, they could board and capture the opposing ship. The *korax* enabled them to achieve both these aims at once.

The boarding bridge played a useful part in 256 at Eknomos, but after that it seems to have been temporarily given up (but see pp. 151 and 155, 358–359). Polybios does not mention it again. The reason may be that when Roman shipbuilding techniques and designs improved, as well as handling skill, such a heavy and unwieldy device was abandoned. But on its first appearance it had achieved surprise, and success in giving the first Roman fleet a victory at sea and in creating in Duilius Rome's first, and only, seaman hero.

On a monument set up in Rome he was described (CIL I.95)) as 'the first Roman to perform exploits in ships at sea. He was the first to fit out and train ships and crews and with them he defeated in battle on the high seas all the Carthaginian ships and their mighty naval personnel under the eyes of Hannibal, their commander-in-chief. By his strength he captured one seven and 30 fives and threes along with their crews, and he sent 13 ... He was also the first to bring the people booty from a sea battle and the first to lead free-born Carthaginians in a victory parade'.

(P.1.25.1) Three years later (257) there was an engagement west of Messana on the north coast of Sicily in which the Roman consul, Gaius Atilius Regulus, was given a sharp lesson in fleet tactics. His ships were beached at Tyndaris when he observed the Carthaginian fleet moving east in some disorder. He yielded to the temptation and put to sea with ten escorting ships, ordering his crews (on the remaining ships) to follow those who were leading. The Carthaginians, observing that some of the enemy were preparing to embark, others were putting to sea, while the first ships were far ahead of the others, turned and faced them. They succeeded in surrounding and destroying all the Roman ships except the flagship, which they came close to taking with her crew. The flagship, being fitted out with units of ancillary armament (*ἐξηρτυμένη ὑπηρεσίαις*) and being a fast ship, unexpectedly escaped. The rest of the Roman ships quickly assembled and forming up in line abreast attacked the enemy, capturing ten ships with their crews and putting eight more out of action.

In spite of the initial reverse brought on by Atilius's rashness, the Roman ships now seem to regard themselves as a match for the Carthaginians in tactical movements. The first of the two reasons for the escape of Atilius's flagship is expressed in a difficult phrase. The word *ὑπηρεσία* in naval contexts is most commonly a singular collective noun meaning crew who act in an ancillary capacity (to the trierarch), usually other than the oarsmen, but sometimes including them. The usage here, in the plural, cannot have the common naval meaning but must describe a number of ancillary weapons with which the ship was equipped and which gave her an advantage over her attackers beside her ram and her speed. It would seem likely that these are catapults, and this interpretation is supported by a passage in the *Geoponica* (18.9.3: quoted in LSJ) which speaks of 'hair used in naval *ὑπηρεσίαι*', twisted hair being commonly used in catapults (p. 355). The speed of the flagship is to be noted. She could have been a specially fast five, but since at Eknomos both consuls had sixes as flagships a six is a possibility.

Both sides, Polybios comments (1.25.5), as a result of the engagement at Tyndaris, thinking that they had held their own, threw themselves wholeheartedly into the organisation of naval power and application to naval affairs.

The Roman preparations for the summer of 256 resulted in their going to sea with 330 cataphract warships (P.1.25.7) and beaching the fleet at Messana. They then moved to Eknomos on the SW coast of Sicily where the enemy was. The Carthaginians moved with 350 cataphract warships to Lilybaion, and from there to a beach at Herakleia Minoa.

The Battle of Eknomos and the first invasion of Africa: 256 BC *(Plan 3)*

The summary treatment of Polybios as the source for the battle of Eknomos by de Sanctis (1916) and Tarn (1930) followed by Thiel (1946 and 1954) has been repaired by Walbank (1957: Vol. i p. 85–88) and more recently by Tibbs (1985). In what follows Polybios who gives a perfectly rational account of the battle has been treated with the respect he deserves.

Polybios explains clearly (1.26.1–3) the strategic objectives of the two fleets. The Romans planned to invade Africa and make that the theatre of a war which should concern not only Sicily but Carthage herself, while the Carthaginians, realising that Africa was very vulnerable, aimed at fighting a naval battle to prevent them carrying out their intention. The Roman ships were accordingly disposed tactically both for battle and for invasion, and the Carthaginians were deployed to thwart the invasion. The Carthaginians succeeded in their objective, breaking up the Roman formation and preventing the ships proceeding to Africa. But it was a Pyrrhic victory; in so doing they lost so many ships that they were unable to challenge the Romans' second attempt. Although tactically a defeat, in the long term and more important strategic sense the battle of Eknomos was a Roman success.

Polybios gives a description, also clear, of the Roman formation. There were four divisions, each named both a *στρατόπεδον* (legion) and a *στόλος* (naval squadron). The fourth division was also called the *triarii*. The whole force (P.1.26.7) numbered about 140,000, each ship carrying, Polybios says, 300 (2 × 5 × 30) oarsmen and 120 *ἐπιβάται* (soldiers on deck and *ὑπηρεσία*). The two sixes of the commanders (P.1.26.11) are mentioned separately and the numbers of their crews are not given; but

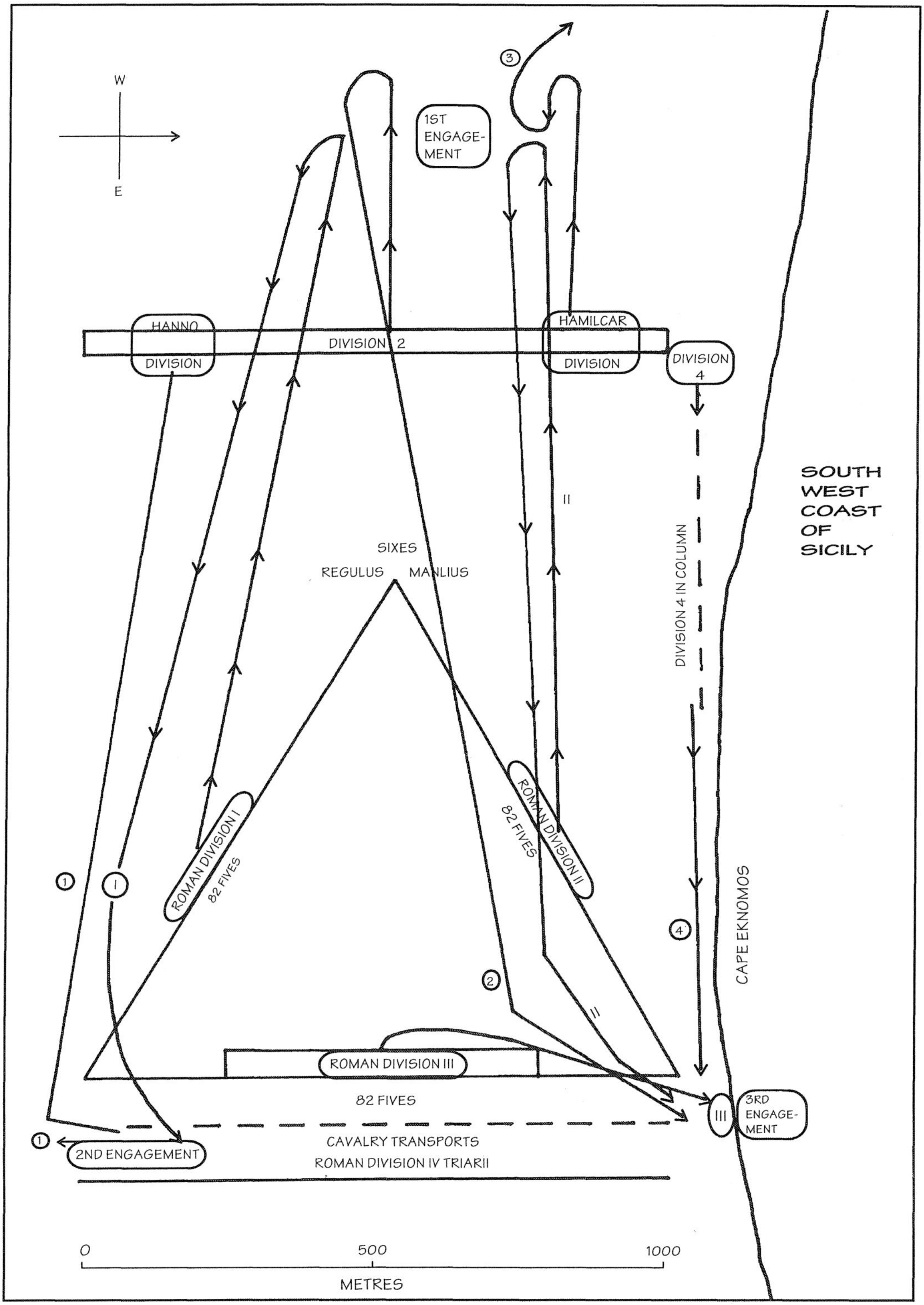

PLAN 3. *Battle of Eknomos 256 BC*

the crew of Pleistarchos's six (p. 34) was 500. It seems likely then that the two sixes were included in the total of ships, 330, given earlier. The crews of the 328 fives then total 13,760 and the crews of the two sixes total 1000 making a grand total of 138,760, which may be described as about 140,000.

In Athenian naval usage the *ὁπλῖται* carried on deck in a three were called *ἐπιβάται*, but the word had a non-technical meaning of any men carried on deck (cf. *AT* p. 132). In Polybios the word has this broader meaning of everyone on board a warship other than the oarsmen, that is to say the entire *ὑπηρεσία*, 30 in an Athenian three, 45 in a Rhodian four, who worked the ship under the captain and included archers and soldiers. There is then no indication in Polybios of how many of the *ἐπιβάται* on the Roman ships were troops embarked with invasion in view. It is perhaps reasonable to guess that such extra troops in the case of the Roman fives were about 80 leaving 40 for the normal *ὑπηρεσία*, and about 100 in the two sixes at Eknomos and in Pleistarchos's earlier six. The cavalry transports mentioned later, unlike the commanders' sixes, are not apparently included in the 330 cataphract ships first mentioned (P.1.25.7) as composing the Roman fleet, because of course they were not fighting ships.

Polybios's total of more than 150,000 men for the Carthaginian force of 350 cataphract ships (P.1.25.9) is reached, he says, on the basis of the number of ships (*κατὰ τὸν τῶν νεῶν λόγον*), but to reach a number of more than 150,000 the ship's company of the Carthaginian ships must be 430, ten more than the figure for the Roman ships. Alternatively, the number of the Carthaginian ships may by the time of the battle have increased by about eight. It is understandable that the Romans, intending a landing in Africa, should have carried a large number of soldiers, but the reason why the Carthaginians should have done the same is not at first clear. However, in a tactical situation where the issue was likely to be decided on the decks of the ships the Carthaginian commander may have felt that he had to match the Roman strength in that area.

The Romans were aware that their ships were the slower. This factor and the necessity to move into the open sea where they could be attacked from all quarters determined their battle formation (P.1.26.10).

The two sixes which were the flagships of the two consuls were ranged side by side at the head of the formation (1.26.11). Behind them the first division on one side and the second division on the other in single file increased the distance between the two files ship by ship, the ships covering each other with their prows as they fanned outwards. When the first and second divisions of the fleet had been arranged in the shape of a ram, the third division was added in line abreast, so that with this addition the whole shape of the formation made up a triangle. Behind the third division they placed the cavalry transports, and paid out tow-lines from them to the ships of the third division. Behind the cavalry transports the fourth division, called *triarii*, was added stretched out one deep so as to overlap those in front on each side (1.26.11–15) . When every part had been joined together in the way described the complete shape of the formation was a ram, the front part of which was hollow but the part at the base was solid, and the whole was mobile and effective and at the same time difficult to break up (1.26.16).

The number of ships in each of the four divisions is not given, and it may be assumed that they were about equal. If precisely equal, the number of ships in each would be 82 and with the two sixes would make up 330, the horse transports not being included. Such precision is perhaps not to be expected, but it may be assumed that the number of ships in each division was about 82.

The Carthaginian battle line (Plan 3) was determined by the Roman formation which was moving out to sea in a westerly direction making for Cape Hermaia (mod. Cap Bon) in Africa (where on their second attempt the Romans landed), that is to say, at an acute angle to the SW coast of Sicily (see Map E, p. 44). As a result the line was drawn up with the ships abreast in three divisions extending southwards from the coast east of the Eknomos promontory, across the path of the Roman fleet's (SW by W) progress, with the intention of surrounding it. A fourth division moved in line ahead along the coast parallel to the Roman course and at a right angle to and adjoining their own main line. Of this the right (seaward) wing commanded by Hanno consisted of regular ships of the line (*ἐπίπλοι*) and also the fastest fives, the latter to effect an outflanking movement (*πρὸς τὴν ὑπερκέρασιν*). Hamilcar, who had fought at Tyndaris, had charge of the ships on the left (of the main line) and on this occasion engaged the enemy in the middle of the line using a stratagem which Polybios proceeds to describe (1.27.7):

'When the Romans saw the Carthaginians stretched out in a thin line and attacked the centre, the battle began in this way. The Carthaginians in the central area, following Hamilcar's orders, soon turned in flight with the intention of drawing out the Roman formation. They accordingly withdrew with speed and the Romans followed enthusiastically. The first and second divisions pressed hard on the retreating ships, while the third and fourth divisions became separated from them, the former towing the cavalry transports and the latter, the *triarii* staying by and protecting them. When the Carthaginians thought they had drawn the first and second divisions out far enough from the rest, the signal was raised from Hamilcar's ship and they all turned together and attacked their pursuers. There was a sharp engagement in which by dint of their superior speed the Carthaginians had a clear advantage being able to move out and round them, easily attack and briskly withdraw. But the Romans by reason of their stout fighting hand-to-hand and their ability to use the boarding bridges to attach firmly ships that had made contact with their own, and because they were fighting under the eyes of both consuls taking part in the battle, had no less hopes of glory. In this way, as far as the divisions were concerned, the fighting developed'.

(P.1.28.1) 'Meanwhile Hanno, on the right wing which had stayed out of the first engagement, went round by the open sea and attacked the ships of the *triarii* and caused much confusion and difficulty in that area. The Carthaginians who were placed on the land side (i.e. the fourth division) changed from their first formation (line ahead) and attacking in line abreast set upon those (the third Roman division) who were towing the cavalry transports. They let go the tow ropes and engaged the enemy.'

(P.1.28.3)) 'There were three parts of the whole engagement and three sea fights were joined far separated from each other in space. And since the squadrons on each side were equal in the first skirmish so the battle turned out to be evenly balanced. Nevertheless the fighting developed logically in each theatre, as is natural when all the factors in the contest are equal. The first engagement was the first to be decided. In the end Hamilcar's men were overcome and took to flight. Lucius Manlius took the captured vessels in tow. Regulus. seeing the fight with the *triarii* and cavalry transports, hurried to their aid with the undamaged ships of the second naval division. When he had contacted Hanno's force and attacked it, the *triarii* quickly regained their spirits, although by this time they were in bad shape, and plucked up courage for the battle. The Carthaginians were thus in a difficult position with some attacking them in front and others in the rear, and were surrounded by the unexpected reinforcements of their opponents. they turned and beat a retreat to the open sea.'

(P.1.28.10–11) 'At the same moment Manlius, now moving up and seeing that the third squadron (which had been towing the cavalry transports) was boxed in against the shore by the Carthaginian force on the left wing (not the actual left wing of the main line) and Regulus also after he had seen the *triarii* and transports to safety, both came to the aid of the endangered third squadron.'

'What happened next was just like a siege ; and the third squadron would clearly have perished before this if the Carthaginians had not been afraid of the boarding bridges, and while keeping the ships hemmed in against the shore were cautious of approaching to ram. The consuls however came up quickly and surrounded the Carthaginians taking 50 enemy ships with their crews, some few only escaping along the coast.

(P.1.28.13) 'Such was the character of the battle in its various theatres. The outcome of the whole was in the Romans' favour. They lost 24 ships, the Carthaginians over 30 destroyed. None of the Roman ships was captured with her crew, 64 of the Carthaginian ships were so captured. In his verdict Polybios is in general right, but it must be admitted that the Carthaginians achieved their objective and the Romans failed. The invasion fleet was prevented from crossing to Africa.'

In many ways Eknomos was a remarkable success for the Romans, and displays well the strengths and weaknesses of both sides at sea. The impression given by Polybios's account is that the Carthaginians were the better seamen, and their ships were, as is stated categorically, faster and more manoeuvrable, whether because they were better rowed and managed or because they were better designed and built. Tactically also they seem to have had a better grasp of the principles of fighting oared ships. Neither is surprising in view of the Carthaginians' long mastery of the sea. Nevertheless, 30 of their ships were put out of action, presumably by ramming, as against 24 of the Romans. The Romans therefore, in spite of their recent apprenticeship, were not unskilled in the use of their slower, less manoeuvrable, fives. The outstanding statistic, which underlines the Roman strengths, was that 64 Carthaginian, but no Roman, ships were taken with their crews, 50 of them in the last part of the battle, when they were caught and surrounded because they had been afraid of approaching to ram Roman ships equipped with the boarding bridge. The Romans had a clear superiority in hand-to-hand fighting, and had the means and the skill, at this stage of their naval experience, to reduce a sea battle to that.

The outcome of the battle was to enable the Roman consuls, when they had rested their crews and fitted out the captured fives, to make the crossing to Africa. They sent a small force first to Cape Hermaia (Cap Bon), and then the rest of the fleet followed. Moving southward in the direction of Carthage, they established a base, hauling their ships ashore and protecting them with a ditch and stockade. After a siege they captured the town of Aspis on the eastern side of the promontory. Then on instructions from Rome Manlius returned, leaving 40 ships, 15,000 footsoldiers and 500 cavalry under the consul Regulus and taking with him the crews of the ships left behind and the prisoners taken.

After some early successes Regulus's army was ultimately defeated and its remnants besieged in Aspis. In the winter of 256 the Romans prepared their fleet for a rescue operation, while the Carthaginians refitted the ships they had and laid down others, finally manning a fleet of 200.

In the following summer (255) the Romans launched 350 ships and dispatched them to Sicily en route for Africa under the command of the new consuls Aemilius and Fulvius. Near Cape Hermaia they fell in with the Carthaginian fleet and routed them easily on the first encounter. Polybios (1.36.12) says that the Romans captured 114 ships, Diodoros (23.18.1) says 24. The fact that later the Roman fleet is given by Polybios as numbering 364, 14 in addition to the original 350, suggests that 14 Carthaginian ships had been captured in the battle. Furthermore, the Carthaginians were able to refit 200 ships a year later. The Roman fleet then took on board the force at Aspis and returned to Sicily.

(Polybios 1.37.1) 'Crossing the strait in safety, the fleet made a landfall near Kamarina, but there met with such a storm, and such disasters that beggar description. Of the 364 ships only eighty survived. Of the rest some were swamped, others were battered by the breakers on the reefs and promontories and filled the beaches with bodies and wreckage'.

Polybios ascribes the disaster not so much to bad luck as to bad leadership, since 'the consuls had been repeatedly warned not to take the route along the outer (SW) side of Sicily which faces the Libyan sea because it was exposed and inhospitable and because one constellation had not yet set and another had not yet risen (for they were at sea between the (heliacal) rising of Orion (30 June) and that of Sirius (28 July)). The consuls took no notice of these warnings and did not realise their exposed position, but were anxious to win over some of the cities which would be amazed at the parade of their recent success.'

This Roman maritime disaster encouraged the Carthaginians to throw another force into Sicily. They also made ready 200 ships (254/3). The Roman reaction was to lay down 220 ships and build them in three months. The consuls for the year 254/3, Aulus Atilius and Gnaeus Cornelius, prepared the fleet and took it to sea. At Messana they picked up the 80 ships that had survived the disaster and moved to besiege and take the Carthaginian naval base of Panormos, then returning to Rome. In the following summer (253/2) the consuls Servilius and Sempronius took the fleet of 300 ships to Sicily and Africa. As they were moving along the coast they ran into difficulty near the lesser Syrtis, (P.1.39.3) 'where owing to their inexperience (of local conditions) they ran on to some shoals; and the water retreating and the ships grounding they were in utter dismay. However, when after some time the sea rose unexpectedly they managed to lighten the ships by throwing all heavy objects overboard. On their return they took the route round Cape Lilybaion to Panormos. From there they took the risk of crossing the open sea on their way back to Italy, were caught again in a storm and lost 150 ships'.

The Romans were so discouraged that they abandoned their naval policy the following year and manned only 80 ships for carrying supplies to the legions in Sicily.

The Siege of Lilybaion and the Battle of the Aegates Islands (*Map F1*)

The election of two consuls with naval experience, Gaius Atilius and Manlius, the following year marked a reversal of policy. In 250/49 50 ships were built, and after the Roman troops at Panormos had fought a successful land battle a fleet of 200 ships was sent to Sicily. They beached near Lilybaion, joined the land forces and laid siege to the city, the last Carthaginian base in Sicily.

There appears to have been a first attempt to relieve Lilybaion by a force under Adherbal (Diodoros 24.1.2). Polybios (1.44.1) tells how later the Carthaginians put together a relief force under Hannibal, son of Hamilcar, 'collecting what was necessary for a besieged city and filling 50 ships with soldiers. Instructed to hurry, he set out with 10,000 soldiers [200 on each of the 50 fives] and beached in the Aegates islands lying between Carthage and Lilybaion, waiting for favourable weather [to run his ships in]'. The islands are in fact north west of Lilybaion, and not on the direct route, but Hannibal found them a convenient stopping place where he could wait for a wind in his favour for the dash into Lilybaion. 'When Hannibal succeeded in getting a stiff breeze in the right direction he spread sail with all his tackle (*ἐκπετάσας πᾶσι τοῖς ἀρμένοις*), and went before the wind to the actual harbour mouth with the men on deck under arms and ready to fight. The Romans were afraid of being carried into the harbour by the force of the wind if they attacked Hannibal's ships, and did nothing to prevent them'. The wind may have made action under oar unsafe.

(P.1.46.1) After unloading the men and stores, Hannibal slipped out of the harbour with his 50 ships by night unobserved, and joined the Carthaginian commander Adherbal at Drepana. Later (1.46.4) Polybios relates a similar success by 'a leading Carthaginian also called Hannibal, nicknamed the Rhodian'. He had offered to run the blockade and report on the state of affairs in Lilybaion and the offer was accepted. He fitted out his own ship, and arrived, like his namesake, at one of the islands off Lilybaion. On the very next day he was fortunate in getting a favourable wind and 'at the fourth hour' (about 10 am) sailed in before the eyes of the Romans who were amazed at his audacity. Soon after he was preparing his departure.

That night, taking steps to guard the entrance more carefully, the Roman commander prepared ten of his fastest ships, and with the whole army awaited the outcome. The (ten) ships, (five) on each side of the harbour mouth and as near as they dared get to the rocks, waited with oars at the ready (*ἐπτερωκυῖαι* 'making wings'), to ram and capture the ship that was about to emerge.

'The Rhodian' left the beach openly and challenged the enemy in audacity and speed so successfully that not only did he row out with his ship and crew unharmed, leaving his opponents' ships standing, so to speak, but when he had pulled away a short distance he stopped with his oars at the ready (*πτερώσας τὴν ναῦν* 'giving the ship wings'), as if challenging the enemy to a contest. But since no one dared to put out against him, because of the speed of his oars, he moved off after challenging the whole enemy fleet with a single ship. 'The Rhodian' did this many times, his local knowledge enabling him to choose the right route through the shallows which it was only possible to take with a favourable wind. Polybios describes it in detail. The Romans tried to prevent access by blocking the channel, on the whole unsuccessfully. At one point they did succeed with great difficulty, so that a four 'particularly well built' ran aground and was captured. The Romans manned it with a picked crew and kept a look-out for ships entering the harbour, in particular 'the Rhodian's'.

(P.1.47.7) It so happened that one night after this incident 'the Rhodian' sailed in and openly put to sea again. When he saw the four deliberately putting out at the same time he recognised the ship and was nervous. At first he tried to outstrip her, but overtaken by the crew's better training he was at last forced to turn and fight. Overwhelmed by the decksoldiers because of their numbers and picked quality he surrendered. Getting possession of this second well-found ship and fitting it out with what was necessary for the duty, the Romans prevented any more daring entries to Lilybaion.

On a later occasion in the second Punic war Livy (30.25.6: p. 68) describes an engagement between a

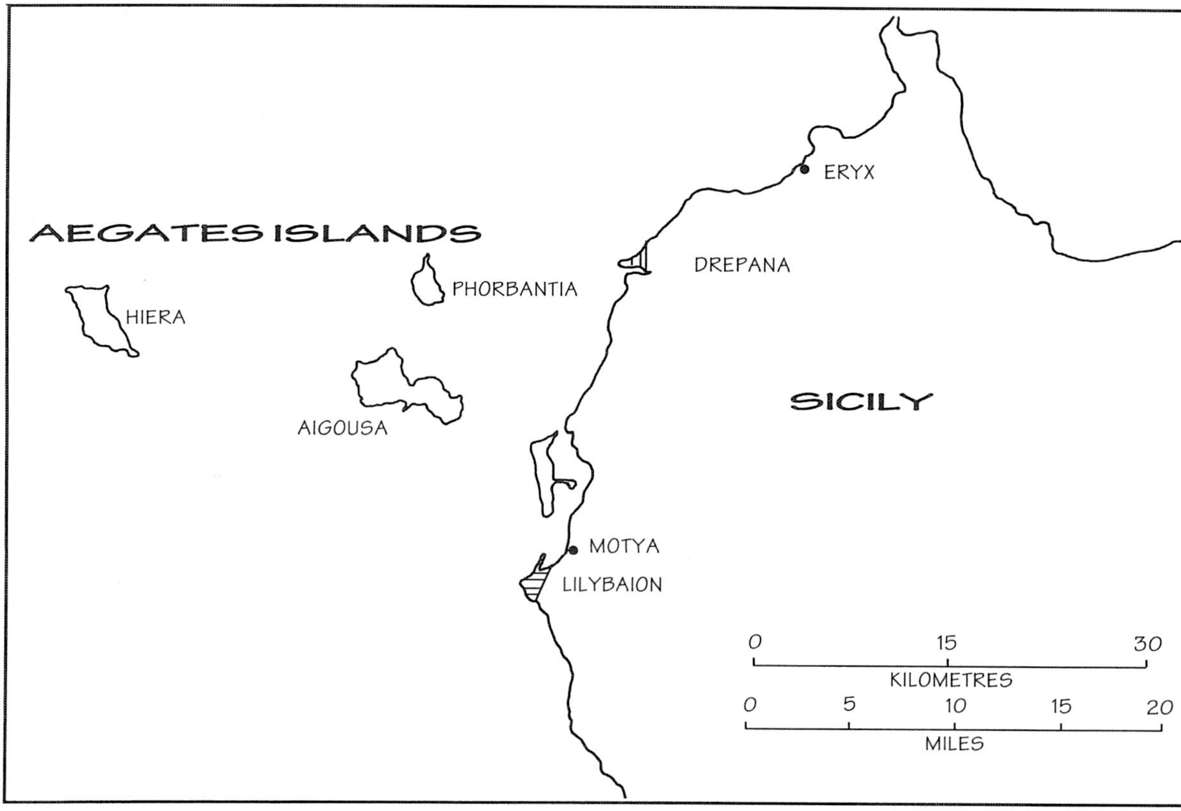

MAP F (i). *Lilybaion, Drepanon, Aegates islands*

Roman five and two Carthaginian fours. The deck-soldiers in the fours were unable to board the five because of her greater height. It seems to follow that if 'the Rhodian's' ship was boarded and captured by a four, that ship, the type of which is not specified, must have been a four also, rather than a five. The moral of the story is that fours were faster than fives, and the reason must have been because they were more lightly built. Fours had been invented at Carthage and were much used by the Rhodians (p. 102, 110). Alternatively, the 'Rhodian's' ship may have been a *τριημιολία*, another Rhodian speciality and equally fast. Hannibal's nickname, 'the Rhodian' may have arisen from his skilful handling of a well-known Rhodian ship-type.

When Hannibal 'the Rhodian's' ship was captured, she 'was fitted out with what was necessary for the duty' of stopping blockade runners. Since her failure to escape the previously captured Carthaginian four had been partly because the latter had a larger number of deck-soldiers, it seems that the refit consisted in making the necessary structural alteration, stouter deck, bulwarks, which would enable her to carry such a number of deck-soldiers.

(P.1.49.1) In 249 BC, when the siege of Lilybaion had reached a deadlock, the consul Publius Claudius received reinforcements of 10,000 sailors from Rome and decided to attack Drepana, where the Carthaginian commander Adherbal was based, with his whole fleet. To achieve surprise he moved at midnight northwards along the coast in close order. At first light the leading ships were visible from Drepana, and Adherbal was determined to do everything possible to avoid a siege. He led his ships in single file to the north side of the harbour opposite the enemy's southern point of entrance. This move caused the Romans some confusion, and in changing direction from entering the harbour to ranging themselves along the coast the

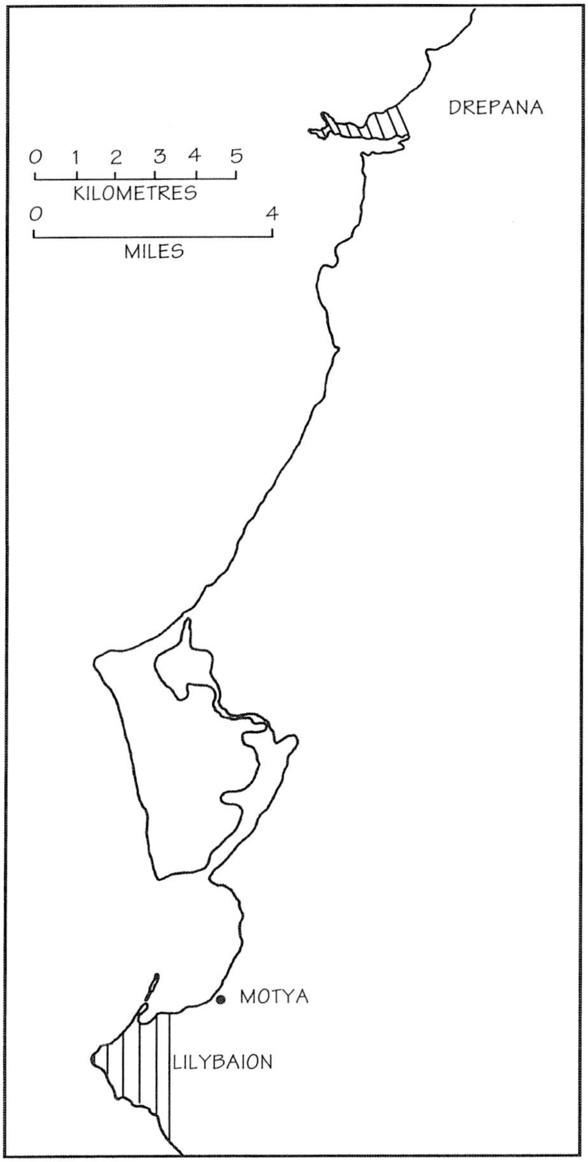

MAP F (ii). *Lilybaion, Drepanon, from Admiralty Chart*

ships collided with each other and broke some oars. Eventually the Roman commanders succeeded in forming up the ships line abreast along the shore facing the enemy who had emerged from the harbour and were drawn up facing them and with their sterns to the sea.

(P.1.51.2) At first the fighting was evenly balanced since both sides had embarked their best soldiers to fight on deck. But before long the Carthaginians gradually got the upper hand having the advantage in many respects. Their ships were much superior in speed because of their superior construction and of their better trained crews; Publius's reinforcements were presumably novices. Further, the Carthaginians were attacking from the open sea while the Romans had their sterns to the land. When Carthaginian ships were in trouble from an enemy, they could easily withdraw seawards and then come round and either get behind their attackers or ram them in the beam. The Romans found turning their heavy ships difficult with untrained crews, so that the Carthaginians rammed them repeatedly and caused many to swamp (*ἐβάπτιζον*). The Carthaginians also could easily go to the aid of hard-pressed comrades, passing behind the sterns of the ships in their own line. The Roman ships could not withdraw, running aground by the stern, or move behind their own line running aground by the bow.

(P.1.51.9) 'To achieve a breakthrough (*διέκπλους*) of the enemy line and appear astern of ships engaging others (which is the most effective naval manoeuvre) was impossible for the Romans because of the heaviness of their ships and their crews' inexperience. Nor were they able to come up astern of their own ships in trouble and aid them because they were pressed against the shore and there was no space for such a manoeuvre'. Publius who was on the left wing saw what was happening and slipped away with thirty ships which were near him, while Adherbal captured the remaining 93, with their crews except for those men who escaped when their ships ran ashore.

The Roman reaction to this defeat was to send supplies to their forces in Sicily with an escort of 60 warships under Publius's colleague. But in the following year there were further Roman losses by action and storm; and for a period of five years (247–242 BC) Rome virtually abandoned the sea, deciding to bring the war to an end on land.

(P.1.59.1–8) When this strategy had no success they resolved in 242 BC for the third time to build a fleet and by cutting off supplies from the Carthaginian army in Sicily finally to end the war. The money to build 200 fives was raised from private sources on the understanding that it would be repaid if the fleet achieved its purpose. Single ships were built and fitted out each by one, two or three wealthy men, the construction pattern being the ship of Hannibal 'the Rhodian' recently captured, which seems likely to have been a four.

Some have seen here a 'doublet' of the story (p. 43) of the capture of the Carthaginian cataphract (probably a five) which served as a model of the first Roman fleet, but this seems unlikely since the circumstances were very different. In the first case a model was needed for the first cataphracts built by Rome, in the second a model was specially chosen because the Romans realised that the Carthaginian ship was lighter and more manoeuvrable than theirs. On this latter occasion what they were interested in was improvement of hull design.

(P.1.59.8) When the fleet was ready it was dispatched to Sicily under Gaius Lutatius in the summer of 242. Appearing unexpectedly he succeeded in capturing the harbour of Drepana and the beaches near Lilybaion, the Carthaginian fleet retiring to Carthage. Realising that the decisive action of the war would be fought at sea, Lutatius spent every day in trials and practice manoeuvres with his crews, at the same time paying attention to their diet and getting the oarsmen into perfect training for the task ahead. In so doing he was remedying the second point in which the Roman ships at Lilybaion had fallen behind the Carthaginian blockade runners, training and fitness of crews.

(P.1.60.1) At Carthage the challenge was accepted and a fleet was sent out under Hanno with the task of ensuring supplies for the Carthaginian army at Eryx. Hanno arrived at the island of Hiera, 48 km. WSW of Eryx, intending to make the final stage unobserved by Lutatius; and then after putting ashore the supplies for the army and taking on deck the best mercenary soldiers and their commander Barcas, to engage the Roman fleet. Lutatius was however aware of his arrival and intention, and took the Roman fleet, with the best soldiers on deck, to the island of Aigousa between Hiera and the Sicilian coast. There he gave the soldiers appropriate encouragement and told the helmsmen that there would be a battle the following day.

(P.1.60.6) Very early the next morning Lutatius saw that there was a fresh breeze, in the enemy's favour (viz. SW), but difficult for the Romans who would put out against the wind with a rough steep sea. At first he was at a loss what to do in the circumstances. But calculating that if he took the risk of an engagement in bad weather he would be fighting only against Hanno and his naval forces, and ships which were still loaded, but if he waited for fair weather, and by his delay let the enemy go ashore and join up with the land force, he would be fighting against ships which were fast-moving and cleared for action, as well as against troops which were the pick of the land army, and in particular against Hamilcar who had a formidable reputation (as a naval commander).

(P.1.60.9) 'He decided accordingly not to let pass the opportunity offered. Perceiving the enemy ships under sail he put out as quickly as possible (under oar). With his crews skilfully managing the swell by dint of their state of physical training, he quickly deployed his ships in a single line and then drew them up facing the enemy prow-to-prow. (1.61.1) When the Carthaginians saw the enemy preventing their passage they lowered their masts and shouting encouragement from ship to ship set about engaging the enemy.' The forces of each side were in the opposite position to that which had prevailed at the battle of Drepana, and the outcome of the battle was correspondingly the opposite. The Romans had both changed their technique of ship construction and also were leaving ashore all the heavy gear apart from that which was needed in battle. The crews, trained to a harmonised stroke (*τὰ πληρώματα συγκεκροτημένα*), were in addition putting up a superior performance for the ships. The deck soldiers also were a body of picked fighters from the infantry legions.

The opposite was the case with the Carthaginians. The ships being laden were in an awkward posture for battle, the crews were quite untrained and recruited at random, while the deck troops were newly enrolled and unused to any hardship or danger. It was because they never expected that the Romans any more could dispute the sea that they had contemptuously neglected their naval forces.

The result was that from the first contact they were worsted at many points and quickly defeated. 50 of their ships were swamped and 70 captured, all with their crews. The rest, raising their masts and meeting a favourable wind, sailed back to Hiera. By unexpected good fortune the wind helped them, changing direction at the right moment. The Roman consul moved away to Lilybaion and occupied himself with the management of the captured ships and men, which was no small matter. Those captured alive in the battle were not much less than 10,000 men. The oarcrews of 70 fives (@ 300) would have themselves, apart from the additional deck-soldiers, amounted to 21,000 men. Having lost command of the sea the Carthaginians were unable to supply their army in Sicily, and being unable to live off the country were forced to come to terms with Rome.

(1.63.4) Polybios gives the following summary of 'the war about Sicily'. It lasted 24 years without a break. It was the longest and most continuous and the greatest of the wars heard of up to his time. On one occasion (Hermaia: P.1.36.9–10) the two sides fought each other at sea with more than 500, at another time (Eknomos: P.1.25) with very nearly 700 fives. In this war the Romans lost as many as 700 fives including those lost by shipwreck, the Carthaginians as many as 500. So that those who admire the battles and fleets of Antigonos and Ptolemy and Demetrios would reasonably, when they take account of previous fleets, be amazed at the scale of the operations.

'If one should wish to consider the superiority of the five over the threes with which the Persians fought against the Greeks, and again the Athenians and the Spartans against each other, one could not anywhere find forces of such power fighting at sea. Consequently the proposition I put forward at the outset, that it was not by good luck that the Romans, as some Greeks think, nor by mere chance, but very naturally, after gaining experience in matters of such a kind and magnitude, not only had the audacity to aspire to world domination and rule, but actually achieved their ambition'.

3. THE EASTERN MEDITERRANEAN: 256–219

The Egyptian Naval Defeat c.256 BC

Polyainos (5.18): 'The Rhodians were waging war with king Ptolemy [II] in the neighbourhood of Ephesos. Chremonides, the *ναύαρχος* of Ptolemy, put out to sea to give battle. Agathostratos led the Rhodians out in single file (*ἐπὶ μίαν ναῦν*), and when he was in sight of the approaching fleet changed formation into line abreast (*μετέστρεψε μετωπηδόν*); and after a short pause returned to the same mooring. The enemy thought that (the Rhodians) had no heart for fighting it out; and singing the paean went back into the harbour. Agathostratos turned to face the enemy; and thickening his line towards both flanks moved against them as they were disembarking near the sanctuary of Aphrodite. By the unexpected assault he won a victory'.

The picture is clearly drawn. The Egyptian fleet in their harbour of Ephesos came out under the Athenian Chremonides, whose defiance of Macedon had led to exile in Egypt, to meet the Rhodian fleet under Agathostratos who were at moorings nearby. As the Egyptian fleet approached, the Rhodians who were in single file formed line abreast (one ship deep) in the usual manner of a fleet offering battle . But they soon retreated to the mooring from which they had put out. The Egyptians concluded that the Rhodians were declining battle, sang a song of victory and went back to their harbour. But Agathostratos's retreat was a ruse, qualifying the engagement for a place in Polyainos's *Book of Stratagems*.

Since Agathostratos's ships had come out in single file, the deployment to the left of the commander's leading ship (see below p. 95 and p. 103) resulted in a line abreast only one ship deep, a very weak formation, but correspondingly wide. To strengthen his line, and also probably to negotiate the entrance to the harbour, he made it deeper (i.e. with more than one file) and so shorter, by moving the ships in the centre towards the flanks on each side. He then moved into the harbour and attacked the Egyptian ships as they were putting their crews ashore by the sanctuary of Aphrodite. Disembarkation and embarkation, which take a little time, are vulnerable moments for an oared warship.

In spite of this reverse on top of the defeats at Kos and Andros and the loss to Antigonos of control of the Island League at Delos, Egypt managed to retain her naval base at Samos and a strong military and naval presence at Ephesos (P.5.35.11).

The action near Ephesos has an additional interest because, as Ellen Rice (1991 p. 33) has noticed, the Rhodian *ναύαρχος* Agathostratos appears as a trierarch in an inscription on a monument probably set up in a prominent position on the ascent to the acropolis at Lindos. The inscription records the dedication of the first fruits of spoils taken by the crews of two *τριημιολίαι* under the command of a *ναύαρχος* and two trierarchs one of whom is named Agathostratos. The monument represents a prow which under the circumstances can hardly be other than the prow of a *τριημιολία*. The prow and the inscription will be discussed below (**11**, p. 203–4).

His naval base at Samos and a stronghold in Ephesos still provided Ptolemy III Euergetes with the confidence to celebrate at Delos his accession in 246 BC and to seize from Seleukos II Seleukeia Pieria at the mouth of the Orontes (P.5.58.11).

When Antigonos Gonatas died in 239 and was succeeded by his son Demetrios II (239–229), Macedonian naval power declined, although it still maintained supremacy over Delos, Keos and the Kyklades; and Demetrios extended Macedonian influence to Crete in 237. This essentially naval power continued to be exercised after Demetrios's death during Antigonos Doson's regency (p. 215), and the latter's expedition in 227 to Karia, an important area of naval recruitment in Hellenistic times, must have owed its purpose to naval competition with Egypt. It was not however until a few years after Philip V's succession in 221 at the age of seventeen that Macedonian sea power revived in face of Rome's.

After the defeat of Carthage Rome was, in terms of ships, potentially the strongest naval power in the Mediterranean, but her almost total reliance on her 'naval allies' for oarsmen and skilled personnel made her unwilling to exercise it except in defence of Italy and her commercial interests in neighbouring countries. Hannibal's invasion of Italy by land after 219 concentrated her attention on land warfare apart from a small but important naval presence in Spain, Sicily and Sardinia, until the move of Scipio to Africa in the later stages of the second Punic war.

These circumstances, attesting a weakened interest in the exercise of naval power among the 'Great Powers' of the region, Egypt, Macedon and Rome, led to naval activity on a minor scale among the lesser maritime states, in particular Illyria, Akarnania, and the Aetolian and Achaean Leagues; Rhodes, whose strategic situation on the route from Egypt, Phoenicia and Syria to the Aegean and the west made her a maritime power out of proportion to her resources, was for a number of years *hors de combat* as the result of the devastating earthquake of 224 BC. Polybios comments that the Rhodians 'made such sensible and practical use of the event that it was for them more an opportunity for reconstruction than a source of harm'. (5.88.4) 'The Rhodians at any rate in their treatment (of the earthquake) making out the catastrophe was great and terrible and behaving at audiences in their embassies and in their individual contacts with seriousness and dignity, made such an impression on the cities and in particular on the kings that they not only received very large donations but the donors also felt gratitude to them'.

The scale of this international aid, without parallel until modern times, is very remarkable and indicates the respect in which Rhodes was held, as well as the charitable fund-raising skill of the Rhodians to which Polybios draws attention.

Rhodes: Protector of the Freedom of the Seas

(Heinen: 1984 p. 432–3)

The position of Rhodes on the trade route from Egypt, Syria and Phoenicia to the western coastal cities of Asia Minor and the Black Sea as well as to the Aegean and further west gave her an interest in preserving the freedom of trade from piracy and impost. An inscription from the period 250–220 BC records a Rhodian admiral (*ναύαρχος*) appointed 'for the protection of the islands and the security of the Greeks' (*ἐπὶ τῆς φυλακῆς τῶν νήσων καὶ ἐπὶ σωτηρίας τῶν Ἑλλήνων*). Strabo (14.2.5) writes of 'the city of the Rhodians' as being 'in harbours and roads and walls and other installations so far superior to others that I cannot speak of any other as equal or nearly equal to it, much less greater. It is remarkable for its good government and careful administration in general and in particular of maritime affairs in which for a long time it held a dominant position [see Ellen Rice: 1991], getting rid of piracy and becoming the friend of Rome and those of the kings who favoured the Romans and Greeks'. Later, rather surprisingly, he compares Rhodes with Massalia and Kyzikos as a place where 'outstandingly and more than among other peoples there is special interest (*ἐσπούδασται*) in the work of master craftsmen (*ἀρχιτέκτονες*) and the making of machines of war (*ὀργανοποιία*) and the stockpiling of arms and other (such) things'.

Polybios (4.37.8–52 10) gives an account of the hostilities which began in 220 between Rhodes and Byzantion as a result of this Rhodian role. Byzantion, controlling the entrance to the Black Sea through which the supply of corn from the Crimea came to the eastern Mediterranean, exacted dues from the ships passing through which were burdensome and caused much irritation to traders. (P.4.47.1) 'All the merchants plying [on that route] called on the Rhodians because they had the reputation of being foremost in maritime affairs'. The Rhodians were drawn to act on their own account as well as that of their neighbours and made diplomatic representations to Byzantion asking for the impost to be lifted. When this approach was unsuccessful they invited King Prusias, who was known to have had disputes with Byzantion, to join them; and declared war, manning six ships and adding four from their allies. Prusias promised to support them on land. Meanwhile the Byzantines sent a mission to Attalos of Pergamon, whose power had been much weakened by his neighbour Achaios appointed by Antiochos III, the king of Syria, as well as to Achaios himself. Both replied favourably. The Rhodians succeeded however in establishing a blockade at Sestos to prevent traffic from entering the Black Sea. Prusias's land support and diplomatic pressure from Ptolemy in Egypt were successful in bringing the war to an end, the Rhodians sending simultaneously three threes under Polemokles to Byzantion and a mission to negotiate a peaceful settlement. The impost was lifted on ships passing to and from the Black Sea (*διαγωγή*).

The hostilities between Rhodes and Byzantion, in which no action appears to have taken place, have a curiously modern ring, like the international subscriptions to relieve the Rhodian earthquake four years earlier and the Rhodian specialisation in arms manufacture while remaining a city with no 'imperialistic' ambition. A picture is presented of the balance of power, before the entry of Rome, among the various small states of the eastern Mediterranean, with the 'Great Power' Egypt exerting diplomatic pressures from the periphery. Rhodes and her allies used the threat of force by a few ships to gain a purely commercial objective.

The War for Koile-Syria

The capture of Seleukeia in Pieria, at the mouth of the Orontes, by Ptolemy Euergetes in 246 BC was an affront to the Seleucid dynasty of Syria and an assertion of Egyptian sea power. It has become plain that possession of the southern coast of Asia Minor, of Cyprus, Koele Syria, Phoenicia and Palestine was the key to the resources of men, skills and shipbuilding material on which sea power depended. In 219 BC Antiochos III of Syria decided to take advantage of Egyptian weakness at any rate to redress the balance. His first step was to attack Seleukeia. It fell and shortly afterwards Ptolemy's *ναύαρχος* Theodotos surrendered Tyre and Ptolemais (Acre) to him with a squadron of forty ships.

(P.5.62.3) 'Of these there were twenty cataphracts, very well equipped, none of which were of lower rating than a four, and the rest were threes, *δίκροτα* and *κέλητες*. This description of the squadron implies that ships of the rating of four and above were at this time thought worth equipping lavishly because of their importance as warships. Threes were sometimes cataphract (decked) and sometimes not. Here the threes were not decked.The description is interesting because the ships are listed in an order reflecting the number of files of oarsmen on each side of the ship: the four with four, the three with three, the *δίκροτα* with two and the *κέλητες* with one. The *δίκροτοι* in Alexander's Indus flotilla (see above p. 10) were rowed at two levels. A fragment of the 4th century comic writer Ephippos (in Athenaios 8.38) speaks of five *κέλητες πεντέσκαλμοι* 'boats with five tholepins a side' and so ten oarsmen in all (at one level of course), so fast launches. The word *κέλης* also means a racehorse.

Antiochos advanced on Egypt. Sosibios and Agathokles negotiated with him on behalf of Ptolemy while an army and fleet were prepared. The Egyptian *ναύαρχος* Perigenes had a fleet of 30 cataphracts and more than 400 transports (*φορτηγοί*) (P.5.68.4). Nikolaos waited with the army and fleet near Porphyrion, while Antiochos came down the coast accompanied by his fleet under Diognetos. In the resultant battle at Raphia (5.84–86) the issue was decided on land with Ptolemy's now well-trained army successful. Koele-Syria and Phoenicia returned to the control of Egypt.

4. THE SECOND PUNIC WAR: 220/19–203

(John Briscoe: 1989 p. 65–7)

The outbreak in 219 of the second war between Rome and Carthage led to some naval activity in the western Mediterranean. (P.3.33.14, cf L.21.22.4) When Hannibal set out in the summer of 218 for Italy he left his brother Hasdrubal as commander in Spain with a fleet of 50 fives, two fours and five threes. There were crews for only 32 of the fives and for the 5 threes (p. 215, 216). From this order of priority it would appear that a fleet needed both heavy ships and fast ships as the following building programme also testifies, but fours did not qualify as either. At Rome 220 fives were launched and 20 fast ships (*celoces*, Greek *κέλητες:* L.21.17.3: Polybios omits the fast ships). To meet the threat of the Carthaginian fleet at New Carthage the consul to whom the province of Spain had been allotted, Publius Cornelius Scipio, was sent with 60 ships and a land force. At the same time (P.3.41.2 cf. L.21.17.8) a great fleet of 160 fives and two legions, accompanied by 12 fast ships was ordered to Africa under the other consul, Tiberius Sempronius. He reached Lilybaion and began large-scale preparations for the invasion of Africa, but was recalled on the news that Hannibal had crossed the Alps.

(P.3.41.4) Publius Scipio reached the mouth of the Rhone nearer to Massalia in five days making about 430 sm at an average speed of about 5 knots for a 16 hour rowing day. He would have been accompanied by a considerable number of troop and horse transports. He failed to reach Hannibal before he had crossed the river, and accordingly sent his brother Gnaeus on to Spain with half the ships and troops and returned to Italy with the rest.

The Battle of the Ebro (Plan 4)

In the following year (217: P.3.95.2–96.6, L.22.19–20.3) Gnaeus Scipio moved from the Rhone to Emporion and thence along the coast to Tarraco. Meanwhile Hasdrubal had fitted out 40 of the fives (here called *κατάφρακτοι νῆες*) and set out in the early summer from New Carthage, giving the command at sea to Himilco. Gnaeus Scipio, seeing himself outnumbered on land, manned 35 ships with oarcrews and chose the best fighting men from the land force for service on deck.

(Livy's account is now more detailed and will be followed): 'The fleet put to sea from Tarraco and on the following day reached moorings (*stationem*) ten (Roman) miles (14.8 km) from the mouth of the Ebro, From there they sent two Massaliot scout ships (*L.speculatoriae, P.νῆες ταχυπλέουσαι*) ahead, which reported that the Punic fleet was moored (*stare cf. stationem* above), also the account of the Punic ships putting out in the mouth of the river Ebro. Accordingly, to catch them unawares and off their guard, Gnaeus raised anchor and moved to the attack'.

'In Spain there are many towers on high ground which are used as look-outs and defence against pirates. From these the enemy ships were seen and the signal given to Hasdrubal. The alarm was raised on land and in the camp before it reached the sea and the ships, since the beat of oars and the rest of a fleet's noise had not been heard, or the sight of it disclosed by the promontories. Suddenly one horseman after another sent by Hasdrubal told the men wandering on the beach and resting in their tents (expecting nothing less than the enemy and a battle on that day) to go on board their ships immediately and (in the case of the decksoldiers) take up their arms, since the Roman fleet was not far from the port. These orders were given by the widely dispersed horsemen. Soon Hasdrubal appeared with the whole army (from the camp which was some distance from the beach). The scene was a hubbub of different kinds as the oarsmen rushed to board the ships and the soldiers resembled fugitives from the land rather than men going into battle'.

'The men were all scarcely on board when some cast off the shore cables and moved out over the anchors (see GOS 56 n. 'Mediterranean Moor'), while others to avoid delay cut the anchor ropes; and the tasks of the crew were hindered by the military personnel acting quickly and in a great hurry, while the soldiery were prevented from taking up and preparing their weapons [including catapults] by the crew's flurry. And now the Romans were not only coming up but had taken order of battle. The result was that the Carthaginians, put into confusion less by the enemy and the engagement than by their own hubbub, turned away their ships in flight with the battle not so much joined as merely attempted. Since the mouth of the river they now faced could not be entered by such a large number of ships in a wide column, they generally drove their ships ashore and some of the men in shallows others on the dry land, some armed, some unarmed, fled to their own forces drawn up on the shore'.

'However, two Punic ships were captured at the first encounter, and four were swamped (*suppressae*). Although it was enemy territory and they could see the Carthaginian battle line occupying the whole shore, the Romans did not hesitate to pursue the demoralised enemy ships and attaching

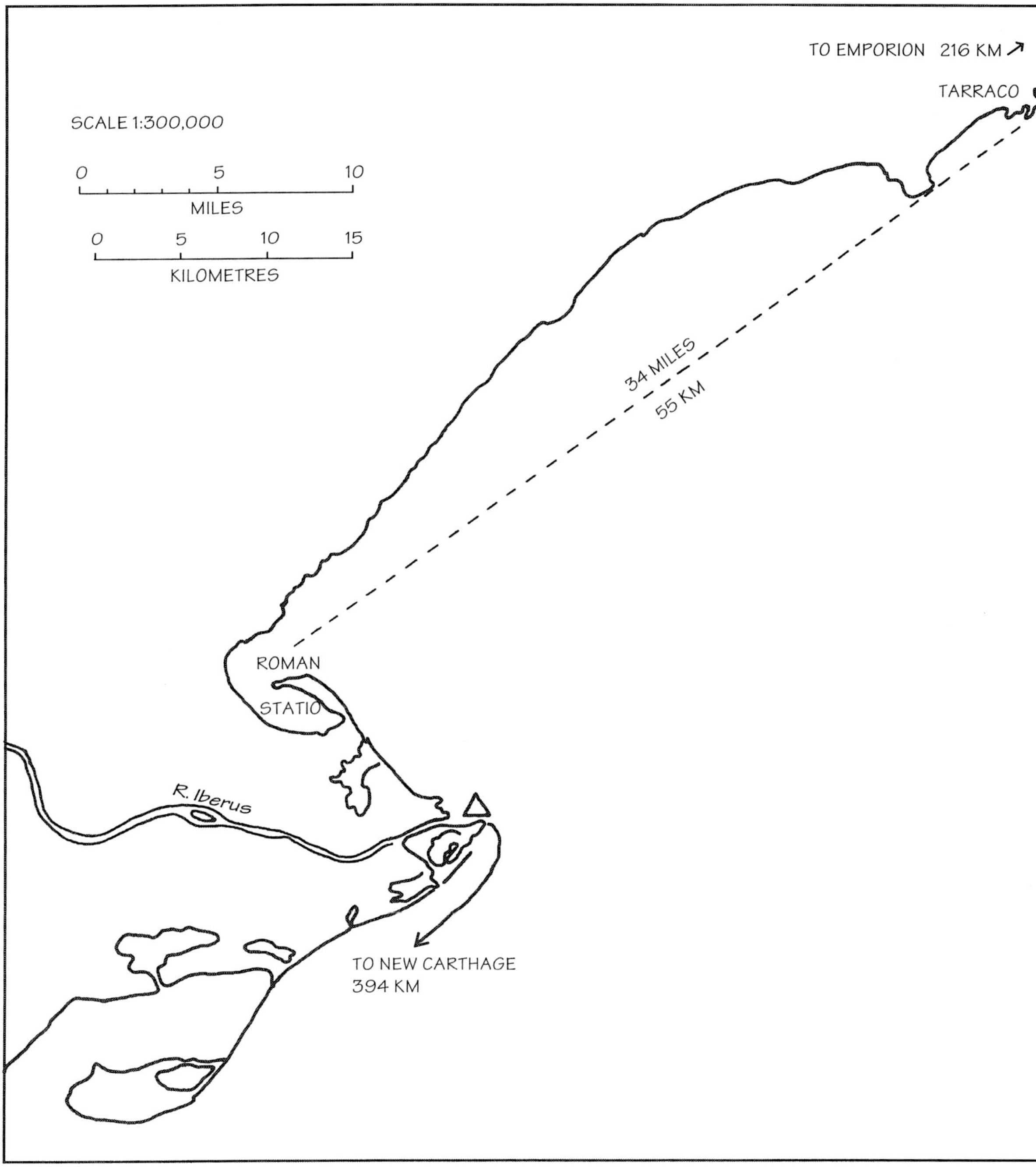

PLAN 4. *The Battle of the Ebro*

Note: The outline of the coast is based on the current Admiralty chart which is unlikely to present accurately the area of the river's outflow as it was at the time of the battle. The main features are nevertheless relevant.

cables to the sterns towed away into deep water all those which had not damaged their prows by running aground or stuck their keels fast in the shallows. Of the 40 enemy ships they captured 25'.

Polybios (3.96.4–6) gives a briefer account: 'After losing two ships with their crews and the oars and decksoldiers of four more, they turned away and made for the shore. When the Romans pursued them vigorously, they ran the ships aground and the men themselves, leaping overboard, escaped to the army's line. The Romans approached the shore with daring, put ropes aboard those ships that could be moved and rowed off in great good spirits, because they had beaten the enemy at the outset, had established command of the sea and had in their possession 25 enemy ships'.

There is an interesting variation between Livy's and Polybios's description of what happened to the four ships lost to the Carthaginians, other than the two lost with their crews (*αὐτάνδρους*), in the initial engagement. Livy's account appears to be a paraphrase of Polybios; but Livy's 'swamped', should be the equivalent of Polybios's 'losing oars and decksoldiers'. However, a ship loses decksoldiers when it has been successfully boarded by decksoldiers from an enemy ship. Loss of oars is the result of breakage through collision. The loss of oars and decksoldiers would make the ship totally ineffective as a warship. 'Swamping' on the other hand is the result of a successful ram, but it has exactly the same effect, putting the ship out of action as a weapon. What happened after the initial encounter to these 4 ships is not told. It is likely that they, like the two captured with their crews and the ships towed off the shore, are included in the 25 ships recorded as captured by the Romans.

A further point of interest is Polybios's remark that support troops on land, which the Carthaginians had, but the Romans lacked, were not conducive to hard fighting at sea. Provision of land support for ships in battle had always been one of the cardinal principles of fighting at sea in oared ships, and was bound up with another cardinal principle, to choose the area for the battle close to land (if possible friendly land). This latter principle is of course associated with a preference for calm water. Polybios's remark is probably not so much iconoclastic as critical of the Carthaginians' lack of appetite on this occasion for the fight.

(P.3.96.8) At Carthage news of this defeat aroused determination not to lose command of the sea 'judging it necessary for all their designs to keep a grip on the sea'. They manned and dispatched 70 ships, first to Sardinia and then to Pisa in Italy to make contact with Hannibal. At the news that 120 fives under Gnaeus Servilius had been sent against them from Rome they made for home. Servilius pursued them, and when they eluded him went on to Lilybaion and from there to Africa where he took two islands (?Cercina and Cossyra: see Map L (ii)) before returning to Lilybaion.

JFC observes: 'This is the clearest indication I have yet read of the importance of sea power to both Rome and Carthage in their struggle with each other. Were the 70 Carthaginian ships all fighting ships intended to link up with Hannibal and then presumably to establish a base in Italy, protected by land by him, so that they could then defend that end of supply routes by sea? Or was it a single supply mission by a mixed fleet of fighting or supply ships? Whichever it was the Carthaginians seem to have underestimated the naval strength of Rome while at the same time having respect for Rome's competence at sea. Servilius's failure to find the returning Carthaginian fleet illustrates the great difficulty naval commanders have always had (before the development of modern technology) in finding their enemy at sea and the reason why fleet actions have taken place close to naval bases or focal points of shipping almost without exception. Servilius's capture of two islands near Africa was presumably intended as a first move towards establishing a forward base, so necessary in permanently limiting the range of Carthaginian seapower. This action indicates how firmly Rome at that time intended to control the western Mediterranean. She presumably felt that she could defend such a forward base'. But no more is heard of it.

(P.3.97.1) At Rome the Senate decided to reinforce Gnaeus Scipio in Spain by sending out 20 ships under his brother Publius who was to join him in command.

From Spain (L.25.36) in the following years 50 ships were recalled to home waters since operations there were on land. They ended in a disaster for the Romans, both Scipios being killed in separate actions in 212. When Capua had been retaken the propraetor Nero and the two legions there were embarked at Puteoli and sent to Tarraco, where the ships were hauled ashore and the crews (*socii navales*) put under arms. He joined forces with what remained of the Roman troops north of the Ebro (L.26.17. 1–3). For the following year the young Publius Scipio, then aged 24, was chosen to take over the command of the Roman armies in what Heitland called 'this almost hereditary war' (i. p. 291). Ten thousand foot soldiers and 1000 cavalry and a propraetor, Junius Silanus, were sent with him: (L.26.19.11) 'So with a fleet of 30 ships, all fives, he set out from Ostia along the coast of the Etruscan sea, past the Alps and the Gulf of Gaul, then rounded the Pyrenaic promontory and landed his forces at the Greek city of Emporion (settled originally by Phokaia). Then, telling his ships to follow, he marched to Tarraco where he held a meeting of all the allies, since embassies from the whole province had poured in at the news of his arrival. He ordered the ships to be hauled ashore there. Four Massaliot threes which had dutifully accompanied his fleet from Massalia were sent home'.

During the winter he evolved a plan, communicated only to his fleet commander Laelius, for the capture of the Carthaginian naval base of New Carthage, with its excellent port facilities. (L.26.41.1) In the spring of 409 he launched his (35) ships, called up his allied auxiliaries to Tarraco by proclamation and ordered the fleet and transports (*onerarias*) to make for the mouth of the Ebro, telling the legions to meet there from their winter quarters and bringing the allies with him from Tarraco. The whole force then moved on New Carthage. (L.26.42.5): 'Laelius was instructed to moderate the progress of his ships so as to enter the port at the same time as the army appeared. The force arrived at (New) Carthage by land and sea seven days out from the Ebro', a voyage of about 215 sm at an average speed of 3 knots in a 12 hour day at sea. The city was captured after some fierce fighting. Scipio sent a five to Rome to announce his success.

(P.10.17.6–16) Scipio seized the opportunity offered by his conquest of New Carthage to increase his fleet of fives, which numbered 35, by manning with prisoners of war 18 captured ships, also fives. There is a briefer passage on the same subject in Livy (26.47.1–3), which gives the number of captured ships as 8, plainly a scribal error.

The total number of prisoners taken, Polybios says, was nearly ten thousand, from whom Scipio separated two groups, first citizens, men and women with their young children, and secondly craftsmen. He freed the first group, and made the second group, numbering about 2000, public slaves of Rome. Livy does not mention the first group and the prisoners are said to be ten thousand free men. As in Polybios the citizens are said to have been set at liberty and the 2000 craftsmen made public slaves. In Polybios Scipio is said to have selected from all those not in the first two groups 'the strongest, the fittest looking and the youngest and mixed them up with his own crews. And making the whole body of oarsmen (*ναῦται*) half as many again as before, he succeeded in manning the captured ships as well as his own, so that in each ship the original crewmembers were twice the number of those who had been added (*τῶν προσγενομένων*) (i.e. from the prisoners taken). For the captured ships were 18 in number and the original ships 35.

The current texts of the passage (Büttner-Wobst (1901), Walbank (1967), Paton (1922)) print the Mss reading *τῶν προγενομένων* 'twice the number of those that had previously been crewmembers'. This reading presents a physical impossibility. Fives were built for a crew of 300 oarsmen (P.1.26.7), 600 could not have been fitted in. Reiske saw in 1753 that *προγενομένων* is a scribal error for *προσγενομένων* which makes sense. The only way Scipio thought it would be safe to man ships for his service with prisoners of war was by using two of his own men to one prisoner-of-war. His *socii navales* would be able to produce the further skilled personnel needed in addition to the oarsmen, and the legions, as usual (cf. P.3.95.5), could provide the decksoldiers.

The Revival of Macedonian Sea Power under Philip V of Macedon (*Maps G and K*)

In the summer of 219 (see above p. 57) Demetrios of Pharos, previously ruler of Illyria, found refuge with the young Philip V of Macedon. In the following winter Philip decided to prosecute the war against Aitolia by sea. As Walbank said (1940 p. 51) 'behind this naval policy there stood a new figure, Demetrios of Pharos'. 'This, he was convinced', says Polybios (5.2.1), 'was the only way by which he could quickly be in contact with his enemies from every direction, while they could have the least opportunity of giving aid to each other, being geographically dispersed and each fearing for their own safety because of the unexpectedness and speed of a descent upon them by sea, since he was fighting against Aetolians, Spartans and Eleans. Upon making this decision he concentrated the Achaean ships and his own at Lechaion (the port of Corinth), and by continuous practice trained the soldiers of the phalanx and accustomed them to pulling an oar'. 'The Macedonians', Polybios added, 'were very ready to undertake sea service in an emergency'.

Philip spent some time in practising his crews and in collecting his ships from various quarters. There is no indication of the number or type of his ships at this stage. (P.5.2.11) 'Then, when the ships were assembled and the Macedonians trained, he distributed victuals and pay and took his force, consisting of 6,000 Macedonians and 1,200 mercenaries, to sea, arriving on the following day at Patrai and leaving a force of Achaean mercenaries at Dyme on the way'. He had sent written instructions to the Messenians, Epirots and Acarnanians and to Skerdilaidas to meet him at Kephallenia.

The reason for choosing Kephallenia as his first target was primarily because that island had afforded the Aetolians naval aid in 220 and might do so again, but also because it was a rich and fertile island and could provide Philip with victuals for his forces. A third reason was that it was well situated geographically in regard to the Peloponnese and to Epeiros and Akarnania and, like Kerkyra, was a stepping stone to the west, Italy and Sicily. He had begun to besiege Palus when 15 *λέμβοι* arrived from Skerdilaidas, unable to send the greater part of his fleet because of disturbances in Illyria. Ships from Epeiros, Akarnania and Messene also arrived. Philip moved his fleet to Leukas and through the channel into the Ambracian gulf to Limnaia from where he took a land force into Aitolia and sacked Thermos. He then returned to Limnaia took his fleet to Leukas and then back to Corinth. After a swift incursion into Lakonia he returned to Macedon by way of the port of Demetrias.

(P.5.95.1) In the following year (217 BC) Skerdilaidas deserted Philip and sent 15 *λέμβοι* to seize four ships under the command of Taurion and their Corinthian commanders in Leukas. The *λέμβοι* then moved south to Malea to prey on merchantmen as they rounded the promontory. Philip, who was engaged in the siege of Thebes, was now able to man and equip, presumably in Demetrias, 12 cataphracts, eight aphracts and 30 *ἡμιόλιοι (λέμβοι)*. He moved south through Euripos to intercept the Illyrian squadron of Skerdilaidas. Failing to contact him he took his fleet to Kenchreai. From there the cataphracts were dispatched to Aigina, and round the Peloponnese to Patrai while the rest were hauled over the Isthmos to Lechaion (Werner 1993–4). It may be inferred that the cataphracts, being possibly fives, were too heavy to be taken over the Isthmos, while the aphracts and *ἡμιόλιοι* were not.

When news reached Philip of the Romans' defeat at Lake Trasimene (P.5.101.6), he began, encouraged by Demetrios of Pharos, to think in terms of the conquest of Illyria and an invasion of Italy. He and the Achaeans made peace with the Aetolians (P.5.110.5), and engaged on a successful land campaign against Skerdilaidas.

In the winter of 216, Polybios says (5.109.1), Philip realised that for the accomplishment of his plans for the invasion of Italy he would need 'ships and naval support (*ἡ κατὰ θάλασσαν ὑπηρεσία*), not so much to challenge Rome at sea, but rather for the purpose of transporting troops, of distributing them quickly to the desired place and of taking the enemy by surprise. Accordingly, concluding that the type of ship built in Illyria was the best for this purpose, he decided to fit out 100 *λέμβοι*, almost the first Macedonian king to take such a step'. This fleet is presumably that which is described, more precisely as usual, by Livy (24.40.2) in the context of Philip's later attack on Apollonia, as *lembi biremes centum viginti* '120 *λέμβοι* with two files of oars a side'. These files were probably at two levels (p. 264).

Philip fitted these vessels out, gave his Macedonian crews some training, and at the beginning of summer brought them, possibly from Kassandreia (formerly Potidaia) where he built warships in 207 (L.28.8.14), through Euripos and round C. Malea to Leukas and Kephallenia. Hearing that the main Roman fleet was still at Lilybaion he moved north against Apollonia, but on the false alarm that Roman fives had left Rhegion on their way to support Skerdilaidas he withdrew to Kephallenia in a 24 hour voyage arriving the next day (P.5.110.5). The Romans had in fact sent a squadron of ten ships to aid Skerdilaidas.

After the second Roman disaster, the defeat at Cannae in the late summer of 216 BC, Philip began to negotiate a treaty with Hannibal which was signed the following year. (L.23.33.4) Since Brundisium and Tarentum were both in Roman hands, Philip's envoys had to land at a hidden beach by the temple of Juno Lakinia near Kroton. On their return a ship was waiting for them there, but when they gained the open sea they were seen by a Roman squadron of 25 ships patrolling the Calabrian beaches. Valerius Flaccus sent *cercuri* to pursue the ship and bring her back. Philip's envoys first tried to escape but when they saw that they were overhauled then surrendered. The prisoners first tried bluff, but letters from Hannibal to Philip were found on them together with the terms of the treaty.

Five specially chosen, very fast, ships (*celerrimae quinque naves delectae*) of the patrol were detailed to take the prisoners back to Rome. 'While they were passing Cumae under sail and it was not certain whether they belonged to enemies or allies, the consul Gracchus who had raised the siege of the city sent ships of the Roman fleet there to meet them'. The ships continued their voyage to Ostia while the letters were sent up to Rome under seal. Both arrived at about the same time. These events show two things, the similarity in appearance of the first line Carthaginian and Roman warships, both fives, and the comparative speed of the most urgent communication by sea and road.

(L.23.38.7) Under the threat of war with Macedon the Senate ordered 25 ships to be prepared for service. These were launched and with the five ships of the detail joined Valerius Flaccus at Tarentum where he took on board available troops. He was instructed 'not merely to defend the coast of Italy (his normal duty) but to get information about the (possible) Macedonian war'. This fleet (P.8.1.6) kept a watch on the Greek coastal region and Philip's movements. It moved later to Brundisium under the command of the propraetor Marcus Valerius Laevinus (L.24.20.12).

(L.23.39.1) During the voyage to Ostia the ship captured with the Macedonian envoys escaped and returned to Philip. He then sent further envoys who went and returned successfully. The treaty was concluded, but by that time it was too late in the year (215) to be immediately effective.

(L.24.40.1–2) In 214 Philip used his new fleet of 120 *λέμβοι* to invade Illyria. These ships, in the role of transports for which they had been built, took a force up the river Aous to Apollonia, while another force captured Orikon in the bay of Aulon. Marcus Valerius Laevinus, the pro-praetor, in command of the fleet now at Brundisium, reacted immediately by setting out with his ships which were prepared and ready. Those of his land force that could not be accommodated in the warships were embarked in transports, *onerariae*, and arrived at Orikon on the following day.

The town was recovered after a short engagement, and when a mission arrived from Apollonia saying that the city was under siege from Philip, Laevinus sent 2,000 picked troops in warships to the mouth of the Aous under an experienced commander. The warships were sent back. Then making their way to the city at a distance from the river where they would not be observed, they succeeded in entering Apollonia secretly, and in leading a sally which caught the Macedonians unawares and routed them. Laevinus then moved his fleet to the mouth of the river and blocked it. Philip was forced to bring his ships ashore and burn them, retreating to Macedon with the remains of his army. Laevinus wintered at Orikon and thereafter a naval squadron remained in Illyria. This adventure was virtually the end of Philip's aspirations in the west, although his capture of Lissos in 213–2 (P.8.13) may indicate his intention still to have a naval foothold in the Adriatic.

The Last Years of the Second Punic War

At the beginning of the year 208 (L.27.22.7) the Roman Senate expected an attack by a great Carthaginian fleet of 200 ships on the coasts of Italy, Sicily and Sardinia in support of Hannibal. Accordingly they instructed Scipio to send 50 of his 80 ships from Spain to Sardinia. To the Sicilian squadron of 70 ships were added the 30 from Tarentum to make up the 100 ships which constituted its normal strength at this time; and the commander was ordered to seize any favourable occasion for a raid on Africa. The urban praetor was given the task of refitting 30 old warships at Ostia and manning 20 new ones with *socii navales*, to provide a fleet of 50 ships for defending the coastal area near Rome. In addition there was a squadron, probably of 25 ships, under P.Sulpicius in Greek waters in view of the threat from Hannibal's ally Philip.

That summer (208 BC) the Sicilian fleet of 100

ships (L.27.29.7) raided Africa and was met by a Carthaginian fleet of 83 ships. In the battle that followed near Clupea (Aspis) the Romans routed their opponents and captured 18 ships, returning to Lilybaion with much booty. A similar raid was mounted in the following year on Utica (L.28.4.5–7) and the Carthaginian fleet, now 70 ships strong, was again defeated with the loss of 17 ships captured and four swamped at sea (*in alto mersas*). The Roman ships again took much booty back to Lilybaion. More importantly the sea was now safe for a large consignment of Sicilian corn to be sent to Rome. It was also safe for the Senate in 206 to order the proconsul Laevinus to return to Rome with 70 ships of the Sicilian fleet, handing over the remaining 30 to the praetor Gaius Servilius.

Livy devoted some chapters to the events in Spain of this year (28.12.10 ff). There, after the capture of New Carthage by Scipio, the Carthaginians under Hasdrubal, son of Gisgo, and Mago with the support of the Numidian king Masinissa had been restricted to the extreme west of the country. They raised a large land force, but were decisively defeated, Hasdrubal summoning ships from Gades to take him back to Africa and Mago retiring to Gades. Masinissa also returned to Africa, but not before he had had conversations with the Roman general Silanus about his defection to Rome.

'Already Scipio had his eyes on Africa and Carthage' (L.28.17.3, confirmed by the fragment of P.11.24a). In an attempt to bring over to Rome the important Carthaginian ally Syphax, he first sent Laelius with presents, and then, the reply being not unfavourable, he and Laelius set out in two fives from New Carthage and arrived, probably at Siga after a crossing 'with a calm sea, most of the way under oar but occasionally with the help of a light wind' (i.e. under oar and sail). 'It so happened that Hasdrubal was in the harbour with seven threes, which immediately made preparations to surprise and overpower them with superior numbers before they could reach the harbour. But a slightly fresher breeze caught their sails and brought them in before the Carthaginians weighed anchor, and no one dared to start a fight in the king's harbour'. Hasdrubal and Scipio were accordingly received together by the king.

A (draft) treaty between Rome and Syphax was drawn up. Scipio's subsequent illness and rumoured death caused a mutiny in the Roman army, which Scipio on his recovery succeeded in suppressing.

The Naval Action at Gibraltar

Livy (28.30.3: 206 BC) at this point describes with his customary good understanding of naval matters (as Tarn HMND 1930 p.127 observes), an incident which throws interesting light on the relative qualities of threes and fives.

Laelius moved his fleet 'out of the strait' between the Pillars of Hercules 'into the Ocean and entered Carteia' expecting to move on to Gades which was to be betrayed to him. The plot was revealed to Mago who arrested the conspirators and handed them over to the magistrate Adherbal for conveyance to Carthage.

'Adherbal embarked the conspirators on a five and sent her off in advance because she was slower than a three. He followed with eight threes not far behind. The five was already entering the strait when Laelius himself in a five, with seven threes following, came out of the harbour of Carteia and attacked Adherbal and the 8 threes. Adherbal was confident that the five, caught in the fast-moving water of the strait, would be unable to come back against the current. In the sudden moment of decision the Carthaginian was briefly at a loss and hesitated whether to follow the five or to turn his rams against the enemy. The delay itself made it impossible for him to decline battle, for the enemy ships were already within missile range and were threatening him on all sides. Also the current removed the choice of what course to steer; nor was the fight like a naval battle, as there was nothing deliberate, nothing the outcome of skill or plan'.

'One thing alone, the physical character of the strait and the current controlling the entire struggle, forced the men, as they vainly tried to row in the opposite direction, on to their own ships or those of the enemy. You might have seen a ship in flight turned back and carried against the victors, and a ship in full pursuit, if she encountered a current in the opposite direction, turning away as if in retreat. Now in the actual engagement one ship, when she was attacking an enemy ship with the ram, would (involuntarily) offer her quarter and would receive the impact of the ram of the other ship. Another when it was offering its beam to the enemy would be suddenly turned inwards and swing round (head on) against the enemy's prow. While the battle joined between the threes was indecisive, the Roman five whether because her progress was steadier or because by reason of her weight she was more easily steered, swamped two threes and as she was carried past one of them swept away the oars of one side. She would have damaged the rest of the ships with which she came in contact, if Adherbal had not crossed to Africa under sail with the four remaining ships'.

In this description it appears:

1. That under oar the five in question was slower than the threes, and probably that all fives were slower than threes.

2. That fives (naturally) were heavier, and also because of their weight more responsive to the helm than threes.

3. That in water subject to variable currents the five (under oar) was steadier than the three, i.e. kept her course better.

(L.28.36.4) Mago launched an unsuccessful attack on New Carthage, using his sailors as well as soldiers in the assault and putting them ashore by means of ladders, i.e. 'brows' over the bows (see *AT* p. 163). These are mentioned (28.36.11) by Livy in describing the hurried withdrawal in which the crew cut the shore and anchor cables (see above p. 58). On his return to Gades, which soon after came over to the Romans, he found the gates closed against him and moved to the Balearic island of Ebusis (Iviza).

The Invasion of Africa *(Map L (i), p. 142)*

In 205 BC (L.28.45.13) Scipio was in Rome organising the building and manning, from sources other than the Roman treasury, of the 30 ships, the core of the force he was to take to Sicily and in the following year to Africa. He was given permission to enrol volunteers and accept subscriptions from the allies to build new ships (p. 354). Livy says (28.45.21) that thirty keels were laid down, 20 fives and ten fours and that on the 45th day afterwards the ships, rigged and equipped, were launched. He says later that since the wood used was green the ships had to be hauled up in Sicily the following winter (for attention to the hulls). When all was ready he set out for Sicily with 30 *naves longae* and 7000 volunteer soldiers. Most of the soldiers as well as the stores and gear would have been conveyed in *onerariae* not here mentioned.

The Carthaginian reaction was to attempt to support Hannibal by withdrawing Mago from Spain, which was now given up, and sending him from the Balearic islands, where he had wintered, to the north Italian coast. (L.28.46.7) With nearly 30 warships and a great number of transports, 12,000 infantry and 2000 cavalry, he attacked and took Genua (Genoa). 80 transports were captured off Sardinia by the Roman squadron based there. Later that year (L.29.4.6; 5.2) 25 warships were sent to Mago from Carthage, with 6000 infantry, 800 cavalry, seven elephants and a large sum of money for recruiting auxiliary troops in the region. He was ordered to advance nearer Rome and to join up with Hannibal. He enrolled a large force of Gauls and Ligurians.

On arrival in Sicily Scipio made elaborate military preparations for the invasion of Africa. He laid up the new ships at Panormos. He refitted the 30 old ships (mentioned L.28.45.8: and above); and sent them under Laelius to raid the farms in Africa. There Laelius met Masinissa who urged him to persuade Scipio to invade as soon as possible, and returned with much booty.

Lokroi, a Greek city on the mainland of Italy, had gone over to Hannibal, but a Roman garrison still held out in one citadel while the Carthaginians occupied the other. Scipio felt obliged to go there and restore the situation in favour of Rome, and having done so in spite of Hannibal's attempt to take the city withdrew leaving his legate Pleminius in command. Pleminius proved a corrupt and oppressive officer and dissension broke out among the Roman garrison. Scipio was forced to go again, this time in a six (L.29.9.8). Sixes were said to have been invented in Syracuse (p. 2) and had been mentioned as used in the first Punic war by the consuls as flagships. It is possible then that the tradition of building these ships continued at Syracuse. Scipio may have taken advantage of the opportunity to use one to make an impression at Lokroi. There is no evidence that such a ship took part in his coming expeditionary force, and had he used one as a flagship the fact would certainly have been recorded.

Accusation by the Locrians reached Rome and Scipio was accused in the Senate of complicity in the misdeeds of Pleminius. A praetor with a number of assessors were sent out to enquire into the suitability of Scipio for his responsibilities. When they arrived, Scipio took the opportunity to lay on at Syracuse army manoeuvres and a sham sea battle. as well as a tour of inspection of the stores of equipment and victuals. On their return Scipio was exonerated and his command confirmed.

The fleet and naval transports were concentrated at Lilybaion (L.29.24.7) and preparation made for departure to Africa. Laelius was in command of the fleet. He ordered the crews on board with provisions for 45 days, cooked provisions for 15 of them. When all were on board he sent ships' boats (*scaphae*) round the fleet with orders that from each ship the helmsman, the ship-master and two decksoldiers should assemble in the square (*forum*).

(L.29.25.8) 'When they were all assembled, Scipio asked if they had taken on board for men and animals water for as many days as there was corn. They confirmed that there was 45 days' supply of water. He then gave orders that the soldiers must remain quiet, obeying the seamen and not getting in their way as they performed their tasks. He and Lucius Scipio (his brother) would protect the transports on the right wing with twenty warships, Gaius Laelius, the fleet commander, and Marcus Porcius Cato, quaestor, on the left wing with the same number of ships. Warships (*rostratae*) should have single lights, transports two and the flagship be distinguished at night by three lights. He ordered the pilots to take a course to the Emporia'.

The raids on Africa in the summers of 208 and 207 BC, and the resultant engagements at sea in which the Carthaginian navy had been worsted and lost ships, established for the Romans (L.28.4.7) 'a safe sea' in which they could not only transport corn to Italy from Sicily but also invade Africa, without a major naval force to protect them. In 256 BC (p. 46 and 50) 330 warships and in 255 BC 350 warships had invaded Africa.

Scipio had brought 20 fives and ten fours from Rome, all newly built of green timber. They had to be laid up and given attention when they reached Sicily, and 30 old ships were refitted for raids on Africa in 207 and 206. The expeditionary force in 205 consisted of a convoy of nearly 400 transports escorted by two squadrons each of 20 ships with rams (*rostratae*). Later *speculatoriae* are mentioned in the Roman fleet at Utica. These would have moved in front of the convoy and be the ten new fours, thus not mentioned by Scipio. His two squadrons on either wing were then fives, selected as the most efficient of the 20 new and 30 refitted older vessels.

In addition to the 40 fives and ten fours there were 'nearly 400' transports, carrying most of the troops and all the cavalry as well as siege engines and supplies. Livy (29.25.3) does not venture a number of the infantry and cavalry on board.

The fleet, meeting patches of fog which caused some confusion, but otherwise enjoying fair winds, and completely unchallenged, actually made for, and landed near, Utica (L.29.27.1–13: 28.11). Scipio was joined by the Numidian king, Masinissa. (L.29.29.4) In the siege of Utica which followed (L.29.35.6) the *socii navales* were given military duties. A winter camp was constructed on a promontory (Castra Corneliana), and supplies brought from Sicily, Italy and Sardinia, without naval interference, to supplement those acquired from pillage of the local farms.

In the following year (203 BC: L.30.2.2) the Sicilian fleet was brought up to strength with 13 new ships from Rome, the rest of the 40 being made up of old ships repaired. Since Scipio brought 30 ships from Rome and took away 40 to Africa, it may be assumed that ten at any rate of the new ships replaced those taken from the regular fleet detailed to guard the coasts of Sicily. (L.30.2.4) 40 ships were assigned to Gaius Octavius for the defence of Sardinia, 2000 soldiers (@50) being put aboard the ships. The same number of ships but with 3000 soldiers (@75) were allocated to the propraetor Marcus Marcius for the defence of Italy. The total number of ships at sea in 203 was accordingly 160, with the African fleet of 40.

At the beginning of spring (L.30.4.10) Scipio drew his ships down into the water, putting siege engines and missile-launchers (*machinae, tormenta*) on board as if he was going to renew the siege of Utica, while moving his troops to attack the camps of Syphax and the Carthaginians under Hasdrubal. He succeeded in burning the camps and defeating Hasdrubal and then was proceeding to march on Carthage, having already captured Tunis when he saw the Carthaginian fleet moving towards Utica, where the Roman ships were in siege positions with their bows towards the land.

Polybios (14.10.9) puts the position succinctly: 'Being aware that his cataphract ships, while well and properly equipped to take out and move forward siege engines and in general for siege operations, were not at all prepared for a sea battle, whereas the enemy's fleet was in a condition resulting from the whole winter spent in preparation for just such an engagement. Scipio gave up the idea of going out and fighting; but mooring his cataphract ships together he placed the transports (*φορτηγοί*) around them three and four deep; and then, lowering the masts and yards, used them to link the ships to each other, leaving a small interval for it to be possible for the auxiliary vessels to move out and through (*ἐκπλεῖν και διαπλεῖν*) (cf. the *διέκπλους* p. 360–363)'.

Livy (30.10.4ff) gives more detail: 'Scipio... did the opposite of what is usually done in naval warfare and gave those warships (*rostratae*), which might have protected the others, a place behind them near the shore. The transports in a fourfold system of ranks (*ordinem*) he placed like a wall facing the enemy. The ships themselves, lest their ranks should be disturbed in the melée, he linked together as if by a single bond, throwing masts and yards across from ship to ship and lashing them together with strong ropes. He laid down planks on top of the transports so as to form a gangway across the whole rank (*ordinem* or system of ranks) of ships and under the planks forming actual bridges (*sub ipsis pontibus*) between ships he made gaps through which the *speculatoriae* could make a sally against the enemy and return safely. When these arrangements had been hurriedly completed as well as time allowed, about a thousand picked defensive soldiers were put on board the transports and a great stock of missile weapons.'

The use of the word *ordo* in this passage gives an instructive parallel with the use of the word in connection with the oarsystem of oared ships. Here as there it can either mean a single file or rank, or all the ranks or files as making up a single system. On one occasion above the use of the word is ambiguous: the gangway described could either cross only the gaps between the transports in one rank or provide a passage between the ranks in the whole system.

The ships used for carrying the siege engines, and thus placed behind the 'wall' of transports with their bows directed to the city walls were the 40 fives of the escort squadrons; and the scout ships, which were low enough to pass under the bridging laid on the transports, are likely to have been *λέμβοι* which alone would have been narrow enough, as well as being low enough to pass through the gaps covered by planks. The 'other light vessels' could be the *scaphae* mentioned at the embarkation in Lilybaion.

The Carthaginian fleet spent a day sailing slowly from Carthage, put in for the night at Rusucmon (mod. Porto Farina), and thus lost the advantage of surprise. The following day only after forming a battle line at sunrise and waiting in vain for the Roman ships to come out did they go in and attack the merchant ships.

Some interesting points arise from the description of the battle. Livy states that 'the transports', presumably unladen, 'were somewhat (*aliquantum*) higher than the Carthaginian warships'. If the Carthaginian ships were fours this would not be surprising (p. 267). But they are perhaps most likely to have been fives, the normal first line Carthaginian type, and the one likely to have made up the fleet prepared during the winter to challenge Scipio's fleet, mainly composed of fives. If that is the case, the comparison introduces an interesting fact. Unladen transports stood significantly higher in the water than fives. The difference of height was apparently sufficient for 'the Carthaginians from their warships (*rostratae*) to throw most of their missiles ineffectively against a higher position, seeing that they had to do it leaning back, while a missile scoring a hit from the transports above did more damage, deriving its force from its mere weight'.

'The *speculatoriae (naves)* and other lightly built craft which were darting out through the gaps under the planks of the bridges, at first were overwhelmed as ships by the impetus and size of the warships. Later they became a nuisance to the defending (Roman) soldiers on the transports because in the melée of enemy ships they often prevented them from launching their missiles in case they hit their own side in the uncertainty of where the blow might land'. The Carthaginians began to use grappling hooks and thereby towed away about sixty of the transports.

On the capture and death of Syphax the Carthaginians asked for an armistice and sent envoys to Rome to sue for peace, at the same time recalling Hannibal. Scipio sent Laelius with booty and captives to Rome accompanied by envoys from Masinissa. The Carthaginian envoys were sent home without an answer.

(L.30.24.5) Two fleets of transports accompanied by warships were sent in 203 to supply Scipio's forces in Africa. The first from Sardinia consisting of 20 *rostratae* and 100 transports arrived safely. The second, from Sicily, of 30 *naves longae* and 200 transports under the command of Octavius got into difficulty. (30.24.7) 'When he had been brought on a prosperous voyage almost within sight of Africa, the wind at first failed and then veered into the south (African), threw his ships into confusion and scattered them widely. With the *rostratae* he struggled, by dint of great efforts by the oarcrew against head seas to reach the promontory of Apollo. The greatest number of the transports made a landfall at the island of Aegimurus thirty miles from Carthage while the rest reached Aquae Calidae opposite Carthage itself'. Hasdrubal with 50 ships went out and brought in the transports, deserted by their crews, towing them by the stern.

(L.30.25.2–8) To protest against the breaking of the armistice Scipio sent three envoys to Carthage. Receiving rough treatment from a mob they asked for ships to escort them back to the Roman camp (Castra Corneliana). Two threes were sent which turned back at the river Bagradas when the Roman camp was in sight. The Carthaginian fleet was moored west of the promontory of Apollo inside the bay (Ap. *Pun.* 34: L.30.10.10 Rusucmon); and three fours from there, whether because a message had been sent clandestinely from Carthage or because Hasdrubal, the fleet commander, risked the crime without public consent, suddenly attacked the Roman five from out at sea as she was rounding the promontory. But they (the three fours) were unable to make a strike with the ram as she slipped swiftly from under their bows; and the armed men could not leap across from the lower ships on to the higher one which was very expertly defended as long as the missiles lasted. When the missiles ran out nothing else could save her but the proximity of the shore and the crowd of men pouring out of the camp on to the beach. When the crew at the oars was able to drive her ashore at speed and with as much impetus as possible, the ship alone was lost but the men escaped.

In the autumn of 203 BC Hannibal returned to Carthage.

(L.30.27.5) In the new year the consul Tiberius Claudius was assigned to the province of Africa with a fleet of 50 ships, 'all of them fives'. For some reason he set out from Sardinia where he met a storm; and his year of office had expired before he could reach Africa. Livy's wording suggests that it was unusual for a fleet to be composed all of fives (apart from transports).

(L.30.27.8) The Sicilian fleet of 40 ships was divided equally between the propraetor Tremellius who was to protect the coast of Sicily with 20 ships and 1000 soldiers (@50) and Pomponius who was to return to Rome with 20 warships and 1500 troops (@75). 50 seems now to have been the regular manning of the deck of a five on active service, while 75 could be accommodated when the ship was not expecting action.

At the land battle of Zama (L.30.32–6) Scipio brought the second Punic war to an end. After the surrender a fleet of 50 *rostratae* arrived from Rome with a hundred transports. In the final naval movement of the war Scipio took his original fleet of 40 ships, reinforced by the 50 warships newly arrived, out from Utica 'to view the site of Carthage'.

In the second Punic war the main actions were on land, but, John Briscoe writes, (1989: p. 65–67), 'it would be wrong to conclude that sea power was not a dominant factor in the war. Indeed it is clear that Rome's continuous numerical dominance was of vital importance for the whole course of the war. Hannibal and Hasdrubal could not transport their armies by sea. Rome could transport her troops to Spain and safely import grain from Sicily, Sardinia and Egypt' (see also Thiel: 1946 p. 32–199).

5. PHILIP V'S NAVAL AMBITIONS

(Maps G, H and I)

In the last decade of the 3rd century BC the conflict between Philip V of Macedon on one side and Rome and her allies Pergamon and Rhodes on the other for the control of the seas of mainland Greece, the Aegean and western Asia offers an informative picture of the use and deployment of the new types of warships. Practically all the evidence on which the story is based comes from Polybios's history, for this period fragmentary, and from Livy, who writes from the Roman point of view. Both, but particularly Livy, are reliable on naval matters.

Rome's re-involvement in Greek affairs, stimu-

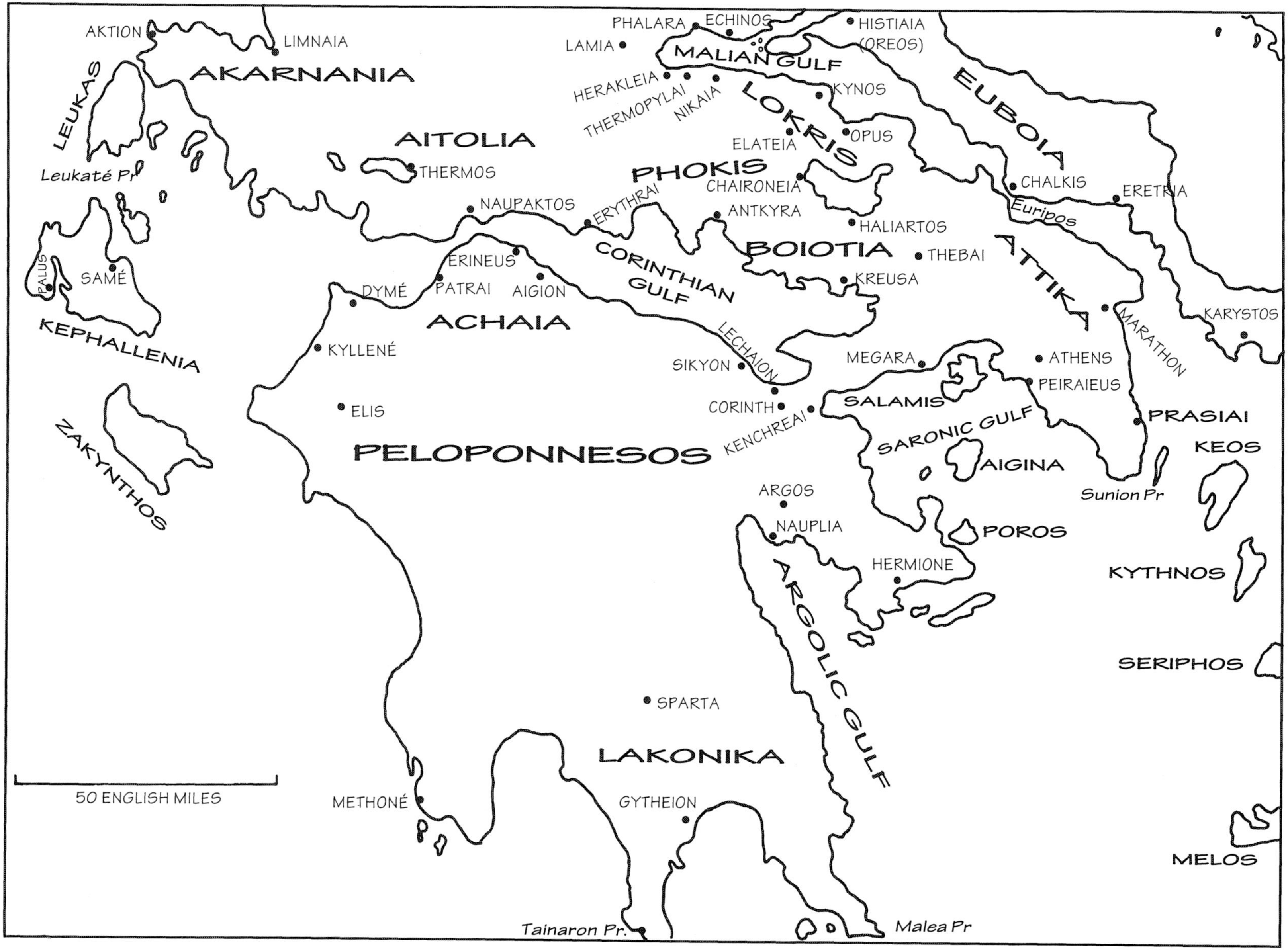

MAP G. *Central Greece*

lated by Philip's alliance with Hannibal and fear of a Macedonian invasion of Italy, began as the outcome of her own alliance with the Aetolians, who headed a League and whose military qualities must have appealed to the Romans. They are characterised by Livy twice, first (27.30.5) as 'a people more warlike than can be expected of the Greek character' (*ferocior quam pro ingeniis Graecorum gens*) and (27.32.1) 'a race always good for a sally' (*promptum ad excursiones genus*). They were also a naval power on a small scale, with a base on the Gulf of Corinth at Naupaktos (Lepanto) convenient for raids across the water on their enemies the Achaeans at Aigion. The Aetolians operated in the Aegean from Herakleia (L.28.5.13) on the Malian gulf and had installed governors and garrisons in the cities of Lysimacheia and Kios in the vital strategic area of Propontis.

In 211 BC (L.26.24.1) 'Marcus Valerius Laevinus who became consul in the following year, having previously tested the attitude of the leading men in secret meetings, came with a fleet of fast ships (*classe expedita*) to a council of the Aetolian League previously summoned for this purpose...'. He offered an alliance on favourable terms between Rome and the Aetolians and their allies, including the Eleans and Spartans, Attalos of Pergamon and Skerdilaidas with his son Pleuratos, of Illyria.

The Romans were to participate with a fleet of at least 25 fives, the Aetolians with ten. There was some delay as the Aetolian envoys went to Rome for ratification, but the parties acted immediately. (L.26.24.15) Laevinus occupied Zakynthos, also some cities in Akarnania which he handed over to the Aetolians. Then 'thinking that Philip had his hands sufficiently full of border warfare to keep his mind off Italy and the Carthaginians and treaties with Hannibal' he withdrew to Kerkyra. In the spring of the following year he moved his fleet to Naupaktos and declared his intention of attacking Antikyra which was a short distance away by land or sea, inviting the Aetolian land forces under Skopas to meet him there. Besieged by land and sea the city fell after a few days. (L.26.26.3) 'The assault by sea was the heavier, because there were catapults and engines of all kinds on board the ships and the Romans were attacking from that side'.

When Laevinus went home on election as consul, the proconsul Publius Sulpicius Galba took over the fleet. He moved round the Peloponnese to seize Aigina which was a member of the Achaean League, and handed it over to the Aetolians who sold it to Attalos for 30 talents (P.9.42.5 and L.22.8.10). Aigina soon became an important naval base for Attalos and the Romans.

Continuing his campaign Sulpicius took his fleet to the Malian gulf to give sea support to the Aetolian general Dorimachos in his attempt to relieve Echinos which Philip was besieging. It is interesting that in spite of the presence of the Roman fleet Echinos surrendered to Philip, since Dorimachos was unable to prevent Philip's supplies coming to him by sea (Cf. λέμβοι p. 111).

Sulpicius's command in Greece was prolonged for a further year (209: L.27.7.15) 'with the same legion and the same fleet' and he was given a similar prolongation for 208 (27.22.10) but without mention of the legion. Livy reports (27.15.7) that in the year 209 the seas around Tarentum were clear of the Carthaginian fleet 'which had been sent across to Kerkyra, since Philip was preparing to attack the Aetolians'. This would account for the continuing Roman anxiety about Greece.

In 209 BC (L.27.29.9) Philip gave help to the Achaeans, who were being harassed by their southern neigbour Sparta under the tyrant Nabis, and subject to raids across the gulf by the Aetolians. There was also a report that Attalos, whom the Aetolian League had elected to their highest office, was preparing to cross to Europe. The Aetolians, supported by Pergamene auxiliaries and soldiers from Sulpicius's fleet tried to bar Philip's way south at Lamia. He defeated them on two occasions, but retired eastwards to Phalara on the Malian gulf where envoys from Ptolemy IV Philopator, Rhodes, Athens and Chios awaited him, anxious, as trading nations, to bring the war to an end.

These cities seem to represent the older 'powers' who now, unlike the parvenus Macedon, Rome, and Pergamon, profited from trade and peaceful conditions. Their motive was also to prevent Philip, and Rome through the Aetolians, from getting involved in Greece. It was agreed to defer discussion of the peace to the meeting of the Achaean League at Aigion on a date already fixed (L.27.30.10). The 30 days truce was used by Philip to garrison against Attalos the vital city of Chalkis at the Euripos strait. At Aigion 'the ending of the Aetolian war was discussed to prevent it being the cause of either the Romans or Attalos entering Greece'.

When the Aetolians heard that Attalos had reached Aigina and that the Romans were at Naupaktos they heightened their demands. Philip dissolved the council. He left 4000 men with the Achaeans and received four ships in return, since he was now determined, with those ships which king Prusias of Bithynia had promised him and with the fleet sent by Carthage, to provoke a battle with the 25 strong Roman fleet (L.27.30.16) 'which had for a long time ruled the sea in that area' (i.e. the Gulf of Corinth).

From Aigion Philip went to the Nemean games at Argos; but hearing that Sulpicius was looting the rich countryside between Sikyon and Corinth, he took a force against them and going on ahead with his cavalry caught them unawares and drove them back to their ships. (L.27.31.3) 'The Roman fleet returned to Naupaktos far from happy with their booty'. This incident is a reminder that looting played an important, and then considered highly respectable, part in naval as well as military operations as a means of maintaining morale and providing victuals.

After the completion of the Games (L.27.31.9-33.5) Philip took his army to Dyme with the intention of launching an attack on Elis which had admitted an Aetolian garrison. But Sulpicius arrived first with 15 ships and 4000 men. They entered Elis by night and caused dismay among Philip's men when the attack was launched. Philip had to content himself with taking an Elean fortress containing much booty, before returning from Achaia to Demetrias on news of trouble on his borders between Macedon and Illyria. On his departure from the area Sulpicius took his fleet out of the Gulf back to Attalos at Aigina where they spent the winter of 208/7.

In the early summer of the following year (207 BC: L.28.5.1) Sulpicius and Attalos took their fleet of 60 cataphract ships (25 Roman and 35 Pergamene) out from Aigina into the Aegean on a voyage which had little serious strategic objective but great effect as a demonstration of sea power. As such it had great consequences, driving Philip to the realisation that he must build and operate a fleet of similar if not greater potential. It also marked out Attalos as Philip's enemy, second only to the Romans.

The allied fleet moved across the Aegean to Lemnos, where Attalos had a base at Myrina. From there they attacked Peparethos, garrisoned from Demetrias where Philip was watching developments. (L.28.5.13) Hearing that Attalos was attending a meeting of the Aetolian council at Herakleia Trachinia, Philip made a forced march to catch him there, but arrived just too late. From Peparethos the allied fleet moved to Nikaia on the southern shore of the Malian gulf and from there attacked Oreos on the north coast of Euboia. It was betrayed to them and sacked. (L.28.7.1) Fire signals from Oreos warned Philip too late: 'but in any case it would have been difficult for him to cross to the island, being inferior in naval strength'. Sulpicius then took the Roman ships to the Macedonian stronghold of Chalkis; but in view of the strength of the place and the dangerous mooring in Euripos, he moved across to Cynos, while Attalos proceeded to sack the seaport of Opus since it was the turn of his men to take booty. The Roman ships returned to Oreos.

When Philip received the fire signal from Chalkis, since approach to it was easy he moved eagerly from Demetrias. (L.28.7.7) 'Attalos, unaware of Philip's approach, was occupied in exacting money from the chief men of Opus, and would have been taken unawares if some Cretan foragers had not given the alarm. 'His men, unarmed and in disorder, made for the sea and the ships in crowds; and as they were manhandling the ships into deep water Philip came upon them and even from the land caused confusion among the seamen. He went back to Opus, railing against gods and men because he had lost the chance of such a coup, snatched away almost before his eyes'.

(L.28.7.10) Attalos returned to Oreos where he had word that Philip's ally Prusias was invading his territory, and moved his fleet back to Asia, 'abandoning the Roman cause and the Aetolian war'. Sulpicius retired to Aigina, while Philip, after some minor operations on land marched to Corinth and from there to Aigion for the Achaean council (L.28.7.17) 'thinking that he would there find the Carthaginian fleet which he had sent for in the hope that he might achieve some naval capability.' The Carthaginian ships had in fact crossed from Italian waters to some small islands off the coast of Akarnania and instead of entering the Gulf to meet Philip had moved to Acarnanian ports, afraid of being caught inside the gulf when they heard of Attalos's and the Romans' move from Oreos.

Philip's plan to assemble at Aigion a fleet of

Carthaginian and Bithynian ships around an Achaean core had plainly miscarried. 'He was distressed', Livy says (28.8.1), and irritated that although he had himself met all his challenges with forced marches he had on no occasion arrived in time, and fortune had mocked his rapid movements by removing every prize out of his sight. Nevertheless, he made a fighting speech at the council and received from the Achaeans three fours and three twos and crossed over to Antikyra in Lokris which had fallen to Laevinus and the Aetolians in the spring of 210 but was now in Philip's hands. From there with seven fives and a squadron of more than 20 λέμβοι which he had previously sent into the Gulf as auxiliaries for the Carthaginian fleet, he moved to Erythrai in Aitolia. There they drove aboard their ships the flocks which in their haste to escape the inhabitants had abandoned. The booty was sent back to Aigion.

Philip proceeded to Corinth from where his land forces marched back to Macedon through Boiotia, while he went by ship along the coast of Attika round Sunion, almost through the enemy's fleet, to Chalkis and from there to Oreos, which he appears to have retaken, and so to Demetrias.

In the past campaigning season Philip had brought aid to his allies and inflicted some losses on the Aetolians; but in spite of his eager forced marches he had failed to meet and destroy his chief enemies. The Romans and Attalos were able to take their forces by sea without interference when and where they wished for booty or for the capture of strongholds. His attempt to assemble significant naval forces had been thwarted by the timidity of the Carthaginians, Prusias's preference for action nearer home, timely though that had been, and the poverty of his mainland allies. There was only one solution, to build a fleet matching the combined fleets of Rome and her allies.

(L.28.8.14) 'At Kassandreia (Potidaia) at the end of 207 Philip laid down the keels of 100 longships and recruited a large force of naval constructors to carry out the work entailed by the programme; and since Greece was quiet following the withdrawal of Attalos and the timely aid Philip had brought to his troubled allies, he returned to Macedon to wage war against his Dardanian neighbours.

Detailed specification of the 100 longships is not given. Later it emerges that the fleets he took to Propontis and Asia in 201 and 200 ranged from tens downwards to a large force of λέμβοι. Most of the cataphract ships and some of the λέμβοι were probably among the new ships. In those years some ships must have been left at Corinth (Lechaion) and at Chalkis and Demetrias. When he took Samos he acquired the Ptolemaic squadron there and used some of them at the battle of Chios. To add to the uncertainty there is no indication of the extent to which the programme was completed. It would have required very considerable resources to pay the constructors and buy the materials needed. There is some suggestion that his maritime allies were called upon to provide manning, as was the case with Rome and probably had been the case with the Persian empire in earlier centuries.

Writing of the year 205 BC Livy (29.12.1) says: 'In Greece affairs had been ignored for those two years' (207 and 206 BC) – ignored, that is to say, in Rome. Sulpicius's command had been renewed for 207 BC. The Aetolians feeling themselves abandoned by Rome, made peace with Philip on his own terms in 205 BC. That year a deputation of five distinguished Romans, including Marcus Laevinus, was sent to king Attalos in five fives, since, although there was no state in Asia allied to Rome, 'on account of the common war against Philip friendly relations had been developed with king Attalos'. The purpose of the mission was to arrange for conveyance to Rome of the image of the Idaean Mother-goddess from Pessinos to allay a plague. Attalos courteously received them and the arrangements were made.

At the same time (205 BC), without any apparent connection, Publius Sempronius arrived at Dyrrachion as Sulpicius's successor (L.29.12.2) with 10,000 infantry and 1000 cavalry and a fleet of 35 warships (*rostratae*). It must be assumed that Sulpicius had been prolonged in his command for 206 BC, although nothing is said to have occupied him in that year. This unexplained inactivity, taken with the prestigious but peaceful mission to Attalos, must have been enough to persuade the Aetolians, who were men of action, that Rome had lost interest in the eastern Mediterranean. To this must be added the awareness that Philip's power at sea was growing daily.

When Sempronius arrived at Dyrrachion with his substantial force, he was angry to find that, in breach of the treaty with Rome and without her consent, the Aetolians had made peace with Philip. He directed his attention in a more promising direction to an Illyrian tribe which had revolted from Philip. On Philip's approach Sempronius withdrew to Apollonia, sending his legate with 15 ships and some troops to Aitolia to assess the situation and the chance of upsetting the peace. Philip looted Apollonian territory; and since neither side wanted an engagement withdrew to Macedon.

At this juncture the Epirots, after sounding out Sempronius, called a peace conference at Phoinike in their territory; and both Sempronius and Philip attended. Peace terms were agreed, put in writing and accepted by the Roman people, since not surprisingly (L.29.12.16) 'now that the (Punic) war had moved to Africa, the tribes wanted at the present time to get rid of the burden of other wars'. Parties to the agreement on the Roman side were Ilion at the Hellespont, Attalos of Pergamon, Pleuratos of Illyria, Nabis of Sparta, as well as the people of Elis, Messene and Athens, while on the side of Philip were Prusias of Bithynia, the Achaeans, the Boeotians, the Acarnanians and Epirots. The Rhodians, Appian says (*Mak.* 4), acted as mediators and as such incurred the enmity of Philip. The peace was clearly viewed all round as a holding operation, by Philip as a breathing space while his armaments were growing, by Rome as an opportunity to concentrate on the pressing requirements of the termination of the war in Africa.

With the peace made Sempronius left for Rome where he was consul for 204 BC. No events in Greece are recorded for that year. In 203 representatives of Rome's allies in Greece came to the Senate to complain that Philip's forces were looting their territory, and that he had declined to give an audience to envoys sent by them to Macedon with their complaints. They also reported that Sopater, an eminent Macedonian, with 4000 troops had crossed to Africa to give aid to the Carthaginians. The Senate sent three envoys in three fives to Philip to say that by these acts he had violated the treaty. One of these, Marcus Aurelius, stayed on in Greece after the others had returned and was later (L.30.42.3) accused of having engaged in military actions in aid of the allies of Rome who were defending themselves against the incursions of Philip and his allies. The latter, though anxious not to provoke an outright war until they were ready, seem to have found that the maintenance of forces on land and sea led, as an economic necessity, to a certain amount of looting.

At the end of 202 BC (L.30.40.4–6) Philip's envoys came to Rome to give his reply. They were told that the new consuls for 201 would hear them in the Senate. (L.30.42.1–10) When the hearing took place, Marcus Aurelius was accused of aggressive actions against Philip's allies, but he was defended by a legate specially sent from Macedon by Aurelius. Philip's envoys were sent back with the message that the king was clearly asking for war and that if he continued on those lines he would soon find it.

Two factors must be noticed affecting the period between the peace of Phoinike and Rome's final declaration of war in 200 BC. The first is the effect in two directions of Philip's naval incursion into the Propontis (Map H). The peace terms did not include an endorsement of his agreement with the Aetolians in 405 BC. He thus felt free as far as the Romans were concerned to break faith with the Aetolians. In the fragment (P.15.21–3) concerning Philip's treacherous capture, with Prusias's co-operation, and cruel treatment, of Kios in the Propontis, Polybios expands on the theme of the damage Philip unwittingly caused to his reputation by his actions and by the deceit which he practised with envoys sent to him at Kios from cities friendly to her (Aetolians and Rhodians presumably) and by the envoy he himself sent to Rhodes. Rhodes earlier had shown her interest in the cities of the Hellespont and Propontis (p. 56–57), and now had besides Byzantion other allies in the area, Kyzikos and probably Abydos.

Polybios continues: Philip did not realise that 'he had made the Rhodians so savage in their hatred of him that they would hear no defence'. From that day 'when his envoy had deceived the Council (*πρυτάνεις*) the Rhodian people' (*δῆμος*, popular assembly) 'considered Philip as an enemy and made preparations to this end' i.e. eventual hostilities, 'and he generated in the Aetolians a similar hatred towards himself by this operation' against Kios. 'For when he had just made peace with that nation and held out his hands to them, without any excuse, when they, the people of Lysimacheia, of Kalchedon and of Kios, were friends and allies a moment before, he first of all brought over the city of Lysimacheia, detaching it from the Aetolian League, then the city of Kalchedon, and thirdly he enslaved the city of Kios when an Aetolian general was in residence and presiding over its affairs. In so far as this plan had been carried out Prusias was

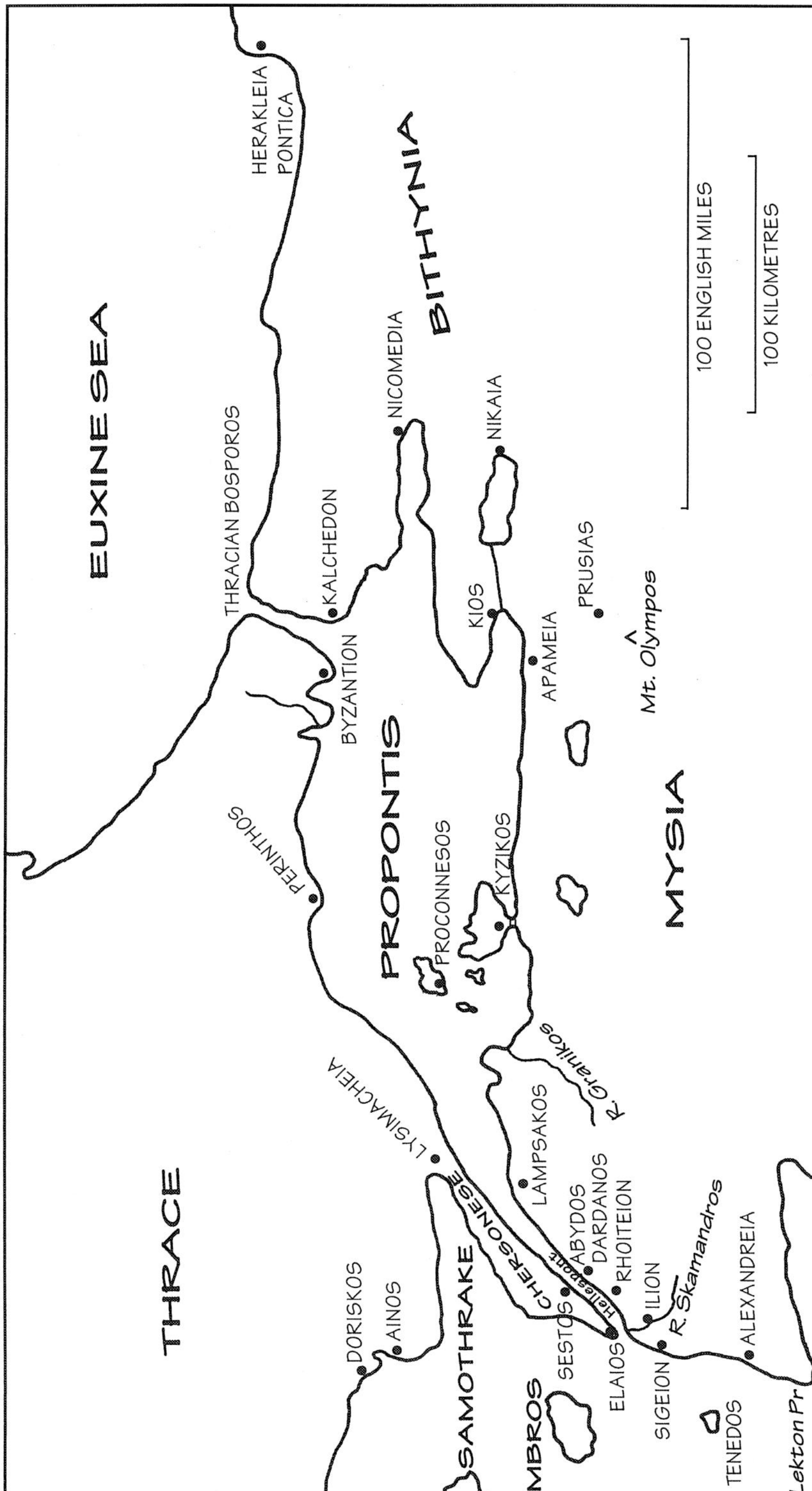

MAP H. *North East Greece*

delighted, but in so far as another took the proceeds while he had as his share of the operation the deserted site of the city, he was not well pleased but could do nothing about it'.

This passage clearly places soon, at the most one or two years, after the peace of 205 the first of Philip's campaigns of expansion which his new fleet enabled, the incursion into the Propontis. Besides attacking Kios and subverting Lysimacheia and Kalchedon, he probably also detached Perinthos (P.18.2.4) from its political union (*συμπολιτεία*) with Rhodes' ally Byzantion. The effects of this campaign are also clear. Philip had established himself firmly in the area which had always been of central importance for aspirants to sea power, as commanding both the sea route from corn lands of the northern Black sea coasts to the hungry populations of the Aegean and also the military land route between Europe and Asia. He had however by his methods alienated the Aetolians, made active enemies of the Rhodians and cooled the friendship of Prusias. All three side-effects, in varying degrees, bore upon the outcome of his naval plans.

The Polybios fragment (15.24) begins: 'Philip, on his return voyage, committing one breach of faith after another, put in about noon at the city of Thasos and enslaved it although not an enemy'. It seems then likely that the previous breaches of faith were those committed in the Propontis and that the capture of Thasos belongs to the concluding stage of that campaign. It is possible that Philip also captured Myrina on the west coast of Lemnos either on his way to Propontis or like Thasos on the return voyage. Lemnos was in Attalos's hands in 207 when the allied fleet moved there from Aigina, but Myrina is among the cities freed from Philip in the peace of 196. There is however another Myrina, a coastal city of Aiolis.

The second factor, strongly influencing the objectives chosen for Philip's second naval campaign, arose from the death of Ptolemy Philopator which was announced in November 205 BC but probably occurred earlier in the year. His successor was a young boy. In the preface to his history (3.2.8) Polybios says that he will tell of the troubles of Egypt and of how when king Ptolemy IV died Antiochos III and Philip conspired together for the division of the realm of his surviving son, how they began to act wickedly and lay their hands, Philip on his possessions in the Aegean, Karia and Samos, Antiochos on the cities of Koile-Syria and Phoenicia. Polybios reaches this subject in 15.20: 'Ptolemy when he was alive never asked for the help of Antiochos and Philip, but when he died leaving an infant son it was surely their duty to unite in preserving his kingdom intact. Who would not be shocked that instead they egged each other on, hastening to divide the child's kingdom and destroy the heir'. Later in the same fragment Polybios refers to an agreement (*συνθήκη*) between them.

A fragment of Appian (*Mak.* 4) gives a very brief but useful summary of Philip's campaigns in this period. The fragment begins with the phrase 'Not long afterwards...' which may refer to the peace of Philip with the Aetolians and then with the Romans, which is the subject of another fragment (3.2). It is however more likely that fragment 4 refers to the notorious Propontis campaign, a record of which does not survive in his history. The fragment continues with the moves leading up to the arrival at Dyrrachion of Sempronius's fleet and army. Here the concluding paragraph is relevant: 'And there was a report that Philip and Antiochos, king of Syria, had made promises to each other: Philip to Antiochos that he would aid him in a campaign against Egypt and Cyprus, both ruled by Ptolemy who was still a boy, and Antiochos to Philip that he would aid him in a campaign against Kyrene and the Kyklades and Ionia'. Appian continues by saying that the rumour (*δόξα*) which dismayed everyone was conveyed by the Rhodians to Rome at the same time (200 BC) that envoys came from Athens complaining of Philip's siege of their city.

Livy (31.14.4) mentions the agreement as a formal treaty (*foedus ictum*) between the two rulers: 'After his naval battles with the Rhodians and Attalos, on neither occasion successful, there was to sustain his morale, apart from his naturally fiery temperament (*ferocia*), the treaty struck with Antiochos king of Syria, the wealth of Egypt already divided among them and which both were poised to seize (*imminebant*), when the news of Ptolemy's death reached them'. It is unlikely that the pact was a formal treaty, but since it is attested as an influential factor in all three sources it must be taken seriously as a motive for the actions of both rulers. Each no doubt mistrusted the other and had reason to do so. But there was a strong community of interest arising from each king's expansionist ambitions. For the invasion of Egypt, and still more of Cyprus, Philip now could provide the naval support which Antiochos lacked, while Antiochos could give the supplies and land support which Philip needed for his campaign in Ionia and which he would otherwise have had to draw from the Black Sea. In the event neither party fulfilled what seem to have been their promises, but the opening moves of a joint campaign were made.

At the conclusion of his description of the battle of Chios, in which the Rhodian *ναύαρχος* Theophiliskos received fatal wounds, Polybios gives a eulogy of him (16.9). It must be remembered that in Rhodes the *ναύαρχος* had a political as well as a naval importance (see Walbank III p. 422). It contains the following passage.

'He was a man who showed himself brave in battle and in policy (*κατὰ τὴν προαίρεσιν*) worthy to be remembered, since if he had not had the courage to take the lead in attacking Philip all the rest would have missed the opportunity in fear of Philip's audacity. As things were, by making a beginning of war (*ἀρχὴν πολέμου ποιήσας*) he compelled his own countrymen to rise to the emergency with him, and he compelled Attalos not to waste time continuing preparation for war but actually to fight boldly and take the chance of battle.'

These words seem to refer to the same circumstances as Polybios (15.23), which describe the exposure of Philip's attempt through an envoy to deceive the Rhodian Council (*πρυτάνεις*) on his treatment of Kios. From that day the Rhodian people (popular Assembly) considered Philip an enemy and made preparation with this end in view i.e. war with Philip. This occasion, the attempt to deceive the Council followed by a decision of the popular Assembly to prepare for war with Philip might well be described as 'the beginning of war' with him; and Theophiliskos as *ναύαρχος* with a political role resembling that of the *στρατηγός* at Athens took a leading, and apparently a Churchillian, role in the debate on the issue. If Theophiliskos was responsible for putting Rhodes on a war footing, after observation, possibly at first hand as one of the Rhodian envoys to Philip at Kios, of his Propontis campaign, the next challenge he faced was to bring Rhodes, and Attalos who was already making preparations for war with Macedon, both together to commit their fleets to battle. This he succeeded in doing off Chios in 200 BC[1].

Philip returned to Macedon for the winter of 202/1 BC; and in the following year mounted a full-scale naval expedition against the Kyklades and Ionia. These were the Macedonian objectives mentioned in the report of his agreement with Antiochos. Polybios (18.54.8) speaks of Dikaiarchos being appointed by Philip to command all his fleet when he decided on treacherously attacking the Kyklades and the cities in the Hellespont. Although he did not lay siege to Abydos in the Hellespont until after the battle of Chios, it is possible that he took Sestos (L.32.33.6) and attempted to take Abydos in 201, and consequently that the attempted subversion of the Kyklades was begun earlier. This is suggested by Marcus Aurelius's report in 201 to the Roman naval commander 'of large armies and a great number of ships the king (Philip) had brought together, and the methods he was using to rouse men to arms, not only throughout the cities of the mainland but in the islands as well, partly by his own presence and partly through his officers'. The Kyklades were, nominally at least, under Ptolemaic control from the Egyptian naval station of Samos.

From the Kyklades Philip's fleet moved to Samos, which was taken and together with it a number of Egyptian warships, some of which had been incorporated into the Macedonian fleet by the time of the battle of Chios. Samos, like Kaunos, Myndos and Halikarnassos, was a city, Livy says (33.20.12), allied to Ptolemy, the liberty of which the Rhodians had taken the responsibility for preserving. He then laid siege to Chios, which was an important, advanced, neutral state (Walbank II p. 205). With Rhodes, Athens, Egypt and Athamania she had sent envoys to Philip at Phalara in 207 and again with Egypt, Mytilene and Athamania in 205. Like Rhodes she was concerned for peace for commercial reasons.

In Appian's summary the first item is, without mention of the Kyklades, Philip's capture of Samos and Chios. In fact he besieged but did not take Chios. Nevertheless, the item fairly represents his attack on Ionia.

Polybios states quite clearly (16.2.4) that 'when the siege of the city did not go well and the large enemy fleet [of Attalos and the Rhodians] took up stations against him (*ἀνθορμούντων*) his chief object was to put to sea quickly, convinced that he would thus get ahead of the enemy and make a safe passage along the coast to [his new base at] Samos'.

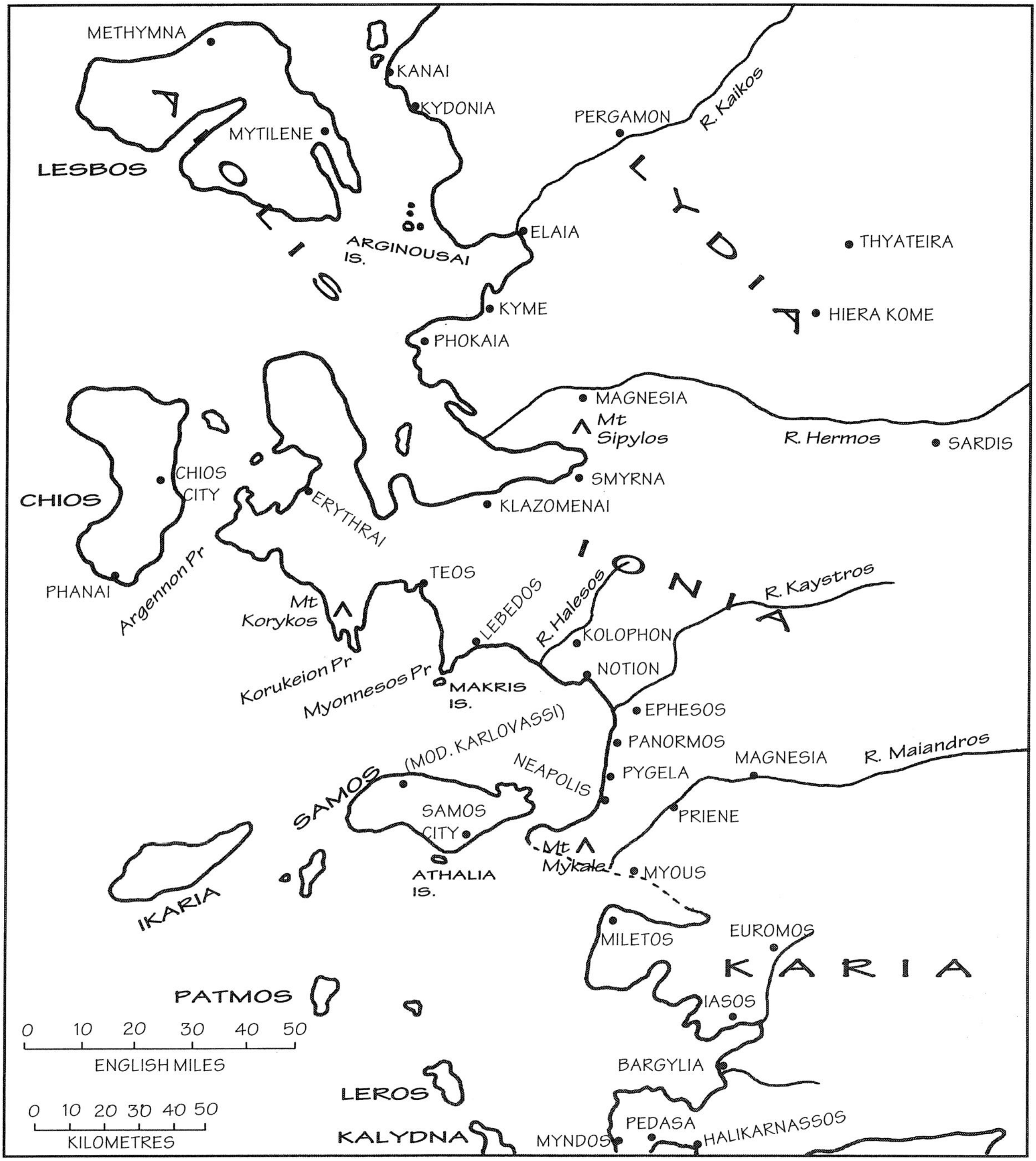

MAP I. *Aiolis, Lydia, Ionia, Karia*

This was a reasonable calculation, since if the opposing fleets were taken by surprise and could only order embarkation when they saw his ships ready to emerge it would be at least an hour, probably more, before they could be at sea.

Philip's decision to abandon a siege which promised to be lengthy, and make a quick get-away to Samos, avoiding a naval engagement, is revealing. It should be taken with Polybios's comment after Philip's subsequent engagement with the Rhodian ships off Lade (Miletos), which had retired to Kos before making their triumphant voyage with Attalos's fleet to Aigina. The short fragment (16.10) begins: 'After the sea-battle around Lade was ended, the Rhodians being out of the way and Attalos not yet with them, it was plain that the way was entirely open for Philip to *complete* his voyage to Alexandria, from which one may well understand that Philip was a madman to take this course'. 'This course' was the action he did in fact take, the return north to attack Pergamon in a fit of temper.

Polybios is in no doubt that Philip's original plan was first to conquer the Kyklades and Ionia (Samos, Chios and Miletos) with Antiochos's acquiescence and, where he needed it, assistance; and then carry out his part of the bargain and move south to provide naval support for Antiochos's invasion of Phoenicia and Palestine. There is evidence that Antiochos besieged Gaza in 201 BC (P.16.18.2 and 16.22a: Walbank II p. 543) and took Sidon about the same time. Both cities marked steps made by Alexander and Antigonos in their invasions of Egypt. But Philip was twice diverted from this original plan and in the end failed to play his part. Polybios regarded both diversions as acts of a madman.

In Appian's summary (omitting the battles) the second event after 'the capture of Samos and Chios' is 'the looting of part of Attalos's territory and the attempt on Pergamon, without respect for sacred things and tombs'. The third is the ravaging of the Rhodian mainland province. Walbank argues (II p. 497–500), after a careful summary of the evidence, that the likely order of events, over which there has been much argument, is: the battle of Chios, the attack on Pergamon, the battle of Lade and the attack on Karia and the Rhodian Peraia. This order fits the Appian summary.

The course of Philip's second naval campaign may now be considered in detail. He set out from Demetrias in the spring of 201 and made his way across the Aegean by way of the hitherto Ptolemaic Kyklades, confirming his control where force was needed. He took the Ptolemaic base of Samos and spent some time refitting for his service some of the Egyptian ships there. He then moved north to Chios and laid siege to the city. When news of Philip's movement across the Aegean reached Attalos he took steps to prepare the defences of Pergamon and, it now being summer, to bring in the harvest and all moveable property so that an invader would have little loot or food. His ships were launched and after a rendez-vous with the Rhodian fleet he proceeded to Chios which Philip was now besieging. The siege was unexpectedly abandoned when Philip attempted to make good an escape to Samos (P.16.2.1–4).

This then is the first stage (Map J (i)): the sudden, unexpected, putting out of Philip's fleet composed, it will appear, of 53 cataphract ships, an unspecified number of aphracts and 150 λέμβοι (p. 62). There is nothing to indicate where his ships were moored. The cataphracts would have been in the harbour, the rest as near as possible outside. The former would have taken the most time to man but manning could have taken place before dawn. The rest, being mostly aphract and small, could have been manned quickly. The allied fleet on the other hand had 65 more cataphracts but fewer units altogether. JFC writes: 'If Philip had posted light defensive forces on vantage points round his moorings and the city, the enemy would have had only a distant view. He might not then have seen any conclusive signs of embarkation until a ship left the shore and then another and another. Communication with Attalos and Theophiliskos could have been by heliograph but even so in these circumstances Philip would have had about an hour's start, say 5 am'. It is remarkable that even with the considerable start his sudden, planned, departure gave him he expected to avoid engagement.

Polybios continues (16.2.5): 'Philip's calculations, however, were a long way out. Directly the men of Attalos and Theophiliskos saw him putting to sea they at once grasped the situation. But it happened that their putting to sea was separate (διαλελυμένον), since they were of the opinion that Philip was still remaining at his siegeworks'. The word διαλελυμένον which Walbank and Paton (Loeb ed.) translate as 'in loose order' contains the clue to the situation meaning, not 'in loose order' which is irrelevant to the subsequent course of events but 'from separate points'. The allied fleet was divided because no departure and so no engagement was expected (which would have required a united fleet) but instead a blockade (cf. Polyxenidas's ships at Panormos (p. 98–99)) requiring ships on both sides of the harbour mouth, the Rhodians north and Attalos south.

Philip's fleet, moving south in column at the initial stage when he still hoped to get away without fighting, was attacked at the head by Attalos's ships and in the rear by the Rhodians, and since some of the Macedonian ships in the middle of the column turned back to help the rearguard, the action resolved itself into two separate battles (so described by Livy p. 75 and later p. 83).

(P.16.2.7) Nevertheless (in spite of the separation of their forces) the allied forces attacked with vigorous rowing, Attalos the right and leading wing of the enemy, Theophiliskos the ships of the left. The enemy 'right' wing was leading because the fleet was in column (of several files). Line abreast, with actual right and left wings, was the basic defensive formation of soldiers and (hence) of ships. The formation in column as reached by turning right or left and moving 'to the wing ἐπὶ κέρας'. Thus a column was usually, but not always (see *AT* p. 59, 88–89), defined as 'right wing leading' since that is the commander's place, and it was so here. By the same usage the 'left' wing of the column generally is, and was so here, the rearguard.

(P.16.2.8) Philip unfortunately found himself hemmed in, and giving the signal to the right wing ordered them to put their ships in line abreast and engage the enemy strongly, while he himself retired with a few λέμβοι to the shelter of the few islands lying in the middle of the channel. There he watched for the outcome of the battle.

The distance between the harbour of Chios and the islands mentioned (off the Argennon promontory) is about 6 sm (11 km) (Map J (i)). The speed of Philip's larger ships, which would have set the pace for the rest in his fast get-away, is unlikely to have exceeded 5 knots, so that the leading ships of his column would have reached the vicinity of the islands and been attacked by Attalos rather more than an hour after they had put out, and say two hours after his departure was noticed by the enemy. This would have given Attalos time to get to sea from a beach, say, 2.7 sm (5 km) north of the point where his ships, rowed vigorously, forced Philip to order a battle line to face them. At the other end of the column, which must have been a long one, Theophiliskos's leading ships, putting out from a beach about 2.36 sm (4.35 km) north of the harbour were using their greater speed to catch up with and attack Philip's 'left wing', the rearguard.

Polybios takes the opportunity at this point of giving a summary of the ships on both sides.

(P.16.2.9–10) 'The total of Philip's ships which participated in the battle was 53 cataphracts and with them ...[say 15] aphracts and 150 λέμβοι with πρίστεις (p. 263). This was because he had been unable to fit out all the ships in Samos. The vessels of his enemies were 65 cataphracts with (σύν) the Byzantine vessels, and with these there were 9 τριημιολίαι and 3 threes'[2].

The 100 ships which Philip laid down at Kassandreia in 207 would have included vessels of all types including λέμβοι which Philip much used, and in large numbers, before 207. Beside the fleet he took to Asia for the second expedition, he would necessarily have provided ships for two, possibly three, naval stations on the mainland of Greece, Corinth (Lechaion), Chalkis and Demetrias, the three 'fetters of Greece'. He may also have needed ships to patrol his recently garrisoned cities in the Propontis and Kyklades. Taking account of all these demands it is surprising that he could muster as many ships as he did for the second expedition.

The fleet of 65 cataphracts provided by Attalos and Rhodes is large. Attalos had taken 35 across to Greece in 210 and may have added a few more since. But it looks as if the Rhodians under their Themistokles, Theophiliskos, built warships during the winter and sent as many as 30. The nine τριημιολίαι were most probably theirs. Walbank (quoting P.16.31.3 and L.31.17.6, 37.11.13 and 37.22.2) notes that Kyzikos and Kos may have contributed ships to the allies.

The First of the Two Battles

The Macedonian right wing was now re-formed in line abreast to face the ships of Attalos attacking from their beach on the coast south of Chios city.

(P.16.3.1) 'The engagement taking the initiative

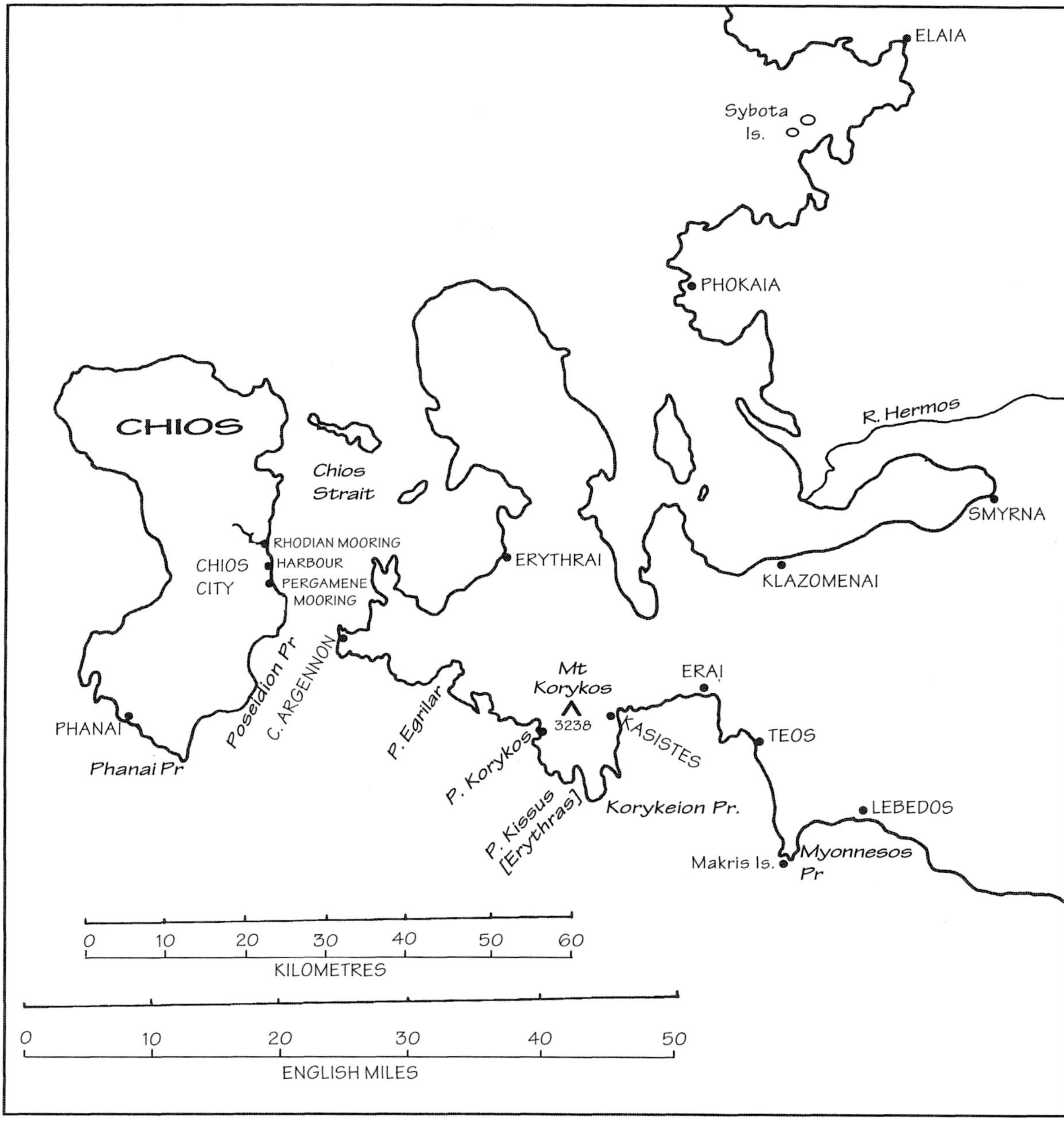

MAP J (i). *Chios and the Erythraean Peninsula.*

from Attalos's ship, all those near him closed without (further) instructions. Attalos came to grips with an eight and first getting in a fatal blow on her below the waterline finally swamped her, although the men on deck fought for a long time. Philip's ten, the flagship, fell into enemy hands in a strange way. A *τριημιολία* crossed her path; and she gave her a powerful blow in the middle of the hull just below the thranite thole, and stuck fast, since the helmsman was not able to check (*ἀναλαβεῖν*) his ship's impetus in time. The result was that the flagship was utterly disabled with the *τριημιολία* impaled on her ram, and was unable to move in any direction' (p. 266).

(P.16.3.6) At this moment two fives attacked the flagship and holing her on both sides destroyed both the ship and her deck complement, including Philip's *ναύαρχος* Demokrates. At the same moment Dionysodoros and Deinokrates, two brothers holding posts of *ναύαρχος* in Attalos's fleet, closed, the one with a seven, the other with an eight, and had strange experiences in this battle. 'Deinokrates, who closed with the eight, took a blow above the waterline himself, since the enemy ship had a high ram (*ἀνάστειρος* see Glossary), but holed her under the weaponry and was at first unable to disengage, although making several efforts to back down. So, since the Macedonians were fighting with great spirit, he faced extreme danger [from boarding]. But when Attalos came to his aid, and by ramming the enemy ship succeeded in breaking loose the two ships, Deinokrates was unexpectedly freed, while the decksoldiers of the enemy ship were all killed still fighting with great spirit'. The ship herself, left defenceless, fell into Attalos's hands.

Dionysodoros, violently closing in to ram (a seven), missed ramming her, but passing along her side lost his own starboard oars; and the turret stanchions (p. 357 *πυργοῦχοι* P.16.3.13) underneath were also carried away. At the same time the enemy surrounded him on all sides. There was much uproar and shouting and the rest of the men on deck were lost together with the ship, but Dionysodoros with two companions swam away to a rescuing *τριημιολία*.

'For most of the other ships the battle was evenly balanced, since the numerical advantage of Philip's *λέμβοι* was matched by the advantage of Attalos's men in the number of cataphract ships'.

The Second of the Two Battles

(P.16.4.4) 'The Rhodians at the outset were, immediately on putting to sea, far removed from the enemy, as I have just said; but being much superior to their opponents in speed of movement closed with the Macedonians of the rearguard'.

All Polybios had in fact said earlier was: (16.2.6) 'It so happened that Attalos and Theophiliskos's putting to sea were separate' and it has been suggested above that this separation meant that the two fleets were beached the one north and the other south of the city. Since the contact south of the city between Attalos and Philip's right wing, his vanguard, has been described, this second passage, describing how the Rhodian ships on first putting out had to row fast in order to catch up with the rearguard of Philip's column, adds confirmation of the second part of the assumption, that the Rhodian fleet was beached north of the city.

(P.16.4.5) 'At first the Rhodians making their attacks on the sterns of the ships as they went ahead carried away the oars from the stern. But when Philip's men began to turn round together and help those in danger, and when those of the Rhodians who were late in getting off the beach joined up with Theophiliskos's men' (i.e. those who got away quickly with their commander), 'then both sides drawing up their ships to face each other's line prow to prow', i.e.both sides forming line abreast, 'fought with great spirit, encouraging each other with trumpets and shouting'.

The description is quite explicit. First the pursuing Rhodians under Theophiliskos came up with Philip's rearguard and sheared off their oars from the stern. The helpless ships then caused their comrades to turn back to help them and form a line of battle and the Rhodians now reinforced did likewise. A formal initial battle situation was thus created separate from the formal battle situation further south. As Polybios observes at 16.5.8, 'At this stage there were two battles at some distance from each other'.

(P.16.4.8) 'If the Macedonians had not placed their *λέμβοι* in between the cataphract ships, the' (northern) 'battle would have had an easy and short conclusion, but as things were these vessels impeded the Rhodians' efficiency in many ways. When the original order of battle had been dis-

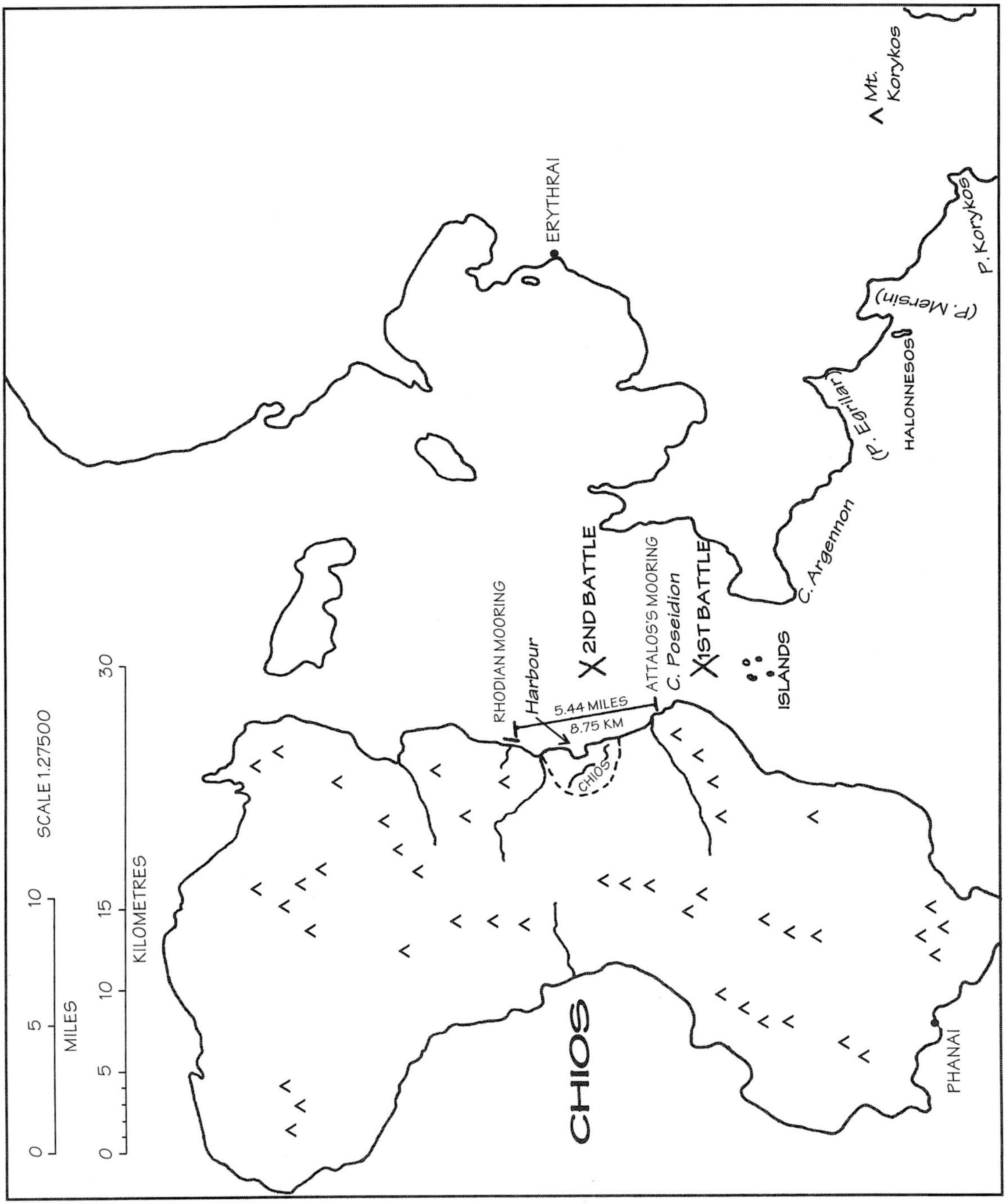

PLAN 5. *Battle of Chios*

turbed after the first clash, there was a general melée. As a result the Rhodians could neither employ the break-through (*διέκπλους*) neatly nor turn their ships nor in short use their usual superior skills, since the *λέμβοι* attacked them, sometimes in the oar-systems so that it was hard to row, sometimes, turning back, in the prows, occasionally in the sterns, so as to get in the way of the work of the helmsmen and the rowers'.

Polybios represents the Rhodians as inheriting the classical doctrine of naval tactics as practised by Phormio and as described by Thukydides in a speech put in his mouth before the battle of Naupaktos (2.89.8).

He says he will avoid fighting in the Gulf of Corinth. 'I see plainly enough that a confined space is a disadvantage to a few ships, even if they are used with skill and are faster, against many ships inexpertly used. The fact is that one cannot move against a ship to ram it, if one cannot get the enemy in one's sights from some way off, and if one cannot retire if need be in a difficult situation. There are no opportunities for carrying out a break-through (*διέκπλους*) or a sharp turn (*ἀναστροφή*) which are the manoeuvres of a faster moving fleet...'.

Like the Athenians the Rhodians concentrated on speed, the break-through and quick turns, avoiding encounters from which extrication was difficult.

Polybios continues (16.4.11): 'The Rhodians made technical provision for close prow-to-prow engagement (*ἐποίουν τι τεχνικὸν κατὰ τὰς ἀντιπρώρους συμπτώσεις*). For their part, they made their ships low in the bows (*ἔμπρῳρα*); and taking blows above the waterline while giving blows below it, they caused damage which could not be repaired. Yet they did not resort to this practice often, in general avoiding engagement of ship to ship from which it was difficult to break free (*συμπλοκάς*), since the Macedonians fought back valiantly from the deck in close combat. They usually employed the break-through and (first) swept away the oarsystems of enemy ships and put them out of action; after that moving round and back, and ramming some in the stern, attacking others amidships; and while their opponents were still turning they would succeed in holing some and damaging on occasion some necessary item of gear in others. Indeed employing this method of fighting the Rhodians accounted for a large number of enemy ships'.

This account of the breakthrough is discussed in Chapter 8 (p. 362).

(P.16.5.1) 'Three Rhodian fives fought with the greatest distinction: the ship with Theophiliskos on board, with her the ship of which Philostratos was trierarch, and the third, the ship of which Autolykos was helmsman with Nikostratos on board. The last-mentioned rammed an enemy ship and left the ram in the hull with the result that the ship struck was lost with her crew, while Autolykos's men (on deck), the sea pouring in through the prow, being surrounded by the enemy at first fought bravely, but Autolykos finally fell wounded into the sea in full armour and the rest of the decksoldiers were killed fighting nobly. At this moment Theophiliskos, coming up to help with three fives, was unable to save the ship which was full of water, but holed two enemy ships and drove off the decksoldiers. When he was surrounded by enemy *λέμβοι* and cataphract ships he lost most of his decksoldiers fighting nobly and was himself three times wounded. Fighting with extraordinary bravery he succeeded in saving his own ship with difficulty, Philostratos coming to his aid and taking part in the current fight with great spirit. Theophiliskos rejoined his own ships and engaged the enemy in another incident, with his physical strength ebbing away through his wounds, but in his nobleness of spirit more splendid and outstanding than before.'

The fact that Theophiliskos 'rejoined his own ships' at the conclusion of these incidents and that Autolykos's ship which lost her ram was immediately surrounded by *λέμβοι* and cataphract ships but received support from Theophiliskos with three fives seems to indicate that the incident was the first move in an unsuccessful breakthrough.

(P.16.5.8–9) 'At this stage there were two formal battles *ναυμαχίαι* at some distance from each other. The leading right wing of Philip's column, according to his original plan was all along aiming for the mainland and was not far distant from Asia (when formal battle was joined), but the left wing since some of the mid-column ships had turned back to help the rearguard cannot have fought the Rhodians far from the coast of Chios.'

The Conclusion of the Battles

(P.16.6.1) 'However Attalos's men were gaining a considerable advantage over the (Macedonian) right wing and were by this time nearing the islands under the shelter of which Philip was moored awaiting the outcome. Attalos noticed one of his own fives outside the battle area holed by an enemy ship and taking water. He went to her aid with two fours; and when the enemy ship gave way and retreated as if to the shore (of Asia) he pressed his attack more eagerly with the intention of capturing the vessel. But Philip, seeing that Attalos was separated a long way from his own men, taking with him (from the main fleet) four fives and three *ἡμιολίαι* as well as those *λέμβοι* as were his escort (see 16.2.8), put out; and cutting off Attalos from his own ships compelled him in great discomfiture to run his ships ashore, (his own unspecified flagship, at least a five, and two fours). When this had taken place, Attalos and his crews escaped to Erythrai.'

He did this safely because the crews of the *λέμβοι* and then the rest turned to looting the royal flagship on which the royal trappings had been displayed to tempt them to give up the pursuit.

(P.16.6.9) 'All things considered Philip had been by a long way the loser in the engagement, but he was encouraged by the reversal of fortune that had befallen Attalos. He put to sea again and was everywhere getting his ships together and exhorting his men to be of good heart as they were the victors in the sea battle. The fact was that there came over the men a certain idea and notion that Attalos was dead because Philip's men had come to shore with the king's ship in tow. However, Dionysodoros, (Attalos's *ναύαρχος*) guessing what had happened to his king, collected his own (Pergamene) ships by raising the signal, and when they had rapidly rallied to him he moved off unchallenged to the moorings on the mainland of Asia.'

Their retirement to moorings in Asia was presumably a temporary measure so that they could make contact with Attalos and his crews at Erythrai. Later these ships joined the Rhodians in Chios.

(P.16.6.12) 'At the same time the Macedonians who were fighting the Rhodians, and for some time had been in trouble, detached themselves from the fighting with the excuse, as they retreated in groups, that they were anxious to bring assistance to their own ships (which were conveniently fighting in their rear, since the retreating groups had previously put about to face the pursuing Rhodians). The Rhodians, taking in tow some of the ships and putting others out of action with their rams moved away to [the city of] Chios.'

(P.16.7.1) 'In the sea battle against Attalos (*ναυμαχία*) Philip's ships put out of action were: one ten, one nine, [one eight see above p. 81], one seven and one six, of the remaining ships ten cataphracts and three *τριημιολίαι*, also 25 *λέμβοι* with their crews. In the sea battle (*ναυμαχία*) against the Rhodians his casualties were: ten cataphracts and about 40 *λέμβοι*, while two fours and seven *λέμβοι* with their crews were captured'. Of Attalos's ships there were put out of action one *τριημιολία*, two fives while two fours and the royal ship were captured. Of the Rhodian ships two fives and a three were put out of action but not a single ship was captured. Up to 60 Rhodians died, and up to 70 of Attalos's men. Of Philip's men up to 3,000 Macedonians (i.e. decksoldiers) and up to 6,000 crewmen died. There were taken prisoner up to 2,000 Macedonians and their allies and 700 of their opponents.'

The lists of ships enable the following points to be made. Ships from the six upwards get a special mention, yet the eight which Deinokrates attacked is omitted and Attalos's 'royal ship', probably at least a six, is not specified. Below these in importance are unspecified cataphract ships. In lists which contain this category fives, fours and threes are not separately mentioned but *τριημιολίαι* and *λέμβοι* including *ἡμιολίαι* are. Fives, fours and possibly threes are thus cataphract. *Τριημιολίαι* and *λέμβοι* are either aphract or cataphract named more specifically because they are separately unique. The small number of losses in ships and men on the side of Attalos and the Rhodians may indicate Rhodian bias, as has been suggested (P.16.14.6).

(P.16.8.1) 'Such was the outcome of the battle off Chios. Philip claimed victory on two counts: by forcing Attalos ashore he had obtained possession of his ship, and having moored at the place called Argennon he was patently mooring where the wrecks were. He followed this up the next day by collecting the wrecks together and picking up the corpses that were recognisable with a view to adding strength to his aforesaid fantasy (*φαντασία*).'

Possession of the wrecks, which did not sink, after a sea battle was recognised as a mark of victory.

'But that not even Philip himself was convinced of his victory, the Rhodians and Dionysodoros proved to him shortly afterwards. For on the following day, when the king was still busy with his tasks, the allies communicated with each other and moved out against him. They drew up their ships in line abreast, and then, when no one came out against them, they moved back to Chios.'

The fact that they 'communicated with each other' before uniting their fleets in a single line of battle, shows that the Pergamene commander was still at the moorings in Asia which he had taken up after the battle. Then, after the unanswered challenge to Philip, the allied fleets withdrew to Chios.

(P.16.8.6) 'Philip had never lost so many men in battle either on land or sea. He was much distressed at what had happened, and his enthusiasm was much diminished. Nevertheless, he tried to conceal his mood from outsiders in every way possible, although the facts themselves did not permit concealment. Apart from anything else, conditions after the battle dismayed all observers. As a result, not Philip alone but all the Macedonians fell into no ordinary state of confusion (*διατροπή*).'

(P.16.9.1) 'Theophiliskos survived for one day; and after writing a dispatch to Rhodes about the events of the battle and handing over his responsibilities to Kleonaios as his successor in command, he died of his wounds.'

The eulogy of Theophiliskos which follows concludes with the account (p. 76) of how he brought his own country and Attalos into the war with Philip.

Philip's moves after the battle

Philip's 'extraordinary confusion' after the battle seems to have turned him aside from his original plan of campaign into an irrational diversion which is described in another fragment of Polybios (16.1). He moved north to attack the city and territory of Attalos:

'King Philip arriving at Pergamon and thinking to deliver Attalos a death blow (after his narrow escape in the battle) began to exhibit every kind of shameful conduct. Yielding to anger like a madman he spent most of his rage not on man but on the gods. In skirmishes, owing to the strength of the terrain, the garrison of Pergamon easily kept him at a distance, and he was getting no profit from the countryside because of the careful provision Attalos had made in these respects. Finally he proceeded to direct his rage to the temples and sanctuaries of the gods, bringing shame, in my opinion, not on Attalos but on himself'.

After a description of his frantic destruction Polybios continues: '... at first he went to Thyateira and moving his quarters from there he invaded the plain of Thebe thinking that he would get good booty in this area. Being disappointed in this hope and reaching Hiera Kome, he sent a message to Zeuxis (Antiochos's governor at Sardis) calling upon him to supply him with corn and co-operate in other respects according to the terms of the agreement [with Antiochos]. While pretending to act according to the terms of the agreement, Zeuxis was not willing to give Philip any real support in the way of victuals.'

The concluding sentence gives an important clue to what one may suppose to be Philip's state of mind at this moment. After the relief of Chios his insane fury against Attalos had been frustrated. The coolness of Antiochos's governor must have led him to doubt the value of the agreement. It remained for him to punish his other enemy, Rhodes, and for that objective he needed entry to Karia and the Rhodian territory on the mainland via Miletos. He apparently rejoined his fleet at some point on the Lydian coast and moved southwards encountering the Rhodian fleet which was moored on the island of Lade off Miletos.

The Battle of Lade

In criticising the Rhodian historians Zeno and Antisthenes (16.14–15) Polybios refers to the subsequent naval engagement between the Rhodians and Philip for the island of Lade.

'In the first place both of them agree that the naval battle fought for Lade was not a lesser event than the battle fought for Chios, but was greater in its effects and in the issues at stake, and that both in the incidents of the battle and in the general outcome victory was with the Rhodians. I would agree that historians should be biassed in favour of their own country but not that they should make statements contrary to the facts'.

'The aforesaid writers admit that among the individual actions in the battle for Lade there were these. Two Rhodian fives with all their crew were captured by the enemy, and when a ship in the battle raised her *δόλων*, foresail, because she had been rammed and was taking water, many of those near her did the same and made for the open sea. In the end the *ναύαρχος*, left with a few ships, was compelled to do the same as those mentioned. Then, finding a favourable wind, the fleet came to a mooring on the coast of Myndos; and the next morning put to sea and crossed to Kos. The enemy took the two fives in tow, moored on Lade and bivouacked in the Rhodians' camp. Furthermore, these historians say, the Milesians, under the impact of the event, not only crowned Philip but also Herakleides (his *ναύαρχος*) by reason of the attack. After recording the facts which clearly attach to (i.e indicate) the defeated side, they notwithstanding declare that in the individual actions and in the general record the Rhodians were the victors, and this although there is a dispatch still preserved in the (Rhodian) *πρυτανεῖον*, which concerns these matters and was sent at the selfsame time by the *ναύαρχος* to the Council and the *πρυτάνεις* and does not agree with Antisthenes' and Zeno's statements but with mine.'

There is a second brief reference to the battle for Lade in Polybios (16. 10.1). 'After the battle for Lade was over and the Rhodians were out of the way, while Attalos had not yet joined up with them, it is clear that Philip was in a position to complete his voyage to Alexandria, from which it is perfectly clear that Philip was a madman when he acted thus' (i.e. invaded Karia).

The wider importance of this second passage in revealing the motive which at the outset was behind Philip's naval expedition to Asia in 200 BC has already been discussed. But taken with the facts which Polybios gives in the first passage it indicates the issue at stake in the battle: possession of Lade, as the key to the domination of Miletos, was the gateway to Karia and Rhodes's mainland province. Polybios invariably calls the engagement 'the battle for Lade *περὶ τῆς Λάδης*' just as he calls the earlier engagement the battle *περὶ τοῦ Χίου* and the First Punic war the war *περὶ τῆς Σικελίας*. In all these three cases the preposition is used with 'the genitive of the object for which one does something', its most common usage. By emphasising that the Rhodians, for one reason or another, as a result of the battle, moved 'out of the way' and left Lade, and their camp, to Philip, and that the Milesians recognised Philip as the victor and hence as their master, Polybios indicates that the battle was indeed for the possession of Lade and hence of Miletos. Philip now had the option of moving into Karia against Rhodes or of proceeding unimpeded with his voyage to Alexandria. He chose the former.

Polybios continues (16.10.2): 'What was it that took hold of his purpose? Nothing else but the nature of events. At a distance many men sometimes aim at impossible goals because of the magnitude of the hopes they entertain, their ambition overriding the calculation of detail; but when they are immersed in actions they go back on their planned strategy, their minds clouded over and calculating falsely, because of the difficult and intractable nature of the circumstances they meet.'

This is a good analysis of why Philip gave up the grand strategy of participation with Antiochos in the invasion of Egypt. It was the cumulative effect of many frustrations on a man of mercurial temper, *ferocia*, to use Livy's word – acts of madness according to Polybios.

The Invasion of Karia and the Rhodian Peraia (mainland province): 201 BC (Map D, p. 33))

Appian's third heading is: '(Philip) ravaged the Rhodian Peraia because the Rhodians had been mediators for him' (in the peace treaty of 405 BC). The reason given for his hostility to Rhodes may have been the first but certainly was not the only one. After the battle of Lade Miletos and the surrounding country came over to Philip: also the Carian cities of Iasos (described in P.16.12), Pedasa and Bargylia, where he spent the winter. In the Rhodian Peraia he took Prinassos. His state of mind during this time is described by Polybios (16.24). He could have expected that the fleets opposing him would have been dispersed to their home ports and laid up during the winter, but 'he was aware instead that more ships were being commissioned and patrols (*φυλακαί*) mounted in a spirit of competition' 'He was uneasy, and his schemes (*ἐπίνοιαι*) of future action were many and various. In the first place he was anxious about moving out to sea from Bargylia and foresaw an engagement. In the second place he was worried about the state of affairs in Macedon and not at all happy to spend the winter in Asia, being afraid both of the Aetolians and the Romans. For he was aware of the envoys sent to Rome against him... and that the war in Africa was now over. As a result he was seriously disquieted, but for the present was compelled to remain where he was' preying on the countryside for food and getting some from (Antiochos's agent) Zeuxis.

Eventually Philip succeeded by a trick in getting to sea without a fight. Polyainos (4.18.2) tells the story. 'Philip... when he was at war with king Attalos and the Rhodians, planned to escape by sea. He sent an Egyptian 'deserter' who informed the enemy that Philip was preparing to fight his way out, and that night he lit many fires as if the fleet was intending to remain. The fleet of Attalos prepared for battle and called off the patrol (*φυλακή*) mounted against Philip's escape by sea. Philip then moved his ships away (by night) without being noticed'. By this time, probably early in 200BC, Attalos had rejoined the Rhodians.

The next information comes from Livy. In March 200BC war was declared by Rome on Philip (L.31.5.1). The reports from Marcus Aurelius and Marcus Laevinus about the state of affairs in Greece had arrived in Rome, as well as a new embassy from the Athenians saying that 'King Philip was approaching their borders and that soon not only their territory but their city as well would be in his hands' (L.31.5.5). Appian's fourth heading runs: 'With another part of his army Philip destroyed Attika and besieged Athens'. When the consul assigned to Macedonia for the year 200, P.Sulpicius Galba, arrived late in the year in Epeiros with his fleet (L.31.14.3) he was met by Athenian envoys asking him to raise the siege of their city. He immediately sent 20 threes with 1000 troops to Athens. The force was small because he had heard 'that the king was not conducting the siege in person but at that particular time was assaulting Abydos, having already tried his strength in naval engagements with the Rhodians and Attalos, in neither case successfully. However he was in good heart partly because of his warlike nature and partly because of the treaty with Antiochos'. Shortly afterwards Livy (31.14.11) speaks of 'King Attalos and the Rhodians arriving at Aigina after pursuing Philip as he retired to Macedon'. It appears then that Philip after his escape from Bargylia had set out for home with Attalos and the Rhodians on his tail. They lost him and he had time to get back to Macedon and out to Abydos (L.31.15.9), and to be reported as there to Sulpicius when he arrived in Greece. The reference to Philip 'trying his strength in naval engagements against the Rhodians and Attalos in neither case successfully' refers to the two simultaneous battles of Chios.

Polybios (16.28.3) is critical of the laziness of the Rhodians and Attalos and contrasts it with the kingly and great-hearted conduct of Philip and his steadfastness of purpose.

'Galled by the failures that had befallen him and driven on by anger and passion, he adapted to the current circumstances in a mood of desperate and inspired courage. Thus he rose superior to the Rhodians and Attalos, and achieved the successes which followed. His aim was to remove the bases and stepping stones for the Romans in that area [NW Greece and the Hellespont] and give himself a stepping stone in Abydos, should he wish again to go to Asia'. Livy is more specific (31.15.9): 'And Attalos and the Rhodians, although if they had increased the pressure on Philip they might have won the honour of having liberated Greece, by letting him cross again to the Hellespont and increase his forces by occupying strategic places in Thrace, drew out the war and left the credit of finishing it to the Romans'. Philip, Livy continues, had a more kingly spirit. Though he had not been a match for Attalos and the Rhodians he was not afraid even of the threat of war with Rome.

Philip defied the Roman ultimatum delivered after an earlier attack on Athens to his general Nikanor (P.16.27.1, L.31.14.10) by sending an army under Philokles to ravage Athenian territory. He then mounted an attack on the Ptolemaic cities in Thrace by land and sea, and then upon Abydos and Sestos. Herakleides who commanded the fleet at Lade was again *ναύαρχος* with orders to proceed to Maroneia while he himself marched there with a small army of 2000 light infantry and 200 cavalry. Maroneia fell to the first assault, Ainos after a laborious siege was betrayed by Ptolemy's prefect. Philip occupied a number of fortresses in the area and a number in the Chersonese surrendered. Abydos, to which Attalos had sent a garrison and Rhodes a single four from their fleet lying close by at Tenedos, closed its gates and only fell after a long siege (P.16 29–34). Leaving a garrison in Abydos, Philip returned to Macedon. By this time Sulpicius had taken his army from Epeiros to Apollonia, sending his fleet to Kerkyra to winter.

(L.31.22.4) The 20 threes, which Sulpicius on arrival in his province had sent under Claudius to Peiraieus, had done much to strengthen the morale of the Roman allies. The raids from Corinth through Megara ceased, and pirate ships from Chalkis no longer dared to come beyond Sunion or even the Euripos strait. Additional coastal defence was provided by the arrival of three Rhodian fours to support three Athenian aphracts (*apertae naves*).

Claudius (L.31.23.1) was advised by refugees from Chalkis that there was an opportunity for an attack on that city by sea. He anchored west of Sunion till dusk and moved by night to Chalkis arriving just before dawn. He succeeded in taking, sacking and devastating the city, but had not sufficient troops to garrison it. This would have deprived Philip of Euripos 'the gateway to Greece'. Instead, Philip arriving too late from Demetrias was provoked to launch an attack on Athens by land, which was held off until troops arrived from Attalos in Aigina and the Romans in Peiraieus. Philip then moved to attack Eleusis but was again thwarted by troops from Peiraieus. He then went to attend the autumn meeting of the Achaean League (at Aigion). Meanwhile his general Philokles was plundering Attika from Euboia, and Sulpicius was invading the borders of Macedon from Apollonia. The autumn meeting of the Aetolian League at Naupaktos (L.31.40.9) was addressed by representatives of Philip and the Romans but deferred a decision. They were awaiting the outcome of the imminent hostilities.

(L.31.28.3) Attalos wintering in Aigina sent envoys to Sulpicius who told him to await the Roman fleet there and then co-operate in naval warfare on Philip. In expectation of this, Philip, now back in Macedon, sent ships to Peparethos and Skiathos to destroy their usefulness to the allied fleet.

(L.31.33.1) Philip was diligently (*impigre*) preparing for war on land and sea. He assembled his fleet at Demetrias, and expecting that Attalos and the Roman fleet would move from Aigina at the beginning of spring (199 BC), he put Herakleides in command of the fleet and of the coast.

Leaving winter quarters, he engaged Sulpicius on land and was worsted in a cavalry battle at Mt Ottolobos. On his retreat Sulpicius returned to Apollonia to hand over his command to the consul for 199 Villius (L.31.40.12). (L.32.28.5) 'Sulpicius had taken up the greater part of his year in trying to find the king and his army. Villius made contact with the enemy but was recalled before he could do anything'. This verdict on Sulpicius's land campaign against Philip is certainly unfair, as Livy's own narrative shows (31.33.4 - 40.6) but his mention of Villius's short tenure of command is chronologically useful.

The allied naval campaign (L.31.44.1) in 199 BC began when the Roman fleet under the legate Apustius left Kerkyra, and rounding Malea joined Attalos near Skyllaion in the territory of Hermione between the Argolic and Saronic gulfs. The joint fleet spent a few days at Peiraieus and then moved to Andros where they were joined by 20 Rhodian cataphracts . The city and garrison surrendered on terms, and the fleet moved to Kythnos, the siege of which was abandoned as not worth while. Returning to the mainland they were joined at Prasiai by 20 *λέμβοι* from the island of Issa in the Adriatic off Illyria. These were dispatched to collect booty from the territory of Karystos in Euboia while the fleet waited at Geraistos. They then moved north past Skyros to Ikos and from there to Mende for an attack on the Macedonian naval base and stronghold of Kassandreia (Potidaia). They encountered bad weather and their attack was unsuccessful. After some successful plundering in the Chalcidic area, their ships being full of booty they returned via Skiathos to Euboia. (L.31.46.1) Attalos and Apustius, leaving the fleet in Euboia (?Geraistos), went with ten *λέμβοι* into the Malian gulf to attend a council of war with the Aetolian representative Pyrrhias. The Aetolians asked for 1000 soldiers from Attalos but were refused because they had not invaded Macedonia when in the previous year Pergamon was invaded by Philip, and went away with promises only.

On the return of Attalos and Apustius to the fleet, an attack on Oreos on the northern coast of Euboia was discussed. The 20 Rhodian ships were sent to a mooring at Zelasion 'a promontory of Phthiotis very conveniently overlooking Demetrias' (*super Demetriadem... peropportune obiectum: Map K*) to mount guard in case Macedonian ships moved from there. Attalos and the Romans attacked Oreos from different sides, and the city was taken.

The effect on the Aetolians of Sulpicius's operations on land, and in particular of the naval campaign, was dramatic. (L.31.40.9) The same praetor Damokritos who had been responsible for the Aetolians' delay in declaring war (on Philip) at Naupaktos (the previous year) had at the next council (autumn 199 BC) stirred them up to war. He had heard of the cavalry battle at Ottolobos, the invasion of Macedon by the Dardanoi and the Illyrians, and in addition of the arrival of the Roman fleet at Oreos and the naval blockade of the Macedonian coast.

(L.31.47.1) The autumn equinox being near, the Euboean gulf became dangerous for ships and the allied fleet withdrew to Peiraieus. Apustius, leaving 30 ships, went on to Kerkyra, while Attalos crossed to Asia after sending the Rhodians home, but not before he had attended the Eleusinian mysteries.

Mare in potestate habent Romani: The Romans have the sea in their power

Among the first duties of the consuls for 198 BC was to present to the Senate envoys from king Attalos who complained that king Antiochos III of Syria was invading his territory while his own army and fleet was in Greece aiding the Romans, and that he could not continue aiding the Romans unless the Romans aided him against Antiochos. The Senate's reply was that they would tell their ally Antiochos not to invade the territory of another of their allies, Attalos.

The consul whose province was Macedonia, Titus Quinctius Flamininus, took a large army of 8000 soldiers and 800 cavalry across from Brundisium to Kerkyra earlier than was usual, although Livy later (32.28.6) says he was delayed 'for the greater part of the year' by religious duties. He crossed immediately in a five to the Roman camp in Epeiros and moved inland to an engagement with Philip on the Aous river. There is an air of urgency about the actions of him and of his brother Lucius, who was given the command of the fleet and of the coastal regions (L.32.16.2). This is likely to have been generated by the need to conclude the war with Philip, before meeting the greater threat from Antiochos.

Lucius Quinctius crossed to Kerkyra with two fives when he heard that the fleet had left, and catching up with it at Same (Kephallenia) on its way to Peiraieus sent back his predecessor in the command. From there he reached Malea in a slow passage towing the supply ships which accompanied the fleet. From Malea he made the passage to Peiraieus with three fast (*expeditis*) fives, and took over the ships which had been left there to guard Athens by Apustius. Two fleets came from Asia, 24 fives under Attalos and 20 cataphracts from Rhodes under Agesimbrotos. They met at Andros and proceeded to Euboia where they ravaged the territory of Karystos. Then, since Karystos had been garrisoned by a force sent rapidly from Chalkis, they moved on to Eretria where they were joined by Lucius Quinctius with the ships from Peiraieus. He had left an order at Peiraieus that each ship of his own fleet (from Malea) as it arrived should proceed to Eretria. All the ships carried artillery of all kinds and siege engines. Eretria surrendered and then Karystos. The fleet then made for Kenchreai, the port of Corinth in the Saronic gulf, which was eventually taken (L.32 23 3), and preparations were made for an attack on Corinth itself (L.32.19.3).

The allied fleet at this point is detailed by Livy (32.21.27) as follows: 100 cataphracts (*naves tectae*), 50 lighter aphracts (*leviores apertae*) and 30 Issaean *λέμβοι*. The number of cataphracts may be broken down into 24 fives (Attalos), 20 cataphracts (Rhodian) and 56 (Roman). Of the last at least three, probably most, were fives and the rest fours or threes. 20, at least, of the whole fleet were threes and these are likely to have been cataphract. There is no clue to the rating of the 50 lighter aphracts. Some could have been threes since aphract threes are known later (p. 113); and some *τριημιολίαι* or *ἡμιολίαι*, although it has been noticed that these like *λέμβοι* are usually specifically named. The pro-Roman praetor of the Achaean league states at the autumn meeting of 198 BC (L.32.21.32): 'The Romans have the sea in their power; whatever land they approach they immediately subject it to their rule'. The Achaean league voted to go over to Rome, and their army was sent to Corinth in support of the allies. But Attalos and Lucius Quinctius, when Philokles brought large reinforcements into the city, decided to abandon the siege and Attalos returned to Peiraieus and the Roman fleet to Kerkyra. Meanwhile, the consul who had been unsuccessfully besieging Atrax on the upper reaches of the river Peneios in Thessaly abandoned the siege and prepared to go into winter quarters further south in Phokis.

(L.32.18.3) 'Because there was no harbour in the whole coast of Akarnania and Aitolia which could at the same time hold the supply ships (*onerariae*) carrying victuals for the army and also provide winter accommodation for the legions' the consul took Elateia where he wintered and, further south, Antikyra with its harbour on the Gulf of Corinth. The passage gives an interesting and rare insight into the problems of supply in winter quarters when military operations did not enable a Roman army to live off the country.

During the winter Philip met the Roman consul at a beach on the Malian gulf near Nikaia. He remained in a ship at anchor. The terms offered were accepted with certain reservations. He was not prepared to withdraw all his garrisons from Greece or from the cities of Karia he had taken. Philip's answer was brought to Rome by his envoys, whom the Senate dismissed. Titus and Lucius Quinctius Flamininus were confirmed in their commands for 197 and preparations were made for the final battle. Lucius Quinctius (L.33.17.2) with the fleet from Kerkyra, by taking Leukas, brought Akarnania under Roman control and Philip's general Androsthenes was defeated by the Achaeans near Corinth (L.33.14.1). At the same time the Rhodians with Achaean help attacked the Macedonians in the Rhodian Peraia. Finally, at Kynoskephalai in Thessaly (L.33.7–9) Philip was decisively defeated by the consul. After a conference with his allies the consul met Philip, who agreed to all the terms of peace which had previously been offered him. Livy comments (33.13.15): 'It is said that the consul (*imperator*) had no more pressing reason for concluding peace quickly than the general opinion that Antiochos was planning war and the invasion of Europe'.

(L.33.24.3–7) The defeat of Philip was reported to the senate in Rome at the end of 197 BC and ten commissioners were appointed to advise the consul on the final terms of peace. They were as follows and provide *inter alia* a summary of Philip's conquests in his two naval expeditions (L.33.30.1–11 cf P.18.44): (i) All Greek cities in Europe and Asia to enjoy their liberty and laws; (ii) All cities in Greece under Philip's control to be handed over to the Romans free of Macedonian garrisons by the time of the Nemean Games; Philip (iii) to withdraw from the following cities in Asia: (In Karia) Euromon, Pedasa, Bargylia and Iasos; (in Lemnos?) Myrina; (in the Hellespont) Abydos; Thasos; (in Propontis) Perinthos and Kios, the latter after an approach by the consul to King Prusias; (iv) to surrender all prisoners and deserters; (v) to surrender all *naves tectae* except five and one royal ship of almost unmanageable size (*inhabilis prope magnitudinis*), driven by sixteen oar-files (*versus remorum*) (a side); (vi) to pay an indemnity of 1000 talents, half immediately.

There was criticism of the peace terms from the Aetolians who had noticed that the cities of Greece in Macedonian occupation were to be handed over to the Romans, not given freedom. In the end it was agreed that the three 'fetters of Greece' as Philip had called them (L.32.37.4) Demetrias in Thessaly, Chalkis in Euboea and Corinth in Achaia should be held by Rome while the threat from Antiochos lasted. It should be noted that the strategic importance of these three strongholds rested on their position on the sea. Corinth controlled the Isthmos with her ports Lechaion on the Corinthian and Kenchreai on the Saronic gulf. Chalkis controlled the Euripos strait, the maritime 'gateway to Greece', while a fleet operating from Demetrias (mod. Volo) controlled the sea routes to the north east and the Hellespont. If Antiochos were to capture these he would have Greece in the power of his fleet.

In the parallel passage in Polybios (18.44.6) Philip is to surrender his *νῆες κατάφρακτοι* except five vessels and the *ἑκκαιδεκήρης*. Polybios's Greek version is enlightening in two ways. It shows that *tectus* is the latin equivalent of the Greek *κατάφρακτος*. It also shows that a ship driven by sixteen *'versus remorum'* is in fact a sixteen (*ἑκκαιδεκήρης*) which on the analogy of the three is a ship with sixteen files (*versus*) of oarsmen on each side of the ship at three levels. The Latin poet Vergil corroborates this use of the word *versus* in a well-known description of a three (*Aeneid* 5.119–120) 'which Greek youths row in triple files (*triplici versu*), and the oars rise in three rows'. Vergil describes thus the three in her two aspects: it has three files of oarsmen a side and it has three levels of oars. It is the files of oarsmen a side which give the sixteen her name, and hence also the three. The Roman attitude to warships 'of unmanageable size' is well shown.

Endnotes

1 It has been argued that the phrase in Polybios's eulogy 'making a beginning of the war' means an actual sea-battle in which Theophiliskos took the greatly outnumbered Rhodian fleet on its own into battle with the Macedonian fleet. There is a record of an engagement of Rhodian and Macedonian ships off

Lade near Miletos, which is usually taken to have occurred when Philip, having suffered considerable losses of men and ships off Chios, was on his way to invade Karia and the mainland territory of Rhodes. It seems most unlikely that Theophiliskos would have thus hazarded his ships at the outset; and that Philip, having made his way on his planned southward voyage as far as Miletos, should have then returned to besiege Chios; or that the Rhodian fleet, which after the battle of Lade went south to Kos (on its way home), should then have turned round and moved north to join Attalos. The preferable alternative is that 'making a beginning of the war' refers to Theophiliskos's part in the Rhodian decision to prepare for war with Philip.

2. The problem presented by the list of casualties in ships at the battles of Chios was earlier raised (p. 62) when Polybius wrote (5.101.2) of Philip in 217 BC that he commissioned a force of 12 cataphracts, 8 aphracts and 30 *ἡμιολίοι λέμβοι*. It is certain (p. 255) that the words aphract and cataphract mean 'undecked' and 'decked' (and later 'boxed-in'). Since ships must be one or the other, it follows that *ἡμιολίοι λέμβοι, hemioliai,* are regarded as exempt from the classification 'decked' or 'undecked' because of their unusual oarsystem; and that they may be either one or the other. *Λέμβοι* may be (p. 263) without or with rams; and if the latter they are sometimes called *pristeis*. Casson (*SSAW* Ch.6 n.107) points out that in the Illyrian war (P.2.10.2–5) and at the battle of Chios *λέμβοι* appear to have the ability to ram (P.16.4.8–12). *Λέμβοι* are also (like *scaphae*: p. 135, 136) sometimes decked and boxed-in; e.g. by Demetrios at the siege of Rhodes (p. 34).

His numerous *λέμβοι* were used by Philip at Chios in the front line between the bigger ships, and they played an effective role against the Rhodians in the second battle (p. 83) 'impeding the Rhodian efficiency' in many ways when a melée developed 'since the *λέμβοι* attacked them'. It must be remembered that some of these *λέμβοι* were *ἡμιόλιοι*, described in the casualty list as *ἡμιολίαι* (p. 84); and it is difficult to believe that if they attacked Rhodian ships they were not decked, boxed-in and equipped with rams. The same must have been true of the *τριημιολίαι*, one of which is said to have been rammed by Attalos's flagship in the first battle and so was in Philip's front line. Three are grouped with cataphracts in Philip's casualty list, and one in Attalos's.

The remaining text to be considered in this connection (p. 113) is the passage in Appian (*Pun.* 75) describing the force sent to Utica at the outset of the third Punic war: *ναῦσι δ' ἐφέροντο πεντήκοντα μὲν πεντήρεσιν ἕκατον δ' ἡμιολίαις ἀφράκτοις δὲ καὶ κερκούροις καὶ στρογγύλοις.*

'They were conveyed by 50 fives and 100 *ἡμιολίαι*, also by aphracts and *κέρκουροι* and many round ships', the army consisting of 80,000 footsoldiers and 4000 cavalry'. The record of the presence of *ἡμιολίαι* in a Roman fleet is unique and the number is surprising though not greater than Philip's fleet of *λέμβοι*. It seems that the Romans had taken a leaf out of Philip's book. In the Roman fleet the *ἡμιολίαι* are grouped with the cataphract ships and distinct from aphracts and infantry and cavalry transports. If Philip's *ἡμιόλιοι λέμβοι* at Chios were boxed in and equipped with rams, it would then seem reasonable to accept the 100 Roman *ἡμιολίαι* as such, cataphract and armed with rams. Livy 36.42.8 (p.84) is evidence that in a Roman fleet aphract ships could be with or in the case of scout-ships without rams; but it is unlikely that an aphract ship with a ram could take part in a formal *ναυμαχίας* as a ship of the line.

3

CHALLENGES TO ROMAN SEA POWER: 2ND AND EARLY 1ST CENTURIES BC

Philip's defeat at Kynoskephalai in 197 BC left Antiochos III heir to his ambitious plans of expansion, to which naval power was central. With Philip as partner he had planned the invasion of Egypt, by his capture of first Gaza (200 BC) and later Sidon. In 198 (L.33.19.8) he had 'brought over all the cities of Koile Syria from Ptolemy's rule to his own'. The transfer of his naval base probably from Tarsus to Tyre in 198 is indicated by his issue of Tyrian coinage (**19**).

In the early spring of 197 he planned to send to Asia Minor a fleet of 100 cataphracts, and 200 lighter ships to win over the coastal cities of Kilikia, Lykia and Karia. He also (P.15.41.a) had designs on Ephesos as a convenient naval base. The Rhodians became alarmed (L.33.20) and courageously gave Antiochos a warning not to pass in his westward advance beyond the traditional boundary of Hiera Akra, but decided not to confront him if he did. They did not however give up their responsibility for the Ptolemaic cities of Kaunos, Myndos, Halikarnassos and Samos. Antiochos took Ephesos in 197 and wintered there 197/6 (L.33.38). From Ephesos troops were sent to attack Smyrna in Ionia and Lampsakos in the Hellespont. He realised the importance of that area for his prospective invasion of Europe.

In 194 (L.34.49) when the Romans withdrew from Greece the Aetolians (L.35.12.2) were hoping that Antiochos would come 'to take possession of the vacant premises'. (L.35.20.13) In Rome steps were taken in 192 to lay down 30 new fives, launch seaworthy older ships and enlist *socii navales*. (L.35.22.2) The praetor Atilius was ordered to take the fleet to Greece to protect Rome's allies and legions were sent to Brundisium and Tarentum to be in readiness if needed. Finally in 192 (L.35.43.2) learning of the defection of Demetrias Antiochos set out from Ephesos via Ilion to Imbros with 40 cataphracts and 60 aphracts followed by 200 supply ships. He landed on the coast of Achaia, was welcomed at Demetrias and disembarked his force of 10,000 foot, 500 horse and 5 elephants. (L.35.43.6): 'Scarcely enough of an army to seize a defenceless Greece, let alone for mounting a war with Rome' (formally declared at the beginning of 191 (L.36.2.2). So it turned out. In spite of Antiochos's capture of Chalkis (35.51.9–10), possession of two of the three 'fetters of Greece', and his superiority at sea, the Romans rightly calculated that their superiority on land was enough. The consul Acilius advanced rapidly from the west with a large army, and caught Antiochos in a trap at Thermopylai. After a crushing defeat he returned to Asia where the war was finally decided in a naval campaign. Antiochos now appreciated the importance of his garrisons in the Hellespont in keeping a Roman army out of Asia.

1. THE NAVAL WAR WITH ANTIOCHOS

The Campaign of 191 BC (Map J (i))

Livy (34.1.1) represents Antiochos, back in Ephesos, as 'unconcerned about the Roman war', in the belief that the Romans would not cross to Asia, but advised by Hannibal to expect them. 'The fact was that the Romans were not less powerful at sea than on land'. He had heard that their fleet was 'around Malea' and that a new fleet under a new commander was on its way from Italy. Taking his advice, Antiochos sent the ships that were ready in commission to the Thracian Chersonese to prevent a crossing there, ordering Polyxenidas to fit out and launch the rest of the ships. Scout ships were also sent around the islands to investigate all enemy movements.

(L.36.42: 191 BC) The new fleet commander, Gaius Livius, set out from Rome with 50 cataphracts for Naples where he had ordered the allies of that coast to assemble the aphracts due under treaty. From there he moved to Sicily and passing through the strait of Messana he added six Carthaginian ships and exacted the ships owed by the people of Rhegion and Lokroi and suchlike allies. The Carthaginian ships may have been cataphracts, but not the others. Arriving at Kerkyra he heard that the old fleet was in Peiraieus. He first plundered Zakynthos and Same (Kephallenia) which had sided with Aitolia, and then moved round the Peloponnese 'in a voyage of a few days under favourable conditions' and reached Peiraieus. 'At Skyllaion he met Attalos's son and successor Eumenes with three ships. He had been at Aigina in doubt whether to return to defend Pergamon, since he had heard that Antiochos at Ephesos was preparing sea and land forces, or stay on with the Romans on whose fortunes his own depended'.

Atilius handed over 25 cataphracts to Livius and returned to Rome. 'Livius with 81 cataphract ships (*constratis*) and many lesser ships (*minoribus*), either aphract ships with rams or scout ships without rams, crossed the sea to Delos'. The total of cataphracts was made up of 50 new arrivals and 25 already in Greece. The further six are some of the nine ships of which the rating is not given, six Carthaginian and three with Eumenes. Since Eumenes' main fleet was in Asia (see below), it seems likely that his ships were aphract and that all the Carthaginian ships were cataphract. By this time Antiochos had withdrawn and the consul Acilius was besieging Naupaktos, but the ships were needed more urgently in Asia than there.

(L.36.43.1) At Delos adverse winds delayed Livius for some days; 'that area round the Kyklades is very windy indeed'. Polyxenidas's scout ships told him that Livius was delayed at Delos and he informed Antiochos at the Hellespont. The king returned as speedily as he could to Ephesos with his ships equipped with rams (i.e. cataphracts and ram-equipped aphracts); and held a council to decide whether to fight a pitched battle or not. Polyxenidas advised him to fight before Eumenes's fleet and the Rhodian ships joined the Romans, 'when they would be about the same in number (as the Syrians) but superior in everything else both speed of ships and the varied potential of their support vessels (*varietate auxiliorum*). The Roman ships were inexpertly built, thus clumsy (*immobiles*) and came as well laden with supplies as ships are coming to an enemy country. The Syrian ships on the other hand were putting out from an entirely peaceful country and would have on board nothing but soldiers and arms. Their own knowledge of the (local) sea and land conditions, as well as of the winds, would also be a great advantage. The enemy was ignorant of all these and would be confused. The proposer of the plan convinced them all, particularly as he was also the man who was going to carry it out'.

Two days were spent in preparation; and on the third they moved from Ephesos to Phokaia with 100 ships, all of smaller size (*minoris formae*), of which 70 were cataphract and the rest aphract. Appian (*Syr*.22) gives 200 ships, 'very much lighter than the enemy's, which was a great advantage to Antiochos since the Romans were still inexperienced at sea'. On news of the approach of the Roman fleet, Antiochos was not minded to be present at the battle, but went inland to Magnesia (*ad Sipylum*) to muster his land forces, 'while the fleet moved quickly to Kissus, the port of the Erythraeans, supposing it to be a more convenient place in which to wait for the enemy'.

(L.36.43.11) 'As soon as the north winds dropped – they had been blowing for several days – the Romans put out from Delos towards Phanai which was a Chian port facing the Aegean (west). From there they took their ships round to the city (of Chios) and taking on victuals crossed to Phokaia, which Appian says received them through fear. Eumenes had gone to Elaia and returned a few days later with 24 cataphracts and a slightly larger number of aphracts. Appian says that he had fifty ships of which half were cataphract. He joined the Romans at Phokaia, who were preparing themselves and making ready for a naval battle'.

(L.36.43.13) 'From Phokaia the Romans put out with 105 cataphracts and about 50 aphracts. When at first they were driven towards the shore by north winds on the beam the ships were forced to move in a thin column with ships almost in single file. When the wind abated a little they tried to cross to the harbour of Korykos which lies north of

Kissus (*super Cissuntem est*), the harbour of the Erythraeans' and otherwise known as Erythras.

(L.36.44.1) 'When Polyxenidas learnt that the enemy was approaching he was delighted at the prospect of fighting. He himself extended the left wing towards the open sea and ordered the trierarchs to open out (*explicare*) the right wing towards the land and thus advanced to engage in an even line'.

'When the Roman commander (of the column under sail) saw what was happening, (leaving his foresail up) he furled his mainsail and lowered his mast, and stowing away the tackle awaited the ships that were following'. (He had to stop to allow the ships in the column behind him to catch up if he was to form line abreast).' By this time about 30 ships (of the Roman, leading, right, wing) were in line (abreast) (*in fronte*); and to bring the left wing (i.e. the following ships of the column) level with them (in the line) he raised (i.e. gave orders to the ships of the right wing to raise) foresails[1] and stood out to sea (to cover the enemy's left wing under Polyxenidas) while ordering the ships (of his left wing) behind him to point their prows towards the shore (and move) against the enemy's right'.

The foregoing passage is a most accurate and detailed account of the manoeuvre by which a fleet moving under sail in column (ἐπὶ κέρας) is transformed into a line-abreast formation (*frons*, μέτωπον). With plenty of sea room the column could all take up stations on the left of the flagship, normally at the head of the right wing, without her having to alter course; but where, as here, sea room is tight, the right wing had to move some distance to the right out to sea so that the left wing had room to fan out as it moved towards the shore. It is interesting to note that in this description of a manoeuvre, as in the description of the battle of Chios, there is no mention of a centre, only of the two wings.

(L.36.44.4) 'Eumenes was the rearguard; but, since the process of lowering sail initially caused some confusion, he also' (like his commander Livius) 'urged his ships forward with the greatest possible speed' to get them into their place at the far end of the line . The reason why Livius used his foresails is indicated. He had to move quickly; and in suitable wind conditions the foresail would add to the speed achieved by the oarsmen. Here its use also indicates that since the north wind favoured Livius's move away from the land to his right the lines of battle must have run roughly north east and south west with the northern ends close to the shore (which here ran roughly north west and south east) and the south western ends towards the open sea. The course being set by the Roman column was then from north west to south east and Polyxenidas's ships were drawn up in a line of battle with the right wing near the shore. Behind them and to the east was the west-facing Erythraean port of Kissus from which they had put out. Identification of the 'harbour of Korykos' in which the battle took place must satisfy these conditions (see note on Maps J1 and J2).

The Battle of Korykos

As the two lines faced each other, 'now (the combatants) were visible to all'. (This last remark suggests that until the lines were formed, one or other of the fleets was, at any rate partially, hidden from the other).

There were two of the Carthaginian ships, probably fives, out ahead of the rest of the allied fleet as the line formed up. Three of Antiochos's ships came to meet them, and as was natural with the unequal numbers, two of Antiochos's ships (probably threes) attacked a single Carthaginian ship first, brushing off the oars on each side. Then the decksoldiers boarded and seized the ship throwing overboard or killing the defenders. The one that fought on equal terms saw that the other ship was captured and withdrew back to the fleet before it could be surrounded by 3 ships.

(L.36.44.8) 'Livius angrily moved against the enemy with his flagship. When the two ships that had surrounded the single Carthaginian ship began to attack him in the hope of giving him the same treatment, he ordered his oarsmen to let their oars down into the water to stabilise the ship, and grappling-irons to be thrown on to the approaching enemy ships. Then when the fighting had been reduced to the level of a land battle, he told them to remember their Roman courage and refuse to treat the king's slaves as men. The two ships were then captured by the one as easily as the one had been captured by the two'. There was then a general *melée*.

Eumenes, who was the last to come up, after the battle had been joined, saw that the enemy's left

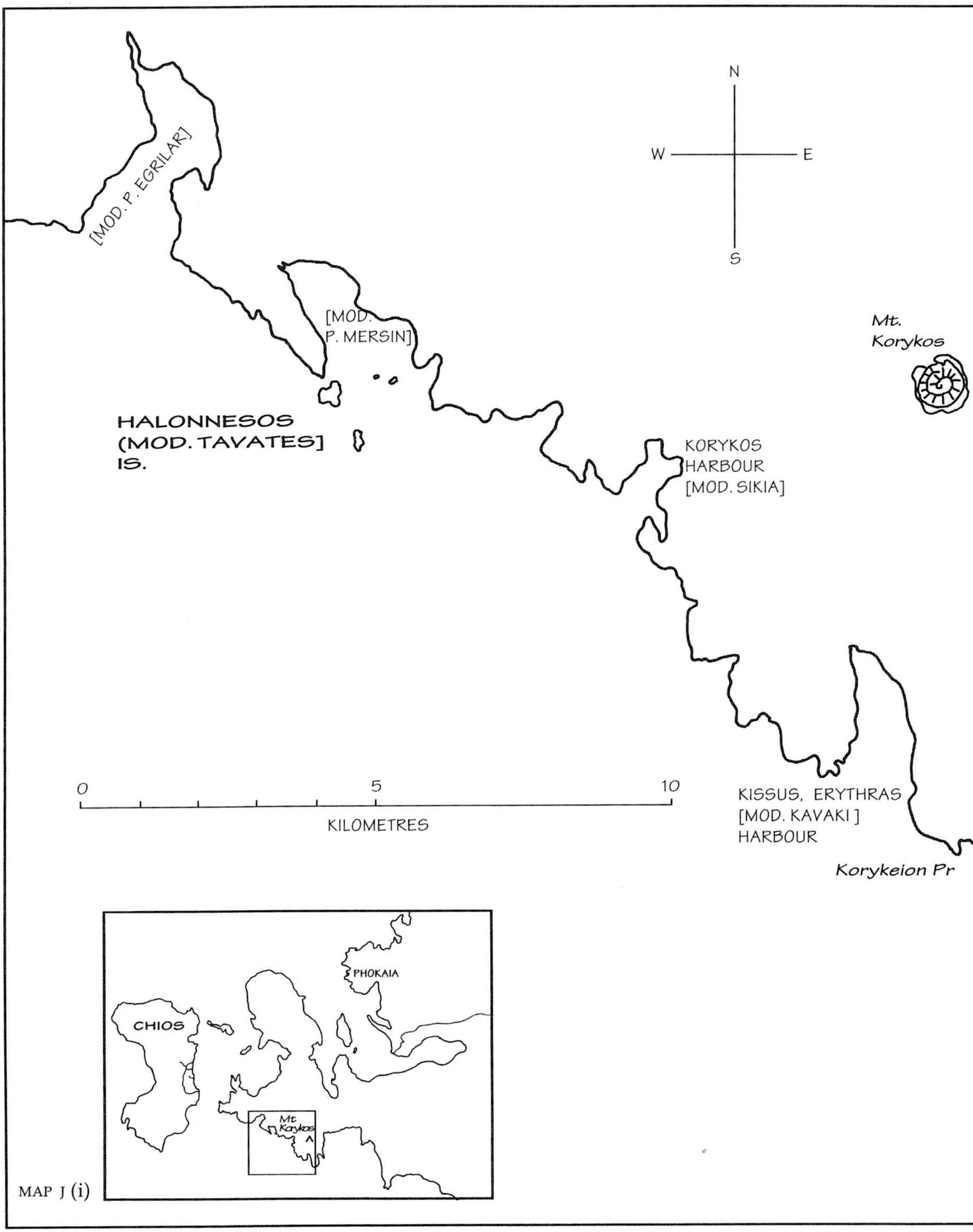

MAP J (ii). *The Korykos Promontory*

wing was being thrown into confusion by Livius, and proceeded against the (enemy's) right wing, where the battle was more evenly balanced. And it was not long before flight of enemy ships began from the left wing. In fact, the moment Polyxenidas recognised that he was undoubtedly inferior in the courage of his decksoldiers, he raised his foresails and began a precipitate flight; and soon even those who had engaged Eumenes near the shore did the same.

The Romans and Eumenes pursued doggedly enough as long as the oarsmen held out and there was some prospect of harassing the men of the (fleeing) column. But they saw that the speed of the enemy ships, being light, enabled them to elude the allies' own vainly struggling ships which were laden with supplies. Appian speaks of the heaviness of the ships which prevented them catching an enemy escaping in light vessels. 'At last they gave up the pursuit, after capturing 13 enemy ships, oarsmen decksoldiers and all, and ten swamped'. Of the Roman fleet only the one Carthaginian ship was lost.

(L.36.45.4) Polyxenidas went straight back to Ephesos. The Roman fleet remained on the day of the battle at the place from which Antiochos's fleet put out, the Erythraean port of Kissus. On the following day it followed the enemy to Ephesos, meeting on the way 24 Rhodian cataphracts (Appian *Syn.*22 says 27) under the *ναύαρχος* Pausistratos. Together they drew up a line of battle off the harbour of Ephesos. After the exercise had sufficiently demonstrated that the enemy fleet admitted inferiority, the Rhodians and Eumenes were sent home. The Roman fleet then, setting a course for Chios, sailed past the west-facing Erythraean port of Phoinikos (see note to Map J (ii) and anchored for the night (offshore) and on the following day crossed to the island and the city (of Chios) itself. When they had stayed there for a few days to give the oarsmen as much rest as possible they crossed

---

Note to map J (ii): Livy gives an account of the fleet movements leading up to the battle, after Antiochos had approved the decision to seek naval confrontation with the Roman and Pergamene fleets.

Polyxenidas took the Syrian fleet out of the base at Ephesos north to Phokaia. There he appears to have had intelligence that the Roman fleet at Delos was waiting for favourable weather to move on Ephesos. He chose Kissus as the best harbour in which to wait and from which to intercept the enemy. The location of Kissus has to be inferred from what follows.

The Romans, when the weather became favourable, moved first to Phanai on the south-west coast of Chios (which Strabo 14.1.35 calls a 'deep harbour' confirmed by Admiralty Chart 2836 B) and from there went to meet King Eumenes of Pergamon and his fleet at Phokaia. For the allied fleet to move on Ephesos it was first necessary to move due west (with a strong beam wind) before turning south through the Chios strait. The north wind slackened (and probably their scouts told them of the Syrian fleet's ambush); and they were attempting to turn east to find shelter in the harbour of Korykos, when Polyxenidas brought his fleet out and formed line abreast with his right wing towards the land and the left extended 'into the open sea'. The reaction of the allied fleet was to down sail and form line abreast with the right wing extended 'to the open sea'. The references to the wings and to the open sea indicate that both Kissus and Korykos were harbours in a west-facing coastline south of the Poseideion/Argennon strait.

Strabo's account of the relevant area (14.1.31) begins with mention of the 'isthmus of the Chersonese (i.e. peninsula) of the Teians and Clazomenians'. The journey (from south to north) across the isthmus is, he says, 50 stades (in fact 10 km) but the passage round is more than 1000. At about the middle of this circuit lies Erythrai, an Ionian city with a harbour and four adjacent islands. (32) On the way [from the south coast of the isthmus] to Erythrai there is first Erai, then Korykos, a high mountain [2328 ft], and a harbour below it called Kasystes, and then [after rounding the Korykeian promontory] another harbour called Erythras [= Kissus: mod. Kavaki Bay] and several others in order [mod. P. Sikia, P. Mersin, P. Egrilar as marked on the Admiralty chart]. The modern P. Sikia, which is nearest to Mt Korykos on the west side, is then to be identified with Livy's Korykos harbour, lying a little more than 4 sm north west of Kissus. (Strabo continues:33) [Northwestwards] after M. Korykos there is a small island, Halonnesos [mod. Tavates], and then the Erythraean Argennon promontory [mod. Cape Bianco], which is very close to the Chian Poseideion (promontory) making a strait about 60 stadia (10.6 km) wide (in fact 6.5 km).

The conclusion to be drawn from Livy's and Strabo's text and corroborated from the Admiralty chart is that the battle of Korykos took place off the west coast (running NW and SE) of the Erythraian peninsula between Korykos harbour (mod. P. Sikia) and Kissus/Erythrias (mod. Kavaki) bay, but nearer to Korykos, which accordingly gave the battle its name.

It may be noted here that, when the Roman fleet retired northwards to Kanai (Strabo 13.1.6: the promontory on the south side of the gulf of Adramyttium) after a successful demonstration off Ephesos, (Livy 36.45.4 p. 150) they 'set course for Chios sailing past the west-facing Erythraian port of Phoinikos'. Since Kissus is the Phoenician name (Erythras being the Greek name) for the harbour, this may be the port Livy means.

to Phokaia. With four fives left there as a garrison for the city the fleet moved to Kanai, and since winter was approaching the ships were hauled up and surrounded by a ditch and a rampart.

The Campaign of 190 BC *(Maps J (iii), J (iv) and Note)*

(L.37.1.10) In the winter of 191–190 both sides prepared for a further campaign on land and sea. Lucius Scipio received Greece as his consular province with his famous brother Publius Scipio Africanus as his legate. They were to lead a large army into Asia. (L.37.2.10) The maritime province was allotted to Lucius Aemilius. He was to take over from the previous praetor 20 *naves longae* and himself enrol 1000 *socii navales* and 2000 infantry 'to serve on board the ships' (@ 100). They would have been light warships, *λέμβοι* with rams, i.e. liburnians, or possibly *ἡμιολίαι*. With these he was to proceed to Asia and take over the fleet there from C. Livius. (L.37.4.5) On rumours that Antiochos after the naval battle was building a larger fleet, 30 fives and 20 threes were to be built at Rome.

(L.37.8.1) Antiochos 'kept the whole winter free for preparations, chiefly concentrating on refitting his fleet so that he should not be driven wholly from command of the sea'. He reflected also that he had been defeated at sea in the absence of the Rhodian fleet and that the Rhodians would not let this happen again. 'He would need then a great number of ships to equal the enemy fleet in power and size (*viribus et magnitudine*)'. (Polyxenidas's fleet at Korykos had all been *minoris formae*) Hannibal was therefore dispatched to (Koilé) Syria (Appian *Syr*.22 ad fin.), Phoenicia and Kilikia to recruit Phoenician ships; and Polyxenidas, who had not been particularly successful, was ordered to take all the more pains to refit those he had, and to acquire others.

Antiochos himself wintered in Phrygia recruiting allies from all quarters. 'He had left his son Seleukos with an army in Aeolis to prevent the defection of cities in that area which were being canvassed on the one side by Eumenes at Pergamon and on the other by the Romans from Phokaia and Erythrai'. The Roman fleet (of 30 ships) was at Kanai (Map I), from where in the middle of winter they made a successful foray after booty with Eumenes' infantry and cavalry.

(L.37.9.5) In the early spring the Rhodians sent out a fleet of 36 ships under Pausistratos, and Livius took 30 of his ships from Kanai and moved with seven fours of Eumenes to the Hellespont to make preparations for the prospective crossing by the Roman army which was coming by land. Livius was met at Ilion by envoys from the local cities of Elaia, Dardanos and Rhoiteion offering assistance. He left 10 ships off Abydos, crossed to Sestos, which surrendered, and then returned to Abydos. Appian (*Syr*.23–24) says that Pausistratos, (whom he calls Pausimachos), left behind at Kanai in command of some Roman ships in addition to his own, organised various trials and exercises and devised fire-buckets. 'He attached to long poles iron buckets containing fire, to hang the fire over the sea in such a way that it was clear of his own ships but would fall on to enemy ships as they approached'. A description of the device *πυρφόρος* employed by Pausistratos is given in a fragment of Polybios (21.7) preserved in [Suidas]. There is also a sketch of such a device in an Alexandrian tomb graffito (**28**).

The Panormos engagement *(Note on Map J (iii))*

(L.37.10.10) Polyxenidas (who was a renegade Rhodian and had a score to settle with Pausistratos) prepared a trap for him. He sent him a man, whom Pausistratos knew, with an offer to betray the king's fleet to him if he Polyxenidas could be restored to Rhodes. Pausistratos moved to Panormos in Samian *περαία* or mainland territory and waited there to investigate the matter, carelessly splitting his fleet up, with some ships sent to get supplies at Halikarnassos and others to the city of Samos. A soldier of Antiochos's army visiting Samos was arrested by the Rhodians as a spy and betrayed the plot, but the information was not believed.

At Ephesos Polyxenidas hauled up some ships close to the water and made preparations as if he was going to haul up others for repair. He summoned oarsmen from winter quarters not to Ephesos but secretly to Magnesia. Then quickly launching from the beach (*deductis*) the ships which had been hauled up (*subductae*) and summoning the oarsmen from Magnesia, he set out after sunset with seventy cataphract ships and in spite of a head wind arrived at the harbour of Pygela before daylight. There he rested (for the day) and crossed to the nearest part of the Samian mainland territory by night.

Meanwhile the pirate captain Nikandros had been given orders to take five cataphract ships to Palinuros and then conduct the armed men to Panormos to take the enemy in the rear, while he himself in the meantime with his fleet in two squadrons, so that he could hold the entrance to the port on both sides, made for Panormos. Pausistratos taken by surprise (and thinking that the enemy ships would try to enter the harbour) manned with his troops the horn-like promontories on each side of the entrance 'preparing to drive off the enemy easily with missiles from both sides. But then when Nikandros's troops appeared he ordered his men aboard the ships and tried to break out, his flagship leading the column. Polyxenidas surrounded his ship with three fives as she emerged and she was rammed and swamped. The deck-soldiers were overwhelmed with missiles and Pausistratos was killed. Some of the other ships were captured outside the harbour and some within it, others were taken by Nikandros as they were being manhandled off the beach. Only five Rhodian ships and two Coans escaped, terror produced by the flashing fire making a path for them through the press of ships. Each ship with poles projecting from her prow carried before her in iron buckets a quantity of ignited fuel'. Appian (*Syr*.21) says that seven ships escaped and that Polyxenidas towed 20 back to Ephesos (the number of Rhodian ships he gives is 27) .

(L.37.11.14) Erythraean threes met the escaping Rhodian (and Coan) ships, which they were on their way to assist, not far from Samos and turned back to the Romans at the Hellespont. It will appear that the escaping Rhodian ships did not go north with them, but stayed on Samos, it must be assumed, with the ships which Pausistratos had sent to Halikarnassos and Samos city and which therefore had escaped the disaster. Polyxenidas, it appears, had returned to Ephesos.

Phokaia which had for some time been finding Roman occupation burdensome (P.21.6), was betrayed to Seleukos IV at this time, and other Aeolian cities, including Kyme, followed. Abydos was discussing terms of surrender with Livius when the disaster to the Rhodian fleet caused him to raise the siege and move south to protect the rest of his fleet at Kanai, which he then launched. Eumenes at the same time came down to his fleet at Elaia. (L.37.12.5) 'Then the whole (Roman) fleet with the addition of two threes from Mitylene moved to Phokaia. When he heard that this city was occupied by a strong royal garrison and that Seleukos's camp was not far away, he plundered the coastal area; and quickly embarking the booty, particularly the men, he waited only until Eumenes with his fleet caught up, and then set out for Samos'.

(L.37.12.7) Rhodian grief at their disaster turned to anger when they realised that the Rhodian Polyxenidas was responsible for it. They dispatched ten ships, and shortly after ten more, under a new and more cautious commander Eudamos, presumably to join the other Rhodian (and Coan) ships probably at Samos city.

(L.37.12.10) (Map J3 and Note): 'The Romans and Eumenes moved first to a mooring in Erythraean territory. They stayed there one night and on the following day reached (a mooring for the night at) the Korykos promontory. Since they wanted to cross from there to the nearest part of the Samian coast without waiting for sunrise when the helmsmen could take account of the condition of the sky, they put out into uncertain weather. In mid voyage the north-east wind (*aquilo*) veered north and the ships began to be tossed about as the sea became rough'.

(L.37.13.1) 'Polyxenidas, thinking that the enemy would make for Samos to join the Rhodian ships, set out from Ephesos and first moored (for the night) at Myonnesos. From there (the next day) he went over to the island called Makris so that as the (allied) fleet passed by he could attack any ships that strayed from the column, or take an opportunity of attacking the rearguard. When he saw the fleet scattered by the gale (see above), he first thought that that was a good moment to attack (since they would not be in defensive formation); but a little later when the wind increased and was now raising bigger waves, since he saw that he could not reach them, he went across to the island of Aithalia, so that on the following day he could attack the ships making for Samos from the open sea'.

A small number of the Romans reached a deserted harbour on Samos at the beginning of dusk, while the rest of the fleet spent the whole night tossing on the open sea and ran into the same harbour (probably mod. Karlovassi). There they

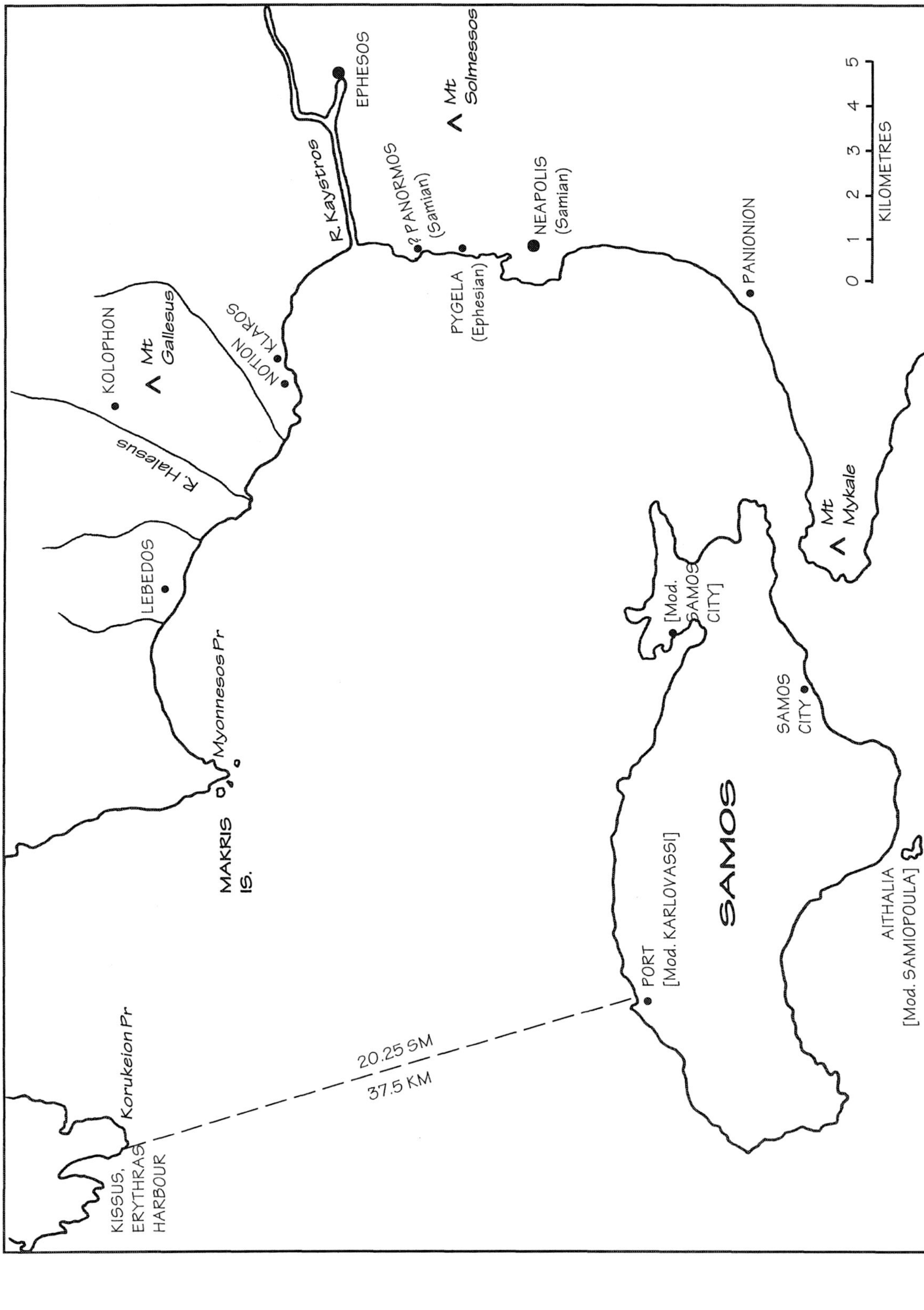

MAP J (iii). *Naval movements in 190 BC*

learnt from local people that the enemy's ships were moored on Aithalia and discussed whether to engage the enemy at once or wait for the Rhodian fleet. Postponing action they went across to Korykos from where they had set out. Polyxenidas also, after waiting fruitlessly, returned to Ephesos, whereupon the Roman fleet crossed to Samos city, since the sea was clear of the enemy. The [new] Rhodian fleet also arrived there a few days later'.

(L.37.13.7) To show that they had been waiting for the Rhodians' arrival, the allied fleet set off at once from Samos city for Ephesos either to decide the issue in a naval battle or, if the enemy refused to fight, a thing which would have most effect on opinion in the cities, to extract from him an admission of cowardice. They stood drawn up in battle order of line abreast in front of the entrance to the harbour (of Ephesos at the mouth of the river Kaystros). When no one came out to meet them, the fleet split up. Part rode at anchor in the open sea at the entrance to the harbour and part landed the decksoldiers on the coast. Since they were al-

---

Note on Map J (iii): In answer to Polyxenidas's false offer of defection Pausistratos took part of the Rhodian fleet at Samos to Panormos 'in Samian territory' (L.37.10.6: Samiae terrae*), where it was trapped by Polyxenidas and largely destroyed or captured. Since the battle is referred to later as taking place at Samos* (ad Samum)*, the location of a Samian Panormos (only mentioned in this connection) is in question.*

Strabo (14.1.19-20) gives the useful information that some of the mainland coast opposite Samos was Samian territory, in particular Neapolis which had once been Ephesian. Then proceeding north he mentions Pygela, then Panormos. He clearly puts Panormos on the mainland and Livy's phrase 'Panormum Samiae terrae' *suggests it.*

Livy begins his account of the battle by saying that Polyxenidas in spite of a head wind took his fleet by night to Pygela and the following night 'crossed to the nearest Samian territory' proceeding to blockade the harbour of Panormos. The word 'crossed' (trajecit) is often but by no means exclusively used of crossing water, and here may well mean crossing the boundary between Ephesian and Samian territory. Polyxenidas's choice of Pygela for his first nocturnal move suggests that it was Ephesian.

On news of the betrayal of Phokaia to Antiochos's son Seleukos, Livius abandoned the siege of Abydos and returned to Kanai. He took the whole fleet to Phokaia which he found too strongly defended. He accordingly moved on to meet the Pergamene fleet from Elaia, and proceeded to Samos city where the ships of the Rhodian fleet which had survived the disaster at Panormos were awaiting reinforcement.

Livius's first night's mooring was in Erythraian territory and the second 'at the Korykos promontory'. Polyxenidas's fleet had come up from Ephesos to Myonnesos and then to the island of Makris with the intention of harassing the Roman and Pergamene ships on the next leg of their voyage to Samos city, presumably round the eastern end of the island which would have brought them close to Makris.

Here Strabo again gives useful information. He describes the city of Samos (14.1.14) as (unlike the modern city) facing south and with a harbour and a mooring place (ναύσταθμος). (By contrast he describes Ephesos as having a harbour and shipsheds (νεώρια)). He says that the island has no harbours, only (ὕφορμοι), anchorages or possibly mooring places. He speaks of a promontory which extends westwards (with headlands Drakanos (mod. Drakoi) and Kantharios) and which was thinly inhabited at that time, being mainly used by the Samians for grazing their cattle.

Livy (Strabo's contemporary) says (37.12.11) that the allied fleet starting from Korykos before sunrise and making for 'the nearest Samian territory' (i.e. the north west coast of the island 20.25 sm away), ran into bad weather, the wind veering from north east (where the land gave shelter) to north, and were scattered. Polyxenidas decided that the sea was too rough for him to attack and 'saw that he could not reach them', [because their course was not the one he expected]. He then 'crossed to the island of Aethalia, so that from there he could attack the ships as they attempted to reach Samos city from the open sea', that is to say from the west after rounding the western end of the island. Aithalia was an early name of Chios; but at this date no island of that name is recorded.

Some ships of the Roman/Pergamene fleet reached a deserted haven (? mod. Karlovassi), presumably, as they intended, on the NW coast of Samos; and the rest joined them the following day. They learned from farmers (agrestes, Strabo's graziers) that the enemy fleet was moored on the island of Aethalia which can now be identified as modern Samiopoula off the south coast of the island and west of Samos city. This identication of the island explains why they then 'had a council of war to decide whether they would immediately fight or wait until the Rhodian fleet' (the ships in Samos harbour and the reinforcements on their way)' could join them. Being outnumbered they opted to wait, and returned (the 20.25 sm) to Korykos.

Polyxenidas lost patience and returned to Ephesos, giving the Roman/Pergamene fleet a clear run to Samos city by either route on its second attempt. The Rhodian reinforcements arrived at Samos city a few days later.

ready collecting a vast amount of booty from the widely looted countryside, Andronikos of Macedon, one of the garrison, made a sally against them when they approached the walls and taking a large part of the booty drove them to the sea and their ships.

'On the next day the Romans set an ambush at about the halfway point and marched in column up to the city'. Naturally enough there was no reaction. The men returned to their ships, and the ships to Samos, the Romans having made the point that the enemy avoided fighting by land as well as by sea.

(L.37.13.11) At this point Livius sent four threes, two from the Italian allies and two from Rhodes, with a Rhodian, Epikrates, in command, to deal with piracy in the strait of Kephallenia. Young Kephallenians led by a Spartan with the appropriate name of Hubristas (Lawless) had already succeeded in closing the supply route from Italy. The incident is interesting in showing the extent and serious effect of piracy and also indicating the wide responsibility of the praetor who held the *provincia maritima*.

(L.37.14.1) Epikrates did not accomplish his mission because at Peiraieus on the way he met the holder of the naval command (*imperium*) for 190 BC Lucius Aemilius. When Aemilius heard of the defeat of the Rhodians, anxious for his own safety since he had only two fives, he took Epikrates and his four ships back to Asia with him accompanied also by some Athenian aphracts. They crossed to Chios, where the Rhodian Timasikrates arrived on a stormy night with two fours from Samos. Brought to Aemilius he said he had been sent as escort because Antiochos's ships in frequent raids from the Hellespont and Abydos made that stretch of the sea dangerous for supply ships. On the crossing from Chios to Samos Aemilius fell in with two Rhodian fours sent by Livius and king Eumenes with two fives.

(L.37.14.4: 191–90 BC) When Aemilius reached Samos and the fleet was formally handed over, there was a council of war. The new Roman commander, Eudamos of Rhodes and Eumenes of Pergamon had to deal with a number of demands on their limited naval resources. The Hellespont crossing had to be secured for the approaching Roman army under the Scipios, an attack on Pergamon by Seleukos had to be met; and, most important of all, the fleet of Hannibal, newly built in Phoenicia and now approaching along the coast of Asia Minor must be prevented from joining Polyxenidas's fleet at Ephesos.

(L.37.22.2: August 190) 'Against the fleet which was rumoured to be coming from Syria the Rhodians with 13 ships of their own, a five from Kos and another from Knidos set out (under Eudamos from Samos) to Rhodes to be on guard there'. Two days before they arrived 13 ships from Rhodes under the commander Pamphilidas, with the addition of four ships which had been on guard in Karia, had been sent against that same Syrian fleet. By attacking the Syrian forces they had relieved from siege Daidala and a number of other fortresses in the Peraia. Eudamos agreed to move on at once. Six aphract ships were assigned to him in addition to the fleet which he had. On departure (from Rhodes) he had hurried as fast as he could, and caught up with the advance ships at the harbour called Megiste. When they had reached Phaselis in one column, the best plan seemed to be to await the enemy there.

Phaselis was excellently situated for sighting the enemy from some way off, but they had not realised that it was unhealthy in midsummer. So they moved on to the mouth of the Eurymedon river. There they were told by the people of Aspendos that the enemy was at Side.

(L.37.23.4) 'The king's men had moved rather slowly because the season of the etesians is unfavourable, being given to north-westers (*favoniis*). The Rhodians had 32 fours and four threes; the royal fleet was of 37 ships of larger size including three sevens and four sixes. Besides these there were ten threes. The Rhodians saw from a watchtower that the enemy was close'.

The Battle of Side

(L.37.23.6) 'At first light on the following day each fleet moved out of harbour ready to fight that day; and after the Rhodians had passed the promontory which stretches out to sea from Side they were immediately visible to the enemy and the enemy was visible to them. On the king's side the left wing which blocked the way on the side of the open sea was commanded by Hannibal, on the right wing Apollonios, one of the wearers of purple, was in command; they had already (when sighted) formed their ships in line of battle (i.e. abreast). The Rhodians were approaching in a long column. The leading ship was Eudamos's flagship. Charikleitos was rearguard and Pamphilidas commanded the centre. When Eudamos saw the enemy's line drawn up and ready for engagement, he also (as well as Hannibal) moved out to sea and ordered those that were following him one after another preserving their station to move into line abreast'.

(L.37.23.10) 'That movement at first caused confusion, for Eudamos had not yet moved out to sea far enough [each ship following him in making a 90° turn *in succession*] for it to be possible for all the ships [making a 90° left turn *together*] to effect a line [abreast stretching] towards the shore[2]. Moving too fast himself, he found himself meeting Hannibal with only five ships; the rest, having been ordered to form line abreast, were not following him. At the end of the column there were no slots left [for the rearguard ships] adjoining the shore and while the ships there were sorting themselves out in a panic (*trepidantibus*) the battle had already started on the right wing'.

Livy's statement (at L.37.23.5) that the Rhodian fleet at the mouth of the Eurymedon R. consisted of 32 fours and four threes can be reconciled with his earlier account (37.22.2) of the movement of ships from Rhodes, if four of the six aphracts there mentioned were threes and if the other two, smaller than threes, are not mentioned being, in the later context, of insignificant rating; and if further the four guardships from Karia were fours and in the later account the two fives are mistakenly given as fours. With those provisos the total in both cases was 38.[3] It is an interesting indication of Rhodian naval policy that her ships were all fours, in the first case 30 and in the second, with the mistaken addition of the two allied fives, 32. A squadron of fours appears to consist of 12 ships with the commander's flagship in addition. The Carian guardships were a detachment of four ships on special duty.

The manoeuvre described is the normal way of forming line abreast from column with the ships in column taking up stations in line abreast by first turning *successively* by 90° to the right (or left) and then turning *together* 90° to the left (or right) to form a line of ships abreast facing the enemy. But the column in this case had not sufficient sea room, since it had been moving too close to the shore. To rectify this Eudamos moved rather too quickly seaward. The fact that he now became separated with four other ships indicates that the column was (as often cf. Thuk.2.90.1) of four files and the leading ships of each file stayed close to him leaving a gap between them and the next four who were acting as ordered. The effect of his action had not yet filtered through to the shoreward end of the line-in-making where there were not enough slots for the rearguard. The clarity and precision of this description is remarkable.

(L.37.24.1) 'However, in a short space of time the good performance of their ships and their naval experience took away the Rhodians' nervousness. The ships moving out to sea quickly each gave a place on the left (landward) side to the ship coming after her (in the files of the column); and if a ship had engaged an enemy with the ram either she damaged the prow or she carried away the oars or by a free (i.e. unchallenged) movement along between the files (*libero inter ordines discursu praetervecta*) she made an attack on the stern'.

The description is again precise. If 'each ship gave a place on the landward side to the ship *coming after her*' in the column and there were four files in the column the line abreast formation must be *four longitudinal files deep*, a much stronger formation than a single line abreast.

The next description, after that of the successful establishment of the battle line, is of what happened when the two lines met. This is not a particular account but a generalised statement of the various possibilities.

'When one ship engaged another she could either smash the prow or carry away the oars or passing right through between the files would attack a ship's stern'. The 'files' (*ordines*) here are not the longitudinal files but the short files composed of individual members of the longitudinal files ranged one behind the other (four deep) and between which ships making a διέκπλους would have to pass once a gap had been made.

(L.37.24.3) 'The greatest consternation was caused when a royal seven was swamped by a single blow of a much smaller Rhodian ship, so that now the enemy right wing in no uncertain manner turned to flight. Out at sea Eudamos was hard pressed by the number of Hannibal's ships although he was superior in other respects.

Hannibal would have surrounded him had not a signal by which a fleet is usually concentrated been displayed from the flagship; and if all the ships which had been winning on the (royal) right flank had not hurried to assist their own men. Then Hannibal and the ships with him started to withdraw, but the Rhodians could not pursue them since their oarsmen were sick (p. 102) and for that reason rather quickly tired. In the open sea where they had come to a stop they refreshed themselves with food'.

The details given in this and the following passage confirm the impression that Livy has been deriving his account from a Rhodian source; and this would also explain why the account of the royal fleet and its moves is abbreviated to the point of obscurity. Although the names of the commanders of the right and left wings of the royal fleet are given (Apollonios (R) and Hannibal (L)) there is no mention of a commander for the centre as in the case of the Rhodian fleet. Nor is it formally stated that Hannibal was the overall commander and that his ship was the flagship, although it is difficult to believe otherwise. Then, Livy says, Hannibal was on the point of surrounding Eudamos and raised a signal which meant that the fleet should come together at one spot (presumably to the flagship so that he could capture Eudamos and the Rhodian flagship). The effect of this signal was to undermine the winning posture of his left wing by withdrawing the victorious ships from there; (and thus produce a deterioration of the whole position of the royal fleet including the left wing) so that Hannibal himself began to withdraw.

The outcome of the battle for the Rhodians was the capture of the one damaged royal seven which they towed to Phaselis. (L.37.24.6) 'Eudamos' while his crews were recovering 'watched the enemy towing away with their aphracts their lame and damaged ships and scarcely more than 20 (of the 37 ships of larger size and ten threes of smaller size) moving off undamaged'. Since the aphracts of the Rhodians were not mentioned in the fleet inventories, it is reasonable not to identify the aphracts mentioned here with the threes in the royal inventory but to suppose that they were not mentioned there either.

From Phaselis they returned to Rhodes 'not so much pleased at their victory as accusing each other of missing the chance of swamping or capturing the whole enemy fleet'. The effect of their victory on Hannibal was important. Although he wanted to join Polyxenidas at Ephesos as soon as possible, 'he did not then dare to pass Lykia'; and to prevent the possibility the Rhodians sent Charikleitos with 20 ships with rams to Patara and the harbour of Megiste, while Eudamos was sent with the seven largest ships of the fleet he had commanded (at Side) to join the Romans at Samos with instructions to use his powers of persuasion to the utmost to make the Romans attempt the capture of Patara. The seven largest ships would have been the Coan and Cnidian fives, the four threes and his own flagship, the last either a specially powerful four or a five. If the two fives were wrongly classified as fours in the inventory of the Rhodian fleet before the battle, it is possible that the two flagships of Eudamos's and Pamphilidas's squadrons of 12 fours were also wrongly so classified.

Antiochos's Final Effort at Sea: The Battle of Myonnesos 190 BC *(Map J (iv) and Note)*

The move of Antiochos to Sardis made it impossible for the Romans to move from Samos to Patara as the Rhodians wished, (L.37.25.2–3) and 'give up protecting Ionia and Aiolis'; but the Rhodians found it possible to send four cataphract ships to join the fleet there. The diplomacy of the consul Scipio prevented Antiochos bringing Prusias over to his side to help him keep the Romans out of Asia. Antiochos accordingly (L.37.26.1) went to Ephesos from Sardis to review the fleet which for some months had been assembled and prepared 'more because he realised that with his land forces the Roman army and the two Scipios could not be resisted than because naval action had ever been attempted by him with much success or that he had any great or certain confidence in it'.

Antiochos thought however that with a large part of the Rhodian fleet at Patara and Eumenes having taken all his ships to the Hellespont to meet the consul there was a hopeful opportunity for him. He was encouraged also by the Rhodian disaster at Samos (Panormos). His plan was to attack Notion, a coastal town in Colophonian territory, which was uncomfortably close to Ephesos, in the hope that the Roman fleet would come to support an ally and an engagement might ensue.

The last thing Aemilius at Samos expected was that Polyxenidas, after twice refusing to fight, would now come out. He wanted to move to the Hellespont but was detained by Eudamos and all his other advisers, who urged him either to stand by his allies or, if Polyxenidas offered battle, to defeat him again and win command of the sea. This was better than abandoning the allies, surrendering Asia to Antiochos by land and sea and making a quite unnecessary voyage to the Hellespont when his role in the war was to be at Samos.

(L.37.27.1) When victuals ran out there, Aemilius set out for Chios where the Romans stored their supplies, Chios being the destination of the supply ships from Italy. The fleet first moved round to the other (i.e. south) side of the island, the (north) side towards Chios and Erythrai being open to the north wind. Samos city is on the south side; the fleet must have been beached on the north side from which Ephesos and Notion could be observed. From the south side they could first tack north east. As they were preparing to cross, Aemilius learned that a large consignment of grain had arrived at Chios from Italy but that the ships carrying wine had been storm-bound. At the same time he was told that the Teians had generously supplied the king's fleet with victuals and promised 5000 casks of wine.

When half way to Chios (on a NW tack) Aemilius suddenly changed course (NE) for Teos, 'intending, if the Teians were willing, himself to use the stores prepared for the enemy, or, if they were not, to treat the Teians as enemies'. However, they were diverted by the sight near Myonnesos of about fifteen ships, which they first took to be part of the royal fleet but which turned out to be pirates with booty from Chios. They pursued them fruitlessly to Myonnesos and on the next day continued their voyage to Teos; and mooring the ships in the harbour called Geraistikos behind the town, presumably on the other side of the peninsula (Strabo 14.1.30) on which the town was built, began to ravage the countryside around it.

(L.37.28.4) By chance on that day Polyxenidas with the royal fleet left the siege of Kolophon (Notion) 'and, learning where the Roman fleet was, dropped anchor off Myonnesos at a hidden harbour in an island which sailors call Makris'. From there, reconnoitring (*explorans*) the enemy's movements from close at hand (the distance from Makris to Teos being 9.72 sm), 'he was at the outset in high hopes of destroying the Roman fleet in the same way as he had destroyed the Rhodian fleet at Samos (Panormos), by stationing his ships round the harbour passage at the point of exit. The nature of the place (Geraistikos) was not unlike, the promontories on either side of the harbour mouth coming together so closely that two ships could scarcely go out at the same time. He had devised the plan of seizing the exit by night, and of attacking, as at Panormos, from land and sea at the same time. Ten ships standing at each exit would attack the ships in the beam as they came out and armed men would be landed from the rest of the fleet'.

(L.37.28.9) 'The plan would not have failed him if the Romans, when the Teians agreed to do as they had been told, had not moved their fleet round to the other harbour in front of the city to take the supplies on board. There was also the fact that Eudamos had pointed out a fault in the other harbour when two ships broke their oars, getting them tangled together in the narrow entrance; and among other things the fact that there was danger from the land side gave Aemilius a motive for moving the fleet over, Antiochos's camp being not far away'.

(L.37.29.1) The fleet had moved round to the city without anyone's knowledge and the soldiers were on shore engaged in sharing the victuals and in particular the wine among the ships, when at about midday a man from the country was brought to the praetor with the news that already for two days a fleet was moored at the island of Makris and shortly before some ships had been observed moving as if to set out. Alarmed by the sudden development the praetor ordered the trumpets to sound, giving notice to return if any men had wandered off into the country, and he sent the tribunes into the city to collect the soldiers and crewmen for embarkation.

There was the usual confusion and the conflicting orders of a hurried embarkation but (L.37.29.5) 'in the end they were assembled at the ships. In the tumult it was difficult for a man to recognise his own ship or go on board it, and there would have been a dangerous confusion (on the ships) at sea and on the land if a division of duties had not been made (among the commanders): if Aemilius in the flagship had not first moved out of the harbour into open water taking out those that followed him and had drawn them up (in column) each in his own file (there were then several files), and if

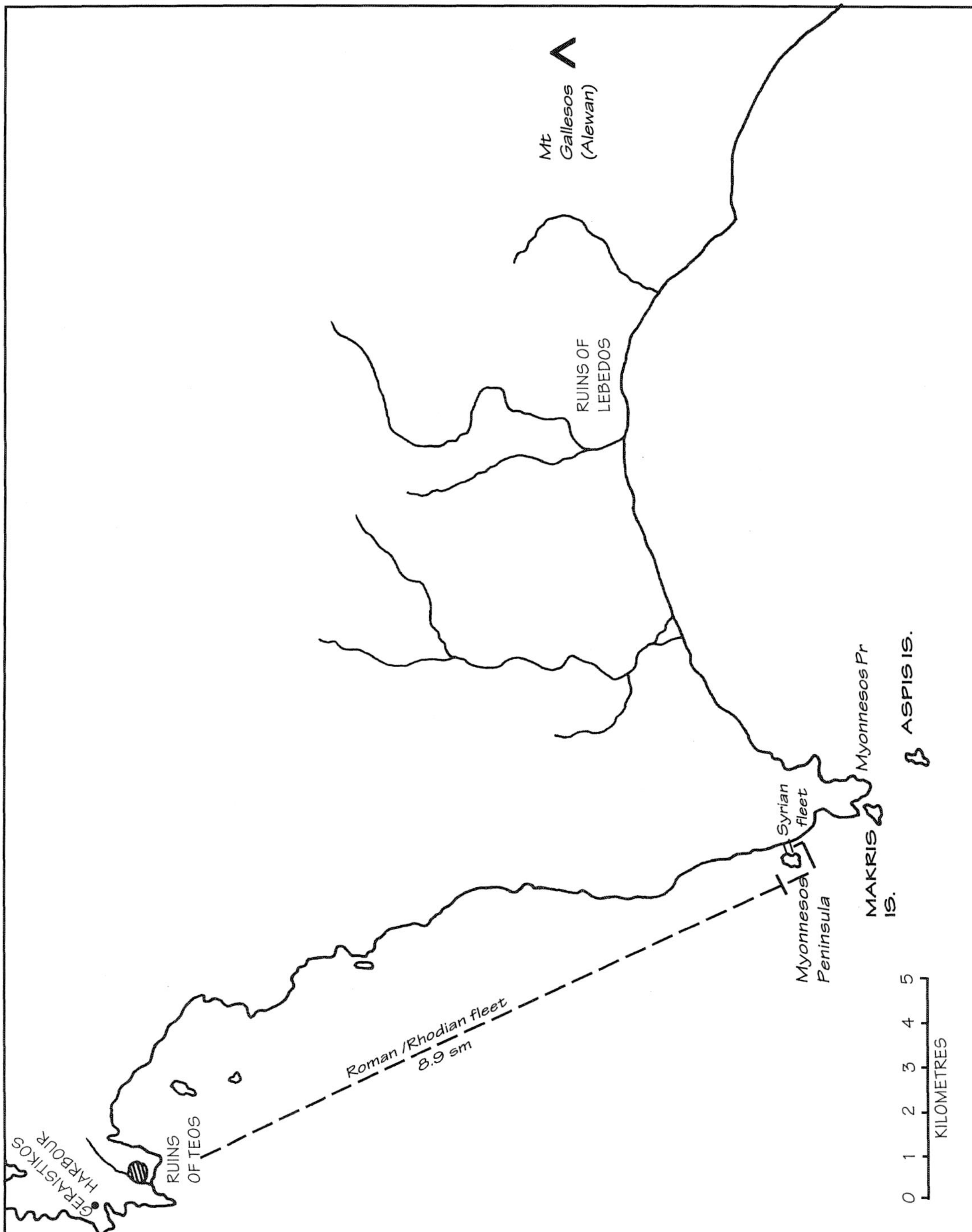

MAP J (iv). *The Teos and Myonnesos Promontories. After Admiralty chart 3346 (see note opposite).*

Eudamos and the Rhodian fleet had not remained in position towards the shore'.

The Battle of Myonnesos: September 190 BC *(Map J (iv))*

'The result was that the embarkation took place without undue hurry and that each ship moved out as it was ready. Thus the first ships (to emerge) extended their file under the eye of the praetor and the Rhodians brought up the rear of the column, and the battle order, drawn up as if the royal opponents were in sight, moved out to sea'. The final sentence, with a brevity which suggests an effortless and orderly manoeuvre unlike that attributed to the allied fleet at the battle of Korykos, describes the move from column (*agmen*) to the battle order (as if the enemy was in sight) of line abreast (*acies*) in the same number of files as in column.

(L.37.29.7) When the allied fleet of 80 ships (83 including 23 from Rhodes: Appian: *Syr.*27) was between Myonnesos and the Korykos promontory they sighted the enemy (they had moved due south about 7½ sm towards Myonnesos). 'The royal fleet' (L.89 ships: A.90 cataphracts) 'came on in a long column of two files, and it likewise deployed a line to face the enemy with its left wing extending so far that it was able to embrace and go round the Roman right wing'. The fact that the royal fleet approached in 'a long column' of two files resulted in the line of battle being long, and two deep. It was also considerably longer than the allied line,

---

Note on Map J (iv): Teos and Myonnesos play a part in the events leading up to the battle named after the latter. Myonnesos had earlier (191 BC) featured in Polyxenidas's plan for a surprise attack on the Roman fleet on its passage from the Korykos promontory to Samos. Livy (37.13.1) says that Polyxenidas then moored first at Myonnesos and then went over to the island called Makris with the intention of making a surprise attack (ut adoriretur) on any ships of the fleet that strayed from the column as it passed by or if opportunity offered on its rear. The island then, it appears, gave the cover for such a surprise attack which Myonnesos did not and was closer to the route which Polyxenidas appears to have expected the Roman fleet to take to Samos city.

Livy next mentions Myonnesos in the following year when a Roman fleet under Aemilius, on passage from Samos to Chios for supplies (and taking the easterly route), suddenly changed course for Teos and was diverted by the sight of about fifteen ships in the neigbourhood of Myonnesos which turned out to be fast and light pirate ships returning from a raid on Chios. They fled to Myonnesos on Aemilius's attempt to capture them, giving Livy an opportunity to describe their refuge (37.27.6).

'Myonnesos is a promunturium between Teos and Samos. The promunturium itself is a hill shaped like a cone and culminating in a sharp point from quite a broad base. It is approached from the mainland by a narrow path (arta semita), while its boundary seawards is formed by cliffs eroded by the waves. Livy's description shows that what he describes is not a promontory but a peninsula to which the present island on the west side of the promontory answers. The result is that in some places the overhanging rocks reach higher than ships at their moorings. The Roman ships wasted a day, not daring to get close in case they were damaged by the pirates manning the top of the cliffs, and when night fell they gave up'. It appears then that the anchorage or mooring facility at Myonnesos was on the seaward side at any rate for the larger ships and was not therefore concealed. Strabo's brief description (14.1.29) 'an inhabited height forming a peninsula' confirms Livy's. The name Myonnesos suggests that it was once an island. These clues have enabled the makers of the Admiralty Chart 3446 to suggest that what appears now be a small island very close to the western side of the main promontory, 2 km from its end, was the ancient Myonnesos, and there seems to be no alternative. They propose also as Makris an island 500 metres SW of the end of the promontory. About 1250 m SE of Makris is another similar small island which may be the one called Aspis or Arkonnesos which Strabo (14.1.29) mentions as lying 'between Teos and Lebedos'.

When a few days later Polyxenidas arrived in the area with the royal fleet he anchored again at Makris. On this occasion Livy describes the anchorage as hidden. He was able to reconnoitre the Roman fleet's position without revealing his fleet's presence.

Aemilius when his pursuit of the pirates proved fruitless had next day continued his intrrupted voyage to Teos and moored his ships 'in the harbour at the back (a tergo) of the city and called by the inhabitants Geraistikos. He sent his troops to loot the cultivated land round Teos. The Admiralty chart shows that between the ancient city and the sea to the west there was a strip of high ground so that the cultivated area must have been to the east and north and that the bay north of the city making with the ancient harbour of Teos a peninsula must have been Geraistikos. Strabo says (14.1.30) that Teos was also (i.e. in the context like Myonnesos) settled on a peninsula and possessed of a harbour.

The harbour which appears to be Geraistikos has now an entrance about 750 metres wide. The horns which Livy says would scarcely allow two warships to enter side by side must have been artificially extended.

for which the reason was partly that the royal fleet was more numerous by nine (or ten) ships, partly (and perhaps mainly) that the allied line was in more than two files, possibly four.

(L.37.29.9) 'When Eudamos (Eudoros: Appian), who was bringing up the rear of the column, saw this, viz. that the Romans (led by Aemilius on the right wing) was unable to make the line equal (to the enemy's) and thus not be turned on the right wing, he speeded up his (22 or 23) ships – and the Rhodian ships were far the fastest in the whole fleet – and bringing the wings equal put his own ship in the path of the flagship with Polyxenidas aboard'. Appian says that the Rhodian commander 'on the left wing saw Polyxenidas outflanking the Roman line and quickly sailing round' (behind the allied line) 'since his ships were light and his oarsmen had sea-experience, sent his fire-ships against Polyxenidas, with flames blazing all round'.

The impression given in Livy's account has been that the allied fleet completed the manoeuvre from column to line abreast before the enemy was sighted. But this impression is inconsistent with Eudamos's manoeuvre just described. The place of his ships as the rearguard of a column deploying into line abreast to the left of the flagship was at the end of the line on the far left. But in the last paragraph Livy says that *he was bringing up the rear* when he saw the disparity of the battle lines and took the instant decision to move quickly to a place on the right of the right wing which would thus be extended sufficiently to bring the two lines to equality. In Appian's description there is no such inconsistency.

(L.37.30.1) 'Now in all the fleets at once the battle began. On the Roman side 80 ships were engaged of which 22 were Rhodian, while the enemy fleet was of 89 ships. They had, of ships of the largest size (*maximae formae*), three sixes and two sevens. The Romans were far superior in the sturdiness of their ships and the courage of their decksoldiers, and the Rhodian ships in agility and in the skill of their helmsmen and expertise (*scientia*) of their oarsmen. Yet those ships scared the enemy most which carried fire before them (**27**); and that which alone saved the ships surrounded at Panormos on this occasion made the greatest contribution to victory. For when the royal ships nervous at the threat of fire turned aside from an encounter prow to prow, they were unable themselves to strike the enemy with their rams and offered themselves sideways to (such) blows. They were more afraid of the fire than of the fighting. Yet, as usual, it was the courage of the decksoldiers which carried most weight in the battle'.

'The fact was that when the Romans had broken through the middle of the enemy's battle line, they swung round and threw themselves from behind on the royal ships which were fighting the Rhodians; and in a short space of time Antiochos's centre and the ships on the left wing were surrounded and swamped. The undamaged part of the fleet on the right was terrified more by the destruction of their comrades than by their own peril; but after they saw others surrounded and Polyxenidas's flagship raising sail and deserting her comrades, they quickly raised their foresails – there was a wind favourable for those bound for Ephesos – and fled'.

Appian, after describing the fireship attack on Polyxenidas, continues: 'Polyxenidas's ships had not the courage to attack the fireships because of the fire, but circling round them heeled over and were filled with water. They were hit on the *ἐπωτίς* constantly. At last a Rhodian ship rammed a Sidonian and the blow was a strong one, so that the anchor of the Sidonian ship fell off and stuck into another ship, bonding the two together. The ships being impossible to separate the battle became like a land fight. Many ships rallying to each of the two ships there was a notable contest and as a result the Roman ships rowed through the centre of Antiochos's line, that area being thinned out because of this incident; and they encircled the enemy before they realised what was happening. When they did there was flight and pursuit'.

It is interesting that both sources attribute the defeat to a classical 'breakthrough' (*διέκπλους*) at the centre of the enemy's line. Whether the weakness there was the result of the incident described by Appian or not, the abnormally long column, becoming an abnormally thin battle line in order to achieve an outflanking movement (the classical *περίπλους*), certainly risked offering the enemy the chance of a massive breakthrough, which was decisive. The moral which the reader is meant, by the Rhodian source, to draw is that Rhodian quick thinking and Rhodian quick rowing in light warships thwarted the *περίπλους* and led to the effective *διέκπλους* of the heavier Roman vessels.

(L.37.30.7) 'Antiochos lost 42 ships (Appian:

*Syr.*29), ten of which fell into possession of the enemy, the rest were burnt or swamped (*demersae*). Two Roman ships were smashed (*fractae*), a number received damage (*volneratae*). One Rhodian ship was captured in a remarkable manner'. Then Livy tells the story of the Sidonian ship which Appian also uses, concluding: 'the anchor cable, (*ancorale*), being pulled out and becoming entangled with the oars, carried away one side of them. The crippled ship was then captured by the very ship which had been struck by her and become attached. These were the tactics employed in the naval battle off Myonnesos'.

(L.37.31.1) The effect on Antiochos of the defeat was traumatic. 'He doubted whether he could protect his distant fortresses and ordered his garrison to be withdrawn from Lysimacheia'. He also withdrew from the siege of Kolophon (Notion) (p. 105 and 104 above) and from Sardis, concentrating his efforts on preparation for the land battle with the Scipios which could not now be long delayed, since there was now nothing to prevent the Romans crossing the Hellespont into Asia. By the end of the year he had been heavily defeated in a great battle near Thyateira which put an end to his ambitions in the Mediterranean.

The peace treaty which followed (188 BC) the defeat contained a naval clause which is given by Polybios (21.42.13) and by Livy (38.38.8) but in both cases the text is imperfect. Walbank's (McDonald and Walbank: 1969, Walbank: 1979 III p. 159) amended versions give the following sense: (Antiochos) must surrender both his long ships and the gear and rigging (*ἄρμενα καὶ σκεύη*: *armamenta*) belonging to them, and he must keep no more than 10 aphracts (Livy: *naves actuarias*) and none of them rowed by more than thirty oars; and he may not keep those for the purpose of a war started by himself.

2. PERSEUS OF MACEDON

Under the year 185 BC Livy (39.23.5) mentions the threat of war with Perseus, the son of Philip V of Macedon. He says that the beginnings lay not with Perseus but with his father, who would have waged it if he had lived. Quintus Marcius, sent to Macedon in 183 to investigate the state of affairs there (P.23.8 and 10), reported similarly. At Rome by 172 (L.42.26.2–5) Genthios, son of Pleuratos, of Illyria was under suspicion as a Macedonian sympathiser, and Perseus was known to have sent envoys to ask for the support of Eumenes II, Antiochos IV and Ptolemy V, but all three had remained loyal to their treaties with Rome. Rhodes sent envoys to protest her loyalty in the face of suspicions to the contrary.

The reaction of the Senate (L.42.27 1–8) was to resurrect the fleet which had been laid up in the dockyards since the end of the Syrian war. 50 fives were to be inspected for seaworthiness and the Sicilian squadron was to be repaired and made ready for service if additional ships were needed. In the event 38 fives were launched at Rome and 12 in Sicily. Naval personnel were to be enrolled for the 50 ships, half from the freedmen and half from the allies, and an army of 8000 infantry and 400 cavalry put in readiness. In 171 (L.42.29.1) 'all the kings and states in Europe and Asia were turning their minds to reflect on the Macedonian and Roman war'. Antiochus IV saw in it an opportunity, while the Roman attention was directed elsewhere, to wage war against the young Ptolemy and his guardians, who in turn were preparing for war against Antiochos to defend their right to Koile-Syria, at that time in Antiochos's possession. The previous year (P.27.3, L.42.45) Rome had sent an embassy to Asia and among the islands to encourage her allies to join her in a war against Macedon. Rhodes was particularly important because it could provide material help, her president Hagesilochos 'having advised the Rhodians to commission (*ὑποζωνύειν*, literally to fit hypozomata to: p. 356) 40 ships', so that they could act instantly as the occasion arose.

(L.42.48.5) The praetor in charge of the fleet, Gaius Lucretius, left Rome with 40 ships of the fleet that had been prepared, his brother Marcus going ahead with one five to collect those due from the allies under treaty, and with orders to meet the rest of the fleet at Kephallenia. These were: one three from Rhegion, two from Lokroi and four from the district of Uria. At Dyrrachion he met ten local *λέμβοι*, 12 Issaean *λέμβοι* and 54 belonging to king Genthios (which Marcus 'pretended he thought had been assembled for his use'), took them with him 'on the third day' to Kerkyra and from there to Kephallenia. (L.42.48.10) Gaius made the voyage from Naples to Kephallenia in five days; and waited there not only until the land force had made the crossing from Italy but also for the supply ships to catch up, 'which had been scattered from their column over the open sea'. His brother also must have joined him as ordered. Polybios says (27.7) that the Rhodian ships were also summoned at this point.

(L.42.56) Gaius then left the fleet under Marcus's command with orders to move round the Peloponnese to Chalkis, while, with the intention of getting to Boiotia first, he took a three through the Corinthian gulf, rather slowly 'because of illness'. Marcus reached Chalkis first and took a large military force, including a substantial Pergamene contingent, inland to besiege Haliartos, where he was joined by his brother coming up from Kreusa on the Gulf. (L.42.63.3 ff) The praetor captured it after a stubborn siege and 'after these achievements in Boiotia returned to the sea and the fleet'. It is surprising that the 'maritime province' exended so far inland.

Other allied ships also assembled at Chalkis (L.42.56.6): two Carthaginian fives, two threes from Herakleia on the Euxine, four from Kalchedon, four from Samos, and then five Rhodian fours. Polybios (27.7.1) describes the mixed reaction at Rhodes to Gaius's letter, 'entrusted to a gym trainer' (*ἀλείπτης τις*), but finally six fours were sent in support of Rome, five to Chalkis and one to Tenedos, the latter to protect commerce through the straits. The absence of Eumenes and his fleet is not significant, in view of his contribution of land forces and, together with his brother Attalos, his presence with them (L.42.57.4). In the following year his fleet took part in the naval operations off Macedonia.

However, since there was at present no naval activity anywhere, the praetor (P.27.7.16) after receiving kindly all the allies who had come by sea, relieved them of their obligations explaining that in the present state of affairs naval assistance was not required. The legate Quintus Marcius, who after he made his report had been sent back to Greece the previous year with a number of fives (L.42.47.9) and a roving mandate, appeared at Chalkis with his ships, and presumably then returned to Rome.

The assembly at Chalkis of ships of various kinds in support of Rome in 171 is interesting as indicating the standing, economic as well as political, of the various states in naval terms. The piratical *λέμβοι* of the Adriatic, from Issa and Illyria, are at the bottom of the table. At the top are the fives of Rome and Carthage, and in between the threes of Herakleia, Chalkedon and Samos. Although Rhodes had fives, the type of ship she used most at this period was the four, from preference probably as Walbank observed (1979: III p. 336) as much as from necessity.

In 170 there is mention in Livy (43.4.8) of an assault by the fleet commander Hortensius, who had succeeded Gaius Lucretius, on the city of Abdera in northern Greece, which, being a free ally of Rome, complained to the senate. (L.43.7.10) Other cities in the area, Emathia, Amphipolis, Maroneia, Ainos, are said to have closed their gates to him. These cities must have been the objects of a naval raid similar to that reported for 169, but, perhaps because of its disreputable nature, not mentioned directly by Livy. There were complaints of the behaviour of Romans in Chalkis and the billeting of seamen in private houses.

At this time the loyalty of Genthios of Illyria was again suspect and (L.43.9.4) eight armed ships (*naves ornatae*) were sent from Brundisium to the island of Issa where there was a legate in charge with two Issaean ships (probably *λέμβοι*) in support. A force of 2000 men, raised locally in that part of Italy, which had been garrisoned the previous year (L.42.36.9), was sent on board the eight ships. The type of ship is not given; they are said to be 'armed' in contrast to the *λέμβοι*. 250 is rather a large number of passengers even for a five used as a troopship, and it has been suggested that '8' may be a scribal error for '18'[4]. The voyage is of 174 sm and at least 30 hours with favourable conditions, say a comfortable two day voyage with a stop for the night halfway on the Italian coast. In more adverse conditions speed would have been more like 4 kn overall, i.e. 45 hours or three days with stops for rest in the middle of the day.

(L.43.12.9 and 15.30) For the campaign of 169 reinforcements for the *socii navales* were sent, 1500 from Rome and Italy and as many from Sicily. Gaius Marcius Figulus was put in charge of the fleet at Chalkis, which went north in the spring in support of the Roman army in Thessaly and was in sight off the coast (L.44.7.10), but victualling arrangements were less effective, the supply ships having been left further south in Magnesia.

The capture of Herakleia Tracheia by the army

(L.44.9.10) in the autumn provided the fleet with a forward base from which Marcius proceeded to ravage the country between there and Thessalonike, the site of the royal dockyards. It was besieged but proved too strongly garrisoned, and he moved north against the second Macedonian naval base, Kassandreia. There he was joined by Eumenes with 20 cataphracts and by five cataphracts from Bithynia. The joint forces besieged the city but abandoned the siege when it was relieved by ten *λέμβοι* slipping along the coast at night from Thessalonike. The fleet then retired south to Iolkos for an attack, after ravaging the fields, on the third Macedonian naval base of Demetrias in the gulf of Pagasai, while the army besieged Meliboia 25 miles north (L.44.12.8–13.3) 'conveniently theatening' its communications. Both attacks were given up and the army went into winter quarters. While Eumenes took his ships back to Pergamon, Marcius sent part of his fleet to Skiathos for the winter and went with the rest to Oreos (in Euboia) as a good base from which to send supplies to the army in Macedon and Thessaly.

(L.44.17) Concern in Rome for the slow progress of the war in Macedonia led to a more rapid choice of the consul to hold that province, Lucius Aemilius Paulus, and of the praetor in charge of the fleet, Gnaeus Octavius. Aemilius immediately suggested that legates should be sent to Macedonia to inspect the army and the fleet and to report on the loyalty of the allies, the supply position and the achievement of army and fleet in the past year.

Their report severely criticised leadership of the army (L.44.20.2); its present position was dangerous and the supply position critical. Their report on the fleet (L.44.20.6) was that some of the *socii navales* had died of sickness; that some of them, especially the Sicilians, had gone home, with the result that the ships were undermanned; those in Macedonia had not been paid, and lacked suitable clothes (for the winter); Eumenes's fleet had come and gone; he, unlike his brother Attalos, seemed wavering in his loyalty to Rome. As a result very substantial reinforcements were ordered for the army and 5000 *socii navales* for the fleet (L.44.21.11).

During the winter of 169/8 (L.44.23.2–10) Perseus engaged in widespread diplomatic activity, first gaining the formal adherence of Genthios through a special envoy Pentauchos (P.29.3–4) who asked him particularly to prepare for war by sea, since the Romans were entirely unprepared in this sphere in the regions of Epeiros and Illyria and he would be able to carry through easily every scheme he proposed. With Genthios he then approached Rhodes 'with whom alone at that time resided *rei navalis gloria*, the prestige of seapower'. He sent letters also to Eumenes and Antiochos.

Perseus also sent his fleet commanders Antenor and Kallippos with 40 *λέμβοι*, to which were added 5 *πρίστεις* (*λέμβοι* with rams) to protect from Tenedos the ships scattered throughout the Kyklades on their way (from the Black Sea) to Macedon with grain. These ships, launched at Kassandreia, went by way of the harbour under Mt Athos on a calm sea to Tenedos. There they came upon some aphract Rhodian ships under Eudamos which they sent away unharmed. On the other side of the island there were 50 Macedonian grain ships blockaded in a harbour by warships with rams (*rostratae*) belonging to Eumenes. Antenor promptly moved round and with threats removed the enemy ships. Ten *λέμβοι* then convoyed the grain ships to Macedon with instructions to return to Tenedos when they had arrived safely. On the ninth day they rejoined the fleet which was now at Sigeion (at the entrance to the Hellespont).

From Sigeion they made a passage to Sybota, an island lying between Elaia and Chios. Next day they intercepted 'between the cape of Erythrai and Chios where the strait is narrowest' 35 horse transports taking Galatian horses and cavalrymen which were being sent by Eumenes from Elaia to Attalos with the Roman army in Macedonia. Eumenes's commanders had no idea that there was a Macedonian fleet in those waters. 'But when the lines of the approaching *λέμβοι* were clearly visible and the acceleration of the oars and the prows pointing at them showed that enemy ships were approaching, then panic hit them'.

Resistance with ships of that nature was impossible; some who were nearer the mainland swam ashore on Erythraean territory, others raised sail for Chios and ran their ships aground. Abandoning the horses (which it would have taken too long to disembark) they fled in disorder to the city. But since the *λέμβοι* had disembarked their armed men nearer the city and at a more convenient landing place (*commodiore accessu*) the Macedonians caught the Galatians and cut them down, some on the road as they fled and others, shut out, in front of the gate. For the Chians, not knowing who were fleeing or who pursuing, had shut their gates. 'Antenor ordered 20 especially fine horses and the 200 prisoners taken to be conveyed to Thessalonike by the same ten *λέμβοι* that had been sent back before'. If the horses were taken on two of the *λέμβοι*, the remaining eight *λέμβοι* would have taken 25 prisoners each. They must have been substantial light craft. He said he would wait for them at Phanai. The fleet moored for nearly three days before the city of Chios and then moved on to Phanai. When the ten *λέμβοι* arrived back sooner than they had expected they put out and crossed the Aegean to Delos.

(L.44.29.1) Three Roman envoys who had been sent by the Senate to Alexandria apprehensive of an invasion of Egypt by Antiochos (p. 109) set out from Chalkis in three fives and, arriving at Delos, found there Antenor's 40 *λέμβοι* and five fives of Eumenes. 'The Roman, Macedonian and Pergamene seamen mixed freely under the truce afforded by the sanctity of the place'. Nevertheless Antenor sent his ships out commerce raiding 'at night mostly in detachments of two or three ships'. His operations had their effect at Rhodes.

At this time (P.29.11 cf. L.44.29.6) envoys from Perseus and Genthios came to Rhodes. The pro-Roman party were 'dismayed at what was happening. The presence of the *λέμβοι* (of Antenor), the size of the (Roman) losses of cavalry (in the previous year) and Genthios's change of allegiance, were wearing them down'. The Rhodian answer was that they were determined to bring about peace.

In the spring of 168 (L.44.30.1) Aemilius was in Macedon facing Perseus, the praetor Gnaeus Octavius at Oreos with some of the fleet and the rest at Skiathos, and Anicius with Appius Claudius at Apollonia to deal with Genthios. The latter (L.44.30.13–14) had 80 *λέμβοι* plundering the coast of Epeiros. At 44.30.15 Livy's text is faulty, but supplemented by Appian (*Illyr.*9) it appears to indicate that Anicius captured some of Genthios's ships, defeated him on land and shut him up in a fortress in which he captured him and all his family, thus ending the war on that front (L.45.43.4) 'in a few days'.

In the meantime (L.44.32.5) Perseus was in great fear not only of the new consul on land but also of the new praetor at sea. 'He had no less fear of the Roman fleet and the dangerous situation of the sea coast' as a result of the admittedly often unsuccessful raids in the previous two years. He accordingly diverted forces to strengthen the garrisons of Thessalonike and other cities of the area. (L.44.35.1) When Aemilius was ready to move he planned a feint towards Thessalonike employing the fleet, when his attack was inland. It culminated in the battle of Pydna in which Perseus was heavily defeated and the war brought to an end. (L.44.44.3) Perseus fled to Samothraké from where Octavius brought him to Aemilius at Amphipolis. By this time the end of the campaigning season was reached and the army and fleet went into winter quarters.

As a postscript to the naval war it may be noted (L.45.35.3) that in the following year when Aemilius Paulus returned in triumph to Rome it was on board 'a royal ship of huge size, which was rowed by sixteen oar-files (*versus remorum*), up the Tiber to the city'. This was (L.33.30.5) the 'ship of almost unmanageable size with sixteen oar-files' which Philip V was allowed to keep after his defeat nearly thirty years before (cf. Plutarch *Aemilius Paulus* 30.2–3).

(L.45.42.12) Also a number of royal ships seized from the Macedonians 'of a size not previously seen' were hauled up on to the Campus Martius. (L.45.43.10) 220 *λέμβοι* formed part of the booty from Illyria. Genthios seems to have taken seriously Perseus's advice to concentrate on sea power.

3. THE THIRD PUNIC WAR

The reasons why the Roman Senate decided that Carthage must finally be destroyed are not stated clearly in Polybios, Livy or Appian. Carthage had a running dispute with Rome's African ally Masinissa in which he was usually the aggressor. But it seems likely that the cause was maritime rivalry, fear of Carthage as a commercial and potentially as a naval threat, with her shipsheds for 220 warships (Appian *Pun.* 96). In 152 or possibly early in 151 (Livy *epitome* 48) the Senate resolved not to go to war if the Carthaginians burnt their fleet and demobilised their army, which would have left them at Masinissa's mercy. In the following year (Appian *Pun.* 70) they defeated Masinissa (ib. 71–3), but suffered a severe defeat in Numidia; and then, putting the blame for the war on their commanders whom they condemned to death, agreed to terms of a settlement with him.

In 150 the Senate decided on war and declared

it formally the next year. Polybios (36.2–7) says that the Romans had long made up their minds on this course. Utica immediately came over to Rome, providing her with a friendly naval and military base. The Carthaginian envoys then in Rome to make complaints about Masinissa had no option but to offer Carthage's surrender. 300 hostages were requested and sent. On arrival they were detained all together in 'the shipshed of the sixteen (warship)' (*εἰς τὸ τῆς ἑκκαιδεκήρους νεώριον*), presumably the largest available building.

'After the hostages had been brought to Rome the Roman commander landed at Utica'. Appian (*Pun.*75) gives details of the expeditionary force. The army was under the command of one consul, M. Manilius, and consisted of 80,000 infantry and about 4000 cavalry 'all the best', and the fleet was commanded by the other consul, L. Marcius Censorinus. They had secret orders not to end the war until Carthage had been razed to the ground.

The force was taken to Utica 'in 50 fives and 100 *ἡμιολίαι*, also in many aphracts and *κέρκουροι* and *στρογγύλοι*'. The unprecedented appearance of a very large number of *ἡμιολίαι* in the Roman fleet is surprising. Even more surprising is their apparent rating with fives as cataphracts. JFC suggests that they may in fact have been *τριημιολίαι*. On the other hand they may have been designed on the pattern of the *ἡμιολίαι (ἡμιόλιοι λέμβοι)* employed by Philip V in his fleet at the battles of Chios, which were not classed as either cataphract of aphract but were apparently armed with rams (p. 91 note 2) and like Octavian's liburnians at Aktion were probably cataphract (p. 317). In any case they indicate a radical change in Roman ship construction in the direction of a lighter warship brought about perhaps by the experiences of the Roman navy in the Aegean working alongside Rhodian ships. Livy often draws attention to the advantages of such ships. The second main category contains 'aphracts, cercuri and round ships'. The first two types are open, oared, long ships (the aphracts including (Ap.*Pun.*114) open threes), the former with rams, the latter not. These could keep up with a fleet under oar or sail. The round ships are what Livy habitually calls *onerariae*, supply ships, and are likely to have been ordinary commercial cargo ships built to carry grain and wine throughout the Mediterranean and remains of which have been frequently found on the sea bed by underwater archaeologists.

Envoys met the consuls on their arrival and were told that the Carthaginians must surrender their arms and missiles, which they did. They were then told that they must surrender their city and withdraw to any place they liked at least ten miles from the sea 'for we are resolved to raze your city to the ground'. At this demand the Carthaginian senate decided to fight, and in desperation the manufacture of arms and the building of ships was put in hand.

Appian (*Pun.*95–96) gives a description of Carthage's two harbours: 'The harbours had communication by water from one to the other and the entrance from the sea into them was 70 ft (21 m) wide, which they could close with iron chains.[5] The first harbour was for merchants and there were thick mooring ropes of various kinds in it. In the middle of the inner harbour there was an island; and the (sides of the) island and the harbour were set about with great quays extending from them at intervals. These quays were tightly packed with accommodation constructed for 220 ships and with stores for warship gear adjoining the accommodation. A pair of Ionic columns stood in front of each shipshed, giving the impression to the eye of a continuous colonnade round both the harbour and the island. On the island a tent (*σκηνή*) had been made for the *ναύαρχος*, from which the trumpeter had to give signals, the herald issue orders and the *ναύαρχος* keep a look-out'.

'The island was situated near the entrance to the harbour and had a steep elevation so that the *ναύαρχος* could observe anything coming from the seaward side, while for those coming in by water a clear sight of the interior was obscured. Not even incoming merchants could see the warship accommodation ahead because a double wall surrounded it; and there were also gates which conducted the merchants from the first harbour to the city without passing through it.'

It is not surprising that the Romans were suspicious of Carthage as a continuing sea power.

Neither Manilius and Censorinus in 149 nor their successors in 148, Calpurnius Piso and Lucius Mancinus, had much success against the determined Carthaginians. (Appian *Pun.*113) The young Scipio, consul for 147, and his *ναύαρχος* Serranus arrived in Utica one evening at a critical moment. Piso was besieging towns inland. Mancinus had made a bold attack from the sea with scaling laders against an ill-defended part of the wall at the top of a cliff. His soldiers entering through a gate opened by the enemy for a sally established a position inside, but were trapped and had to spend the night there without food.

Learning about the situation at midnight 'Scipio immediately ordered the trumpet to be sounded for action and the heralds to collect on the beach those who had come with him from Italy and some young Uticans; the older men also to bring provisions down to the threes'. The absence of the consul with the army caused a shortage of men; and it appears then that the ships Scipio had come with were threes, an indication of the urgency of his voyage, perhaps of the fact that his force was recruited mainly from the allies (cf.Ap.*Pun*.112 *ad fin*) and the ships of the Sidetai' (Ap.*Pun*.123). Coming from Side in Pamphylia they distinguished themselves later in the campaign.

'He himself put to sea (with his threes) at the last watch (very early in the morning) and gave orders to the soldiers that as they approached the city they should stand up on the decks to make the enemy think them more numerous than they actually were'. On threes, which lacked the stability of the bigger ships, the soldiers on deck were normally made to sit down when they were proceeding under oar; they were also less numerous than those on the bigger ships. Mancinus was being attacked on all sides by the Carthaginians at daybreak when 'Scipio's ships came in sight moving up with a fearful splashing (of oars, indicating speed) and packed with soldiers standing on every inch of deck'. He rescued Mancinus.

(Ap.*Pun*.120) Scipio succeeded in cutting off supplies to Carthage coming by land. But some came by water: 'Scipio's ships were blockading Carthage but they kept station neither continuously nor in close order since the seashore was unapproachable and invariably steep and they were unable to ride at anchor beside the city. The walls were manned by Carthaginians and waves pounded on the rocks there more than anywhere else. The result was that the supply ships of Bithyas, and an occasional merchantman made reckless by the chance of making money, looking out for a strong on shore wind, ran the blockade under full canvas. Threes were unable in those conditions to catch up with merchantmen (*ὁλκάδας*) carried along by sail and wind. But these chances occurred infrequently and only when the wind was blowing strongly on shore'. Threes are mentioned because they were the fastest cataphract ships the Romans had, and light as well.

(Ap.*Pun*.121–122) 'The Carthaginians also built fives and threes of old timbers, probably old frames which were kept on account of scarcity; and they made a new entrance to the harbour from which they moved out with their ships, fifty *τριηριτικαί* (p. 262), *κέρκουροι* and *μυοπάρωνες* and many other smaller ships. The sudden appearance of the harbour mouth, and of the fleet there, so dismayed the Romans that if the Carthaginians had immediately attacked their ships, neglected during the siege and with no seamen or oarsmen available, they would have taken the whole station (*ναύσταθμος*). On that occasion they merely came out on parade' and went back again. 'However, on the day after next they were drawn up for a pitched battle, and the Romans put out against them with their ships and everything else in good order.... There was much shouting of encouragement on both sides and enthusiasm of oarsman, helmsmen and decksoldiers since this was the Carthaginians' chance of salvation and the Romans' of complete victory'. The fight went on till midday.

'In the fighting the small Carthaginian vessels ran up under the big Roman ships into the oarsystems, and holed (*διετίτρη*) the sterns. They cut away the rudders and oars and did much further detailed damage, escaping easily and attacking easily. While the issue was still in doubt and evening drew on the Carthaginians decided to retire, not because they were worsted but so as to put off the decision to the next day. (Ap.*Pun*.123) The smaller vessels retired first; and taking the entrance first, because they were many, they bumped into each other and jammed the mouth tight. The result was that the larger ships following them were unable to enter and took refuge at the mole, a wide area in front of the wall which had been built long before for merchants to unload their cargoes. A low parapet had been built on it during the present war so that it should not ever be used by the enemy as a wide space for bivouacking. The Carthaginian ships took refuge there in default of the harbour and moored with their prows facing outwards, and when the enemy attacked from the sea they fought back some from the ships themselves, some from the mole and others from the parapet'.

'It was easy for the Romans to attack (with the

ram) and fighting stationary ships was simple, but the withdrawal of the ships by turning round, since they were long, was slow and difficult, with the result that they received equal damage in this manoeuvre, for when they turned they were struck by the Carthaginian ships moving against them. This went on until five ships of the people of Side [in Pamphylia] who followed out of friendship for Scipio dropped their anchors some distance out at sea and after attaching long ropes to them attacked the Carthaginian ships under oar and when they had rammed withdrew stern first hauling in the ropes, and once more moving in at a high rate of striking again withdrew stern first. Then the whole fleet, seeing and imitating the Sidetans gambit, inflicted much damage on the Carthaginians. Night put an end to the action and the Carthaginian ships, as many as survived, fled to the city'.

There was no further fighting by sea and in 146 after much stubborn fighting on land Carthage was taken. Scipio was able to send 'the fastest ship' to Rome to announce the end of the war.

4. MITHRIDATES VI AND THE PIRATES *(Map AE)*

The First Mithridatic War

(Ap.*Mithr.*10–15) In the first decade of the 1st cent. BC a power struggle developed in the southern coastal area of the Euxine Sea between Rome and her allies on the one side and Mithridates VI Eupator of Pontos on the other, centering on naval control of the Hellespont and Bosporos. Mithridates' father had been a 'friend of Rome' sending ships and auxiliaries to her aid against Carthage. But his son became the bitterest and potentially the most formidable of her enemies.

By the outbreak of war in 88 BC Rome's allies, the kings of Kappadokia and Bithynia, had been driven out. Mithridates had an army and many allies (250,000 foot and 40,000 horse), a fleet of 300 cataphracts for which he had recruited *πρωρᾶται* and *κυβερνῆται* in Phoenicia and Egypt. Rome's forces in the area consisted of three armies each of 40,000 men, and a fleet on guard at the Bosporos. Her ally Nikomedes, the expelled ruler of Bithynia, had 50,000 foot and 6,000 horse.

It was not surprising that in the first engagements the Roman generals and Nikomedes were defeated and the former captured. Mithridates was able to take the whole of Asia Minor including the important naval bases of Magnesia, Ephesos and Mitylene. Rome declared war, allocating the province of Asia and the conduct of the war with Mithridates to Cornelius Sulla. Mithridates spent the winter of 88/7 in the construction of a large number of ships for an attack on the last important Roman ally in the region, Rhodes, where those Italians who could, and the Roman governor Lucius Cassius, took refuge from the general massacre of Romans and their allies which followed. Even Athens went over to Mithridates.

(Ap.*Mithr.*24) In the spring of 87 Mithridates led his fleet against Rhodes. The Rhodians put to sea in battle order with some of their ships in line abreast (with one flank protected by the shore as will appear) and some ships facing (out to sea) towards the flank (*πλάγιαι*). The king (at the head of the column) in a five, beginning a *περίπλους*, ordered his men to go out to sea in column (*ἐπὶ κέρως*); and increasing the rate of striking to encircle the enemy who were fewer in number. The Rhodian L-shaped formation was adopted as protection against a *περίπλους*. The manoeuvre progressed until the Rhodians, nervous of the encirclement, began to retire gradually (by backing down); and then turned round and fled into the harbour. They placed booms across the harbour mouth and began to fight Mithridates from the walls. The king encamped near the city. After trying in vain to gain entrance to the harbour, he decided to wait for his army to arrive from Asia. There was some skirmishing which encouraged the Rhodians to keep their ships in readiness for a sortie.

On one occasion (Ap.*Mithr.*25) when a merchant ship (*ὁλκάς*) belonging to the king passed by under sail and a Rhodian *δίκροτος* put out to bring her in, a violent sea fight took place. Mithridates's ships attacked with greater fury and numbers, while the Rhodians skilfully moved round his ships and holed them (*ἀνατιτρώντων*). They took in tow one three with its crew and returned to harbour with many trophies (*ἀκροστόλια*) and much spoil. On another occasion, a Rhodian five had been captured, unknown to them, and they sent out 6 of their fastest ships under Damagoras, their *ναύαρχος*, to find it. The king sent 25 ships against them. Damagoras backed down (as slowly as possible in line abreast) till sunset; but when it was twilight and the king's ships (which were also in line abreast) turned to move away, he attacked them, swamped two and pursued two others to Lykia (the mainland opposite), returning to Rhodes after spending a night at sea. This latter incident emphasises the danger for an oared ship in turning away (or round) and exposing her side, abandoning the line abreast formation in face of an enemy in similar formation even if fewer in number (though superior in speed).

(Ap.*Mithr.*26) Again, when Mithridates' land forces on board *ὁλκάδες* and threes, the latter probably towing the former, were coasting along (the mainland) a wind from Kaunos (NE by N) drove them towards Rhodes. The Rhodians quickly put out against them, while they were still in confusion from the rough sea and scattered (i.e. with towing abandoned); and took some (of the *ὁλκάδας*) in tow, rammed some of the other of the two kinds (*ἑτέρας* and so threes) and burned others (*ἄλλας* others of either kind). For the use by the Rhodians of firepots slung over the prows of warships see p. 98 and **28**. The result was unexpected, to the Rhodians because of their few ships and to Mithridates because of his many. In revenge he prepared for another sea fight and a siege. For the latter an ingenious siege engine was devised. In the end he gave up and moved along the coast against the naval city of Patara.

Meanwhile (Ap.*Mithr.*28) Mithridates had sent his commander Archelaos to Greece with large supplies and a large fleet. On the way he took Delos and other places which had previously revolted from Athens and restored them to her as his ally. The Roman general Bruttius from Macedonia fought at sea against Mithridates's general Metrophanes swamping 'one vessel (*πλοῖον*) and a *ἡμιολία*'. He then withdrew to Peiraieus which Archelaos subsequently captured. In late 87 (Ap.*Mithr.*30) Sulla arrived from Italy and immediately attacked Peiraieus. Sulla's lack of ships enabled Archelaos (Ap.*Mithr.*32) to receive a new army by sea from Mithridates, while Mithridates' son invaded Macedonia. Sulla was greatly handicapped in his siege of Peiraieus by naval weakness, but he succeeded nevertheless in taking both Peiraieus and Athens, and Archelaos was defeated at Chaironeia (Ap. *Mithr.*44) in the following spring (86 BC).

Archelaos was able to move freely among the islands and ravage the coastal areas. He laid siege to Zakynthos, but abandoned it and retired 'more like a pirate than a soldier' to Chalkis. At Orchomenos (Ap.*Mithr.*50) he was defeated again by the Romans and again escaped to Chalkis. (Ap.*Mithr.*51) Sulla found winter quarters in Thessaly while he awaited the arrival of Lucullus and his fleet, even beginning himself to build ships. At Rome Sulla's enemies secured his outlawry, and sent Flaccus and Fimbria to command the Roman forces in Greece and Asia. Sulla, unmoved, offered terms of peace to Mithridates, which he accepted. To both the peace was no more than a truce.

(Ap.*Mithr.*56) Lucullus's fleet on arrival (at Peiraieus) was dispatched to Abydos. On several occasions avoiding capture by pirates, Lucullus had succeeded in collecting ships from Cyprus, Phoenicia, Rhodes and Pamphylia. He had ravaged the enemy's coasts and had skirmished with enemy ships. The presence of this fleet, taken in the context of the land defeats at Chaironeia and Orchomenos, convinced Mithridates that for the moment at any rate his hostilities with Rome were better ended. On his conclusion of the treaty of Dardanos with Sulla in August 85 BC Lucullus took over Mithridates's ships and the latter retired to Pontos, his sole remaining possession.

At this point Appian (*Mithr.*63) comments on the miserable condition of the Asiatic province: 'which hordes of pirates, resembling naval fleets rather than pirates, openly assaulted. Mithridates had first let them loose upon the seas when he was ravaging the whole area, thinking that he would not have it under his control for long. Increasing in number, they had captured Iasos, Samos, Klazomenai, this last when Sulla himself was there'.

Peace made, Sulla was now able to turn to reestablish his position at Rome. He left Patrai for Brundisium (Appian *CW* 1.79) with his army in 1600 vessels.

The Second Mithridatic War

(Ap.*Mithr.*64: 83 BC) Murena 'whom Sulla had left with Fimbria's two legions to settle the rest of the affairs of Asia found minor excuses for war, being keen on a triumph'. Mithridates did in fact build a fleet and raise a large army nominally against the peoples of the Bosporos. The scale of his preparation quickly aroused the suspicion that it was being assembled not against them but against the Romans'. The war started by Murena, after his defeat, was quickly terminated by Sulla (81 BC).

In 76 BC Mithridates made a treaty with the rebel Sertorius and in the following year declared war on Rome. Lucullus who had been the praetor in charge of Sulla's fleet was given the command against Mithridates, a clear indication of the kind of war that was expected but did not immediately take place. (Ap.*Mithr.*69) Mithridates had spent the rest of the summer of 75 BC and the whole of the winter in cutting timber, building ships and manufacturing arms. And in the beginning of the spring of 74 he was exercising his fleet (Ap.*Mithr.*70). (Ap.*Mithr.*71) He invaded Bithynia forcing the Roman governor Cotta to flee to Kalchedon opposite Byzantion on the Bosporos, where the Roman fleet of 64 ships under Nudus was in harbour; he burned four of them and towed away the rest.

Lucullus's first act (Ap.*Mithr.*72) was to take his five legions to Propontis where Mithridates was besieging Kyzikos, using among other siege engines, 'a tower carried in the harbours on two fives linked together from which a bridge by mechanical means sprang out when the tower was near the wall'. Here Lucullus (Ap. *Mithr.*76) contented himself with successfully denying the enemy supplies by land, while Mithridates had command of the sea and was thus able to evacuate Lampsakos when it was besieged by Lucullus. Eventually 'leaving 10,000 picked men and 50 ships under Varius, the general whom Sertorius had sent him, Mithridates went with most of his force to Nikomedia', many being destroyed in a storm.

Lucullus then set about mustering a fleet from the province of Asia in three squadrons, one of which took Apameia, the second Prusias and Nikaia, while with the third Lucullus captured 13 enemy ships in the Troad. He then caught up with Varius and his ships at an uninhabited island near Lemnos and took him and his fellow commanders prisoners. A second storm (Ap.*Mithr.*78) caused Mithridates the loss of 60 ships on his way to Pontos, and scattered the rest. His original fleet at Kyzikos must then have been in excess of 120, a number which explains Lucullus's reliance on land forces alone at Kyzikos and the reason for his delay in mustering a fleet until Mithridates had divided his ships into two squadrons, taking one east to Nikomedia and then Pontos and sending the other under Varius west through the Hellespont.

In the second storm Mithridates' ship was damaged and he went on board a small pirate vessel, in spite of his friends' warning, but the pirates took him safely to Sinope from where he went under tow to Amisos. It seems unlikely that he would have gone under tow unless he had returned to his own ship. Amisos (east of the river Halys in Pontos) was the port he was making for, since it was close to Eupatoria which Mithridates had built and named after himself as his capital city. Lucullus turned and followed him, besieging both cities, as well as Themiskyra on the coast further east. It was now winter, and Mithridates withdrew inland to Kabeira.

In the spring (Ap.*Mithr.*79–82: 71 BC) Lucullus marched inland and eventually defeated Mithridates, who took refuge with Tigranes of Armenia. Lucullus then (70 BC) returned to his fleet and captured a number of cities on the southern coast of the Euxine Sea including Amastris and Herakleia, and, after a siege, Amisos and Sinope. In the following year, demanding the surrender of Mithridates by Tigranes, Lucullus marched against him, capturing Tigranokerta after a battle. But the campaign ended indecisively. 'The Romans' (Ap. *Mithr.*91) 'troubled by the revolt of Italy and hard pressed by famine caused by pirates on the seas, thought it the wrong moment to wage another war of such importance before they had disposed of their troubles'. They accordingly ordered the disbandment of Lucullus's army. Roman pressure removed, Mithridates regained Kappadokia for the second time and strengthened the defences of his own kingdom, while the Romans concentrated their attention on the pirates who for some years had been virtually taking from them the command of the sea.

The War against the Pirates

Appian's account of the pirates (*Mithr.*92) is worth notice.

It begins with the statement that Mithridates, at the beginning of his war with the Romans, 'employed the pirates. In the early stages they gave trouble (to the Romans) moving around in a few small ships as pirates are accustomed to do. But as the war was prolonged they became more numerous and took to large ships. They made big gains; and even when Mithridates was defeated and made peace, they did not cease their activities. Deprived, owing to the war, of their livelihood and homelands, and having nowhere else to turn, instead of the land they harvested the sea, first in *μυοπάρωνες* (ones) and *ἡμιολίαι* (one-and-a-halfs), subsequently in *δίκροτα* (twos) and *τριήρεις* (threes), they moved around in squadrons, led by pirate chiefs just like fleet commanders'.

They took and plundered unfortified cities, and besieged others, holding wealthy citizens to ransom. 'Regarding the name of pirates as unworthy they called these gains naval prize-money. They kept craftsmen chained to their work-benches and brought in a continuous supply of timber, brass and iron. Encouraged by their profits and determined never now to give up piracy, they likened themselves to kings and autocrats and powerful armies; and thinking that when they were all united they would be invincible, built ships and manufactured arms of all descriptions, particularly in the part of Kilikia called Tracheia, which they adopted as their common mooring ground and encampment'. 'Hence they were all called by the common name of Cilicians. The evil may have originated with the inhabitants of Kilikia Tracheia, but Syrians, Cypriots, Pamphylians and *Ποντικοί* and practically all the eastern tribes...' participated.

(Ap.*Mithr.*93) 'The result was that very quickly there were many tens of thousands of them and they dominated not only the eastern Mediterranean but also the whole sea within the Pillars of Herakles. They even defeated some of the Roman commanders in battles at sea'. 'Murena (83 BC: Sulla's governor of Asia) had attacked them but had accomplished nothing noteworthy, nor had Servilius Isauricus his successor; and now the pirates, treating Rome with contempt, were making landings on the coastal areas of Italy, in particular Brundisium and Etruria.'

Appian is perhaps unfair to Servilius. He gained his cognomen of Isauricus for his successful attack in 82 BC on Isauria which was a part of Kilikia Tracheia. It was not his fault that his success was not followed up. Florus (I.41.6.4–6) speaks of him as 'having been sent against the pirates; and however much he threw the light and elusive *μυοπάρωνες* into confusion, the victory he won was not bloodless. He was not happy only with having driven them from the sea but also overthrew their cities, Phaselis and Olympos, which were extremely strongly fortified and full of booty assembled there for many years, as well as Isaura, the stronghold (*arcem*) itself of Kilikia. Conscious of this great exploit he was supremely fond of the cognomen Isauricus. In spite of these many disasters, the pirates could not keep to the land ... but immediately the enemy withdrew, finding the land unbearable, they sprang back to the sea; and determined rather more widely than before to terrorise the coasts of Sicily also and by a sudden incursion our own Campania'. The attack on Sicily is to be connected with the defeat of the Roman praetor (and the Sicilian squadron) by them.

The first Roman to be given a roving command against the pirates was Marcus Antonius (74–71 BC). He was defeated off Crete and forced to come to terms with them. Q. Caecilius Metellus plundered Crete in 70, destroying a harbour which has been recently excavated, it having been raised by an earthquake above sea level. In the following year the pirates sacked Delos. With that the patience of the Romans was at last exhausted and in 67 Pompey was given a wide ranging command on land and sea, a large army and a fleet of 'ships with *ἡμιολίαι*' numbering 270. In a rapid and well-organised campaign he defeated the pirates (Ap. *Mithr.*96). The Cilician pirates surrendered a large quantity of arms, some ready for use, others still at the forge, also ships, some under construction, some already at sea. They surrendered also stocks of bronze and iron, sail cloth, rope and timber of many kinds. (In Kilikia) Pompey took 71 ships by capture and 306 by surrender. This was the result of Pompey's own operation there. The result in the other operational areas would have been proportionate.

After his success against the pirates Pompey was given the task of bringing the war with Mithridates to an end. (Ap.*Mithr.*99) In 66 BC Mithridates was defeated on land and fled again to Armenia and from there round the Black Sea via Kolchis to Skythia. Pompey pursued him as far as Kolchis and then turned back to invade Armenia in 65. In the subsequent year he brought under Roman rule the vital naval areas of Koile-Syria, Phoenicia and Palestine. In 63 Mithridates was betrayed by his son Pharnakes, killed and his body sent in a three to Pompey.

At Pompey's triumph in 62 the naval importance of his campaigns was emphasised. '700 fully-equipped ships were brought into the harbours of Rome' (Ap.*Mithr.*116–7), and a tablet was carried with the inscription beginning '600 ships with bronze rams were captured'. Mithridates's power at sea in the eastern Mediterranean had constituted the most formidable of the succession of external challenges to Rome from that quarter.

5. THE FLEETS OF JULIUS CAESAR *(Map AW)*

In the eastern Mediterranean Pompey won reputation by conquering for Rome, first the pirates, then Mithridates, and thus all the areas which under him had constituted an empire based on sea power. His rival Caesar saw in the conquest for Rome of the west, Spain, Gaul, and Britain the means of achieving an equivalent reputation and consequent political power.

For the reduction of Britain, where (*CBG*.4.20) the Belgae of the south east had given aid and comfort to the Belgae of the continent in their resistance to his armies, Caesar needed to defeat the Veneti, an Armorican people of Brittany, who would otherwise, Strabo says (4.4.1), have had the naval strength to interfere with his British invasion fleet. To defeat the Veneti he needed a battle fleet. The descriptions of the formation and use of this fleet, and of some of the fleets subsequently deployed by Caesar in his campaigns, possess for us a quality of authenticity which in antiquity only the descriptions of the formation and use of Nearchos's fleet can share. They are written by the man who assembled and used them, Caesar himself. This does not mean that they are written without bias, but personal bias is unlikely to affect his account of the ships he employed or of their navigation.

Towards the end of the second book of his *Commentaries* on the Gallic war (*CBG*.2.34) Caesar records the report of the young Crassus whom he had sent with one legion to the western maritime states that all these had been 'brought under the power of the Roman people'. However, (*CBG*.3.7–8) when Caesar went off to Italy and Illyria, and Crassus who was wintering (57/56 BC) at Angers on the Loire sent officers to collect supplies of corn from the maritime states, these states conspired under the leadership of the Veneti, who inhabited the south-west facing coast of modern Brittany, to retain the officers as hostages; and Crassus was told that if he wanted them back he should return the hostages he had taken from them.

Caesar describes the Veneti as having by far the widest influence (*amplissima auctoritas*) of the states on the Atlantic coast, by reason of their possession of very many ships on which they used to sail to Britain and of their superiority over the other maritime states in knowledge and practice of the sea (*scientia et usu nauticarum rerum*). Further, they held tributary almost all those who sailed that sea, since it was violent and open, with few harbours here and there and those in their possession.

When the sudden revolt was reported to Caesar (*CBG* 3.9.1), he instructed Crassus to employ the time until his return 'in building warships (*naves longas*) on the Loire which flowed into the Atlantic, training oarsmen recruited from the province, and enlisting seamen and helmsmen'. The seriousness with which Caesar immediately took the revolt of the Veneti and the acquisition of a fleet may be explained if he was already contemplating the invasion of Britain and realised that the Venetian fleet would be a threat to that operation unless destroyed. Speaking of the Belgae who lived on the Atlantic coast, Strabo (4.4.1) says 'there are, first, the Veneti who fought the naval battle with Caesar; they were already prepared to hinder the voyage to Britain, since they used the trading station there (*Emporion*)'. As soon as weather conditions permitted (i.e. in the early spring of 56 BC) Caesar returned from Italy to his army in Gaul.

(*CBG*.3.9.3) On news of his arrival the Veneti and their allies 'prepared for war, and particularly began to see to everything relating to the deployment of ships, with the greater optimism because of their great reliance on the nature of their country. They were aware that access on foot was restricted by tidal inlets and access by sea was made difficult by ignorance of the terrain and the infrequency of harbours; and they were sure that the Roman armies could not, through lack of supplies of corn, remain long in their territory. And if the unexpected were to happen, they had greater sea power, while the Romans were not trained seamen and knew nothing of the local conditions in which they would be fighting, shallows, harbours, and islands; furthermore they realised that navigation in an enclosed sea was quite a different matter from navigation in the completely open and quite limitless Ocean. They fortified their cities, brought in supplies from the fields and concentrated their ships at Venetia where they expected Caesar would open the campaign'.

(*CBG*.3.11.5) 'Caesar put the young Decimus

Brutus in command of the fleet and of the Gallic ships which he had ordered to assemble from the Pictones and Santones and the other pacified areas and instructed him to proceed against the Veneti as soon as possible'.

Caesar does not detail 'the fleet'. The Gallic ships are presumably those built on the Loire and manned with locally trained oarsmen, seamen and helmsmen. The territory of the Pictones and Santones lies on the coast south of the Loire.

He proceeds to describe the difficulties encountered by the Romans in their first attacks on the Venetian towns and how when one town was threatened with capture the Veneti brought a large number of ships and evacuated their possessions and themselves to the neighbouring towns: (3.12.3) 'and this they did more easily for a great part of the summer because our ships, i.e. the fleet', as opposed to the Gallic ships 'were detained by storms' (on their way from the Mediterranean). Dio Cassius (39.40) gives the position rather more clearly: after speaking of 'the vessels, *πλοια,*' which Caesar had built inland, hearing that they were of a type suitable for use in tidal waters, and brought down the Loire, he speaks of Caesar wasting almost the whole summer in fruitless attempts 'until Decimus Brutus arrived with fast ships for him from the Mediterranean'.

Caesar gives a detailed description of the ships of the Veneti (3.13.1). 'The hulls were more flat-bottomed than in our ships, so that they could more easily meet shallow water at low tides (cf. Tacitus *Annals* 2.6.2). Their prows rose fairly sharply, and their sterns as well, to suit big waves and stormy weather. The ships were built entirely of oak (cf. Strabo 4.4.1) to withstand any violent treatment, the thwarts being fastened to knees a foot thick with iron nails as thick as a thumb. Their anchors are fitted with iron chains instead of ropes, and instead of canvas sails they have hides, and pieces of leather[6] finely sewed together, perhaps because of the scarcity of canvas and ignorance of its use, or, as is perhaps more likely, because they thought that with canvas the great storms of the Ocean and the strong winds could not be faced satisfactorily, and the great weight of the ship could not be held on course'.

(*CBG*.3.13.5) 'The engagement between our ships (i.e. again 'the fleet') and these was such that one side was superior in speed and oarpower, while for them the remaining factors were more suited and more favourable, because of the nature of the land and the violence of the weather'. It appears also that the Veneti had the advantage of greater numbers.

(*CBG*.3.14.4) 'The fact was that our ships ('the fleet') could not damage theirs with the ram, so solid in build were they (with timbers a foot thick). Nor, because of their height, could they effectively be reached by missiles. For the same reason they were, conveniently for them, less vulnerable to rocks. Furthermore, when the wind began to blow violently and they had to run before it, they both withstood rough weather more easily and in shallows remained upright more safely, and when they were left (on shore) by the (retreating) tide they had nothing to fear from rocks and reefs. Our ships had to fear all these eventualities'.

(*CBG*.3.14.2) 'When the Roman fleet under Brutus at last arrived' (the fleet which Dio called 'the fast ships from the Mediterranean') 'and was seen by the enemy, the Veneti, with nearly 220 ships ready for action and equipped with weapons of all kinds, put out from harbour and took up position opposite our ships. Neither the fleet commander Brutus nor the tribunes of the soldiers nor the centurions to whom the individual ships had been assigned had any idea what they should do or what tactical plan they should follow. They realised that they could inflict no damage with the ram. Towers (p. 358) were raised but they were overtopped by the height of the sterns of the Venetian ships, and missiles could not be satisfactorily hurled from a lower position, while those thrown by the Gauls fell with more deadly effect'. Dio's description of the ships as 'fast' suggests threes, but the use of towers makes it likely that at any rate some, probably the greater part, were at least fours and fives, which might be considered fast in comparison with the Gallic craft.

'There was one device of great effectiveness prepared by our men, very sharp hooks inserted in, and nailed to, long poles, resembling in shape a pick-axe. When the ropes which held the yards to the masts [of the enemy's ships] were engaged by these and pulled, they were cut through as the [attacking] ship increased its speed under oar'. Plato, in the *Laches* (183D), gives a rather scornful account of the use of this weapon, the *δορυδρέπανον*, against a merchantship. 'When the halyards were severed the yards of course fell[7]. The result was that since the whole hope of success for the Gallic ships lay in the sails and rigging their removal took away at once the whole usefulness of the ships'. (*CBG*.3.14.8) 'The rest of the fighting depended on courage in which our men were far superior, particularly because the battle was in full view of Caesar and the army ...'.

'With the yards (of the Venetian ships) dismantled ... when individual ships were being set about by two or three, the soldiers put all their efforts into boarding. When the Gauls saw this happening and several ships had been captured, there being no help for this situation, they tried to reach safety in flight. After the ships had been carried by the wind into one area, there was suddenly such a dead calm that no movement was possible, a circumstance which was extremely fortunate in bringing the business to an end. Our men had followed and captured individual ships so that of the whole number only a few reached land at nightfall, the battle lasting from about the fourth hour till sunset. This battle finished the war with the Veneti and with the whole coast, since all the men and ships available had been assembled for the engagement'.

This is the only battle at sea between ships under oar and ships under sail recorded in antiquity. If the wind had strengthened instead of failing, the Romans might have suffered a defeat or been forced to withdraw.

Dio Cassius's account (39.40–43) of the battle, written four centuries later, is more logical and detailed than Caesar's. It is hardly more authentic, but it may derive from other sources which filled out, in some cases gratuitously, Caesar's military brevity. Dio speaks of the Roman ships being kept by Brutus in harbour so long as the wind blew.

'He was afraid of the number and magnitude (*magnitudo* = size and weight) of the enemy ships, both the impetus given (to them) by the wind and their impact [on the Roman ships]; but when the wind fell to a calm and the heavy enemy ships became motionless, no longer moved by their sails, Brutus plucked up courage, came out and attacked. Moving round and through their opponents, now ramming one ship and now withdrawing, where and when he liked, he did them much severe damage with impunity..., and then, using the *δορυδρέπανον*, the Romans cut down their opponents' sails and rigging, so that if the wind rose again they could not escape'.

It is remarkable, in any case, that we should have an eyewitness's description of an unusual battle between two quite different kinds of warship, developed to suit quite different conditions of sea, land and winds. It is not surprising that Brutus and the subordinate Roman officers were initially at a loss for tactics when their light and manoeuvrable oared warships (the 'fast ships' from the Mediterranean, probably threes with a number of fours and fives and one or two sixes as flagships) (p. 271) were faced by large heavy warships moving about under sail in a strong wind with hostile intent. According to Dio it was only after the wind dropped that the Romans came out and that they used the *δορυδρέπανον* as a precaution against the wind rising again. By Caesar's account they came out with the wind still blowing, disabled the enemy ships with the *δορυδρέπανον* so that they were driven together helplessly into a corner where they were at the mercy of the fast and agile Roman ships. Dio's mention of ramming and of the normal tactical manoeuvres connected therewith suggests the introduction of traditional material unsuitable in a context in which ramming was ineffective. The geographer Strabo, who was a younger contemporary of Julius Caesar, has the last word (4.4.1). When speaking of 'the Belgae who live on the coast of the (Atlantic) ocean', he says that Caesar easily defeated them in a naval battle 'not using the ram, for their timbers were thick, but as they sailed before the wind against his fleet the Romans pulled down their sails with the *δορυδρέπανον*'. Caesar's account is accordingly to be preferred, even if it does attribute a greater degree of courage to the Roman ship masters.

Strabo repeats some of the information found in Caesar's account of the ships of the Veneti, and adds other points. 'Because of the strength of the wind their sails are made of leather and instead of ropes they use chains' (anchor chains, clearly not halyards). They build their ships with flat bottoms and high bows and sterns because of the ebbing of the tides, and of oak timber of which they have plenty. For this reason (because the ships are made of oak) they do not fit the plank-fastenings (*ἁρμονίαι*) tightly, but leave gaps. These gaps they caulk (*διανάττουσι*) with seaweed to prevent the wetted surface drying out when the ships are hauled out of water, since the seaweed is habitually rather moist, whereas oak is dry and lacking sap'.

Julius Caesar's Invasions of Britain

The destruction of the fleet of the Veneti opened the way for Caesar to invade Britain without a naval threat to his communications, and at the end of the summer of 55 BC he decided to do so, (*CBG*.4.20.1–2) 'because they had supplied auxiliaries to the Gauls'.

Although the campaigning season was nearly over, 'he thought it would be very useful for him merely to reach the island, see the people, and gain knowledge of the lie of the land, the harbours and the approaches, all of which were almost unknown to the Gauls. Hardly anyone except traders went there and these themselves knew nothing except the sea coast and the country lying opposite Gaul'. He invited the traders from everywhere to meet him, but was not able to discover the size of the island, their military practices, political system, or what harbours were suitable for the reception of a large number of the bigger ships (*multitudo maiorum navium*).

(*CBG*.4.21.4) He sent an officer, Volusenus, in a warship (*navis longa*) to collect information, and moved to the territory of the Morini 'which is nearest to Britain' i.e the coast on each side of Cap Gris Nez. Here he ordered the ships from the neighbouring regions to assemble and 'the fleet which had fought the Veneti'.

The phrase 'a large number of the bigger ships' indicates that Caesar was intending to take across the Channel some at least of the fleet that Brutus had brought up from the Mediterranean against the Veneti. He says then (3.11.5) that Brutus's eventual command against the Veneti consisted of a number of *naves longae* built on the rivers of Gaul and 'the fleet'. The former had not proved effective by themselves and (3.14.1) he had decided to postpone the final confrontation at sea until the fleet arrived. Dio (39.40) describes the latter as 'fast ships'. It seems then that the Roman warships in the Veneti campaign fell into the two familiar categories: the smaller and less powerful *naves longae* mostly built on the rivers of Gaul and warships of the larger category (*maioris formae*), fours and fives, possibly even Brutus's six, all from the Mediterranean. Larger ships are referred to in the account of the landing, and it is therefore confirmed that Caesar actually took them across. In the fleet from the Mediterranean there would also have been some ships of the smaller category probably threes in view of the difficult voyage from Spain through the straits of Gibraltar and the Bay of Biscay. Volusenus's *navis longa* was probably such a ship, and there is a later reference to *speculatoria navigia*.

Caesar stayed at the assembly point (later referred to as a harbour) and for some time engaged in diplomacy and preparation of the invasion ships. (*CBG*.4.22.3) 80 *onerariae* (carrying 150 men each: see below) were provided as sufficient for carrying two legions (@ 6000). His force of warships (*naves longae*) was put under the command of the quaestor (Brutus), the legates and the prefects. 18 (necessarily specialised) transports which had been detained by unfavourable winds eight miles away (at a place later referred to as a more northerly harbour *superior portus*: p. 123) were allocated to the cavalry. In the Athenian fleet converted threes carried 30 horses each (AT p. 226).

When weather conditions were favourable (*CBG*.4.23.1) Caesar set out at the third watch (3 am), instructing the cavalry to go to the distant harbour, board ship and follow him. He arrived in Britain with the first ships at about the fourth hour of the day (10 am). Observing the cliffs (of Dover or Folkestone) and the British manning them, he thought it unwise to attempt disembarkation there and waited at anchor for the rest of the ships to arrive. He held a meeting of the legates and tribunes, and told them Volusenus's intelligence and his own intentions. Then, finding a combination of favourable tide and wind, he gave the signal and raised anchor. At about seven miles (north or west)[8] he moored his ships on an open level shore. The British disputed the landing with cavalry and chariots. This caused great difficulty, because the *onerariae* (used as troop transports) because of their size could only stand in deep water'. while the heavily laden soldiers had to jump down and keep their feet in rough water, at the same time fighting an enemy who was on dry land or had advanced a short distance into the water.

(*CBG*.4.25) 'When Caesar saw what was happening he ordered the warships to whose appearance the enemy was more unaccustomed and which could be moved more easily to go a little way apart from the *onerariae*, row at speed, place themselves on the enemy's open flank and from that position to harass the enemy and drive him away with slings, arrows and catapults. This was of great help to our men.

The enemy came to a halt and retreated a little at the appearance of the ships, the movement of the oars and the unaccustomed kind of catapult'.

Finally a landing was effected with some fierce fighting. (*CBG*.4.26.4) The warships' boats, *scaphae*, and scoutships, *speculatoria navigia*, filled with soldiers were sent to aid groups outnumbered by the British. Unfortunately the cavalry had been unable to reach the landing place. The enemy, defeated in the engagement, sued for peace. The warships to the sight of which the British were more unaccustomed are shown by the presence of *scaphae* (p. 135, 265) to have included some in the category of larger warships (*maioris formae*).

Four days later the 18 ships with the cavalry on board set out from the upper (i.e. more northerly) port in Gaul with a gentle breeze (*CBG*.4.28.1). As they came in sight of the camp such a storm arose that most of the ships could not hold their course. Some returned to port, others were taken to a lower (more southerly) part of the island towards the setting sun (i.e. SW) and were in great danger. When at anchor they were filling with water, they necessarily put out to sea as night came on and returned to the continent.

(*CBG*.4.29) 'On the same night' (as the storm i.e four days after the landing) 'there was a full moon, which unknown to the Romans usually causes the highest tides in the Atlantic. Accordingly, at the same moment, the tide had filled with water the warships with which Caesar had safeguarded the transportation of the army and which he had drawn up on dry land, and the storm was battering the *onerariae* riding at anchor; nor was any means available to our men to meet or save the situation. Many ships were damaged and since the rest, without their ropes, anchors and remaining gear were useless for service, there was naturally great anxiety throughout the army. The fact was that there were no other ships for the return voyage and everything needed for repairing the ships was lacking; also since it was accepted that the winter was to be spent in Gaul, no provision had been made for winter supplies of corn in this territory. When the situation became known to the British, they planned revolt.

(*CBG*.4.31.2) The soldiers, however, succeeded in repairing the rest of the fleet with materials taken from the 12 ships worst damaged, and the revolt was suppressed. As the equinox was approaching, Caesar did not delay to settle terms of peace. Doubling the number of hostages he took with him to Gaul, he put to sea in favourable conditions a little after midnight and arrived safely. Two *onerariae* were unable to make the harbours reached by the others and were carried a little further south. The 300 soldiers (@150) put ashore from them were attacked by the Morini. Caesar sent the cavalry from his camp to support them and arrived in time to drive off the Morini, inflicting many casualties'.

The report of this final incident is important as confirming that Caesar's invasion troops were taken to Britain, at any rate largely, in transports, not warships. The two passages before this in Caesar's account of the invasion are these: the first (*CBG* 4.22.3), which seems clear enough, says that Caesar assembled 80 *onerariae* 'which he thought sufficient for the transport of two legions'; the second (*CBG* 4.29.2) is ambiguous and speaks of 'long ships by means of which he had secured (*curaverat*) the transport of his army (*exercitum transportandum*)'. He could have secured it either directly by transporting the army in them or indirectly by ensuring the safety of their transport in *onerariae*. The report of the two stray cargo ships with 150 men in each suggests that the latter, if it can be applied generally, is the right interpretation of the second passage.

Julius Caesar's Shipbuilding

(*CBG*.5.1.1) In the winter of 55/54 BC, leaving Gaul for Italy, Caesar instructed the legates whom he had put in command of the legions, to use as much of the winter as they could in building new ships and repairing old ones. He indicated the shape and design. For speed in loading and for hauling ashore he made them 'a little lower than those we have become accustomed to use in our sea', and the principal reason for this (change) was his observation that because of frequent alterations of tide less big waves are generated there (i.e. in the Channel); for the transport of cargoes and of great numbers of baggage animals he wanted them a little broader than is the custom in other seas. He ordered all these (*onerariae*) to be of the type of *actuariae*, for which service a low profile is very useful. His new transports were to be broader, lower in profile and oared. He ordered materials for rigging ships to be brought from Spain (e.g. esparto grass for making ropes: *AT* p. 191).

(*CBG*.5.2.2) On his return (to Gaul from Italy) in the spring of 54 BC he found 600 of the type mentioned above, and 28 warships (*naves longae*) fitted out and within a few days of launching. He ordered them all to assemble at the port of Itius (Gesoriacum, Boulogne) which is most convenient for the crossing to Britain of about 300 stades. He himself moved there with the legions. There he learnt that the 60 ships which had been built among the Meldi (on the Seine) had been unable to keep their course because of a storm and had returned (to the Seine). The remaining ships were all ready for service and completely equipped. (*CBG* 5.7.3) He was detained at Itius by the Caurus (NW) wind for 25 days.

(*CBG*.5.8.1) 'Caesar left Labienus in charge of Gaul, with three legions and 3000 cavalry to protect the harbours and ensure supplies of food. He himself with five legions and equally 3000 cavalry put out about sunset. Carried by an African (south) wind, about midnight, when the wind dropped, he did not hold his course and was taken a long way by the tide. At sunrise he saw Britain on his left hand side. Then, again following a change of tide, he tried under oar to gain that part of the island where the previous summer he had noticed the best landing. In this voyage the soldiers' courage was very praiseworthy. They rowed without a break in the heavy transports (*vectoriis gravibusque navigiis*) and kept up with the warships. At about midday they reached Britain'.

These oared *vectoria navigia* must be the new, purpose-built transports, distinct from the *onerariae*, he had had built during the winter.

(*CBG*.5.8.5) 'There was no enemy in sight, but as Caesar learnt later from prisoners, although a large band had gathered, they had been frightened by the number of ships which, swelled by the annual private adventurers, had reached more than 800 to be seen at one time'. Caesar disembarked his army, left a guard for the camp and the ships, and made his way inland, the less anxious for the ships because he left them on a soft, open beach with anchors dropped (out at sea), and Atrius in command of the camp guard. He advanced 12 miles during the night and sighted the enemy. He attacked and defeated them. On the following day he sent three bands to pursue the fugitives, but was overtaken by messengers on horseback from Atrius 'to say that a great storm had arisen on the previous night and that almost all the ships were damaged and cast up on the shore, because neither the anchors nor the ropes had held and the seamen and helmsmen had not been able to control the force of the storm. The result was a great deal of trouble from that assemblage of ships'.

This disaster suggests a landing at Walmer or Deal exposed to easterly gales.

On his return Caesar saw that about 40 ships were lost, but that it seemed possible to repair the rest with a great deal of work. He wrote to Labienus asking him to lay down as many ships as he could, and decided, although it involved a great deal of labour, that the best plan was to haul all the ships right out of water (*subducere*) and make them part of the camp with a single fortification. He did in fact learn the lesson that the Mediterranean mooring practice was unfit for northern waters.

(*CBG*.5.22.1) After a repulse of an attack on the naval camp, Cassivelaunus, the British leader, offered peace, and Caesar took the decision to winter on the continent. (*CBG*.5.23.1) When he brought his army to the coast he found the ships repaired. They were then hauled down to the sea. Since many of them had been lost, he decided to take the army back in two journeys. It so happened that of the whole number of ships in many journeys this year and the year before, no transports at all were lost, but of those which were returned to him empty from the continent, after disembarking the troops of a previous voyage, as well as the 60 ships which afterwards Labienus had had built (and were therefore sent across the channel to him empty), very few reached Britain, and almost all were blown back. Caesar waited for them in vain for some time, but to avoid being prevented from sailing by the season, since the equinox was near, he was forced to pack the soldiers aboard rather tightly; and finding very calm weather put out at the beginning of the second watch (9 pm) and reached land at dawn, bringing all his (surviving) ships in safely.

Endnotes

1. *dolones* = *ἀκάτεια, foresails* Xenophon *HG* 6.2.27. cf. Polybios 16.15.2 for their use at the battle of Lade (p. 83).
2. JFC observes: 'It looks as if Eudamos ordered the left turn together into line abreast before the right turn in succession had been campleted by the ships still in column'.
3. L.37.22.2: 1st Dispatch (Pamphylidas: 13 + 4 Rhodian ships = 17. 2nd Dispatch (Eudamos): 13 Rhodian fours + 2 allied fives + 6 aphracts: 21.
   L.37.23.5: Rhodian fleet assembled at the Eurymedon R, 32 fours + 4 threes (+ 2 ships of lower rating unmentioned) = 38.
4. JFC calculates that if the ships were fives the further 130 men in addition to the 120 men normally carried as well as the oarcrew would have been too many, thus reinforcing the argument for reading 18.
5. Wide enough for one oared ship to pass through with a clearance of about 14ft 9in (4.5 m) on each side of the blade tips.
6. JFC notes this as curious because leather becomes fairly weak when wet, though weakening can be delayed by greasing.
7. JFC draws some interesting conclusions about the ships of the Veneti from the Romans' use of the *δορυδρέπανον*: 'One man can handle a 10ft pole just as four men might manage a pole $(10 \times (4)^{1/4})$= 14ft long, of which 10ft could extend outboard. In that case (if the ships were close alongside each other) the beam of the Venetian ship could not have been more than 20 ft (6 m) if the halyards were belayed at the foot of the mast, which is the most likely place. A sailing ship with a high hull, if twenty ft wide, would have been about 60–70ft long'.
8. JFC: 'north if he first anchored off Dover, since there is a flat coast from Walmer about seven miles from Dover; or west if he anchored off Folkestone since seven miles west there is a shelving shore (probably more so in those times) at Hythe or Lympne'.

4

FLEETS OF THE ROMAN CIVIL WARS: 50–31 BC

Between 50 and 31 BC, in the civil wars which followed Caesar's march into Italy, there occurred a number of naval campaigns and engagements culminating in the battle between the fleets of Octavian, by then calling himself Caesar, and of Antony and Cleopatra at the entrance to the Ambracian gulf.

The first of these, in 49 BC, were minor engagements between Caesar's fleet under Decimus Brutus and the fleet of Massalia, a Greek colony of Phokaia, under the Pompeian Domitius. The next was the Dyrrachion campaign in the following year when Pompey's naval commanders tried to prevent Caesar's army crossing to Epeiros. The third, in the same year, after the defeat of Pompey at Pharsalos and his death in Egypt, was Caesar's capture of Alexandria, followed, in 46 BC, by his African campaign against the Pompeians.

After Caesar's assassination in 44 BC a largely naval campaign in the eastern Mediterranean ended in the defeat of Brutus and Cassius on land by Antony at Philippoi. This was followed by Octavian's naval war in Sicily against Sextus Pompeius ending, in September 36, in the battle of Naulochos. Finally, in September 31 BC, Octavian's fleet trained in Sicily under Agrippa defeated the fleets of Antony and Cleopatra at Aktion in a battle which led to the establishment of Egypt as a Roman province directly under the new Caesar. The outcome of the battle left Rome as the sole naval power in a sea, command of which had been disputed since the death of Alexander, briefly by Athens, then by Egypt, Macedon and Syria, by Carthage and Rome, against Macedon, by Rome in alliance with Pergamon and Rhodes, by Mithridates and the pirates, and latterly by the rival claimants to the mastery of Rome herself.

1. THE BATTLES OFF MASSALIA *(Map AE)*

When Caesar arrived in Gaul (*CBC*.1.34) he learnt that Pompey, whose province Spain officially was, although he had administered it from Rome by deputies, had dispatched Vibullius Rufus there, and that Domitius Ahenobarbus had set out with seven *naves actuariae* to take charge of Massalia. These ships had been assembled by private citizens of the island of Igilium (mod.Giglio: off the Tuscan coast) and of the territory of Cosa (in Tuscany). Domitius had manned them with his own slaves, freedmen and tenants (*coloni*). Also, some envoys from Massalia at Rome had been sent home ahead of the others with messages from Pompey to keep the city loyal to him. As a result when Caesar arrived in Spain the Massaliots closed their gates to him. They summoned to their aid the Albici, *barbari* on whom the Massaliots had relied from early times and who lived in the hills above their city.

During the ensuing negotiation Domitius's squadron arrived. He was appointed governor and put in charge of defence. On his instructions the fleet was sent out in all directions; they seized cargo ships wherever they could and brought them into harbour, using those lacking sufficient or adequate metal fastenings, timber and rigging to repair and rig the rest. Whatever corn they found they brought into the common stock; the rest of the food in the shops was requisitioned against a siege.

Angered by this hostile attitude, Caesar led three legions against the city; he brought up towers and mantlets for an assault and laid down the keels of 12 warships at Arelate (mod.Arles) on the Rhone. These ships, type unspecified, were constructed and fitted out in thirty days from the date on which the wood was cut, and brought to Massalia where

Caesar put them under the command of Decimus Brutus, while he left C.Trebonius as legate in charge of the siege. Caesar himself went to confront the commanders of Pompey's armies in the province. It may be noted that when on one occasion (*CBC*.1.54.2) he needed to take his men across a river, his experience of Britain stood him in good stead. He built British coracles for the purpose.

(*CBC*.1.56.1) Encouraged by Domitius's arrival the Massaliots prepared for an engagement at sea with Brutus's fleet. They made ready 17 warships (*naves longae*), of which 11 were cataphract (*tectae*). They added a large number of smaller vessels 'so that our fleet should be frightened by very numbers. They placed on board a great number of archers and a great number of Albici', (described above); 'and these they spurred on with presents and promises. Domitius asked for certain ships for himself and manned them with tenant farmers and shepherds (*colonis pastoribusque*). As a result with a fleet complete in all respects they faced very confidently our ships under the command of D. Brutus'. These, which are likely to have been cataphract, like the Massaliots' 11 ships, were stationed at an island opposite Massalia.[1]

(*CBC*.1.57.1) 'In number of ships Brutus was greatly inferior', though in heavy ships he was slightly superior; 'but Caesar had assigned to that fleet men chosen for their strength from all the legions, *antesignani* and centurions, who had asked for this privilege. These men had prepared iron claws and grappling-hooks and had provided themselves with a great number of javelins of different kinds and other missiles'. It appears that they planned to exploit their superiority in heavy ships to the full. 'Thus when the enemy's appearance was observed they brought their ships out of harbour and fought the Massaliots…'. The Albici are described as ' not far short of the Romans in courage', while Domitius's shepherds, hoping for their freedom, tried by their bearing to catch their master's eye.

(*CBC*.1.58.1) 'The Massaliots themselves trusted to the speed of their ships and the experience of their helmsmen. They eluded our men and sustained their attack. Since there was plenty of sea room, they attempted by extending their line to surround our men, or to attack single ships with many, or to brush off the oars as they ran across them. When they came too close inevitably they had to rely rather on the courage of their mountain-dwellers than on the skill and manoeuvres of their helmsmen. We had fewer practised oarsmen and skilled helmsmen, since both had been promoted from cargo ships and had not yet even learnt what the different items of gear were called; and our men were further handicapped by the slowness and weight of our ships which had been hastily built from unseasoned timber and had not the same turn of speed as theirs. So long as there was room for hand-to-hand fighting our men happily drove single ships in the way of a pair. Then, throwing the iron hand on them and holding each ship fast, they fought on two fronts and boarded the enemy's ships. Some of the ships they swamped (*deprimunt*), killing a great number of Albici and shepherds; some they captured with their crews, some they towed into harbour. On that day the Massaliots lost nine ships including those that were captured'.

The second battle

(*CBC*.2.3) Later in the siege Pompey sent L. Nasidius from Greece in support of the Massaliots with 16 ships, 'of which few were equipped with rams'. Another ship was added to the squadron by a daring raid on the dockyard of Messana as Nasidius passed through the straits. He sent on ahead a small ship advising the Massaliots of his approach and urging them to prepare to fight Brutus's fleet again with his support. They brought their numbers up to their earlier total by repairing old ships and putting them into service. They had also added fishing vessels (*piscatoriae*) which they had equipped with protection for the oarsmen against missiles. Joining Nasidius's squadron they prepared for an engagement. Brutus's twelve heavy ships were now reinforced by the six captured Massaliot ships which had been repaired and put into service when Nasidius was expected.

The ensuing engagement went much as before. As it proceeded, the Roman ships left gaps in their line which gave sea room for the skill of the (Greek) helmsmen and the agility of their ships. The Romans seized opportunities to throw grappling irons and attach enemy ships, and went to the aid of their ships in trouble. The smaller Greek ships gave the Romans much inconvenience from missiles thrown from a distance. One incident is reported in which Brutus's flagship attacked by a three on each side accelerated suddenly and caused the two attackers to collide with each other with serious results, one three breaking her ram and disintegrating. The two were then quickly swamped by ships supporting the flagship. Nasidius's ships proved useless and withdrew from the fight with none lost. The Massaliots lost five swamped and four captured, one ship escaping to Further Spain with the squadron of Nasidius.

Lucan's account of the battle
(De Bello Civili 3.509–762)

Marcus Annaeus Lucanus, the nephew of Seneca, was born in AD 39 and at the age of 26 he was forced, like his uncle, to take his own life in AD 65 when it was discovered that he was involved in a plot against the emperor Nero. His poem, an unfinished epic on the civil war, contains an account of the sea-fighting at Massalia which is remarkably informative in spite of its tiresomely baroque style. He had very probably read Caesar's description of the fighting, and if so he has certainly embellished it very liberally from his own imagination. That imagination, however, was certainly charged, less than a century later than the fighting he describes, with images of warships belonging to the contemporary scene. In his time there were still examples of the larger warships he mentions, fives and sixes, in the fleets at Misenum and Ravenna (Appendix B); and liburnians, threes and fours were in general use. There is no reason to think that the types of warship underwent any great alteration in that period. Whether one or another of them actually took part in the battle is a question impossible to answer unless their presence is otherwise corroborated; but if, as is the case, the reader is more interested in the types of ships than in the details of the battle, except in so far as the details illuminate those types, an answer is not of great importance. What is important is the description given of the various types by an apparently sharp-eyed observer intent on giving, admittedly in a somewhat peculiar style, a vivid picture, often too vivid, of a sea battle as he imagined it to have taken place.

Caesar's siege of Massalia, Lucan says (3.509), was not successful on land, so confrontation at sea followed: 'No gleaming figurehead graced ships adorned with painted planks, but raw timber was joined together just as it fell on the mountain side, to make a stable deck for sea-fighting'. There can be no clearer, or blunter, statement of the objective of Roman heavy warship construction than this, and it points directly to the ships of larger design, *maioris formae*, that is to say, the ships of higher rating than threes.

(3.514) 'And now the fleet accompanying the tower-carrying (flag)ship of Brutus had arrived on the swirling water (*gurges*) of the Rhone to the waves (of the sea) and was moored (*arva tenens*) at the Stoichades'. These three islands were off Gallia Narbonensis 70 miles east of Massalia. The reason for their mooring so far away may have been either to prevent reinforcements reaching Massalia by sea from that direction or because the immediate vicinity of Massalia was hostile. It seems likely, but not certain, that since Lucan describes the newly built fleet as accompanying the flagship down the Rhone the flagship, subsequently described as a six (which Roman flagships often were: cf. p. 271), was not one of the newly built ships, and she alone carried towers (or a tower). If that is so the total number including the flagship was 13.

(3.516–520) 'The Greek fighting men (*iuventus*) also were ready to commit to the fates their whole strength, and they put under arms together aged seniors and youths. Not only the fleet moored on the seashore (*quae stabat in undis*) took crews on board, they also sought out from the dockyard ships (*alnos* alders: cf. Vergil *Georgics* 2.451) too old for service'. This passage indicates that Lucan is putting together the two engagements described by Caesar.

(3.521–528) The morning was fine and the sea undisturbed by wind from the north or south. The fleets are rowed out from their moorings (*statione*) to the high seas. This description implies that the Massaliot fleet had moved out from the harbour of Massalia against Brutus and had spent the previous night at least encamped nearby on the mainland. 'The keels shudder at the impulse of the oars, and the repeated strokes shake the lofty sterns'. Since sterns in all these warships are high-rising, Lucan probably means 'stern' here by the word *puppis* which very often in Latin poetry is used to mean 'ship' by *συνεκδοχή*. The adjectival noun *tonsi* 'things shaved' used by Lucan here for 'oars' is probably derived, together with the noun *pinus* in line 531, from the Homeric phrase *ξεσταί ἐλάται*, lit. 'shaved spruce trees' with the meaning of 'shaved oars' in Odyssey 12.172 and Iliad 7.5. It recalls a passage in Theophrastos (5.1.7) speaking of 'men shaving wood to make oars' and an inscription relating to Kos (SIG 1000.18) and mentioning oar-shavers. These words throw a light on the way oars were made with a tool known in modern times as a spokeshave. Lucan's description of the effect of powerful rowing on the ship is no exaggeration, as anyone who has been on board *Olympias*, the modern reconstruction of the three, will confirm.

(3.529–537) 'The wings of the Roman fleet' (drawn up in line abreast with the islands behind them) 'were outflanked by ships of various types, powerful threes, ships which were moved by a rising, fourfold, system of built-up oarsmen, and ships which dip more oars in the water. This power (*hoc robur*) barred access to the open sea'. The Massaliot heavy ships on each wing of their battle line abreast, by outflanking the Roman line, effectively prevented them from getting to the open sea by a *περίπλους*, moving round the enemy's wings.

'In the crescent shaped line (*lunata classe*) the liburnians receded, content to have been built up in a two-fold (oar)system (*ordine gemino*)'. The liburnians' 'recession' in a crescent-shaped line means that they were at the centre with the bigger ships on the wings. 'But higher than all these ships the flagship of Brutus is driven by sixfold strokes, carries her mass upon the deep and reaches the water far below with her topmost oars (*summis longe petit aequora remis*)'.

The implication of this final clause, since the superlative 'topmost' is used, is that the ship had more than two levels of oars, and that alone. It also states that the water reached by the topmost oars was afar, that is to say, far below. It says nothing about the length of the topmost oars in relation to the others.[2] Whether, without her towers, the six stood higher in the water than the equally three-level threes and fives is a question which will be discussed below. Her greater height could be the result of the tower(s) she alone carried, or of her sixth file of oars, probably the former.

The general picture Lucan presents is clear. The Roman line (composed, according to Caesar, of 12, possibly 13, ships) all cataphract, was drawn up seawards of the Stoichades from where the ships had emerged. Facing them is the more numerous Massaliot fleet in a crescent-shaped formation (like the Persian fleet at the battle of Artemisium: *AT* p. 54), with its heavy ships on the wings overlapping the wings of the Roman line and its liburnians further back in the centre. Brutus's flagship six showed higher in the water than all the other ships (on both sides).

The descriptions of the various types of ships in the lines 529–537 are to say the least enigmatic.

The three is explained as owing her name either to the number of fore-and-aft files of oarsmen on each side of the ship or equally to the number of oarsmen in each unit (comprising a thranite, a zygian and a thalamian). A ship with double-manned thranite, zugian and thalamian oars would then be properly named a six (*ἑξήρης* in Greek), and such a ship be described, somewhat enigmatically as 'driven by six strokes' i.e. the strokes of six men, two thanite, two zygian and two thalamian oarsmen on each side, or by the strokes of six files of oarsmen on each side. The phrase 'driven by six strokes' used of a *ἑξήρης* is latin for an adjective in the *κρότος* series, *δίκροτος*, *τρίκροτος*, up to *ἑξκαίδεκάκροτος* 'with sixteen beats' used of a ship by Aelian (*Tactica* 4).

Brutus's tower-carrying six, as flagship, was the only six. The other enigmatic definitions of types, resembling clues to a crossword puzzle, are given by the lines 530–1: 'ships which were rowed by a rising, fourfold, system (*ordo*) of built-up oarsmen and ships which dip more oars in the water'.

In the first definition Lucan is tortuously making two points: the ships he means have an oarsystem which is fourfold and which has more than one level. If the numeral is to be explained in the same way as the numerals in the names of other oared warship types are explained, it refers to the number of files of oarsmen on each side of the ship or to the number of men in each rowing unit or 'room' on each side. A ship with four men in each such 'room' at more than one level could seat them at two or three levels. Four levels are ruled out on a number of considerations. A reasonable conclusion is then that Lucan in his phrase describes an oared ship with two levels of oars with two oarsmen at each oar. It is argued below that the four depicted in the Alba Fucentia graffito (**38**) is likely to have had 140 double manned oars (p. 88) and consequently an oarcrew of 176 (p. 268–269).

Threes are described by Lucan in a straightforward phrase 'strong threes', which encapsulates the chief characteristic of the classical three, the favourable power/weight ratio which gave her remarkable speed and manoeuvrability in battle, as well as usefulness in towing ὁλκάδες laden either with grain, military stores, or soldiers.

There is a description of a further type of ship in the Massaliot fleet, 'those which dip more oars in the water', more than the fours which Lucan has just mentioned, possibly also more than the threes mentioned before the fours. Since twos are shortly to be described, this further description can only relate to fives. It will be argued (p. 270–271) that the five was a ship of three levels of oars with the oars of two levels double-manned and one level single-manned. Since the fives at Eknomos were said to have had 300 oarsmen, with such a system they would each have had 180 oars, ten more than a three and 92 more than a four which had 88.

There remains the description of the Massaliot liburnians. It is possible that the Massaliots called them by that name, but as Phocaean Greeks they are more likely to have called them pentecontors, which were originally of one file but in time adopted two, like the triacontors, and like the fast pirate galleys, the ἡμιολίαι. The Romans came to know liburnians in their dealings with Illyricum, of which Liburnia was a part. It is probable that liburnian is Lucan's name for the Massaliot pentecontors, a recognition that they were of the same design. He describes them as 'ordine contentae gemino crevisse liburnae' (cf. the similar use of *creverant* by Florus: p.163) 'content with the growth of a double oarsystem' (i.e. the modest achievement of two levels, eschewing the over-ambitious third level) is mildly humorous. It makes two points, growth, i.e. increase in height leading to doubling. Mere doubling of what could be (and once was) single would leave two possibilities: either a single level ship with oars double-manned or a two-level ship with one man to each oar. The word growth (*crevisse*) leaves no doubt that the second possibility is the one Lucan describes[3].

An account of the battle follows (3.538–762). The two lines advanced upon each other until there was space separating the ships which could be crossed with one oarstroke. Then the shouting drowned the noise of the oars and the trumpets. 'Then the oarsmen brought the oars forward to the catch (*caerula verrunt*) and fell back on the seats hitting their chests with the oars. The rams clashed and the ships backed down. Missiles thrown darkened the air and, as they fell, the empty sea. And now the prows (i.e. the ships as seen by the enemy) left gaps and the wings extended. As the fleet formation loosened vessels of different kinds were allowed to pass through... But for the Greeks their ships were handy both to attack and to retire, and with a quick turn to change course and rapidly answer the helm. A Roman ship, on the other hand, was more reliable for keeping a stable keel and in conditions similar to warfare on land'.

'Then Brutus said to the master in the poop where signals were made: 'Are not you letting the line straggle in the open sea and fighting with manoeuvres suitable there? Join battle now, put the hulls amidships in the path of the Phocaean rams'. He obeyed, and offered the ships across the enemy's path. Then every ship that tried Brutus's timbers was caught by her own strike and captured as it stuck to the ship that was struck, but other ships were tied with grappling irons and smooth chains and trapped by their oars. On the sea thick with ships the battle was stationary'.

The description of rowing style is unique. Lucan is likely to have formed his picture from watching oarsmen in Roman warships, fours and fives, which were double-manned. The 'master' in the poop of Brutus's flagship which was also the source of signals to the rest of the Roman fleet, is the man in command of the ship (*navis magister, τριήραρχος*)); but he is also, since the ship is a flagship, the fleet commander (*ναύαρχος*) under the praetor Brutus. He would direct the tactics of the fleet in battle, unless, as here, over-ridden by the praetor. Lucan emphasises the tactic Brutus adopted as the result of having ships built massively as floating platforms for specially chosen deck-fighters. This tactic may have been, at least partly, the outcome of the battle with the Veneti when he was fleet commander under Caesar. Brutus's unnamed fleet commander was trying the classical tactic of *περίπλους* getting round the enemy's wing to the open sea which was 'loosening' his line, against which the enemy had made tactical provision, and for which his slow heavy ships were not suited. The conversation is certainly imagined, but the point good.

The fate of a Roman ship (LC 3.627–633) 'Piled high with the carnage of men and full of blood' is described: 'she had taken many blows (of the ram) on her side and let in the sea by her broken plank fastenings. Then filled up to her top oarports she sank low taking in the water around her in eddies. Divided, as the keel sank, the surface was parted and the sea fell into the place of the ship (or of the stern *puppis*)'. It is possible that Lucan is describing the sinking of the ship below the surface, but if he had meant that dramatic moment the likelihood is that he would have expressed it more clearly. Since ancient warships usually floated when holed, swamping is more likely, on the other hand the timber of which she had very recently been made was green and heavy; and Lucan emphasises that she was heavily burdened. She might then have lost her usual positive buoyancy.

Lucan describes (3.647–652) another disaster, at least of an unusual kind since capsizing is not elsewhere recorded of warships (except possibly in Plutarch *Moralia* 338A (p. 18). He does not say to which fleet the ship belonged or what its type was. 'When the massed soldiers (*turba*) of one ship, over-eager for the fight, leaned over on to the tilted side and left empty the side where there was no enemy, with the weight all in one place the ship (*puppis*) overturned and covered the sea and the seamen within the hollow hull. There was no possibility of striking out in the open sea, but they died in their watery prison'. In view of what Lucan had said about the stability and weight of the Roman ships it seems likely that he is thinking of one of the smaller Greek ships, probably decked, since a deck would enable untrained but warlike decksoldiers (e.g. the Albici) to move all to one side.

Another incident is described (3.661–666) which illustrates the instability of some of the smaller, open, Greek ships.

'Their ship wrecked, most of the crew (*turba*) avoided death by striking out and went together for aid to a ship of their allies; but when they grasped the upper wales with their arms, though forbidden to do so because the ship was heeling and likely to sink if a crowd were taken aboard, the crew wickedly cut their arms through with the sword...'

Finally the use of fire as a weapon (**28**) may be noticed (3.680–90), and the statement (3.683) that pitch and wax (*ζώπισσα* Pliny *NH* 16.56) used on the hulls of warships helped the blaze.

The outcome of the battle is given at 3.753–760: 'Most of the Greek fleet was swamped (*mergitur*), other (Greek) ships with changed oarcrews carried their captors; only a few reached the dockyards in hurried flight... Brutus as victor at sea first added naval renown to Caesar's arms'. Lucan gives no indication of any losses in Brutus's fleet of 12 newly built ships, beyond the one described.

2. THE CAMPAIGN OF DYRRACHION *(Map K)*

(*CBC*.3.3) During 49 BC Pompey, left at peace by Caesar's operations in the western Mediterranean, set about collecting his forces. In first place he had summoned a great fleet, from the province of Asia and the Kyklades, Kerkyra, Athens, Pontos, Bithynia, Syria, Kilikia, Phoenicia and Egypt. The list gives an interesting register, not quite complete, of the large and small naval powers of the immediately pre-imperial years. He also had put in hand the building of a large fleet of new ships in all those places. Plutarch (*Pompey* 64) speaks of his irresistible fleet consisting of 500 fighting ships (*μάχιμοι*) and a vast number of liburnians and reconnaissance ships (*κατάσκοποι*)[4]. He had, further, demanded money 'from the kings, dynasts and tetrarchs of Asia and Syria, and from the free peoples of Achaia, as well as from the provinces allotted to him by the Senate'.

(*CBC*.3.4–5) Eight legions of Roman citizens backed by supporting troops and a large number of auxiliaries constituted the core of his army. A great quantity of corn had been collected from Thessaly, Asia, Egypt, Crete and Kyrene.

Pompey (49/48) had decided to winter his forces at Dyrrachion, Apollonia, and at all the coastal towns (facing Italy) with the intention of preventing Caesar from crossing to Epeiros. With that end in view (*CBC*.3.5.2) 'he deployed his fleet throughout the whole coastal district'. He appointed a number of fleet commanders: his son Cnaeus to the Egyptian ships, Laelius (Balbus) and Triarius to the Asian, Cassius to the Syrian, Marcellus and Coponius to the Rhodian; to the Liburnian and Achaean fleet Libo and Octavius. The reason why the sources of ships in the last two commands are not included in the list of those from whom additional ships had been demanded must lie in the presence with Pompey already of sufficient ships from them. Bibulus as supreme commander was in charge of the whole coastal operation.

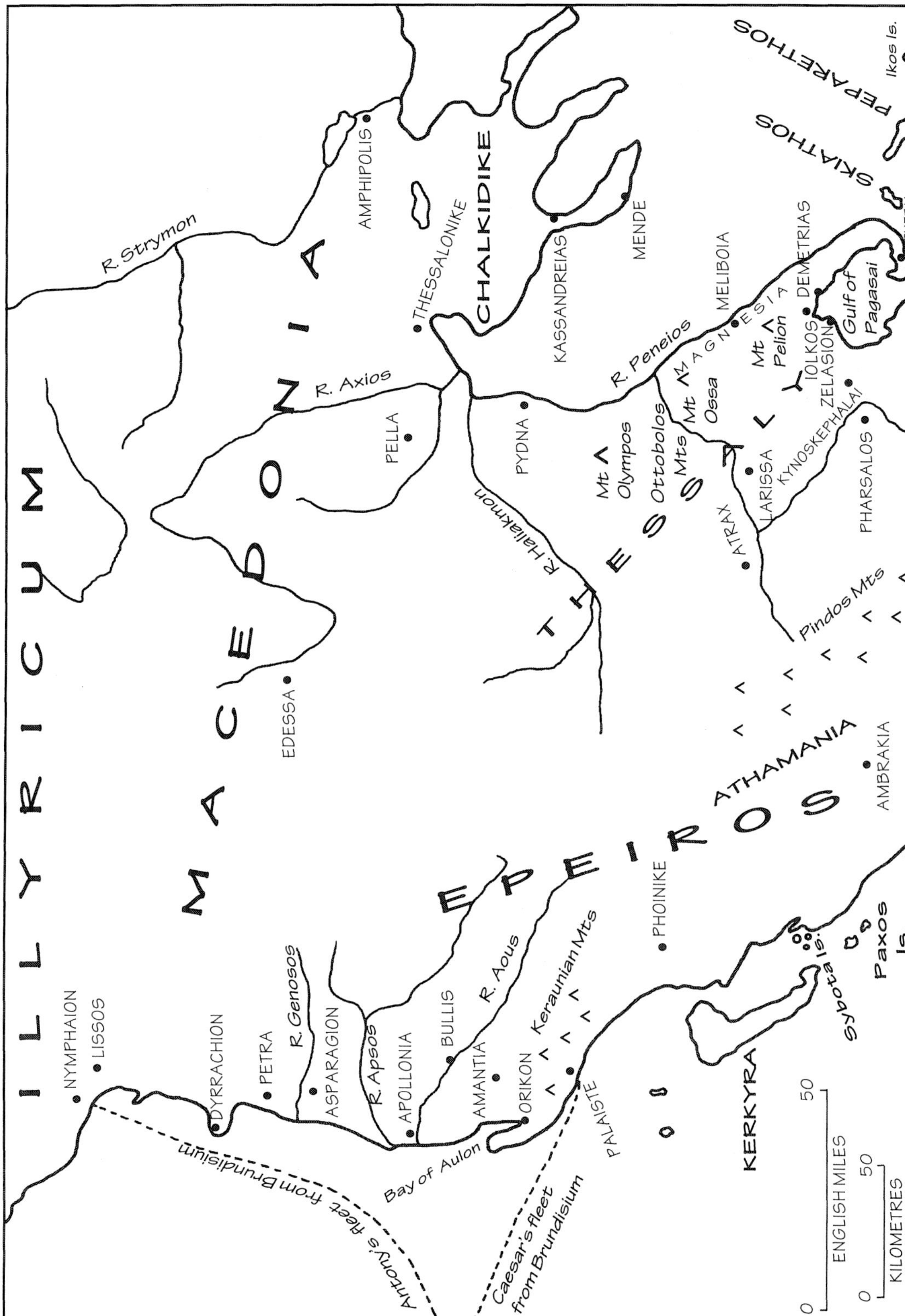

MAP K. *Campaign of Dyrrachion: Macedonia and Epeiros*

In the face of this formidable opposition, after a previous attempt at a crossing (*CBC*.3.2.1–3) had been abandoned through, among other things, inadequate ships for his twelve legions and accompanying cavalry, (*CBC*.3.6.1) early in January 48 BC Caesar came to Brundisium and spoke to his troops. He told them that they were near the end of their toils and dangers. They must happily leave their possessions and baggage behind and go without them (*expediti*) on board ship, so that the maximum number of soldiers could be taken. Seven legions were embarked. They put out on the third of January and made a landfall the following day. They found moorings near a place called Palaiste in a rocky and otherwise dangerous area, since they feared all harbours thinking that they would be occupied by the enemy. There he landed the troops with all the ships without exception safe and sound. Caesar seems to have had a liking for sea-crossings in January (p. 41).

(*CBC*.3.7) 'The two commanders, under Laelius, of the 18 (Pompeian) ships from Asia were at Orikon about 25 miles south of Apollonia, and Bibulus was at Kerkyra about 50 miles south of Orikon. But neither did the former have enough self-confidence to venture out of harbour, although Caesar had under him twelve warships in all, of which four were cataphract; nor did Bibulus, whose ships were unready and his oarsmen scattered, arrive in time, since Caesar was observed on the mainland before the news of his arrival was brought to him at all'.

(*CBC*.3.8.1) 'When the troops had been landed, the ships were sent back by Caesar the same night, so that the remaining legions and the cavalry could be brought across'. But the ships were late in leaving; and missing the night breeze fell in with the enemy. Bibulus captured about thirty of the empty ships and vented on them the anger arising from his own slackness and distress, burning them all and killing in the same fire the seamen and shipmasters, hoping to discourage the rest by the magnitude of the punishment'. Thereafter Bibulus held all the moorings and beaches with his fleets and with patrols tirelessly deployed, he himself keeping watch on board ship in the worst winter weather and thinking no toil or duty beneath him, nor looking for help, provided he could get Caesar in his grasp. Appian (*CW*.2.56) speaks of 'Pompey's threes putting out frequently on patrol'. These are presumably among the *κατάσκοποι* mentioned by Plutarch.

(*CBC*.3.12–13) Immediately after landing, Caesar had marched the 25 miles north to Orikon and then to Apollonia. Both admitted him. Appian (*CW*.2.54) says that when Caesar entered Orikon the Pompeian commanders, Lucretius and Minucius, were on the other side of the town with 18 warships convoying ships carrying grain for Pompey and that they sank the ships to avoid Caesar seizing them, and fled to Dyrrachion. Caesar marched on to Dyrrachion but Pompey got there first. Appian adds that Pompey then sent a fleet to recover Orikon.

When Caesar heard that Pompey was at Dyrrachion he decided to spend the winter in camp (under leather rather than canvas, *sub pellibus*) at the river Apsos in Apollonian territory and await there the arrival of the remaining legions from Italy. Pompey took the same course and brought all his forces into camp across (i.e north of: see *CBC*.3.19.1) the river.

(*CBC*.3.14.1) At Brundisium according to Caesar's instructions his commander Calenus put the legions and cavalry on board, as many as his ships allowed, and put to sea, but he had hardly left the harbour when he received a letter from Caesar telling him that all the harbours and beaches were held by enemy fleets. He himself accordingly returned to harbour and recalled all the ships. One which went on and did not obey Calenus's order because it had no soldiers on board and was privately owned was taken to Orikon and boarded by Bibulus who killed all in her. The position now was that Bibulus with his fleet at Orikon (now again in Pompey's hands) denied the sea and the harbours to Caesar, while Caesar denied Bibulus all the beaches, which he held under guard, so that Bibulus had to be supplied with victuals, firewood and water from Kerkyra, and on one occasion when the weather was bad he had to rely on fresh water collected as dew in the skins with which the ships were covered at night. In this stalemate, talks were initiated but broken off. Bibulus himself succumbed to the hardships of the blockade in midwinter.

At this point Libo took the 50 ships under his command at Orikon to Brundisium and occupied an island opposite the harbour.

'He reckoned that it was preferable to keep under guard this one place where was the necessary egress for the Caesarian ships, rather than the beaches and harbours of all (the others). At his sudden appearance he caught and burned some cargo ships and took away one with a cargo of grain'. He caused great panic and, by landing troops at night, some damage. He sent a letter to Pompey suggesting that the rest of the fleet should be hauled up and refitted, since he could prevent reinforcements going to Caesar with the fleet he had'.

(*CBC*.3.24) 'Mark Antony, who was at Brundisium at this time, took nearly 60 boats (*scaphae*) belonging to the big ships (e.g the fives) and covered them with mantlets of basketwork (*pluteis cratibusque*). He put élite crews on board and distributed them along the shore in many different places. Then he orderd two threes which he had had constructed at Brundisium, to go to the entrance of the harbour for oarcrew training. When Libo saw them coming out rather boldly he sent five fours in the hope of intercepting them. When the fours approached our ships our veterans took refuge in the harbour and Libo's ships followed them rather incautiously in hot pursuit. Antony's boats then suddenly emerged from all quarters and captured one of the fours with its oarsmen and decksoldiers and compelled the rest to flee ignominiously. Adding to this loss Antony posted cavalry around the coast and prevented Libo from obtaining water'. He was thus forced to give up the blockade and withdraw.

(*CBC*.3.25) Caesar says 'many months had passed and the winter had nearly come to an end' since his own crossing (4 January) and his encampment north of the Apsos river a few days later. In fact it can hardly have been more than three months. Communicating presumably by a light vessel crossing by night he wrote impatiently to Brundisium telling them not to miss a chance of crossing and saying that the beaches of Apollonia were the most free of enemy patrols since they did not dare to go very far from the harbours (principally, Kerkyra, Orikon, Dyrrachion, Lissos).

(*CBC*.3.26) At last 'Antony's ships obtained a favourable south wind and put out to sea' (presumably at night), 'on the following day moving past (Dyrrachion and) Apollonia'. Since they were moving north they would have passed Apollonia first, as Appian says, and since Apollonia was in Caesar's hands the alarm would not have been given from there.

'When they were seen from the mainland the commander of the Rhodian ships at Dyrrachion, C. Coponius, led his (war)ships (20 according to Appian) out of harbour and when they were now drawing near our (mainly transport) ships with a slackening wind, the same south wind increased and served to protect our ships. Not indeed for that reason did Coponius give up his effort; but by the hard work (rowing) and determination of his crew he had hopes that the force of the gale could be counterbalanced; and when our ships had passed Dyrrachion thanks to the great force of the wind he followed none the less. Our men while taking advantage of the kindness of fortune were nevertheless anxious, in case the wind fell. They reached harbour, a place called Nymphaion three miles beyond Lissos, and took the ships in. The harbour is shelterd from the SW but exposed to the south wind. They thought the danger from the wind was less serious than the danger from the fleet. As soon as the ships got in, by great good fortune, the wind which had been southerly for two days veered west'.

The change (and strengthening) of wind put the Rhodian ships in danger (on a lee shore or in heavy swell). All 16 cataphract ships were lost, and some of the great number of oarsmen and decksoldiers (if the ships were fives: 4,800 and 1,920 respectively) were drowned, the rest were rescued by Caesar's men and sent home.

(*CBC*.3.28) 'Two of Caesar's (transport) ships lagging behind and benighted, anchored off Lissos. Otacilius Crassus, in command at Lissos, sent out *scaphae* and a great number of smaller ships and prepared to assault them. At the same time he negotiated their surrender, promising them their lives if they did. One of these ships had 220 men from the legion of recruits, the other a little less than 200 from a veteran legion. The recruits were frightened by the number of ships and in poor shape from the tossing at anchor and nausea. They surrendered to Otacilius under oath that the enemy would not harm them. All these were brought before Otacilius and put to death in the cruellest fashion in his presence without regard to the sanctity of the oath. The soldiers of the veteran legion on the other hand, similarly affected by the discomforts of the gale and the bilgewater, thought they ought to relax nothing of their former courage; and prolonging the early hours of night in negotiating conditions and pretending to surrender, they compelled the helmsman to put the ship ashore. Then finding a suitable place they spent the rest of the night there and at first dawn when Otacilius sent against them nearly 400 cavalry, which patrolled that part of the coast, and armed men from the garrison who followed them, they put up a defence and escaped safely to our men after killing a number of the enemy'.

Lissos then went over to Caesar and Otacilius escaped to Pompey. When Antony had put all the troops ashore (at Nymphaion), three veteran legions, one legion of recruits and 800 cavalry, he sent a number of the ships back to Italy to bring over the remaining footsoldiers and cavalry; but he left at Lissos the *pontones*, a kind of Gallic ship, in case, if Pompey decided to invade Italy, Caesar should have some ships with which to follow . He also sent Caesar a report of the area in which the troops had been landed and details of them.

(*CBC*.3.30) Antony's arrival at Nymphaion was known by Caesar and Pompey simultaneously and both moved, Caesar to join forces with him, Pompey if possible to intercept him. When Pompey learnt that they had met he moved to Asparagion in the territory of Dyrrachion, 'so as not to be surrounded by two armies'.

The arrival of Antony with the greater part of Caesar's remaining forces altered the pattern of the war, placing the emphasis on the land rather than on the sea. Withdrawing the legion from Orikon, placed there to safeguard the coastal area, Caesar sent Domitius Calvinus with two legions to Macedonia where (*CBC*.3.57) he came to face the Pompeian Scipio who brought an army from the province of Asia. Other legates brought over Thessaly and Aitolia including Naupaktos, but Achaia remained Pompeian.

Pompey's naval strength continued to make itself felt, to remove from Caesar the means of withdrawal to Italy. (*CBC*.3.39) Caesar left three cohorts at Orikon under Acilius, who had brought the 12 warships there (*CBC*.3.7) into the inner harbour and moored them fast. He sank a merchant ship at the entrance and attached to her another, on top of which he built a tower and and kept it manned against a sudden attack, which soon came.

(*CBC*.3.40) 'Pompey's elder son Cnaeus, the commander of the Egyptian squadron (of 60 ships: Appian *CW*.2.71), went to Orikon. He towed away the sunken ship with a winch (*remulcum*) and a number of ropes, and attacked the other one with many ships on which he had built towers to match. The result was that, fighting from a higher level and constantly sending in fresh troops to relieve those that were exhausted, as well as attacking the town walls in the other areas with ladders from the land and with the fleet, so as to divert the enemy's detachments, he overcame the Caesarians; and with hard work and a great many missiles he drove down the defenders, who were all taken off by *scaphae* and escaped. He captured that ship and at the same time occupied the natural spit on the other side which had made the town a peninsula. He then brought into the inner harbour 2 twos' (probably *κέρκουροι* as Egyptian) 'under small shields and propelled by poles. Thus making for the warships, which had been tied up to the land and were empty, from both directions' (by the harbour entrance and by the spit) 'he towed away four of them and burned the rest'.

When this operation was completed Cnaeus Pompeius left Laelius, detached from the Asian fleet, to prevent supplies reaching Orikon from Amantia and Byllis. He himself went on (north) 'to Lissos', from which the previous Caesarian garrison had probably been withdrawn (*CBC*.3.30.1) 'entered the harbour and burned the 30 *pontones* left there by Antony. He tried to take the city by storm, defended by the Roman community and soldiers sent by Caesar' (presumably after the attack on Orikon). He stayed three days, lost some men in the attack and withdrew.

(*CBC*.3.43) Pompey seeing Dyrrachion, his main supply base, threatened, moved to a camp outside the city where he was besieged by Caesar and Antony. The siege of a perimeter, Caesar says, of 16 Roman miles extended the Caesarian army to the utmost and eventually (*CBC*.3.65) involved it in serious losses. Caesar finally decided to change his strategy, moved inland to join Domitius; and Pompey followed to join Scipio. The two armies finally fought the decisive battle of Pharsalos (6 June 48 BC), in which Pompey was defeated.

While these land operations were in progress (*CBC*.3.100) Laelius took his squadron to Brundisium and, like Libo earlier, occupied the island opposite the harbour. Similarly the commander at Brundisium with specially protected *scaphae* (*tectis instructisque scaphis*) lured out Laelius's ships and captured one of them, a five which came out too far, and two smaller ships at the harbour mouth.

He also with cavalry patrols prevented the men from the fleet getting water. But Laelius, taking advantage of a season more suitable for navigation, was bringing supplies of water for his men in *onerariae* from Kerkyra and Dyrrhachion, now Pompey's main naval bases. 'He was not deterred from his operation; nor before news of the battle in Thessaly came through could he be driven away from the harbour and island either by the disgrace of losing the ships or by shortage of necessaries'.

(*CBC*.3.101) Another Pompeian fleet commander, C. Cassius, 'with the squadron of Syrian, Phoenician, and Kilikian ships' went to Sicily. Caesar's fleet in that area was in two divisions, one under the praetor Sulpicius at Vibo in the straits and the other under Pomponius at Messana. Cassius descended on Messana before Pomponius knew of his arrival and catching him unawares sent *onerariae* packed with combustible materials on to his fleet before a strong favourable wind and burned all 35 ships, of which twenty were cataphract. He could have taken the city if news of Caesar's victory had not arrived in time to encourage the defence. Cassius then moved on to the squadron at Vibo, which was beached, since the Caesarian seamen were in a panic similar to that of the other squadron previously. Finding the wind favourable Cassius sent in the prepared fire-ships, and five ships were burnt, the fire catching each wing. When the wind was spreading more widely due to the strength of the wind, the soldiers on the sick list from the old legions who had been left to guard the ships did not put up with the ignominy, but on their own accord boarded the ships and put out to sea. They attacked the Cassian ships and captured two fives, in one of which was Cassius, but he was taken off in the ship's boat and escaped. Two threes also were swamped. Not long afterwards news arrived of the battle in Thessaly and Cassius and his fleet left the region.

Pompey, after the battle, went from Larisa to Mitylene, where his wife was. Although he still had strong naval and military forces in Kerkyra and Africa, he decided to go from there to Kilikia with his entourage in four threes sent by Rhodes and Tyre with the intention, concealed from his friends, of continuing eastwards to Parthia. His friends dissuaded him and agreed, Appian (*CW*.2.83) says, to go to Egypt 'which was near and was a great kingdom, still prosperous and powerful in ships, grain and money, while its rulers (Ptolemy and Cleopatra), although under age, were family friends of Pompey's'. He sailed to Egypt by way of Cyprus.

Cleopatra, daughter of Ptolemy Auletes and by his will joint regent with her brother Ptolemy, had quarrelled with him and she had retired to Syria. Ptolemy was at Kasion with an army expecting her invasion, when Pompey's ships appeared at Pelousion. His guardians Achillas and Pothinos (in charge of the army and of the treasury respectively) took the advice of the king's tutor Theodotos to lure Pompey ashore and kill him, thus finding favour with Caesar. And this was done 20 September 48 BC.

The Division of the Pompeian Navy

(Appian *CW*.2.87) On Pompey's march inland Cato had been left in Kerkyra 'with a second army and 300 threes'. Here Appian is almost certainly using the word *τριήρεις*, as it was used in his time (p. 37), as a general word for warships. As has been seen, Pompey's fleet contained, probably a large number of fives, as well as threes employed where fast ships were required. The fleet was divided among the leaders. Cassius moved to Pontos to enlist Pharnakes against Caesar. Scipio and Cato took their ships to Africa, where they relied on Attius Varus and Juba, king of Numidia. Pompey's elder son, Cn. Pompeius, went quickly to Spain, with Labienus and Scapula. Since, as will be seen, a part of Cassius's fleet subsequently numbered 70 ships, it seems reasonable to suppose that the 300 ships were divided into three fleets of 100, one going to Pontos, one to Africa and the third to Spain.

3. CAESAR'S WARS IN EGYPT AND AFRICA

Alexandria (Plan 6)

Caesar arrived in Alexandria on the 2nd of October 48 BC with a force of two legions, one that had followed him from Thessaly and a second brought by Calenus from Achaia, 800 cavalry, ten Rhodian and a few Asian warships. The legions were not up to strength, 3,200 men in all, and the ships were few; but Caesar had faith in his now formidable reputation. In fact (*CBC*.3.110) Achillas had an army not contemptible either in numbers (twenty thousand foot and two thousand cavalry) or in quality and training, and despised the few Roman soldiers.

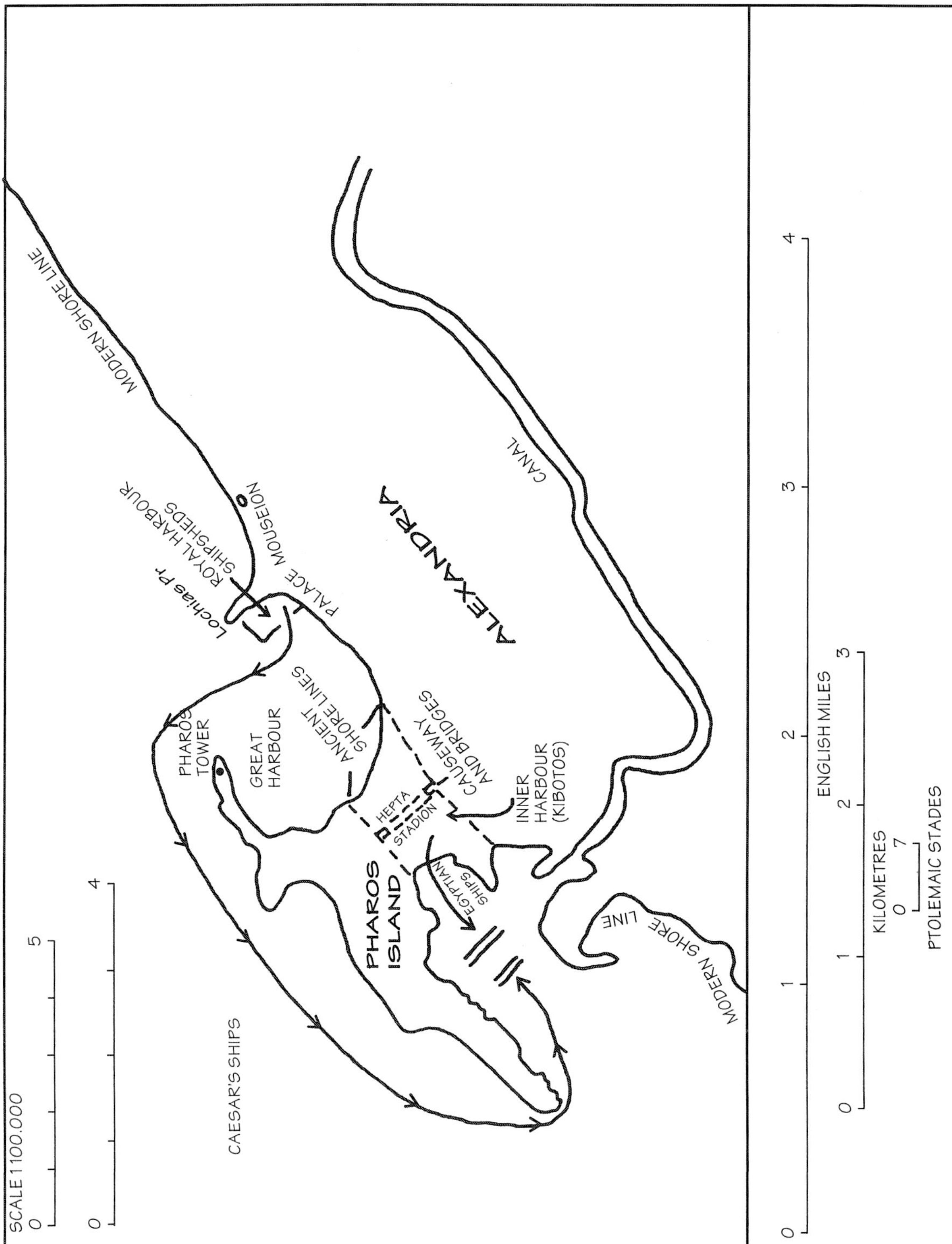

PLAN 6. *The Battle of Alexandria*

Caesar immediately found himself besieged in the part of the city which his forces occupied.

The centre of fighting was the main harbour, since the Egyptians tried to seize the warships, 50 of which had been sent to assist Pompey and had returned to their home port after Pharsalos.

These were: (*CBC*.3.111.3) 'all fours and fives fully equipped and manned in all respects for sea service'. In addition there were the 22 ships, all cataphract, which formed part of the normal Alexandrian garrison. If Achillas had seized these, he would have been able to expel Caesar's ships and control the harbour and the whole area of the sea, preventing provisions and reinforcements from reaching him. The vital issue was bitterly contested, but Caesar succeeded in burning all the ships mentioned and the remaining ships in the dockyards, since they occupied too wide an area to be guarded with his small force.

'He lost no time in landing troops from his ships near Pharos, [*CBC*.3.112.1] the high tower which gave its name to the island lying opposite Alexandria and forming the harbours. Earlier rulers had made a causeway by which, with a bridge, the island was connected to the land. Those who held Pharos controlled the eastern harbour entrance. Caesar accordingly, when the enemy was fighting the battle, put troops ashore, seized the island and garrisoned it. (*CBC*.3.112.8). Caesar fortified this district which contained a small part of the royal palace in which he had been given living quarters, and a theatre adjoining it which took the place of a citadel and had access to the harbour and the rest of the dockyards. In the following days he increased the fortifications'.

The *Bellum Alexandrinum*, which is attributed to Caesar's legate Aulus Hirtius (*HBA*), continues the narrative. The year was still 47 BC and Caesar consul. It begins with the statement that Caesar sent for 'ships of all kinds from Rhodes and from Syria and Kilikia'. These were the nearest possible sources of naval units. 'He also summoned archers from Crete and cavalry from Malchus king of the Nabataeans; and gave orders that catapults should be supplied from all sources, corn should be sent and reinforcements brought'. He also enlarged and improved the defences of his sector. The Alexandrians on the other hand pressed on with hostilities believing (*HBA*.3.4) that if they did not drive Caesar out Egypt would become a province instead of a kingdom; and they must do it quickly, since he was cut off by bad weather, and, because of the season, could not get help from overseas.

(*HBA*.9.3) Ships, sent by Domitius Calvinus, arrived with the thirty-seventh legion made up of surrendered Pompeians and with corn, arms, missiles and catapults; but they had to anchor 'above Alexandria' (i.e. west) on the coast of Africa, since a south-east wind, blowing for many days without ceasing, prevented them making harbour. They sent Caesar a *navigium actuarium* (under oar) to tell him they were delayed and were short of water. (*HBA*.10.1) To decide what to do he took his whole fleet out to meet them, with no decksoldiers since they could not be spared from the fortification. He sent oarsmen out to find water, and a number of these going too far after booty were taken by the enemy's cavalry. From them the enemy learnt of the presence of Caesar and the absence of decksoldiers, and decided not to forgo the opportunity. They accordingly manned with decksoldiers all the ships they had in service and met Caesar on his return voyage.

(*HBA*.10.6) Because of the absence of decksoldiers and the lateness of the hour when local knowledge would help the enemy, Caesar declined battle and pulled up those vessels he could in a place he thought inaccessible to the enemy.

'One Rhodian ship on Caesar's right wing was separated a good distance from the others; the enemy saw an opportunity and 4 cataphract and a number of open ships made a strong attack. Caesar had to give her help to avoid a shameful rebuke in face of the enemy, although he thought the Rhodians would deserve it if anything serious happened to them. Battle was joined with great spirit on the part of the Rhodians. Although in all encounters they shone in skill and courage, on that occasion in particular they did not bear the whole brunt, lest what was caused by their fault should turn out to be a reverse. So the engagement became a most favourable one. One enemy four was captured, another swamped and two cleared of decksoldiers, while a great number of decksoldiers besides in the other ships was killed. If night had not brought the engagement to an end, Caesar would have captured the whole enemy fleet. With the enemy in panic at this disaster and a light adverse wind blowing, Caesar brought into Alexandria the *naves onerariae* (carrying the 37th legion etc) under tow to his victorious ships'.

(*HBA*.12) The Alexandrians decided to concentrate on building up a fleet as a means of depriving Caesar of reinforcements and supplies. 'Furthermore the men of the city and coastal region were seamen, and those who had from youth up been trained by daily use were keen to go back to an asset which was natural and domestic; and they realised how proficient they were in the use of small boats. As a result they threw themselves as one man into the preparation of a fleet. They brought back to Alexandria the ships posted at all the mouths of the Nile to exact dues, and repaired old ships in hidden docks of the palace, which had not been in service for many years. Oars were made from roof timbers and poles.' As a result contrary to expectation they completed in a few days 22 fours and five fives; to these they added a number of smaller and open ships (by implication the fours and fives were cataphract). 'In the harbour having trials under oar to see what each of these could achieve they put on board especially good soldiers and prepared for fighting in every possible way'.

Caesar had nine Rhodian ships (for although ten were sent one went ashore in Egypt on the voyage out), eight Pontic, five Lycian, and 12 from Asia. Of these ten were fives and fours, the rest below this size and for the most part open.

This list of 34 ships implies that the ten fives and fours were in a class of larger ships all cataphract, and that the class of smaller ships included threes, and probably others e.g. *τριημιολίαι*, which were cataphract, although these were in a small minority (say ten, leaving 14 open vessels). Yet trusting in the courage of his soldiers, Caesar was preparing himself for battle knowing the (strength of) the enemy forces (i.e. 27 to ten in the larger class and an unknown number to 24 in the smaller).

(*HBA*.14) (Plan 6: Plutarch *Caesar* 49.3, Strabo 17.1.6, Ammianus 22.16.10) Caesar took his ships in column out of the eastern harbour where the (royal) *νεώρια* were and round Pharos. He offered battle with the Rhodians on the right wing and the Pontic ships on the left. Between these two (columns) he left a space of 400 paces (296 m: 17.4 m a ship) which seemed sufficient for deploying the 17 Rhodian and Pontic ships. Behind this line (i.e. when the two columns had been deployed in line abreast) the remaining 17 ships were distributed in support: he arranged and gave orders as to which ship should follow which, and which ship each should support.

(*HBA*.14.3) The Alexandrians did not hesitate to bring out and draw up their fleet. They put in the front line 22 ships (of the 27 fours and fives) and the rest they put in the second line in support. They brought out in addition a great number of smaller craft (*navigia*) with fire-bearing missiles in an attempt to scare our men by the number and noise and flame. (*HBA*.14.5) In between the two lines were shallows with a narrow crossing (Strabo characterises the western harbour (Eunostos) as difficult to enter); and men waited for some time to see which side would cross first because those who (first) entered the shallows to deploy their line or to withdraw in case of misfortune would seem to be the more at a disadvantage.

(*HBA*.15.1) The Rhodian commander Euphranor 'in greatness of spirit and in courage more like a Roman than a Greek' volunteered to go first, and Caesar gave the signal for battle. 'Four Rhodian ships advanced beyond the shallows and were surrounded and attacked by the Alexandrians. They stood up to the attack and deployed with skill and cleverness; and their experience was so effective that in spite of the unequal numbers none was broadside on to the enemy. None had her oars brushed off; but they were always coming head on in their movements. In the meantime other ships followed them. Then of course the lack of sea room led to the abandonment of skill, and the whole engagement was a matter of courage'.

'The battle was not a fair one, because if our men were driven back there was no refuge on sea or land for the defeated; while if we won, everything in the future was still at risk. On the other hand if they had gained the mastery with their ships, they would win completely; and if they had been mastered, they could yet try their luck again. The result was one five captured, and a two with its soldiers and oarsmen, and three swamped. All our ships were safe. The rest of the enemy ships fled to the town [on the island of Pharos] and men from the moles [not the Heptastadion] and the overhanging buildings protected them and prevented our men from approaching'.

It appears that the Alexandrians had retaken Pharos on which Caesar (*CBC*.3.111.6 and 112.4) says he placed a garrison on his arrival and which he describes as an island on which 'there are the houses of Alexandrians and a village the size of a town' connected by a causeway (the Heptastadion) to the city. It is this island and the attached moles, from which the Alexandrian ships were protected, that Hirtius now (*HBA*.17) says that Caesar decided to attack 'lest this should happen more often'. He puts ten cohorts (@ 600), selected light-armed troops and men of the Gallic cavalry he thought suitable on smaller vessels and *scaphae;* one part of the island he attacked with cataphract ships to distract the enemy's attention, offering large rewards for the first to take the island.

'At first they stood up equally to our men's attack; at the same time they were both fighting from the roofs of the houses and defending the beaches under arms, while for our men there was no easy approach because of the roughness of the ground; and with mobility and cleverness they protected the narrow places from *scaphae* and five warships. But as soon as a few of our men, trying known places and shallows, gained a footing on the beach and others followed them and regularly attacked those who stood on the level beach, all the Pharites fled. When these had been driven away and a guard of the harbour left, our men moored ships on the beaches and near the village and landed from the ships to keep a watch over the buildings'.

(*HBA*.25) The last sea battle of the Alexandrian war was caused by an attempt of the Alexandrians to cut off Caesar's seaborne supplies by sending ships to Kanopos. In reply Caesar ordered his whole fleet under the command of Tiberius Nero to move there. Euphranor went with the Rhodian ships, and the only incident recorded by Hirtius in the battle which follows was the death of Euphranor. When the two fleets met, and 'Euphranor, as was his custom, was the first to join battle and rammed and swamped an enemy four, he pursued the next ship rather far and his own followers did not come up fast enough so that he was surrounded by the Alexandrians. No one came to his aid either because they thought he had enough protection in himself from his courage and good luck or because they feared for their own safety. So he, who alone in that battle distinguished himself, was the only one to perish togther with his victorious four'. It does not sound as if the battle was otherwise notable.

(*HBA*.26–33) The arrival overland of Mithridates of Pergamon (in March 48 BC) with a large army raised in Syria and Kilikia, and his immediate capture of Pelousion, 'the gate of Egypt by land', Hirtius says, 'as Pharos is her gate by sea', led to the surrender of the Alexandrians and the establishment as rulers of Egypt of Cleopatra, the elder of the two daughters of Ptolemy Auletes, and his elder son. Caesar left for Syria, and then the province of Asia. After defeating Pharnakes of Pontos at Zela he settled the affairs of the province, and after giving Syria his attention returned to Italy in July and to Rome in October.

Caesar's invasion of Africa *(Map L (i))*

The invasion of Africa is the third in a remarkable series of naval operations beginning with Julius Caesar's fight for Alexandria. In the African invasion, what must have seemed to Caesar's officers and men a careless neglect of obvious precautions and a reckless abandonment of the rules of naval movement, turned into a recipe for success which could hardly have been achieved in any other way. The writer of the commentary on the African war, possibly Hirtius, gives enough information to enable the reader to appreciate Julius Caesar's strategy; but he does not appear to understand fully what was in his mind.

(*HBAF*.1) Caesar arrived in Lilybaion on the 19th of December and announced that he wished to embark immediately for Africa, although he had only one legion of newly recruited men and six hundred cavalry. He set up his tent beside the shore with the waves breaking beside it. He did this to prevent anyone hoping that there would be any delay for him; and so that everyone should be prepared (for embarkation) every day and hour. At that time of year it happened that there was no weather suitable for a sea voyage; nevertheless he kept the oarsmen and soldiers on board and lost no opportunity of setting out. This was particularly in spite of the messages from inhabitants of Africa that the Pompeians' forces consisted of an infinite number of cavalry, king Juba's four legions and a great force of light-armed men, Scipio's ten legions, 120 elephants and a number of fleets (i.e. those under Attius Varus, Cnaeus Pompeius, M. Octavius and the main fleet under Scipio). Nevertheless he was not deterred and 'put trust in his heart and his expectation'. His staff must have thought that he had taken leave of his senses.

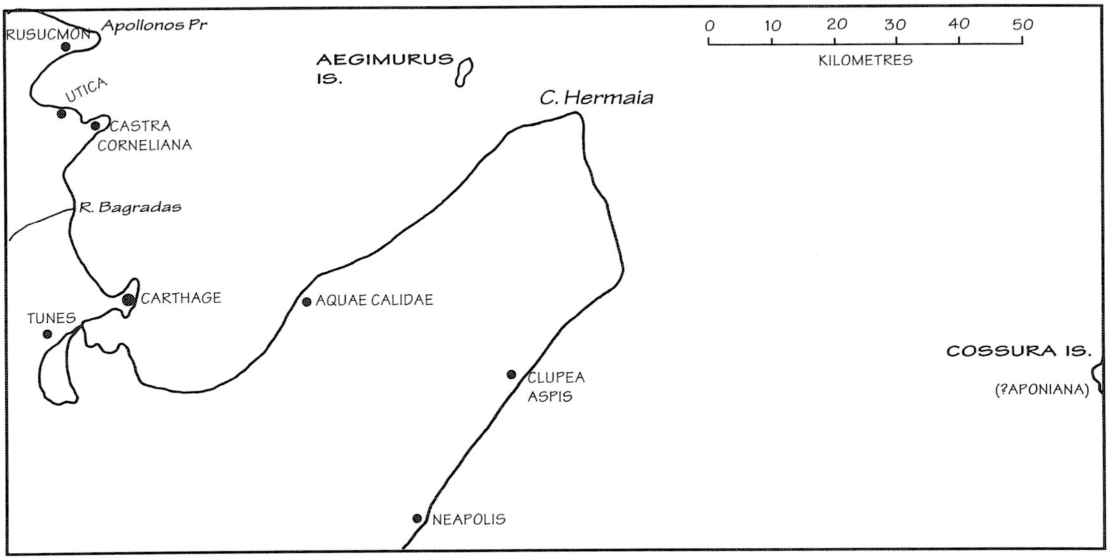

MAP L (i). *Julius Caesar's invasion of Africa*

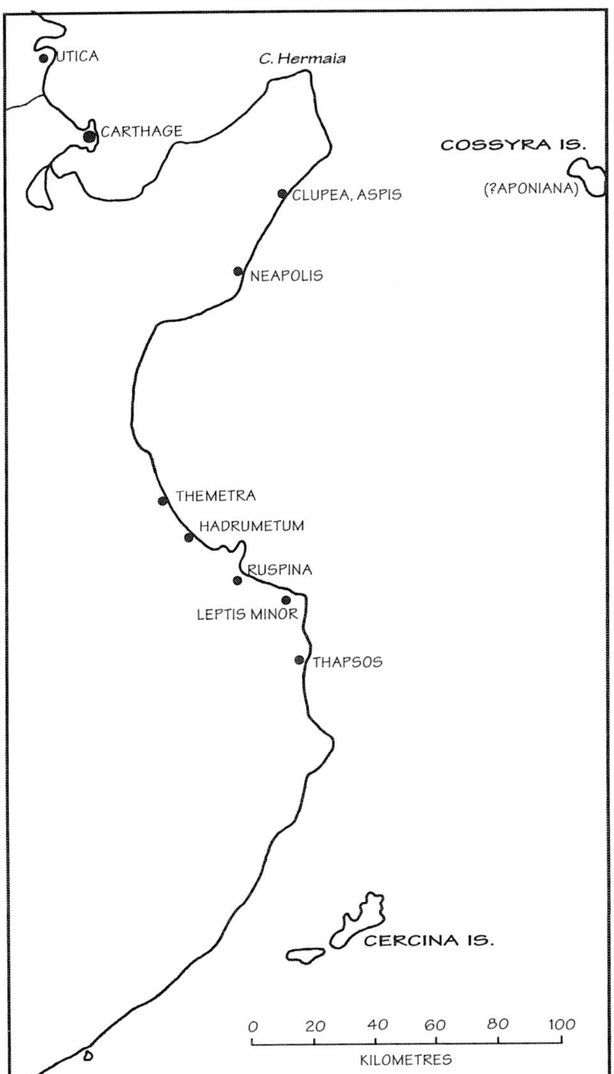

MAP L (ii).

As he necessarily waited for the weather to improve 'day by day the number of warships increased and more *onerariae* were assembled at a rendezvous: four legions of newly recruited men arrived, a veteran legion and up to two thousand cavalry'.

(*HBAF*.2) As soon as each legion arrived it was embarked on the warships and the cavalry on *onerariae*. He ordered the greater number of ships to go on ahead and make for the island Aponiana[5] at a distance of (...) from Lilybaion. To the praetor Alienus, whose province Sicily was, he gave orders about all the details and in particular about speedily embarking the rest of the army. After giving his commands he went aboard on the 27th December and immediately caught up the rest of the ships. Carried by a steady, fast, wind after four days[6] he came within sight of Africa with a few warships. The *onerariae*, except for a few, had been scattered by the wind, and wandering had made for different places. The fleet passed Clupea (Aspis) and then Neapolis. It left (behind) a number of fortified places and towns not far from the sea.

(*HBAF*.3) 'He reached Hadrumetum, where there was a Pompeian garrison under the command of C. Considius and where Cnaeus Calpurnius Piso appeared from Clupea along the shore with cavalry and about 3,000 Mauri. He stayed there a short time in front of the harbour, until the rest of the warships should catch up and disembarked his army, numbering at that time 3,000 footsoldiers and 150 cavalry. Pitching camp in front of the city he settled down without giving any provocation and forbade his whole force to plunder. Meanwhile the townspeople manned the walls (of Hadrumetum) with armed men and placed themselves in numbers in front of the gate to offer resistance: their strength was the equivalent of two legions. Caesar rode round the city, examined the terrain and returned to camp'.

'Quite a number blamed Caesar and said he was imprudent and had not told the helmsmen and commanders what precise place to set course for, or as had been his custom on previous occasions given them sealed orders so that when the time came they should read them and all without exception make for a certain place. Caesar had not forgotten this; as a matter of fact he was expecting that no harbour on the coast of Africa to which fleets might go would be for certain safe and free from enemy garrison, and after disembarking he was looking out for an opportunity offered by chance'.

This last paragraph shows the extent of Caesar's gamble. He knew that all the harbours would be defended and the coastal towns garrisoned by Pompeian troops. On the other hand the main armies were in winter quarters and the main fleets hauled up; hence his haste to be in a position in Lilybaion to take advantage of any break in the weather and a favourable wind. This window of opportunity had occurred and he had begun the invasion with such forces as were ready. But he was unable to inform those that followed of a rendezvous, since he reckoned that he had to get across and then look for 'an opportunity offered by chance'. His first attempt was at Hadrumetum, but in spite of his unprovocative behaviour the city appeared hostile. Since his force was outnumbered, and reconnaissance offered no solution, he tried negotiation with Considius which was rejected, and decided that he had to try elsewhere.

On 1 January Caesar pitched camp near Ruspina, and then after a few days moved to Leptis Minor where the citizens were friendly. (*HBAF*.7.3) Further 'quite a number of warships and *onerariae* had chanced to arrive at that same place; the rest, as he was told, not knowing where they were, had been seen to make for Utica'. In the meantime, because of the straying ships, Caesar did not leave the seacoast or move inland and kept all his cavalry on board probably to prevent the land being ravaged: he gave orders for water to be brought to the ships. The oarsmen in the meantime who left the ships to find water were wounded and a few killed by sudden and unexpected attacks of the Maurish cavalry... (*HBAF*.8.1) He sent messengers to Sardinia with letters asking for immediate supplies and reinforcements. He also unloaded some of the warships and sent them back to Sicily for the second load of supplies under Rabirius Postumus, whom in the meantime he sent out with ten warships to look for the stray *onerariae* and at the same time keep the sea free of enemies. He also sent Sallustius Crispus to the island of Cercina which was rich in grain (*HBAF*.8.3, Polybios 3.96.12, Strabo 17.3.13).

Caesar's situation was improving but it was still precarious. (*HBAF*.9) 'He moved to Ruspina from where he foraged for grain and then returned, so as not to leave the maritime cities (of Leptis and

Ruspina) behind him without garrison and to preserve them as garrisoned home ports for the fleet. He accordingly gave orders for all available wood (*ligna*) to be brought into the city; and left Saserna there with one legion while he himself went by night on board the ships in the harbour (2 miles away) with seven cohorts. He was preparing next morning to go in search of the straying ships himself when suddenly the ships about which he was anxious began coming in'. (*HBAF*.11.2) He immediately ordered the troops to disembark and parade under arms on the beach to welcome the arrival of the soldiers. The ships were quickly brought in and the soldiers and cavalry returned with him to Ruspina where camp was pitched. Caesar then went out with 30 light-armed cohorts to bring in corn. His plan was then understood: he intended without the enemy's knowledge to go with the fleet to bring help to the *onerariae* which had gone astray in case by chance they had fallen in with the Pompeian fleet. He also did not want those of his own solders who had been left on guard (at Leptis and Ruspina) to know what he was doing lest they would surrender through fear, realising their own small numbers and the large numbers of the enemy. His foraging expedition ended in an engagement.

(*HBAF*.20) Caesar continued to fortify Ruspina, connecting the city with the harbour (2 miles away) by a wall and the camp to the harbour by another wall, to ensure safe communication and enable reinforcement to reach him safely. Missiles and catapults were brought into the camp from the ships. He armed some of the oarsmen from Gaul and Rhodes and some decksoldiers and sent for them to come into the camp to place them in the enemy's fashion in between the cavalry. He also increased the numbers of his forces with many archers from Palestine, Syria and elsewhere (who had presumably been serving in the fleet). Expecting a second engagement, he made other military preparations, which included sending for iron and lead from Sicily.

(*HBAF*.21.3) Caesar's *onerariae* were dangerously astray, not knowing the area and the position of the camps. Individual ships were being attacked and burnt by numbers of *scaphae* which put out. Caesar accordingly placed squadrons around the islands and harbours to enable supplies to get through more safely.

(*HBAF*.23 3) Cn. Pompeius urged on by Cato in Utica took a fleet of small ships, 'including some with rams' against the Mauretanian king Bogus and made an unsuccessful attack on Ascurum. Thereupon he withdrew to the Balearic islands.

Scipio brought his army to Hadrumetum and confined Caesar within his fortifications, thus presenting him with an acute supply problem since nothing had yet come from Sicily or Sardinia; and at that time of year (January) ships could not safely move at sea. He sent urgent commands to Alienus and Rabirius Postumus in Sicily to send him an army without delay or excuses about winter or winds. Vergilius, the Pompeian of praetorian rank who was governor of the maritime city of Thapsos, noticed that individual *onerariae* with troops of Caesar's on board were wandering uncertain of their position or of their camps. Seizing the opportunity he put soldiers and archers on board an *actuaria* which he had and attached to it *scaphae* belonging to warships. He then began to pursue the individual Caesarian ships. He put out against a number and had been driven off and put to flight; but he did not cease his attacks.

(*HBAF*.34) When Sallustius Crispus reached Cercina the Pompeian governor fled. Finding a sufficient number of *onerariae* there he was able to load them with grain and send them to Caesar at Ruspina. 'Meanwhile Alienus at Lilybaion had embarked two legions, 800 Gallic cavalry, 1000 slingers and archers and the second consignment of suppies on *onerariae* and sent them to Caesar in Africa. The ships had a favourable wind and reached safely the harbour near Caesar's camp at Ruspina'. Thus Caesar, fortified at the same time with grain and reinforcements, at last laid aside his anxiety, with his men encouraged and the supply position eased. He gave orders that the legions and horsemen should be rested from their weariness and seasickness, and sent them to their quarters in the various forts. (*HBAF*.37) Hirtius describes the reinforcement supplied by 'the second consignment' as consisting of 'two veteran legions, cavalry and light armed soldiers'. He says also that Caesar ordered the *onerariae* to return at once for the transport of the rest of the army. On 27 January Caesar began his moves from Ruspina to engage Scipio's army. His gamble had been successful. He was now within sight of a position in which he could meet Scipio in battle on land and sea.

(*HBAF*.44.1) From the second supply fleet one

ship, a three, blown off course to Thapsos, was intercepted by Vergilius with warship *scaphae* and other small craft. A second ship, a three from the same fleet blown off course to Aegimurus, was captured by the fleet of Varus and Octavius. On board were veteran soldiers and a centurion. There was apparently a squadron of Caesar's warships, riding at anchor and maintaining regular patrols off shore, detailed to protect Caesarian ships coming into the area of Thapsos. Caesar ordered the punishment of those responsible for letting the first ship fall into Vergilius's hands (*HBAF*.46.4). This squadron is mentioned later (*HBAF*.53) when two legions, the tenth and the eighth, (which were not those sent by Alienus from Sicily with 'the second consignment' the thirteenth and fourteenth), 'setting out from Sicily in *onerariae*, were not far from the harbour of Ruspina, when they caught sight of the Caesarian ships moored near Thapsos, which they took to be Pompeian. Being anxious not to come unawares upon enemy ships waiting there in ambush, they made for the open sea under sail; and, after some time and a lot of tossing about, many days later reached Caesar, enduring thirst and hunger'. These units must have been part of 'the remaining army' for which the ships which brought 'the second consignment' went back.

(*HBAF*.62.1) The main Pompeian fleet, apart from the ships of Varus and Octavius mentioned in 44.1 and the fleet of Pompeius which had withdrawn to Spain, had been laid up for the winter at Utica; but was launched when news came of the arrival of the legions from Sicily. Scipio manned them with Gaetulian oarsmen and decksoldiers; and their preparation for action, luckily for Caesar, took some time.

Varus moved 55 ships from Utica to Hadrumetum to lie in ambush for the Caesarian fleet.

'Unaware of their arrival Caesar sent L. Cispius with 27 ships to the Thapsos area to take up station as a guard for his supply fleet. He sent Q. Aquila also with 13 warships to Hadrumetum for the same purpose. Cispius reached his destination quickly, Aquila tossed about by rough weather was unable to round the promontory and took himself and his fleet rather a long way out of sight in finding a bay sheltered from the high wind. The rest of the fleet, beached near Leptis, stood without guards, the oarsmen ashore and widely dispersed on the coast, some going to the town to buy victuals'.

(HBAF.62.5) 'Varus had learned all these facts from a deserter and seizing the opportunity emerged from the docks at Hadrumetum in the second watch. He reached Leptis at first light with his whole fleet, burned two *onerariae* which had anchored at a distance from the harbour and captured two fives without guards and unopposed'.

'When Caesar heard what had happened he immediately rode to Leptis and told all the ships to follow him. He went on board a small boat, and, meeting Aquila at sea frightened and in a panic at the sight of such a large number of enemy ships, started following the enemy. Meanwhile Varus, disturbed at Caesar's speed and boldness turned his whole fleet and tried to flee to Hadrumetum. Caesar followed for four miles, recovered a captured five with all her decksoldiers and 130 enemy guards and captured nearby the three which had stayed to fight with her complement of oarsmen and decksoldiers. The rest of the enemy ships rounded the promontory and all reached Hadrumetum and the dockyard. Caesar was unable to get round the promontory with the same wind and remained at anchor that night. Next day he went to Hadrumetum, burned the *onerariae* outside the dock, the other ships having been either hauled out of water or taken into the dockyard, and remained a short time in case the enemy wished to fight at sea. Then he went back to camp'.

Caesar had established his fleet's superiority.

After this spirited action no further naval activity is reported in the African war, brought to an end a few weeks later at the land battle of Thapsos. On the Ides of June (13th) Caesar went on board his fleet for the voyage to Sardinia; and fifteen days later took ship from there. 'Sailing along the coast and delayed by bad weather in various ports, he arrived on the 28th day in Rome'. Before the end of the year he had left to deal with the last Pompeian resistance, in Spain. In March of the following year (45 BC) that resistance was defeated at the land battle of Munda at which Cnaeus Pompeius fell, and in October he was back in Rome. On the Ides of March in 44 BC he was assassinated in the Senate house.

4. COMMAND OF THE SEA: 44–31 BC

There is a turbulent period of 13 years (for which Appian is the main source) between the assassination of Julius Caesar in March 44 and the naval defeat by Octavian, Caesar's adopted son, of Antony and Cleopatra in September 31 BC. It covers a struggle by a few ambitious men for the autocratic rule, to which Caesar had shown the way, of a Roman empire now stretching from Phoenicia to Spain and embracing all the countries on the Mediterranean seaboard. In this struggle deployment of naval forces naturally played a significant, and in the end a decisive part.

The fleets by which Caesar had moved, reinforced and supplied his armies against Pompey himself in Macedonia, and after Pharsalos against Pompey's supporters in Asia and Spain, in Egypt and north Africa, remained in being for his successors to find and use.

At Caesar's death Antony was at the centre of power, and succeeded in obtaining from the Senate the crucial province of Macedonia which was both near Italy and the station of an army of five legions which Caesar had been making ready for the invasion of Parthia. Dolabella, Caesar's fleet commander and his recent choice as consul, given Syria by the Senate, was opposed on landing by Trebonius the governor of Smyrna and one of Caesar's murderers. Dolabella succeeded in seizing him and putting him to death. The chief conspirators, Brutus and Cassius, rewarded by the Senate with the minor provinces of Crete and Cyrenaica, (Ap.*CW*.3.24) decided to go to Syria and Macedonia where Caesar had previously sent them (Ap.*CW*.4.57), and take control by force. They were 'collecting troops and money' and Trebonius had been fortifying the towns of Asia in their interest.

(Ap.*CW*.4.60) Dolabella and his lieutenant Phigelus gathered a hired fleet from the usual Asian sources, Rhodes, Lykia, Pamphylia and Kilikia. Dolabella advanced on Syria by land and sea, making his base at Laodikeia in coastal Syria on a promontory with an adjacent harbour. Cassius besieged Dolabella there and sent to Phoenicia, Lykia and Rhodes for ships, being ignored by all except the Sidonians. A naval engagement followed in which a considerable number of ships were put out of action on each side, Dolabella capturing five with their crews. Cassius renewed his requests for naval aid writing also to Cleopatra and Serapion, her commander in Cyprus. The people of Tyre, Arados, and Serapion (not knowing beforehand what Cleopatra wished) sent 'all the ships they had'. Cleopatra excused herself on the grounds of plague and famine in Egypt, but in reality she was in league with Dolabella because of her loyalty to Caesar. For the same reason she had sent Dolabella the four legions (left by Caesar in Egypt: Ap. *CW*.4.63) through Alienus (see above p. 143, 144) She had another fleet to send him, but the weather kept it in harbour. The Rhodians and Lycians said that they would not help either Cassius or Brutus in civil wars: the ships they had sent to Dolabella were escort vessels and they were not aware that they were fighting on his side. In another sea battle Dolabella was defeated; when Cassius took Laodikeia, Dolabella committed suicide.

(Ap.*CW*.4.63) Hearing that Cleopatra was about to move to Octavian and Antony with 'a fleet of heavy ships' (*βαρεῖ στόλῳ*), Cassius turned to Egypt with the intention of preventing the expedition and punishing Cleopatra for the plan. His intervention was prevented by a sudden summons from Brutus with the information that Octavian and Antony were at that moment crossing the Adriatic. (Ap.*CW*.4.65) The two leaders conferred, Brutus wanting to move to Macedonia, Cassius to reduce first the Rhodians and Lycians, both with fleets, which might attack them in the rear when they were facing Octavian and Antony. They decided to move, Brutus against the Lycians, Cassius against Rhodes. 'As Cassius was going to join battle with men who were very strong in naval warfare (*κρατίστοις τὰ ναυτικά*) he fitted out his ships, manned and trained them at Myndos'.

The Battle of Myndos

The most respected Rhodians were anxious at the prospect of battle with the Romans, but the common people were confident recalling past actions against men of a different sort. They launched 33 of their best ships' (against Cassius's 80 heavy ships). They sent a message to Cassius telling him not to despise them or disregard the treaty between Rome and Rhodes. They would give assistance if asked to do so by the Senate. (Ap.*CW*.4.71) They put to sea with 33 ships against Cassius at Myndos intending to alarm him by their sudden attack. Appian describes the battle as follows.

'Using their oars to show off their skill they bivouacked for the first day on Knidos and on the following day they were seen by Cassius's men (at

Myndos) coming in from the open sea. Cassius put out against them in astonishment; and the action was a contest of physical strength and naval power on both sides. The Rhodians, with their light ships, were accustomed to move through the enemy's line quickly and then round them and to employ manoeuvres of return. The Romans on the other hand, on their heavier ships, when with their weightier impetus they made contact, bore down upon the enemy as in a battle of footsoldiers. Cassius surrounded the enemy with a great number of ships, so that the Rhodians were unable to move round or through the line, but rammed them only bow to bow. As they pulled back their skill was destroyed by the lack of sea room in the confined space, while the ramming and turning manoeuvres (*ἀποσιμώσεις* p. 363) were feeble against the heavier Roman ships, whereas for the Romans they were effective against the ships with lighter build. In the end three Rhodian ships were captured with their crews and two were broken up (*ἀνερράγησαν* cf Thuk.7.34) and swamped; the rest escaped to Rhodes in a damaged condition. All the Roman ships retired to Myndos and most of those that were damaged were repaired'.

(Ap.*CW*.4.72) Cassius then moved to Loryma on the coast opposite Rhodes and sent troops across to the city on *ὁλκάδες*, thus showing confidence that the Rhodian ships would not dare to challenge the move. In person he put out at the head of eighty ships equipped in a formidable manner. The Rhodians did come out, lost one more ship and were surrounded. The town was then besieged, Cassius using collapsible turrets (*πύργοι ἐπτυγμένοι*) which he put up on his ships; and was finally taken after betrayal. (Ap.*CW*.4.74) Cassius then sent a subordinate commander Statius Murcus with 60 cataphract ships to lie in ambush near Taenaron (in the Peloponnese) for Cleopatra, who was (still) planning to sail across to help Octavian and Antony with a large fleet of very heavy ships (*μεγάλῳ στόλῳ καὶ παρασκευῇ βαρυτάτῃ*).

(Ap.*CW*.4.75) With the troops he had collected in Macedonia (8 legions, a large force of cavalry) and the treasure from Thrace Brutus subdued Lykia; and with the Lycian fleet as well as his own ships he moved to Abydos to await Cassius who was coming with his fleet, so that they could both cross to Sestos together. Murcus at Tainaron learnt that Cleopatra's fleet, on its way to Octavian and Antony, had been damaged by a storm and that Cleopatra had returned to Egypt. He accordingly took his ships to Brundisium and moored at the island opposite the harbour to prevent the armies of Octavian and Antony crossing to Macedonia. Nevertheless, with the help of a strong wind in his favour and a few warships and towers mounted on rafts, Antony, who was still at Brundisium, was able to secure the passage of detachments of troops in *ὁλκάδες* which he sent across from time to time.

(Ap.*CW*.4.83–4) Sextus Pompeius, the younger son of Pompey the Great, had remained in Spain after his elder brother's death at Munda and built up a following there. On Caesar's assassination he had been recalled by the Senate and given his father's 'command of the sea'. He came to Massalia and added to the ships he had brought from Spain those he found in various harbours. When the second triumvirate was established he moved his already considerable fleet to Sicily which the governor Bithynius surrendered to him. There he was joined by many refugees from the proscriptions at Rome. He now had the Sicilian fleet under his control and a considerable army. His forces included many seamen from Africa and Spain. He was then well off for officers (*ἡγεμόνες*), ships and infantry. (Ap.*CW*.4.85) 'Thinking that it would be an easy task to remove Sextus from the province', on his way to answer Antony's request to help him against Brutus's commander Murcus at Brundisium, Octavian sent Salvidienus with a fleet to the straits of Messana (Map M2, p. 151) and he himself marched down through Italy to Rhegion.

A sea battle followed between the two fleets around the Skyllaion promontory, in which Sextus's ships 'being lighter and crewed by more skilled men were superior in speed and seamanship' (and unlike the Rhodians at Myndos, to whom the same description applies, were not outnumbered more than two to one). The Roman ships were in trouble being heavier and bigger. When the usual rough sea developed and the water was driven this way and that by the current, one side was in less trouble being accustomed to the rough sea, but Salvidienus's men[7] neither steady on their feet nor any longer able to recover their oars (i.e. the oarsmen, who 'caught crabs'); nor finding the rudders responsive '(i.e. the helmsmen) 'were in a state of confusion'. Salvidienus was the first to withdraw his ships; and Sextus followed. A roughly equal number were put out of action on each side. Salvidienus returned to his harbour of Balaros 'in front of (πρό) the crossing' to repair his damaged and strained ships. Octavian, leaving the threat from Sextus on one side for the present as less urgent than the threat from Brutus and Cassius, was forced to sail round Sicily on his way to Antony at Brundisium.

(Ap.*CW*.4.86) On Octavian's approach Murcus withdrew a short distance from Brundisium and kept watch for the *ὁλκάδες*. They had an escort of threes but made the passage without anxiety having the benefit of strong and favourable wind. The transports returned, embarked the rest of the army and returned under full sail, together with Octavian and Antony. It is clear that the threes were there not only to protect the *ὁλκάδες* but to tow them if necessary (p. 267). Brutus and Cassius then sent Domitius Ahenobarbus the younger with 50 ships to join Murcus in his useful work. 'Murcus and Domitius, with 130 warships and a greater number of auxiliaries (*ὑπηρετικαί*) and a large force of soldiers moved about causing trouble'.

(Ap.*CW*.4.87) Octavian and Antony had sent in advance into Macedonia and Thrace beyond Philippoi eight legions under Decidius and Norbanus to block the passage of Brutus and Cassius's army moving westwards after the passage of the Hellespont. The latter had 19 infantry legions as well as other troops. Marching through Lysimacheia (Kardia), the gate of the Thracian Chersonese, towards Ainos and Maroneia, they successfully by-passed the army under Decidius and Norbanus and accompanied by a second fleet under Tillius reached the sea coast south of Philippoi where Tillius met them. Since Appian (*CW*.4.133) gives the total number of ships in Brutus and Cassius's fleet as 'above 200' Tillius's squadron is likely to have been more than 70 ships. This number would have been thought sufficient for the Aegean where no naval confrontation was to be expected. If Brutus and Cassius were to win the prospective land battle they would need strong naval protection in the Adriatic to secure the crossing of their armies to Italy. (Ap.*CW*.4.106) Brutus and Cassius made their camps on each side of the 'gate between Europe and Asia'. Their supply base was Thasos and their fleet (*τριήρεις* = warships in Appian's usage) were moored at Neapolis (70 stades away: 12.4 km). Antony's base was at Amphipolis which Norbanus had fortified. He tried to cut off Brutus and Cassius's supplies from Thasos, while his own supplies were threatened by Tillius's fleet.

The first battle of Philippoi (October 42) resulted in Cassius's suicide but was not decisive. (Ap.*CW*.4.115) On the same day, Appian says, Murcus and Domitius Ahenobarbus with their 130 warships in the Adriatic met a convoy of *ὁλκάδες* protected by a few *τριήρεις*. The transports carried two legions of infantry, a praetorian cohort of about 2000 men, four squadrons of cavalry and a large body of picked men. The first few transports escaped under sail; but the wind suddenly dropping the rest drifted on the open sea in a dead calm 'delivered up to their enemies by some god'. They attacked each ship at no danger to themselves, and broke it up; nor could the accompanying threes surrounded in their small number do anything to help. The greater part of the men surrendered to their enemies. 17 threes surrendered and Murcus's men accepted the crews' oath of allegiance to themselves. Their commander Calvinus returned to Brundisium five days later in his own ship.

Brutus, who realised that Antony and Octavian were facing starvation, was unwilling to fight a second battle, but was forced by his men and defeated. He committed suicide.

Sea power after Philippoi

(Ap.*CW*.5.1) After the defeat and death of Brutus and Cassius the victors divided the land forces between them; and Octavian returned to Italy while Antony went first to Ephesos and then to Kilikia where he joined Cleopatra at Tarsos.

Cassius Parmesius had been left in Asia by the Republicans with ships and the task of raising money. After the first engagement he selected 30 Rhodian ships, burning the others so that Rhodes would be powerless in a possible revolt, added them to his own and departed. Clodius, sent by Brutus to Rhodes with 13 ships, found the Rhodians in revolt after the second battle and Brutus's death. He removed the Roman garrison of 3000 and joined Parmesius. They were joined by another Republican commander, Turulius, with a large fleet and a large sum of money extracted from Rhodes.

'To this fleet, seeing that it was now a powerful one, there gathered all those who were in charge of naval services (*ὑπηρεσίαι*) and manned it with decksoldiers from wherever they could and oarsmen from slaves, prisoners of war and, as they moved to the islands, from the islanders. Others joined them, including Cicero's son, and leading men from Thasos'. (It would seem likely that Tillius's fleet also did so.) 'They soon had a large number of officers (ἡγεμόνες) of the army and ships. They also added a force which had brought Crete over to Brutus and moved to the Ionian sea (Adriatic) to join Murcus and Domitius Ahenobarbus who were there in command of a large force'.

The Republican fleet now split into two parts, one under Murcus moving to Sicily to join Sextus, the rest remaining with Ahenobarbus. Appian later (Ap.*CW*.5.25–26) reports Murcus's force as having consisted of two legions, 500 archers and eighty ships, and Ahenobarbus as moving round the Adriatic with 70 ships, two legions of soldiers and a force of archers and slingers, light-armed troops and gladiators. There he devastated the regions under the triumvirs, attacked Brundisium, capturing some of Octavian's 'τριήρεις' and burning others. In reply Octavian could only send a legion to Brundisium.

Antony, after spending the winter of 41–40 in Alexandria, moved to Asia and from there to Athens where he joined his wife Fulvia, who had come from Brundisium, and his mother Julia, who had taken refuge with Sextus and had been sent by him with warships from Sicily. She was accompanied by some leading Pompeians whose aim was to bring Antony and Sextus into alliance against Octavian. Antony's reply was that he would ally himself with Sextus in a war against Octavian, but so long as Octavius kept his side of the bargain would try to bring the three of them together.

At this point Appian says (*CW*.5.53) that 'Octavian considered himself to be far superior to Antony, Sextus and Ahenobarbus in military strength since he had more than 40 legions, but as he had not a single ship and no opportunity to build any, while they had 500, he was afraid that they might bring famine to Italy by patrolling the coasts' and setting up a blockade. As far as Sextus was concerned this possibility was a real one. If Octavian really had no ships then, in addition to the loss of his ships at Brundisium, he must have lost those sent under Salvidienus.

(Ap.*CW*.5.55–71) Antony moved from Athens to Kerkyra and from there into the Adriatic 'with a small army and 200 ships which he had built in Asia'. Learning that Ahenobarbus was coming to meet him with a fleet and a large number of soldiers, Antony advanced to the encounter with five of his best ships, ordering the others to follow at a distance. Ahenobarbus came on with his whole army and all his fleet rowing at a high rate of striking (μετ' ὀξείας εἰρεσίας). The two fleets approached each other with flags flying. Antony's lictor, as was customary when a superior commander met one of inferior rank, requested Ahenobarbus to dip his flag. He did. The two moved amicably to Brundisium, which closed its gates against them. Antony laid siege. Octavian arrived and eventually a reconciliation was effected. In the treaty of Brundisium (October 40 BC) the two leaders divided the empire between them, and in the following year Octavian and Antony met Sextus at Aenaria near Puteoli. Sextus came 'with many ships of the best kind, himself on board a splendid six (λαμπρᾶς ἑξήρους)'. The agreement known as the treaty of Misenum was recognised by all parties as a temporary truce; but it may have gone some way to alleviate Sextus's blockade which had led to acute famine in Rome.

Octavian against Sextus at sea

(Ap.*CW*.5.77) Urged by his fleet commander Menodoros to consider the treaty as no more than a truce, Pompeius immediately began to build ships and recruit crews. Piracy, possibly stimulated by Pompeius, was again common. Menodoros, in the meantime, came over to Octavian with Sardinia and Corsica, three legions and a large number of light-armed troops. Octavian brought warships from Ravenna, an army from Gaul and all the rest of his military and naval equipment hurriedly from Ravenna to Brundisium and Puteoli. He built towers on the coast 'to prevent Sextus raiding it again'. Also, 'he ordered the building of new 'τριήρεις' at Rome and Ravenna and sent for a large army from Illyria. (Ap.*CW*.5.80) 'He then ordered Cornificius from Ravenna to bring with him to Tarentum the complete expeditionary force (παρασκευή).

(Map M1) Early in 38 BC when everything he had in hand was ready, Octavian moved against Sicily, going himself from Tarentum, while Calvisius Sabinus and Menodoros moved from Etruria. The infantry marched round to Rhegion; and everything was done with speed and enthusiasm. Sextus heard

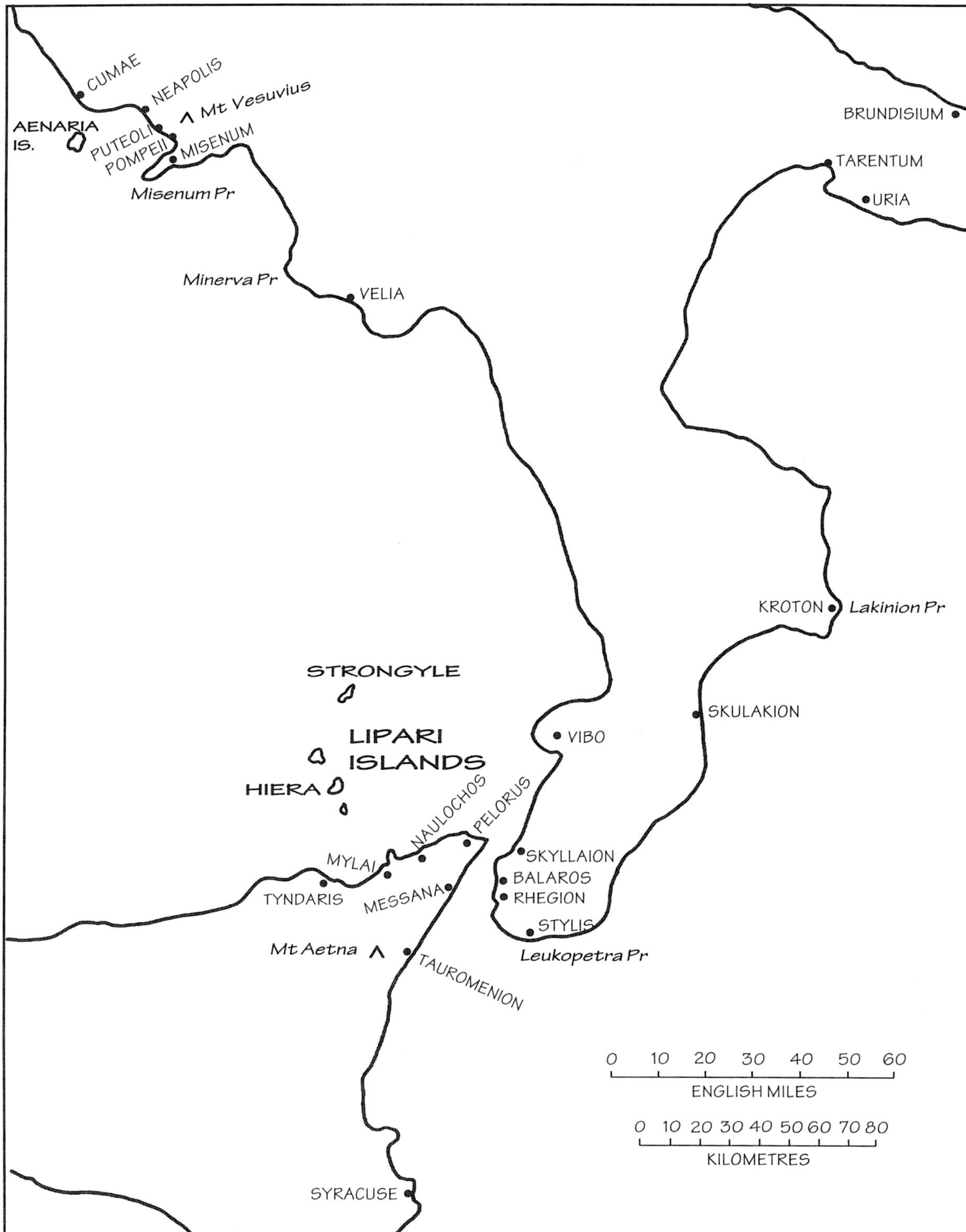

MAP M (i). *Octavian's naval campaigns 38 and 36 BC*

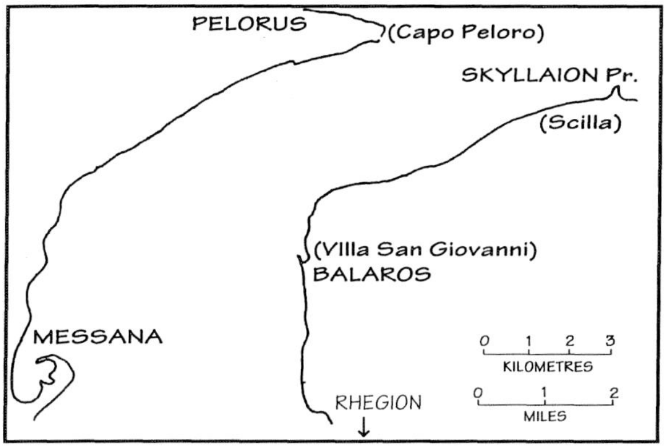

MAP M (ii). *The Straits of Messana*

of Menodoros's desertion as Octavian was already moving to the attack. In face of the attack from both quarters he himself awaited Octavian at Messana, while he ordered Menekrates, who was a particular enemy of Menodoros, at the head of a large fleet to confront Calvisius and Menodoros. Menekrates accordingly came in sight of his enemies about the late evening out at sea. They withdrew into the bay north of Cumae and rested for the night, while Menekrates passed on to Aenaria.

The battle of Cumae

(Ap.*CW*.5.81) At first dawn Calvisius and Menodoros moved along the gulf very close to the shore in a crescent-shaped order (στόλος) to prevent the enemy from making a breakthrough (διέκπλους). Menekrates again came into sight and immediately approached at speed with a rush. Having nothing much to achieve against enemies not putting out to sea, he was trying to force them ashore by exerting pressure (ἐγχρίμπτων), while they moored their ships and at the same time fought off the rams. This gave his ships the opportunity of withdrawing and attacking again whenever he wanted and using other ships turn and turn about. His opponents were at a disadvantage from the rocks on which they ran aground and from the immobility of the ships. It seemed as if they were fighting on foot against an enemy fighting at sea, having no ability to pursue or disengage.

(Ap.*CW*.5.82) 'In these conditions Menodoros and Menekrates caught sight of each other; and giving up their other fighting immediately attacked each other with angry shouts, putting on the issue of this contest, which of them should win, the whole outcome of the battle. Their ships fell upon each other with a violent impact; and the one ship shattered the ram of Menodoros's ship and the other the oars of Menekrates. Then when grappling irons were thrown and the ships were locked together, there was nothing more for them to do, but the men fought as on the land and did not fall short in energy and courage. There was a rain of javelins, stones and arrows on each and boarding-bridges

---

Note on Map M (i): Octavian's strategic plan for the attack on Sextus Pompeius in Sicily in 38 BC relied on the meeting in the strait of Messana of a fleet under Calvisius and Menodorus 'from Etruria' and Octavian's from Tarentum. But the interception of the former at Cumae with a fleet sent north by Sextus delayed Calvisius's arrival in the straits. Octavian got there first and, though outnumbering Sextus's ships remaining at Messana, refused to join battle with them until the arrival of Calvisius. He was accordingly himself attacked before Calvisius appeared, and then lost the greater part of his ships in a severe storm. The campaign was abandoned.

Two years later the strategic plan was more complex, the result perhaps of Agrippa's appointment as fleet commander. Octavian brought his main fleet south from Puteoli to Vibo without interference. 102 of the ships contributed by Antony were made ready at Tarentum under Taurus with a force of infantry and cavalry. The third member of the Triumvirate, Lepidus, was required to invade Sicily in the west from Africa. The plan then appears from the course of events to have been the following. The main fleet with two legions was to invade the north eastern coast of Sicily under Agrippa while Taurus's force moved to Skulakion, was reinforced there with three legions from Vibo and moved again to Leucopetra where (at Stylis) a further three legions were awaiting the opportunity to cross to Tauromenium. Landings were then made from two directions; the legions put ashore by Agrippa were to effect a junction with those from Tauromenium, reinforced by Lepidus's forces moving up from the west. The lines of supply for Sextus's forces at Mylae and Messana were thus to be cut.

In spite of some reverses, and delays caused this time by the interception of Lepidus's ships approaching Sicily from Africa and by the engagement at Mylae the plan appears to have been carried out and Sextus consequently forced to risk everything on the outcome of a final battle at sea off Naulochos.

were thrown out so that the men could go from one ship to another. Since Menodoros's ship was higher than the other the bridges made boarding easier for those who risked it and the missiles thrown from a higher point more deadly'.

This fighting in which there were many casualties took place on the left wing (of Menodoros). Menekrates was wounded and Menodoros, more seriously wounded, threw himself into the sea. Menekrates towed away his ship. On the right wing Calvisius had some success in cutting off some ships and pursuing them out to sea, but Menekrates's second in command, Demochares, fell on the the rest of Calvisius's ships. Sextus's fleet was more successful by far. Calvisius waited at his station as long as he expected Demochares to attack, but was unable to fight a battle since his best ships had been destroyed and the rest were unserviceable. When he learnt that Demochares had returned to Sicily, he repaired his ships and moved along the coast keeping close to the shore in the bays (*ἐξελίσσων τοὺς κόλπους*).

Octavian, in the meantime, had moved from Tarentum to Rhegion with a large fleet and army; and had caught Sextus with 40 ships only. He was advised to attack him while so greatly outnumbered and before the rest of Sextus's fleet came up. He refused, waiting for Calvisius. ... When he heard of what had happened at Cumae he went out to meet Calvisius but when he was nearly there, Sextus sprang out from Messana and attacked the rear of his column. In pursuit of his scouts he attacked the whole fleet, challenging it to a battle. But although Octavian's ships were harassed they did not turn round into battle line as Octavian forbade it, either because he was afraid to fight in a channel or because he was abiding by his first decision not to fight until Calvisius appeared. By his tactic all the ships took shelter by the shore and rode at anchor, defending themselves from attack prow to prow. With Demochares setting two ships against one they were already in confusion, and being dashed against the rocks and each other were beginning to be filled with water. They were being destroyed without striking a blow, these too like the ships at Cumae moored and being rammed by the enemy moving in to attack and then backing out'.

'Octavian had to scramble ashore. However, Cornificius and other commanders there encouraged each others not to wait for orders but cut their anchors and put out against the enemy, preferring to do and die rather than stand by passively and succumb to attack. Cornificius first with extraordinary bravery crashed into Demochares's flagship and captured it, Demochares jumping on to another vessel. In the middle of the fight Calvisius and Menodoros came in sight approaching from the open sea. Demochares's men saw them first and retreated. It was already getting dark and being weary they did not want to face men who were fresh. Octavian and his men who had escaped on shore were succoured by the chance arrival of a legion of his troops. He was repairing his ships on the following day under the protective screen of Calvisius's ships when a great storm got up. It shattered Octavian's ships which were 'dashed against the rocks and against each other, not being fully manned (*ἐντελῶν*) and under control'.

(Ap.*CW*.5.89) 'However, Menodoros, expecting when the storm began that it would increase, put out into the more open sea and rode it out at anchor, experiencing a less rough sea because of the depth of the water. Nevertheless even against this he began strong rowing to avoid being driven ashore, and some others followed his example. But most of them thinking that the wind would soon go down, as it does in spring, held their ships with anchors at bow and stern, from the sea and from the land; and kept other ships off with poles. As the wind grew more violent everything was in confusion and the ships were in collision with each other, breaking their (bow) anchor cables and being cast on to the shore or against each other'. Appian continues with a vivid description of the scene of death and destruction, and concludes: 'The storm was unparalleled and it destroyed the greater part of Octavian's ships and men'. Later (Ap.*CW*.5.92) he is more specific: less than half of Octavian's ships were saved and these were badly damaged.

There is a gap in Appian's text covering the year 37 and our information comes from the less reliable, and later, Dio Cassius. However, Appian says that by the spring of 36 Octavian was again making preparations, even more ambitious than the previous ones, for the defeat of Sextus. Dio gives some details. He says (48.2–4) that the year 37 and the following year Octavian spent in building ships and gathering and training oarsmen; also that he entrusted Agrippa with the equipping of the ships, which Agrippa did very enthusiastically. The introduction into the naval sphere of Agrippa, who had previously distinguished himself as a military commander in Gaul, marks the turning point in Octavian's naval affairs, which under his own direction had hitherto been disastrous.

The ships were built along the coast of Italy, but because of Sextus's raids and the absence of natural safe harbours Agrippa cut channels to the Lucrine Lake to produce a large and safe inland harbour. (Dio 48.50–53 and 51.5) There he assembled his ships and oarsmen. He made the ships cataphract (*κατέφραττε*). This is a most interesting statement, indicating that these new warships on delivery from the shipyard, at any rate those which had been built in the Italian coastal cities, were 'open' *apertae* and that they were given their decks and (wooden) protective armour in a naval dockyard[8]. This protection was not a mere canopy deck which the Italian shipyards would have had no difficulty in adding but a more sophisticated kind of protection against missiles, the complete 'boxing in' of the oarsmen shown on all the representations of the larger Roman warships.

At the new harbour, Dio adds, Agrippa not only fitted protective armour to his ships, he also trained his oarsmen on *ἴκρια*, mock-ups of the oarsystem set up on land.

Dio (49.1.2) says that Octavian 'was chiefly confident because of the height of his ships and the thickness of their timbers, since they had been built especially thick and high so as to carry as many decksoldiers as possible (and they carried towers (p. 154, 155) as well, so that the decksoldiers might fight from a commanding height as from a wall); and so that the ships' (by dint of their thick hulls) 'might resist the ramming of the enemy and bend back their rams, the more violent they made the collision'.

Appian's narrative continues: (Ap.CW.5.93) 'At the beginning of spring (37 BC) Antony moved from Athens to Tarentum with 300 ships to join Octavian in the campaign' (*συμμαχήσων*) '(against Sextus) as he had promised. Octavian however wished to postpone the attack until his (new) ships were built and added to his existing fleet. Antony replied that his forces were ready and sufficient, but Octavian delayed further. Antony stayed at Tarentum and sent to Octavian again, since he was burdened with the expenses of the fleet and needed Italian soldiers for his prospective campaign against Parthia, expecting to exchange ships for Italian soldiers'.

(Ap.CW.5.94) The two triumvirs met at the river Taras; and the outcome was that Octavian postponed his campaign against Sextus to the following year (35 BC), while Antony set off for Syria, giving Octavian 120 ships then and there and gaining a promise of 20,000 Italian legionaries.

Octavian's sister Octavia secured from her husband Antony a present for her brother of ten *phaseli trieritici* described as of mixed design, cargo ship and warship. Taking into account Appian's use of the word *τριήρης* as a general word for warship (p. 37), it does not necessarily imply that these *phaseli* had three levels of oars, only that they had rams. But they may have had three levels since Catullus's *phaselus* 'claimed to be the fastest ship afloat'. They are likely to have been fast ships for fleet communication, yet with a ram for use in tight corners.

The triumvirate was renewed for a further five years, and Antony left for Syria on his way to Parthia. Menodoros now went back to Pompey taking 7 ships, without Calvisius's knowledge. Octavian took the opportunity of appointing Agrippa in his place as fleet commander.

(Ap.CW.5.98–99) The kalends of July (1/7/36 BC) was the date fixed for the beginning of the campaign against Sextus. Lepidus by agreement moved from Africa with 1000 *ὁλκάδες*, 70 warships, twelve legions, 500 Numidian cavalry and much gear (*παρασκευή*)[9]. Taurus moved from Tarentum with 102 of Antony's 130 ships (120 + 10 *phaseli*), the oarsmen of 28 having died during the winter. Octavian himself moved from Puteoli with his scouts (*πρόπλοι*) ahead reconnoitring the bays and Appius following with a strong rearguard. On the third day after setting out a gale from the south hit Lepidus's ships and capsized many of his *ὁλκάδες*, but he succeeded in reaching moorings in Sicily and besieged Sextus's commander Plenius in Lilybaion. Taurus returned to Tarentum when the wind started to blow. When Appius was rounding the promontory of Minerva, some of his ships were driven on to the rocks and smashed, others ran violently aground on the shoals and the rest were scattered with some damage.

Octavius's fleet found shelter in the gulf of Velia, except for one six which was wrecked on the promontory. A south-west wind followed the south wind and the water in the gulf became rough, being open to the west. It was impossible either to move out against the wind or for the oars and anchors to keep the ships safe. They were driven on to each other and on to the rocks. At night the peril grew worse. The limited holding strength of Roman anchors is well illustrated.

Next morning Octavian had his whole fleet to repair with such means as they had on board. Six heavy ships, 26 of the lighter ships and a greater number of liburnians had been lost. Since repairs would take thirty days, he came to the conclusion that the campaign must be postponed to the following year. However, it appears that he changed his mind, since (Ap.*CW*.5.100) Sextus learnt 'that Octavian was building more ships and intending to move against him again in the current summer'. After raiding Octavian's corn-ships at anchor and dockyards to show his value as a defector, Menodoros came over to Octavian once more, in time for the renewed campaign against Sextus.

(Ap.*CW*.5.103–5) Putting out again (from Puteoli) Octavian landed safely at Vibo. He ordered Messala to cross to Sicily with two legions, join Lepidus and proceed to the bay in front of Tauromenium. He sent three legions to Stylis at the far end of the strait to await events, and ordered Taurus to move round from Tarentum to Mt Skylakion opposite Tauromenium. 'Taurus made the voyage prepared equally for an engagement and for a voyage under oar; his infantry also moved along in company, reconnaissance being made on the land by the cavalry and at sea by the liburnians'. Sextus placed guardposts at all the landing places in the island and concentrated his ships at Messana so as to be able to send them where they were needed.

Four more legions were on their way from Africa to Lepidus. Papias, otherwise known as Demochares, intercepted them. They took his ships for a squadron sent by Lepidus to meet them, and consequently suffered severely. Lepidus's squadron, putting out slowly, met some survivors who fled thinking them enemies. Some of the troop transports were burned, some captured and some were capsized. The rest returned to Africa.

After a reconnaissance Octavian crossed with his whole fleet from Vibo to Strongyle (mod. Stromboli: the northernmost of the Lipari islands). He was aware of a large force on the opposite shore at Pelorus, Mylai and Tyndaris and guessed that Sextus had moved his fleet there. Leaving Agrippa in charge of the fleet he returned to Vibo. Moving rapidly from there with Messala and three legions to Taurus's camp, he intended to seize Tauromenion while Sextus was away, and thus make attacks on him from two directions. Agrippa accordingly moved nearer the coast to the island of Hiera (?Lipara, where Dio places him before the battle), with the intention of attacking Papias who had a fleet of 40 ships at Mylai. Seeing the threat from Agrippa, Sextus sent him 45 ships under Apollophanes and then followed himself with 70. The Pompeian force at Mylai thus totalled 155 ships, under Papias since Sextus observed the ensuing battle from high ground ashore.

The Battles of Mylai and Naulochos

(Ap.*CW*.5.106) While it was still dark Agrippa put out from Hiera with half his ships intending to engage Papias alone (i.e. 70 ships). When he saw the fleet of Apollophanes also (45 ships) and on the other side the seventy ships, he informed Octavian that Sextus was at Mylai 'with the larger fleet'. This latter phrase is ambiguous since the numbers of Agrippa's fleet are not given by Appian or Dio. 'The larger fleet' could mean either that Papias's fleet contained the larger number of Sextus's ships or that Papias's fleet was larger than Agrippa's. Since Agrippa fought with only half his fleet, and the other half from Hiera did not come up until the battle was over, the latter alternative seems likely. On the other hand Dio says that 'one side was more numerous, the other' clearly Papias's 'superior in the skills of the seamen'. Dio may be including the late-comers in the total of Agrippa's fleet.

'Agrippa led the heavy ships at the centre' (of the line) 'and called out the rest of the fleet from Hiera urgently. In both fleets everything was magnificently ordered, and at bow and stern they had towers on deck'[10]. 'When they had had the usual encouraging speeches and the standards had been raised on each ship they moved out against each other, the one side in line abreast (*κατὰ μέτωπον*), the other' (in column) 'for an encirclement (*ἐς περικύκλωσιν* Thukydides 3.78). The moves were accompanied by shouts and the noise of the oars and a variety of terror'.

'As to the ships, Sextus's were smaller' (than their opponents: probably both shorter and lower p. 269) 'and light and fast for attacking and encircling tactics'(Dio 49.3.2 speaks of their *διέκπλοι*). 'Octavian's ships were bigger and heavier', (Dio mentions their greater height, their towers and the thickness of their *ἐπωτιδες*), saying that for that reason they were slower as well, but causing more damage when ramming and less vulnerable when rammed. Dio (50.23.1–2) adds that Antony believed that Sextus had been defeated because Octavian's ships were larger and hence had a greater number of soldiers on deck.

(Ap.*CW*.5.106 continued) 'As to the men, Sextus's were better seamen than Octavian's, but Octavian's were more powerful. Accordingly, the one side' (Sextus's) 'was not successful in ramming but only when carrying out encirclement, and they bent back the oarsystems of the bigger ships, or their rudders (by a stern attack), or cut off oars, or entirely separated the ships' (from their supporting craft) 'and did them no less damage than by ramming. Octavian's men sought with ramming to cut into or shatter or break up enemy ships and they threw missiles from a height to ships at a lower level and cast boarding bridges or grappling irons on them more easily. The Pompeians, when they were worsted jumped into the sea, and the auxiliary vessels (*ὑπηρετικά*) moving around picked them up'.

(Ap.*CW*.5.107) Agrippa made a direct set at Papias and smashed into him at the *ἐπωτίς*, shattering the ship and breaking into the hull. The ship threw off the men in the towers and began to take in a great deal of water. Of the oarsmen the thalamians were all cut off, but the other of the two levels of oarsmen (*οἱ ἕτεροι*) breaking through the canopy-deck swam away. Papias was taken up into a ship alongside, and continued to fight the enemy.

This last paragraph is of particular interest. It illustrates the point made by Dio that Agrippa's heavy ships had thick *ἐπωτίδες* able to smash the weaker *ἐπωτίδες* of Papias's ships in a head-on encounter. Agrippa's flagship was at least a five, probably a six. Sextus's flagship was a six (see above p. 149) but his fleet, including naturally his flagship, was at Messana, while he was observing the battle from high ground. In view of the emphasis on the lesser height and lightness of Papias's fleet as a whole Papias's ship is likely to have been a four; and this identification is borne out by the result of the attack, in which the thalamians were trapped and drowned, while *the other of the two categories* of oarsmen managed to escape. The Greek *ἕτεροι* indicates that there were only two categories of oarsmen in the ship; had there been three the word *ἄλλοι* would have been used. A four, with two categories of oarsmen, *θαλάμιοι* and *ζύγιοι* would have had four files of oarsmen on each side of the ship, the thalamian and zygian oars being double-manned. Papias's flagship seems also to have been boxed in since to escape from the rapidly filling hull the zygians had to break through the canopy deck (*κατάστρωμα*). If it had not been boxed in (**38**), but with an open side like the 5th and 4th centuries three, the upper oarsmen could have escaped sideways from under the deck.

'Sextus saw from his vantage point that his ships were gaining little success, that whenever there was close fighting they were cleared of decksoldiers and that the other half of Agrippa's fleet was approaching from Hiera. He accordingly gave the signal to withdraw in good order'. They started to do this but when hard pressed by Agrippa turned and fled, not to their beaches but to muddy shallows. (Ap.*CW*.5.108) 'Agrippa's helmsmen stopped him taking his big ships into shallow water[11] and he rode at anchor at sea to show his readiness to blockade the enemy and fight if necessary at night'. He reluctantly took the advice of his friends not to tire his men out or take risks in waters liable to storms, and withdrew in the evening.

'The Pompeians moved along the coast to their harbours. They lost 30 ships and swamped five of the enemy. There was considerable damage inflicted on either side'. After praising and rewarding his men 'Papias encouraged them to believe that being lighter they would have the advantage in the strait because of the current, and he promised that he would make some addition to the height of their ships'.

He may have been contemplating the addition of towers if most of his ships lacked them.

(Ap.*CW*.5.109) Suspecting that Octavian was at Taurus's camp with a view to attacking Tauromenium, Sextus left his forces at Mylai where they were and moved to Messana. Octavian had moved from Skylakion to Leucopetra ready to cross to Cornificius when he heard the result of the battle; and delayed until the following day. He then crossed with all the troops he could carry and was making camp when Sextus appeared unexpectedly from Messana with a large fleet accompanied on land by a force of cavalry, while infantry came up on the other side (the south).

Octavian's force consisted of three legions, 500 cavalry without their horses, 1000 light armed men and 2000 colonists serving as allies. There was also the fleet. To prevent being blockaded from the sea as well Octavian took his fleet to sea before daybreak and drew up a line of battle, going round the ships in a liburnian to give them courage. There were two engagements and Octavian's ships were defeated and dispersed; some ships disobeyed orders, put up their small sails (*τὰ βραχέα τῶν ἱστίων*) and fled to the Italian coast. After a night spent among 'the auxiliary craft' he made his way to Messala's camp from where he sent a liburnian to Cornificius and ordered the three legions from Stylis to cross as soon as they could. He sent also a letter to Agrippa who had been attacking Tyndaris and other maritime cities on the Sicilian coast telling him to go to Cornificius's aid.

Cornificius was without supplies and was forced to march to meet the three legions under Laronius which Agrippa sent. These moves enabled, and were probably planned to enable, Octavian to threaten Sextus's supplies (see Note on Map M1), and it became apparent to Sextus (Ap.*CW*.5.118) 'that the issue must be decided by a great battle' and that this must be at sea. He issued a challenge in those terms to Octavian, who felt he must accept. Off Naulochos '300 ships were made ready in their own fashion on each side. They carried missiles of all kinds and towers and all the engines (*μηχαναί*) they could devise. Agrippa devised one called *ἅρπαξ* which was a spar five cubits (2.22 m, 7ft 3in) long bound with iron and with rings at each end. The *ἅρπαξ*, an iron hook, was fastened to one of the rings and a large number of ropes to the other. These ropes, after the *ἅρπαξ* had been hurled by a catapult and had engaged an enemy ship, were hauled in by mechanical means'.

(Ap.*CW*.5.119) As usual the account of the battle first mentions the shouts of the oarsmen on each side, then the accompanying shower of missiles, some thrown by catapult (*μηχανή*) others by hand, stones, firebrands, and arrows.

'Then the ships themselves crashed into each other, some into the side, others at the *ἐπωτίδες*, others at the ram, where the impact is most violent in shaking the decksoldiers and making the ship less ready for battle. Others moved through each other's line discharging missiles and javelins, while the auxiliaries rescued those who fell overboard. There was hand to hand fighting (*ἔργα χειρῶν*), strenuous rowing (*βία ναύτων*), skilful action, and shouted commands, of the helmsmen (*τέχνη κυβερνήτων καὶ βοαί*), the encouraging cheers of the commanders (*παρακελεύσεις στρατηγῶν*) and (the operation of) all the engines (*μηχανήματα πάντα*)'.

'The *ἅρπαξ* was the star turn. It hit ships from a long range, being light, and took a firm hold especially when it was hauled in by the ropes. It was not easily severed by the victims by reason of the iron binding, and its length made it difficult for them to cut the ropes. Since this device had never been known before (and thus they were unable to deal with it by mounting hooks on spears), they could think of only one thing to do in this unexpected situation, by backing water to pull against it, but with the enemy doing the same the efforts of the oarsmen were equal, and the *ἅρπαξ* did its work'.

There follows (Ap.*CW*.5.120–1) a vivid account of the resultant hand-to-hand fighting.

'From the colours of their towers, by which alone the ships differed from each other, Agrippa concluded with difficulty that more of the Pompeian ships had been destroyed; and encouraged those near him as having already succeeded. He then attacked the enemy, pressing on them unceasingly until all those within range were overcome and threw down their towers, turned their ships round and fled towards the straits. Seventeen of these managed to get away, but the rest, intercepted by Agrippa, were pursued and driven aground. Their pursuers also running aground pulled off some of the enemy and burned others. Those that were still fighting surrendered when they saw what was happening to the others'.

Appian reports that three of Octavian's ships were swamped, Sextus lost 28 swamped in the battle, the rest were burned, captured or running aground were wrecked. Only 17 escaped.

The account of the battle is interesting, but probably owes as much to Appian's imagination as to trustworthy sources. It nevertheless has some value since his imagination would have been coloured by direct observation of the types of naval unit involved. In view of what has been said by him of the differences between the ships of Octavian and those of Sextus in the battle of Mylai it is difficult to believe that in the short time between the battles of Mylai (summer 36) and Naulochos (Sept.-Oct.36) the Pompeian ships could have been so transformed that the only difference between the two fleets lay in the colour of their towers. It is possible that what Appian means is that that was the only difference within the categories of big ships (sixes, fives and fours); and that Sextus had fulfilled his promise of heightening his ships and had done it by equipping with towers his warships in the bigger and heavier categories. These, apart from Sextus's six appear to have been mainly fours. Towers were it seems pieces of equipment that could be jettisoned in an emergency (p. 168).

All Sextus's land forces in the area surrendered. Plenius was summoned from Lilybaion, but Sextus, afraid of being prevented from leaving Sicily by Octavian's fleet in the strait, went with his seventeen ships from Messana to Antony. Plenius reached Messana later and surrendered. At Antony's hands, indirectly, he met his death in the following year.

Octavian, finding Lepidus now with strong military forces in Sicily, succeeded in taking over the island and eliminating him as a political rival. In the next four years, with Octavian in Italy and Dalmatia and Antony in Armenia, Syria and Greece, events were leading up to the final engagements of the civil wars, fought at sea.

5. THE CAMPAIGN OF AKTION

In the year 33 BC (Dio 50.2) Antony and Octavian began open preparations for war with each other. Yet no actual moves appear to have been made in either 33 or the summer of 32.

The First Phase *(Map N, Plan 7)*

Octavian, having settled affairs in Italy as consul in 33, was unable to confront Antony before the winter of 32–31. Antony had returned from his campaign in Armenia with much treasure (Orosius 6.19.4). He moved to Ephesos with Cleopatra. 'It was there', (Plutarch *Antony* 56.1), 'that his fleet was assembling from all sides, 800 ships including ὁλκάδες. Of these Cleopatra provided 200, as well as 20,000 talents and supplies for the whole force during the war. Later (*Antony* 61.1) Plutarch gives more detail: 'when the forces came together for the war Antony had no fewer than 500 fighting ships. They included many eights and tens, fitted out in an imposing and ostentatious manner. He had in addition 100,000 infantry and 12,000 cavalry'.

(Dio 50.9.2) Antony moved, with Cleopatra, to Kerkyra in the late autumn of 32 with the intention of taking the war into Italy; but discovering that the scout ships sent to watch his movements were lurking near the Keraunian mountains (on the coast of Epeiros) he concluded that Octavian had crossed with his whole fleet and proceeded no further. He returned to Patrai and spent the winter there. (Dio 50.11.1) In fact Octavian put out from Brundisium and had gone as far as Kerkyra intending to attack Antony's naval forces moored off Aktion, but he met with a storm and returned with some damage. Antony appears then already to have sent his fleet to Aktion.

(Dio 50.11.2) When the spring of 31 came Antony did not move at once: 'the fact was that his crews (τριηρῖται) were of different races wintering some way away from the ships. They had not gone through any training, and were diminished in numbers by sickness and desertion'. Orosius says that when Antony visited his fleet at Aktion he found that a third of the oarsmen had died of hunger, and was unmoved saying: 'So long as the oars are safe (all is well), there will be no lack of oarsmen while there are men in Greece'. Plutarch's account (*Antony* 62) is rather different, that in spite of enrolling crews of the most unsuitable material from 'long-suffering Greece' his and Cleopatra's ships 'were not fully manned and most of them were lacking a full crew and moved badly'. Octavian on the other hand assembled his fleet in Brundisium and Tarentum composed of ships not built for height and bulk but responding well to the tiller, fast and properly manned.

Octavian's first move (Dio 50.11.3) was to send Agrippa ahead to Greece where in spite of a very strong Antonian garrison he took Methone on the south west coast of the Peloponnese, near the end of the promontory of Messenia. From there (Orosius 6.19.6) Agrippa was able to intercept *onerariae* with cargoes of arms and grain for Antony from Egypt, Syria and Asia. His activity there was undoubtedly responsible for the shortage of food in Antony's fleet at Aktion.

(Dio 50.11.4) Octavian now took the whole of his land forces, and a fleet of 230 warships (Orosius 6.19.6), over to Epeiros (Torune: Plutarch *Antony* 62.3: see Map K for the ports available). He was

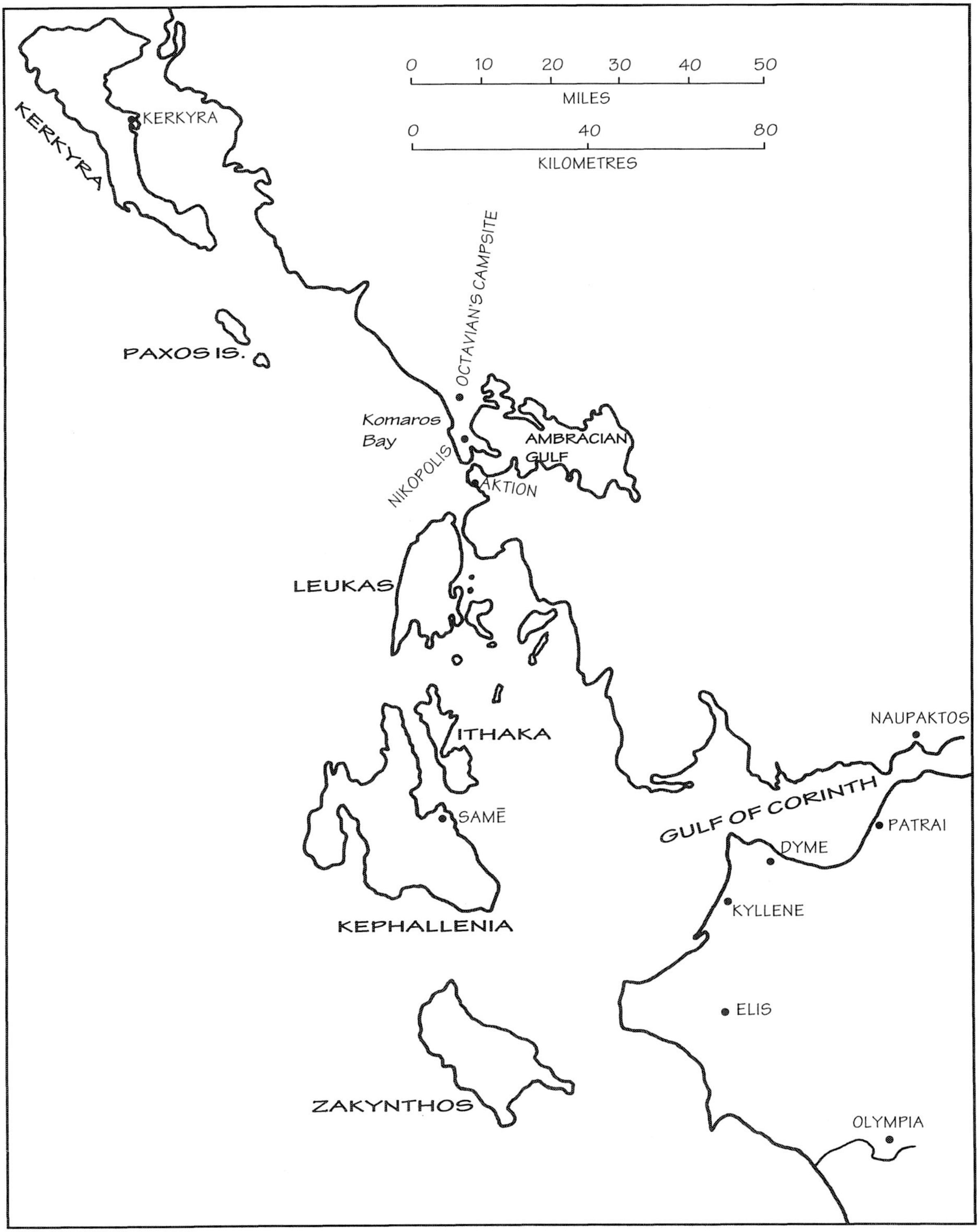

MAP N. *The Aktion Campaign*

leading them', Dio (50.12.1) says, 'not to the Peloponnese or against Antony but to Aktion where the greater part of Antony's fleet lay; and waited to see if he could bring Antony's forces over to his side either willingly or indeed unwillingly'. There is no information about the location of Antony's land forces (his camp) at this time. It appears to have been not yet at Aktion. From Methone Agrippa moved north against Kerkyra which had been deserted by its governor; and set up a naval base (*ναύσταθμον*) in one of the island's harbours. In Orosius's account (6.19.7) 'he pursued the fugitives from Kerkyra and defeated them in a naval battle; and after many actions involving much bloodshed joined Octavian'.

Dio puts these moves differently and adds details. He says (50.12.1–2) that Octavian disembarked his infantry[12] at the foot of the Keraunian mountains (Strabo 6.3.5: Map K) and sent them to Aktion while he himself (rather than Agrippa) with his ships took Kerkyra which had been abandoned by its garrison, established a naval base in one of its harbours and from there sent ships against Aktion. He challenged Antony's forces either to come out to battle or to discuss terms of surrender, but met with no response. He then seized the site of the later Nikopolis, (which his cavalry had reconnoitred, and moved his forces there).

Octavian, Dio says (50.12.3–4), 'established his headquarters on a point of vantage from where he could see over the open sea as far as the Paxos islands (Map N), and both the water inside the gulf and the water in between in which are the harbours adjacent to the Nikopolis site. He fortified this area and led walls from it down to the outer harbour called Komaros. From this point he besieged and blockaded Antony's forces at Aktion by land and sea'.

Orosius records Antony's reaction: 'Antony was disturbed by the defections and hunger of his soldiers and decided to quicken the pace of hostilities. He suddenly marshalled his forces, marched to Octavian's camp and suffered a defeat. On the third day after the battle Antony transferred his camp to Aktion, prepared to seek a decision in a naval engagement'.

Florus abbreviates as follows: (2.21.4) Octavian 'on the first report of new movements' of Antony 'crossed from Brundisium so as to be in the path of the coming attack. He had placed his camps in Epeiros and had surrounded with hostile naval forces the whole of the shore of Aktion, the island of Leukas and Leukate Pr as well as the horns of the Ambracian Gulf'.

A detail in Dio (50.12.5) is interesting, if hardly relevant: 'In fact I have heard that Octavian actually carried threes over from the outer sea into the gulf by way of the fortifications, using newly flayed hides treated with olive oil in place of runways; but I cannot report any action of these ships within the Gulf and so find it difficult to believe the story. It would not have been a small operation to bring threes across on land over so narrow and uneven a path. Yet it is said that this was done'.

Dio describes the site (Plan 7): (50.12.7) 'Aktion, an area dedicated to Apollo, lies in front (south) of the mouth of the strait leading into the Ambracian Gulf and opposite the harbours near Nikopolis. The strait extends for some distance through narrows, and itself and the approaches to it are (good for) mooring and ambush'. 'Antony's men' (that is to say the fleet) 'occupied the position in advance and built towers on each side of the entrance' (to the strait), 'stationing ships in the area in between' (the towers), so that they were able to go in and out safely. They encamped on the far (southern) side of the strait in the sacred site on ground which is level and wide but in fact more suitable for a battle than for a camp. The result was that they were afflicted by sickness in winter, and much more so in summer'.

The 'sickness', added to the shortage of victuals, became a major factor in the deterioration of Antony's position.

Dio, like Orosius, places Antony's arrival at Aktion after Octavian's bold seizure of the site of the future Nikopolis (50.13.1): 'As soon as Antony learned of Octavian's arrival he lost no time but hurried with his company to Aktion, arriving not long afterwards'. Dio makes no mention of any preceding land battle. Antony's company (lit. 'those with him') did not include his whole force which was some time in arriving. 'Octavian drew up his infantry in line of battle in front of the Antonian camp and often moved his ships against them, and (captured and) brought in their transports, with the intention of joining battle before Antony's whole strength assembled'.

It is likely that in this period occurred the daily desertions to Octavian and 'finally before the face

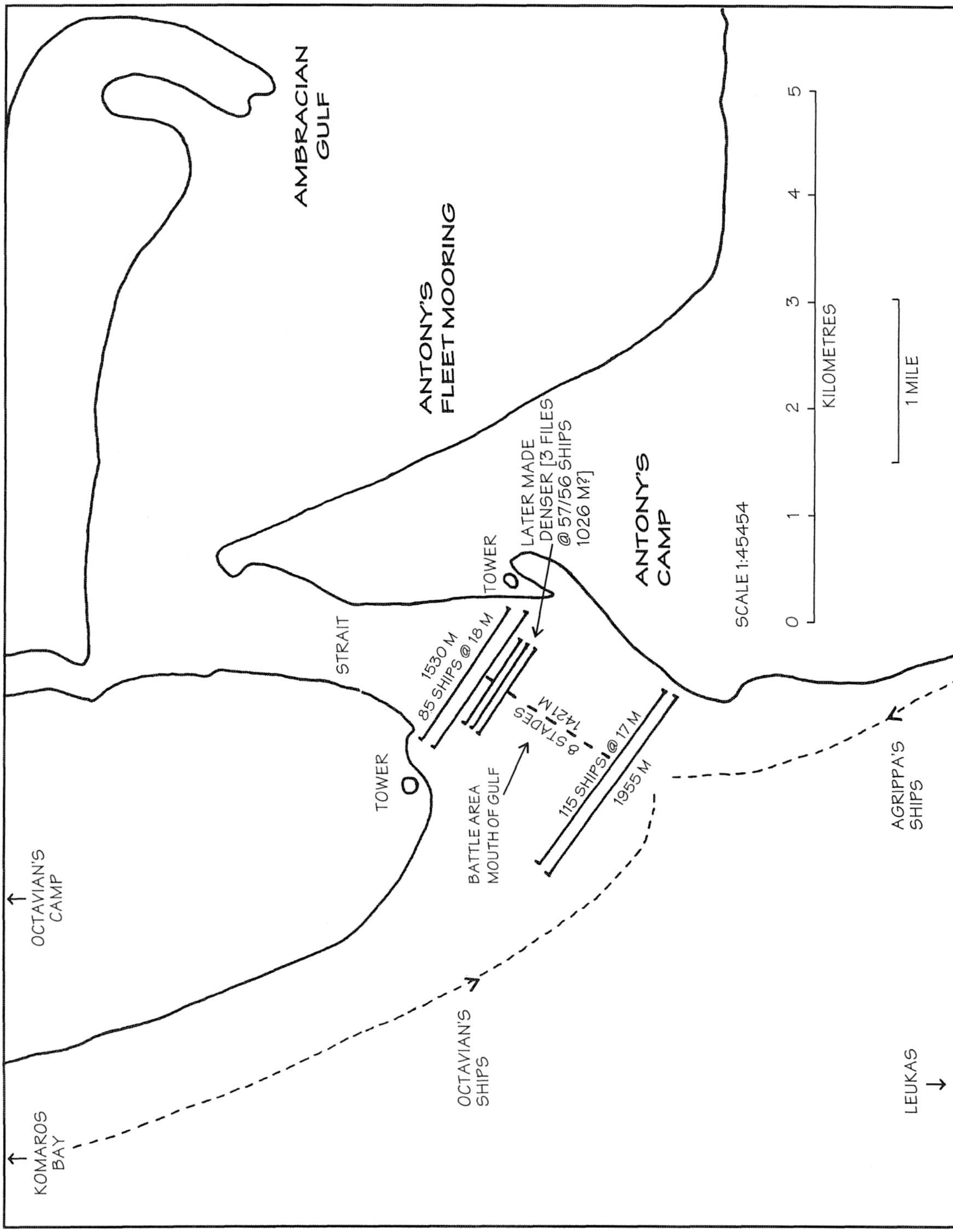

PLAN 7. *The Battle of Aktion*

Note on Plan 7: The succession of moves by Octavian (O) and Antony (A) on the day of the final battle may be summarised as follows:

Source		Move
Dio	1.	*On Agrippa's advice O. abandons his plan to allow A. to move out and then to overtake and attack A's column. Instead he packs his ships with decksoldiers for a fight at the mouth of the Gulf and waits for A. to come out.*
Dio	2.	*A.'s trumpets signal his movement through the strait and formation of lines a short distance outside it across the mouth of the channel*
Plutarch		*A. instructs his helmsmen to accept attack without movement.*
Vergil, Dio	3.	*O. leads his ships from Komaros, Agrippa from Leukas.*
Plutarch		*They form lines 8 stades away from and facing A's.*
Plutarch, Dio		*There is a pause (P. till noon, D. a short time).*
Plutarch		*O. amazed at seeing A.'s ships stationary.*
Dio	4.	*A. makes his lines denser (and shorter), as defence against periplous which is likely to follow his forward movement.*
Dio	5.	*[O. gives signal to advance both wings and turn them inwards. This move prompts A.'unwillingly' to attack in fear of periplous. This initiative by O. is unlikely. P.'s account is more likely with periplous coming later]*
Plutarch		*A.'s men are impatient at delay and advance left wing.* *O.pulls back right wing.*
Dio, Plutarch	6.	*The result is fighting at the mouth of the Gulf.* *Agrippa extends left wing for periplous*
Vergil,Plutarch, cf.Horace, Propertius	7.	*At this point Cleopatra (at anchor behind A.'s lines) sounded order to form columns, is seen raising sails. Cleopatra, followed by Antony, move left (south to Peloponnese and Egypt). Overtaken by Eurycles's liburnians.*

and eyes of the Antonian fleet the storming of Leukas, the capture of Patrai, the occupation of Corinth and the two defeats of the enemy fleet by Agrippa' of which Velleius (84.1–2) speaks.

Dio (50.13.3) says that while waiting for his forces to arrive Antony engaged in skirmishes, advanced his camp beyond the channel and sent forces round the gulf (to put pressure on Octavian and cut off his supplies), while Octavian (recollecting perhaps the Dyrrachion campaign and Philippoi) sent forces into Greece and Macedonia to draw Antony's troops in that direction.

During this time (Dio 50.13.5 enlarging on Velleius) 'Agrippa made a sudden seaborne attack on Leukas and took it with the ships there, and took Patrai after a sea battle with Q. Nasidius. Later he brought Corinth over to Octavian'. Dio also (50.14.1–3) records another naval battle which ended in an Antonian defeat, and a defeat of Antony himself by Octavian's cavalry. As a result of these reverses the decision was taken to abandon the advanced camp beyond the channel. Then, as victuals began to run out because of the blockade, Antony held a council to decide whether to risk an engagement at sea or to move elsewhere. It was decided, Dio says (50.15.1–4), to move. 'They did not want to move out secretly, or openly like fugitives, lest they alarmed their allies; but they wanted to get away as if preparing for a sea-fight so that they might at the same time force their way through. As a result of this decision, since the seamen had become fewer through sickness and desertion, they (Antony and Cleopatra) chose the best ships and burnt the rest and secretly put on board all their most valuable possessions'. Plutarch (*Antony* 64.1) enlarges saying that Antony burned all the Egyptian ships with the exception of 60; and manned the largest and best from threes to tens.

Our sources do not agree in precise detail on the succession of events in the preliminary phase, but the main features of the picture are clear. Octavian's fleet under Agrippa had won the campaign before the final battle began. The capture of the heavily defended fortress of Methone meant that the main supply line for the fleet at Aktion, from Egypt, Syria and Asia, was effectively cut from the outset. Then, when Agrippa moved up to Kerkyra, Leukas and Patrai, not only was the screw significantly tightened but their capture, certainly in the case of Leukas and Patrai, most probably also in the case of Kerkyra, was achieved with loss of ships to Antony. It is not surprising that hunger and desertion are repeatedly mentioned, as well as sickness, as the main causes of Antony's inability to maintain the pressure on Octavian by land, but also of his diminishing naval effectiveness.

Agrippa's continued successes at sea, the two naval actions, must have had a serious effect on Antonian naval morale; and perhaps almost as much the occasions when Antony, waiting for soldiers to arrive to man the capacious decks of his large ships, refused to let his fleet accept the challenge of Caesar's ships drawn up outside the channel. The reason for Antony's lack of decksoldiers at Aktion is never given. Antony mustered large land forces at the outset. It is possible that the blockade was effective not only in the supply of victuals and arms but of men as well. The many defections would also have played their part. There is also the possibility that the unhealthiness of Antony's Aktion camp was a reason for keeping the army at a distance (in Epeiros) and that it took some time to bring them up by land.

Under the circumstances it is difficult to disbelieve Dio's account of the final council, difficult also to disbelieve the accounts which follow of a hard fought battle at sea. Antony's tougher and more seasoned commanders, loyal to the republican tradition if not to Octavian, some of whom must have attended the council, might have reckoned that Cleopatra and Antony were best away; and that if their disappearance could be kept from the rest of the fleet, victory at sea was not impossible, while on land, if not actually at Aktion, there was still a formidable force as yet uncommitted. As Romans they were accustomed to win their battles. At any rate, there was no surrender. Even Antony might have hoped that if the battle went well at the outset there might be no need to run away.

The Ships

Dio (50.16–22) represents Antony making a speech to his men in which he shows contempt for Octavian's fleet. 'With their ships they will not even be able to put out against us. In fact you see the size and solidity of our hulls (*τὸ μέγεθος καὶ τὸ πάχος τῶν ἡμετέρων σκαφῶν*), which are such that even if by dint of number their ships were a match for them, yet under these conditions they would not damage them either by ramming or other forms of attack (προσβολαῖς). For the thickness of the timbers and the height itself of the ships, even if there were no defenders on board, would deter them. At what point will anyone be able to attack them (our ships), with so many archers and slingers on board, and seeing that they have the additional advantage of being able from towers to attack the enemy from above? If anyone should get near, how would he not be sent under by the very multitude of oars, or drowned hit by all those who are fighting from the decks and towers?' Antony tells his men not to be worried because Agrippa won a sea battle against Sextus, since Sextus's equipment was far inferior. Later in the speech he reminds them that 'the whole issue in this war for both sides hangs on the naval side. If we are superior in this, we shall suffer no harm from anything else'.

(50.23.1–2) Dio observes: Antony 'embarked great numbers of archers, slingers and heavy-armed troops. Since Sextus was defeated chiefly by the size of Octavian's ships and the great number of his decksoldiers, Antony built his hulls much higher than those of his opponents. He had produced few threes but rather fives[13] and tens and all the remaining types in between. On top of them he had constructed high towers and put on board a great number of men so that they could fight as it were from walls'. The distinction here between threes as ships of smaller size and the bigger ships, fives to tens, on which 'high towers' are built, is to be noticed.

Florus (in a style recalling Vergil and Lucan, and with equal accuracy) gives a more detailed account of the two fleets.

(2.21.6): 'We [i.e. Octavian] had four hundred ships or more, the enemy had less than two hundred, but size compensated for the small number, since they ranged from six to nine [files of oarsmen a side]. In addition Antony's ships, given height by towers and storied (fore-and-stern) castles (*tabulatis castellorum*), looking like cities, made their way to the groaning of the sea and the exhaustion of the wind. Indeed size itself was their undoing'.

At 2.21.2. Florus calls these additional constructions *propugnacula* (cf. Pliny NH.32.1).

Octavian's 'ships', Florus continues, 'ranged in height (*creverant*) from two [files] of oarsmen each [i.e. liburnians] to six but not more. They were thus agile performers of the roles required of them, attacks and withdrawals and turnings. In numbers they attacked single enemy ships, which were heavy and handicapped for all manoeuvres, with missiles and rams at the same time, and in addition with thrown firebrands. Then, when they wished, they made themselves scarce. Nothing showed up the size of the enemy naval units more than the scene after the victory, as the wreckage of a vast fleet caused by the battle drifted over the whole surface of the sea'.

Orosius's account of the opposing fleets (6.19.8–9) is this: 'Octavian's ships were 230 with rams and 30 without, 'τριήρεις' equal to liburnians in speed. Eight legions were put on board the fleet and (there were men) from five praetorian cohorts'. The first part of this statement is puzzling. The phrase 'τριήρεις equal to liburnians in speed' can hardly be taken to describe the foregoing phrase '230 (ships) with rams and 30 without', still less to the latter part of it '30 (ships) without (rams)'. It may be a dislocated phrase, relic of a description of a separate category of auxiliary warships used for reconnaissance (either actual threes or τριήρεις used as a general word for warships). His fleet is known to have included such vessels. Florus gives Octavian 400 ships from twos (liburnians) to sixes.

It is possible therefore that Orosius's statement gave him 230 ships from fours to sixes with rams, and 30 big transports without rams, also, to make up Florus's 400, a category of 140 smaller warships (with rams) including threes and liburnians. This is a reasonably balanced battle fleet.

If the eight legions and five cohorts had been up to strength (48,000 + 3,200 = 51,200) there should have been an average of 128 decksoldiers on each vessel. But since fives carried 120 into battle, sixes possibly 150, the 230 big ships if there was an equal division of categories would have carried an average of 135 decksoldiers (= 31,050), the ramless ships @ 100 3,000 and the threes @ 40 (5,600) making 39,650 in all, a good deal too few. With the legions @ 4,500 and the praetorian cohorts up to strength (36000 + 3,200) the figures would just about balance at (@ 98). There are many variables and estimates in this calculation but it does perhaps show that the proposed loading is possible and fits the numbers recorded.

Orosius continues: 'Antony's fleet was of 170 ships making up as much in size as they lacked in number. They were in fact in height ten feet from the waterline'. With a Roman foot of 295.7 mm the height above the waterline of a nine or ten would then have been 2.957 m or 9ft 3½ins comparing with the height above the waterline of the reconstructed three of 8ft 2½ins. These are very revealing figures. Ships of nine or ten ft above the waterline, their visible height increased by towers of six feet or so on deck, would not seem very high to us, but they clearly did so to the eyes of antiquity.

In the speech Dio attributes to Octavian before the battle there are of course references to Antony's ships (50.24–30). He does not make any new points, but the words are perhaps a useful summary of the case against the big ships which had always persuaded the Romans that fives were big enough for fighting with, or rather from, while the impressive six was useful for diplomatic occasions and as a flagship.

'Will they not by their very size and solidity be more difficult to move for those who row them, and less responsive to the helmsmen? What help is it to those who fight from them not to be able to make a breakthrough or an encirclement, which are the manoeuvres of fighting at sea? ... For if their ships stay in the same place as if rooted there, we shall be at liberty to break into them (*ἀνά-ρρηγνύναι*) with our rams, we shall also be at liberty to damage them at long range with our engines, we shall also be at liberty to burn them down with our fire-carrying missiles. And if they actually have the courage to move anywhere, they could not succeed in catching any ship they pursue or escaping if they turned to flee, being extremely slow to do anything because of their weight, and extremely vulnerable to damage because of their size'.

It does nevertheless appear that they could outsail the lighter ships (see shortly below).

Octavian's plan of battle, Dio says, was based on the assumption that Antony and Cleopatra intended less to fight a battle than to break out of his blockade. (50.31.1) 'He planned to let them come out so that he could attack them in the rear as they escaped. He expected that in a fast ship he could quickly catch them; and that when they had made plain their intention of escaping somewhere, the rest of their forces would come over to him without fighting'. Octavian, unlike his adoptive father, shows himself to have had a natural preference for 'jaw jaw' rather than 'war war' and this plan, like the intelligence report of the intentions of his opponents on which it was based, was good. It was also a humane one, designed to spare the lives of as many of his Roman opponents and their allies as he could.

Dio adds that his plan was thwarted by Agrippa's practical objection that they would not be able to catch up with Antony and Cleopatra (if they were allowed to break out) *since the enemy planned to use sails*. Octavian's plan like Agrippa's objection seems to derive from a piece of hard information provided either by observation of Antony's preparations for the battle or by a deserter: viz. that mainsails, not merely the small sails (which were probably always taken into battle as they took up little room and might be useful afterwards) had been put on board at least some of the ships in Antony's fleet (Cleopatra's). Agrippa, who did not share Octavian's aversion from fighting at sea, also thought that he would win without difficulty since Antony's fleet, unlike Octavian's, had been hit by a storm of wind and rain which had thrown them into confusion. The remark about the storm which hit Antony's fleet but not Octavian's is puzzling. It suggests either that Antony's fleet was afloat the night before in the gulf (which is unlikely), or that Octavian's ships or a number of them were moored further away than the Komaros harbour, for example, on Leukas.

Accepting Agrippa's objection Octavian prepared his ships, not for hot pursuit with as few men as possible on deck but with a very large number (*παμπόλλους*) of infantry aboard. He also 'placed all his friends in auxiliary vessels so that they could sail around quickly and both give encouragement to the combatants and tell him what he needed to know'. Then he waited for the enemy to come out.

Fleet numbers recapitulated

Florus's numbers for the opposing fleets are: Octavian 400, from twos to sixes: Antony less than 200, from sixes to nines. Orosius's numbers are: Octavian: heavy 260 (230 with rams, 30 without) light ?140 (threes and liburnians): Antony 170 making up in size what they lacked in number. Both these sources are regarded as reliable as being based on Livy, and are not irreconcilable.

Plutarch's figure for Antony's fleet at Ephesos (*Antony* 56.1) is 800 ships including *ὁλκάδες*, of which Cleopatra provided 200 (warships and ὁλκάδες). Since he says that sixty of Cleopatra's warships were selected and the rest burnt immediately before the battle, it is reasonable to guess that her original fleet was half ὁλκάδες and that 80–100 warships survived until the battle, to be reduced by selection to 60. Using the same proportion Antony's warships at Ephesos would have been 300. At the next count (*Antony* 61.1) 'when the forces were collected for the war' Plutarch gives Antony not less than 500 fighting ships and does not mention Cleopatra's which were then presumably, as under Antony's command, counted with his. Plutarch at that point gives Octavian 250 ships of war. So, the warships under Antony's command will have increased from 400 (300 + 100 of Cleopatra's) to not less than 500, Octavian's from 230 to 250.

Alternatively, if two thirds instead of a half of the 800 ships at Ephesos were warships (533 instead of 400) Antony's ships would have remained steady at about 533 on the second count. More than half of Cleopatra's original 133 warships would not have survived (intermediate casualties and deliberate burning) until the battle. This alternative is preferable.

Orosius (6.19.6 and 8) gives Octavian 230 (big) ships with rams when he left Brundisium for Epeiros and the same number before the battle. He gives Antony 170 (war)ships at the battle. These are likely to have included the surviving 60 ships provided by Cleopatra.

By the spring of 31 (Dio 50.11.3) Antony's crews had been diminished by disease and desertions; and in clashes with Agrippa's fleet at Methone; and elsewhere he would have lost ships. If all the uncertainties are taken into consideration there is no reason to doubt Orosius's final figure of 170, which may be assumed to include only cataphract, turreted ships from fives to nines. Florus (2.21), also probably based on Livy, roughly corroborates Orosius giving a figure of 'less than 200 ships, from sixes to nines, heightened with turrets and floors'. But he disagrees with Dio who speaks of Antony as having few threes, rather fives to tens. This hints at the presence of some lighter vessels in his fleet: Florus's range of fives to nines is more likely. Florus's figure of 400 ships for Octavian's fleet, is made up in Orosius's account by 230 warships of large design, 140 of smaller design (fast threes and liburnians) and by 30 large transports.

The engagement: primary sources

Up to this point the authorities quoted for the Aktion campaign have been late, although some may reflect material from the lost books of Livy. Primary sources are however available in references to the campaign and battle of Aktion by contemporary Roman poets. The first published collection of Horace's poems, the *Epodes*, belongs to the decade before the battle; and the first four lines of the first poem in the collection refer directly to the campaign. He addresses his patron Maecenas who was a trusted friend of Octavian: 'You will go, my friend, aboard liburnians among the lofty fighting towers (*propugnacula*) of warships, ready to meet every risk that Caesar takes, Maecenas, at your own'.

The poem was certainly written at the outset of the campaign when Maecenas with other friends of Octavian was expecting to accompany him abroad. Liburnians, in Roman fleets, were light two-level oared auxiliaries with decks and rams (p. 264). It has also been seen (Dio 50.31.3) that in his preparations for the battle he put on board auxiliaries 'all his friends (staff officers) who could move around quickly in the battle area and give necessary advice to the combatant ships and communicate appropriate information to Octavian himself'. The story of Eurykles (p. 170 below) shows that there were liburnians in Octavian's fleet, as well as liburnians for staff communication, as would be expected. Before the battle of Naulochos (p. 156) he used a liburnian to communicate with his commanders and went round the ships in a liburnian to give his men encouragement. His fleet had turrets in the Sicilian battles (p. 154, 156); and it had them, naturally, at Aktion. It is this customary role given by Octavian to his friends which Horace envisages Maecenas performing in the coming battle. Dio (51.3) says that Maecenas was in the event given the important post of taking charge of affairs in Rome during Octavian's absence. If that is correct, and it may well be so, it does not in any way affect Horace's expectation and the interpretation to be given of it, except to show that the expectation was unfulfilled.

The passage has been taken as contrasting Octavian's fleet of liburnians with the ships of Antony with their lofty towers. This is quite mistaken, as is now generally recognised. Liburnians were among the auxiliary vessels present in all fleets; and both fleets had towers (*propugnacula*, where the *propugnatores* were stationed) on their bigger ships.

Since Antony's first line fleet though fewer in number (170 against 230) contained ships larger in size (sixes to nines as against fours to sixes), these could have accommodated higher towers although the decks of his sevens, eights and nines were not necessarily higher than Octavian's fives and sixes. It is the height of the towers on Antony's ships which is emphasised in the accounts of the battle. Dio says that Antony tried to gain greater height for his ships by the construction of towers.

A second reference by Horace to the Aktion campaign is in *Epodes* 9.7–20. and concerns the battle itself, being written after the news of it had reached Rome. 'Just as (Sextus Pompeius) was driven from the strait (of Messana) and his ships burnt...so 2000 Gallic cavalry came over to Caesar's side and the sterns of the enemy ships bidden to move to the left remained in harbour'. The reference in the last sentence is enigmatic and will be considered in connection with the later detailed accounts of the battle. Here it may be explained that the 'stern' of the ship is said to be 'bidden' because that was the seat of command. So in a modern description of an engagement 'the bridge' can be used for the officer in command of a ship. Horace plainly believed that in a battle, which could only be Aktion (although Kromayer 1931 doubted it), some at any rate of Antony's ships remained 'in harbour' (as Ferrabino 1924, Tarn 1931) after 'receiving an order to move to the left'.

Chronologically the next reference to Aktion in contemporary poetry is in *Aeneid* 8.671–713, where Vergil describes the scenes of the battle wrought by Vulcan on the central, circular, panel of Aeneas's shield. The artist appears to have selected five discontinuous moments to give, so-to-speak, a 'strip cartoon' of the engagement and its outcome. The first three lines give the subject of the picture as a whole: the (two) fleets of bronze-armed warships and the whole sea of Leukates disturbed by the battle lines (*instructo Marte*).

The first scene is of Octavian's fleet assembling: 'On one side (*hinc...*) there is Octavian leading the Italians to battle, attended symbolically by the Senate and people (of Rome), the Penates and the Great Gods. Suitably adorned with twin flames and the Julian star he stands in a high stern. Apart is Agrippa also suitably adorned, high up leading a column (of ships)'.

Whereas battle lines are mentioned in the general picture, and Octavian 'leads the Italians', Agrippa is 'apart' leading a column (*agmen*). It looks as if Agrippa is depicted approaching from the side at the head of a separate squadron in column ('high up' could mean that he was in the distance). This treatment may reflect his operations against the Antonian fleets, or more likely, his arrival from a mooring on Leukas (where he escaped the storm), since the mooring in the Komaros bay would not have been large enough for the whole fleet.

The second scene is of Antony and his fleet: 'On the other side (*hinc...*) there is Antony in rich barbaric style and varied arms, the conqueror from the peoples of the Dawn and the red shore' (the Indian ocean), 'bringing with him Egypt and the powers of the Orient and farthest Bactra; and there follows (for shame) his Egyptian wife. As one they all rush forward (*una omnes ruere*) and the whole sea foams shaken by the oars' stroke and the trident rams. They seek the deep water'.

Unlike Octavian's Antony's line is already formed, the ships are together (*una*). They are 'seeking the deep water' but are by implication still in the shallows of the strait through which they advance with vigorous rowing. Vergil is aware that Antony's purpose was to break out.

The third scene is of the fighting in brief: 'You would think that the Kyklades had been torn loose and were moving in the water or that lofty mountains were joining battle (*concurrere*) with mountains. In such massive numbers[14] do the men attack the turreted ships (*tanta mole viri turritis puppibus instant*). Flaming tow is thrown by hand and flying iron in missiles. Neptune's fields grow red with new slaughter. In the midst the queen calls up her columns (*agmina*) with her country's timbrel'.

Cleopatra's use of the timbrel instead of the Roman trumpet to transmit orders at sea is something which Propertius later (3.11.43–44) notes with disapproval. It is however here a matter of fact rather than a 'good example of a propagandist smear' (Gransden: 1976). She uses it 'to call up her columns', that is to say, to convert the lines of her ships abreast into columns to move away to a wing.

The fourth scene is of the war in heaven (698), and its corollary on earth:

The divinities in Homeric fashion, are depicted

as mirroring the human battle, the monstrous Egyptian gods against the Roman. At line 704 'Apollo of Aktion, seeing this, draws his bow', whereat the eastern contingents in Antony's fleet turn in flight and 'the queen herself was seen summoning the winds, raising sail and letting out the loosened sheets' i.e. preparing to sail before the wind.

The final scene is of Nile receiving back her conquered children and of Octavian's triple triumph at Rome.

In the light of Vergil's picture the last two lines of the second reference in Horace's *Epodes* (9.19–20), written immediately after the battle, may be looked at again. 'The sterns of enemy ships ordered to the left remain in port' (*Hostiliumque navium portu latent/puppes sinistrorsum citae*). Page (1853) suggested that the 'sterns of ships bidden to move' could indicate backing down, but there is no parallel to the usage nor any indication of backing down in the tradition. On the other hand Vergil's picture clearly indicates that it was believed in Rome within a decade of the battle that at a critical point in the action Cleopatra gave the signal to move to the wing in column. The order would have been then 'to the left wing' as the ships were facing west and were to sail south for Egypt. This then fits Horace's enigmatic remark, since, as the secondary sources say, the greater part of Antony's fleet did not follow Cleopatra and the few ships that accompanied him. Tarn (1931) argued that there was virtually no battle. Cleopatra's ships and a few others with Antony got away, while the rest of Antony's ships surrendered and were burnt. Kromayer (1928) had accepted from the tradition that there was a substantial battle. In reply to Tarn later (1931) he argued that Horace Epodes 9.19–20 might refer to one of occasions when Antony's fleet declined to come out to fight before the final battle.

The difficulty with that explanation lies in the undoubted fact that the poem's subject is Aktion, and the words 'ordered to the left' (*sinistrorsum citae*) cannot refer to an order to come out of harbour which was disobeyed, only to supposed disobedience to an order to ships in line abreast to move to the left in column. Vergil's picture shows that Cleopatra's order to her ships to form columns (inevitably to the left) had become notorious. Propertius (3.11.43–44) speaks of Cleopatra 'the queen daring to rout the Roman trumpet with the shaking timbrel' which suggests that the timbrel on one notorious occasion was thought to have attempted to take the place of the trumpet in issuing orders to a Roman fleet. It is hardly possible for something suggesting this to have happened and become notorious on any other occasion than Aktion. If that was the occasion then her order given by the timbrel to form columns was given, as Dio says, 'to her subjects'. The fighting all took place, after Antony's ships had moved out of the strait, at the mouth of the channel into which 'the strait' leads (see Plan 7). That is probably a sufficient foundation for Horace's words written when accurate versions of what occurred on 2 September 31 had not yet reached Rome. '*Portu latent*' is an unfriendly interpretation of the fact that Antony did at any rate at first keep his ships in the channel mouth at the SW end of the strait which could be described as his 'portus' with towers on each side of the entrance as distinct from the 'deep water'. Plan 7 shows that his battle lines would just have fitted into the width of the channel's mouth and would have been protected neatly on both flanks as long as he remained there. Plutarch (*Antony* 65.2–4) says, as will be seen, that when the battle lines were drawn Antony instructed the ship masters 'to receive the enemy's attacks ...and keep their station within the mouth of the gulf', and that Octavian 'was astonished to see the enemy motionless in the strait' (not distinguishing between the strait and the channel's mouth). He was astonished because he knew what Antony's intention was. Remaining in the channel's mouth was good defensive tactics, but did not serve that intention, 'to seek the deep water'.

The battle: the secondary sources

Dio had said (p. 164) that Octavian on Agrippa's advice had abandoned his plan to let Antony escape without fighting and then pursue him, putting instead large numbers of decksoldiers on board his ships for close fighting and 'waiting for Antony to come out'. Accordingly (50.31.4): 'When Antony's men put out at the trumpets' signal and drew up their line of closely packed ships a little outside the straits and came out no further, Octavian came on, as if to join battle with them if they remained where they were, or even to force them to withdraw. But when they neither came out to meet him nor turned about, but remained where they were and in addition actually made their line considerably denser' (and thus shorter), 'he didn't know what to do'.

'Octavian paused for a short time ordering the oarsmen to lower their oars into the water. Then suddenly at a signal he brought forward both wings and turned them inwards', a reaction to Antony's move shortening his line, and so making it denser, which was rightly interpreted as a preparation for moving out. The deep formation of the Athenian line at Arginousae (*AT* 87–92) was adopted against the *περίπλους*. Octavian 'hoped if possible to surround them', (with a double *περίπλους*), 'but failing that, at any rate to break up their line. Accordingly, anxious about the wings bending inwards on him, and about being surrounded, Antony went out to meet the challenge as far as possible; and came to grips with Octavian although he did not want it...'. That is true in the sense that he wanted, as Dio had said earlier, 'to get away, as if preparing for a sea fight'. And that is what in fact he and Cleopatra and some ships succeeded in doing. But the rest of Antony's fleet must have fought either still in or at any rate just outside the channel. They could be said, by an unsympathetic reporter, to 'skulk within harbour, though ordered to move to the left in column' after Antony and Cleopatra.

Dio (50.32.2) now turns to the details of the fighting: 'The contest was not the same on both sides. Octavian's men, having smaller and swifter ships, accelerated noisily and put in the ram, being themselves protected all over (*πεφραγμένοι πάντῃ*) from wounding (by missiles)'. That is to say, their ships were totally boxed-in. 'And if they swamped a ship, so much the better; but if not, they would back down before a hand-to-hand fight developed. They would then either quickly ram the same men again, or would let them be and turn to others. Doing as much damage as they could in a short time, they would then turn to others, and again to others, so that they would attack enemies as unexpectedly as possible'.

'In so far as they feared the long range offensive of the enemy (by missiles) and feared as well hand-to-hand fighting, they spent no time in the approach or in the encounter; but ran in suddenly to get there before the archers could shoot. Wounding an enemy soldier or causing only enough disturbance to avoid being caught, they would retire out of range'.

'The other party' (Antony's men) 'pelted those on board the approaching ships with a thick hail of stones and arrows, and hurled grappling irons onto the attackers' ships. If they hit them, they got the upper hand; if they missed, their own hulls would be damaged and they would go under; or if they wasted time in trying to avoid this result, they would find themselves an easy target for others. Of two or three ships attacking one ship at the same time, one or two would achieve their aim while one or two were damaged. On the one side the helmsmen and oarsmen did the hard work and took the punishment, on the other the decksoldiers. ...The one party would run in over the oars and smash them, while the others above tried to swamp them with stones and missiles from catapults'.

The practice of using large stones to be thrown on to attacking vessels from a height is corroborated for Aktion by Propertius (4.6.49).

The battle was indecisive. Cleopatra on board a ship riding at anchor behind the Antonian line suddenly turned to flight herself and gave the signal to the others, her subjects (engaged in fighting) '*τοῖς ἄλλοις τοῖς ὑπηκόοις σημεῖον ἦρε*'. When they raised their mainsails, since the (shore) wind by chance blew favourably, and made for the open sea, Antony 'thinking that they were fleeing not on Cleopatra's orders but in fear because they had had the worst of it in the fighting, followed. The rest when this happened were disheartened and afraid; and some raised their sails while others lightened their ships by jettisoning the towers and gear'.

The implication is that Cleopatra's ships had formed part of Antony's line albeit in the rear. Octavian's ships did not pursue those who had fled because they had brought no sails. The fight continued and was only brought to an end when Octavian used fire against the vessels that still resisted. Dio gives a long, detailed and gruesome account of this part of the battle.

Plutarch's account of the engagements is different from Dio's in some respects and contains additional details. Nothing in either is inconsistent with the little the primary sources provide. He begins with one of the challenges offered by Octavian in the days before the battle:

(*Antony*: 63.1) 'When the enemy moved against him at daybreak', that is to say left their mooring to challenge him to fight, 'Antony was afraid that Octavian would catch his ships with their decks unmanned by soldiers, because the infantry had not yet arrived. He put the oarsmen under arms on the decks for display, and then raising the oarblades and 'making a wing' on each side he held the ships at the mouth of the Gulf near Aktion with their prows pointing seaward as if they were under oar and ready for action'.

Octavian was deceived and withdrew.

'It had been Cleopatra's decision that the war should be decided by the ships, although she had already planned to make a dash for the open sea and had placed her ships where she could easily get away' i.e. on the left flank. 'When the decision was taken to fight at sea Antony burned all the Egyptian ships except 60, manning the best and biggest [in his whole fleet] from threes to tens, putting on deck 20,000 hoplites and 2000 archers'. 'The helmsmen protested at the order to put sails on board but were overruled by Antony saying that they would prove useful in preventing the enemy escaping'.

(65.1)'On the first and following three days the sea was too rough to allow a battle; but on the fifth day, with the weather fine and the sea calm, battle was finally joined. Antony had Publicola with him on his right wing, Coelius on his left wing with M. Octavius and M. Insteius in the centre. Octavian placed Agrippa on the left wing, [Arruntius in the centre: see 66.3] and took the right wing himself... Antony went round all his ships in a small rowing boat urging the soldiers, because of the weight (*βρῖθος*) of their ships, to be content to fight from fixed positions, as if they were on land; and ordering the helmsmen to receive the rams of the enemy with their ships immobile as if moored to the land, while they held their difficult position at the mouth of the gulf'.

'After inspecting the rest of the line Octavian was taken to the right wing [the position of the commander-in-chief]; and was amazed to see the enemy ships lying in the narrows without moving, and giving the impression of riding at anchor. For quite a long time he thought this was so, and kept his ships about eight stades'(three-quarters of a sea mile) 'away from the enemy. It was now the sixth hour [noon] and the [shore] wind and sea were getting up. Antony's men were impatient of the delay [in breaking out] and confident that the height of their ships would make them difficult adversaries. Accordingly they put the left wing in motion. Octavian was pleased to see this, and backed down on his right wing. He wished to draw the enemy still further out of the gulf and the narrows, and effecting an encirclement (*περιπλέων*) with his own expertly rowed (*εὐήρεσι*) ships to come to grips with those ships which by dint of their size and undermanned condition were sluggish and slow'.

It is to be noticed that Plutarch says that Antony's ships took the initiative after forming a line and then remaining stationary at the mouth of the channel. Dio's account makes Octavian, who with more ships is likely to have formed a longer line, take the initiative by turning inwards his two wings, and that this caused Antony unwillingly to advance his whole line. It seems likely that Plutarch is right. There is no doubt that Antony's purpose was to break out and that his initial posture was indeed safe but in fact a pretence of preparation for a pitched battle. Since Plutarch attributes the move of the left wing to the impatience of Antony's men at the delay (in breaking out) rather than to Antony himself he implies that his men were privy to the plan. If the first, if delayed, step after forming his line step was to thicken it, a move to lessen vulnerability to *περίπλους*, that showed his purpose; and the following signal to advance his left wing a little way showed it again since the left wing would lead a column heading south. Octavian's reported reaction of withdrawing his right wing to allow Antony to emerge further is a likely one if he knew Antony's purpose.

(*Antony* 66.1) 'When the fighting began to be hand-to-hand, there was no ramming or breaking of ships' timbers, because Antony's ships from their weight were unable to get up momentum, which is what principally results in violent blows with the ram, while Octavian's ships not only avoided engagement prow-to-prow against solid, abrasive, bronze rams but did not even have the heart to ram on the side. Their rams would easily have been broken off when they hit hulls lashed together and made of massive squared timbers fastened with iron (nails?). The contest was like a land battle or, more accurately, like a siege. For three or four ships jointly assailed one of Antony's, the men employing wicker shields, spears and poles as well as flame throwers, while Antony's men fought with catapults from wooden towers'.

(*Antony* 66.3) 'When Agrippa extended the other (left) wing to effect an encirclement, Publicola [with Antony on the opposite right wing] was forced to go out against him and broke away from the centre. The men there were in confusion and there was hand to hand fighting with Arruntius's men. Then suddenly, while the fighting was still undecided and on equal terms, Cleopatra's sixty ships were observed raising their sails to move out and escaping on a course through the middle of the melée of fighting ships. They had been placed in the rear of the big ships, and caused confusion as they pushed their way through. Their opponents looked on in amazement as they saw them taking advantage of the (shore) wind and setting a course for the Peloponnese'.

Dio says (50.33.1–2) that Cleopatra was 'riding at anchor behind the combatants' and from there signalled her subjects to escape; and that they took advantage of a favourable wind and raised their sails. It is perhaps reasonable that Cleopatra would not be expected to take a part in the battle herself, but inconceivable that her sixty selected ships should also have been non-combatant (out of a total of 170). They would have been used as a support squadron with other similar squadrons behind the front squadrons to deal with encirclements and penetrations. But they were near enough to Cleopatra to hear her signals. Although Cleopatra had stationed herself and her ships so that they could 'easily get away', they had as it turned out to make their way out of the channel's mouth through the fighting on the left wing.

(*Antony* 66.5) 'As soon as Antony saw Cleopatra's ship sailing away,... he transferred' (from a larger ship) 'into a five' (as being faster) 'with Alexas the Syrian and Scellius as the only fellow passengers; and went after the woman who had already destroyed him and was to add to that destruction'.

(*Antony* 67) 'Cleopatra recognised Antony' (on board his five) 'and raised a signal from her ship. He came alongside and was taken aboard; but he neither saw her nor was seen (by her), but went forward alone to the prow and sat by himself with his head in his hands. Thereupon liburnians came in sight, sent in pursuit by Octavian. Antony ordered the ship's prow to be turned round to face them. He made the other ships withdraw, but not the ship of Eurykles the Laconian. He attacked with a rush and brandished a spear on the deck as if he was about to hurl it at Antony... However Eurykles did not ram Antony's ship but hit the other flagship (for there were two) with the bronze ram and swung her round. Then he caught this ship in the side as she turned and one of the others in which there were valuable personal belongings...Antony and Cleopatra made their escape to Alexandria'.

Eurykles's ship, which had both a ram and a deck, may, as flagship of a liburnian squadron, have been a three, but some liburnians (πρίστεις: see p. 263), probably all those in Roman naval service, had rams and there is no reason why some should not also have had decks (p. 264). However, a ship that was able to put out of action a flagship, i.e. at least a five, by ramming may be thought to have been heavier than a two, although that conclusion is far from necessary. A second point to notice in this incident is that a liburnian squadron, possibly led by a three, was able to catch up with a group of heavy ships under sail with a favourable wind and a start of an hour or so, but unable in fact to capture Antony and Cleopatra. This would have required some heavy ships to achieve. Agrippa, it seems, was right.

(*Antony* 68.1) Plutarch gives no details of the losses on either side except to remark that 'three hundred ships were captured, as Caesar (Octavian) himself has written'. Antony's land forces surrendered to Octavian after their commander Canidius had left them.

Appendix A

The evidence of Tacitus 31 BC–AD 117

A number of ship portraits included in Chapter 5 (Iconography) derive from, or shortly before or shortly after, the period of the early Roman Empire in which the Roman historian Tacitus wrote (bn.c.AD 56 or 57, d.AD 117). The part of his *Annals* which survives covers the years from the death of Augustus (AD 14) to AD 66, two years before the death of Nero, while the only preserved part of his *Histories* deals with the turbulent years from the death of Nero to AD 70, a year after the accession of Vespasian. His other two historical works, the *Agricola* and *Germania* were written the first in and the second shortly after AD 98. His evidence is therefore of great value in the attempt to determine the types of warships represented in the early Empire.

After the accounts of great ships taking part in the naval engagements leading up to and including the battle of Aktion the reader when he comes to Tacitus is struck by the fact that Tacitus mentions no type of warship of higher rating than a four, and that he only mentions fours once, as taking part in a mock sea fight staged by Claudius in the Fucine lake (*Annals* 12.56.2).

The fact is striking but not inexplicable. After Aktion the big ships were not only discredited but unnecessary. Tacitus refers to them in the *Annals* (4.5.1) in a review of the naval scene. He says that there were two Roman fleets, one at Misenum and the other at Ravenna; that the *rostratae naves* captured by Augustus at Aktion (which must have at least included fives to tens, as well as a few threes: p. 164–165), were sent by him to Forum Julii (Fréjus) 'under strong oarcrews' (*valido remige*) the latter phrase indicating the types of ship they were; while *sociae triremes*, threes manned and possibly also built by the allied cities, were posted at strategic points in the provinces. Inscriptions (see Appendix B) show that the Misenum and Ravenna fleets were composed mostly of threes, some liburnians and fours, and one or two fives and sixes. Tacitus compares Claudius's mock sea battle with the one put on 'with light ships' by Augustus (in 2 BC) on an artificial lake on the far side of the Tiber. These light ships, drawn presumably from the Misenum fleet, are specified in the *Res Gestae Divi Augusti* (4.4.3) as 30 triremes and biremes (the latter liburnians) and more smaller ships.

Except on one occasion when in the year of the four emperors (AD 69) Tacitus speaks of Otho's sea power and his ability to blockade the Adriatic (*Histories* 2.12.1) the principal function of warships was now to serve the Roman armies on the Rhine and Danube frontiers. In AD 16 Germanicus built a fleet of 1000 ships (*Annals* 2.6) for use on the Rhine. His flagship was a three. Later (*Histories* 5.22–23) in AD 70, also on the Rhine, Cerialis's flagship was a three (*praetoria triremis*), while the ships mustered by the rebel Civilis were twos (*biremes*) and single banked craft, also small craft with crews of 30–40 men 'fitted out like liburnians'. These specifications are interesting because the 'biremes' are clearly full-sized liburnians (with an oarcrew of fifty) while there were also smaller craft with the oarsystem of liburnians (two levels of single manned oars) but smaller, like the two-level triacontors in Alexander's Indus flotilla (p. 9).

In the Rhine fleets the threes were the big ships. Corbulo in AD 47 (*Annals* 11.18.2) brought his threes up river through the main channels and the other craft (shallow by a shorter route) through the creeks and canals. Similarly when the Misenum fleet was trying to round C. Misenum in AD 64 in a storm the losses are described (*Annals* 15.46.3) as 'threes and a great number of smaller ships'.

Threes were used for swift transport (*Annals* 16.2.2) and dangerous situations where a 'strong' ship was needed as on the occasion (*Ann.* 2.55.3) when Germanicus sent them to rescue Cnaeus Calpurnius Piso in danger of shipwreck on a lee shore. They were also the most prestigious. A governor setting out for his province of Galatia and Phrygia was assigned two threes from the Ravenna fleet as escort (*Hist.* 2.9); and Agrippina was given a three manned by *classiarii* i.e. Roman soldiers rather than *socii navales* (cf. *Ann.* 14.4.6) to take her about.

Tacitus speaks of detachments of three twos (*biremes*) as used independently as in *Ann.* 4.27.1 for the protection of commerce. Furneaux (*Ann.* 16.14.5) recognises the term *liburnicae* used of a detachment of ships sent by Nero in AD 66 to arrest Sosianus as 'equivalent to *biremes* but sometimes used more generally, as we have a '*trierarchus liburnicarum navium*' in *Hist.* 2.16.2'. This recognition is right, but it is *biremis* which is the more general and *liburnica* as a distinct kind of *biremis* the more specific term in Tacitus's usage, as has been seen above, and 'τριήραρχος' is often used for a commander of ships other than threes (e.g. p. 205).

Liburnicae appear frequently in the Histories, first in Otho's fleet at the first battle of Cremona (2.35.4), then at Ravenna (3.12 and 14 'the soldiers of three liburnians') and (3.42.3) as a squadron used by the Othonians on the east coast of Italy. Mucianus, in command of the Black Sea fleet, concentrated all the best liburnians at Byzantion, leaving the rest of the area undefended (3.47.15), from which it may be concluded that the fleet consisted of liburnians. To meet Otho's naval ascendancy Vespasian built liburnians quickly (3.48.4). When Tarracina, occupied by the rebel Misenum fleet under Claudius Apollinaris, fell to Vitellius's brother Lucius, Apollinaris escaped with six liburnians and the rest of the fleet (apparently all liburnians), were captured or put out of action (3.77.12). Liburnians also appear in Tacitus's later *Agricola* (28.5) where he tells the story of three liburnians hijacked in Britain by a cohort of Usipi.

From these passages the conclusion must be drawn that in the provinces the liburnian was the predominant warship of the early empire; that the three was present in strength in the home fleets but used for special purposes. Fours were used, perhaps as a deliberate archaism, in AD 52 for Claudius's mock battle. Augustus in his mock battle used nothing larger than threes. Fours are not mentioned by Tacitus as in naval service, yet nineteen of them appear in the inscriptions of the early empire. It must be supposed that Antony's larger ships, fives to tens, which were sent to Forum Julii in 31 BC were laid up together with most of Octavian's fives and sixes, only one or two fives and sixes being kept in commission for special service. It is not therefore surprising that ships of higher rating than fours are rarely represented in inscriptions after the first half of the first century AD.

Appendix B:
Roman fleets after Aktion

The following table gives the mainly epigraphical evidence for the composition of the two main fleets of the early Roman empire, one at Misenum and the other at Ravenna, and of three or four of the provincial fleets. The table is based on Miltner in *RE* Supplement band V pp. 951–956 (1931) and embodies the corrigenda and addenda given by Casson *SSAW* Ch. 15 n. 57 (1971) and further addenda provided in the paperback edition of SSAW (1986). Relevant entries have also been included from *L'Année épigraphique* after 1979.

The references are to the *Corpus Inscriptionum Latinarum (CIL)* and to *L'Année épigraphique (AE)*, *Berliner griechische Urkunden (BGU)*, *Corpus papyrorum latinarum (CPL)*, *Ephemeris Epigraphike (Ephem. Epigr.)*, *Inscriptions grecques et latines de la Syrie*: L. Jalabert et R. Mouterde: Paris (1929–) (*Jal.-Mout.*), *Revue archéologique (RA)*, Panciera (see *SSAW* Ch.13 App.n.13).

THE FLEET BASE AT MISENUM

Established 27–18 BC (Viereck: 1975: p. 252–279)

LIBURNIANS	
Aesculapius	X 3651
Aquila	X 3361; 3641
Armata	VI 3145; X 3589, 3634, 3668
Clementia	X 3511
Diana	*AE* 1975.271
Fides	VI 1063,20; X 3423, 3593, 3632;
Hept...	VI 32761
Juno	*AE* 1979.161
Justitia	X 3492; 3632; 3657: *AE* 1978: 2nd-3rd cent. AD
Libertas	X 3590
Margarita	*AE* 1974.261: 1st cent. AD
Minerva	X 3607
Neptunus	X 3412, 3475, 3647
Taurus Ruber	X 3421
Virtus	*RA*. VI 1905 477 nr.126: *Jal-Mout.* 1162 (see Casson *SSAW* Ch.15 n.57)

THREES	
Apollo	VI 3139; X 3383, 3471: *RA* iv 1916.478 nr.109
Aquila	X 3562, 3564
Asclepius	X 3377
Athenonice	X 3403, 3408, 3602, 3623, 3662
Augustusi	X 3446. 3450, 3560, 3649, 3650
Capricornus	VI 3095; X 3597
Castor	X 3582
Ceres	X 3517, 3540, 3546, 3554, 3592
Concordia	VI 3094, 3144; X 3370, 3427, 3462, 3498, 3565: *AE* 1980.487: end 3rd cent. AD.
Cupido	X 3442, 3484, 3642, 3664, 3667
Danuvius	X 3508, 3546, 3553
Diana	X 3381, 3523,
Euphrates	X 3477, 3484, 3510
Fides	VI 3117, 3124, 3128; X 3501, 3591, 3599, 3625: *AE* 1949.208
Fortuna	X 3589, 3636: *AE* 1946.145, *Jal-Mout.* 1171
Hercules	VI 3102, 3143, 32774; X 3379, 3432, 3505, 3575, 3583
Isis	VI 3123; X 3615, 3618, 3640
Juno	X 3374, 3482
Juppiter	X 3638, 3664: *Ephem.Epigr.* viii p.116 nr.444
Juventus	VI 3107
Liber pater	X 3535, 3540, 3563, 3579, 3595: CPL 120 restored in *Jal-Mout.* 1168
Libera	VI 32771
Libertas	X 3422, 3588, 3597
Lucifer	X 3384, 3394, 3395, 3579
Mars	X 3507, 3584, 3627
Mercurius	X 3338, 3401, 3452; XIV 239: *Ephem. Epigr.* viii p.116 nr 444
Minerva	VI 3136; X 3406: *Ephem.Epigr.* viii p.116 nr.444: *AE* 1949.206: *AE* 1988.311 (end 2nd cent. beginning 3rd cent. AD)
Neptunus	X 3375, 3378, 3656
Nilus	VI 32764b; X 3578
Oceanus	X 3437, 3496
Parthicus	VI 3121; X 3454
Pax	VI 3105; X 3380, 3470, 3515, 3533, 3652: Jal-Mout, 1159

Perseus	VI 3146; X 3399, 3466, 3664
Pietas	X 3497, 3610, 3613: *Jal-Mout.* 1165
Pollux	VI 3106; X 3514
Providentia	X 3636: *AE* 1929 142: CPL 120
Rhenus	VI 3115, 3138; X 3407, 3467
Salaminai	VI 3112: *AE* 1946 146
Salus	VI 3134, 3147, 3699; X 3402, 3639, 8119: CPL 120
Salvia	VI 3094; X 3532, 3580, 3600
Satyra	X 3400a, 3459, 8210
Silvanus	X 3398, 3408, 8211: *AE* 1983 189: 2nd-3rd C AD
Sol	X 3405, 3503, 3603, 3617, 3658, 3666
Spes	VI 1063,17; X 3381, 3510
Taurus	X 3447, 3648: RA vi 1905, 477 nr.126: *AE* 1929.147: *Jal-Mout.* 1162
Tiberis	X 3476
Tigris	X 3393, 3400a, 3443, 8210; XI 3737: CPL 120
Triumphus	X 3555, 3629, 3645: *AE* 1980.486: early 3rd cent. AD
Venus	VI 3110; X 3382, 3458, 3460, 3461, 3468, 3472, 3539, 3596, 3598,3635,3652,6800: *AE* 1965 145: AD 127–129
Vesta	VI 3097; X 3483, 3572, 3585 *AE* 1929 146
Victoria	III 7327; X 3445, 3545, 3577, 3612
Virtusi	VI 3137, X 3397, 3400, 3406, 8208: *RA* vi 1905.477.nr.126

FOURS

Annona	X 3495
Dacicus	X 3426, 3439, 3480, 3482, 3490, 3569, 3647:
Ephem. Epigr.	viii p.101 nr.383: *RA.* iv 1916, 213 nr.52: *Jal-Mout.* 1167
Fides	VI 1063 15; X 3485, 3546; XIV 237
Fortuna	VI 3126, 3127, 3133; X 3465, 3566
Libertas	X 3598
Mercurius	VI 3114
Minerva	VI 3136; X 3406: *Ephem.Epigr.* viii p.116 nr.444: *AE* 1949 206; 1987.261
Venus	X 3391, 3420, 3478, 3491, 3605, *RA.* iv 1904, 448 nr.171: *Jal-Mout.* 1178
Vesta	X 3365, 3372, 3404, 3454, 3481, 3489, 3495, 3531, 3534, 3534, 3566, 3653.
Victoria	VI 3142,

FIVE

Victoria	X 3404, 3410, 3455, 3463, 3523, 3539, 3568, 3580, 3606, 3637

SIX

Ops	X 3560, 3611

MISENIAN SHIPS OF UNSPECIFIED TYPE

Danae	XIV 234.
Hercules	XIV 241
Jupiter	XIV 233, *Jal-Mout.* 1158
Minerva	VI 3140.
Minervia ratis	*AE* 1964.105
Ops	VI 3119
Venus	X 3509, 3618
Vesta	X 3464a.
Victoria	X 3670

RAVENNA

navalia since 35 BC: Home Fleet base 27–15 BC

LIBURNIANS

Ammon	XI 3735
Diana	VI 3149; XI 111
Pinnata	*AE* 1979. 248: 3rdQtr of 1st cent. AD
Satura	*AE* 1967 114

THREES

Aesculapius	X 3486; XI 68, 78, 109
Apollo	X 3527, XI 101, 109
Aquila	XI 90
Arcina	XI 100, 102, 3735 (*SSAW* Ch.15 n.60)
Augustus	VI 3151; XI 46
Castor	XI 44, 53
Constantia	XI 55
Danae	XI 30, 120
Diana	XI 31, 85
Mars	II 4063; X 3524; XI 51, 52, 67
Mercurius	XI 122
Minerva	XI 35, 36, 72, 119
Neptunus	VI 3161; XI 94, 97
P...	*AE* 1980.488: end 3rd cent. AD
Pax	XI 103
Pietas	XI 64, 343
Pinnata	XI 28
Providentia	XI 39, 91
Triptolemus	*AE* 1966.97: cf.CIL IX 41
Triumphus	XI 60
Victoria	XI 59, 65, 113.
Venus	*AE* 1980.488: end 3rd cent. AD
Virtus	VI 3148, X 3645, XI 95

FOURS

Fortuna	XI 47, 63, 82, 92
Mercurius	XI 106

Neptunus	XI 45
Padus	XI 70, 99, 110
Vesta	VI 3158; XI 62
Victoria	VI 3159; XI 89: *RA* vi 1905 492 nr. 201

FIVES

Augustus	XI 58, 343, *RA*. xvi 1922 406 nr. 135 5
Victoria	XI 50, 54, 77, 112

The Hercules (Ravenna) is mentioned without specification of type:

PROVINCES

Britain

Radians (Three): XIII 3564

Alexandria

Draco (liburnian) CPL 210

Fides (liburnian) CPL 191

Lupa (liburnian) BGU 741 7–8

Mercurius (liburnian) CPL 125

Neptunus (liburnian) CPL 250

Taurus (probably a liburnian) CPL 223

Syria

Capricornus (liburnian) *Jal-Mout.* 1163

Gryps (liburnian) III 434

Moesia

Armata (liburnian) *AE* 1950.175

Sagita (liburnian) *AE* 1967.429

Mauretania

Nilus (liburnian) VIII 21025

WARSHIPS OF UNKNOWN STATION

LIBURNIANS

Augustus	V 1048, Panciera 325
Clupeus	V 1956
Lucusta	*AE* 1980.689
Murena	III 2034
Sphinx	Panciera 329 n.55
Triton	IX 42
Varvar(ina)	XI 104

THREES

Aesculapius	V 2833
Apollo	V 2840
Aquila	VI 32777a
Augustus	VI 32776
Capricornus	VI 32776
Crocodilus	V 960
Diana	VI 3172
Diomedes	IX 1631
Juppiter	XIV 233
Libertas	XIV 4133: *RA*. xiv 1921 456 nr.33
Neptunus	VI 3165
Ops	VI 3168
Perseus	VI 3169
Phryx	*RA*. xxxvii 1900 508 nr.105
Providentia	*RA*. viii 1906 485 nr.163
Quadriga	IX 43
Sol	XIU 242: BGU 455
Venus	V 8819

FOURS

Fortuna	III 3165
Ops	*RA*. xxvi 1927, 348 nr.3
Padus	V 541

SIXES

Ops	VI 3163, 3170; XIV 232

SHIPS WITHOUT SPECIFICATION OF STATION OR TYPE

Amila Augusta Felix *Ephem. Epigr.* IX 1319

Clementia	VI 3167
Mars	V 1959
Triptolemus	*AE* 1966.97
Victoria	XI 3736

The tombstones and papyri which record the ships in the foregoing lists derive for the most part from the first two centuries of the early Roman empire. They thus present a useful picture of the regular composition of the imperial fleets.

The picture shows the three as the most numerous type and as a 'strong' ship (in Lucan's characterisation) most suited to the demands of contemporary naval service, secure and rapid communication, protection of the food supply, suppression of pirates; and, often most urgent if not in the long run most important of all, maritime and riverine support for the imperial armies in the provinces and in particular those dealing with provincial rebellions on the Rhine and Danube.

The liburnian, economical in manpower and suitable by reason of its light draught for the 'creeks and canals' of the low countries of Europe and the Delta of Egypt, played an important supporting role to the three, but is also seen operating on her own in very small detachments.

The four was again more economical in manpower and, as double-manned, in skilled oarsmen; and she had also the advantage of a broader deck for fighting men. But her role in the imperial fleets is not attested. In the last days of the Republic the four appears in

Sicily as a flagship to a fleet of small vessels engaged in the suppression of piracy (p. 269). That may have remained her role in the empire, a second class flagship in a number of minor fleets. It would explain her small but not insignificant numbers.

The single fives and sixes were plainly the first class, but normally unused, flagships for the potential major fleets retained in commission to convey members of the imperial house. Pliny the Elder (NH 32.1.4) speaks of Caligula's five as having 400 oarsmen. Since ten regular oar-files @ 40 men is unlikely, the ship was either a five carrying spare oarsmen or a six (12 @ 33–4). In any case she shows the use to which were now put the few examples in commission of the great warship types of the previous century.

Endnotes

1. Peskett (1908) says in a note: The 'island opposite Marsalia' is 'probably the island of Ratonneau just opposite the port'.
2. As JSM wrongly said in LSRS p. 45. In JFC's reconstruction of the Isola Tiberina ship (**27**) the deck is 1.4 ft higher than the deck of the same ship reconstructed as a five.
3. JFC: 'It would also follow that these ships were light and fast, therefore as narrow as possible. Otherwise a single level of double-manned oars would be adequate, cheaper and easier to man – and slower'.
4. An interesting example of the current classification of warships into first and second line. It will be seen that these *κατάσκοποι* included threes, not therefore included in the *μάχιμοι*.
5. Pantellaria 31 sm from Lilybaion is a reasonable candidate but in antiquity that island is called Cossyra elsewhere.
6. JFC notes that four days is a very long time to cover the 113 sm from Lilybaion to the African coast 'with a steady, fast, wind'. The narrative, or our text of it, seems faulty.
7. Casson (*SSAW* p. 104) says that the men who could not keep their feet in rough weather were 'the men on deck', since the helmsman and the oarsmen are said to have other difficulties. The decksoldiers are required to sit (p. 000) when the ship is under oar in battle, so would probably be sitting then. That leaves the other members of the *ὑπηρεσία* in particular the two deck gangs who might well have duties to perform which required them to move about on deck.
8. JFC observes that the shipbuilder would have had to allow for the weight of the structure to be added if the waterline was eventually to be correct for the oar rig.
9. JFC notes that 12 legions (9600 men @ 50 a ship would have filled only 182 *ὁλκάδες* and the 500 cavalry only 33, leaving 785 for the 'much gear'. It seems that more than half of them must have been sent over empty for use on other occasions.
10. JFC observes: 'That towers were at bow and stern indicates that boarding was normally made and received from the ends of ships. Towers so placed would have been valuable for both attack and defence'.
11. JFC: This shows that there was a significant difference in draft between Papias's fours and Agrippa's fives and sixes.
12. Not 'cavalry' as E. Cary (1917).
13. It appears that here as on another occasion (p. 2 and 16) in Diodoros the text which reads *πεντήρεις* has been the victim of the logic of editors who have replaced 'fives' with 'fours' in the belief that there was a steady increase in height from threes onward.
14. For *moles* meaning a mass of armed men cf. Vergil *Aeneid* 12.575, Livy 26.6.9, Tacitus *Histories* 1.61 and *Annals* 2.46.4

5

ICONOGRAPHY

FOREWORD

The reconstruction of the Athenian three was based on two main hypotheses: the first was that, apart from minor differences brought about by the tapering of the hull fore and aft, the oars at all three levels were of the same length: the second was that the Greek name *τριήρης* did not indicate the number of levels of oars but the number of files of oarsmen on each side of the ship irrespective of level (as in the case of the names of types of oared galley in medieval times). This latter hypothesis provided an answer to the serious objection to a three-level *τριήρης* that it implied the absurd consequence that the *τετρήρης* had four levels of oars, the *πεντήρης* five, and so on to the forty. A further hypothesis was that the introduction of oars manned by more than one oarsman (*a scaloccio*) enabled the number of files on each side to be increased to produce ships of higher denomination than three without physical impossibility. Nevertheless the belief is still common that the word *τριήρης* means a ship of three levels of oars, and accordingly that a ship-portrait showing three oar-levels can only be a representation of a three. The belief is also general that ships depicted in antiquity with two levels of oars must have two files of oarsmen a side only (i.e. the common *liburna* as Panciera p. 154), while the possibility that they may be *τετρήρεις*/quadriremes/fours with the oars at each level double-manned, or ships of much larger denomination with oars pulled by gangs of men, is not generally recognised.

In the period 399–31 BC Mediterranean fleets were composed of increasing numbers of ships of denominations higher than three. The fleets of the Hellenistic kings had a great number of such ships ranging from fours to Ptolemy Philopator's forty, and the Romans and Carthaginians fought the first Punic war with many hundreds of fives, while the three became in the latter part of the 4th century a ship of lower rating (*minoris formae*), no longer a ship of the line but a scout for communication and lesser operations, the roles of the frigate of sailing navies.

There are many warship representations datable to the period, deriving particularly from Rome and Italy. Apart from coins where the oarsystem is in most cases indicated by unrealistic convention, they show oarsystems occasionally of one, usually of two or three levels. None show oarsystems of more than three levels. Where fives, sixes, sevens etc are mentioned in contemporary literature it is their height which is emphasised, as is to be seen, e.g., in the accounts of the battle of Cypriot Salamis, of an incident in the 2nd Punic war and Lucan's account of the battle of Massalia. This feature is noted in the case of some ships as the result of the erection for battle of towers at bow and stern and sometimes amid ships, in the case of others as the result of their higher decks.

The only conclusion that makes sense under these circumstances is to include the types from five to, say, eight with the three in the category of ships of three levels of oars, to include the four and the ships bigger than the eight with the twos (triacontor, pentecontor and liburnian) in the category of ships of two levels of oars, and to accept in the case of the types from four upwards the (*a scaloccio*) practice, which is attested in the case of the forty at the end of the 3rd century BC (p.274–277), of rowing more than one man to an oar. On the basis of this conclusion the iconography of the warships of the period will be interpreted. The graffito of a four (**38**) is fortunately so labelled. It will be possible also with some degree of certainty to identify among the other representations at least a pentecontor (**vii**) and liburnians (**44, 45–49**), Athenian threes (**ixa, ixb, ixc, x**), *τριημιολίαι* (**11, 20, 21, 26, 36**), fives (**12, 18 I, 18 II, 35, 43**), more tentatively a six (**27**), and two of the bigger ships (**25, 29**). Practical designs of a liburnian (**72**), a *ἡμιολία* (**73**) and a *τριημιολία* (**74**), a four (**59**), fives (**57, 61, 63, 65, 66, 71**) and six (**67**), will be offered.

Much of the material which will be examined in the following iconography, in particular the ship-portraits on coins and in some of the reliefs, defies rational interpretation. A quotation from Lepper and Frere's introduction to their *Trajan's Column* (p. 36) gives very relevant advice on how to set about the interpretation of the Column's sculpture, which is applicable *mutatis mutandis* throughout the field of the representations of oared warships.

> 'Somehow the reader must try to get the wavelength of these reliefs for himself, an operation which calls for patience and humility, as well as imagination. He must not be too quick to claim an intuitive insight into their messages. Only after prolonged and repeated study should he ask himself what sort of activities and behaviour or attendant circumstances seem to get special individual treatment, what methods are used to furnish them with a particular identity.'

Before examining the representations of the oared warships of the period in which the new types may be shown it will be worthwhile to look at the representations of the two-level pentecontors and the threes about whose oarsystems something is known, and thus to gain some clues to the artists' method and technique of representation.

THE PRECURSORS: THE EARLY TWOS AND THREES

Innovations in Mediterranean naval construction made during the 4th and 3rd centuries BC arise from two types evolved from the Homeric long ship (*GOS* p. 7–72, pls 1–7) which was rowed by oarsmen in two files one on each side. The evolution answered the need for a better power/weight ratio in warships when the ram became the main weapon in confrontation at sea. The first of the new types is the pentecontor with two files of oarsmen a side at different levels (the two). The second is the three, with three files of oarsmen a side at different levels. This latter type was evolved possibly in two forms, one in Phoenicia of the 8th century BC without a *παρεξειρεσία* (the survival of this type into the 5th century is by no means clear), and the other in mainland Greece with a *παρεξειρεσία*. Threes, and occasionally twos, were used as first-line ships in large numbers towards the end of the 6th and throughout the 5th and the greater part of the 4th century BC.

An iconography of the types of warship developed from the three needs accordingly to be prefaced by showing such clear representations as survive of the two-level pentecontor and the three.

The invention of the ship with two levels of oars is attributed to the Ionian city of Erythrai by the historian Damastes of Sigeion writing in the late 5th century BC (*FGrH* 5F6). Such ships are first shown in a group of fragments of vasepainting from the Late Geometric (735–710 BC) and early Archaic (700–650 BC) periods and identified as showing ships of two oarlevels by R. T. Williams (*GOS* Geom. 42, 43, 44 and Arch. 1 p. 36, 37 and 73: Pl. 7.d, e, f and 8.a). Ships rowed at two levels appear shortly afterwards in the relief from the palace of Sennacherib at Nineveh (**ia, ib**) depicting the evacuation of Tyre in 701 in a fleet composed of longships (with armed forefoot) and auxiliaries (with upward curving bows). The vertical line (in the case of the example shown in **1b** the vertical band) indicates the termination of the the metal (bronze or exceptionally iron) sheath of the forefoot, constituting the ram (Torr 1894). This line is absent in the pictures of longships in Geometric vase painting (e.g. *GOS* Geom. 2 Pl. 1). The line or band occurs regularly in Archaic representations and is most clearly visible for what it is in the early 5th century r/f vasepainting of Odysseus and the Sirens (*AT* pl. 47). The simultaneous first secure appearance of the ram and the multiple level oarsystem on the Nineveh relief confirms the likely causal connection between them, the former leading to the latter.

In the last two decades of the Archaic period (510–490 BC) pentecontors employing the two-level oarsystem are well and consistently documented on Samian coins (**ii**), a gem (**iii**) and on Attic b/f vases (**iv-vi**); and the type is corroborated two hundred years later by the detailed representation of the stern section of the *Argo* on the Ficoroni bronze casket (**vii**). From these six representations of the type (both aphract and cataphract) its main characteristics may be clearly seen. The type is important as leading to the four with double-manned oars at two levels, developed at Carthage in the latter half of the 4th century BC; and as matched by the λέμβοι with two oar-levels, in particular the liburnians, of the Adriatic. The biggest types of warship developed in the later Hellenistic period were also probably rowed at two levels.

i. (a) and (b) Fragments of the Nineveh Relief (after 701 BC) and (c) Fragment of Geometric Vasepainting (735–710 BC)

(**a**) Detail showing fleet auxiliaries *LSRS:* 14b, B.660. By courtesy of the British Museum

(**b**) Detail showing an oared warship: *LSRS* 14a, B.379, 664–5. By courtesy of the British Museum.

(c) Fragment of Geometric Styled Attic pottery from the Acropolis Athens: National Museum 265. Kirk (1949) 32 Pl. 40 4, Williams (1958) Pl. XIV c, *GOS* Geom. 44 Pl. 7f.

The relief in Sennacherib's palace at Nineveh showed the evacuation in 701 BC by Luli, king of Sidon, of people from Tyre by sea to Cyprus under threat from Sennacherib's land invasion. The ships of the evacuation fleet are under oar and of two distinct types with certain common features. All are rowed at two levels *en échelon*. The uppermost oars are worked over the topwale, the lower through oarports in the sides of the hull. Oarsmen, disproportionately large, are visible at the upper oars in the open-sided 'rooms'. All the ships have a canopy deck with a disproportionately high bulwark hung with shields outboard, over which appear the heads and shoulders of correspondingly large human figures.

One type of ship (shown in (**a**)) is upward-

i a

curving in the bow as well as in the stern. Being fleet auxiliaries designed to keep up with oared warships they have a two-level oarsystem which sacrifices some cargo-carrying capacity for greater power and a shorter hull.

The other type (shown in (**b**)) also shows oars, sixteen, worked at two levels, but here the bow is sharply pointed at water-level and the forefoot is armed with a (bronze) sheath indicated by the fastening band. These ships, identified by their rams as warships, also stand higher than the other type, having a course of rectangular hatched areas alternating with open spaces below the bulwark with its shields and above the stanchions rising between the visible upper oarsmen's 'rooms'. This puzzling additional course visible in the Phoenician warship is fortunately explained by the near-contemporary group of Late-Geometric fragments of vase paintings, which have been shown to depict undecked longships with two-level oarsystems. The most important of these is shown in (**c**). It depicts a course of alternate hatched areas and open spaces similar to that in (**b**) but with the difference that the open spaces are the 'rooms' of visible oarsmen.

It seems that the otherwise inexplicable open course appearing in the Phoenician warship is the unmanned thranite oarlevel of a three. It is unmanned since the qualities, speed and manoeuvrability, which characterise the three were unnecessary in an operation (a voyage of about 27 nautical miles) where no naval challenge was expected (Sennacherib having no fleet) and speed would have been restricted to that of the two-level auxiliaries. Furthermore the topweight of the unusually large number of deck passengers made an unmanned uppermost oar level desirable. Further, it is likely that oarsmen rather than ships were in short supply.

The two features, the ram and the additional course leading to greater height above the waterline, which distinguish from each other the two types of ships shown in the relief, express the difference between a two-level fleet-auxiliary and a front-line three.

i b

i c

If this interpretation is correct, it appears that in the late 8th century BC there was a Phoenician type of decked three with no *παρεξειρεσία*, with *two* open side courses, (at the zygian as well as at the thranite level), and with the thalamian oars rowed through ports in the hull. This three-level oarsystem, as will be seen, by the 5th century was superseded in Phoenicia by another which may be called Corinthian or Greek, but reappears in the late 4th century with the development of the five. Its occurrence in Phoenicia in the 8th century explains the hitherto puzzling attribution by Clement of Alexandria (*Stromateis* 1.16.76) of the invention of the three (*τρίκροτος ναῦς*) to the Sidonians. Clement is a late and perhaps not very reliable witness, but he is likely to have derived his information from a respectable source, the *Inventions* of Philostephanos of Cyrene who lived in the 3rd century BC and was a pupil of the poet Kallimachos.

The political and naval pressures which caused the development of a three-level oarsystem in Phoenicia in the 8th century would have been felt at about the same time, and equally strongly at 'wealthy' Corinth with her western colonial expansion against Phoenician competitors. The difference in the resulting designs suggests independent development. Thukydides says (1.13.2) that 'threes are said to have been built first at Corinth in Greece' and 'it appears that Ameinokles, the Corinthian shipwright, built four ships' (in the context threes) 'for the Samians; and it is about three hundred years to the end of this (i.e. the Peloponnesian) war (421 or 404 BC) when Ameinokles went to the Samians'. There are uncertainties about the date of the Corinthian 'invention': the date Thukydides is giving for Ameinokles' visit may be at the earliest 704 or 721 (depending on which peace Thukydides chose; or, it has been argued, fifty years later in each case). Ameinokles' reputation would, further, have taken some years to spread. However the Corinthian invention must have been round about the end of the 8th or the beginning of the 7th century BC. Her thalassocracy (period of dominating the seas, whatever that might mean) was given (Forrest 1969) as 730–669 BC; and it is likely that the invention occurred nearer the beginning than the end of that period. Salmon (1984: p. 223) puts the naval developments at Corinth after the fall of the Bacchiads there in 650. This dating seems later than the evidence suggests.

ii. Tetradrachm of Zankle-Messana 490/89–484/2. Photo: The Ashmolean Museum Oxford: Barron (1966) *The Silver Coins of Samos* Pl. VI–VII: *GOS* Arch. 89 p. 111 Pl. 20e, B.520.5

The tetradrachms struck by the Samians at Zankle (Sicily) between 490/89 and 484/2 BC give on the reverse side a clear representation of the prow of the *σάμαινα* described by Plutarch (*Perikles* 26): 'The *σάμαινα* is a boar-prowed ship as regards its *retroussé* snout, rather roomy and bellied, built for the open sea as well as for fast movement.' The ship got her name from her first appearance in Polykrates's shipyards in Samos towards the end of the 6th century. The lexicographers add further information: Hesychios says that the ships called *σάμαιναι* were decked throughout (i.e. right across). and quotes his earlier fellow Alexandrian Didymos to the effect that '*σάμαιναι* have a rather individual build compared with other ships. They are in fact broader in the beam; and their rams are turned up so that they look as if they imitated a boar's snout. That is the reason for the line: a swift Samian ship in the shape of a boar'.[1] The lexicographer Photios and [Suidas] both add that the *σάμαινα* was *δίκροτος*, with two oar levels.

The *σάμαιναι* which Polykrates built combined the speed and quick acceleration needed in battle manoeuvres and raids with the broad deck for carrying decksoldiers and broad beam to accommodate cargo as well as the thalamian oarsmen. They were built for the open sea to extend

ii.

Polycrates' influence beyond the neighbouring waters of Samos; and in fact the Zankle coinage shows that they took Samian exiles to western Greece.

The stempost curving forward above the boar's head prow is short and stumpy. The ram, the snub of which is likely to have had a practical purpose, is given support by a pronounced downward-sloping wale. The band indicating the fastening of the ram sheath to the hull curves forward from the base of the sternpost and back aft to the keel. Aft of the stempost the foresail is shown with its multiplicity of square pieces of cloth (*φάρεα*: Od.5 243–261) as in some Geometric vasepainting (*GOS* 2c and d). The foredeck sidescreen is ornamented with a circle, probably an eye as in (**iv**). Below the deck there is the forward end of an open course with dividing stanchions. Below the open course there are, as in (**v**), four wales. Comparison with the ship on the Delphic *μετόπη* (*GOS* Arch.38 p. 66 pl. 12a: 600–550 BC)[2], and with the pentecontors in (**v**) suggests that between the topwale and the second wale below it and between the third and fourth lower wales ran courses of oarports for the samaina's two levels of oars.

Polykrates's *σάμαινα* type with its distinctive boar's head with snub nose may be recognised in a late 6th century gem (**iii**), in spite of the ship's formalised oarsystem (oarsmen without oars, and a single oarbank). It may be noted that the ram fastening is clearly marked in the gem where it has been inferred in the Delphic *μετόπη*. There is also a number of Attic b/f vasepaintings of ships with two levels of oars (but without the snub snout ram) dated around 510 BC indicating that the two-level type had been adopted in Athens (**iv-vi**).

iii. Engraved gem 520–480 BC. Metropolitan Museum New York 4.2.11.21: *GOS* Arch. 107 p. 117, *SSAW* pl. 84. B473.

The boar's head prow on this gem resembles very closely the prow on (**ii**). Above the snub snout, tusks and eye two wales terminate in projections as in (**ii**) and (**vi**). At the base of the stempost is a second eye again as in (**ii**) and (**vi**).The stem-post rises in elegant S curves recalling stemposts in geometric vasepainting. There is no foredeck. The deck carries five formalised decksoldiers with shields and below it in the rooms formed by deckstanchions (cf. **vi**) are five formalised oarsmen (at the catch but with invisible oars). The topwale is in relief and from under it emerge thirteen oars in a single formalised row. There is a helmsman of disproportionate size holding the tiller of a single large rudder. The boar's head prow identifies the ship represented as a *σάμαινα*.

This representation of an oared warship of the 6th century BC is valuable as an example of the code used later by engravers of gems and coins to show warships by emphasising the significant features noted above, which are nevertheless in no realistic relation to one another either functionally or in size, number and position. The picture is otherwise most informative and some of its details are confirmed by reference to the more realistic b/f representations of cataphract *σάμαιναι*.

iii

iv. Attic b/f amphora c.510 BC. Tarquinia 678; *GOS* Arch. 86 pl. 20b, *AT* pl. 25, B470.

The aphract ship represented has a stempost only slightly curving upwards, a foredeck with side screens or bulwarks stretching down to the topwale. Aft of the foredeck the topwale encloses a course of oarports. There is no deck. Below a broad wale the lower course of oarports runs aft. Oars are visible emerging from the oarports. The human figures are exaggerated, the figure of Dionysos enormously. The boar's head prow (**i** above) terminates in the ram.

iv

v. Attic b/f cup c.510 BC. British Museum 436: *GOS* Arch. 85 pl. 19 and 20a, *AT* pl. 26, B462/3.

Of the two cataphract warships on this cup both with boar's head prows the former (**va**) has a stempost and foredeck with bulwark similar to those on (**i**). A cloth is draped over the foredeck sidescreen (and may conceal the eye present in vi).

v a

The outsize sitting figures (cf. below 40 and 45–9) disguise the presence (as in **ii**, and **vi**) of a railed deck under which is an open course. Over the lower sill of the topwale the upper level of oars is rowed, while the lower level of oars emerges through a course of oarports below it.

The second warship (**vb**) resembles (**va**) in most respects. The upper oar-level is only half-manned, probably because some of the oarsmen (again over-size) are attending to the sails. The open course below the deck is deeper than in (**va**) and the oars-men sit lower.

vb

vi. Attic b/f jug c.510 BC. British Museum 508: *GOS* Arch. 88 pl. 20d, B469.

The forward section of a boar-prowed cataphract ship is shown with a straight stempost and a fore-deck with side bulwark/screen stretching down to the topwale and decorated with a large eye. Aft is the deck (with no guard-rail) and below it an open side with 'rooms' separated by deck-stanchions. Below the open side the topwale terminates for-ward, like the lower wale, in a projection above the ram's eye. Between the topwale and the lower wale runs a course of oarports. No oars are shown. If, as is likely, the ship is a pentecontor with oars at two levels the upper level is worked over the topwale as in **va** and **vb**, and the lower through the oarports shown. There are (as in **va** and **b**) grossly exaggerated figures disguising the presence (as in **ii** and **v a** of the deck. The outsize, but less grossly exaggerated, heads of oarsmen unrealistically fill the 'rooms'.

vi

vii. The Ficoroni bronze casket 325–300 BC. Villa Giulia Rome: *SSAW* Fig. 106 (photo Alinari) Beazley (1947) 58ff B 579 and 580.

A drawing of the engraved scene, depicting the stern section of the *Argo* as a cataphract pentecontor of two oar-levels moored, is shown by A. Köster (1923) and again in *AT* Fig. 27. Reference to the Alinari photograph of the original (in *SSAW* and B) shows that two thalamian oarports visible on the original are omitted in the drawing. They are restored here. One can be seen through the rungs of the ladder and the other behind the head of the Argonaut seated on the ground.

Reading from left to right, one figure facing half-left comes down a ladder with a can in one hand and a basket (of clothes) in the other: a second figure (on deck) sits on a cushion in the stern facing half-left: a third, also facing half-left sits on the ground with an oarstrop in his hand and an oar across his thighs: a fourth lies on his back on deck with his head on a cushion: the fifth sits behind him on deck with his wrap floating in the breeze. All the figures are, as usual, in relation to the ship disproportionately large.

The starboard side of the stern and part of the hull are partially masked by the figure descending the ladder and the figure seated on the ground. Reading again from the left: the starboard rudder is shown raised in the horizontal position (with a very short stock) the deck follows the upcurving

vii

stern and is supported by stanchions on each side with crosspieces connecting each pair at their tops, these supports being visible from the side. The horizontal deck is shown with stanchions curving inboard from the interior surface of the hull to the (edge of) the deck above. The stanchions and crosspieces in the stern explain this. (In the Athenian three (**ix**) the deckstanchions rest on the upper wale outside the hull).

The upper end of the ladder rests on the edge of the deck and is prevented from slipping sideways by a chock placed between its forward side and a stanchion at the point where the ladder also touches the topwale. The position of the ladder touching both gunwale and deck as it slopes upward indicates that the deck is narrower than the ship's beam[3]; and that there is of course no outrigger. Two rows of oarports are shown one above the other *en échelon* and between three narrow wales. There is a still lower wale (terminating out of sight in the ram) but no oarports at that level.

The *Argo* thus displayed is a cataphract warship with two levels of oars. Since there were 50 Argonauts, she must be a pentecontor, apparently decked but open-sided like the ships **i-iv** above, a larger version of the two-level triacontors used by Alexander on the Indus (see above p. 9–10) at about the time the casket was engraved. The design and size of the oar shown rules out the possibility of double-manning and hence of her being anachronistically a four as the Ruvo vase *Argo* (**x**) a century earlier was painted anachronistically as a three. The artist may have used a contemporary *λέμβος*/ *liburna* as model. It may be noted that the picture of a complete single-manned oar, unshipped, is unique. Unlike most representations of one-man oars, however, it is monoxylous.

viii. The Vienna Fragment of a r/f cup c.450 BC. The Museum of the University of Vienna (503.48): *CVA* pl. 21 8; Furtwangler drawing, *GOS* pl. 26b, *AT* pl. 43 B 575.

The fragment shows part of the side of a three of the mid 5th century which differs from those of (**ix**) and (**x**) in having a deck rail and (probably) a narrower deck (*AT* p. 154–5). Below the deck is an open side as in the two-level pentecontors. There

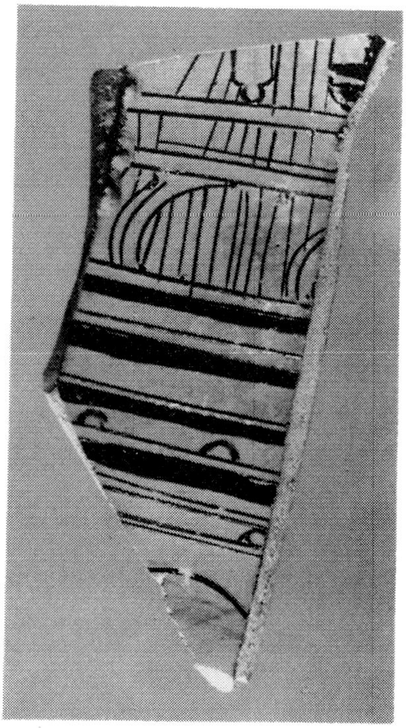

viii

are similarly deck-stanchions, curving inboard to give perspective as in (**vii**). But here there is an outrigger. Below an upper horizontal there is a lower horizontal; and between the two there is space for the thranite oars to emerge. No tholepins are shown. The oarports for the zygian and thalamian oars appear to be set between thin horizontal wales, as in the two-level pentecontors (**iii-vii**).

ix. (a) The Lenormant Relief c.400 BC. The Acropolis Museum at Athens: *GOS* pls. 23 and 24, *AT* Figs. 13 and 14, B.604. Line drawings (**55, 56, 57**).

The relief shows a section of the starboard side of an oared warship with three levels of oars and a *παρεξειρεσία*, certainly a three in view of its date. Part of the uppermost file of oarsmen is clearly visible through the open side between the edge of the deck and the upper horizontal of the *παρεξειρεσία*. Together with the stern depicted on the exactly contemporary Ruvo vase (**x**), which corroborates it in detail, the relief presents a clear picture of a late 5th century BC Athenian three from which

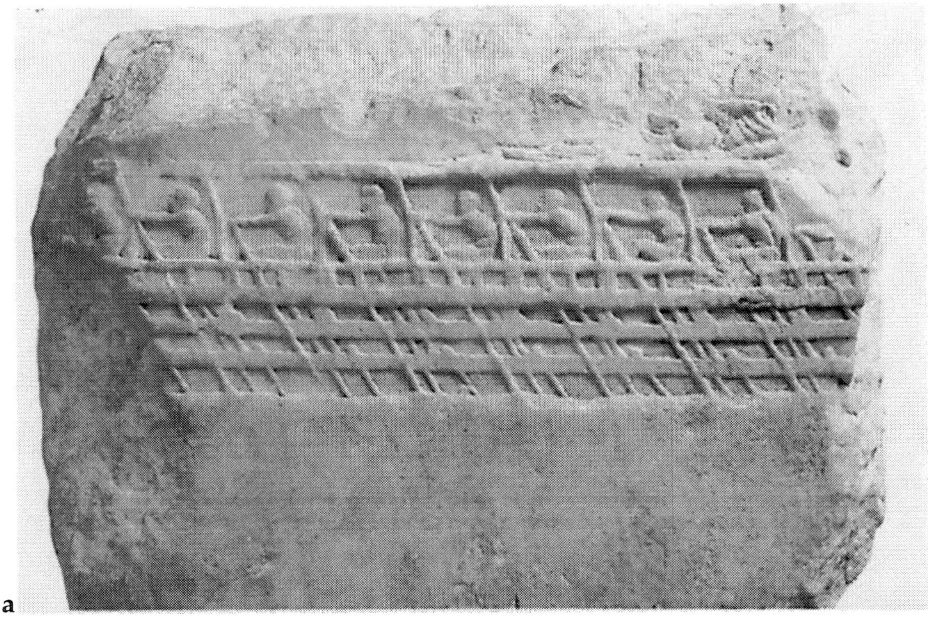

ix a

ix b

ix c

some of the later types of Greek warship developed.

Further illumination on the appearance of the Athenian three is provided from subsidiary sources: (**b**) the dal Pozzo drawing in the British Musuem and (**c**) the Eleusis relief.

(**b**) The drawing, now in the British Museum, was made in Rome between 1610 and 1635 for the Cavaliero dal Pozzo. Its subject, which has since disappeared, was a relief depicting the bow section of a ship apparently similar to that partially depicted in the Lenormant relief. The artist fails to understand and hence to represent the oarsystem. Five thranite oarsmen are shown as in the relief, but have no tholes although their oars are fully visible. The upper parts of the stocks of the zygian oars have been presented as slightly short posts between the three wales, while the thalamian oars emerge from the lower hull and reach the water from behind the lowest wale. The lightly aft-curving deckstanchions mark the separate rooms but are not recognised as butting on to the lowest wale. The upper two horizontals, recognised as belonging to a *παρεξειρεσία* by Assmann in the Lenormant relief, are in the drawing not so recognisable. Two positive contributions are made by the drawing, the *reclining* bow officer (*πρῳρεύς, πρῳράτης* signalling aft to the (invisible) helmsman; cf. *GOS* Arch.35 Pl. 11); and the apparent position of the oarsmen's head *outboard* of the edge of the canopy deck. This would be the case before the decks were extended *δι' ὅλης* right across (p. 185).

(**c**) The Eleusis relief was discovered recently by Lucien Basch on the back of the fragment of stone in the Eleusis museum. The side previously exhibited showed part of a relief featuring the goddess Artemis. The side now discovered shows crudely part of a three-level oared warship and is dated after 350 BC. Its great merit is that it corroborates usefully the presence of a *παρεξειρεσία* in such a ship, not at this date necessarily a three.

x. The Ruvo Vase. c.400 BC. the Jatta Collection, Ruvo: *GOS* pl. 26a, *AT* 41 a and b, B.576.

x

The Attic r/f volute krater by the Talos painter shows the port side of the stern of an oared warship representing the Argo and resembling in detail the ship shown in (**ix**).

Representations (**ix** and **x**) show greater realism than those of the 6th century BC except in two respects. The human figures of the Ruvo vase and, to a much lesser degree, of the relief are exaggerated in size. In the case of the Ruvo vase the figures are the actors in the mythological scene depicted and thus earn greater attention. The attempts to give perspective in all three cases lead to departure from realism in showing the deck-stanchions (and in two cases brackets), actually upright, as curved in various ways. In the relief the brackets also take on the angle of the oars which are shown at the catch. An *ἄσκωμα* is shown in the larger, lower, thalamian oarport.

xi. Coins of Sidon 5th century BC

In the 5th century BC the Phoenicians and Palestinian Syrians (Herodotos 7.89.1) were the leading naval powers of the eastern Mediterranean providing the largest contingent, 300 threes, for Xerxes' invasion fleet in 480. The next largest, 200 threes, was provided by Egypt. In Phoenicia (Herodotos 8.67.2, 7.44: Diodoros 16.44) Sidon was the leading naval city with Tyre in second place. Herodotos relates (8.99.1) that Queen Artemisia of Halikarnassos rated her ships in Xerxes's fleet second in performance to the Sidonian. Towards the end of the century the reputation of Sidon for possession of the best ships and oarsmen was no less (Euripides *Helen* 1451–4, 1530–4: 412 BC).

Fifth century literature provides no evidence that the Phoenician threes of that time differed from the Greek in any important respect (e.g. in their oarsystem as has been suggested). When the

xi a

xi b

xi c

Greek fleet was moored at Artemision in 480 BC and Xerxes' fleet was arriving at Aphetai on the other side of the strait, some Persian late arrivals mistook the Greek ships for Persian, went to join them and were captured. For this to occur the mistake must have persisted until they were very close to the ships; but this incident is no evidence for the similarity in appearance of Greek and Phoenician ships since the latecomers may have thought the ships they saw belonged to Asiatic Greeks whose ships would have been of the Corinthian rather than the Phoenician pattern (p. 181). There were certainly some superficial (i.e. non-structural) differences between the two but the absence of the outrigger in 5th century and 4th century Phoenician threes is possible though not certain. The Phoenician three of the Nineveh fresco finds no echo in the 5th century Phoenician coins.

Evidence for Sidon's pride in her ships (and the best of her ships were her threes and thus the most likely to be exhibited) is shown by their appearance on almost all the coins minted there before Alexander entered the Phoenician scene in 332 BC. These coins provide the only extant representations of them. The sharp bow profile of the Phoenician warships in the Nineveh relief is continued in these ships.

(**a**) 450–435; Betlyon Pl. 1, 1 (No.1: Obv.): BM cast.
(**b**) End of 5th century: *SNG* IV Fitzwilliam 6043 Ba'alshallim I (420–410 BC: first king to add his initial)
(**c**) Betlyon: Pl. 1.7 (No.7: Obv.): American Numismatic Society, New York

In the last half of the 5th century, when Sidonian ships were no larger than threes, they appear without oars, first (**a**) with a deck hung along its edge with a row of shields and with an unfurled triangular sail (or a square sail brailed up to that shape), then later (**b**) with a partially furled sail and (**c**) with no mast or sail.

They show large eyes aft of the characteristic sharp ram, a bow ornament and a *στυλίς* rising across the upward curve of the stern. Below the line of shields there is an open space divided into 'rooms' by the deck-stanchions, and below the topwale a line which may indicate the lower edge of a *παρεξειρεσία*. There is no sign of zygian oarports below that line or of thalamian oarports between the two narrow parallel wales which are seen strongly marked running fore-and-aft lower still (cf. **viii** the Vienna fragment c.450 BC). Oarports are small details which a coin engraver might reasonably omit.

xii. Coins of Arados 5th and early 4th century BC

(**a**) end of 5th century: Babelon pl. 116.5: B.684
(**b**) early 4th century: *BMC* 1: B.685
(**c**) 380: *SNG* V Lockett 3806, B.687 BM cast
(**d**) 380: *SNG* V Lockett 3807, B.685 BM cast

These four Arados coins represent ships of a common type dating from the end of the 5th century and the first two decades of the 4th century when the three was the only first-line warship in use in the eastern Mediterranean. It is therefore reasonable to infer that the warships shown were threes which the city would have been proud to exhibit.

Coin (**a**) gives a crude and conventional representation of the starboard side of a three-level ship. The deck hung with shields in the Phoenician manner is shown supported by stanchions dividing a recessed area. The stanchions stand above three horizontal courses, the lowest of which is a wale terminating forward in a ram. Above this wale there is a recessed slit in which are a number of very short uprights (? brackets of a *παρεξειρεσία*). Above is a course surmounted by a similar recessed slit with short uprights , and above that the course on which the stanchions butt. This last horizontal may reasonably be taken to represent the upper course of the outrigger terminating forward in the eye/*ἐπωτίς*. There are no oars shown. The picture may be admired as concise shorthand for a three, probably with a *παρεξειρεσία*.

Coins (**b**), (**c**), and (**d**), show ship portraits similar to those on (**a**). The horizontal courses are less strongly marked and there are no short uprights shown between them. There is a deep recess below the deck hung with shields and the stanchions are clearly visible. In (**b**) there is a large stern rug (cf. a similar rug hangs in the stern of the ship on the early 5th century r/f stamnos depicting Odysseus and the Sirens (*AT* pl. 47) and in the bow of the ship in **v b**.).

xii a

xii b

xii c

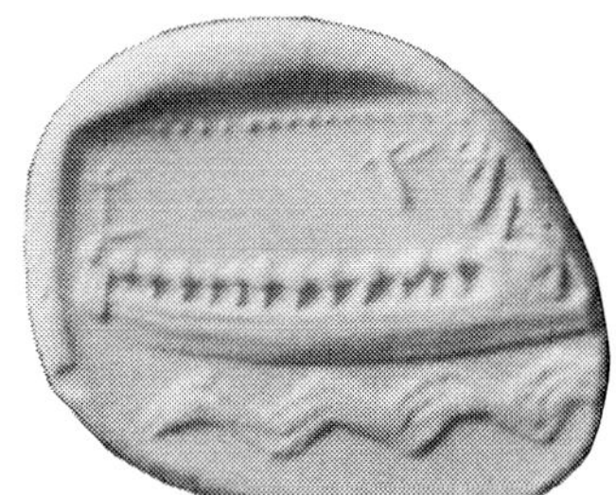

xii d

The detail of which the coin designer was capable included the deck and its stanchions, the outrigger with its internal uprights and bracket supports, these detracting from realistic presentation of the hull. It did not, however, extend to oarports.

THE AGE OF INNOVATION

1. Coins of Sidon 386/5–332 BC

(**d**) Fitzwilliam Museum, McClean Collection 9490

Ba'alshallim II (386/5–372)

(**e**) Betlyon: Pl. 2.4 (No.18: Obv.): *AT* 28a; BM 1918 2–4 156

Abd'astart I (372–362/1)

(**f**) (Silver); Betlyon:Pl. 2.7 (No.23: Obv.):*LSRS* 33c; *BMC* 29

Tennes (357/6–348/7

(**g**) (Silver); Betlyon: Pl. 3.6 (No.34: Obv.): *BMC* 64

Abd'astart II (342/2/341–340/339)

Abd'astart III (340/339–332)

(**h**) (Silver): Betlyon: Pl. 4.5 (No.42: Obv.): BM 1987 6–49 462

The Sidonian coinage of the period 385–332 (**d, e, f, g** and **h**) shows (with a few exceptions e.g. Basch: 1969 p. 149 12, 13, 14: dated 380–374)) a marked change in its depiction of warships. Oars are now shown; they do not emerge realistically or semi-realistically from the ship's side; but are placed quite unrealistically (yet as a formalised row of oars) under the keel, as in the Persian seal (**2a**). Both on the seal and on the Ba'alshallim II coins (**d, e**) the oars are stepped in three rows thus suggesting a ship of three levels of oars. In the stern there is a στυλίς. In the coins (**f**) of his successor Abd'astart I, the Philhellene, otherwise called Straton, the oars are similarly shown, but the stepping suggests two levels (similarly a pentecontor or a four).

1 d

1 e

1 f

1 g

1 h

After Abd'astart I's minor revolt had been put down by Persia and Tennes installed as king , the standard of workmanship in the coins declined: Betlyon p. 17 'the lack of definition and the poor execution of minute details, which once were perfectly clear, is proof of this'. This decline accounts for the abandonment of stepping (as in **g**), in rendering the oars of ships which are not likely to be of lesser type as a single, unstepped, bank. When Tennes joined the major revolt of Egypt and Cyprus, her front-line ships in 351/0 BC consisted of 100 threes and fives (D.16.44); but on Tennes' betrayal of the city to Ochus, the Sidonians burnt all their ships (D.16.45.4). Tennes continued to rule Sidon for a short time until Ochus put him to death and the city then appears to have been ruled directly by a Persian satrap until the reigns of Abd'astart II and III in the last decade before Alexander's invasion.

The abandonment of accurate detail characterises the later coins of the period before Alexander (for example **h**). The lack of pride in her warships which her coinage seems to reflect in this period may account for the fact attested by Diodoros that when Alexander invaded Phoenicia in 332 BC and chose Sidon as his naval base for the siege of Tyre the Sidonian fleet consisted solely of threes (Arrian 2.20.1).

In the coinage of the 4th century, apart from the addition of oars, the characteristics of the 5th century Sidonian threes are usually present, a row of shields on the edge of the deck, the open area below the deck divided into 'rooms' by deck-stanchions, the *παρεξειρεσία* terminating forward in an eye/*ἐπωτίς* and below it a recessed line for thalamian oarports, the zygian oarports being imagined under the *παρεξειρεσία*. The engraver may perhaps be pardoned for compressing the complex system into what has become an often obscure pattern, in other words, a code.

2. Persian seals 520/15–331 BC

(**a**) *SSAW* 105, Basch (1969) pl. 10A, B.699,
(**b**) Basch (1969) pl. 10B, B.700

(**a**) On one impression of a Persepolis seal a warship is depicted, identified by Casson rightly as a three since the ends of the oars are 'stepped' to indicate three levels. These oars emerge from beneath what appears to be a *παρεξειρεσία* terminating rather uncertainly in an *ἐπωτίς*.

They continue to be placed unrealistically (influenced by the Sidonian practice **1** above) beneath the hull. On the deck there are four armed men of greatly exaggerated size. Above them is part of the yard with sail furled. The helmsman and two rudders are visible in the stern.

The die has been moved and slightly twisted while the impression was being made with the result that there are two masts close and not parallel to each other and the markings on the ship's side are distorted.

(**b**) An impression from another seal shows a warship with oars in the full Sidonian practice placed symbolically under the ship. Since there is damage to the base of the impression it is not possible to say whether or not the oars are 'stepped'. On the side of the ship under the deck, on which there are four outsize figures, there are wide vertical structures resting on a wale and under them a second row of the same resting on another wale very close to the ship's keel. The impression is much damaged in this area; it does however appear that there are two open courses one above the other with no sign of a *παρεξειρεσία* . In respect of its double open courses and its wide vertical structures separating the rooms the ship recalls the Phoenician three of the Nineveh palace relief and foreshadows the ships of the Arados (**3f**) and (**3g**), Byblos (**4e**) coins, the Amathus gem (**5**) and the Erment model (**6**). The very wide dating given to the seals makes it difficult to relate them to one or other of the sets of coins.

The ships depicted on the seals are of course not Persian warships except in so far as they would have been built and manned by the maritime peoples, including Phoenicia, rather loosely subject to her during the latter period of the seals' dating.

The absence of the row of shields along the edge of the deck in (**a**) makes it unlikely that the ship portrayed is Phoenician, probably therefore from one of the Greek Asiatic cities. The ship in (**b**) may have a row of shields although the damage to the seal makes it uncertain. But the oarsystem appears to be Phoenician.

It is remarkable that these two seals, as with some difficulty interpreted, contrast (**a**) the Corinthian three with the uppermost oars rowed through a *παρεξειρεσία*, below an open course of

2 a

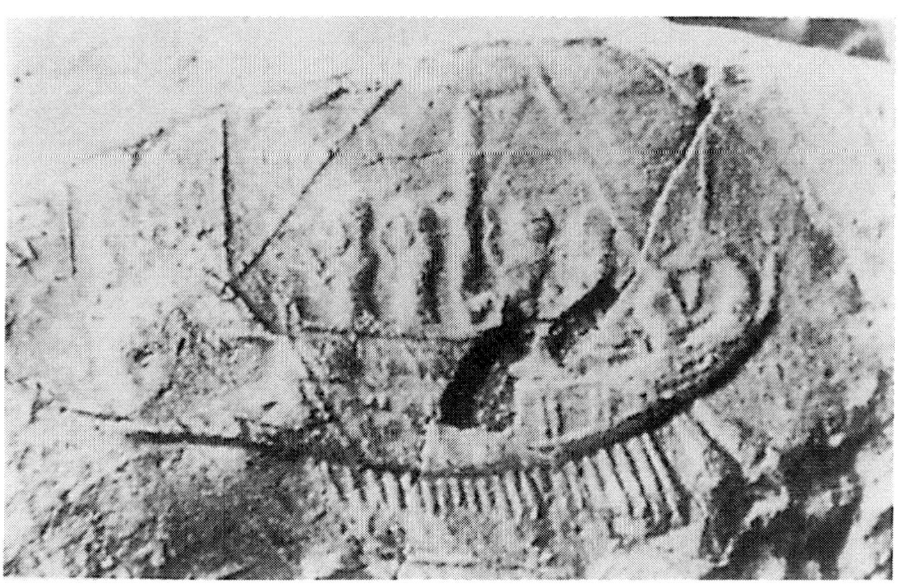

2 b

oar-rooms and terminating forward in an ἐπωτίς, with (**b**) 'the Phoenician design' of a three-level ship with no *παρεξειρεσία* and two open courses on the ship's side one above the other.

3. Coins of Arados late 4th century BC

(**e**) 350–332: *BMC* 54; B.692
(**f**) 350–332: *BMC* 62: *LSRS* 33a; *AT* 28b: B.693
(**g**) 350–332: *BMC* 67: *LSRS* 33b;*AT* 28a: B.694

(**e**) Resembles the earlier Arados coins (**xiia, b, c,** and **d**), but the inference that it represents a three is less safe by reason of its date, since after about 350 bigger ships may have been in use in the Phoenician cities since they had been present briefly at Sidon. This city however is likely to have taken a lead then in naval building. The coins of the second group, (**f**) and (**g**) show ship portraits surprisingly different from those on coins of the first group, but bearing a striking resemblance to those of the Persian seal (**b**), the Byblos coin (**4e**), the Amathus engraved gem (**5**) and the Erment model (**6**), all likely to belong to the last half of the 4th century In them there are two levels of open rooms and no sign of a *παρεξειρεσία*.

4. Coins of Byblos 4th century–c.333 BC. M. Dunand (1937), Kraay (1966) 685, Jenkins (1972) 330–1.

(**a**) Reign of Ozbaal: c.348–40: *BMC* 4: B.697A
(**b**) Reign of Adramalek: c.340: BM 75 2/1323 B.697B
(**c**) Reign of Ayinel: 340–333: BM 1951 10 7–8
(**d**) Reign of Ayinel: 340–333: *SNG* IV Fitzwilliam 6029
(**e**) Reign of Ayinel: 340–333: B.697 C.

Some examples (**a, b, c, d**) of the period 348–333 (the reigns of Ozbaal, Adramalek and Ayinel) show three armed men, disproportionately large in size, on a deck with a bulwark hung with shields. The deck is supported by a large number of stanchions resting on a bulging hull beneath which is a conventional indication of the sea. In (**b**) and (**d**) there is some indication of an oarbox.

A coin (**e**) dated in the seven years of Ayinel's reign shows again three armed men on a deck hung with (very small) ?shields, but above this course there is a post-and-rail bulwark. Below the course deck-stanchions divide an open course into oar-rooms, at the base of which there is a course of larger shields, and below them again stanchions dividing a lower open course above a bulging but shallow hull. This coin seems to bear the same relationship to (**a, b, c,** and **d**) as Arados coins (**f** and **g**) bear to (**a-e**). It shows the Phoenician oarsystem in contrast to the Corinthian.

3 e

3 f

3 g

4 a

4 b

4 c

4 d

4 e

5. The Amathus engraved gem 340–330 BC. British Museum No. 449: B702

Amathus was a Phoenician city on the south coast of Cyprus. The gem shows, like the Byblos coins, three armed men of exaggerated size on the deck of a ship. Like the Arados coins (**f** and **g**), the Byblos coin (**e**) and the Erment model (**6**) the ship has a row of shields at the edge of the deck and two courses of open 'rooms' beneath the deck. Her date is likely to be the decade before the siege of Tyre where the king of Amathus served in Alexander's fleet (p. 12). His flagship like those of other Cypriot kings is likely to have been a five.

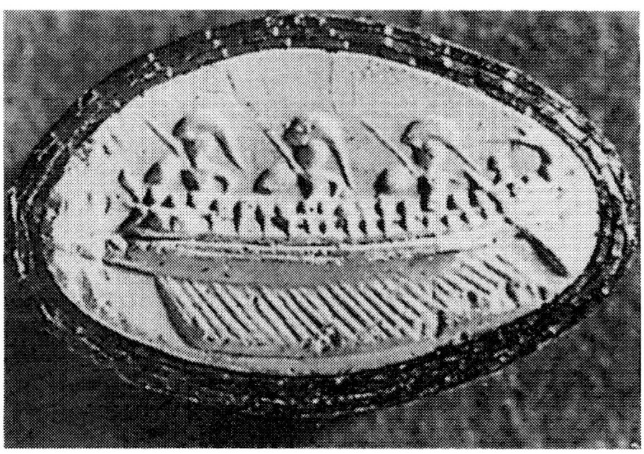

5

6. The Erment model 350–300 BC. Danish National Museum of Copenhagen no. 5487: Breitenstein (1941) pl. 63 fig. 520: *LSRS* 34, *SSAW* 103–4, B.708–11. Line Drawings (**58**).

The model was bought in the Egyptian market. Its date and provenance is thus uncertain. The seller said it had come from Erment in Upper Egypt, hence the name it enjoys.

The model depicts a warship with a pronounced ram and an aft-curving stem. There are the stubs of oars at three levels. At the top and middle levels

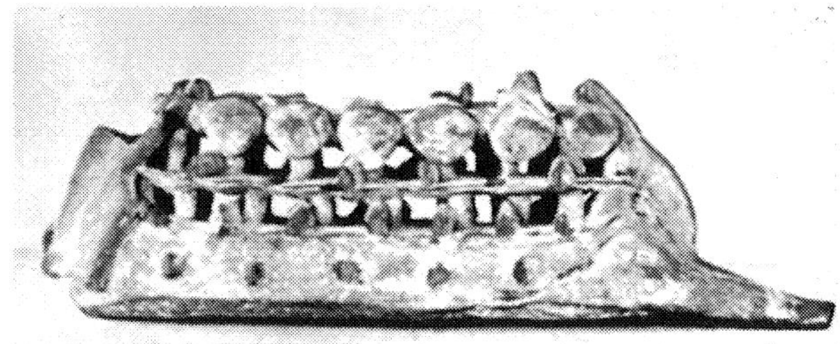

6

the oarsmen's rooms are open and the oars are rowed over sills. The oars at the lowest level are rowed through oarports. There is a deck and bulwark with a row of shields hung over its edge in the Phoenician manner. That and its resemblance to the warships of the Nineveh palace relief and to the Arados coins (**f** and **g**), the Byblos coin (**e**) and the Amathus gem (**5**) make a Phoenician connexion certain. There is a difference between the coins and the model and gem. In the former the shields hang on the side of the bulwark and the two open courses run beneath them, while in the model and gem the shields both cover the bulwark and hang over the edge of the deck. There are rudders on the port and starboard sides in the stern. The six holes in the deck (visible in *SSAW* 104's and B, 707's view from above) are likely to be slots into which the figures of disproportionately large armed men were fitted, another Persian/Phoenician feature. The ship represented may be either a three or a five.

Note on figures 2–6

The ship portraits and model reasonably dated to the last half of the 4th century BC, which have been described in **2–6**, present problems of interpretation for which we can offer not solutions but suggestions, out of which solutions may be constructed, since certain interpretation of the evidence does not yet seem to us possible.

In that period the engravers of the Sidonian coinage, the Persian seals, the coinage of Arados and Byblos, the Amathus gem and the maker of the Erment model aimed to represent warships with three, on one or two occasions with two, levels of oars. So much is generally agreed, although the only quite certain representation of a ship of three oar-levels of the period is the Erment model.

Before about 350 BC, since the first line oared warships in the eastern Mediterranean were then threes, representations which are apparently intended to show warships with three levels of oars can safely be recognised as threes. In 351/0 a short-lived Sidonian fleet was composed of threes and fives, in 332 the Tyrians, and the Cypriot and Phoenician kings (but not the Sidonians), had fives as flagships at Alexander's siege of Tyre; and in 326/5 there are fives in the Peiraieus naval inventories. Since it can be accepted that fives had an oar-system of three levels like the three (p. 270–271), representations of warships with three levels of oars after 350 BC can accordingly be of either threes or fives. Threes with 170 oarsmen are likely to have differed from fives with 300 (as at Eknomos 256 BC). But in the latter half of the 4th century BC their points of difference are difficult to establish safely.

The appearance of the famous Sidonian threes on coins of the 5th century is well established (**xi**), and Sidonian 4th century coins (**1**) present the same design except that oars are added symbolically. Whether or not these threes actually had a *παρεξειρεσία* is a matter of opinion since the portraits on Phoenician coins do not settle the matter one way or another. Only the Persian seal (**a**) suggests, rather unclearly, the presence of an *ἐπωτίς* and consequential *παρεξειρεσία*, but this ship has not the row of shields which mark a Phoenician ship. Fortunately the uncertainty does not affect seriously the problem of differentiating the three from the five.

That problem centres on the appearance of a design of a warship with three levels of oars, very probably in the Nineveh palace relief of the early 7th century, most clearly and tangibly in the Erment Model (**6**: dated after 350 BC), equally clearly but two-dimensionally in the Amathus gem (5:340–330 BC) and Arados coins (3:350–332 BC), and less clearly in a Byblos coin (4:340–333 BC and a Persian seal (**2b**: dated before 331 BC). The absence of the 'Phoenician design' from the Sidonian coinage may have an historical explanation (p. 192). The question at issue is whether this Phoenician three-level design of the late 8th century in its reappearance in the last half of the 4th century represents a three or the newly introduced five.

Compared with the representations of the Corinthian three (**viii-x**, and also probably on most of the 5th and 4th century Phoenician coinage), the three-level design of the Nineveh warships, Persian seal **b**, some Arados and Byblos coins, the Amathus gem and the Erment model, has two distinct features: the absence of a *παρεξειρεσία* and and the presence of a second open side divided into oar-rooms for the zygian oarsmen. The bulwark on the Erment model is damaged; but it appears here and there. The irregularities of the deck surface and the four holes on each side of it are likely to be the relics of the decksoldiers (on each side in the three dimensional model) which appear in all the other ship portraits of the later group (**2–6**) . There is a bulwark in the ship shown on the Byblos coin (**4e**) but not on the Amathus gem (**5**) or the Arados coins (**3f** and **g**) and probably not on the Persian seal (**2b**) although it may lie behind a scarcely discernible row of shields.

What reasons can be given for the reappearance of this three level design? The reason for the presence of the *παρεξειρεσία* in the Corinthian-Athenian three is understood to have been the economical addition of the thranite oarsman to a previously two-level oared ship with the aim of achieving greater speed and manoeuvrability (*AT* p. 25–36). If a three-level ship could now dispense with a *παρεξειρεσία*, the hull must have been modified to satisfy new and different tactical and strategic aims, the requirement of more fighting men on deck either for transport or in battle or both.

Plutarch in his *Life of Kimon* (12.2) says that when Kimon in 467 BC was in command of the fleet of the Delian League in SW Asia Minor he 'set out with 200 ships which had originally been well built by Themistokles for speed and easy turning and which he had then made broader and given crossings (i.e. over the central gangway) (*πλατυτέρας ἐποίησεν αὐτὰς καὶ διάβασιν τοῖς καταστρώμασιν ἔδωκεν*), so that they might proceed against the (Persian) enemy with greater fighting power exercised by many *ὁπλῖται*'. Taken with Thukydides's remark (1.14.3: *SSAW* 5.55) that the ships, built on Themistokles's advice, with which the Athenians fought at Salamis 'were still without decks throughout their whole breadth' Plutarch's account of Kimon's modification of the Themistoclean three is corroborated and the modified three must have been one Thukydides was familiar with (and commanded) in the Peloponnesian war. Plutarch's indication of Kimon's tactical objective is however ambiguous. It is not clear whether the increased fighting power was to be exercised on land or at sea. The former is perhaps more likely under the circumstances and with Kimon's tendency to fight on land. The widening of the deck to transport more troops would have created the category of *ὁπλιταγωγοί, στρατιώτιδες* leaving a separate category of specially built (*AT* p. 152) 'fast threes'.

If the 'Phoenician design', like Kimon's modification of Themistokles's ships, aimed at greater transport potential, further hull modification would be needed and that might well make a *παρεξειρεσία* unnecessary, but reduce naturally the effective power, the speed and manoeuvrability which had been the three's forte. Part of the hull modification would be the strengthening and heightening of the deck-bulwark. The possible absence of the bulwark from the Erment model and three of the other ships in the group (**2–6**) somewhat weakens the case for the transport hypothesis. Relevant also is the description in Arrian (21.1) of the ships which Sidon provided for Alexander's fleet at Tyre 'threes which were not fast', that is to say 'transports'. Sidon however, unlike Arados and Byblos, does not show the new design on her coinage in the period before the siege.

The reason for the second feature, the additional open course, is again a practical one. Lack of the outrigger would have meant that its open underside would have been lost as a source of ventilation. Experience of *Olympias* has shown that, with 170 oarsmen packed tightly together, good ventilation is of great importance. It seems likely that ventilation was a reason for the additional open side seen so clearly in the Erment model.

The two open sides would in battle certainly have exposed the oarsmen to missiles. Screens however were used to protect the oarsmen of a 5th century Athenian three and presumably did so effectively. If so screens would also be effective at the lower level in 'the Phoenician design'.

The 'Phoenician design' may have aimed, in addition, at balancing the increased weight of the hull (resulting from the achievement of the higher transport potential) by increasing the oar-power, double-manning the thranite and zygian oars and thus producing a five. Such a development would have made the need for a further open side all the more pressing, with 300 instead of 170 oarsmen. Alternatively the Erment model may represent the three as it appeared originally in the Nineveh reliefs and the Persian seal.

At this point it is to be recollected that no picture recognisable as showing a five is extant before 'the Phoenician design' reappeared. Later there is a number of candidates for recognition as fives with deep oar-panels which will be considered in due course. These deep flat-sided oar-panels, standing out from the side of the hull in different degrees according to the artist's method and physical point of view, show three levels of oars quincunx-fashion: e.g. the Nymphaion ship (**13**), the ships on the Calenian dishes I (**18**), the Ostia frieze (**35**), the Aula Isiaca fresco (**40**) and the Pompeii Shipshed fresco (**43**). Louvres above, and probably beneath as well though invisible, provide ventilation (impressively in the Nymphaion ship); so that it is possible to see these oarsystems as descended from 'the Phoenician design' and belonging to fives. Strong arguments in favour of this line of descent are brought forward by JFC in Chapter 7 (p. 284 ff.). It must be remembered also that Rome built her first fleet of fives in imitation of the Carthaginian cataphract which she had captured, and that Tyre had strong links with Carthage.

Different types of bigger ship (including the five), exhibiting the *παρεξειρεσία*/oarbox of the three from which they are descended, are also to be considered (**10**, **27**).

These then are the possibilities which 'the Phoenician design' offers in the 4th century: either (i) it belongs to a Phoenician type of three which is attested in the 8th century, or (ii) it is a late 4th century revival of that design. In the latter case it may have been used (iia) as a design suitable either for a transport three or (iib) for a heavier three-level ship on which more soldiers could be carried on deck in battle, with power correspondingly increased by double-manning at two levels, a five in fact.

Objections to (i) and (iia) are that such ships were no novelty, were lacking in prestige and accordingly unlikely to motivate exhibition on coins in the 4th century (iia) further suggests no reason why a type of three which had long been superseded should then have been revived. The five (iib) on the other hand was a novelty in Phoenicia, as the flagship of Phoenician kings it was undoubtedly prestigious and with the increase of the oarcrew from 170 to a number probably not far short of the 300 which manned the Roman fives at Eknomos (p. 46) providing a very cogent explanation of the revival of the additional open side, correspondingly increased ventilation.

7. Coins of Kios 340–300 BC

(**a**) 340 BC: Babelon (1901) Pl. 180.4: *AT* 39
(**b**) 330–302 BC: Berlin Museum: B.583
(**c**) 330–302 BC: *SNG* IV Fitzwilliam: McClean 7458
(**d**) 321–300 BC: *BMC* 1

Kios was a colony of Miletos founded at the head of the gulf of the same name on the south west coast of Propontis (p. 74 Map H). Coins (**a**) and (**b**) show prows of oared warships not inconsistent with the Greek threes of the late 5th century The S shaped typically Greek stempost, suggested in the dal Pozzo drawing ((**ixb** p. 186) of a three, is fully attested here (**a** and **c**) for the first time and reoccurs in the coins of Phaselis, and an early coin of Leukas.

As they represent a type of ship known in her main features, they provide a good introduction to the representational technique of the engraver when faced with the problem of showing warships' prows. The bow section (like the stern section in other cases but unlike the whole ship) can be shown realistically in some detail.

In (**a**) the foredeck continues aft without break and is shown supported by a deckstanchion before

7 a

7 b

7 c

the picture ends at the coin's edge. Below the open side (large enough to accommodate a view of the thranite oarsman if the ship had been shown manned) there is an outrigger: and beneath it two narrow wales and below a broad wale curving downwards to the ram.

(**b** and **c**) are a little more explicit. Although they do not show a deckstanchion, the ἐπωτίς is clearly defined and in the lateral face of the outrigger in **b** there is a succession of oblong spaces in which tholepins are visible. Brackets supporting the outrigger are shown. There are no oars. The outrigger brackets butt on to the broad lower wale. No oarports are shown in **a** or **d**, but the wales are visible, between which they appear in threes (cf. **viii**) and in two-level pentecontors (**vii**).

8. Octobols of Histiaia (Oreos) 340–338 BC. F. T. Newell (1921)

(**a**) *TINC* (1936) p. 23 Fig. 1: B.587
(**b**) *BMC* 24: B.588
(**c**) *BMC* 27: B.589
(**d**) Cabinet des Médailles Paris (Babelon) pl. 198.28 B.590

8 a

8 b

8 c

8 d

8 e

(e) Cabinet des Médailles Brussels: Hirsch Collection 1266 B.592.

Newell argues convincingly that this series of coins was issued at Histiaia in the period of two years after the expulsion by an Athenian naval expedition of the ruler installed by Philip II of Macedon and before the defeat of Athens at Chaironeia and Philip's recovery of Euboia. They celebrate the expulsion.

In all five coins a nymph is shown half front seated on the deck in the stern of an oared warship. She is of a size quite out of proportion to the ship.

The starboard deck railing is shown above the port deck railing of the deck. Except in the case of (a) where the deck railing appears planked, they are of the post-and- rail kind. The nymph sitting on the deck has her right hand behind her resting on the starboard deck railing and the near port deck railing appears from under her right thigh. Her right hand holds the *στυλίς*.

Below the port deck railing the edge of the deck is shown in high relief and in some depth. In (b) and (e) the open side of the ship under it shows most clearly, divided into 'rooms' by stanchions perpendicular in (b) and (c) slanting (for perspective) in (e). Below the open side the *παρεξειρεσία* is marked by horizontals between which an oar emerges in (b). The three oars are shown most clearly in (e), the uppermost through the *παρεξειρεσία*, the lower beneath it and the lowest from the hull a good deal lower. They can be recognised as the thranite, zygian and thalamian oars of a Greek three.

As is to be expected the Athenian naval intervention in Histiaia was effected by a squadron of troop-carrying threes as attested by the deck railing (cf. **viii**). Fives are not recorded in the Athenian navy until 326/5, though owing to the absence of records for the three previous years they may have been present a year or two earlier.

9. Coins of Phaselis 4th–3rd century BC

(a) BM 81 14
(b) BM 1979 1–1 826
(c) *BMC*? no. cf. B 584, 585

9 a

9 c

9 b rev.

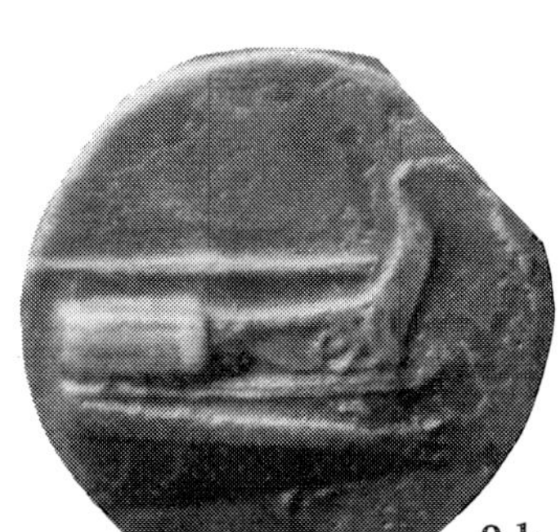

9 b. obv.

(**a**) A warship's prow is shown with the elegant Greek stempost. On the foredeck stands? a figure and behind it the letter *φ* standing for Phaselis? (p. 268). The deck is supported by stanchions over the *ἐπωτίς* and oarbox. Brackets of the *παρεξειρεσία*/ oarbox are indicated.

(**b**) A warship's prow is shown. The deck has no bulwark or rail?. The narrow space between deck and oarbox bears traces of stanchions. There is a deep oarbox with brackets, and possible indication of oarfiles using it (cf. **13b** and **c**), an *ἐπωτίς* and a pair of wales below.

Rev. The stern of a warship: the deck is supported by stanchions. The *ἄφλαστον* is of unusual size.

(**c**) A warship's prow is shown in great detail. The foredeck is supported by stanchions. Slung along its side is the club of Herakles. There is a puzzling object (?a shield) between the after end of the club and a deck stanchion at the coin's edge. As in (**a**) and (**b**) the *ἐπωτίς* is seen aft of a stylised eye and is supported as in (**b**) by brackets.

The obverse of these coins portrays the sterns of types of warship with a projecting deep oarbox. There is no reason to believe the ships represented in **a**, **b**, and **c** are other than Greek threes. Phaselis was a Doric city founded from Lindos in Rhodes.

POLYREME FLEETS OF THE THIRD AND SECOND CENTURY BC

10. Coins of Demetrios Poliorketes c.300–c.295 BC. The coins are in various denominations but silver tetradrachms are largest in scale and easiest to study. Of these there are about 51 dies.

Newell (1927), Kraay 1966 574, Jenkins 1972 536–7, Lockett *SNG* 1518–21. Also Bellinger (1962) 29–30, and cf. B 727, 728.

(**a**) *SNG* IV Fitzwilliam: McClean Collection 3574
(**b**) Newell (1927) pl. 3.3
(**c**) *SNG* III Lockett 1519: BM cast.

These coins represent a series introduced by Demetrios after his father's defeat and death at the battle of Ipsos. They show on the reverse the prow of a warship. The first noticeable feature is the idiosyncratic stubby, slightly *retroussé*, stempost, distinct from the upright Phoenician and S-shaped Greek. A winged female figure, probably the goddess Nike

10 a

10 b

10 c

or Tyche (Victory or Fortune), has alighted on the foredeck. With her right hand she holds a trumpet to her lips and with her left a *στυλίς* with a crossbar at the top. The trumpet is a piece of naval equipment regularly used in battle in the Hellenistic period to signal close encounter with the enemy (D.20.50), and the *στυλίς* and crossbar is another, regularly seen in the stern slightly raked aft across the rising forward curve of the stern ornament (cf. **7**, **39**). Although frequently seen in warship pictures this *στυλίς* is mentioned recognisably only once or twice. Plutarch (*Pompey* 24) says that the pirates at that time were so prosperous that they had golden *στυλίδες*. In his glossary Casson *SSAW* describes it as an identifying device carried in the stern which was set up alongside the *ἄφλαστον* and which bore either a device symbolising the guardian deity of the ship or 'his' (or her) 'name written out '(on the crossbar or a pennant). The *στυλίς* was then an object to which a certain sanctity attached, worth decorating with gold if that could be afforded.

Newell rightly saw the introduction of the series by Demetrios in 301 as reflecting a personal motive 'to remind his rivals as well as his subjects that 'in spite of Ipsos' he was still the unchallenged master of the sea. But Newell proceeded to suggest that the ship on which the goddess alighted represented a unit of Ptolemy's defeated fleet (because its stem had been truncated) and the *στυλίς* in her right hand was a trophy seized from such a ship in the moment of victory.

It is true that the *ἀκροστόλιον* was taken from the stern of a captured ship (p. 115) but not the *στυλίς* from the stern.

It is also most unlikely that the coinage had any close connexion with the battle of Cypriot Salamis which had taken place five years before the issue began. The goddess Nike (or Tyche) proclaimed with her trumpet blast not that victory which by 301 needed no announcement; but Demetrios's resultant mastery of the sea, which at this critical moment in his affairs it was necessary to declare to the world. The Histiaian coinage (**8**) demonstrates the connexion of a protecting deity with the *στυλίς*; and the goddess in Demetrios's coinage holds it in her hand to symbolise that protection.

The ship portrayed is accordingly not, as has been suggested, the largest ship in his fleet with which Demetrios was said to have sent the news of the Salamis victory to his father, nor a particularly fast ship to do that errand better, still less an enemy ship whose *στυλίς* Nike holds as a symbol of the famous victory which she is by now unnecessarily proclaiming (by rather ineffectual means).

After his father's death Demetrios went in for the construction of the big warships for which the long timber he now controlled in Cyprus gave him the material (p. 30). It is likely therefore that the ship portrayed on his propaganda coins would have been one of them.

The prow, with its deck over the forward part of a usually protected but here open side, under which a substantial oarbox runs aft from the *ἐπωτίς*, initiates an otherwise common type. The large eye-panel at the base of the stempost is also a typical feature. There are in one at least of the surviving examples (**b**) traces of oarports in the side face of the deep oarbox. The open side under the deck (in battle protected with screens) would give ventilation for an oarcrew working their oars at three levels, as in the three and in the ships (a five, six or seven) reconstructed by JFC (**65**), (**67**), (**69**) on the basis of the Isola Tiberina monument (**27**). There is a course of two narrow wales separated by pairs of short uprights immediately below the oarbox which could provide oarports for zygian oars and below it a broad wale, which in (**c**) appears to show circular oarports for thalamian oars, curving down to the ram. The ship then appears to have three levels of oars. She could be one of the larger types based not on the 'Phoenician design' of the Erment model which shows no *παρεξειρεσία* but on the three with her *παρεξειρεσία* having become an oarbox.

11. The Lindos Prow c.265–260 BC. Blinkenberg (1938), *LSRS* pl. 29, Morrison (1980), Rice (1991), B.780, 781. Reconstruction: Ch. 7 p. 374–377: (**74**)

At the approach to the acropolis of Lindos in Rhodes a number of blocks of stone have been found which appear to form part of a large monument in the form of a ship's prow once surmounted by a statue (of Victory). It shows the terminal bow section of an oarbox with a boxed-in superstructure. There is a blank vertical panel between the edge of the deck and the downward sloping top of the oarbox. In the

11

ship of the Demetrios coinage (**10**: c.300 BC) the place of this blank vertical panel is taken by an open side, entirely necessary for ventilation. Here, as in the later Samothrace prow (**20**: 200–180 BC) which shows a blank vertical panel in the same place, the necessary ventilation course must be assumed. Such a course is to be seen in the ship of the Nymphaion fresco (**13a** and **c**: 3rd-2nd century BC).

On the lateral face of the oarbox, where oarports might be expected, there is an inscription, of which a good deal remains. It can be seen to have contained the names of 288 men who served in *τριημιολίαι* together with their commander and two trierarchs. Blinkenberg dated the monument to about 265–60 BC. One of the trierarchs, Agathostratos, commanded the Rhodian fleet at the battle of Ephesos (p. 55).

In view of the inscription it seems likely that the ship represented is a *τριημιολία*; and it is possible, though Blinkenberg did not draw this conclusion, that the 288 names it could record form the crews of the two ships of that type of which the trierarchs are named. If that is so, the inference can be drawn, allowing 24 men in each ship as *ὑπηρεσία* (compared with 30 in a three and the 45 of a four p. 349), that the files on each side of the ship were 24 + 22 + 14 = 60 oarsmen, an oarcrew of 120 which with the 24 *ὑπηρεσία* made a crew of 144 all told (so in two ships 288). The files of these sea-going, two-level, cataphract, ships with oars arranged on the *ἡμιολία* principle (p. 261–62) would have been more than twice as long as the open, *ἡμιολίαι* (with 1½ files ten and five men strong) which Alexander built for service on the Hydaspes (p. 10).

12. Coins of the Roman Republic: the Prow Series

The earliest Roman coins to show the prow of a warship are the public issues of the heavy bronze (*aes grave*) units which were cast not struck and were of the pound weight (the *as*). The types of the last issues of *aes grave* (Crawford 714 and 718 34/36 Table LX Vol. II p. 172) show on the obverse the Janus head (looking both ways) and on the reverse a warship's prow. These coins mark the beginning of what Crawford terms the Prow series and the types remain those of the Roman bronze coinage for over a century, later struck rather than cast. They are a clear public proclamation of Rome's awareness of her position as a naval power and are accordingly likely to date from the First Punic War (264–241) or at least soon after it.[4]

The Prow Series of reverse types shows three significantly distinct variants, each with minor variations.

The first kind is shown here by examples (**a**) and (**b**).

- (**a**) *Aes Grave*: Crawford 36/1 Pl. H, BM 1919.12.22–41 (264–241 BC)
  Rev, a warship's prow: left
- (**b**) *As*: Crawford 110/2 Pl. XX1/3, *BMCRR* 326 (211–208 BC)
  Rev, a warship's prow: right

The stempost curves forward and then (in (**a**) slightly) aft. Across its base there are visible in (**a**) two oblique lines marking the fitting of its butt to the hull. Aft of the stempost butt there is the eye panel, and aft again the *ἐπωτίς* and deep oarbox. Above the eye panel and oarbox in (**a**) there is the planked side of the deck which has a guard-rail and post from which the rail slopes down to the stempost. In (**b**) the foredeck post is replaced by a tower and the rail is double. In both the *προεμβόλιον* ends the middle wale, below which the lowest wale (in **b** doubled) slopes down to the main ram. In both (**a**) and (**b**) the oarboxes are of a depth suitable for the five rather than the three. But above the oarbox there is not the open space between it and the deck which is found in the three and in the second and third variants of the Prow series.

The second variant is shown by examples (**c-f**).

- (**c**) *Sextans*: Crawford 38/5 Pl, VII 1, *BMCRR* Rome 59: B.899B (217–215 BC): right
- (**d**) *Aes grave*: *BMCRR* 18.68.5–14 133, B, 960: right
- (**e**) *Aes grave*: uncia struck: Crawford 43/5 Pl. VIII 12, *BMCRR* Aes grave 9, 1878.6 (2.1, B.899A (214–212 BC): right
- (**f**) *Uncia*: Willers III 7, cf. Crawford 85/4 Pl. XVI 12 dated 211–210 BC: right

The main features of (**a**) and (**b**) are repeated in these four prows. In (**c**), (**d**) and (**e**) a club of Hercules is displayed on the vertical side of the foredeck. On the foredeck in all four prows there is a tower with guard-rails. This deck in (**c**), (**d**) and (**e**) reaches the edge of the die and may be regarded as continuous

12 a

12 b

12 c

12 d

12 e

12 f

12 g

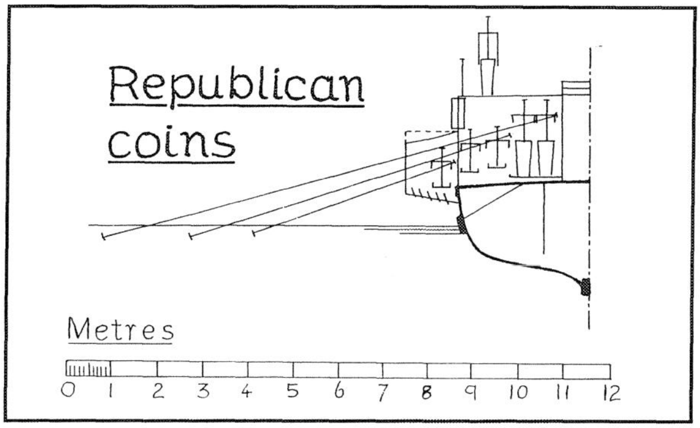

Half section of **12** *as fives.*

with a main deck after its planked side gives place to an open side. This open side distinguishes these prows from those in (**a**) and (**b**). There is a significant difference between (**c**), (**e**) and (**d**), (**f**). In (**c**) and (**e**) the oarbox is shallow resembling the *παρεξειρεσία* of a three (or *τριημιολία*), while in (**d**) and (**f**) it is deep and could accommodate the three levels of oars of the Roman five.

If, as is likely, the absence of the open side between deck and oarbox in (**a**) and (**b**), both of which appear to be fives, reflects a real difference in design of some ships rather than the carelessness of the coin designer, a reason must be sought. The open side, screened when necessary against weather and enemy missiles, provided ventilation in threes. In fives ventilation would have been even more essential; but at the same time since fives were developed with close combat much in view, defence against missiles was even more necessary. It is then possible that some ships were designed in the interest of defence with a reduced area of open side (cf. in particular the five shown on the Ostia relief (**35**)).

The third variety in the design of the ships of the Prow series is to be seen in example (**g**).

(**g**) As Willers IV 12: cf. Crawford 240/2a, 241/3, 244/3 Pl. XXXVI 13, 15, and 21 (134 BC), 337/5 Pl. XLIII 19 (91 BC) and 339/1a Pl. XLIV 1 (91 BC).

Comparison of these prows with the Alba Fucentia graffito (**38**) which is labelled a four suggests strongly that the ships presented, in several cases rigged with towers as in (**g**), are fours. The latticework sidescreens in the open side beneath the deck give some protection. The zygian (upper) oars would emerge from the hull over the topwale while the oarports shown below would serve the thalamian oars.

As the historical evidence for the fleets of the period covered by the Prow series leads one to expect, the ships portrayed are mostly fives, with a few *naves speculatoriae*, threes and fours.

13. The Nymphaion fresco: 284/3–245 BC. N. L. Grach: *Vestnik Dreveistorie* 1. (1984) 81–88; L. Basch (1987) App. 1 pp. 493–6, MM 71.2 (1985).

In the Cimmerian Chersonese (Crimea) Nymphaion was the least of three important maritime cities of a kingdom which had close commercial ties with Athens in the first quarter of the 4th century The capital Pantikapaion, like Nymphaion to the south of it, faced east across the Cimmerian Bosporos (the strait of Kertsch). Strabo (7.4: late 1st century BC-early 1st century AD) says that Pantikapaion had a harbour and shipsheds for about thirty ships; and that Nymphaion also had a good harbour. He says that Pantikapaion was a colony of the Milesians and for a long time was ruled autocratically by the dynasty of Leukon, Satyros and Pairisades, as were all the neighbouring colonies around the mouth of Lake Maiotis (the Sea of Azov) on both sides of the strait ...The last of these autocrats was also named Pairisades (V) but he was unable to hold out against the native population, who kept exacting more and more tribute; and he therefore gave up the sovereignty to Mithridates Eupator (of Pergamon). After him the kingdom became subject to Rome.

The third seaport of the Bosporan kingdom was Theodosia 530 stadia (94 km) west of Pantikapaion along the south coast of the Cimmerian Chersonese. Theodosia, Strabo says, 'is situated in a fertile plain and has a harbour that can accommodate as many as 100 ships'. She also was a colony of Miletos.

The Spartokid dynasty had united the Greek cities of the Cimmerian Bosporos by the end of the 5th century and Theodosia became one of the chief exporters of wheat in the Greek world, in particular to Peiraieus. In the reign of Satyros I (407–393 BC) the Athenians were granted exemption from export-duty and the privilege was renewed under his successor Leukon. An Athenian trading post was established at Nymphaion and, notably about 425, it had become prosperous enough for its annual tribute to be assessed at one talent..

An inscription of 348 BC (*IG*^{2} 212 +: M. N. Tod (1948) II 167) found at Peiraieus records honours voted by the Athenian Assembly to Spartokos II (347–342 BC), Pairisades I (347–309 BC) and Apollonios, the two eldest sons of Leukon and now joint rulers (until Pairisades' death) of the Bosporan kingdom. The decree is in response to a letter from the two rulers offering to Athens the privileges previously given by Satyros and Leukon and making certain requests. One of these is for permission to recruit at Athens officers for their warships (*ὑπηρεσίαι*). The decree grants this permission subject to the accompanying Bosporan envoys making a list for the Secretary of the Council of the names of the officers taken, 'in whose orders it is to serve the sons of Leukon to the best of their ability'.

Rostovtzeff (1930) wrote of Pairisades II whose envoys to Ptolemy II are mentioned (with those of Argos) in the Zenon papyrus 1973 dated 21 September 254 BC. He noted that there is no literary reference to him nor does he appear in Athenian inscriptions, but that he had trading connections with Rhodes, Egypt and Delos and 'it is probable that close commercial relations of the Bosporos kingdom with Rhodes began much earlier than this time (254 BC) and lasted into the 1st century BC. At that moment Egypt was the chief naval power in the Aegean and her hostility would be a fatal handicap to Pairisades' trade'. He implies that Pairisades had sent envoys to gain Ptolemy's favour. As an indication of later Bosporan connection with Antigonos, Rostovtzeff refers to the dedication by Pairisades of a bowl at Delos in the year 250 BC, when Antigonos and Stratonike made their appearance at Delos to reassert his control of the Island League.

Skeat (1974) is more cautious in comment on the papyrus. He identifies the Pairisades mentioned as Pairasades II (reigning from 284/3 until shortly after 250) and speaks of 'the semi-Hellenised Bosporan state' as being in 254 BC 'now at the height of its power and prosperity'. He refers to Rostovtzeff and continues: 'Although Pairisades normally used, and was accorded, the title of *βασιλεύς* it is noticeable that he is not so designated here: possibly Ptolemy II and his ministers did not condescend to recognise the Crimean kinglet as an equal. The reasons for the mission from Pairisades are unknown, although it is conjectured' (by Rostovtzeff)' that some form of economic cooperation between the two greatest grain-producing areas of the Near East may have been involved. Nor do we know if the mission was successful. According to Rostovtzeff Pairisades soon after turned against Egypt: but the evidence based on dedications at Delos is inconclusive'.

Excavations in 1982 on the site of ancient Nymphaion on the western side of the Cimmerian Bosporos revealed in the stratum of the Hellenistic period 15 m^2 of plaster fallen from the wall of a room. The presence in the room of a fine stone altar and a large amount of votive material showed it to have been used for religious purposes.

The word *nymphaion*, since nymphs are regularly water deities, is frequently used as the name for a fountain with an architectural background (Philostratos *Vita Apollonii* 8.12) of which the Nymphaia at Delos (*IG* 11^2.144 A 91) and at Miletos are well known examples.

The building (300–250 BC) in which the fresco was found had been constructed on three terraces of a steep slope facing the harbour. On the lowest level there are stone altars of various designs and on the upper terrace a yard paved with square slabs and a cloister, as well as 'huge cisterns for storing water'. The latter suggest that the building is indeed a Nymphaion, from which the city took its name (cf. Nymphaion near Lissos on the Adriatic), the architectural background to a natural spring. The room containing the fresco was reached from the courtyard; and wide steps led to the lower levels.

The plaster indicated that a considerable part of the wall surface had been covered with drawings, symbols and inscriptions. When reconstructed it showed a coloured panel made with an undercoat of white throughout, while in places there were traces of a nearly lost pinkish top coat. The middle part of the fresco is composed of five horizontal bands of unequal height. Below a narrow decorative band of 3 cm there is a broad (47 cm) band evenly coloured in bright yellow on a smooth polished surface which contains throughout its length (1.20 m) a representation of an oared warship. On the ship's bow is inscribed boldly the name of the Egyptian goddess ISIS, which Grach takes to be the name of the ship and an indication that she is Egyptian[5].

On the after end of the deck there are four oblong shields. Grach says: 'One can recognise with certainty that the other drawings, carelessly executed, (one of which shows a man with his arm raised over a shield (the forward one of the four) and a bird over the ship (threatening him with a trident) appeared later and are not connected with the original concept of the composition'. With this opinion we may readily agree, although the four shields may well belong to the original ship-portrait, which Grach thinks was engraved on the wall (plaster) first and may well have been originally the only engraving (there).

Among the illustrations to Grach's article are:

(a) The ship shown without oarports: Grach 7, B.1128
(b) Prow section in full: Grach 8, B.1129
(c) Stern section in full: Grach 9, B.1130.

Casson (*SSAW* Ch. 15: see also Torr (1894) p. 65–6, 148) treats the subject of name devices on a ship's bow and stern very fully. 'The device forward was most important, for this identified the vessel; it was its *ἐπίσημον* or *παράσημον*, 'name-device'. It was not a written name but a symbol, and in the Nymphaion ship this symbol was the framed picture of the heads of a horse and a rider immediately forward of the eye (**1b**). This device depicts one of the twin *Διοσκόρω*. Since there is a *Castor* (*CIL* X 3582) and a *Pollux* (VI 3106, X 3514), both threes, later in the imperial fleet at Misenum, *Διόσκορος* or *Διοσκόρω* may be assumed to have been the name of the ship, not *Isis*. *Διοσκόρω* was a common name among merchantmen (cf. *Acts* 28.11 St Paul's ship) but is not recorded for a warship. There was no practice of inscribing actual names on a ship's hull until much later (seamen being normally illiterate). The inscription 'ISIS' may have been added, like the magnificent bird and trident, after the completion of the fresco. There is apparently a tutelary deity worshipped in the stern.

The presence of shields on the deck's edge has been noted as a Phoenician peculiarity. In Phoenician contexts the shields are round and form a continuous course from bow to stern, indicating, presumably a full complement of armed men. These shields are four in number, and are oblong, in shape unlike the similarly placed Phoenician shields but like those at the edge of the deck of the ships on the coins of Hasdrubal (**17**) and on Calenian dishes (**18 I**).

The fresco of the Nymphaion, Grach writes, is dated by the accompanying material, its content and the nature of the script of the inscriptions, to the first half of the 3rd century BC, or even to the second quarter i.e. to the time of the reign of Pairisades II of the Bosporos (the years 284/3–245), whose name appears repeatedly in the inscriptions. The reliability of the date is confirmed by a stamp with the inscriptions *ΒΑΣΙΛΙΚ* and *ΒΑΣΙΛΙΚΟΣ* on a tile from the Bosporos and a slightly earlier potter's stamp with an emblem in the form of an eagle and a dolphin on an example from Sinope (the relevance of the items mentioned by Grach is obscure). Among the remains of the tiled roof which fell on to the floor before the plaster...(there was) a large fragment of a marble altar (which) by the nature of its ornamental decoration and analogues corresponding to it can be dated to the last quarter of the 4th century BC. It is possible that the construction of the sanctuary itself dates from the same time.

13 a

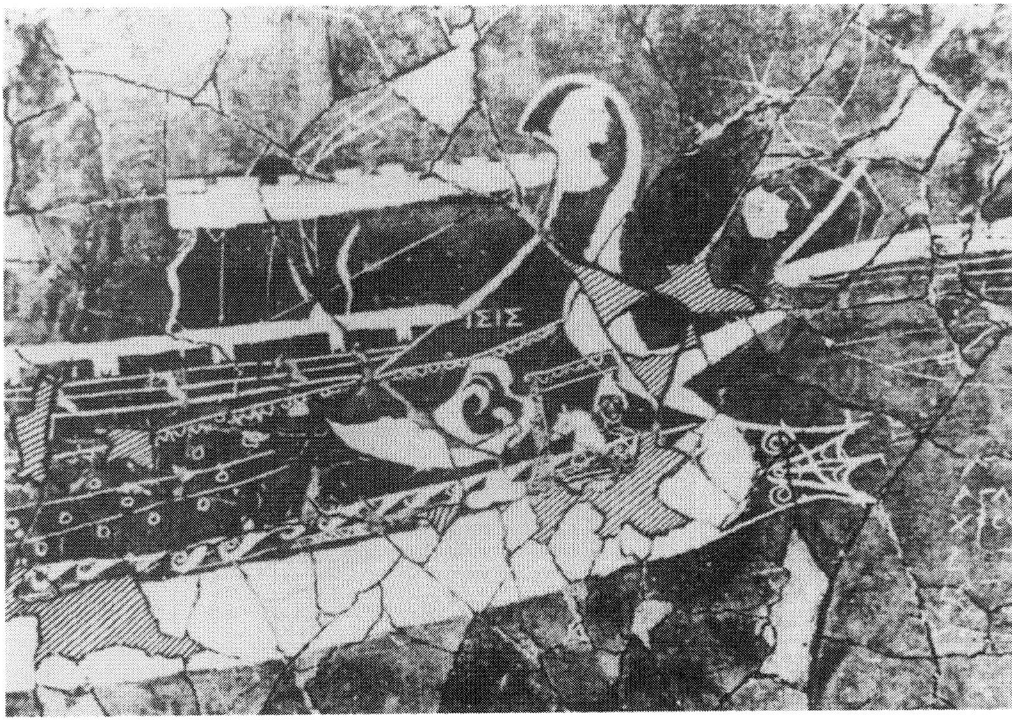

13 b

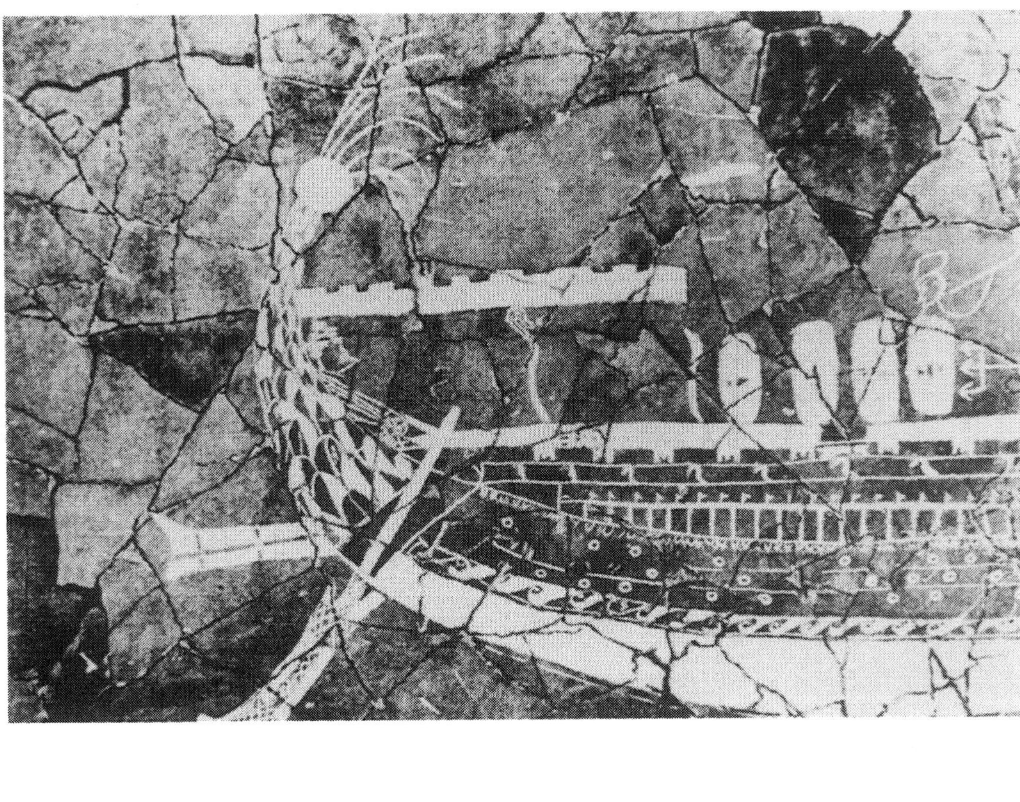

13 c

The occurrence of the names of three of the months in the Milesian calendar in the inscriptions in Greek visible on the plaster fragments confirm Miletos as founder of the cities of the Bosporan kingdom. Spartokos I was the founder of the Bosporan dynasty (see Tod: 1948 II p. 43). That the name Pairisades in the inscriptions on the fresco refers to the second rather than the first king of that name is not at first sight certain. If the sanctuary was built in the last quarter of the 4th century, reference to the first (347–309) becomes more probable. On the other hand Grach also reports that the 'new' name 'Satyros' appears among the many inscriptions twice 'before' (i.e. presumably linked with and to the left of) the name Pairisades. The inscription of 346 BC (*IG*2[2] 212: Tod II 167) honouring Spartokos II and Parisades I refers thrice to a Satyros and his son (Tod II 115 387–47 BC) Leukon as their predecessors in the Bosporan kingship. Since the kingship seems to be often shared, the Satyros in the fresco may then be Satyros II sharing the kingship with a Pairisades who must then be the second king of that name. Athens in 287 BC sent envoys to a Bosporan king Spartokos asking for corn (*IG* ii 311 = *Syll*[2] 194) and Spartokos was thanked in a decree passed the following year. This Spartokos II must have preceded Pairisades II and Satyros II to whose reign the fresco belongs.

Basch (1987) includes a brief notice of the fresco in an Appendix (**1**) and later in an 'étude approfondi' (*MM* 1985) 'of the *Isis* of Ptolemy II Philadelphus', he reaches three conclusions: '(a) that we are in the presence of a galley with three tiers of oars, (b) that it does not correspond to any known type and (c) that by reason of its upperworks it was not a lightly built vessel such as a *τριήρης*' as Grach assumes. He, like her, takes Isis to be the ship's name and that she is an Egyptian ship of Ptolemy Philadelphos's fleet.

No one could quarrel with the first and third of Basch's conclusions, but the second is a different matter. Many would come to the first and third conclusions regarding the ships on the Calenian dishes of Canoleios (**19**: 250–180 BC) also, as well as to the ship on the Ostia relief (**35**: shortly after 20 BC), and to the ships on the Pompeii shipsheds fresco (44 AD 64–58). In all these we are in the presence of ships *maioris formae* (excluding fours which have been seen to have two levels of oars only). The second conclusion accordingly does not stand.

It can further be seen that the upperworks of *Dioskoros* follow the pattern, though differing in some details, of the upperworks of ships which can be recognised as fives.

There is however one factor in her representation which distorts the picture and has to be discounted. It is the unrealistically strong curvature of the 'rockered' keel, resulting in the increased distancing from the water of the three rows of oarports as they approach bow and stern (Grach recognises this as an Egyptian feature, on what ground for Egyptian warships of this period is not obvious). No oars are shown. If they were shown, it would be clear that no practicable long ship could have been built with such a strong curvature of the keel. The resultant unrealistically heightened bow and stern cause the horizontal courses, the lines of the guard rail of the deck, of the louvres, and of the wales, running the length of the ship, to have an unnecessary amount of space between them because the line of the guard-rail and of the deck have become too high and short. To gain a proper idea of the actual ship represented the observer must in imagination pull bow and stern apart so that the deck becomes lower and longer and the curvature of the keel is greatly reduced, if not eliminated altogether in the area of the oarsystem. Then the oars do not become further from the water as they approach bow or stern (which of course would have been impossible in an actual ship), and the oarbox with its three rows of oarports *en échelon* takes up its proper position parallel to the waterline of the ship, as reason requires.

The strong curvature of the rockered keel has produced another but less confusing anomaly. The ram is the normal square termination of a wale on each side of the hull, but in the Nymphaion fresco the curvature causes it to be shown as fitted at an angle, awkwardly, so that the function of the wales is defeated.

The larger warships commonly have turrets in bow and stern (p. 359). In *Dioskoros* instead of turrets there is in each area, serving the same purpose, a high deck, with a guard-rail and supported by stanchions, abutting the stempost in the bow and the *ἄφλαστον* in the stern, in both cases near the top. Below these runs the regular deck with a guard-rail. Outboard of the guard-rail there is the normal *πάροδος* supported unusually by brackets butting on to a wale. The beam of the forty (late 3rd century: p. 274–277) is given as from *πάροδος* to *πάροδος*, which suggests that the *πάροδος* had by then become a regular feature of the bigger warships.

Below the brackets and wale there is a featureless area above a course of uprights framed by wales. This course of uprights is the ventilation panel which normally appears under the *πάροδος*, but here supports a second, lower, *πάροδος*. On the upper side of the frame there is a row of hooks (implying the second *πάροδος* as a means of access to them, cf. *Syrakosia* p. 357 which had three *πάροδοι*). Below it there is the panel showing three rows of oarports quincunx-fashion, the rows separated from each other by two wales.

Here the prows on the Roman Republican coins **12b** and **c** may be compared. In **12b** there are bollards on a *πάροδος* (cf. the hooks), and below it (cf. **29**) a ventilation panel above the panel framing two parallel wales. The prow in **13c** shows similar features except that here there is only one wale in the oarbox, implying two levels of oars instead of three as in **12b**. The difference between the Nymphaion ship and that on **12b** is that the former has two *πάροδοι* with a row of hooks on the lower *πάροδος*. The purpose of the row of hooks may be explained as the means of rigging before an engagement the necessary screening over the ventilation panel below them.

The Nymphaion ship displays a remarkably fine 'eye' immediately aft of the *παράσημον*. This like the *παράσημον* on the Isola Tiberina prow (**27**) and on the Praeneste relief (**29**) faces half forward. The *παράσημον* here as on the Praeneste relief takes the place of the absent *ἐπωτίς* and indicates the outward position of the oarbox aft of it. The Phaselis (**9**), Demetrios (**10**), and Roman Republican (**12**) coins show similar large eyes forward of an *ἐπωτίς*.

There is perhaps a greater similarity between the Nymphaion ship and the ship on the Ostia frieze (**35**) which belongs to the last quarter of the 1st century BC. The latter has a *πάροδος* surmounting a ventilation course, beneath which is a narrow, recessed oarbox. She has no *ἐπωτίς* and forward of the oarbox is a framed *παράσημον* taking its place, and forward of that a formalised eye. The two ships have all these several elements in common, but in the Nymphaion ship the *παράσημον* is forward, and in the Ostia ship aft, of the eye.

The ship on the Nymphaion fresco, thus interpreted, is certainly one of the larger types of Hellenistic oared warship. She is, as Basch recognised, certainly not a three. Nor, with three levels of oars, is she a four. Her spacious bow and stern 'turrets' and her two *πάροδοι* suggest a five. She belongs to the group of ships represented with deep oarboxes accommodating three levels of oarports *en échelon* (Group B). JFC sees difficulties in fitting such an oarsystem into a ship larger than a five. She can only therefore be recognised as a five – with some idiosyncrasies.

Finally, what was her connection with the Bosporan kingdom? It may seem unlikely that the Bosporan kingdom possessed a five, not however impossible, since it was then at the height of its prosperity and in the last half of the previous century the kings of the Cypriot and Phoenician cities had fives as their flagships. If Pairisades had one, that would be a very good reason for inscribing a portrait of her on the temple wall. Strabo says that the capital Pantikapaion had a harbour (for merchantmen) and *νεώρια* for 30 (long) ships. Such a modest fleet would have been mostly threes , and officers for them had to be recruited in Athens and no doubt elsewhere. It may seem more likely that the ship was a visitor.

Her aft curving stempost, in spite of the shields on deck, rules out a Phoenician but not a Macedonian, an Egyptian or Greek (e.g. Kios **7**) origin. The motive for a visiting warship of the bigger kind would have been diplomatic or commercial, or both. Dionysios I of Syracuse used the five he had invented for a diplomatic visit to Rhegion (p. 2).

Within the Euxine Sea there were at this period two naval powers. On the south coast Herakleia, which was, in Tarn's words, a 'great maritime city', had been acquired by Lysimachos in 289 BC to give him a base in the Euxine while Lysimacheia, which he had founded to dominate the Hellespont, had on the site of Kardia before that enabled him to levy taxes on commercial traffic in and out of it. The second was Byzantion which also had a financial interest in the commercial traffic from the Euxine (p. 56–57). Rostovtzeff noted the effect on the corn price at Delos according to whether Lysimachos closed or opened the Hellespont to traffic. He might well have felt that the accession of two new men to the kingship of Bosporos, from where the traffic came, was the moment for showing the flag and making a diplomatic visit from Herakleia in a ship of the larger sort. This visit could only have taken place in the first three or four years of the new reign. Byzantion, whose fleet would certainly have contained a five, might well have had the same idea. Kios, a sister colony of Miletos, was not far away in Propontis and had a fleet of threes, but advertised no five on her coinage. The new Seleukid ruler Antiochos I had no fleet at this time. After 280–79 'he encountered great difficulties with the tribes and cities of the northern coast of Asia Minor particularly at Herakleia Pontika, which continued to oppose him for many decades' (p. 74 Map H; Heinen: 1984 p. 415).

Lysimachos had a second motive for a diplomatic mission from Herakleia. He was at the height of his power in 285 BC (Tarn: 1913 p. 116) since Demetrios's 20 years of naval supremacy had just come to an end. Lysimachos took over not only part of his fleet at Pella (the Phoenician contingent at Ephesos under Philokles falling to Ptolemy) but Macedon as well, much of Thessaly and the Thracian coast up to the Danube mouth, much of Asia Minor with nearly all the great coastal cities from the Hellespont to Kilikia and Aegean islands including Imbros and Samothrake (from Ptolemy). It has been shown (Tarn: 1913 p. 220) that the islands and the coastal cities of Asia Minor, including Pantikapaion's mother city Miletos, were importers of corn. He might well have wished to approach the kings from a position of strength with a request for the special privilege in the import of corn which Athens had enjoyed in the past.

Athens' close connection with the Bosporan kings was of long standing and vital to her survival. She also might have thought that a polite visit at that moment was called for; but for the opening years of the new reign at Pantikapaion Athens and Peiraieus were under siege and the resultant loss of Peiraieus to Antigonos would have made such a mission impossible in the following years.

The other sea powers who might wish to send a five on a diplomatic visit to Pantikapaion during the years 284/3 to shortly after 250 BC (which Grach puts at 245) are Antigonos Gonatas, Ptolemy II, and Rhodes. Rome had no fives before the First Punic War, and did not end it until 241 within a very few years of the end of Pairisades's reign.

Antigonos, in the early years of Pairisades' reign, was in no position to send a five to the Euxine. While Lysimachos, his arch-enemy, controlled the Hellespont Antigonos would not have ventured to do so; and after Lysimachos's death at Kouropedion in 281 (Will: 1984 p. 113) he was heavily defeated at sea by Ptolemy Keraunos, who had inherited Lysimachos's fleet and proceeded to rule Macedon until he fell to the Celts. Antigonos had no ships until his restoration to Macedon after his victory over the Celts on land at Lysimacheia in 277 BC. Thereafter he was closely preoccupied with Macedonian affairs until he had gathered the resources to build a fleet in the late seventies and early sixties of the 3rd century BC and defeat Ptolemy's admirals at the battles of Kos (spring 261: Walbank: 1982 p. 239) and Andros (?246: Walbank: 1982 p. 248–9, Tarn: 1913 378ff). During the last two decades of Pairisades' reign, when Antigonos possessed Lysimacheia, he might well have sent a five on a diplomatic visit to the Bosporan kingdom. It is most unlikely that Ptolemy alone had Phoenician ships in his service at that time.

The threat to Ptolemy's command of the sea disappeared with Lysimachos, and his control of the Aegean was then complete, stretching as far north as Samothrake, which he had regained. As ruler of a great corn producing country second only to the Bosporan kingdom he would have had that as a common interest with the Bosporan kings; and, as the possessor of the greatest fleet the eastern Mediterranean had seen, would have had plenty of ships to send. A five, which was both prestigious and a strong performer, was a most suitable ship for the voyage. But it is unlikely to have been undertaken after the battle of Kos (261), first of the series of naval defeats suffered by Ptolemy, the second being from the Rhodians at Ephesos 'in the 250s' (Walbank: 1982 p. 233). After Lysimachos's death Byzantion, Kalchedon and Herakleia formed a powerful league, which would have done its best to discourage but could not prevent Ptolemy from penetrating the Euxine. He enjoyed a brief window of free naval movement between Lysimachos's death and the revival of Macedon as a naval power.

Rhodes, at this time, was a sea power of the calibre of Byzantion or Herakleia, and had close commercial links with the Euxine. As the scourge of piracy she was *persona grata* with all the great powers. She herself was an entrepreneur in the corn trade, and might have reason for a diplomatic mission to the greatest producer of 'her vital supply of grain' (Heinen: 1984 p. 432). The five was not however the sort of ship one would expect her to send in that context, rather a four or a τριημιολία, with which she might persuade rather than impress. Her interest in the corn trade was shown 20 years later in her hostile demonstration against Byzantion in protest against the latter's impost on traffic through the Bosporos (p. 90), in the course of which she sent three threes and closed the Hellespont. She also sent a mission which negotiated a peaceful solution.

The identification of *Dioskoros* as an Egyptian ship is claimed by Grach primarily on the ground of her supposed name, ISIS; secondarily by the statement that the letter in the Zenon archive 'mentions in particular the fact that the rulers of the two states, the kingdom of Bosporos and the kingdom of Egypt had a mutual interest during the period in friendly contacts and relations and paid each other visits for discussions'. She has unfortunately been wrongly informed. The letter is evidence for a visit to Egypt by envoys from Argos and Bosporos and for nothing else, not even for a meeting between the envoys and Ptolemy, or for which side initiated the visit. The only points in favour of the ship being Egyptian are the Phoenician features, since it is known that Demetrios's Phoenician contingent went over to Ptolemy. But that does not mean that Ptolemy had a monopoly of Phoenician ships. Antigonos would certainly have recruited some as king of Macedon.

No firm identification of *Dioskoros*'s home port is possible. If the fresco could be dated to the few years before 281 BC, the ship, if a visitor, may have come from Herakleia on Lysimachos's orders. If it can be dated in the seventies or sixties the ship may have been under the Macedonian flag. The least unlikely time for a ship of the Egyptian fleet to visit the Bosporos is after 281 and before 262. A Rhodian ship could probably have made the voyage at any time during Pairisades' reign, but a Rhodian ship is unlikely to have been a five which *Dioskoros* almost certainly is.

The most likely answer is that, like the flagships of the no more important or prosperous Phoenician and Cypriot kings who became Alexander's allies (p. 6), *Dioskoros* was a local ship of Phoenician type acquired by Pairisades as the prestigious flagship of his fleet. Her portrait in meticulous if somewhat eccentric detail was then proudly displayed on the wall of the Nymphaion temple. If so, she may have derived her name from the city where she was built, Dioskourias, a sister Milesian colony in Kolchis at the eastern end of the Euxine, which is described by Strabo (11.2.16–17) as the emporion of seventy surrounding tribes, excellent in everything which relates to ship-building, and as later giving Mithridates Eupator most aid in building up his power at sea.

14. The Cyrene prow 246–241 BC: Anna Lia Ermeti (1983). See Lionel Casson's review *AJA* 87 (1983) p. 418. B.816 cf. 817

The prow shows a προεμβόλιον extending as far forward as the main ram, which is at the waterline. The aim of this remarkable development seems to be to combine the advantages of ships with high main rams (ἀνάστειροι) and those with rams at waterline level, indicated by the dolphin.

14

15. Carthaginian grave stele 3rd century BC. Bartolini (1979A), B.823.

15

The prow shown is interesting because it exhibits in simplified form and larger scale the features which have been visible in the prows shown on contemporary Roman coins. Behind the stem there is the same aft sloping foredeck terminating at the curved deckstanchion and below it the ἐπωτίς as the forward cover to the deep oarpanel. There is however one feature which is not Roman. The stempost curves forward at its extremity forming a drum, not aft as in Roman ships. The ships on the Hasdrubal and similar Carthaginian coinage (**17**) show stemposts which terminate in a forward curve making a bird's head and beak. The forward curve would then seem to be a characteristic by which Carthaginian ships were identified. It is interesting that the Isis fresco (**42**) of the 1st century BC when Roman and African ships might be pictured going into battle together two ships are shown side by side, one with a forward curving and one with an aft curving stempost.

16. Coins of Antigonos Doson 227–221 BC. Tetradrachms with 66 reverse dies showing on the obverse Apollo seated on a prow: I. L. Mevker (1960) 39ff, Kraay and Hirmer (1966) 575–6, Jenkins (1972) 540–1. The example illustrated is BM 1947.4–6.192.

The stempost seems higher than that on Demetrios Poliorketes' coinage because the superstructure here is lower; and it ends with a slight swelling. Although the ship is certainly Macedonian the stempost does not show the notch at its extremity visible on the stempost of Demetrios's ships, appearing close to the Roman stempost. Only on some dies is there an oblique marking at the base of the stempost. The superstructure is not as marked as on Demetrios's coins. It appears just above Apollo's thigh and usually behind his left elbow. In front of his knees two timbers project as a *προεμβόλιον* in line with the oarbox on which he is sitting. A heavy wale ends in the ram. The markings on this represent rivets and clamps fastening the metal sheath to the timber. There are sometimes stylised sharp waves on the ram.

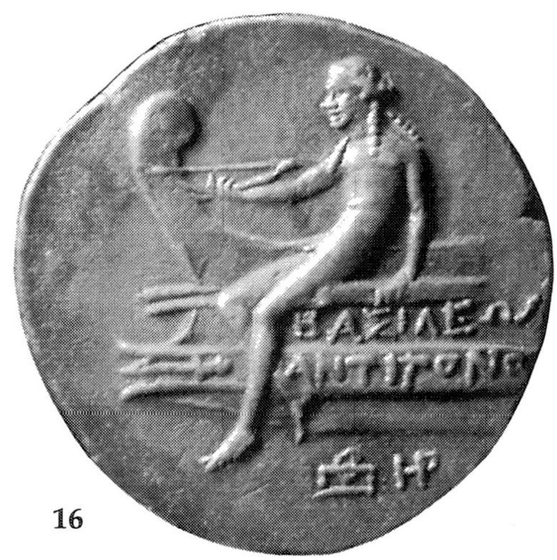

16

17. Coins of Hasdrubal: 228–221 BC

(**a**) Cabinet des Médailles, Paris
(**b**) BM 1878 b. 3 15
(**c**) Jenkins and Lewis (1963) p. 45 pl. 22, no.461 Carthaginian of same period: B.745

17 a

17 b

17 c

These coins show the port side of the prow of a Carthaginian warship with a stempost curving forward in (**a**), and (**b**) to form a bird's head and beak resembling the stempost of the ship on the right in the Pompeii Shipshed fresco (**43**). (**a**) is clear and precise. Large shields are hung outboard of the deck in the Phoenician manner so as to form a substantial bulwark (cf. **19 I**). In the case of (**a**) the shields overlap each other, and the lower wale runs horizontally forward to the ram. In (**b**) and (**c**) only a single shield is shown. There is an open side below the deck. On top of the forward end of the oarbox (*ἐπωτίς*) there is a pair of bollards.

The oarsystem is indicated in (**a**) by five pairs of oars issuing from the side of the oarbox *en échelon* as in the Samothrace prow (**20**), which is identified as a *τριημιολία* (p. 266). (**b**) and (**c**) show indistinctly prows with similar features except that the lower wale curves downward to the ram the oarsystem is indicated formally by four oars emerging under the oarbox. Two wales terminate one in the upper the other in the lower (main) ram.

The area of the side of each ship between the shield bulwark (i.e. the edge of the deck) and the top of the oarbox and *πάροδος* shows some deck stanchions, less distinct (? louvres) in (**a**).

18. Dishes from Cales I 3rd-2nd century BC. Signed by the potter L. Canoleios: c.250–180 BC: *SSAW* 6.75. Pagenstecher (1909) p. 81 nos 126 and 128a.

(**a**) National Museum Naples 117276: *CVA* Italy fasc. XXII 2, B.947.
(**b**) Louvre 4 249

These dishes show the prows of a number of similar warships with remarkable features:

(i) The stemposts are straight and stumpy.
(ii) The prows are massed together as if the intention is to show a fleet rather than, as has been usual, single ships. The oars have been omitted.
(iii) The foredeck shows a low bulwark and continues aft until it is masked by massive shields (cf. **18**). The side wall of the foredeck terminates aft, as in (**29**) with the *παράσημον* (clearly visible in the ships of (**b**)).
(iv) The foredeck continues aft over the usual arching side of the f'o'c'sle cabin to form the maindeck from the side of which the shields hang over a deep space two thirds of the depth of the oarbox beneath it. It is clear that space is a generously designed ventilation course in the position where it is to be expected. Aft of the eye and beneath the ventilation course the deep oarpanel, like that in the Nymphaion ship (**13**: cf. **35**), shows on its lateral face three courses of oarports arranged quincunx fashion.

The period of Canoleios's artistic activity covers Rome's naval victories against Carthage and the extension of her naval power into the eastern Mediterranean, in both of which fives were the ships of the line. The system he illustrates does not admit further development (e.g. to sixes) and in any case

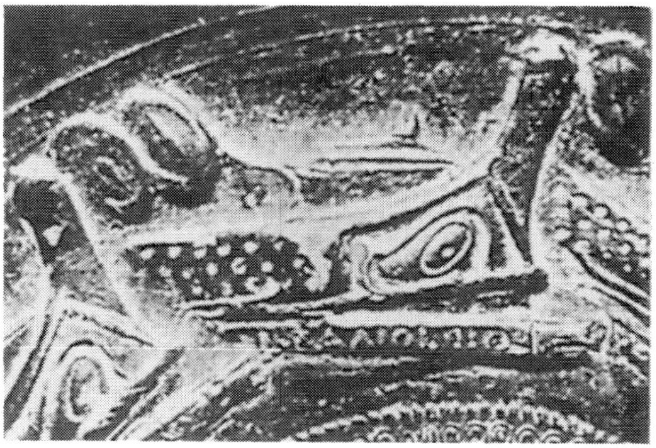

18 Ia

18 Ib

sixes were employed at this time as flagships. There can thus be a strong probability that Canoleios's ships are fives.

The remarkable similarity between the use of massive shields as protection for the deck on these coins and on Hasdrubal's contemporary coinage (**17**) of 228–221 BC suggests the possibility, which would explain the un-Roman stempost and the absence of oars, that Canoleios represents captured Carthaginian fives. The absence of the forward curving top in the shape of a bird's head and beak *ἀκροστόλιον* shown in Hasdrubal's coins (**17**) which appears also in one of the two ships shown in the Shipshed fresco (**43**) may also be an indication that the ships portrayed in Canoleios's dishes are captives (see p. 115: *ἀκροστόλια*).

Dishes from Cales II: Illustrating the Ulysses story: end 3rd century and early 2nd century BC. Berlin F. 3882: Odysseus *φιάλη*: Pagenstecher (1909) 126 26–27: B 951, 952, 953.

This artist, whose work is sufficiently illustrated by the Berlin *φιάλη*, places four ships on each dish with a full complement of oars emerging from the lateral face of the oarpanel at three levels. By a somewhat illogical treatment of them at the for-

18 II

ward end of the system (turning the ship there slightly towards the viewer: cf. **35**) he indicates that they are arranged at three levels quincunx fashion (cf. **35**). As in the case of the Aula Isiaca fresco (**40**) and the Trajan's Column frieze (**45–49**) the grossly exaggerated figures interfere with the ships' structure. Above the oarbox the necessary ventilation course is 'stood through' by the figures. The ventilation course is shown best on the dish from the Martin von Wagner Museum Wurzburg (B 952). The stemposts of the ships on the dishes of (**18 I**), in contrast to those on the dishes of (**18 II**), are of the normal Roman pattern.

The ships could be threes; but unless the Canoleian dishes, the Ostia relief, the Aula Isiaca or the Shipshed fresco depict threes, which in the circumstances is most unlikely, there is no other case of a three with the deep oarbox accommodating all three levels of oars; and later examples of Roman threes are of the 5th and 4th century BC design (**41**). It seems more likely that the artist is anachronistic, as the artists of the Ruvo vase (**ix**) and the Aula Isiaca fresco (**40**) were, and gave Ulysses a modern first-line ship as befitted a Greek hero, that is to say, a five.

19. Tyrian Coinage of Antiochos III 198/7–194/3 BC

When in 198 BC Antiochos III gained possession of Koile-Syria from Egypt he was able to move his naval base to Tyre from Tarsos (Newell: 1941 p. 233 quoting Strabo 14.5.10). He immediately began to mint his own coinage there, indicating his naval presence by a prow on the reverse of the bronze units and a stern on the reverse of the bronze doubles.

(**a**) Newell (1941) No. 1258 Pl. XLV 9 Rev: Bronze unit dated to 198/7 BC by the inscription PIE.

A prow is shown (left). A swan-neck stempost (cf. **17** and **43**, also the Carthaginian coin B.745), from the point of which hangs a streamer or fillet, rises from a strongly marked upper wale, which projects to make a *προεμβόλιον* reaching as far forward as the main ram. Above the wale is a dolphin and above the dolphin the eye aft of the Phoenician letter (a reversed p). Aft of all three is the *ἐπωτίς*. The guard rail of a foredeck and deck at one level begins above the eye etc. Below the deck there is an open side with deck stanchions above an oarbox running aft from the *ἐπωτίς*. The hole at the centre is a common feature of these coins and is not part of the ship picture.

19 a

19 b

(**b**) Newell (1941) No. 1275 Pl. XLVI 10 Rev. Bronze double: dated to 194/3 BC by the inscription PIG

A stern is shown (left). By contrast with (**a**) the deck guard-rail is less and the open side with deck stanchions more strongly marked. The oarbox beneath is also clearly shown. There appears to be a turret with an arch on its forward end. Aft of the turret a hook appears to be the tiller of the starboard rudder which is in the down position. The port rudder is raised.

The turret suggests one of the larger ships, but the oarbox is not deep enough for a five and the solid oarbox such as is seen in the Samothrace prow (**20**) which has been identified as a *τριημιολία* favours the same identification for this ship. Alternatively it is a three, It must be accepted that types *minoris formae* could carry a tower aft.

20. The Samothrace Prow 200–180 BC. Louvre 2369: *GOS* pl. 28, *SSAW* pl. 118, *LSRS* pl. 29b, Rice (1991) Fig. 5. B.747–754. Line Drawing (**74**).

Martin Robertson (1975: p. 535–6) writes: The monument 'celebrates a sea victory probably somewhere in the neighbourhood of the north Aegean, though as the island (of Samothrake) was a centre of worship of the Kabeiroi, gods of the sea and seamen, that does not absolutely follow'. 'A fragmentary inscription associated with the Victory has been related by the letter forms to signatures of a Rhodian sculptor, Pythokritos. The statue has been supposed his, and may in any case be a Rhodian dedication'. Blinkenberg (1938) argued that it represented a *τριημιολία*, Casson (1971) a four, both favourite Rhodian warships.

The prow base. Unfortunately the ram and stempost are missing. Only the point is preserved where the stempost begins to curve up from the hull below the foredeck.

The interpretation of what remains of the prow is greatly helped by the coins of Demetrios Poliorketes (**10**: 300–295 BC) and the Lindos prow (**11**: 265–260 BC) which share with it foredecks merging into maindecks and oarboxes of the same shape and type. The three ship-portraits, although the first two date from an earlier century than the third's, help to explain each other.

Demetrios's coins show a similar winged figure to the Victory, but make it plain that the massive block of stone on which she stands has nothing to do with the ship. Demetrios's goddess alights on a foredeck (without a bulwark) which as it stretches aft becomes a maindeck over an open side below which an oarbox projects. The three-dimensional Lindos and Samothrace prows show how the oarbox projects with an outward and down-sloping upper surface and an outward and up-sloping lower surface, and the Samothrace oarbox shows oarports at two levels *en échelon*.

The side wall of the Samothrace prow is marked with a narrow wale indicating the line of the deck and the base of a bulwark paralleled, e.g., by the similar bulwark on the prow of the Ostia frieze ship (**35**). There is no *πάροδος*; the side drops vertically to the point at which the slope of the oarbox begins. This blank side corresponds to the open side of the Demetrios prow and is to be interpreted with its help. It may be compared with the ventilation course of the Nymphaion ship (**13**) and the latticework of the prow on the Lugdunum coin of Octavian (**31a**). At the bottom of the blank side there is on both sides of the ship a wavelike course of what may be

20

louvres, but they seem too small to provide the ventilation required. It is more likely that the whole blank wall was decorated to indicate a much more adequate ventilation course.

The lateral face of the oarbox on each side: SSAW 128, B.747–758, Rice (1991) Fig. 6. The pair of oarports arranged *en échelon* on the lateral face of the port and starboard oarboxes show tholepins. Since the pins are aft of the middle point of the oarport, the oar must be worked forward of it (by oarsmen facing aft) and the oar rowed against the strop, not against the pin.[6]

If the statue is a Rhodian dedication, the warship chosen to bear on its prow the Victory monument is likely be one of the Rhodian favourites, a *τριημιολία* (see p. 266). The difference in level between the oarports *en échelon* on the oarbox face is too small for the ship to be a four: see (**60**).

Detail of 20

21. The Lindos relief c.190–180 BC. Blinkenberg (1938) 22–30, *AT* 34, *SSAW* 108: Rice (1991) Fig. 7, B.783–5. Line Drawing (**74**)

The relief provides a detailed picture of part of the stern of a Rhodian ship, port side. The wales on the outside of the hull are gathered, continued and brought up and over the helmsman's chair to make, with the *στυλίς*, a fine stern ornament. The deck follows it upward, supported on stanchions as in the stern of the Ficoroni casket (**vii**). Under the upper sections it seems possible to see through the ship while in the lower sections (under the helmsman's feet) there is an enclosed cabin. Round the upward curving stern forward of the port rudder pivot is a plaited rope, as appears, e.g., on the Pergamon monument (B.945).[7] Forward of the handle of the port rudder as it lies in its horizontal position there begins the oarbox with the protected rowing area above it. A deckstanchion represented as curved (for perspective: cf. deckstanchions in **vi**, **vii** and **viii**)) rises from inboard of the oarbox to the deck. Aft of this there is a short stout pillar resting on the end of the solid cross timber (*θρῆνυς*) aft of which the oarbox ends. Forward of the stanchion the rowing area is boxed-in.

Blinkenberg concluded that the relief, like the prow (**11**), represented a *τριημιολία*, and this con-

21

clusion seems probable in spite of the absence of oarports, which might, if it were a *τριημιολία*, not extend as far aft as the relief. It is clearly cataphract but with an air of lightness and elegance which would suit a *τριημιολία* (p. 320).

22. The Athlit Ram 204–184 BC

This bronze ram was found in the sea off Athlit about 12 miles south of Haifa in November 1980. In 1991 a monograph on it,edited by Lionel Casson and J. Richard Steffy, was published by the Texas A & M University Press. It contained articles by Elisha Linder the principal investigator, the editors, and William Murray. Murray had worked on the Actium Campsite monument with Photios M. Petsas and published with him an article 'Octavian's Campsite Memorial for the Actian War' in *Transactions of the American Philosophical Society* Vol. 79 Part 4. Murray there argues tentatively that 'the ram was originally cast in Cyprus in the generation between 204 and 184 BC', and was used on a Ptolemaic warship stationed on the island. From the evidence of sockets in the terrace wall of Octavian's campsite monument he concludes that the ram does not belong to one of the larger ships but to 'either a five or perhaps a four'. It weighs 465 kg compared with 200 kg 'which is an appropriate weight for the ram of a three'.

The importance of the find does not lie only in the shape of the bronze ram which seems to have been carefully designed to perforate, but not to penetrate too far, the hull of an enemy ship (see Ch. 6.4). Steffy argues (p. 38) that the ram was designed only to spring the timbers of the hull not to penetrate them, but see JSM and JFC: *CR* 1992 above p. 365). The timber structure found inside the bronze sheath exhibited the shell method of hull construction, previously observed only in the wrecks of ancient merchantmen and of the large *λέμβος* found off Marsala.

23. Coins of Leukas 3rd–2nd centuries BC

(**a**) *BMC* 69
(**b**) *BMC* 74
(**c**) *SNG* IV Fitzwilliam: McClean Collection 5362
(**d**) *SNG* IV Fitzwilliam: McClean Collection 5363
(**e**) *BMC* 98
(**f**) BM 1876.7–3.225

These coins show two different types of warship,the earlier (**a**) and (**b**) which have Greek (cf. **7**, **8**) and the later (**c**), (**d**), (**e**) and (**f**) which have Roman

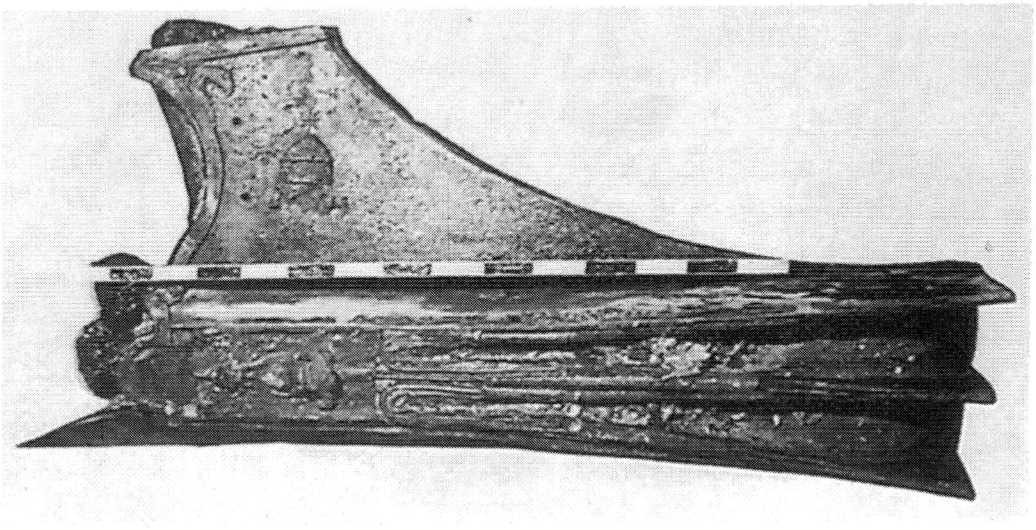

22

characteristics reflecting Roman political influence after 168 BC.

(**a**) Bronze coins with warship prow on reverse are included by Gardner in *BMC* Thessaly to Aitolia (pl. 28 11–14, 68–77) among 4th century issues. Immediately aft of the upper part of the Greek-type (S-shaped) stempost there is a high foredeck the arched side-wall of which curves up to the deck which is shown supported by one deckstanchion before the coin's edge. Aft of the lower part of the stempost there is a large eye forward of the *ἐπωτίς* and oarbox supported by a bracket. Wales terminate in the *προεμβόλιον* and main ram which is at water level.

(**b**) This coin shows the same features as (**a**) with the addition of a foredeck with a rail.

(**c**) This coin shows a typical Roman stempost rising from the foredeck which continues aft without a bulwark over a ventilation showing a pattern of paired uprights separating circles with a central button. Below there is a narrow oarbox (cf. **d**) terminating in the *προεμβόλιον*. Below is a course of herring-bone pattern above the lower wale which terminates in the ram. The ship appears to be *ἀνάστειρος*.

(**d**) This coin is similar to (**b**) except that the course beneath the deck is narrower and shows no pattern while what appears to be a narrow wale in (**a**) is here a much broader course, an oarbox terminating in the *προεμβόλιον*.

(**e**) This coin supplies the omissions of (**c**) and (**d**). There has been much rubbing away on the bottom left hand side but traces of a guard-rail are visible on the deck and of a pattern in the ventilation course below. The course terminating in the *προεμβόλιον* widens to show an *ἐπωτίς*, and below as in (**c**) and (**d**) there is a course of herring-bone pattern between the upper wale/oarbox and the lower wale terminating in the ram.

(**f**) This coin is broadly similar to (**e**). The keel is more obviously rockered and the ship *ἀνάστειρος*. There is a pattern on the wale terminating in the main ram and a pattern other than herring-bone on the hull between the two wales. The artist distinguishes between the upper projecting part of the (oarbox/wale) i.e. the oarbox and the part which is wale and terminates in the *προεμβόλιον*.

If the evidence of the 'Roman' coins (**c**)–(**f**) is pooled, it suggests that the ship portrayed is one of the bigger types, a four or a five.

23 a

23 b

23 c

23 d

23 e

23 f

24. Coins of the Roman Republic: Private types 114–87 BC

I. The Fonteius family

The gens Fonteia belongs to Tusculum,the chief cult-centre of the Dioskouroi in Latium; and they are represented on the obverse of these coins. It has been suggested that the ships on the reverse allude to the overseas origin of Telegonos, the founder of Tusculum and the son of Odysseus and Kirke. The cask slung on the outside of the hull in the stern of the ship on coin (**ii**) is said to be the *doliolum* (small cask) in which the *sacra* were brought from Troy to Italy by Ulysses. Confirmation that sacred objects are carried in that position may come from one of the ships on Trajan's Column. A recessed oblong rectangular vessel carried in the same position on the hull of one of Trajan's ships (**47**) is shown being taken ashore in a later scene (**49**). The men in the procession are wearing wreaths on their heads. A more prosaic and likely interpretation of the cask is that it is a water container carried conveniently over the stern and later shown taken ashore for replenishment.

(i) *Denarius* (silver) issued by C. Fonteius 114 or 113 BC: *BMCRR* 597, Crawford No. 290/1 Pl. XL 5, Sydenham (1952) 555, Viereck (1975) pl. 14, B.902.

In the ship on the reverse the stempost, stern and helmsman are greatly out of proportion to the rest. The helmsman holds the starboard tiller well over the stern tower, which like the bow tower has a pitched top (cf. **39a**). Between the two towers there are three symbolical decksoldiers with shields. There is no deck guard-rail, emphasised in (**ii**). Between the ἐπωτίς and the corresponding side projection in the stern the ventilation course and oarbox have been unrealistically merged together into a space from the upper part of which come five symbolical oars. Below this space the middle wale runs forward terminating in a crocodile head *προεμβόλιον*. Between the middle wale and the upper of the pair of narrow wales terminating in a trident ram there is a course of short uprights. The oarsystem is unrealistic to a degree that makes it impossible to guess the type portrayed. The crocodile may indicate an Egyptian connection.

(ii) *Denarius* (silver) issued by Mn. Fonteius 108/7 BC: *BMCRR* 1230, Crawford No. 307.1a and 1b Pl. XLI 7 and 8, B.904: showing a ship (reverse: right).

This Mn. Fonteius is, Crawford says, probably the brother or cousin of the C. Fonteius of (**i**) and the father of the Mn. Fonteius in (**iii**).

The designer (cf. Crawford also 305/1 rev.) breaks free from the traditional prow of the bronze coins and shows a whole ship. His style also departs from attempted realism and in this coin tries to show both sides of the ship, as regards the bow, the oars and the deck guard-rail. Although the view is mainly from starboard both the starboard and portside 'eyes' are visible and a few of the oars on the port side fan out past the portside eye. Similarly on the deck, which has a tower with a pitched top in the bow, the portside guard-rail is shown *above* the starboard guard-rail, both converging in the stern.

The after end of the starboard deck guard-rail is shown, but the greater remaining part is masked. In one of the casts shown in B.904 the whole length of the bulwark is masked. Below the edge of the deck there is a recessed open side divided by uprights beneath which 12 oars emerge. Comparison with the later Pozzuoli relief (**39a**) suggests that the masking feature is protective sidescreening material (leather or hair as in the Peiraieus naval inven-

24 Ii

24 Iii

24 Iiii

24 II

24 III

tories) rolled up. When needed it would be let down (see *AT* p. 164 for Chabrias's device) to cover both the open side and the oars at the point of emergence from the deep oarbox. Screening does this in the relief. In the similar coin (Crawford No. 307 1b) the oar 'bank' is stepped at its extremity indicating two levels.

The lack of realism makes a guess at the type portrayed hardly profitable.

(iii) Bronze coin (*As*) issued by Mn. Fonteius 85 BC: Willers VIII 5 (here enlarged), cf. Crawford No. 353/3 Pl. XLVI 16 Rev.

This coin being bronze shows (rev) a prow (portside left) in the traditional style with two Dioskouroi caps placed over the name of the moneyer.

At the base of the stempost there is an unusually high eye panel. Aft of this and beneath the deck and its guard-rail there is a screened ventilation course. Below it and above the wale terminating in the *προεμβόλιον* there is an oarbox with two levels of oarports *en échelon* within a 'machicolated' panel. Below this there is a third course of oarports above the bottom wale. For the oarsystem (of a five) cf. also Crawford 350/3a Pl. XLV of 86 BC.

II. Bronze coin (*As*) issued by L. Calpurnius Piso Frugi 90 BC: Willers V 3 rev. cf. Crawford No. 304/4 Pl. XLIV 7 Rev.

A prow (left) of the usual pattern is shown. The figure of Victory stands on the foredeck. Aft of her the deck guard-rail runs aft. Below the deck and aft of the stempost fitting and eye panel the ventilation course (screened in Crawford No. 340/4) runs aft above the wale which terminates in the *προεμβόλιον*. Below the wale there is a course of oarports above another wale and below that a further course of oarports. Here as in I. **(iii)** the artist is attempting to show the three levels of oarports of a five.

III. Bronze coin (*As*) issued by L. Rubirus Dossenus 87 BC: Willers VII 4: cf. Crawford 348/6 Pl. XLVI 3.

The reverse shows the prow of a ship beside a building. This has been held to be a temple; but reference to the Pompeii shipshed fresco (**43**) suggests that the building may be a shipshed, into which a warship is hauled stern first leaving the bow at the lower end. The prow is otherwise unremarkable.

25. Relief of two larger two-level warships c. 100 BC. The National Museum at Naples: A Ruesch (1908) no. 642, *SSAW* fig. 119, Viereck (1975) Bild 5, B.910.

These fragments show two ships either without rams or with their rams a casualty of damage. The latter is almost certain. The workmanship is crude. The ships have two levels of oars emerging from beneath what appears to be a heavy rope girdle. A crowd of heavily armed men, very greatly exaggerated in size, occupy the deck. At a lower level sits the helmsman (quite unable to see where he is going). The sculptor, like the coin designers, was not concerned with realism but only with the image of ships which carried armed men on deck, was rowed by oars at two levels and had a helmsman. It is probable that what looks like a rope is a course in wood acting as a louvre which would be necessary beneath the deck and above the oar-

25

system. The heavy, monoxylous nature of the oars suggests multimanning, and in that case the ship is portrayed is likely to be one of the very large types, a nine or upwards.

POLYREME FLEETS:
1ST CENTURY BC – 1ST CENTURY AD

26. The Palazzo Barberini Mosaic: Early 1st century BC. *LSRS* 30, Morrison (1980) pl. 5, b.969 B.

The mosaic has been much restored (see B.969 A). The restored area in the bottom right hand corner as it affects the oars is marked off here by a line. A Nile scene is pictured in which the bow (port and starboard) and the port side of an oared warship are shown with armed men crowded on deck behind a bulwark. The stempost is in Roman style, as in the case of the other ship likely to be Egyptian, the two-level ship of the Praeneste relief (**29**). There is no ventilation course visible but there would be room for it above the oarsystem and below the deck.

26

From the oarbox below oars emerge at to levels (*en échelon* to judge from the forward pair of which the lower oar is visible forward of the upper). This feature links the ship with the Samothrace prow (**20**) and the Palazzo Spada relief (**36**), whereas the ships of the Praeneste relief (**29**) show the lower of their two rows of oars emerging beneath the oarbox. The latter is most likely to be one of the larger two-level warships, nines and upwards; and the ships, with both levels of visible oars emerging through the oarbox, *τριημιολίαι*. This Egyptian ship, if a *τριημιολία*, with 52 oars a side, a quarter double-manned and an oarcrew of (26 + 26 + 13) × 2 = 130, would have been slightly bigger than the Rhodian ship of the same type (**11**) with 48 oars a side and an oarcrew of (24 + 24 + 12) × 2 = 120, near enough for it to be reasonable to conclude that the type of ship is the same in each case.

27. The Isola Tiberina prow 100–50 BC. Krauss (1944), B.792–801: Photographs by T. A. Morrison. Line Drawings (**60**), (**61**), (**64**), (**65**), (**67**), (**68**), (**69**).

This impressive monument, only partly preserved, is on the downstream end of an island in the Tiber in Rome. It consists of the remains of a large scale model of the prow and part of the hull and oarbox of a ship with the main ram apparently above the waterline (*ἀνάστειρος*). Only the port side has been

27 a

27 b

27 c

preserved. In its complete form it would have been a fine sight as it faced ships coming up the Tiber from Ostia.

The carving of the staff and snake of Asklepios as a *παράσημον* (cf. **14**, **19**, **29**) on the forward face of the *ἐπωτίς* has caused it to be dated to 293, the year when the god was said to have been brought to Rome from Epidauros and his temple built on the island. The date, twenty years before Rome 'took to the sea' in the 1st Punic war is most unlikely for such a grand naval monument. In view of the nearby temple Asklepios's emblem would naturally and properly have been given to the monument as a name-device (*παράσημον*) at whatever time the monument was built.

Friedrich Krauss recognised that 293 BC must be taken as a *terminus a quo*, but dates it firmly in the first half of the 1st century BC by reason of the materials used, travertine marble for the actual ship (*Formteile*) and Sperona and Peperibo for the adjoining tufo walls. Krauss's dating seems conclusive and makes the monument a younger contemporary of the Fonteius coins (**24**). There are no indications of the oarsystem, but the monument's prestigious position makes it virtually certain that it represents a scale model of one of the bigger ships, as corroborated by the fact that the ship is *ἀνάστειρος*, i.e. has its ram above the waterline. It is perhaps most likely that the ship intended was a six, a consul's flagship.

28. Alexandrian tomb graffito 1st century BC. After Schiff (1905) pl. 1: *SSAW* 115.

The rough sketch of a warship shows a firepot rigged over the bow from a tower (p. 358). As an illustration of the firepot it is unique; but the prow itself is interesting with its Roman style and high downward pointing ram.

28

29. The Praeneste relief 50–1 BC. Vatican Museum: Köster (1923) fig. 34, Simon in Helbig-Speier (1963) no. 489, *LSRS* 27, *SSAW* 130–132: Viereck (1975) Bild 22, B. 913–6.

The relief, of which the greater part is preserved, gives a remarkably detailed and, apart from the customary exaggerated human figures and the unrealistic ratio of height to length, realistic representation of one of the larger two-level oared warships, port side. It has lost by damage only the end of the ram and the stern. The crocodile symbol on the wale in the bow forming a *προεμβόλιον* (cf. **24Ii**) has been taken to indicate that the ship is Egyptian.

In the bow the stempost to which the foremast is made fast curves forward and then aft in Roman style. A soldier standing inside the prow with his feet at the level of the *προεμβόλιον* shows that there is (unusually but as in the Orange prows: **34**) no foredeck. Outboard of the soldier standing in the prow and at the level of his chest there is the *παράσημον* a box showing a man's head facing half forward and half sideways. On the after side of the box is a circular symbol. Since there is no eye, this may stand for it, and its unusual position aft of the *παράσημον* is paralleled in the Nymphaion ship.

On the deck there is a tower furthest forward, and a planked bulwark with shield decoration begins. Outboard of the bulwark two armed men with poles stand on a *πάροδος*, and behind the bulwark there stands a number of armed men at a higher level. There is a gap, between the bulwark and the prow wall and *παράσημον*, to allow passage on to and out from the deck (see **14**, **37**, **43**).

In the lateral face of the hull below the *πάροδος* there is a course of louvres, as Casson has suggested (*SSAW* p. 145). The louvre course in cataphract ships, a physical necessity, takes the place of the open side. It stands very slightly outboard of the upper course of oars both merging as they run forward smoothly, without an *ἐπωτίς*, with the side wall of the prow (cf. **44**). The upper course of oars in turn stands outboard of the lower course of oars. The reason for this brief *παρεξειρεσία* accommodating both the course of louvres and the upper course of oars is, JFC suggests, the necessity for a *πάροδος* in such a ship, built for close lateral encounter with an enemy ship. The oarsystem consists of thirteen massive monoxylous oars in the upper level and twelve (or thirteen) in the lower level. Such a system

29 a

29 b

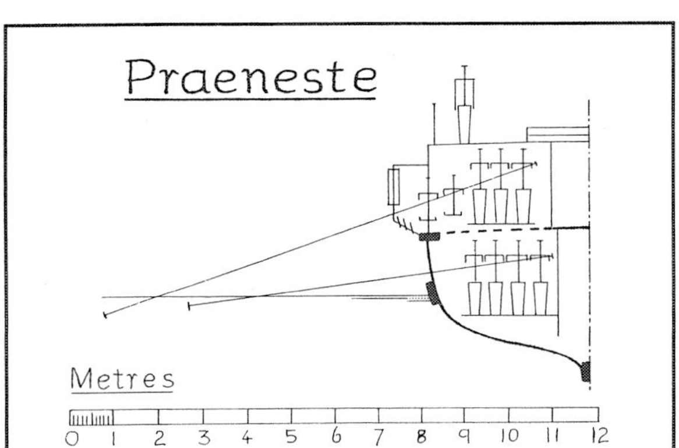

Half section of **29** *as a nine.*

suggests one of the larger polyremes, above an eight, of which there had been many in Ptolemy Philadelphos's fleet.

All the oars are fitted with leathern sleeves (ἀσκώματα) to avoid the entrance of water when the ship is under sail with the wind abeam (see *AT* General Index s.v.); or alternatively when the deck-fighting, as it well might, causing all the decksoldiers to move to one side to repel boarders, makes the ship heel (the oars of course having been pulled in as far as possible).

30. Coins of the Roman Civil Wars: 46–31 BC.

(**a**) *Denarius* of Cn. Pompeius jnr and M. Minatius Sabinus: 46–45 BC: *BMCRR* Spain 77. Crawford 470/1a Pl. LV 18.

Cn. Pompeius jnr, after the death of his father, carried on the war against Julius Caesar in Spain, where his pro-quaestor Sabinus struck silver coinage for him before his defeat at Munda in 45 BC.

Rev. Wearing a turreted crown and holding a sceptre or spear in her left hand, Corduba extends her right hand to a Pompeian soldier who descends from the stern of a ship by the ladder.

(**b**) *As* of Sextus Pompeius (younger son of Pompey the Great) 45 onwards: *BMCRR* Spain 95, Crawford 479/1 Pl. LVI 17, B.900. Minted in Spain or Sicily.

Rev. Ship's prow. Immediately aft of the stempost on the foredeck there is a tower buttressed to the stem-post and forward of the guard-rail. On top of the guard-rail are four ?bollards. Below the line of the deck the ventilation course appears to widen vertically. A very deep protruding oarbox occupies the space above a wale (which terminates in the προεμβόλιον). Although much worn forward the oarbox shows marking of horizontals indicating the oarsystem of a five. Beneath it the three-prolonged ram, to which the keel rises, terminates in a strongly marked wale. The ship is ἀνάστειρος.

(**c**) *Denarius* of Sextus Pompeius 44–43 BC: issued by Q. Nasidius (p. 000). *BMCRR* Sicily 21, Crawford 483.2 Pl. LVII 24.

30 a

30 b

30 c

30 d

30 e

Rev. A warship (right) under oar and sail. The helmsman and *proreta* are shown large. On deck the heads of soldiers are visible above the bulwark. Below the bulwark there is a row of round objects (?louvres: cf. **19 II**); and beneath them twelve oars are shown at the catch. Masked by the oars amidships but visible fore and aft of them is a wale running from the stern to the ram.

(**d**) *Denarius* issued by Cn. Domitius Ahenobarbus in 41 BC. *BMCRR* East 94, Crawford 519.2, Pl. LXII 22.

The coin commemorates the victory of Ahenobarbus over Octavian's fleet commander Cn. Domitius Calvinus (in 42 BC: p. 148) at sea. An armed figure stand on the foredeck of a warship. Beneath the foredeck is the forward continuation of the *πάροδος* as it extends to the stempost. Beneath the forepart of the main deck is a panel containing possibly a *παράσημον*, aft of which is a deep oarbox/ *ἐπωτίς* and above it a ventilation course indicated by uprights. Below is a wale terminating in the *προεμβόλιον*.

(**e**) *Denarius and aureus* 40 BC: *BMCRR* East 111 and 112, Crawford 521 and 2 Pl. LXIII 24 rev.

Rev. (issued by) Cn. Domitius Ahenobarbus. The prow is similar in its general shape to that of (**d**), but the deep panel aft of the stempost and forward of the *ἐπωτίς* is shown latticed and the area between the upper and lower wales has a 'machicolated' pattern. (cf. **24** I iii above for a similar 'machicolated' panel of two levels of oarports *en échelon*). The oarbox is surmounted by a ventilation course of a pattern resembling that shown in the Praeneste relief (**29**) of similar date.

31. Coins of Octavian, later Augustus 44–19 BC.

(**a**) *As* 40–27 BC: minted at Lugdunum (Lyons): two examples. BM Lugdunum 1901 5–3 24OH. Grant *FITA* (1946) pl. vii 22–23, B.901.

Rev. Prow of a warship with star and denomination above. Aft of the short bow section there is a guard-rail along the deck which is shown by a strongly marked horizontal (?*πάροδος*). Below this horizontal there is a panel containing (forward) an eye and aft of the eye a square with central knob (a παράσημον). Aft of the square to the edge of the coin the panel is filled with latticework protecting the open side. At the base of the panel another strongly marked horizontal leads to the weakly indicated προεμβόλιον. From under the lower horizontal a row of oars emerges and forward of the oars a dolphin is shown.

31 ai

31 aii

(**b**) *As* c.40 BC; Gallia Narbonensis: Grant *FITA* (1946) pl. vi 21 p. 208

Rev. Ram's head with circle above bow section with a minimum of detail. Main deck has a post and rail bulwark. Below is an oarbox with no detail and the wale beneath it continues forward to a προεμβόλιον. Below again a lower wale goes forward to the ram.

31 b

(**c**) *Bronze* Gallia Narbonensis (?Arelate) 39–38 BC: issued by Octavian. Grant *FITA*^{2} (1969) pl. II 11.

Rev. The forward section of a warship. On the foredeck there is a dotted line (low bulwark) over a row of four arches under which is the upper wale leading to the προεμβόλιον. Between the wale and the lower wale which terminates in the ram there is a further row of four arches (square-topped). This system of arches is likely to provide ventilation for the cabin under the foredeck.

Aft of this forward section there is the main deck and on it a tower. Under the tower there is a dotted line (low bulwark) and under the dotted line two arches above another dotted one. From their position these arches and the dotted line are likely to indicate the open side and, below it, the παρεξειρεσία of the oarsystem of a three. From the παρεξειρεσία the upper wale leads forward to the προεμβόλιον. Beneath the upper wale there are two round raised areas separated by incisions over the lower wale which with the line marking the keel lead forward to the three pronged ram. The incisions may indicate supports for the outrigger butting on to the lower wale. A tower is unexpected but not unknown in a three (see **19**).

31 c

32. Augustus's coins 25–29 BC

(**a**) *Sestertius*: Macedonian mint 25–23 BC. Grant *FITA*^{2} (1969) pl. III 14.

Rev. A prow. High stempost possibly with animal's head. Aft of it two horizontals with four uprights which could be either a post-and-rail bulwark or, more probably, a tower. The prow's style suggests a big ship; but there are no details except

32 a

32 b

a long *προεμβόλιον* and a three-pronged ram on the waterline.

(**b**) *Sestertius*: Vienne (Gaul) c. 19 BC: Willers *NZ* 34 (1902) p. 117 26.

Rev. A prow. Die (**i**) BMG 0028: Aft of the stempost there is a tower of three stories (cf. *turres contabulatae* on board ship in Livy 24.34.7 and Florus's *tabulatis castellorum* p. 163). Below the top edge of the bulwark (otherwise not shown) there is a wide area extending to the upper wale which runs forward to the *προεμβόλιον*. This area, which is much worn, is where the *ἐπωτίς* would normally be shown. It is featureless except for the large eye occupying its forward part; but implies an oarbox beyond the coin's edge.

33. Two fragmentary reflector plates from terracotta lamps 20 BC–AD 20. Both were acquired by a collector in the Fayoum (Egypt) in 1882 and purchased by the British Museum.

(**a**) British Museum Greek and Roman Department: 1926–9–3054: Hector Williams (1981) p. 23–27 Fig. 1.
(**b**) British Museum Egyptian Department 83.10.18.88: *ibid*. Fig. 2.

Hector Williams gives both pieces a likely date of 20 BC to AD 20, and through the centaur figureheads (Propertius IV 49–52) associates them with the battle of Aktion.

In (**a**) there is a stempost curving up into a centaur figurehead. Soldiers, greatly exaggerated in size, crowd on deck behind a bulwark decorated with at least one shield. A *πάροδος* probably separates the bulwark from the edge of the deck where two wales run parallel to it with a small space between them (? ventilation course), terminating forward in an *ἐπωτίς*, decorated in front, Williams says, with an incised circle (*παράσημον*). Below this pair of wales is a row of oars at the catch. Williams suggests that an incised line at the lower end of the bank may indicate the water or possibly the ends of a second row of oars.

From under the *ἐπωτίς* and the oars an upper wale runs forward to terminate in the *προεμβόλιον*, a ram's head. Below, a damaged wale terminates in a three pronged ram. There are many resemblances to the ship in the Praeneste relief (**29**): the figurehead, the soldiers behind the bulwark, the shield decoration of the bulwark, the possible (see **b**) *πάροδος*, louvres and *παράσημον*, the animal *προεμβόλιον*, and the possible two banks of oars. All suggest that the ship on the terracotta fragment may represent, like the Praeneste relief but less realistically, one of the larger Egyptian warships.

The fragment (**b**) is similar. There is the same centaur figurehead and decksoldiers behind a bulkhead which here is of the post-and-rail variety without shield decoration. In this case there is no doubt about the *πάροδος* with an outboard projection at each end. The outboard projection in the bow is the *ἐπωτίς*, the other is the rudder pivot (see *SSAW* pl. 170). Below the wales there is a bank of oars at the catch and below the level at which they emerge a double wale comes from under the *ἐπωτίς*

33 a

33 b

and terminates in the προεμβόλιον. This second ship-portrait is more crudely drawn but appears to represent the same type of ship as (**a**).

34. Relief Sculpture from the Triumphal Arch at Orange early 1st century AD or earlier. Amy (1962) pl. 551 86 c: Williams, H. (1981) p. 23–27 Fig. 3.

The prows shown in the relief of the Arc d'Orange are about contemporary with the prows of the Praeneste (**29**) and Ostia (**35**) ships and have a number of features in common. The Orange and Praeneste prows are both without the usual foredeck. In the former the stempost terminates on a panel containing the eye, aft of which is the *παράσημον* half facing forward. Above the oarbox and *παράσημον* the deck terminates, surmounting the regular latticework ventilation course, but unlike the Praeneste prow shows no bulwark.

The prow in the Ostia relief is unlike the Praeneste and Orange prows in having a foredeck; and is like the former in showing a deck with fighting figures behind a bulwark and *πάροδος*, and like the latter in displaying an eye forward of the *παράσημον* which performs the function of an *ἐπωτίς* covering the projection of the deep oarbox although presented as facing sideways. In all three cases there is a ventilation course above the oarbox and beneath the deck (or in two cases the *πάροδος*).

In all three cases also there is an animal head for *προεμβόλιον* (two lions and one crocodile) which terminates a wale in the form of a rope in the Orange and Ostia prows.

The Orange and Ostia ships show similar deep oarboxes, in the latter case three levels of oars also, and are fives. The Praeneste ship with a different oarsystem is one of the larger two-level warships. In the Orange sculpture the rams are at waterlevel but in the Ostia relief the ship is *ἀνάστειρος* and the ram is well above the waterline indicted by the oars, with the result that in the Orange prows there is a larger area than in the Ostia prow between the upper and lower wales. Apart from these minor differences the two monuments seem to represent the same type of ship, fives (see **13**).

35. The Ostia relief: soon after 20 BC. Squarciapino (1955), Meiggs (1973), *LSRS* 31, *SSAW* pl. 125, B.949.

This relief belongs to a funerary monument set up on the seashore outside the Porta Marina at Ostia to commemorate C. Cartilius Poplicola, a leading citizen of Ostia (Meiggs *Ostia*[2] p. 39 f and Note K p. 475). The largest of the two surviving fragments shows the bow section of a warship with the usual two rams and back curving stempost, here terminating in a helmeted head, with an oblique line at its juncture with the hull. There is a foredeck with an armed figure standing on it behind a planked bulwark. Outboard of the foredeck bulwark the *πάροδος* begins and beneath the *πάροδος* first a circle with a stud at its centre (? a formalised eye) and

34

35

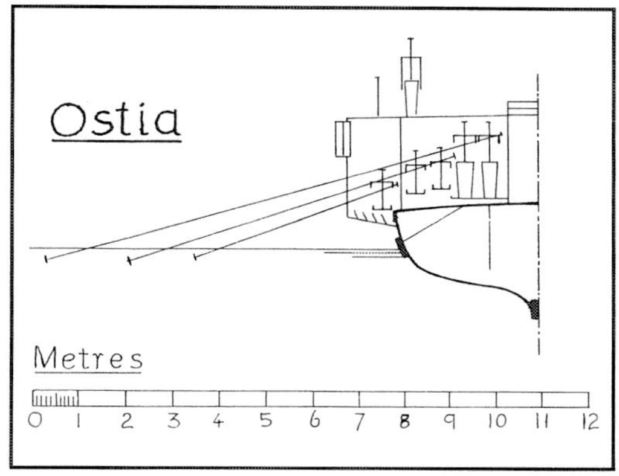

Half section of **35** *as a five*

aft of that a framed ? eagle as the *παράσημον*. Below the 'eye' and *παράσημον* a wale decorated as a rope (cf. **25** and **34**) runs forward to terminate in a *προεμβόλιον* as a lion's head. Below, but above the waterline, there is a large three pronged ram. A raised line runs down vertically from the forward end of the foredeck under the *πάροδος* edge and the upper wale but apparently over the lower wale and under the hull. Its function, except to mark off the bow section of the ship, is not clear. The lower wale appears to have suffered damage before its junction with the ram.

To return to deck-level: the foredeck continues aft as the maindeck, also behind a bulwark, now apparently decorated with a post-and-rail pattern. Another figure, holding a shield, stands behind it. Outboard of the main bulwark the *πάροδος* continues aft. Beneath the *πάροδος* is a deep projection with some worn decoration on its lateral (outboard) surface. In this position there is a ventilation course in other large cataphract ships (cf. **29**, **31a**, **36**, **40**) and the decoration is likely to screen this. The projection connects with the *παράσημον* (cf. the decorated box in the Praeneste relief (**29**) at its forward end). Underneath as it runs aft there is a deep rectangular recessed oarpanel which continues aft to the edge of the fragment. In it three rows of oars emerge at three levels from three rows of oarports, the oarports in each row directly above the oarports in the row below. The oars are shown entering the sea (and thus establish the waterlevel as lower than the ram). There is a smaller fragment showing the stern, the helmsman's head, the port rudder and the surface of the sea. The ship is *ἀνάστειρος* (p. 364, 366), a characteristic of the bigger warships (fives and above).

On the other face of this fragment there is the prow of another three-level oared warship; and other fragments of the memorial showing armed men fighting. The subject of the frieze is concluded to be a sea battle featuring one ship in particular, presumably that of Cartilius Poplicola.

An inscription records Cartilius's services as 'a man of leadership'. He was eight times, absent and present, elected duumvir (chief magistrate of Ostia), three times with censorial power. As Meiggs says, his absence may be explained by military service which his monument recalls. This military service will have included a sea battle with Cartilius on board the ship portrayed.[8]

The date of Cartilius's death and of the subsequent dedication of the monument is not accurately known. He could have lived one or two decades after the battle it records. That would bring his active service at latest into the Aktion campaign, since there was no fighting at sea thereafter in which he could have participated. The ship on which a man of leadership served, at least as trierarch, in these campaigns was certainly a five, not a three.

It has been already seen that the Calenian dishes of the 3rd–2nd century (**18 I** and **II**) give the earliest surviving representations of warships with an oarbox showing three levels of oarports quincunx-fashion. The difference between these ships and the ship on the Ostia relief is that the latter has rows of oarports directly above one another, although the oars themselves are shown *en échelon* in triads and not one on top of another. Since the *en échelon* arrangement is attested in the other examples, it may be that the sculptor of the Ostia frieze in order to show what he knew to be there, three levels of oarports and oars in triads *en échelon*, was forced to present the oarports unrealistically and one above the other, since if the oars were (as e.g. in the Pozzuoli reliefs **39**) shown realistically the oarports would not be seen.

Another example of this sculptor's preference for information rather than realism is in his presentation of the *παράσημον*. On the Isola Tiberina prow (**27**) and the Praeneste relief (**29**) it is given facing half forward; and in the Nymphaion ship the artist uses perspective to give that impression with the *Dioskoros παράσημον*. But in the Ostia ship the *παράσημον* appears to face fully sideways although the observer can see that the forward edge of the frame abuts the inward curving prow while the edge aft abuts the outward projecting oarbox. The half forward-facing position of a name-device is both more practical for identification by ships ahead and abeam and better attested.

36

36. The Palazzo Spada Relief: Roman copy of a Hellenistic original.

There are in Rome two reliefs depicting the stern section (port side) of a Hellenistic galley, one in the Palazzo Spada and the other in the Palazzo Ludovisi. Drawings of both are given in Daremberg, Saglio et Pottier (1877–1919) figs 5273 and 5274 (B.802 A, B) and a (rather dim) photograph (Anderson) of the latter in *SSAW* pl. 114. Since the stern shows Hellenistic features (below) it is likely that the two are Roman copies (2nd century AD) of a Hellenistic original. The Palazzo Spada relief is the more informative copy of the two.

The high curving *ἄφλαστον* of the stempost has two *στυλίδες*, carried on Greek but not (*SSAW* p. 346) on Roman warships. The stern cabin has a flat roof and the gangway outside the stern has no handrail. In the Ludovisi relief the stern cabin (*σκηνή*) has an arched roof familiar in the warships of Trajan's column (**45–49**) and again like those warships a gangway round the stern with lattice handrail. It looks as if the sculptor of the Ludovisi copy has Romanised his original more than his colleague.

On the deck of the Palazzo Spada relief there is a machicolated (?) tower. The bulwark (with three bollards behind or on top of it) stops short of the stern to accommodate the stern landing ladder (cf. **40**). The oarbox projection on the ship's side accommodates at its after end the port rudder. Outboard of the bulwark there is a *πάροδος* on the upper surface of the oarbox into which the gangway round the stern leads. The upper part of the oarbox is the ventilation course protected by latticework (**30d** and **e**, **31a**); the lower part shows pairs of oars *en échelon* emerging from 'rooms' marked, as the ventilation course is, by uprights.

In this ship, unlike the ship on the Praeneste relief (**29**), both sets of oars *en échelon* emerge from the lower part of the oarbox. The ship portrayed is likely to be a *τριημιολία* (cf. **11**, **20** and **21**).

37. The Gytheion model end 1st century BC – 1st century AD. The Sparta Museum: B.936–943: found in the sea off Gytheion: terracotta. Portside shown.

The model is a crude representation of a ship with a ram, hence a warship. The deck is made up of a foredeck with no bulwark (and aft of it a space surrounded by a 'planked' bulwark higher in the bow and becoming lower as it approaches the stern). There is a *πάροδος* outboard of the bulwark. On the port and starboard side the deck is supported by stanchions, which continue downards to rest on the outer wale above the waterline. By curving outwards they also serve to support a *παρεξειρεσία* which is shown in part on the port side with an *ἐπωτίς*. There are signs of the shield-like ornaments on the side of the bulwark such as are found in the Praeneste relief (**49**) and the Fonteius coinage (**24a**).

There are no clues to the oarsystem except possibly the line of holes above the lower wale. They are not large enough for oarports but may indicate where emerging oars could be attached, but since no holes of this kind are visible below the gunwale or in the small piece of the lateral face of the *παρεξειρεσία*, it seems more likely that no oars were represented and that the small holes were for the attachment of another wale.

The type of warship the model represents is not identifiable. Its importance lies in the tangible evidence of a substantial bulwark.

38. The Alba Fucentia graffito 1st century BC – 1st century AD. Noti di Scavi (1953) p. 120, *LSRS* 26, *SSAW* 126, B.903. Line Drawing (**59**, **60**).

The Graffito inscribed *navis tetreris longa* is unique as the only representation of an ancient warship which is labelled as to type, a longship four. It gives a rough indication of what a four looked like from the port side with oars unshipped and mast and sails lowered. The features are (besides the ram):

1. a foredeck unprotected by a bulwark;
2. a main deck again with no bulwark (cf. **34**) surmounting a latticework ventilation course, resembling that in the Palazzo Spada stern (**36**) and another in a prow on a coin of Octavian (**31a**), which can also be seen (in spite of the artists' disturbance of the oarsystems) in the Aula Isiaca fresco (**40**) and the Trajan's Column ships (**45–49**. See also below p. 268–69).

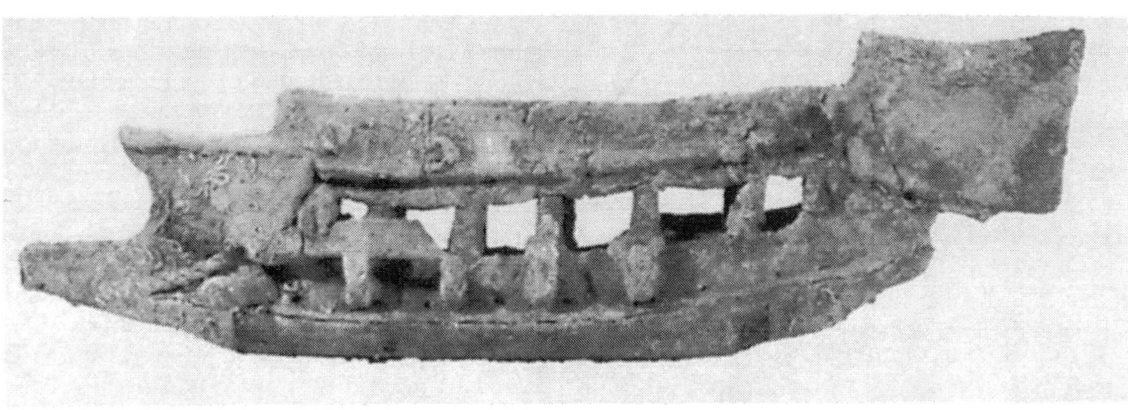

37

38

39. The Pozzuoli reliefs 25 BC – AD 25: The National Museum, Naples: *LSRS* 32 a and b, *SSAW* 129, 131, B.962, 963.

These two reliefs show ships with Roman style stemposts and three levels of oars portrayed in a highly conventionalised manner. The differences between them are interesting recalling the representations of ships on Roman coins (of which they may be copies). The ship on the left (**a**) has a high aft curving stempost resembling that of the Praeneste ship. She has a large main ram and a *προεμβόλιον*. Behind the stempost on the foredeck there is a tower (p. 356–58) indicating that she belongs to one of the larger types. On the main deck there are men facing aft. Since they are on deck they are decksoldiers, not oarsmen. Facing them is a larger (and hence more important) man (*κελευστής* trierarch), behind whose head the tiller is held by the helmsman sitting high in the stern. All the men are as usual quite out of proportion to the ship. There is an *ἐπωτίς* forward of a long rectangular sidescreen (see **24b**) from under which the three 'layers' of very solid oars emerge. The oars lie one on top of the other, and thus presumably emerge from oarports one vertically over the other in a hardly realistic manner, as in the ship on the Ostia relief (**35**). The stern is highly decorated and the *aplustre* large. There is a *παράσημον* at the base of the stempost.

In ship (**b**) by comparison all the features noted in (**a**) are present with one exception, but they are smaller in size. The officer facing the decksoldiers is absent. Instead there is a bow officer (*proreta*) on the foredeck. This ship unlike the other has a *στυλίς* from which a pennant is flying. She is therefore not Roman. In the bow she appears to have two *παράσημα*, one facing forward on the *ἐπωτίς* and one facing sideways. Her oars are shown somewhat lighter, similarly in three layers but *en échelon*, and

39 a

39 b

are seen to emerge from the oarbox on the side of the ship. This is the significant difference between the two ships.

The two identical pieces of stone on which the ships are illustrated appear to belong to a frieze which required that the representations should be of the same size, even if the objects depicted are not. Nevertheless the artist seems, by making the details in (**a**) larger, to suggest that it is a larger ship. The sidescreen, which in (**a**) covers the emergence of the oars, shields the (necessary) ventilation course and oarports, and is fitted to a *πάροδος* on which decksoldiers could stand and fight.[9]

40. The Aula Isiaca fresco 1st century AD.

S. Reinach ((1922) p. 165 fig. 5) calls this a fresco of which there was an 18th C drawing in the Albani collection now lost: B.954. We are grateful to Martin Robertson for the following opinion about the date of the fresco: 'The 1st century AD is the most likely date'; but 'so much of the material from Rome itself (as this is) certainly belongs between the very late Republic and Flavian times that it looks as though that may have been the period when these Greek style pictures were most popular'.

O. Höckmann (1985) pl. 98 gives a version of it under the title 'Fresko von der aula Isiaca Rom' which appears to show a fourth row of oars under an oarpanel from which three rows of oars emerge. This so-called 'fourth row of oars' is to be explained since the ship (bringing Paris and Helen to Troy) is beached, by comparison with a Pompeian fresco (**43**) showing oared warships hauled up in shipsheds. These have the deep projecting oarbox with three rows of oarports quincunx fashion and below it a row of timbers which Assmann (1889, p. 100) identified as shores to keep the hulls upright (see also Basch: 1979, Morrison: 1987).

JFC notes: 'If these (the ships in **43**) were large ships they would have been wide and prone to their sides dropping when supported only on the keel.

40

Hence the rows of shores. Only a few would have been needed to keep the ship upright on a slip. The large number of shores in both pictures indicates that they were large ships.'

The scene (at Troy) shows Paris helping Helen as she descends a ladder from the stern of a ship showing three levels of oarports quincunx-fashion in the portside deep projecting oarbox.

The fresco, which was discovered in the Aula Isiaca, may be accepted as offering another example of the type of three-level ship represented in the Nymphaion fresco (**13**), the Calenian dishes under the signature of Canoleios (**18I**) and the Ostia relief (**35**), i.e. a five. The ship, of which a good, indeed exaggerated, part of the stern section is shown, resembles the Octavian coin (**31a**), the four of the Alba Fucentia graffito (**38**), the Nymphaion and Calenian ships, the three-level ship on Trajan's Column (**47.2**) and the Palazzo Spada stern (**36**) in having a course of latticework above the oar panel. She also shares with the Trajan's Column ships (**45–49**) the characteristic of having human figures grossly exaggerated in size making nonsense of the oarsystem shown.

The Palazzo Spada stern gives the clue to the function of the latticework course as louvres in this ship, in the coin of Octavian (**31a**) and in the Trajan's Column ships. The grossly exaggerated figures have caused the artist in both cases to surrender the deck which with its bulwark would have surmounted the latticework ventilation course. The prow area forward of the oarsystem and aft of the foredeck, usually a narrow gap (cf. **45–50**), is also exaggerated in length for the same reason, to accommodate the large human figures and proportionate ladder.

41. Amandus and Atrio Corinzio frescoes.

(**a**) A fresco in the House of the priest Amandus at Pompeii: AD 54–68 *LSRS* pl. 35a: *SSAW* 124: *AT* 44: B.977.

Part of the starboard side and the bow of an oared warship is shown as she comes into view

41 a

from behind a rocky cliff. There is possibly some indication of oars on her port side.

The following features are to be seen:

i. The stempost curving aft in the Roman fashion.
ii. A high foredeck with a high bulwark and a main deck with a waist-high bulwark hung with shields, the latter crowded with armed men:
iii. Below the deck a course of curved stanchions, as in the Lenormant relief, but unlike the Lenormant relief (**ixa**), the Eleusis relief (**ixc**) and the dal Pozzo drawing (**ixb**), blind with no oarsmen shown in between the stanchions.
iv. Beneath the blind course oars emerging from the ship's hull at three levels. The painting is too rough to indicate whether the uppermost level of the oars emerges through an outrigger (as in a three) or as in (**12**), (**13**), (**15**), (**18**), (**35**), (**39**) and (**40**) i.e. a Carthaginian/Roman five.

(**b**) Detail of a fresco of the 1st century AD in the Casa del Atrio Corinzio at Herculaneum B.974; one of the several oared ships depicted in a naval battle.

The ship resembles the ship in (**a**) in its main features: the decks crowded with men armed with spears and shields, the waist-high guard-rail, the blind course below the deck and the roughly painted oarsystem emerging below the blind course. It differs in certain details: the stempost curving forward in Carthaginian fashion unlike the Roman style stempost of (**a**), the absence of shields on its guard rail, the presence of a tower on deck and the absence of stanchions in its blind course. The general resemblance of the ships in (**a**) and (**b**), the tower and the surer interpretation in (**b**) of the blind course as a permanent louvre/sidescreen makes more certain the identification of both ships as boxed-in fives of the Romano-Carthaginian design.

The battle scene of which (**b**) is a detail is then historical, a naval engagement in the Punic wars which were fought by fives on both sides. The imperial fleets contained very few ships larger than threes (p. 172–74).

41 b

42. Isis fresco (Pompeii) 1st century AD. The National Museum, Naples: *LSRS* 35b, *SSAW* 133, B.973 (Ucelli (1950) fig. 256).

In this fresco two ships advance under oar showing half front bow and port side. The ship on the left has a forward curving (Carthaginian style) stempost with an *ἀκροστόλιον* similar to the bird's head on the Hasdrubal coins (**17**) and the right-side ship of the Shipshed relief (**43**). The ship on the right has a backward curving stem-post Roman style. The two ships differ from that shown in **41** and from the Atrio Corinzio ships in some ways but in both the main deck is packed with men armed with shields and spears.

i. There is a waist-high bulwark stopping short of the bow structure to give access to the *πάροδος* (cf. similar gaps in the bulwarks in the Nymphaion fresco ship: **13**).
ii. The decks are not hung with shields.
iii. The two *ἐπωτίδες* are visible in each case and on the port side clusters of oars at ?two levels emerge through the lower part of the oarboxes. The upper part of the oarbox probably serves as a ventilation course as shown by **29**, **36** and **38**.
iv. The top surface of the oarbox in each case could serve as a *πάροδος*.
v. There is a commodious stern shelter (*σκηνή*) in each ship resembling those of the ships on Trajan's Column (**45–49**).

42

Detail iii is not clear. If it is as described the oarsystem of these ships is similar to that of the Samothrace prow (**20**) and the Barberini mosaic (**27**); they are *τριημιολίαι*.

43. Shipshed frescos from Pompeii 1st century AD. The National Museum, Naples: Nos. 8604, 8605 and 8606: B.955.956 and Basch (1979). Line Drawing (**71**). Photograph kindly supplied by the Soprintendenza alle Antichità, Napoli.

The two ships depicted in the fresco are shown half-front, drawn up out of water in the open (seaward) end of shipsheds. The viewpoint is slightly 'shifted' so that more is visible of the starboard side of the ships than should strictly be possible. The stempost of the left-hand ship (**a**) curves aft in the

43 a

43 b

Roman, that of the right-hand ship (**b**) curves forward in Carthaginian style resembling the stempost of the right-hand ship of the Isis fresco (**42**) and the stemposts of the ships on the Hasdrubal coin (**17**). The deep oarpanel of ship (**a**) shows three rows of oarports quincunx fashion. Over the oar panel there is room for a ventilation course with the πάροδος on the upper surface outboard of a substantial bulwark. On each side of the stempost an eye decorates the side timbers of the bow terminating in the ἐπωτίς on the half-frontal face of which there is a παράσημον (cf. the Isola Tiberina prow). The παράσημον (most clearly on the starboard side ship (**a**)) makes an angle with the edge of the oarpanel and there is a boss or knob at the top of the angle. Two bollards are visible on each side of the upper edges of the foredeck bulwarks, one near the stempost and one further aft. The two ships appear to be ἀνάστειροι (p. 364–66) with rams built above the waterline.

*Note on **10** and **27** in comparison with **13**, **18**, **35**, **40** , **41a**, **41b** and **43***

(see below p. 259 for grouping)

Group DI

JFC's work on the Isola Tiberina monument (**27**) shows that the ship it represents, designed on the pattern of the Greek three, can be reconstructed as a five and the design expanded for a six and a seven. It is likely that Dionysios I's pioneering fives and sixes were so designed. With this ship may accordingly be associated the type represented on the coins of Demetrios Poliorketes (**10**). This appears similarly to be designed on the pattern of the three but is likely to represent one of the bigger ships with which Demetrios's name is associated.

Group DIII

The ship portraits presented by the Nymphaion fresco (**13**), the Calenian dishes I and II (**18**), the Ostia frieze (**35**), the Aula Isiaca fresco (**40**), and the Shipshed fresco (**43**) have in common an oarsystem design quite different from that shown by the ship portraits of Group DI. On the side of the hull there is a panel in which three levels of oarports quincunx fashion are shown, and in the case of (**35**) and (**40**) oars as well. The degree to which the panel appears to be standing out from the ship's side varies according to the viewpoint. Where this is directly from the side (**12**, **13** and **35**) it does not seem to stand out at all. In (**18**) and (**40**) it stands out a little, in (**41a**, **41b**, **43**) rather more. Although the oarbox in this group does not appear to stand out as far as the oarbox in Group DI, JFC's reconstruction (**71**) nevertheless requires it to stand out in Group DIII as far as in Group DI. The apparent difference is to be accounted for by the nature of the representations in each case, two in Group DI being three-dimensional.

The ships in Group DIII are either recognisably Roman (**12**, **35**, **43a**) or Carthaginian (**18**, **43b**) or an anachronistic Homeric illustration probably by a Roman artist (**18 II** and **40**), or of unknown origin (**13**). That Roman and Carthaginian ships have the same oarsystem is borne out by Polybios (1.20.15) who says that the Romans when they first built a fleet designed the ships (fives) on the lines of a captured Carthaginian cataphract. The point of the story presumably was that the Carthaginian design was different from the Greek which it would have been natural for them to copy as they had in the case of the three (and, see below, did subsequently in the case of the six).

Carthage was (*CAH*[1] IV pp. 348–350) 'the last and greatest of the colonies of Tyre' and 'she continued for several century to show her respect by the annual despatch of sacred envoys to the festival of Tyrian Melkart'. Phoenician naval developments would then certainly have become quickly known and followed at Carthage, in particular 'the Phoenician design' of threes and then fives (DIII) which appeared first in the Nineveh palace relief (**i**) and then in the Persian seal (**2b**), the Phoenician coinage and gem, and the Erment model (**2–6**) in the latter half of the 4th century BC (p. 196–99 above). This design of a three-level oared ship without a παρεξειρεσία or oarbox is shown very clearly in the Erment model. Whether or not the ship so designed was a transport three or a five need not be settled, although the balance of probability seems to be in favour of a five. JFC has shown by his reconstructions (**57**, **58**) that it could be either. In either case the ship is the ancestor of the five as it appears in Group DIII, the Carthaginian five which the Romans took as a model for their own.

JFC has further shown that the design of Group DIII, unlike that of Group DI, cannot be developed further to produce ships of higher denomination than the five. The ships in Group DIII must accordingly be threes or fives. Where they are plainly fast-line ships they are fives. The design of the six which had appeared in Agathokles's fleet at Syracuse must necessarily also have been adopted by Rome for her flagships at Eknomos.

44. Tomb relief c. AD 100. British Museum *LSRS* 28, B.918.

In the prow depicted, below a foremast with foresail set, there are two parallel wales terminating forward in a *προεμβόλιον*. As in **29** and **34** there appears to be no foredeck. As the upper wale runs aft it butts smoothly without an *ἐπωτίς* on to an upper 'oar panel'. In it the oars emerge through oarports in rooms marked by uprights (cf. the Spada relief: **36**) and above the projecting sill of the top wale. Above it is a projecting course with (? rope) markings, above which is ? a figure on deck. If the ship is decked the projecting course must represent louvres (cf. **25**: the nautical relief with rope pattern louvres below a deck and above the two-level oarsystem. Cf. also **29**). Below the projecting sill of the upper oarpanel the lower wale butts onto a course of oarports for the lower oars. The two levels of oars are *en échelon*. There is a marked difference between this prow and (**25**) and (**29**) in respect of the oars which here are short and slender (cf. the oar in **vii**), and so single manned; but in (**25**) and (**29**) they are massive and long, plainly multiple manned. The foremast and foresail are visible

The ship portrayed at this date may be identified as a liburnian resembling the twos (certainly liburnians) of Trajan's Column, whose distorted oarsystem this relief helps to explain.

44

45–49. The Trajan's Column relief: completed in May AD 113. Lepper and Frere (1988) (hereafter LF) p. 16. The oarsmen are grossly disproportionate to the ship. No other warship is shown.

THE SHIPS OF TRAJAN'S DACIAN EXPEDITIONS

45. LF Plate XXV, Scene xxxiii, Casts 80–83.

This detail illustrates Trajan's first war against the Dacians (AD 101–2). He and his staff are about to embark on the imperial galley at 'a large and well-established harbour town'. LF suggests on good grounds (one of which is the dolphins present in the seaport in **48**) that it is a riverside harbour somewhere in the Danube catchment area.

The ship here (**45.1**) has a stern shelter (σκηνή), is without sails and rowed by eight oars a side at two levels. The upper level of oars is shown as in (**44**) rowed through a screen, here of latticework (Cf. **40** and LF pl. XXXVI for a latticework fence on land). The screen is made up of a course of units: St Andrew's crosses framed and slightly wider than high with a slit below the lower horizontal side.

46. LF Plate XXVI, Scene xxxiv–xxxv, Casts 84–87. Here Trajan is disembarking. LF suggests that the place of disembarkation is Oescus (Map A East) in Moesia Inferior 'some three miles up the sidestream of the same name' as preferable to Novae on the Danube itself.

Four oared ships (**46.1–4**) are shown. Two (**46.1–2**: in cast 84) are transports. The upper ship is decked and shows two oarsmen and cargo. The lower ship is a horse transport and shows one level of oarsmen. In both cases the oars are rowed over the topwale. The other two (**46.3–4** in casts 85, 86) are longships. The lower ship (**46.3**) is larger, has a stern shelter (σκηνή) and is rowed by 9 oars a side, the other (**46.4**) is smaller and rowed by 7 oars a side, both at two levels *en échelon* with the upper

45

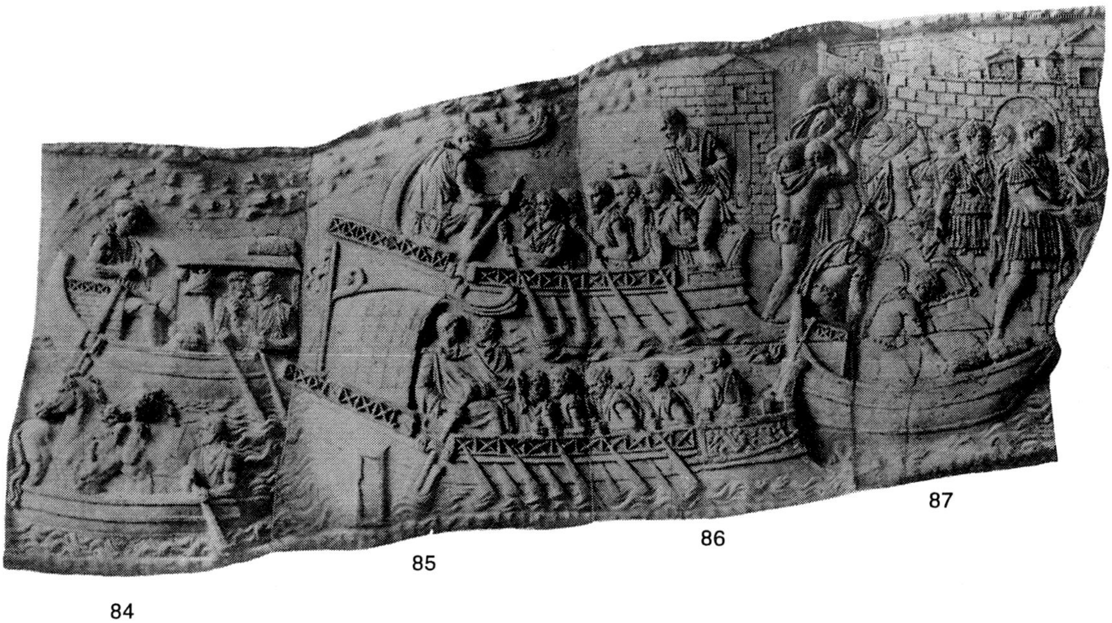

46

level rowed through the screen (see under **45**). In both ships a wale runs from the rudder fitting beneath the screen and is separated from it by a slit running forward to the bow. Under this upper wale the lower level of oars emerges.

Ship **46.3** has an elaborately decorated bow and unusually for a Roman warship a *στυλίς* and pennant in the stern. The foremast leans against the stempost. She appears to have two helmsmen. On the starboard surface of the hull aft of the rudder there is a vertical, rectangular, recessed, oblong container resembling in position but not in shape the *doliolum* in (**24 I ii**) (see **48**). The oarsmen are as in (**45**) grossly disproportionate.

47. LF Plates LVIII and LIX, Scenes lxxix and lxxx, Casts 208–213.

Three longships are shown (**47.1**, **2** and **3**) with the nearest (1) furthest to the left and the furthest (**a**) nearest to the right. They are setting out from a seaport (dolphins in cast 212) which is now generally accepted to be Ancona (Cichorius and LF) at the outset of the second Dacian war.

Ships **47.1** and **3** with seven oars a side at two levels resemble **45.1** with nine and **46.3** and **4** with seven and nine respectively at two levels. In all cases the upper level is worked through a lattice screen (see **45**). Here, each slit (under the screen units) is marked off from the next by a continuance of the vertical sides butting on to a narrow wale.

Ship **47.2** has oars at three levels, the uppermost rowed through a screen (see **45** above). Below each screen unit is a slit. Each slit is marked off from the next by a continuance of the vertical sides butting on to a narrow wale. The middle level of oars is rowed below the slit and above the upper wale, and the lowest level between this wale and the lower wale which terminates forward in the *προεμβόλιον*.

It appears that in the sea-going fleet of Trajan's second Dacian expedition, as opposed to the river squadron, Trajan's flagship was a ship (**47.2**) with three levels of oars quincunx fashion, a three.

LF notes that ship **47.1** 'has its sail brailed up to the yard and lashed to an unshipped mast'. The unshipped mast is visible stowed conveniently on crutches fore and aft (cf. **49** below), a practice shown in a longship with a single level of oars in a mosaic (c. AD 250) in the baths at Themetra (**50**).

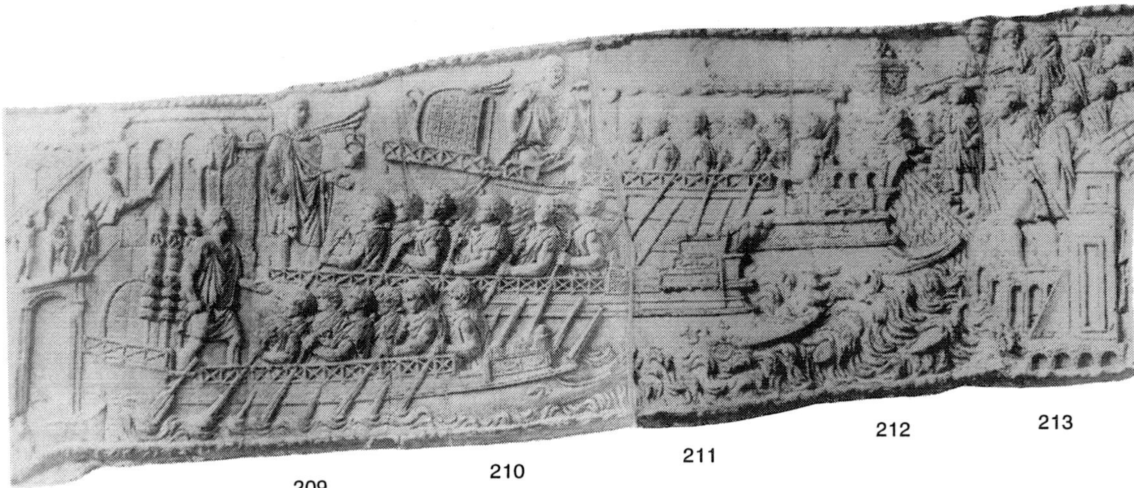

47

LF Plate LX, scene lxxxl, cast 204 shows the oblong recessed container observed in **46.3** carried by Trajan's men in the march after his arrival at Zadar from Ancona (LF p. 133) 'while some of his expedition coasted along by sea'.

48. LF Plate LXI, Scenes lxxxii–iii–lxxxiv, Casts 216–220.

Two ships are shown one (**48.1**) above the other (**48.2**) with oars at two levels as in **45–47** but not worked by oarsmen. In **48.1** the upper oars emerge over the lower horizontal side of the lattice under which the regular continuances of the vertical sides of the lattice units have no wale to rest on as in **45–47**. In **48.2** the frames of the lattice units rest directly on a wide wale with wave? decoration.

Above the latticework there is the foremost end of a mainsail furled round mast and spar and supported on crutches.

The oblong recessed container, observed on the outside of the hull in the stern of **46.3** in the first Dacian war and again carried on the march in LF Plate LX illustrating the second Dacian war is seen again in this scene carried in the midst of a procession of men wearing chaplets on their heads to the rendezvous with the fleet. Like the *doliolum* on Mn. Fonteius's coinage (**24 I ii**) it would appear to be a container of sacred objects (if not merely of water).

49. LF Plate LXII, Scene lxxxvi, Casts 225–8.

The prow section of the ship in cast 225 is without oarsmen. This circumstance allows the mast and sails, unstepped and furled together, now to be shown in their proper position supported on crutches a few feet above the deck (not as high as in **47** where they had to clear the heads of the outsize oarsmen), and the course of lattice screens to be in their proper position below the deck which is properly shown on the level of the foredeck. On the foredeck there is a turret of four arches (cf. **29** bow, **36** stern). Nevertheless, the artist, remembering the other ships on the column in which the grossly exaggerated oarsmen are seated, makes the oars emerge, the upper file through the lattice screens and the lower beneath the upper wale as they have e.g. in **45** and **46**.

48 216 217 218 219 220

49 225 226 227 228

Note on ***46–49***

The oared warships on Trajan's Column present a difficult problem of interpretation. The artist's task was to depict ships of the Pannonian Danube fleet, consisting of liburnians with a three as flagship rowed by oarsmen at two and three levels respectively (Viereck: 1975 p. 225).

Human figures in these scenes, as elsewhere in the relief, were shown in a size which dwarfs not only the ships but the buildings and the whole environment. As far as ships are concerned the constant enlargement of human figures in works of art has always presented problems of interpretation for those interested in forming a practical assessment of the ships in or beside which those figures are depicted. The exception to this rule is the Lenormant relief (**ixa**), but there the ship was the centre of attention and the thranite oarsmen shown were lay figures who were of a size to fit the ship (cf. also **iii**).

In the case of the Ruvo vase (**x**) the vasepainter had a story to tell and indulged his wish to exaggerate the human figures in its interest; but fortunately this indulgence did not bring with it distortion of the picture of the ship. That remained a fairly realistic image; and the ship, once the human figures are discounted, looks realistic.

It has been seen that the Phoenician or Greek engraver of coins, given the task of depicting an oared warship of great complexity, saw that realism was impossible in so small a compass as the coin's face. Instead he chose to select certain features according to his view of their importance and present them by a sort of symbolic code. The selection was bound to be subjective; but the code is not difficult to break once the artist's purpose is understood. It is thus possible to derive a certain amount of information about the ship the coin designer was depicting.

In the relief on Trajan's Column it is clear that in the case of the ships the artist's preoccupation with the human figures has severely distorted his rendering. Trajan and his staff had to be portrayed, the former in more than life size, as commander on board his flagship. The oarsmen apparently had to be shown as well, as human figures in detail, and still quite out of proportion to the ships. To make the oarsmen and not the others proportional to the ship would have been ridiculous; and if the ships were shown proportional to the men they would have taken up more than the available space. The artist seems to have solved his dilemma by giving the ships to a limited extent a realistic appearance on the outside but abandoning realism in what had to do with the link between ship and men, the oarsystem and consequently the internal structure. Two and three levels of oars (rowed by disproportionately large men) necessarily had to emerge from the realistic ship at unrealistic places (cf. to a limited extent **iii**, **5**, and **18 II**).

The two-level warships that would have accompanied Trajan's flagship across the Adriatic are likely to have been cataphract liburnians (**vii** and **44**: and p. 170–72, 264) with deck and bulwark, a ventilation course (because cataphract and boxed-in) and oars emerging at two levels. Trajan's flagship in what was to become a river squadron would have been a three (p. 170–72, 264), again certainly cataphract, with deck and bulwark, ventilation course, oarbox for the thranite oars and zygian and thalamian oars emerging through oarports.

The artist's solution of his problem has a parallel in the treatment given to another oared warship, in this case a five, by the artist of the Aula Isiaca fresco (**40**). There the ship is shown beached, with three levels of oars emerging through the deep oarpanel usual in Carthaginian and Roman fives. Above the oarpanel there is a latticework course.

The artist of the fresco did not have the problem facing the artist of the relief to fit outsize oarsmen to a realistic oarsystem. He could leave the outside appearance of the oars as it was, even if the outsize figures within the ship were inconsistent with the outside appearance, requiring the abolition of the oarsmen's furniture, the deck and bulwark. The section of the ship aft of the oarsystem and forward of the afterdeck (?helmsman's seat) also had to be lengthened to accommodate the disembarkation (outsize figures and ladder).

The problem of the artist of the relief was more difficult. The enormously exaggerated seated oarsmen necessarily led, as in the fresco, the artist to ignore the oarsmen's furniture, deck and bulwark of a normal liburnian and three. However, the oars held by his disproportionate visible oarsmen could not emerge except where in a normal liburnian and three there was a ventilation course screened by latticework as in the Octavian coin (**31a**), the Orange relief (**34**), the Palazzo Spada relief (**36**), the Aula Isiaca fresco (**37**) and the Alba Fucentia graffito (**39**). These disproportionate upper oarmen rowing through the latticework had to stand symbolically not only for the oarsmen they displaced but also for the other one level in the case of the liburnian or two levels in the case of the three. The oars were visible but the happily invisible oarsmen (like all the oarsmen in the Aula Isiaca fresco) could be neither proportionate nor disproportionate but absent.

The screens in (**44**) through the bottom of which the upper oars were rowed present a more solid protection for the oarsmen than lattice; but lattice, backed by loose leather or horsehair curtain (*GOS* p. 302: *παραρρύματα*) in battle, would combine the essential ventilation of a cataphract ship on passage with provision for the necessary protection of the oarsmen when battle was joined. Fortunately the Palazzo Spada relief (**36**) puts the matter beyond doubt. In the Nymphaion ship (**13**) there is a row of hooks from which defensive screens could be fixed over the ventilation course below. The Praeneste ship (**29**) louvres look rather more sophisticated. Trajan's fleet was not however expecting, or prepared for, engagement at sea, and his lattice screens while normally acting as louvres could serve as a framework for protection from weather or missiles if opposition was encountered in river transit.

If this interpretation of the ships in the Trajan's Column relief is followed, the form of the two types of ship represented may be set out thus:

Liburnians:
(**45.1**, **46.1** and **2**, **47.1** and **3**, **48.1** and **2**, **49.1**)
The latticework ventilation course present in all eight cases implies a deck at least. Since (**44**) which is contemporary and is taken to be a liburnian, has no bulwark, a bulwark as well need not be implied. The lattice screen itself is corroborated by the rather more solid version in (**44**) designed for more serious protection than was needed on the Dacian expedition. There is no reason to doubt the emergence of upper oars over the topwale and below the screen as in (**44**), not perhaps in the rather unpractical way shown on the column. Ships **48.1** and **2** show variations. In the former there is no narrow wale to form the slits under the lattice units although the continuations of the frame sides are there, and in the latter no continuations but a broad decorated panel instead. The oarsystem as shown on the outer side of the hull may be accepted roughly as shown.

Three (**47.2**)
In the three as portrayed the thranite oars are worked through the latticework units under each of which is a slit separated from the next by a short upright.

In Trajan's flagship the thranite oars will thus have emerged from the *παρεξειρεσία* beneath the ventilation course; the zygian oars will have emerged (as they do in the relief) immediately below the *παρεξειρεσία* and above the middle wale, and the thalamian oar immediately above the lowest wale. Very little alteration to the picture needs to be made beyond the removal of the giant oarsmen, the restoration of the deck and possibly a bulwark as well and the shifting of the thranite oars from the lattice course to the slits below it.

50. Mosaic at Themetra (Sousse, Tunis) c. AD 250. L. Foucher (1957) Fig. 9, B.1108.

This small warship, with one level of oars manned, is recognisable as a *λέμβος* with no deck, so aphract. The course of black dots running fore and aft in the wale under the oarports cannot be lower oarports since they extend fore and aft well beyond the rowing area. She has a stern cabin and the tillers of the rudders are shown in the stern (*σκηνή*). There is also a high sidescreen. Of particular interest is the foremast stepped and strongly raked with sail partially unfurled ready for immediate use while the main mast with sail furled is on crutches as in ships on Trajan's Column. The absence of human figures has made it possible for the ship and its gear to be realistically presented.

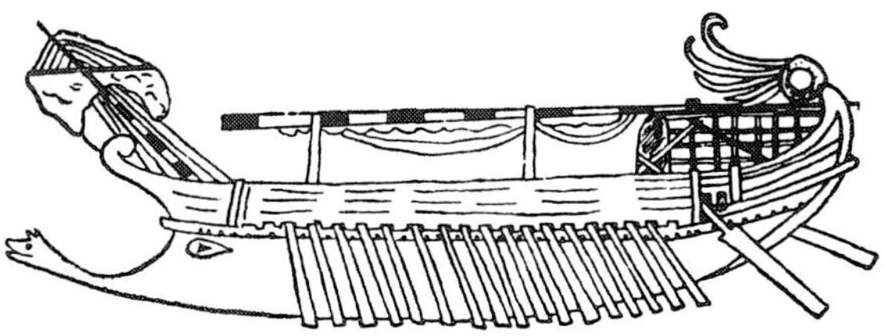

50

Endnotes

1. Prows in the shape of a boar's head were usual in Attic b/f ship-pictures of the 6th century (e.g. *LSRS* Pls. 11 and 12, B. 428–458). The peculiarity of the *σάμαινα* was that the boar's snout was retroussé.
2. There is close similarity between the *σάμαινα* on the Zankle tetradrachm and the ship represented in the Delphic *μετόπη* (GOS Pl. 12a), both of which have an unusual lower bow, convex in silhouette, and a similar but not identical stempost and small 'eye' and pattern of narrow wales. The *μετόπη* which survives in two fragments provides the first unquestionable example of a two-level *longship* (as distinct from the two-level fleet auxiliaries of the Nineveh relief) showing two oarports between the lowest (triple) wale and the middle (single) wale and above that en echelon a further oarport, rather damaged but clearly implied by the oarports above the lowest wale. The kind of ram fastening which appears in the Zankle tetradrachm is not shown in the Delphic *μετόπη* but a fastening further forward is likely to have been masked by the horse of the Dioskouros.
3. The ladder in the Ruvo vase picture (**x**) of *Argo*'s stern is to be compared. There the edge of the deck is immediately above the outer face of the *παρεξειρεσία*, this *Argo* being a late 5th century three with a wide deck.
4. Crawford (p. 42 note 5) accepts the suggestion that the prows shown are of a type 'otherwise first found in the coinage of Antigonos Doson in an issue struck after 227' (**16**); and accordingly dates all these issues to 225 BC. The similarity between the prow of Doson's ship and the Roman lies solely in the shape of the slightly backward-curving stempost. But this Macedonian feature is to be seen in coins of Arados after it had been surrendered to Alexander by Straton in 333 BC, of Demetrios (with a slight variation and of Demetrias soon after its foundation) in 293.
5. The word ΟΡΘΑΙΑ written from right to left on the hull of a ship depicted on an ivory plaque (*GOS* Pl. 10d) may be compared. The plaque was found in the temple of Artemis Orthaia in Sparta.
6. Cf. Aischylos *Persai* 375–6. *ναυβάτης τ' ἀνὴρ τροποῦτο κώπην σκαλμὸν ἀμφ' εὐήρετμον* and Vitruvius 10.3.6. *remi circa scalmos strophis religati.*
7. JFC rightly discounts this rope as the after loop of a *ὑπόζωμα*. Its function could be to secure the strong point around which the *ὑπόζωμα* went under tension in the stern.
8. Lucius Gellus Publicola, whom Plutarch records as with Antony and commanding the right wing of his line at Aktion, may have been supported there by Cartilius who shared with him the cognomen of the Valerii (Meiggs 1973 p. 477) linked with Ostia.
9. There is such a gangway outside the bulwarks and surmounting the louvres on the Praeneste relief (**29**), but there the ventilation course has its own protection and the oarports are protected by *ἀσκώματα*.

6

CATEGORIES AND TYPES

Categories

Longships – Round ships

The broadest warship category is that of 'long ships', (*μακραὶ νῆες, naves longae*), distinguishing warships from 'round ships' (*στρογγύλοι νῆες, ὁλκάδες, onerariae*) which, carrying cargo, and sometimes troops and military supplies , were navigated solely under sail, or towed by longships, being without an oarsystem.[1] They naturally had an important role to play in invasion fleets. There were also certain intermediate types of fleet auxiliary (*πόρια, κέρκουροι*) which had oars to enable them to keep up with warships under oar at ordinary cruising speeds. They may have had a forefoot (cf. the Marsala ship) but no bronze sheath and so were not 'armed', *rostrata*, equipped with rams.

Longships had from the earliest times a forefoot which appears to have been found useful in reducing wave-making resistance by lengthening the entry of the hull. These ships carried men and gear to war, being rowed by the men who subsequently fought on land. When fleets began to seek confrontation at sea the forefoot came to be sheathed with a bronze ram which became the warship's principal armament. When the galley developed a canopy deck (i.e. a deck with no structural function) this accommodated the longship's secondary armament of archers and armed men equipped with hand weapons and missiles, later catapults. All longships were propelled by oars as well as by sails. Oars alone were used in combat, although in exceptional circumstances (p. 85, 95) the smaller foresail was raised in or before battle. Passage was made under sail when the wind was favourable.

Cataphract – Aphract

Odysseus (*Od.* 5.256) protected (*φράξε*) his improvised ship with a wash-strake of latticework 'to keep out the waves'. That this was a common practice is shown by Alkaios (7th-6th centuries BC) when (A 6 7 Lobel-Page), using the metaphor of the ship of state he urges his 'crew' at the onset of a storm to protect the ship with washstrakes (*φράσσειν*) and run for a safe haven (see also late 8th century Geometric vasepaintings, *GOS* 43 and 44). Boisacq gives the meaning of *φράσσειν* as 'serrer l'un contra l'autre, boucher, obstruer; barricader; garnir de defenseurs, protéger'.

In the 5th century Thukydides (1.10.4) writes of the Greek ships that went to Troy as not likely to have had on board many extra men (*περίνεῳ*) for two reasons, first that they were going to cross the open sea with all their gear [and so did not want any extra weight]; and the second that they did not have their ships *κατάφαρκτα* (the Attic form of *κατάφρακτος*). The adjectives *φαρκτός, φρακτός* from the verb *φράσσειν* only occur the former in the *Etymologicum Magnum* 667.23 and the latter in Oppian *Halieutika* 1.641 (2nd-3rd centuries AD); but *κατάφρακτος* becomes common in the Greek historians with *tectus, constratus* its equivalents in Latin writers.

Φρακτός, φαρκτός compounded with adverbial *κατά* means 'protected, fenced-in from top to bottom, from end to end' (see Boisacq s.v). However, the sense in which Thukydides used *κατάφαρκτος* was 'built with a deck (*κατάστρωμα*) 'from end to end', since extra men, other than those who rowed, were in his time carried on deck (*ἐπιβάται*) although he admits (1.14.3) that Themistokles's threes at Salamis had not decks (*διὰ πάσης*) right across. Side screens to protect the open sides, which 5th century threes certainly carried for putting up in an emergency, had no relevance to the carriage of extra men.

The development of side-screens in the 5th century is well attested. Aischylos's reference to them on board an Egyptian ship (*Suppliants 715: παραρρύσεις νεώς*) is not anachronistic, although the word probably is. Xenophon (*HG* 1.6.19) relates that Conon in 406 BC, to disguise his preparations for breaking the Spartan blockade of Chios, put the decksoldiers below deck and threw sidescreens along the open sides (*παραρρύματα παραβαλών*), to hide the soldiers who would normally be on deck and the thranite oarsmen, otherwise visible through the open side (**ix**).

The normal function of these sidescreens was protection of the oarsmen from sun and weather, and in battle. Xenophon (*HG* 2.1.22: 405 BC) describes preparation for battle: 'throwing alongside the sidegear' (*τὰ παραβλήματα παραβαλών*). In the naval inventories under 'hanging gear' (e.g. 2^2 1611 (357/6)) sidescreens (*παραρρύματα*) appear frequently in pairs (port and starboard), some white (i.e. canvas) and some made of hair; on one occasion (1627 of 330/29) there is a sidescreen of leather. It is likely that the canvas was protection against the sun and weather while hair and leather material was protection against missiles. Sidegear is also mentioned (in 2^2 1604 (377/6) 31) less precisely under the name *παραβλήματα*.

Other similar items of hanging gear appear in the inventories, in 1631 (323/2) 418 *κατάβλήματα* of hair, and in 1611 (357/6) a *ὑπόβλημα* and a *κατάβλημα*. Whereas it seems clear that the sidegear (*παραρρύματα, παραβλήματα* (which were apparently nailed down: 1604 31) are the screens to fill the open space between the edge of the deck and the top of the *παρεξειρεσία* in the three, the *κατάβλημα, ὑπόβλημα* gave protection under the *παρεξειρεσία*. JSM noticed in *GOS* (p. 302): 'an interesting thing about the *ὑπόβλημα* is that it is always absent in lists of the hanging gear of *τετρήρεις*: 1627 466, 1628 333 and 605, 1629 1081'. Its absence fits our conclusion (p. 267–69) that the four had two levels of oars and would thus have had no outrigger beneath which to rig a screen.

Devices attributed to Chabrias, commander of Athenian fleets between 389 and 357 BC, as described by Polyainos (3.11.13) explain both the *ὑπόβλημα, κατάβλημα* (two words with the similar meaning of something let down or put under), and the *παράρρυμα*. 'As protection against the impact of waves Chabrias fixed leather under the *παρεξειρεσία* on each side and attaching lattice (*φράγμα*) to the deck fixed it to the *παρεξειρεσία* as a vertical protection'.

The warships bigger than threes whose function, beside ramming, was to provide a firm platform for offensive and defensive action by decksoldiers, developed solid and permanent 'boxing-in' (with louvres for ventilation) to protect the oarsmen as the ships approached each other and while such combat was in progress. Cataphract thus came to be a term covering in the larger ships decking and possibly also the permanent boxing-in with louvres which succeeded the upper and lower temporary protective gear. Of the smaller and lighter cataphracts some threes and some of the others were decked but not boxed-in although they would have had removable screens. Such long ships were used as scouts and for fleet communication, but some, for example liburnians, were armed with rams and boxed-in for offensive action in an emergency. So the three on Trajan's Column serving as the emperor's flagship (**47**) would have been decked and had its open side permanently protected by lattice work as in the case of the ventilation panels in other ships (e.g. **34, 38, 40**).

The latin equivalents of *κατάφρακτος* are *tectus* 'covered' and *constratus* 'decked'. Aphract, the opposite to cataphract and its one latin equivalent *apertus* had the meaning of undecked.

When Agrippa (p. 153) was given command of the fleet being prepared for Octavian's final campaign against Sextus Pompeius, to escape the raids of Sextus's fleet on the coastal shipyards the ships were assembled and fitted out in the newly created base on the Lucrine lake. Part of this final preparation was to make them cataphract (i.e. put in 'dead' work). It is interesting that this task belonged to the commander rather than the shipbuilder, presumably because he would know what he intended to require of his ships in action. Agrippa envisaged engagements in which the decksoldiers of his larger and higher ships would have the advantage over Sextus's lower and smaller fleet in close contact. Since close contact required good protection for the oarsmen, he saw to it that such was provided.

Liburnians appear to have been decked and were possibly boxed in as well and there are occasions when smaller ships (e.g. λέμβοι) were boxed-in for special tasks (e.g. p. 263). Such protection would have been limited by the sinkage resulting from additional weight.

Ships with rams – Ships without rams

The category of ships equipped with rams (*naves rostratae*) is not coextensive with that of cataphracts. All cataphract ships would have been equipped with rams; and some aphract ships also who did not thereby become μάχιμοι (p. 258).

Smaller – Larger Warships

A common division in Livy is between larger and smaller ships (*naves maioris formae, minoris formae*).[2] The line in this division seems to have been drawn between fours and threes. These categories again are not coextensive with the categories cataphract and aphract. Fours are regularly cataphract and among the bigger ships. At the battle of Korykos in 191 BC Antiochos's fleet of 100 ships of smaller size included seventy which were cataphract. These smaller cataphracts would have been mostly threes, which are regularly rated among the smaller ships; and, if as is likely the Lindos prow (**11**) which is cataphract represents a τριημιολία, the smaller cataphracts included τριημιολίαι and on occasion ἡμιολίαι as well.

Lighter – Heavier Warships

Warships are also characterised as light or heavy. Weight would have correlated closely with beam, since length was much the same for most types (three and above) and draft would not have varied very much for reasons of stability. Yet at the second battle of Mylai Agrippa's heavier ships, fives at least, were warned not to pursue Papias's ships, at most fours, into the shallows where they had taken refuge. Ships with multi-manned oars would have been broader and therefore heavier than ships with single-manned oars. (See Ch. 7 Appendix D for displacements.)

Ships of the rating of six and above were certainly 'heavy'. Fives when they were *expediti* (p. 70, 89), i.e. stripped for speed, may have been regarded as among the lighter ships; and the fours, though among the larger ships, would have been among the lighter. Certainly the ship, either a four or a τριημιολία, belonging to the 'Rhodian' at Lilybaion (p. 54) was notably fast and manoeuvrable, usually the virtues of light warships. The four from Centuripi which Cicero mentions (*Verrines* 5.89) was 'incredibly fast under sail'.

Fast ships – Στρατιώτιδες

The phrase 'fast threes' is used by the earlier Greek historians and appears in inscriptions to mean threes with special hull characteristics (*AT* p. 152) enabling them to achieve the acceleration and manoeuvrability which good ramming tactics required, and for the same purpose with the restriction to ten heavy-armed soldiers. Themistokles's threes though built for speed nevertheless had a canopy-deck but not right across. The same sources show that there were also threes called στρατιώτιδες or ὁπλιταγωγοί with different hull characteristics, possibly wider beam, certainly bulwarks and a more strongly built deck to enable them to carry forty or so soldiers.

Diodoros's phrase (20.47.1) 'heavier στρατιώτιδες' in his description of Demetrios's invasion fleet for Cyprus in 307 BC could mean troop-carrying threes which were of course heavier than the fast threes, but since Demetrios's fleet subsequently turns out to have included a large number of ships of higher denomination than threes it seems that the 'heavier στρατιώτιδες' were in fact these ships of higher denomination; and that the phrase means troop-carrying warships heavier than the normal troop carrying threes. They are distinct, as fighting ships, from the πόρια which were not fighting ships but fleet auxiliaries. In the 5th and early 4th centuries troops carried on στρατιώτιδες were for fighting on land. In the 'heavier στρατιώτιδες' of the late 4th century they were carried for fighting at sea, while troops for fighting on land were carried in oared auxiliaries.

One reason at any rate, probably the most important, for the development of the warships of higher denomination than the three was the requirement by the new aspirants to sea power, in the first place the Macedonians, whose forte was hand-to-hand fighting, for a steady platform on which a large number of fighting men could be carried and used in a sea battle. Στρατιῶτις is accordingly a suitable name for such ships.

Πόρια (Troop transports) – Warships

In Demetrios's invasion fleet for Cyprus there is

also a category of πόρια, transports for both infantry and cavalry. In the Athenian fleets of the late fifth and the fourth centuries cavalry were transported in converted threes (30 horses and 60 oarsmen (*AT* Fig. 70 p. 157 and pp. 225–8). But earlier, e.g. in Dareios's invasion fleet, there were purpose-built cavalry transports. In Xerxes' invasion fleet and in the troop-carrying threes later in the century 40 armed men were accommodated on deck, but there are occasions when infantry are recorded as being transported in ὁλκάδες, i.e. 'round' ships (and so usually with an escort of threes and towed, as the name implies, when necessary) as opposed to 'long' ships (moving under oar or sail). The πόρια in Demetrios's invasion fleet may have been, either themselves oared to have a chance of keeping up with the warships, or round ships towed by threes.

Fighting Ships – Auxiliaries

In his description of Pompey's fleet in 49–48 BC Plutarch uses the distinction between fighting ships (μάχιμοι) and others. In the *Life of Pompey* 64.1 he speaks of 500 fighting ships and a vast number of λιβυρνίδες and κατάσκοποι (scouts); and in the *Life of Cato the Younger* of (54.3) fighting ships not less than 500 and a great number of λιβυρνικά, κατασκοπικά and ἄφρακτα [πλοῖα]. As Torr (1894) observed in these two passages 'fighting' (μάχιμοι) is in place of κατάφρακτοι describing ships built and equipped to take their place in the battle line. There is a third passage for comparison describing the Roman fleet under Livius which crossed from Peiraieus to Delos on the way to meet Antiochos's fleet at Korykos in 191 BC. Livy (36.42.8) speaks of 81 κατάφρακτοι and many smaller ships which were either aphracts with rams or *speculatoria* [*navigia*] without.

In the first passage of Plutarch the ships which are not 'fighting' are either liburnians or scouts. Since liburnians are also employed on occasion as scouts (Appian 5.103), it seems that whereas liburnians are, as will be seen, an originally local type of cataphract two-level λέμβος which could have many functions, scouts are ships other than liburnians employed for reconnaissance.

In the second passage the non-fighting category consist of liburnians, κατάσκοποι or aphracts. The implication is that the scouts and liburnians were cataphract. In the third passage by dividing the non-cataphracts into aphracts with rams and *speculatoria* [*navigia*] without rams the reliable Livy shows that Plutarch's second passage is more accurate than the first and that among aphracts in a Roman fleet of the 2nd and 1st centuries BC there was a range of warships with rams (the aphracts of the second passage) as well as ram-less oared ships, i.e. λέμβοι. When the λέμβος is fitted with a ram it is often called a πρίστις (see below p. 263).

The term 'scout' (πρόπλους, κατάσκοπος, *speculatoria* [*navis*]) may be taken to describe a function rather than a type; that is to say, it seems to describe ships of any type which perform the function of reconnaissance. It does however appear that to be of any use they would have to be possibly fast fours or threes, or liburnians which had a reputation of being light and fast.

Capital Ships – Scouts

JFC writes: 'The scope for reconnaissance would be very limited for ships under oars. The speed of a fleet under oar in fair conditions would have been about five knots at most, four knots most probably. A reconnaissance ship, if a τριήρης and manned by an élite crew, could maintain a continuous speed of seven knots at most (except perhaps on a special occasion). That gives the reconnoitring ship a speed advantage of at most three knots over the fleet. If searching ahead of the fleet the scout could therefore be 15 miles ahead in 5 hours and would take 1 hr 20 minutes to return to the moving fleet to report a contact made.

A man at the top of *Olympias*'s mast can just see the deck of a similar ship over the horizon on a clear day (neglecting refraction of light) at a range of 10 miles. His horizon is 7 miles distant. A man on the deck of *Olympias* has a horizon 3 miles distant and could, as above, just see the decks of similar ships 7 miles away.

Fleets generally proceeded along coasts and would be very unlikely to come across an enemy out of sight of a coast except along well-known sea lanes e.g. from Greece to Italy or from Sicily to Africa. Scouts would therefore be deployed ahead of a fleet and would have been ordered to keep in sight of the main body, i.e. not more than 10 miles ahead, from which position they could see at most 10 miles ahead of themselves, 20 miles from the fleet or 5 hours at the assumed fleet speed. The scout again would take about 1 hr to report back to the fleet.

If scouts were smaller vessels (than threes) they would be slower and their masthead lower. No vessel with a continuous speed of less than 6 knots under oar would be much use as a scout. A good height of mast giving extra visual range (7 nautical miles for a three) would have been regarded as essential for a scout which would in any case have to be able to sail at least 2 kn faster than the fleet. The problem would be to find a vessel combining speed under oar and sail with small dimensions.

Oarsystems

(representations in Ch. 5 and Ch. 7 in square brackets)

A. Ships with one level of oars
Eikosoroi, Muoparones, Pentecontors, Triacontors

B. Ships with two levels of oars *en échelon*
I. Triacontors, Pentecontors, Lemboi, Liburnians [**ii-vii**, **44**, **45–49**, **72**, **76** Liburnian]
II. Fours [Alba Fucentia graffito: **38**, **59**, **76**]
III. Nines and above [Relief of two warships: **25**, Praeneste relief: **29**]

C. I. Hemiolia [**73**, **76**]
II. Trihemiolia [**11**, **17**, **20**, **21**, **26**, **36**, **42**, **74**, **75**, **76**]

D. Ships with three levels of oars, threes to eights
I. With a *παρεξειρεσία* for the thranite oars
[The Greek three **viii-xii**, **1**, **2**, **7–9**, **41**, **51–6**, **76**]
[The Syracusan five **57**]
[The prow on Demetrios Poliorketes' coins **10**]
[" " Antigonos Doson's coins **16**]
[The Isola Tiberina Prow **27**, **60–69**]
[Trajan's flagship **47.2**]
II. With no *παρεξειρεσία* for thranite oars and two open side courses, threes and fives
[Nineveh warship **ib**]
[Persian seal **2b**]
[Arados coins **3f** and **g**]
[Byblos coins **4e**]
[Amathus gem **5**]
[Erment model **6**, **58**]
III. With deep oarbox and oars/oarports quincunx-fashion, fives
[Roman Republican coins **12**]
[Nymphaion fresco **13**, **71**]
[Calenian dishes I **18**]
[Calenian dishes II **18**]
[Ostia frieze **35**, **71**]
[?Pozzuoli reliefs **39**]
[Aula Isiaca fresco **40**, **71**]
[Amandus fresco **41a**, Herculaneum fresco **41b**, **71**]
[Pompeian shipshed fresco **43**, **71**]

Note on Groups D II and D III

D II is distinct from D I, the latter being the main line of development of the Greek warship from the three to the forty following what Arrian described as the *Ἑλληνικὸς κόσμος* (p. 11).

D II may originate with the 8th century Phoenician three but the evidence for this is not as clear as one might wish, and the conclusion from it must be speculative. However, a ship of three oarlevels without a *παρεξειρεσία* is shown without doubt by the Erment model.

The Erment model belongs to a group of representations of oared ships of the period between 350 when there is the first record of the presence of a five in Phoenicia and Alexander's siege of Tyre in 332. The model shows oars, while the Arados and Byblos coins and the Amathus gem do not, but the model is linked to them by the common features of shields at the edge of the deck and two open courses of 'rooms' on the hull's side. The row of shields is attested as early as 701 BC in the relief showing the ships of Luli king of Tyre and Sidon escaping to Cyprus (**i**) and is mentioned in Ezekiel's lamentation for Tyre in 586 BC (27.1–11) which likens the city to a ship whose decksoldiers hang 'shield and helmet' about her. This feature establishes the origin of the model firmly as Phoenician.

The other feature which the model has in common with the Arados and Byblos coins and the Amathus gem is the second open course of oarsmen's rooms on the hull's sides. A single course is shown in the representations of the Greek and Phoenician threes (**v-ix**) and is important for ventilation, screens being used to protect the thranite oarsmen in battle. The appearance of a second open course suggests the need for more ventilation and the presence of more oarsmen at the three levels of oars than in the threes.

The Sidonians burnt the fleet, including fives, which they had assembled in 351/0 BC for their unsuccessful revolt against Persia; and Arrian speaks of Sidonian threes sent by Sidon to join Alexander in 332. But Tyre had fives and the kings of other Phoenician cities than Sidon (including

Amathus) had fives as their flagships. It is a coincidence that the presence of these fives in the Phoenician fleets is recorded just in those years when the second open course appears on the Arados and Byblos coins and the Amathus gem. Double manning in fives of their thranite and zygian oars gives the reason why additional ventilation was necessary.

Coins were used then, as throughout antiquity, for national publicity. Ships were shown as national symbols. Earlier Sidon had shown on her coins the threes for whose performance she was famous in the eastern Mediterranean (p. 188). The ship-design which now appeared on the coins and gems would have been the type of ship of which the city had at that moment reason to be proud. The fives, the kings' flagships, introduced into Phoenicia several years before Athens had them (325/4 BC), well qualify for this position. Later, in the first half of the 3rd century BC, Pairisades II at the height of the Bosporan kingdom's prosperity may have possessed a five of the Phoenician type which was proudly displayed in fresco on the wall of the Nymphaion temple.

It seems then likely that the group of representations in D II show a five with three levels of oars, but distinct from the fives of the Greek tradition in having no outrigger for the thranite level.

Less than a hundred years later there begins to appear a second group of representations of warships (D III) with three levels of oars also distinct from the Greek tradition in having no outrigger specially for the thranite oars.

In three cases (**12**), (**35**), and (**43a**) the ships shown are undoubtedly Roman. Of the rest two (**18 I**) and (**43b**) have Carthaginian characteristics. The home port of (**13**) the ship of the Nymphaion fresco, is uncertain. The main characteristic of these ships is a deep oar-panel in which are oarports (in three cases oars as well) at three levels quincunx fashion. In four cases (**13**), (**19**), (**35**) and (**40**) the viewpoint is directly from the side and the oar-panel hardly appears to stand out at all from the hull. In the other three cases (**18**) and (**43a** and **b**) the panel appears as the lateral face of an oarbox standing out a distance from the hull's side.

JFC reconstructs the ships represented in this group as fives but finds that no further development of ships with this main characteristic is feasible.

The link between the Roman and Carthaginian design testified by group III is interesting because it is corroborated by Polybios's story, the truth of which there is no reason to doubt, that when in the 'war about Sicily' Rome decided to 'take to the sea' she built a fleet of fives on the design of a cataphract ship she captured from the Carthaginians. This link leads to the further connexion with the early idiosyncratic but problematical Phoenician five (D II) of the last half of the fourth century. Carthage was a colony of Tyre and although Tyre declined and Carthage prospered she maintained a close relationship with her mother city through the annual festival of Melkart.

The early five which the later evidence of the group D II appears to attest in Phoenicia may have been invented by Carthage, anxious to keep abreast of the similar but not identical invention of her rival Dionysios; and have been derived from her by Tyre; or alternatively it could have been acquired by Carthage from inventive Tyre with the same motivation. Carthage will have developed this early design into a more useful and sophisticated ship in which the original principle was kept but oars were rowed at all three levels through a projecting oarbox. The fact that the outriggerless three with two open sides appears first in the Nineveh warships is a point in favour of Tyre as the inventor of the similar early five.

The realisation of two contrasting lines of development, the Hellenic mode and the Phoenician, beginning possibly with the three in the late 8th and more demonstrably with the five in the 4th century BC has proved most enlightening. Now that the significance of the Carthaginian mode is realised the Roman adoption of it in contrast to the Greek has a new meaning. The fortunate sterility of the Carthaginian and Roman as opposed to the proliferation of the Greek and Macedonian mode may have had some influence on the naval construction policies of each. We have however to remember that the Isola Tiberina prow, built probably to commemorate a consular six, is the best example we have of the later Greek mode.

Types

Naming

The earliest types of Greek warship were named in literature and inscriptions according to the number of oarsmen: *εἰκόσορος* (twenty), *τριακόντορος* (thirty), *πεντηκόντορος* (fifty).

The *τριήρης*, (*AT*) has three files of oarsmen a side. She also seats the files at three levels. The number of files a side could be, and was, increased up to, and in the largest ships well beyond, the limit of usefulness, but in the *τριήρης* the number of levels had reached a practicable limit at three. It follows that the series of names of the warship types from three, *τριήρης*, to forty, *τεσσαρακοντήρης*, reflects the number of files of oarsmen on each side irrespective of level, a practice followed at a later age in the naming of the types of galley.

The Roman practice is described by Casson very aptly (*SSAW* 7.6): 'Roman writers' (except Hirtius p. 139–41) 'consistently use layman's language when referring to warships, instead of naval jargon, *biremis* for *liburna* being but one example. They almost always speak of *triremes*, *quadriremes* and *quinqueremes* whereas the official terms were *trieres* (*CIL* VI 1063 17, 3095, 3277.1; IX 41.43), *quadrieres* (*CIL* VI 1063 15, *AE* 1927 3) and *penteres* (*CPL* 195)'. Casson compares the use of *tetreris* in the Alba Fucentia (**38**) graffito.

The smaller ships

The -krotos series

The correctness of the above interpretation of the type-names in *-ήρης* is corroborated by a similar series of adjectives in *-κροτος*, of which the following occur: *μονόκροτος*, *δίκροτος*, *τρίκροτος*... *ἑξκαιδεκάκροτος*: with one beat, two beats, three beats ... sixteen beats. Xenophon (*HG* 6.2.12) wrote of a ship which had a well-trained oarcrew as *ναῦς συγκεκροτωμένη* (cf. Polybios 1.61.3): it is a ship in which the rowing is in unison. *Κρότος* as a noun is used for the tap of feet in a dance or the clap of hands in applause; and so fittingly in the adjectives and verb for the sound ('clunk' or beat) of the oar at the finish, one on each side of each room in a ship with one file, two on each side of each room in a ship with two files and three on each side of each room in a ship with three (for room see Glossary).

With ships employing multiple-manning of oars the beat is of the oarsman as he operates the oar in the company of others. His ship may be called 'sixteen-beat' although in each half room there are two oars operated each by a gang of eight oarsmen. It is 'harmonised' when all sixteen 'strokes' are made together, in much but not quite the same way as three oarsmen of a three's triad do so. Lucan similarly but rather more accurately describes Brutus's flagship, plainly a six, as 'driven by sixfold strokes' (one 'sixfold' stroke in each half-room). Aristeides however, like Appian living at a time (last half of 2nd century AD) when the word *τριήρης* was used as a general term for warship (as liburna became in the 5th century AD), does not use a single series of terms (*Or*. 25.(43).4) for the '*τριήρεις*' in the harbour of Rhodes. He speaks of *δίκροτοι* and *τρίκροτοι*, presumably simple twos and threes and then ships of seven and nine files (a side), that is to say sevens and nines, without indicating the number of levels.

The word *τρίσκαλμος*, meaning 'with three tholepins', which Aischylos (*Persians* 679) used as a synonym for *τριήρης*, teaches the same lesson. The three differs from the two or the one by having three tholepins instead of one or two in each half-room, just as *τρίκροτος* picks out the characteristic of three oar-beats in each half-room (instead of two or one). The concept of the oar-room and its manning, and hence of the files (*στοῖχοι*) on each side of the ship, rather than the concept of the oar-level or bank, is basic to the determination and naming of the types.

Appian's progressive list

A passage in Appian illustrates the point made at the end of the last paragraph. In describing the growth of the seapower of the pirates encouraged by Mithridates (*Mithr*. 92 p. 117) he says that they first used *μυοπάρωνες*, then *ἡμιολίαι* and subsequently *δίκροτα* and *τριήρεις*. This series is based on the number of oarsmen on each side of the ship in each room.

The *μυοπάρων* is the smallest type of oared warship, mentioned several times in Cicero (e.g. *Verr*.2.5.73) as a pirate craft, but once (ib. 2.1.86–90) as a ship provided by the Milesians from their fleet as escort, when it is said to be 'armed', i.e. equipped with a ram. It is then a long ship of the smallest kind with one file of oarsmen on each side and thus one oarsman on each side of each room .

As Torr noticed (1894: p. 118–9), there is a clue to the nature of the *μυοπάρων* in two parallel passages, one in Appian (*CW*.5.95) and the other in

Plutarch (*Antony* 35). Both write of a gift from Antony to Octavian at the instigation of Octavia, Octavian's sister and Antony's wife. In Appian the gift is ten *φάσηλοι τριηρετικοί*, 'the type a mixture of a cargo ship and a long ship'. In Plutarch the gift is 20 *μυοπάρωνες*. Catullus (4.2) introduces a *phaselus* 'which says she was the fastest ship afloat', while Sallust (*Hist.* 3.8) writes of a large *phaselus* which carried one cohort (600 men). If Appian's half-warship-half-cargoship is the same as a *μυοπάρων*, then the latter is a long ship of fairly broad beam with one file of oars on each side and a ram, occurring in various sizes and ranging from a fast variety to one which was a mixture of a cargo ship and a long ship. Since Phaselis was a city on the border of Lykia and Pamphylia, a locality famous for its pirates, it seems likely that the *phaselus* like the *μυοπάρων* and several other types of fast and commonly light craft derives its name from a connection with piracy rather than as Liddell-Scott-Jones says with beans. It is frequently mentioned by latin writers of the 1st century BC and AD.

The next ship in Appian's list of pirate vessels is the [*ναῦς*] *ἡμιολία*. The rational explanation of the name is that it indicates, like the general numerical series of warship names (into which it could not be conveniently introduced), *τριήρης, τετρήρης, πεντήρης* etc, the number of files of oarsmen on each side of the ship irrespective of level or particular room.

In Arrian's description of *ἡμιολίαι* in Alexander's fleet on the Indus (p. 9–10) it has been noticed that they came under the general term of *τριακόντοροι* some of which were rowed at one and some at two levels of oars. In *ἡμιολίαι* of one oar level the half file of five oarsmen would have provided double-manning for the oars amidship. In *ἡμιολίαι* of two levels the half file would have rowed at the lower level amidships. Since the latter system is likely to be the more efficient and *ἡμιολίαι* were the fastest ships in the Indus fleet, it is likely to have been the system there employed.

In the first quarter of the 4th century Theophrastos (*Characters* 25.2) speaks of the nervous passenger at sea who sees a pirate *ἡμιολία* in every headland; and there is reference to a Carian (i.e. piratical) *ἡμιολία* in a fragment of a probably 4th century Attic orator preserved in the *Etymologicum Magnum* (450.38). These are the first references to the type, suggesting that it was invented by pirates.

Arrian (3.2.3) speaks of Aristonikos the tyrant of Methymna sailing into the harbour of Chios in 332/1 with five 'pirate *ἡμιολίαι*'. As early as 346/5 they had become a respectable warship type, used by the Phocian commander Phalaikos (D. 16.61.4), by Alexander on the Indus and Agathokles of Syracuse (D.19.65.2) in 315 BC. As such they appear not infrequently later (see p. 62 and 84 above for the [*λέμβοι*] *ἡμιολίοι* in Philip's fleet in 217 BC and *ἡμιολίαι* certainly cataphract in his fleet at the battle of Chios).

Casson (*SSAW* 128–31 and *SSAW*[2] p. 445–6) has argued that a sixth century Attic black-figure cup in the British Museum, which shows a two-level ship with the upper level only half manned, is a *ἡμιολία*. The main objection to this identification is that the word *ἡμιολία* does not appear in literature until nearly two hundred years after the date of the cup; and secondly it admits no explanation of the *τριημιολία* (p. 266).

The next in Appian's list is the *δίκροτος* with two men to the room on each side. In Arrian (6.5.2) triacontors which are *δίκροτοι* 'had their lower oars not very far above the water' and therefore undoubtedly rowed the two files of oarsmen on each side at different levels one man to an oar (rather than *a scaloccio* two men to each oar. This is probably then the oarsystem of the ships called *δίκροτοι*, as in the case of the *τρίκροτοι, τριήρεις* the system is of three files rowing one man to an oar at three levels.

There is finally in this section one linguistic point to be made. Appian's phrase *τριηρετικὰ σκεύη* has been translated 'warship gear', since Appian, and other later writers (see p. 37) use the word *τριήρης* in a general sense for warship. Later (*Pun.*121) he speaks of the Carthaginians building fives and threes; but describes the ships when they emerged from the new harbour entrance as *νῆες τριηριτικαί*. The sharp eye of Cecil Torr (1894 p. 119) observed long ago that this phrase must include the fives with the threes and that Appian is using the word *τριηρετικός* in the later general sense.

It should not therefore be used to indicate any particular oarsystem. The word *τριηραρχος* should be compared, which is used for the captain of any warship, e.g. p. 205 of a *τριημιολία*.

Λέμβοι, λιβυρνίδες (νῆες), λιβυρνικά (πλοῖα); lembi, liburnae; pentecontors, triacontors, liburnians

The *λέμβος* is half way between a general category and a specific type. The Greek word *λέμβος* (etymology unknown) first appears in the 4th century BC as the name of a small vessel towed behind a merchant ship (Demosthenes 32.6), necessary since merchant ships normally anchored off shore. It occurs also, with the meaning of 'hanger-on' in a fragment (34.7) of another 4th century comic writer Anaxandrides. The Latin equivalent *lembus* appears in Plautus *Mercator* (1.2.81 and 2.1.35) which derives directly from the *Emporos* of the 4th century Greek comic writer Philemon. A sixth-century cup in the British Museum (**va**) shows a warship with two levels of oars towing another smaller ship with a ram, possibly a larger naval version of the merchantman's boat.

It is a small warship of this kind that the fourth century writer of [Aristotle] *IA* (10.710 a 31) has in mind when he uses the adjective *λεμβώδης* 'like a *λέμβος*'. 'For birds of prey', he says, 'speed of flight is essential for survival. Accordingly their bodies are built for appropriate movement. They have small heads and slim necks but a breast strong and sharply pointed (*ὀξύ*) or projecting (*τὸ εὔτονον*), as in the case of the prow of a ship of the *λέμβος* kind'. The characteristic of the *λέμβος* of which this writer is thinking is hull design aimed at speed and armed with a ram, the Illyrian pirate craft often mentioned in the Hellenistic centuries.

The first mention of this latter kind of *λέμβος* is in Diodoros's description of the siege of Rhodes (305/4: 20.85.3). Demetrios uses 'the stoutest of his *λέμβοι*, after they had been boxed in with planks and fitted with small doors (*θυρίδες*) which could be closed, to bring up to the wall long-range catapults and Cretan archers to harass the defenders and prevent them adding to the height of the walls while he was getting his siege engines ready'.

These *λέμβοι* were then, before adaptation, open, aphract (see also Polybios 16.2.9), but built sufficiently stoutly to serve the purpose in hand. That *λέμβοι* could be of the size of the pentecontor is shown by a passage in Strabo (2.3.4) describing how Eudoxos in his attempted circumnavigation of Africa in the 2nd century BC built 'a *λέμβος* as big as a pentecontor (*πεντηκοντόρῳ πάρισον*)'. Shortly before he had spoken of Eudoxos setting out from Gades 'having built a big ship and also two boats for towing (*ἐφόλκια*) like pirate *λέμβοι*. The greater size of the third *λέμβος*, which he built after he had set out, is indicated by the description, 'as big as a pentecontor'.

In the first Punic War (P. 1.53.9) *λέμβοι* are said 'normally to move in front of a fleet and report on the approach of the enemy', i.e. they were used as scouts. In 195 BC (L. 34.35.5) Nabis after defeat at sea by the Romans agreed to possess no ships other than two *λέμβοι* rowed by not more than sixteen oarsmen, probably the smallest kind. *Λέμβοι* sometimes conveyed horses (p. 112).

A characteristic of at any rate some *λέμβοι* is given by a pair of passages, one in Livy (32.32.9) and the other in Polybios (18.1), both describing the same incident, the voyage of Philip V in 197 BC to meet the Roman consul Flaminius. Livy says Philip went 'with four *λέμβοι* and a ship with a ram (*navis rostrata*)'; Polybios says he went with 'four *λέμβοι* and a *πρίστις*'. *Πρίστις* is also the name of a shark (Torr 1894 p. 121), and its use as the name of a type of ship indicates its character as being itself an offensive weapon, the sense in which this is so being indicated by the parallel phrase in Livy: she had a ram, and by implication the others did not. Elsewhere (40.4.11) Livy mentions an *armatum lembum* i.e. one with a ram. So in the race of warships in Vergil *Aeneid* (5. 119–226) one of the four chosen ships is named *Pristis*, said to be fast and equipped with a ram (116, 187). She finishes a good second.

Torr (1894 p. 115) took the passage in Livy to indicate that all *λέμβοι* were without rams. But *λέμβος* is plainly a name covering a wide range of light warships. *Πρίστεις* are generally mentioned together with *λέμβοι* (Polybios 16.2.9, Livy 35.26 and 44. 29), and they may well be a specialised kind of the general type, those with rams, often given the wider name of *λέμβος*. Casson has argued (*SSAW* Ch.6 n.107) that there are texts in Polybios (2.10.3–5 the Illyrian war and 16.4. 8–12 the battle of Chios) where the manoeuvres of *λέμβοι* indicate a ramming capability.

The term *lemboi* apparently could also include *ἡμιολίαι* since Polybios (5.101.2) writes of Philip V in 217 BC commissioning a force of cataphracts and *ἡμιόλιοι λέμβοι* (p. 62). They were also rowed at two levels. Livy (24.40.2) speaks of Philip having 120 *lembi biremes* in 214 BC. It cannot be a coincidence that Appian in his introduction to his history of the Illyrian war (*Ill*.3) speaks of the Liburnians as a maritime people, 'an Illyrian tribe, who practised piracy in the Ionian sea' (the Adriatic) ' and the islands, with fast, light ships, so that still now' (2nd century AD)' the Romans call their light, fast (or pointed ὀξέα), two-level warships *liburnides'*. Liburnians (lat. *liburnae*) appear in Julius Caesar's fleets in the 1st century BC (*CBC*.3.9.1). Appian (*CW*.5.99 and 111) speaks of Octavian losing a number in a storm and later boarding one himself.

These liburnians, which played a large part in the Roman imperial fleets, the name eventually becoming like τριήρης a general word for warship, are then a local kind of λέμβοι, essentially with oars at two levels. Lucan (3.534 ff) describes the fleet of Julius Caesar's admiral Decimus Brutus in the western Mediterranean in 49 BC. It included many larger types of warship and 'liburnians ...content to have grown to two levels' (p. 131). Two levels is then the characteristic of the liburnian which distinguishes her from other λέμβοι. Livy calls them, in the Illyrian fleet, '*lembi biremes*'.

Propertius (3.11.44) speaks of the liburnian rams (*rostra liburna*) of Octavian at Aktion. Pliny the Elder writes (*N.H.* 10.23) of swans as like liburnians in moving through the air *rostrato impetu* in beaked flight and so cutting the air more easily than if they pressed against it with a flat surface. This interesting remark shows at least the shape of the liburnian's prow as it meets the water, probably also confirms that it was equipped with a ram, as one would expect. It further seems to indicate an awareness that the forefoot, observed from the earliest times in representations of ancient oared ships, contributed to their speed.

Liburnians were also decked and boxed-in, since Plutarch (*Cato Minor* 54.3) distinguishes them from aphracts. Eurykles, the Spartan commander of the detachment of liburnians sent by Octavian at Aktion (p. 170) in pursuit of Antony and Cleopatra, had as flagship a ship which was able to sink one of the two flagships in the escaping squadron and on the deck of which Eurykles is described as standing. In [Suidas], λιβυρνικά (q.v.) are described as cataphract ships. They were then, it seems quite formidable warships of the smaller kind, fast, protected against missiles and armed.

Polybios (1.53.9), as has been seen, describes the Roman fleet moving along the coast of Sicily towards Lilybaion in 249 BC preceded by λέμβοι 'which are accustomed to move ahead of (προπλεῖν) fleets'; and later Appian (*CW* 5.103) speaks of liburnians performing the same function when Octavian's commander Taurus moved his army and fleet from Tarentum to join Octavian opposite Tauromenium. Appian says that reconnaissance was effected on land by cavalry and at sea by liburnians. Liburnians are also spoken of as used for fleet communication by Octavian in the same campaign and later at Aktion.

The Trajan's Column relief (**45–49**) represents a number of two-level oared warships of the Pannonian imperial fleet which are certainly liburnians. The insertion into them of enormously disproportionate oarsmen at the upper level has disguised their cataphract structure (deck, louvres etc).

Λέμβος then is a term covering a wide variety of oared ship, probably originally used in piracy on the east coast of the Adriatic (as the ἡμιολία was in the Aegean). For this original purpose speed, as well as capacity for carrying men, equipment and booty, were important. Speed and agility would be the main requirement for their use as fleet scouts, so that less heavily built ships would be needed. The smallest would be useful for conveyance of dispatches and fleet officers. The largest rowed twenty-five men a side and the smallest eight. These oared ships can be taken, as Casson has rightly argued, to be the cousins of the twenty-, thirty- and fifty-oared ships of the Aegean (and, one may add ἡμιολίαι), developing like them rams, a two-level oarsystem and when cataphract and used in battle a deck and boxing-in.

Naves actuariae

The *actuaria* is the Roman name for a small oared ship used in fleets. Hirtius (*HBA* 44) in recounting the Caesarian Vatinius's actions against the Pompeian Octavius in the Adriatic in 47 BC describes Vatinius, who was short of larger warships, fitting rams to *actuariae*, 'the number of which, but by no means the size, was large enough for a pitched battle'. Other passages make it clear that the *actuaria* was an oared ship. Cicero (ad *Atticum* 16.3.6) writes of three small *actuariae* (*actuariolae*) of ten oars each.

In the terms of peace with Rome Antiochos was allowed to retain no *actuariae* rowed by more than 30 oars (triacontors in the older terminology). The implication is that *actuariae* of more than thirty oars were built. Livy mentions (25.30.10) *actuariae* used as (necessarily rowed) landing craft at the siege of Syracuse in 212 BC.

The most interesting reference to them is in Caesar's description of the vessels he ordered to be built in the winter of 55/4 BC for the second invasion of Britain. The *onerariae* which Caesar had used to transport his troops across the Channel in the first invasion 'stood somewhat higher than warships' (p. 65). Caesar described how his troops, heavily laden with gear, had had to jump down from these *onerariae*, which could only stand in water which was not shallow (p. 122), into a rough sea to face an enemy on dry land or wading into the sea to meet them. They would have been equally inconvenient for unloading cargoes and baggage animals in those conditions. The vessels he designed were a little wider than was customary in the Mediterranean but a kind of *actuaria* with a usefully low profile. As a kind of *actuaria* they would have the added advantage of being oared and thus to some degree independent of wind or towing (p. 139). Casson (*SSAW* Ch. 8 n. 3) quotes Aulus Gellius as (10.25.5): '*actuariae* ships which the Greeks call *ἱστιόκωποι* or *ἐπακτρίδες*'. *Ἱστιόκωπος* signifies a ship with oars and sails. It was the combination of oar and sail which made what was primarily a fast merchantman suitable as a fleet auxiliary.

Scaphae

Roman merchant ships regularly had boats (called *scaphae* in Latin) towed astern and manned for security by a member of the crew (Plautus *Rudens* 1.2.74, Horace *Odes* 3.29.62, Petronius *Satyricon* 102.5: see *SSAW* Ch. 11 n. 94).

The *scaphae*, longboats which belonged to the larger Roman warships appear to have been more substantial craft which are likely either to have been towed astern or to have proceeded in company. They are associated with *naves actuariae* and *speculatoriae* (reconnaissance units p. 258). On one occasion they were, with *actuariae*, 'filled with rubble' (for fortification) 'and light armed troops' (*CBC*.3.62.23). At the first landing in Britain (*CBG*.4.26.4) Caesar ordered them and the *speculatoriae* to be manned with soldiers to assist the difficult disembarkation from *onerariae*. Antony at Brundisium (*CBC*.3.24.1) boxed in about sixty '*scaphae* of the big ships (*navium magnarum*)' and set them in ambush for the Pompeian raiders. Cassius (*CBC*.3.101.6) escaped from a five in a *scapha*, and Octavius (*HBA*.46) similarly transferred from his flagship (a four) to a *scapha* and when that sank from overloading to 'his *muoparo*'. In Africa (*CBC*.2.43.1) Curio's fleet commander Marcius Rufus ordered the masters of his ships (presumably fives) to send all the *scaphae* to evacuate the army from a beach.

The inference from these passages is that *scaphae*, like *λέμβοι*, were a kind of round-ship's boat, but that the name was also used, again as in the case of *λέμβοι*, for longboats of some size which were part of the regular equipment of the larger warships (*maioris formae*) from fives upwards. Vegetius, writing in the early 5th century AD about the Roman navy, says (2.1) that *scaphae exploratoriae* 'scout longboats' were attached to the larger warships (*maioribus liburnis*) and had twenty or so oarsmen a side (*in singulis partibus*). At this date Vegetius uses the word *liburna* as a compendious term for warships in general (*AT* p. 9).

This conclusion has an important bearing on the rating of the ships in the fleet which Julius Caesar sent up from the Mediterranean (through the bay of Biscay) for the campaign against the Veneti and then for at any rate the first invasion of Britain, since *scaphae* were employed then in the landing of the two legions from the 80 *onerariae*. The soldiers manning the *scaphae* would have been from the marine contingent on the bigger ships. That the invasion fleet contained ships of that rating was suggested by Caesar's remark (*CBG*.4.20.4–5) that he had been unable to discover from the traders who had been to Britain among other information 'what ports were suitable for the considerable number (*multitudinem*) of larger ships'. It was not clear whether 'larger ships' indicated the specific category of warships *maioris formae* i.e. fives and upwards or meant merely ships larger than the average.

The presence of *scaphae* suggests that there were certainly some at the landing and probably that the phrase 'larger ships' does specify the category of fives and upwards. If the latter is the case then there was a considerable number of them (*multitudo*). Their original function had been to destroy the Venetian fleet. Their function in the invasion of Britain may have been partly to impress and dismay the enemy in the contested landing. They may also have been given the task, usually assigned to threes, of towing the 80 *onerariae* in the short crossing.

When Caesar invaded Africa in the winter of 47/46 BC the Pompeian fleets were laid up; but their *scaphae* were used to attack and burn Caesar's straying *onerariae* (*HBAF* 21.3); and on one occasion (44 1) a warship convoying the second supply fleet (of *onerariae*) and carrying on board a Roman knight was blown off course to Thapsos and brought in by a fleet of longboats and small *actuariae* (*scaphis naviculisque actuariis*). Since Hirtius goes on to speak of a second three (*altera navis trieris*), the first warship was also a three.

Τριημιολίαι

An interpretation of the *ἡμιολία*, discussed above, rests, and can only rest in the absence of other evidence, on the principle of type naming. This gives an unambiguous clue: that the oarsystem consisted of 1½ files of oarsmen on each side of the ship. The application of this principle to the *τριημιολία* gives a less simple answer. It suggests an oared ship which is both a three and a one-and-a-half.

In JFC's reconstruction of the *τριημιολία* (**74**, **76**) two full files of oarsmen work their oars through an oarbox with their oarports *en échelon*, as seen in the prow of the Samothrace monument (**20**). As in the *ἡμιολία* there is a further half-file of oarsmen taking advantage of the wider beam in the midships section of the ship and rowing shorter oars.

At the battle of Chios (p. 81) Philip's ten rammed a *τριημιολία* 'amidships just below the thranite thole'. This incident indicates that the ten was *ἀνάστειρος* i.e. with a ram above the waterline, but it also shows that the *τριημιολία* was low in the water.The incident fits the *τριημιολία* as reconstructed .

At the outbreak of the third Punic war (p. 113) a Roman invasion fleet destined for Africa contained 100 *ἡμιολίαι* listed among the larger cataphract ships. It is possible that they were actually *τριημιολίαι*, and that *ἡμιολία* was used, at any rate by the Romans, as a general term, covering both types. Nevertheless the *ἡμιολίαι*, distinguished from *τριημιολίαι*, in Philip's fleet at the battle of Chios would, like his other *λέμβοι*, have been cataphract.

The *τριημιολία* was a favourite type at Rhodes, used for commerce raiding during Demetrios's siege. There is evidence in papyri for *τριημιολίαι* in the Ptolemaic navy (Wilcken: 1922–27 II 251.2–4 *τριημιολία μισθοφόρος* 259 BC)) and in the list of ships in the navy of Ptolemy Philadelphos in Athenaios (5.203d). Inscriptions show that *τριημιολίαι* were also present in the Athenian navy (*SSAW* p. 131, Ch. 6 n. 121) at the end of the 3rd and in the 1st century BC.

The Lindos prow (**11**) can safely be taken to represent a *τριημιολία* with an oarcrew of about 120, and the shape of her oarbox is thus securely attested. This attestation is important because there are four ship-representations in particular which have oarboxes of this kind. The first is the relief of about 200 BC cut in the rock beside the ascent to the acropolis at Lindos (**21**). The second, third and fourth share the characteristic of showing oarports or oars or oar levels *en échelon*: the prow on which the Victory of Samothrace stands in the Louvre (**20**) probably dedicated by the Rhodians between 200 and 180 BC, a warship shown on the Palazzo Barberini mosaic of the early 1st century BC (**26**), and the hellenistic Palazzo Spada relief (**36**).

The Lindos relief is likely, as Blinkenberg thought, to represent a *τριημιολία* in view of the predilection the Rhodians had for that type of ship. Its position, like the prow monument, beside the ascent to the acropolis, where there is also a later monument (noted by Ellen Rice n. 37) dedicated by the 'archon of a *τριημιολία*', adds to that likelihood. Ellen Rice has argued convincingly for the Samothrace prow as representing a *τριημιολία*. The Palazzo Barberini mosaic shows a Nile scene in which a large boxed-in warship is depicted with packed fighting men on deck. On the port side twenty-six oars emerge *en échelon* at each of two levels through a boxed-in *παρεξειρεσία*. This ship also may then have a claim to be regarded as a *τριημιολία* with an oarcrew of 130 (2 × (26 + 26 + 13)). None of these monuments provide evidence for the half-file of oars since the Samothrace monument stops short of the midships section, and in the other cases (**26** and **36**) the half-file is masked by the two full files above them.

In the Palazzo Spada relief the oarbox does not

appear to project as far as it appears to project in the Palazzo Barberini mosaic, or as it does in fact in the three dimensional Samothrace prow, but the oars of the full files emerge from the oarbox in pairs *en echelon*. On that criterion it may be recognised as a *τριημιολία*.

Threes (see p. 179–181 and 185–188)

In the case of the three the hypothesis presented in *AT* has been shown by an actual reconstruction, which takes into account all the evidence available, to be a practical solution. *Olympias* comes close to the ancient examples in performance. However, the three's role, and in consequence her build as well, were different in the navies of the Hellenistic age. She was cataphract or aphract and rated among the smaller ships, though fast, as in Demetrios's fleet at Cypriot Salamis.

In the subsequent invasion of Egypt the fast ships (i.e. threes) were used to tow transports and carry troops. Threes were regularly used for escorting (*προπέμπειν, παραπέμπειν*) *onerariae* (*ὁλκάδες*). In the campaign of Octavian and Antony against Pompey *ὁλκάδες* were sent across the strait from Brundisium with an escort of threes (for towing if necessary). They made the crossing in the event (under sail) with a strong wind in their favour. Later (Ap. *CW* 4.115) a similar convoy with an escort of threes was caught and largely destroyed. Lucan's brief characterisation of them as 'strong' is significant and certainly apt. At the siege of Utica in 203 Scipio's reconnaissance units are identifiable as threes; and in Roman fleets of fives and threes the latter would undoubtedly have had this role. It is interesting to note that though fast they are said (p. 114) not to have been able to catch up with merchantmen sailing before the wind. *Olympias* in the summer of 1992 reached nearly 10 knots under sail before a strong wind.

The coins of Kios (**6**) and Histiaia (**7**) in the 4th century and of Phaselis (**9**) in the 3rd century BC almost certainly contain representations of threes which differ in minor respects from the 5th/4th century Athenian three. Bulwarks and *πάροδοι* are added in some; and the *παρεξειρεσία* has become an oarbox projecting beyond the edge of the deck. There is however nothing to suggest that their oarsystem was radically changed.

Fours

By the type-naming practice the four (*τετρήρης, quadriremis*) may be recognised as having four fore-and-aft files of oarsmen on each side of the ship.

Aristotle is quoted by the elder Pliny (*NH* 7.207) as having attributed the invention of the four to the Carthaginians (Preface xii). Dionysios would certainly have been aware of and have copied any invention made by his naval competitors. A Carthaginian connexion might equally have been responsible for a more likely first historical appearance of the four in Alexander's siege of Tyre in 332 BC, both in his own fleet (Curtius 4.3.14) largely derived from his Phoenician allies and among the Tyrian ships.

Two years later (330–329 BC) eighteen fours are recorded in the Athenian naval inventories (*IG* 2^2 1627 24), but their introduction there could have been three years earlier since no lists for those years survive. The number of fours in the Athenian navy had by 325/4 increased to 50; and when Alexander reached Thapsakos in 324 the fleet of threes, fours and fives he had ordered, some brought overland from Phoenicia, were waiting for him. The growing popularity of fours is shown immediately after the death of Alexander when the Athenian assembly voted, in a burst of nostalgic jingoism, to form an alliance to regain the mastery of the Aegean with a fleet which was to include 200 fours. But the dream faded at the defeat of Amorgos.

Naval supremacy in the Aegean was achieved by Antigonos in 315/4 with a Grand Fleet of 240 warships in which of the 113 heavier types 90 were fours. But Antigonos's son Demetrios, who in 306 was given the naval command in the invasion of Cyprus as a preliminary to the conquest of Egypt, did not share the naval preferences of Athens and of his father. His invasion fleet contained 53 of 'the heavier, troop carrying, warships' which with additions in the final battle were 7 sevens (Phoenician), 10 sixes, probably 45 fives, and only 30 (Athenian) fours, whereas the fleet of his opponent Ptolemy contained 'nothing larger than a five or smaller than a four'. Since in the description of the battle the disadvantage at which Ptolemy stood with ships lower in the water than Demetrios's is emphasised, it is likely that fours in his fleet were in a majority.

In the invasion of Egypt that followed there were no major naval engagements. The only heavier ships mentioned were fives and fours; and it was noted that when the fleet was struck by a northerly gale the fours were driven to the dangerous moorings at Raphia, whereas the more powerful fives were able continue to Kasion (where in fact they were not much better off).

Fours seem to have been discredited in these two campaigns as to both their fighting and their sea-keeping qualities. The subsequent struggle for naval supremacy among the greater naval powers in the the eastern and western Mediterranean was fought out by heavier warships from fives upwards. Fours were used by the Romans and Carthaginians but not in the line of battle. The Rhodians retained a preference for the four, and in 47 BC Julius Caesar found himself faced by an Egyptian fleet which was largely of fours. Sextus Pompeius in Sicily met Octavius's heavier fleet of fives and above with a fleet in which his own flagship, a six, was apparently the only ship larger than a four.

For modern enquirers the four is unique among ancient oared warships in one respect. A contemporary representation of her survives, the Alba Fucentia graffito, dated 1st century BC-1st century AD, labelled with her type name in latinised Greek *navis tetreris longa* (**38**). This accident means that the process of discovering the oar-system and other practical details of the four, unlike the same process in the case of the other warship types, begins with the iconographical evidence to which the epigraphical and literary evidence is subordinate.

The graffito shows a long, low, warship with a deck but no bulwark or guard-rail, a ram and no visible oarbox or oarports. The stern also finishes without the normal upcurving *ἄφλαστον*. The absence of the bulwark, oarbox and oarports, and *ἄφλαστον* does not necessarily mean that the ship depicted did not have them, since the sketch is very rough and unfinished, and the ship's side is quite blank except for the course in latticework below the line of the deck and some indication of wales. For the letter *φ* which the artist has written above the ship just forward of the midship point there is a parallel in the Phaselis coin (**9a**) where it probably stands for the city of origin. The graffito has one great virtue, the ship is shown without the distortion of exaggerated human figures.

The Latticework Course

Apart from the prow the most striking, and at first sight most puzzling, feature is the latticework course. This may be explained by reference to two monuments, the Palazzo Spada relief (**36**) (probably representing a *τριημιολία*), which is regarded as a Roman copy of a Hellenistic original, the Praeneste relief (**29**) of the last half of the 1st century BC, and a coin minted by Octavian at Lugdunum (**31a**) 40–37 BC. Three other monuments give support, the Orange Arch relief (**34**) 1st century AD or before, the Aula Isiaca fresco (**40**) 1st-2nd century AD, and the Trajan's Column relief (**45–49**) AD 113. The reader is referred to the interpretation of these in the Iconography (Ch. 5). The conclusion to be drawn from these monuments and coins follows.

In the Athenian navy removable screens of hair or leather were used in battle to protect from missiles the open side of the three, divided into 'rooms' by the deck stanchions and thus above the *παρεξειρεσία*. When with the use of ship borne catapults missile attack became a more serious hazard a permanent course of (usually) crisscross latticework units divided by the deckstanchions was devised instead, backed by or itself forming louvres. It is this latticework course divided into units by the stanchions which the artist of the graffito sketched, leaving out, as well as the oarsystem below, the bulwark and towers above which usually (but not always) made the deck a fortress.

The Oar System of the Four

If the 22 units of the graffito ship's latticework course may be regarded as *interscalmia* (for which Vitruvius gives a Greek equivalent probably *διπηχιακή* or *διπήχυια*, at any rate a word meaning two cubits), useful conclusions result. Taking the Roman cubit of .444 m the length of the rowing area of the four depicted is 19.4 m. The hypothesis may be checked by comparing (1) the ratio between length of rowing area with height of deck above the waterline in the graffito and (2) the ratio of the length calculated on the hypothesis with the actual height of a four estimated on various grounds. Ratio (1) is 1:8.

The height of the four above the waterline is calculated by John Coates from his reconstruction (p. 294) as 2.2 m. A passage in Livy (20.25.2–8 shows a substantial difference in height (not less than, say 0.5 m) between the four and the five. The decksoldiers of two Carthaginian fours were unable to board a higher Roman five because of the difference in height (p. 68). Orosius (p. 163) says that Antony's fleet at Aktion from fives to tens stood 'ten feet' (2.96 m) above the water. The four would then have stood (2.96 m less about 0.5 m) about 2.46 m above the water. This gives a range of 2.2–2.46 m for the four's height above water. The latter ratio is then from 1:9 to 1:79, as near to the former ratio of 1:8 as to make a reasonable confirmation of the hypothesis that the latticework units show *interscalmia* of two Roman cubits.

The substantial difference in height between the five with its three levels of oars and the four makes it likely that the four had only two levels. This is confirmed by a passage in Appian (5.106): the ships of Sextus Pompeius under Papias at the battle of Mylai were 'smaller'[3] than the ships of Agrippa 'who led the heavy ships at the centre'. The decks and towers of Papias's ships were lower than the decks and towers of Agrippa's since the latter 'threw missiles from a height to ships of lower level'. Agrippa in his flagship, probably a five or a six, attacked Papias's ship and damaged it in the bow so that 'the *θαλαμιοί* were all trapped but the others (*οἱ ἕτεροι*): a word meaning the others of two categories) broke through the deck and swam away. The passage makes it clear that Papias's fours were smaller (shorter as well as lower) than Agrippa's heavier ships and that they had two levels of oars.

The conclusion may finally be drawn that the four as it appears in the graffito had twenty-two oars on each side at each of two levels; and, since it is named a four, that the oars were double manned. There were then forty-four oars a side and an oarcrew of 176. There is evidence that the *ὑπηρεσία* of a Rhodian four numbered 45.

An inscription of 325/4 BC (*IG* 2^2 1629.654) gives a valuation of the *ταρρός* (the complement of oars in use) at 665 dr, 7.5 dr apiece if there were 88 oars. Comparison with Andokides' (2.11) price of a rough-hewn trireme oar at 5 dr (850 dr for the *ταρρός*, mounting to say 1105 dr for the finished *ταρρός*: 6 dr 3 obols apiece), shows that, taking account of the higher price of double-manned oars, 88 oars @7.5 dr is proper for a four as envisaged above.

The Qualities of the Four

The virtues of the four which recommended her so strongly to the Athenians of 322 BC, to Antigonos and Ptolemy a few years later, and to the Rhodians and Egyptians in the later centuries appear to be the following.

Compared with the three she was, as a smaller two-level ship, cheaper to build and with double-manning and a smaller crew more economical to run. Although classed with her broad beam as one of the heavier *στρατιώτίδες* she was fast and manoeuvrable (p. 52: the four at Lilybaion). These characteristics also made her at first preferable to the five. She seemed to combine satisfaction of the requirements of the new naval tactics with qualities needed for the older. As the flagship of a Roman fleet commander in Sicily in 73–71 BC, she seemed like a floating city (Cicero *Verrines* 2.5.88: *urbis instar*) to the pirates with their long boats, but under sail she had an incredible turn of speed. This was probably the quality which recommended her as a reconnaissance vessel to the Roman fleets of fives. Her low profile offered less windage and thus easier rowing in adverse conditions, but in encounter with the ships of higher decks it proved her undoing.

Fives to Tens

The iconography has shown that in the period from the beginning of the fourth century BC to the end of the 2nd century AD there is a number of representations of warships with oars rowed at three levels. The historical survey (Chs. 1–4) has shown that during the period from the fourth century to the battle of Aktion a large number of oared warships from fives to tens was built and saw service with a varying degree of success, while others from the eleven to the forty were also constructed but saw no active service; or if they did none is recorded. Fives and sixes were first built as flagships to fleets of threes, but in the eastern Mediterranean later fleets containing significant numbers of ships up to tens were built and deployed in action, and still larger ships were built by Demetrios and Ptolemy Philadelphos though none was used in battle. In the western Mediterranean large fleets of fives, with, at least on the Roman side, sixes as flagships, were built and used in the wars between Rome and Carthage. Later Rome sent large fleets, mostly of fives, against her enemies in eastern waters; and in the Civil Wars there were engagements at sea culminating in the final sea battle at Aktion, all involving fleets of the larger warships.

In these circumstances it is unlikely that *none* of the ships of higher denomination than three were represented in the many coins, sculptured reliefs, models and frescos depicting warships which survive from this period of often intense naval activity. Since no representations of ships of more than three levels of oars survive, the conclusion must be drawn that some of those that survive showing ships with oars at two and three levels represent a few at least of the very widely employed larger types.

A group of representations of Phoenician ships (Ch.5 **i.2–6**: Note: p. 196–199) which display features most clearly visible and tangible in the Erment model (**6**), viz. three levels of oars and open ventilation courses at the upper two levels. The striking difference between this Phoenician design of a three-level oarsystem and that of the Greek threes is that the uppermost level of oars is not rowed through a *παρεξειρεσία* and that there are two instead of one course of open rooms. Representations of the Erment model group are quite distinct from the Phoenician 5th century and early 4th century representations of oared warships (at this date necessarily threes). But it is not clear whether these latter ships had or did not have their uppermost oars rowed through outriggers of the Greek type.

This Phoenician design of three-level oared warship, distinct from the current design of both the Greek and probably the Phoenician threes, coincides in its late 4th century appearance with the historical arrival of the five in the fleets of the Phoenician cities. The coincidence suggests that the late 4th century design is of a five. The alternative suggestion is that it is of a three either fast (as drawn in section in **58**) or modified to accommodate more decksoldiers for battle on sea or on land.

JFC has reconstructed the Erment model in drawings both as a fast three and as a five, both being possible, and has concluded that no development of the design for warships of higher denomination than the five is practicable. He has also reconstructed in drawing the Isola Tiberina prow with its trireme-style *παρεξειρεσία* as a development of the three to become a five. He has further developed the design to become a six and seven.

The Five

It is to be seen that JFC's work on the Erment model and on the Isola Tiberina prow opens the possibility of two different designs for the five (p. 259). The first was pursued (by Dionysios of Syracuse) on the basis of the three and taken further at Syracuse to produce the six which was later adopted by the Romans as a consular flagship. It appears in the Macedonian coinage (**10** and **16**) and notably as a Roman six in the Isola Tiberina prow (**67**). The second design of a five was initiated in Phoenicia, reached Carthage through their close ties with Tyre, and was copied by the Romans from a captured Carthaginian cataphract. It appears first in the Nineveh warship (**1b**), then in the Erment model and then in the frequent portraits of Roman and Carthaginian warships exhibiting the deep oar panel with three levels of oars quincunx fashion.

Fives, then, with 2 × 5 men to the room (at three levels) and five files of oarsmen each side, employed double manning at two of the three levels, single manning at one. An arrangement with not more than two men to each oar is implied by Polybios's description (p. 353) of the training of crews for fives on dry land with a long stroke and seated oarsmen. The Roman five was cataphract and rated as one of the larger ships.

A clue to one dimension of the fourth century five is provided by the account of the measurements of Hephaistion's tomb. Arrian (7.14.8) says that Alexander ordered a tomb to be made ready for Hephaistion at Babylon at a cost of 10,000 talents. Diodoros (17.115.1–5) gives the details which include that 'gilded prows of fives entirely filled up the [outside of the] foundation course (*κρηπίς*) being 240 in number'. He also says that the structure was four-sided and that each side was a stade (196 m on the basis of a cubit of 0.490 m) in length. Each prow thus measured 3,26 m. The prows built into Augustus's campsite memorial at Aktion (p. 311) are shown by the remaining traces to have been measured from *ἐπωτίς* to *ἐπωτίς*. If the prows on Hephaistion's tomb had been measured similarly that dimension of a five was 3.26 m, only 4 cm broader than, and not inconsistent with, a similar measurement of *Olympias*.

In Lucan's account of the battle off Massalia fives are said 'to dip more oars in the water' than the (threes and) fours mentioned by him just before. Fortunately Polybios (1.26.7) gives the number of oarsmen in the fives of the Roman fleet at Eknomos as 300. This is an average of 30 oarsmen a file in each of the 5 files on each side and thus 3 × 30 = 90 oars a side, 180 in all, more than the 44 oars a side, 88 in all (crew of 176) of the Athenian four and more than the 170 of the three).

A five with an oarcrew of 400 is said by Pliny (*NH* 32.1.4) to have carried Caligula. This would give files averaging 40 and oars numbering 240. She seems an improbable ship in point of length (with a rowing area of nearly 40 m), but since the point of the story Pliny is telling depends on the large number of oarsmen it is likely that the mistake in transmission lies rather in the type than in the number of oarsmen. A six with altogether 12 files of an average of 33 oarsmen each and 198 oars is a more practical proposition and more likely.

Polybios (p. 55) regarded it as self-evident that the five was superior as a warship to the three. Livy's account of the engagement in the Straits of Gibraltar involving the two types (p. 64) comes to the same conclusion. The five's greater mass would have caused her to respond more slowly to surface water-turbulence than the three. When fives were *expediti* stripped for action (p. 70, 89) they would be reasonably fast but not as fast as threes similarly stripped. On one occasion (p. 50) it is said that Roman fives were heavier and more difficult to turn than the Carthaginian fives which were better built.

The Six

Xenagoras[4] attributed the invention of the six to the Syracusans. It is a short step from the five to the six by extending double-manning from two to three levels and it is likely that Dionysios I, rather than his son, had taken it before the end of his reign in 367. Antigonos had fives, nines and tens in his fleet, but no sixes. Ten sixes appear in Demetrios's fleet at Cypriot Salamis in 306 to outface Ptolemy I Soter's threes and fours. There were sixes also in the invasion fleet which Agathokles collected in Syracuse shortly before his death (in 289). Ptolemy Philadelphos (283–246) built five sixes, and many larger ships, in competition with his rivals.

Rome's African invasion fleet in the first Punic war was led at Eknomos (p. 46) by the consuls each on board a six. Scipio used a six in the Sicilian fleet on a diplomatic mission to the Locrians (p. 65). Philip's Grand Fleet at the battle of Chios contained at least one six, which was lost (p. 84), among the larger ships. When Antiochos decided that he needed a fleet of big ships, and sent Hannibal to Syria to build one, Hannibal came back with four sixes (p. 102) and three sevens which fought at Side (190 BC) and some of them again shortly afterwards at Myonnesos.

The Isola Tiberina monument of a warship set up in the first half of the 1st century BC to celebrate Rome's command of the sea can be reconstructed as a six, and is then likely to represent one. It stands 1.4 ft higher than the reconstructed five.

When Cato sold up the treasure of Ptolemy XII in Cyprus in 56 he brought the proceeds back to Rome in the 'royal six' (Plutarch *Cato Minor* 39). Brutus's flagship at Massalia was a six (p. 129), and when Sextus Pompeius, whose ships were normally of the smaller kind, came to meet Octavian and Antony in 39 BC near Puteoli it was in a 'splendid six' (p. 149). At Aktion there were sixes on both sides. In Octavian's fleet they were the largest, in Antony's the smallest warships (p. 163). The six then was a not uncommon, and certainly a prestigious, if unwieldy, ship in the fleets of the Hellenistic centuries.

The Oarsystem

There is one possible clue in literature to the detail of the six. Diodoros (20.112.4) says that Pleistarchos, sent by Kassandros with a fleet to support Lysimachos in 302, lost most of his ships and was himself wrecked in his flagship, a six, carrying not less than 500 men. He would have had troops on board, and if they were as many as 90–100 with a *ὑπηρεσία* of 50–40 in a fleet carrying military aid, the twelve files would have contained 30 oarsmen each on average (360 oarsmen + 140 troops and *ὑπηρεσία*). This compares with a three's 30 *ὑπηρεσία* and a maximum of 40 decksoldiers and a five's 300 oarsmen with [40] *ὑπηρεσία* and [80] decksoldiers = 120 *ἐπιβάται*, carried in similar circumstances.

The Romans who clearly regarded the five and the four as the ships in which they felt happy to fight their kind of naval war, included the six in this preference as a conspicuous type of ship suitable for the fleet commander in battle and for prestigious occasions. This fact says a good deal about the qualities of the six. The Romans went no further down this road.

The six, which embodied the full development of double manning, was a glorified five (possibly, if the Pozzuoli relief ship **39a** is a six, with a *πάροδος* screening the oarports); and that, the Romans appear to have thought very sensibly, was enough for them. Triple and quadruple oarmanning present new problems which were alien to the Phoenician type of five which they had copied from the Carthaginians (p. 43). It is interesting that the cautious Ptolemy I Soter and the Rhodians, both of whom did not, apparently, venture into sixes, seem to have shared the Roman distrust of the bigger ships. The Romans and Rhodians may also have doubted their cost effectiveness.

The Seven

Pliny quotes an unknown Mnesigeiton as attributing to Alexander the building of sevens to tens (Preface xii). Curtius gives a detailed account (10.1.17–18) of Alexander's plan to circumnavigate Arabia and Africa, returning through the Pillars of Herakles. For this voyage he ordered a fleet of 700 sevens to be built at Thapsakos and taken down the river to Babylon (p. 12). The addition of a third oarsman to one of the *a scaloccio* pairs of the six would have been no great innovation (p. 68).

The ships above threes in Antigonos's fleet of 315/4 BC were mostly the 90 fours. He had ten fives and from there, taking triple- and quadruple-manning in his stride, went up to three nines and ten tens. But his son Demetrios included seven Phoenician sevens in his fleet at Cypriot Salamis (p. 27) and later Ptolemy Philadelphos had thirty-six sevens in his Grand Fleet (p. 37). They seem to have been a popular and useful type.

Pyrrhos's flagship in his crossing to Tarentum from Epeiros in 280 BC was probably a seven, which proved to have better sea-keeping qualities than the smaller ships. A seven which had belonged to Pyrrhos was the Carthaginian flagship twenty years later at the first battle of Mylai. Philip at the battle of Chios had at least one seven, since one was put out of action; and Antiochos later had three sevens in the fleet Hannibal built for him in Syria.

Silius Italicus (14.384–88), writing in the 1st century AD about a battle between the Romans and Carthaginians in the 2nd Punic war (212 BC) speaks of a ship which stood higher as she moved, frightening to see, among the ships around her. No larger ship than she had left the Carthaginian shipyards. 'In fact she smote the sea with her oars having an oarcrew 400 strong (*nam quater haec centum numeroso remige pontum pulsabat tonsis*). Torr (1894 p. 13) takes the ship to have 400 oarsmen (J. D. Duff in the Loeb translation gives her 400 oars which is impossible). Such a ship if a seven with three levels of oars and files of 29–28 oarsmen would have had an oarcrew of just about 400 ($2 \times 7 \times 28\frac{1}{2} = 399$). More precisely if (like the three) she had 85 oars a side at three levels, but with three men to an oar at the one of the three levels which had 29 men to the file and two at the other two levels, which each had 28 men to the file, the oarsmen would have numbered 398,

Silius was aware of the seven captured from the Carthaginians at the battle of Mylai. Her frightening height, like the height of Brutus's six at Massalia, would have been produced by the towers she was able to carry.

The Eight

The first mention of an eight is (Polybios 16.3.2) at the beginning of the first battle of Chios when Attalos began the action by ramming an eight below the waterline and swamping her, 'although the decksoldiers continued the fight for a long time'. Though immobilised, she must have floated, swamped, with her deck above water.[5] The Grand Fleets of Antigonos and Ptolemy Philadelphos had no eights, though the former had nines and the latter sevens and nines. Antony was said by Plutarch (*Antony* 61) to have had many eights in the fleet he assembled at Ephesos at the beginning of the Aktion campaign.

One eight belonging to Lysimachos (p. 36) and named *Leontophoros* was famous. There is fortunately in existence to give some information about her a fragment of Memnon, the historian of Herakleia, where *Leontophoros* was built. He wrote in the time of Hadrian (*FGrH* no. 434.8.5 Vol. III B p. 344). The fragment gives a description of the ship: '(There was) one eight, which was called *Leontophoros*, remarkable for her size and beauty. In this ship while there were a hundred men rowing each file so that there were eight hundred men from each side (*μέρος*), from both sides there were one thousand six hundred oarsmen. Those who fought from the deck were one thousand two hundred. And there were two helmsmen'.

Leontophoros

This ship, which must have owed her name to her *παράσημον*, is said to be remarkable for her size. Since the number of men in each fore-and-aft file is given by Memnon, the most striking thing about the ship at first sight is the length of the hull which can be estimated from the calculable length of the rowing area. On the basis of a 0.490 m cubit the *interscalmium* or oarsman's room is 0.980 m, and the length of the rowing area 98 m. The overall length of the ship was accordingly about 110 m, 10 m less than three times the length of a three built on the basis of a similar *interscalmium*.

It was the number of oarsmen in each file which, not surprisingly, made *Leontophoros* so remarkable. A five, with an oarcrew of 300 and 120 *ὑπηρεσία* and decksoldiers (in an invasion fleet), and a six, with a crew of 500 including, say, 140 *ὑπηρεσία* and decksoldiers, would both have had files of about 30, but would have had a beam which by comparison with the long thin three was disproportionately large.

It seems that Lysimachos constructed a ship in which the broad beam, resulting from eight files a side, was answered by a corresponding length, thus producing a ship with the lines of a three and files with more than three times the usual number of men in them. A probable distribution of the files (cf. the five) would have been by triple-manning the zygian and thalamian oars and double manning the thranite oars.

In spite of her success in battle, *Leontophoros* was an experiment which, it seems, was not repeated, but the beauty of Lysimachos's ship was remembered.

A single hull of this length would require a certain breadth for stability and great structural strength. Calculation of this necessary breadth may raise the possibility that she had two (or even one) level of oars with four (or eight) men to each oar. The problem is one which must be left to the naval architect to solve with the name (implying eight files a side) and the fore-and-aft file of 100 men (implying a length of 110 m) as the only firm parameters.

Casson (*SSAW* 112–115) has suggested that the ship, like Ptolemy Philopator's monstrous forty, had two hulls, and for that reason, like the forty, two helmsmen. This possibility must be considered. If a single-hulled ship satisfying Memnon's description turns out to be a practical proposition, that would be preferable to the catamaran hypothesis. The example of the forty is not encouraging. It is further difficult to imagine a catamaran warship of that size meeting the requirements of beauty and high performance which Memnon's description of *Leontophoros* sets. On the other hand an oared warship with a single hull nearly three times as long as *Olympias* and with 4.7 times more power might be both beautiful and formidable. Steering a ship of such great length might well require a man at each tiller.

The Nine

There were three nines in Antigonos's Grand Fleet in 315/4 but none in Demetrios's fleet at Cypriot Salamis. Agathokles must have built one at Syracuse since Pyrrhos took over a 'royal nine' there in 278. Ptolemy Philadelphos's fleet contained thirty nines. Philip had at least one at Chios. At Aktion Florus says that Antony's fleet ranged from sixes to nines, but Plutarch speaks of him having earlier at Ephesos only eights and tens.

In the context of the ship built for the Panathenaic procession and kept 'near the hill of Ares' [in Attica], which naturally enough was not particularly large, Pausanias (1.29.1) says that he knows no one who has beaten the vessel in Delos which 'from the deck downwards has nine oarsmen'. If this vessel (*πλοῖον*) is, as the context implies, a vessel carried in procession, it can hardly be a nine as has been believed, rather than a boat with nine oarsmen a side at one level.

No details of nines are known. One of these may be represented in (**25**: 2nd-1st century BC) and another in some detail in the ship on the Praeneste relief (**29**: second half of the 1st century BC). Both show systems of two levels of massive oars.

The Ten

An unknown writer Mnesigeiton attributed the building of warships up to tens to Alexander (Preface xii).

The ten tens in Antigonos's fleet were not taken by Demetrios to Cyprus, and the list of Ptolemy Philadelphos's fleet does not include tens. But Philip's flagship at Chios was a ten and there were many tens in the fleet Antony assembled at Ephesos. As in the case of nines there is no detailed description of them, and their oarsystem is likely to have consisted like the nine of two levels of oars, each oar being manned in the case of the ten by a gang of five oarsmen.

From the Eleven to the Forty

The importance of deck height is constantly emphasised in the accounts of sea battles and the speeches attending them, up to and including Aktion. This importance is corroborated by the use of towers, sometimes collapsible, sometimes of many stories (*tabulae*) on the bigger ships. It seems therefore likely that the ships up to tens took their oarlevels (and hence decks) to the highest practicable height, achieved apparently in the three- or two-level tens which were the highest denomination taken into battle (Tarn: 1905 p. 201 n.101).

In the ships bigger than tens, which were undoubtedly built, the naval architects were likely to have continued to provide the stable platform of ships of two levels with large gangs of oarsmen on each oar, building not so much warships as sea fortresses. The mention of thranite oars however in the detailed description of the Forty of Ptolemy Philopator (221–204 BC) may indicate that this ship, hardly a viable proposition as a warship, was built with the maximum three levels for its forty files of oars on each side of her catamaran hull.

Demetrios's conquest of Cyprus enabled him to get the long timbers needed to build an eleven (Theophrastos *Hist.Plant.* 5.8.1); and in 301 BC after the death of his father the Athenians allowed him to take away from Peiraieus his fleet which included a thirteen. He used her (or a sister ship) later for a diplomatic mission (Plutarch *Demetrios* 32.2) to Seleukos and entertained him on board.

Plutarch also speaks of Demetrios building a great fleet of 500 ships which included fourteens and fifteens and (*Demetrios* 20.4) showing them off to his enemy Lysimachos. 'His enemies would stand amazed as they saw sixteens and fifteens passing along the coast'. Antigonos Gonatas took over thirteens, fifteens and sixteens from him (p. 36). These types at any rate seem to have appeared practical. Ptolemy Philadelphos included 14 elevens, two twelves, four thirteens, one twenty and two thirties in his fleet (p. 37). But there is no extant description of their detail, as there is of the later monstrous forty.

Philip V of Macedon had a sixteen which he was allowed to retain by the terms of peace with Rome (p. 90) when all his other cataphracts were surrendered: Livy (33.30) describes it as 'of almost unmanageable size' (*inhabilis prope magnitudinis*). Yet the ship was brought back to Rome in 167 to grace the triumph of Aemilius Paulus after his defeat of Perseus, Philip's son. The consul (Plutarch *Aemilius Paulus* 30.2) was rowed up the Tiber in her 'the populace keeping up with the splashing oars as they (the oars) slowly took the ship along'. It appears to have been kept in a special shipshed, in which later the 300 hostages sent from Carthage at the beginning of the third Punic war were accommodated (p. 113). Livy's comment, and the absence of warships bigger than tens from naval engagements, are sufficient to indicate that they became progressively less manageable as the denomination increased up to the forty, of which through the good offices of Athenaios Kallixeinos's detailed description has survived.

The Forty of Ptolemy III Philopator 221–204 BC

After speaking of Ptolemy Philadelphos's outlays on the navy and, briefly, on books, libraries and the Museum, Athenaios continues (5.203 e):

'Since we have spoken about the construction of ships, let us mention (for it is worth hearing) the ships built by king Philopator concerning which the same Kallixeinos gives an account in the first book *About Alexandria* as follows: (Jacoby *FGrH* III C (1), No. 627):

'Philopator built the forty with a length of 280 cubits, (a beam of) 38 cubits from side gangway (*πάροδος*) to side gangway and a height of 48 cubits to the (top of the) stem post. From the stern ornaments to the part of the ship [under] the sea (the vertical distance) is 53 cubits. The ship has four rudders of 30 cubits (long), the largest thranite oars of 38 cubits, [which] through having lead inserted in the handles (*ἐγχειρίδια*) and becoming thus heavy inboard were easy to handle in use.'

'The ship had been constructed with two sterns and two bows and had seven rams, one leading and the rest subsidiary, some fitted on the eartimbers (ἐποτίδες). The ship took twelve undergirders (ὑποζώματα), each of six hundred cubits'. [Plutarch (*Demetrios* 43 4–5) confirms the length and height to the stem post.]

The ship was extremely well-proportioned. The rest of the ship's furniture was amazing. It had (figures of) animals of no less than 12 cubits (?long) at the bow (cf. **29** and **33**: an Egyptian characteristic) and stern; and every area of the ship was decorated with wax (i.e. encaustic) painting. The whole area of the oars (τὸ ἔγκωπον) as far as the keel (on the inside of the hull) was wreathed about with ivy-leaf and thyrsus decoration[6]. There was a large equipment of ropes. It filled [all] the ship's space where it was needed.

'When the trials took place, the ship took on board more than 4,000 oarsmen, for the services under the helmsman (ὑπηρεσία) four hundred men and on to the deck 150 less than three thousand soldiers. And separate under the thwarts there was another crowd of men and a large supply of provisions.'[7]

'The ship was launched in the first place from a cradle, which they say was constructed with the timber of fifty fives. She was drawn down with shouting and trumpets. After that the launching was devised by a man from Phoenicia. He prepared, as long as the ship, a ditch, which he dug near the harbour. He built the foundations of this ditch with hard stone to a depth of five cubits, and thrust close together across these foundations over the ditch's breadth cross logs which left a space four cubits deep (on top of the logs). And making an inlet from the sea, he filled with sea water the whole excavated space into which he easily led the ship with the help of bystanders. Then they stopped up the original opening (of the channel from the sea) and drained away the water with pumps. When this had been done, the ship settled safely on to the aforementioned logs.'

The quotation from Kallixeinos continues with an account of Ptolemy Philopator's river craft called a cabin-ship (θαλαμηγός), with which we need not be concerned.

The highly circumstantial account of the launching of the forty adds to the credibility of Kallixeinos's detailed description of the ship herself, which must certainly be taken at its face value. Athenaios is a reliable source, and Kallixeinos was a Rhodian who wrote in Alexandria at the end of the 3rd century BC during the reign of Ptolemy Philopator. Not only had he the opportunity of seeing the ship, but, as a Rhodian, he would have understood the practical details which he gives. The fact is that of this monstrous warship we have a more detailed and reliable description than we have of any other, and the description is well authenticated. If we can make sense of it, sense may be made of the whole range of hardly less monstrous warships produced by the naval competition of the Hellenistic kings from the *Leontophoros* to the thirty.

The dimensions may be set out as follows: A = 532.5 mm, the greater, B = 462.5, the smaller Ptolemaic cubit:

Length	280 cubits:	A: = 149.1 m		B =129.5 m.
Breadth btwn πάροδοι	38 cubits	= 20.235 m	=	17.575 m
Height (bow)	48 cubits	= 25.56 m	=	22.2 m
(stern)	53 cubits	= 28.22 m	=	24.5 m
4 Rudders	30 cubits	= 15.975 m	=	13.875 m
Thranite oars	38 cubits	= 20.235 m	=	17.575 m (longest)
Hypozoma	600 cubits	= 319.5 m	=	277.5 m

The ship's company is given as follows:

Oarsmen	4,000 +
ὑπηρεσία	400
ἐπιβάται	2,850
Stewards	a large number (πλῆθος)
Total naval personnel:	7,250

The implications of these figures may be considered (adopting the lesser Ptolemaic cubit of 0.4625 m):

1. The most remarkable, and novel, feature of the forty is that she had two prows, two sterns and four rudders, from which it may be safely assumed that she had two hulls. Although such construction is unprecedented, at the siege of Tyre (p. 9) two fours were used joined together as a platform for siege engines. (Joining two large hulls together by a common deck on which a huge cargo is piled is a common practice seen on the Nile in modern times.)

2. The breadth of the ship is given as from πάροδος to πάροδος. The πάροδος is well illustrated in the

Roman cataphract warship which appears in the Praeneste relief (**29**) It is a side gangway, on top of the ventilation course and oarbox, for use in combat by decksoldiers climbing over the bulwark to board an enemy ship.

The order in which the initial details are given is significant, first overall length, then breadth, then height at stem and stern, then length of thranite oars, then length of rudders, and only then the fact that she had two prows and two sterns. The breadth must then be the overall breadth, not the breadth of the individual hulls. There are then also only two *πάροδοι*, one on the port side of one hull and one on the starboard side of the other. This conclusion removes the possibility, which has been suggested, that oars were worked in between the two hulls, about which in any case there would be severe structural and operational difficulties.[8]

The ratio of overall breadth to overall length is 1:8.26 which compares with the ratio for a three of about 1:7. The breadth to length ratio of each individual hull is 1:16.5. Such a ratio would seem to preclude anything but close integration of the two hulls. The inner walls of the two hulls could then have a common topwale at an appropriate height. But the convergence of the walls of each hull would have resulted in the separation and divergence of the inner topwales towards bow and stern. The general shape and appearance of the forty now becomes clearer.

3. The four rudders may be assumed to have been rigged two to each hull, one on each side. At the stern hulls would have been somewhat less than the maximum breadth of 7.5 m. allowing space in which the inner rudders could function but broad enough to make it necessary for there to be two helmsmen at least, one for each pair of rudders in each hull. And this doubling (at least) of helmsmen would also have been required by the length of each rudder (13 m) and corresponding weight, too much for one helmsman if all four were 'ganged' with a single tiller.

4. The twelve *ὑποζώματα* carried by the forty were six for each hull. Their function in reducing the tendency of a long narrow hull to hog is now well understood (see *AT* 170–2, 220–1). Their given length 277.5 m is appropriately somewhat more than twice the length of each hull. The number carried compares with the four routinely allotted to each three in the Naval Inventories (six for a long voyage: *AT* p. 170).

5. A clue to the main problem presented by the forty, her oarsystem, is provided by the entry for the thranite oars. The terms in which it is couched are: '(the ship had) thranite oars of thirty eight cubits, the largest...'. This means that the thranite oars, of thirty-eight cubits, were the largest oars, not that the largest of the thranite oars were of thirty-eight cubits, which would have been phrased differently (i.e. of the thranite oars the largest...). The principle of the three's oarsystem was that all the oars were of the same length, that appropriate to an average oarsman, (except necessarily at bow and stern). It appears, not surprisingly, that in the forty this principle was abandoned, as it was likely to have been in the types above the five.

The use of the term thranite implies that there were in the forty also at least one, and there is no reason why there should not have been both, of the two categories of *τριηρῖται* beside the thranite. In the account of the ship's company, after the oarcrew, *ὑπηρεσία*, and decksoldiers, Kallixeinos adds: 'and, apart, the ship took on board under the *ζύγια* another lot of men and no small supply of victuals'. *Ζύγια* is to be taken as an alternative form of the word *ζυγά* which was used by Homer for the seats of oarsmen and ultimately contributed to the name of the middle file of oars in the three and of the men who rowed them, the *ζύγιοι*. In the Odyssey cargo is stowed under the *ζυγά*; and later *θάλαμος* came to be the name for this space and *θαλαμιός* the name for the oarsmen who came to row there. In the forty it seems that stewards and victuals would compete with oarsmen for this area, but the word, 'apart' may explain how it was shared, the oarsmen taking the amidships sections while the stewards etc occupied the not inconsiderable space fore and aft left vacant. There is some indication that in other oared warships there was a cabin under the deck in the stern (*AT* p. 131) and in the bow as well. There is therefore no reason why there should not have been three levels of oarsmen in the forty.

The length of the ship is 280 cubits (129.5 m), and if she is classified as a forty on the same principle as the classification of the oared warships of other denominations, then forty fore-and-aft files of oarsmen must be accommodated on each side of the ship (in this case forty in each hull). Since twenty files of oarsmen overall had already been accommodated in Ptolemy Philadelphos's twenties, it would not seem impossible to accommodate twice that number in two hulls as large as the twenties placed side by side. Ellen Rice (1983 p. 143) ingeniously suggests that the forty could be so called 'because it is a catamaran composed of two twenties'. This would seem only to solve the problem of the oarsystem if oars can be worked between the hulls, and that is very difficult to accept on structural grounds as well as for reasons of oarsmanship.

Kallixeinos says that 4,000 oarsmen were taken on board for the trials. Ellen Rice has suggested that for trials a larger number of oarsmen were taken on board than the number needed. This presents a way of reducing the number to be accommodated, but not by many, since the manning table shows that the ship must have been very crowded and the reason in those circumstances for taking extra oarsmen on board does not seem sufficient. In trials the ship would (indeed could) not have gone far from her home port, so that taking spare oarsmen on board would have been unnecessary. If there were forty files a side, the number of men in each file would have been fifty (2 × 40 × 50 = 4000) (which compares with files of about 30 men in the three and 100 in *Leontophoros*). In the three about four fifths of the hull is used for rowing. Taking that proportion for the forty 224 cubits (103.6 metres) would constitute her rowing area, and the room for each 3–level gang of forty oarsmen would have been 4.5 cubits (2.08 m).

Plutarch remarks that the ship moved laboriously. It is hard to believe that the ship so carefullly described by Kallixeinos could have moved at all.

Endnotes

1. Cf. [Aristotle] *De Incessu animalium* 710 a 15 is relevant. 'The flight of bees and wasps is slow and weak *ὥσπερ ἂν οὖν εἰ ὁλκαδικὸν πλοῖον ἐπιχειροίη κώπαις ποιεῖσθαι τὸν πλοῦν.*
2. In the royal fleet of 37 ships *maioris formae* at the battle of Sidé Livy singles out (37.23.5) the three sevens and four sixes for special mention; and at the subsequent battle of Myonnesos (37.30.2) he says that the enemy (i.e. royal) fleet of 89 ships has three sixes and two sevens *maximae formae*.
3. The Greek word *βραχύς* can mean 'short', 'small', 'low' (as a wall in Thukydides 7.29.), or 'few'. Here the last is ruled out since individual ships are described.
4. Xenagoras was a Greek historian writing in the latter half of the 2nd century BC. See Preface xii.
5. Since this eight and another in the same battle were rammed prow-to-prow by Attalos's ships and holed below the waterline, it has been concluded (p. 364) that they were built with their rams above the waterline (*ἀνάστειροι*) as were the bigger ships from six upwards.
6. Such decoration 'as far as the keel' would have seriously impeded the ship if it was on the outer wetted surface of the hull. The words indicate that *τὸ ἔγκωπον* was regarded as extending to the ship's bottom; so that the separate area under the the thwarts which is mentioned in the next paragraph as accommodation for 'a crowd of men and a large supply of provisions' must have been at bow and stern forward and aft of the rowing area.
7. This apparently vertical separation implies a lower deck. Plutarch (*Demetrius* 42.4) gives the same number of men in the *ὑπηρεσία* and 'nearly three thousand hoplites'.
8. (Livy 24.34.6) Marcellus placed high towers and engines for battering walls on 'pairs of fives with the inner oars removed so that the sides of the ships were brought together and the ships propelled by the outer oarsystem (*ordine*) as if they were a single ship' (*iunctae aliae binae quinqueremes demptis interioribus remis ut latus lateri adplicaretur cum exteriore ordine remorum velut una navis agerentur, turres contabulatas machinamentaque alia quatiendis muris portabant*). The parallel with the forty is remarkable.

7

RECONSTRUCTING THE SHIPS

INTRODUCTION

A naval architect attempting to reconstruct ancient Mediterranean warships is offered scanty literary and iconographical evidence on which to draw. It is, however, generally accepted that these ships were relatively fast for oared vessels, and when the demands of the laws of physics and our present knowledge of human ergonomics are brought to bear, the room for choice in features of their design affecting performance under oar is greatly narrowed. In many cases main hull dimensions, stability, oar power, lengths, gearing and rig, and longitudinal hull structure can be determined within quite close limits by such considerations.

It might be thought that the galleys of the Middle Ages and the Renaissance would point the way to their ancient predecessors, particularly those which employed the same oarsystems. Many students have tried that path back to the earlier ships, but either have met with little success or have returned with misleading conclusions. While more is known about those later galleys and particularly those of Venice and France (Zysberg and Burlet: 1986, Rodgers: 1940, Lane: 1934, Guilmartin: 1974 and Alertz: 1991), they were not as fast as the ancient types. Owing to the very different construction of their hulls, which were also decked, their oarcrews could not be inside the hull but were entirely above it and necessarily on one level. Oars were consequently longer than in the ancient warships (except possibly in polyremes of the higher, and slower, denominations), stroke rates were slower and the 'stand-and-sit' method of rowing was necessary. Hulls were heavier and speeds lower. The later galleys provide therefore some but only limited help.

The Three – The Archetype

The reconstructions presented in this chapter owe much to the experience gained in designing, building and then testing the recent reconstruction of a Greek τριήρης (a three) of the 5th–4th cent. BC. That experience served to confirm with little residual doubt that the cumulative evidence about the Athenian three of that time (Morrison and Williams: 1968 repr. 1995 = *GOS*, Morrison and Coates: 1986 = *AT*), when supplemented by the physical solutions of its attested performance under oar, had become sufficient to define its design (**51** to **54**) in its essentials. The results of the sea trials (Coates, Platis and Shaw: 1990, Shaw: 1993) of *Olympias*, as the reconstruction has been named, did however reveal some shortcomings in speed under oar. The causes of these, also identified during the trials, have been rectified in the adjusted design shown in **55** and **56**. The derivation of the oarsystem and midship structure is described in detail in Appendix A to this chapter to give an example of how the oarsystems of the following reconstructions have been recreated in order to illustrate the interactive elements which make up oarsystems and how these in the reconstructions which follow have been built up.

The three was the first type of oared warship to have files of up to 30 or so oarsmen on three levels and it was the archetype for the polyremes developed from it. Like its successors, it exploited the structurally efficient but labour-intensive ancient Mediterranean method of hull construction to its limits, and its hull was as slender as adequate stability permitted. Hull planking was joined together positively edge to edge by large numbers of closely spaced hard wood tenons fitted tightly into

51 Trieres Olympias – *General view*

52 Trieres Olympias – *Oars at speed*

53 Trieres Olympias – *Part profile for comparison with* ***ix(a)***

individual mortices in plank edges giving the planking the cohesion and shear stiffness of a true shell in the modern engineering sense. The method of joining planks of timber together side-by-side, widely used by carpenters in the ancient world, enabled longer hulls to be built capable of withstanding the bending and shearing forces to which they were subjected: the development of the 50–oared single-level, 35 metre long, pentecontor from its 30–oared predecessor probably depended upon the adoption of tenons in place of sewing to hold the planks together as had been the earlier practice (*SSAW* p. 9–10) which had already been in use in merchant ships, if not in warships, for some time. Long timbers also were required to build threes (Meiggs: 1983) to prevent the greatest of the tensile hogging stresses in the topwales of their hulls, owing to bending in the waves, from being borne by scarfed joints in tension. These stresses were also reduced by the use of prestressing tendons (*ὑποζώματα*), heavy ropes stretched from bow to stern just under the hull beams and kept tight. The hulls, typically 13 times as long as they were deep, may thus have been some of the first examples of pre-stressed beams. Calculations indicate that they were stressed to the practical limit.

The sea trials of *Olympias* demonstrated the importance of an *interscalmium* (the oarsman's 'room') of adequate length to allow the full length of oarstroke and therefore power available from oarsmen working on fixed seats to be developed in favourable sea conditions. Any greater length than that would on the other hand cause the ship to be unnecessarily long, adding to hull wetted area and therefore to its resistance, without enabling the oarsmen to produce any more power. In *Olympias* the *interscalmium* has the length of two cubits of 0.444 metres, understood from the evidence extant at the time of her design and building to be the length of an Attic cubit. More recent metrological finds (Morrison: 1991) have shown that the cubit in use in Peiraios and Salamis in the 5th–4th cent. BC was more likely to have been 0.490 m in length. An *interscalmium* of 0.98 m has therefore been adopted for all the reconstructions which follow. On trial, that *interscalmium* was clearly shown to be too short

54 Trieres Olympias – *Oarcrew interior*

and in consequence about 70% of full sprint oar-power (giving 90% full sprint speed) was realised.

The three and its reconstruction, *Olympias*, have provided a substantial basis upon which to reconstruct other types of ship in a number of important respects, namely hull form and construction, strength and stability, as well as oar power and speed. The trials demonstrated in particular the need for oars to be the right length, gearing and weight if high powers and stroke rates are to be reached when rowing on fixed seats. They showed beyond all doubt that all those matters are critical to the high speeds attested as having been attained by some types of ancient warships and which it may with some confidence be inferred was attained to little less degree by the others. Few reconstructors have paid sufficient attention to oarsystems, and it is probably true to say that none of their past proposals could, if built, have approached authentically required speeds under oar.

The design and mechanics of one-man oars are discussed by Shaw in Appendix B to this chapter, and that discussion has been extended by him to the operation of two-man oars upon which the effective propulsion of the first polyremes so largely depends. The use of two-man oars, particularly at high powers and speeds, is buried in the past. They necessarily played no part in the trials of *Olympias* and there are no known surviving records on this matter. The medieval galleys are of little help and no experiments have yet been made to recover the parameters of their optimum use which, by practice, may be assumed to have been established in polyremes. Shaw's analysis has therefore had to be taken as a basis for deciding the proportions of two-man oars in the following reconstructions of polyremes, in which the principal aim has been to keep their length to the minimum. It is very likely that multi-manned oars were, as shown in ships identified as polyremes (e.g. **19**, **29**), monoxylous and therefore with narrower blades than one-man oars whose blades would be more effective if wider owing to the wider sweep of their stroke in the water. The blades of one-man oars (e.g. the detached oar in **vi**, and oars in *AT* fig. 47) were therefore likely in normal conditions to have been made separately and then attached to the shaft.

On a number of other aspects of the warships of the period, however, *Olympias* has not been able to contribute to our understanding. The *ὑποζώματα* remain enigmas, particularly as regards tightening them (Shaw: 1993): in *Olympias* a modern equivalent had to be used. Operationally, while the trials have yielded some manoeuvering data, practical tactics have not yet been established by using those data in simulating manoeuvres by computer. Fleet manoeuvres and tactics have not in consequence yet been studied with the benefit of an experimental basis, nor has the use of catapults and their various types of missiles as fleets approached for battle, their ranges, accuracy and penetrating power and effectiveness, nor techniques of ramming or grappling an enemy, of laying alongside for boarding, nor the detailed tactics and weapons for the boarding itself. These are all matters on which the outcome of a battle could depend. Such evidence for them as the ancient historians have provided has been given in Chapters 1–4 and discussed in Chapter 8. It requires reexamination in the light of the reconstructed ships.

Oared ships' routine on passage is also largely unknown apart from the knowledge that the crew normally went ashore for a midday meal and at night. Nearly all aspects of logistics remain conjectural. The maximum allowed-for rate of consumption of water, the main and most vital consumable on board an oared ship (p. 286 and 326–7), may be assumed to have been about on the same scale per head as in the later French galleys (Burlet, Carrière, Zysberg: 1986), about 7 litres per man per day. It was probably carried in large *πίθοι*, but how it was replenished and its consumption managed we do not know. What stores and food were carried on board, embarkation drill, defence of the ship and rules for the crew ashore while the ship was moored stern to a beach, what personal gear and weapons were allowed on board, how oars were shipped and the handling of the sailing rig, about these matters and many more necessary for running a ship, there are numerous disconnected hints from time to time from the ancient historians but little or no systematic knowledge. The following reconstructions should be seen in that context and as no more than attempts to deduce what is possible from such ancient evidence as is now available with assistance from the reliable and unchanging natural laws in aiming to derive adequately seaworthy designs likely to be capable, if built and tested at sea, of approaching the performance of their originals.

Evidence from earlier chapters affecting the design of the types of warship considered or reconstructed is collected for each type in Appendix C of this chapter for ready reference. In Appendix D are tabulated the main particulars of the ten types and varieties of ship types of which a reconstruction is presented below.

After a brief discussion of the larger polyremes, the detailed evidence of Murray and Petsas (1989) about the ram sockets of the memorial for the Aktion war is considered. The waterline breadths (BWL) of fives to tens are assessed on that evidence and compared with those of the reconstructions (Appendix E), yielding likely upper and lower limits for that most important dimension in the range of polyreme types that saw battle service. Experiments with multi-manned oars would however be necessary to resolve the differences in these estimates of BWL, which are 1.1 m in the seven reducing to 0.6 m in the five. They arise mainly from the lateral spacing of oarsmen, sitting or standing at multi-manned oars, and second from the necessary breadth to be given to the middle-line gangway in these large ships.

Notes on the Drawings of Reconstructions

The drawings are intended to show reconstructions of ships rather than reconstructions of representations of ships, and apart from purely ornamental features, nothing has been included in them unless a practical purpose has been seen for it. All drawings, except two drawn in perspective, conform to the scales shown in each.

Half of the midship sections are shown with, in most cases, a plan of a short length amidships below it. In the section, oarsmen, their seats and footstretchers, are shown diagrammatically only but to scale. Where oarsmen are canted in plan and therefore not facing directly aft, their seats and bodies in the ship section are placed at the after edge of their seats. Oarsmen are assumed to be 1.73 m in stature, a height 1.5 cm taller than any individuals for whom evidence of their stature has survived from the region and times embracing the period in question (Shaw: 1993), in order that the kind of strong and well-grown individuals, useful in oarcrews but probably bigger than the average in the male population, could be accommodated.

The position of the ὑπόζωμα in ships thought to need one is indicated by two concentric circles under the middle of the hull beams. Expected positions of the loaded ship's centre of gravity (G), and the metacentre (M) are indicated in most cases. The distance by which G is below M is a measure of the ship's stiffness in resisting heeling moments when upright or at more normal angles of heel. The righting moment developed by the ship's weight and buoyancy forces when heeling at an angle φ is GM × the ship's displacement × sinφ.

In the ship sections, oars are shown lying athwartships, and therefore at their true length, in two or three critical positions in that vertical plane, namely,

a. the blade adequately immersed for the pull-stroke in calm water with the ship upright at her loaded waterline (labelled WL)

b. the same when the ship had heeled 3° up on the side of the oar, and

c. the oar raised as far as possible with the loom in contact with a thigh of the oarsman, to clear waves.

In the plans, the arcs swept out by oars during full shallow strokes appropriate in calmer conditions are shown to indicate, in conjunction with their vertical positions shown in the sections, how oars at different levels would mesh with each other. Arcs have been arranged, as far as possible, to minimise the need for blades, particularly if working close to each other vertically, to overtake in the course of a full stroke. The length of a full stoke, achievable in calm or slight seas for full power and measured at the end of the loom (i.e. at the butt) along the chord of the arc is 1.1 m for sitting oarsmen and 1.3 m where they are shown standing. Both lengths are maxima within an *interscalmium* of 0.98 m, a length common to all the reconstructions presented in this chapter.

In the three diagrams by Burlet of the movements of individual oarsmen, the stroke shown is only 0.8 m long at the mid-handle of the only, or the No. 1, man on the oar at the butt end of the loom. The stroke is of the dipping style which has to be employed in rougher water and is suited to longer oars with long narrow blades and strokes having smaller angular arcs. Though normal in latter-day sea-boats, it is less powerful than the longer, flatter, stroke which, however, can only be practised in relatively calm waters. For maximum performance oarcrews must be able to adapt their stroke according to wave conditions. In the roughest water in which it is possible to row effectively at all, the stroke has to be shortened and deepened beyond the proportions shown by Burlet, with further unavoidable loss of effective power. In these three diagrams, a horizontal dashed line shows the level of the mid-handle for the No. 1 man on each oar when the blade is about to enter or has just left the water, assumed calm: it is labelled Blade in Water (BIW) line and it is important for the most effective rowing that this line is within a narrow range of height (0.4 to 0.5 m) above the oarsman's seat.

In the plans, seats are shown in the correct positions relative to the oar stroke: they are canted to the ship as necessary. A rail to carry a foot stretcher similar to that used successfully in *Olympias* is indicated by a line aft of each seat. Oarsmen, seats, foot stretchers, oar arcs, and ship structure are arranged to avoid fouling when oars are worked with up to 3° of heel on the ship or in waves of about 0.8 m in height from trough to crest.

Oars are indicated by a line of the correct projected length and one which represents their axis. They are marked to show the positions of assumed centres of pressure on the blades and the mid-length of the oarsmen's handles. The gearing of an oar is the ratio between the distances of the centre of pressure and the mid-handle from the pivot, the tholepin. All oars are shown being pulled against the oarloop holding the oar to the thole, as the great majority of evidence indicates the practice to have been in the ancient Mediterranean (Shaw: 1993), as it still is there today. The opposite practice has obtained in northern Europe where oars have always been pulled against the thole. The outlines at each end of the full stroke, shown in two internal ship profiles, were obtained photographically from life during the trials of *Olympias*. The positions of oarsmen in other drawings conform to the requirements of those outlines.

In the general arrangement drawings of whole ships, half-plans show the interior with seats and main structure at hull beam level, and the plan of the overhead deck or canopy, or the lines of the hull. Open oarports are shown filled in in black, and of rigging only mast stays and yard braces are shown.

THE RECONSTRUCTIONS

The types of ship reconstructions which are presented below are:

57 A *πεντήρης* (five) developed as simply as possible from the three, as might have been done at Syracuse in the first decade or in Phoenicia in the last half of the 4th cent. BC (Ch. 1).

58 Interpretations of the Erment model (**6**) 350–250 BC:
(i) as a three
(ii) as a five

59 A *τετρήρης* (four) to fit into the Peiraios shipshed (after c. 330/329 BC)

73 A 50–oared *ἡμιολία*, late 4th cent. BC.

74–75 A 120–oared *τριημιολία*, after the monuments of Samothrace (**20**) and Lindos (**21**) c. 190 BC.

Interpretations of the Isola Tiberina monument (**27**), 100–50 BC:
i.(**60**) as a four (rejected)
ii.(**61–66**) as a five
iii.(**67**) the same developed into a six
iv.(**68–69**) the same developed into a seven.

71 A five, after the Nymphaion fresco (**13**), Ostia frieze 1st cent. BC. (**35**), the Pompeii shipshed (**43**) and Aula Isiaca frescoes (**40**) 1st cent. AD.

72 A liburnian, AD 100–200.

The Early Five

In considering the development of the five, the particular improvements or changes in the balance of the characteristics of the three bring sought by the ancient naval commanders and shipwrights should be identified as far as may be possible. The necessarily trial-and-error process of building modified ships while pursuing these changes might then be recreated in the mind, if only tentatively.

The outstanding military difference between the three and five was the number of boarding troops carried, and that may therefore be regarded as the main purpose of the development which amounted to changing the main armament of the ship while keeping the ram as a secondary weapon of opportunity. The invention may have had also a more general purpose. Dionysios's five was said to have been more seaworthy than his threes (see p. 3); and the same quality relative to threes is attributed to the Roman five at the end of the 3rd cent. BC. (p. 64–65).

Fives carried about 70 more troops than threes and that addition, together with a strengthened deck, would have added about 10 tonnes in topweight and raised the centre of gravity of the ship (the three) by 0.4 m, halving its stability. At the same time the moveable weight, the troops, would have been increased eightfold. To make the ship sufficiently stiff to prevent rowing from being impeded by the ship being rocked by unavoidable movements among the numerous troops and others as well as to restore the waterline to a height at which the oarcrew could work, the ship would have to be made wider at the waterline and elsewhere too. Such a modified three, heavier and strengthened, would have been able to carry the troops satisfactorily but she would have been decidedly slower than the original. There would however have been enough extra room inside the wider hull for additional oarcrew to recover some of the loss of speed, not to mention vital windward ability under oar. Increasing the number of files to five would have added another 15 tonnes or so to the total weight of the ship.

The ship would be fighting in denser melées for boarding, besides being slower than threes and decidedly slower to turn. She would therefore be more prone to be rammed by them, so the need to strengthen the hull would have become apparent, calling for more additions to weight and breadth to maintain stability. Ramming, if succeeding in breaching the hull, would trump the five's main armament literally in one blow. That risk must have been evident as soon as the characteristics of the new type had become apparent. The protective wale at the waterline and very likely the framing and stringers behind it inside the hull would have been strengthened to reduce, at least, the proportion of ramming attacks likely to be successful. In (**57**) the waterline wale has therefore been enlarged and in the five of (**61**) where the ship's section exactly follows the evidence upon which it is drawn, that wale is heavier still.

Another consequence of fighting battles by boarding would have been the need for more protection for the oarcrew, so the development of boxing-in would have soon started, adding a little more weight. A heavy screen, which might have been of wooden louvres, and a grating over the (midship) gangway have been included in (**57**). In boarding battles oarcrews must have been in danger not only from missiles but also from enemy boarders fighting on and no doubt occasionally within their ship, as well as from arrows and spear thrusts from troops in enemy ships which could be close and partly alongside. In the threes of the 5th century oarcrews were protected in battle first by the light wooden canopy over them and second by hair sidescreens (see *GOS* p. 302 and General Index) let down from the canopy and secured to the outrigger. Hair sidescreens could well have given sufficient protection against missiles hand-thrown or shot by bow from ranges common in the necessarily more open formations and melées of ship-ramming battles, but they would have been less effective against the later, heavier, catapulted missiles or the closer and more numerous well-armed fighters, no doubt trained and aiming to wound and kill personnel.

Screens, louvres and gratings over openings do however impede the flow of air, and the need to ventilate a sweating mass of men inside a protected ship would never have been forgotten. Experience with the recent reconstruction of the three at sea demonstrated beyond all doubt the importance of ventilation to an oarcrew who, when working hard, would be dripping sweat into the bilges in quite large quantities.

A man working hard breathes out 100 litres of air a minute containing 4–4½% carbon dioxide and his thermal efficiency as a heat engine is about 20%. If therefore he is producing, as a maximum, 400 watts of mechanical work on his oar handle, he will also have to generate about 1.5 kilowatts of waste heat, to be disposed of by evaporating water in the lungs and by sweating at the rate of up to 2 litres per hour. That high rate of working could not however be maintained for more than a minute or so in the enclosed space of a boxed-in ship, whereas a rate of 150 watts, corresponding to a ship speed of about 7.7 knots, could be kept up for more than half an hour.

To ventilate an oarcrew of about 300, each working at about 150 watts on the oar handles, 30 m^3 of air would have to be drawn into and exhausted from the ship's interior every minute to keep the concentration of carbon dioxide down to a practicable upper limit of 2%. But about five times that amount would be needed to carry away the water vapour from the evaporating sweat in the humid conditions often obtaining near water. With the small convective height available about 50 m^2 of effective entry area and a little more exhaust area would be needed. The greatest practicable convective movement or air through the ship would therefore have been sought to prevent conditions becoming impossible for maintaining the faster speeds. The most that could have been done (and by any modern standard it would have been too little) would have been to allow air to enter over the topwale under the sidescreens and to exhaust through the deck by the gratings or louvres over the gangway, which must therefore have been high enough to give walking headroom. Putting the more portable screen, gratings or louvres in place would probably have been part of the drill for clearing a ship for action before battle. Normally it may be expected that, for better oar performance, they would have been kept stowed to keep the vent openings as clear as possible, except when exercising in clearing for action and operating in the action condition.

The net result of the hypothetical development is illustrated in (**57**) in which a ship's midship section is drawn. The weight has risen in total from 45 tonnes of the three to about 90 tonnes, the height of the deck above the waterline by 0.3 m to about 10 Roman feet as attested (p. 163), the breadth on the waterline (BWL) from 3.6 m to 5.1 m to provide the ship with the added stiffness against rolling for which a metacentric height (GM) of about 1.5 m may be estimated to be sufficient (compared with 0.8 m in the three as shown in **55** and **56**). The five was evidently too wide, at an overall breadth of about 6½ m to fit into shipsheds built for threes and its cost compared with a three would have been roughly doubled. The five therefore represented a very considerable development from the three. However, for those who could afford them, it is easy to see that a properly handled frontline core of fives would make a fleet difficult to defeat by an enemy with threes only.

An oarsystem for an early five, as shown in (**57**), calls for no outrigger; but owing to the greater height of the thranite oar, the topwale has had to be raised, with the benefit of added hull depth and therefore of hull bending strength, which would be needed owing to the increased displacement and length of ship compared with the three. The five would be about 10% longer than the three besides being double its weight, so the maximum hull bending moment may be expected to be about 2.2 times that in the three, in which the 'design' bending moment is 90 tonne-metres. In the five, to keep maximum bending stresses to the same level as in the three (about 4.5 Newtons/mm^2) hull planking and other timbers would have to be about 25% thicker than in the three. These stresses in the three, because the three was a fast type but of a mature well-tried design, may be assumed to have been as high as the method of construction, and an acceptable average length of service-life permitted.

It is possible that a somewhat different oarsystem, more like that shown in (**61**), could have been adopted in the first fives. If that was the case, an outrigger would have had to be retained, the zygians with their thole would have been further inboard and their oarport enlarged to allow the necessary oar movement. Such an arrangement may have had the advantages of giving the outer men of each pair a slightly longer stroke and of letting in more air too. It may be doubted however whether ships with open outriggers were suited to boarding battles.

There can be little doubt that in all fives the one-man oar was at the lowest level because if placed above any two-man oars it would have had either to slope down through them and therefore be confined to their much smaller angular arc to mesh with them or be long enough to work above and outboard of them: in the first case about half its possible power would be lost and oar synchronisation would be difficult and fragile in operation; and in the second the oar would be too long to be worked fast enough by one man to contribute any effective propulsive power at eight knots or so.

In (**57**) the oarsmen have simply been added inboard of the positions of the thranites and zygians in the three. Oarsmen in consequence are interleaved with each other. They should be as close as practicable both vertically to keep the total height to the minimum, and horizontally to give the outboard man of each pair of oarsmen the longest possible stroke at his part of the oar loom. The two-man oars would have to be 6–7 metres long, first to give the inboard men on the ends of the looms a gearing of about 2.7, and second to limit the slope of the top oar, when its blade is immersed, to 25° which is the maximum for two-man oars. At greater slopes, the height to which the blade could be lifted off the water becomes too restricted, limiting its use in rough water, unless its handle is set too high for effective pulling in more ordinary conditions. A gearing of 2.7 would be appropriate in a ship likely to be about 15% slower in a sprint than a three. The gearings of the outboard men would necessarily be much higher, between 4 and 5.

To enable ships to be propelled at eight knots or more, oars have to be worked fast, at 35 or more strokes per minute. They should therefore be no longer than is absolutely necessary on account of the muscular effort absorbed in accelerating and retarding them to make each stroke. The masses of similarly shaped oars varies as length × (diameter)^2, and their moments of inertia as (length)^3 × (diameter)^2, the mass of a two-man oar (about 1.5 times as big in both length and diameter as a one-man oar) is 3.3 times and the moment of inertia 6.4 times that of a one-man oar. Any counterweighting added to the end of the loom to balance an oar would increase these ratios still more.

In (**57**) the two-man oars are shown 6.86 m (14 cubits) long. The one-man oars of the medieval triremi, 10 m long, were in use for a very long

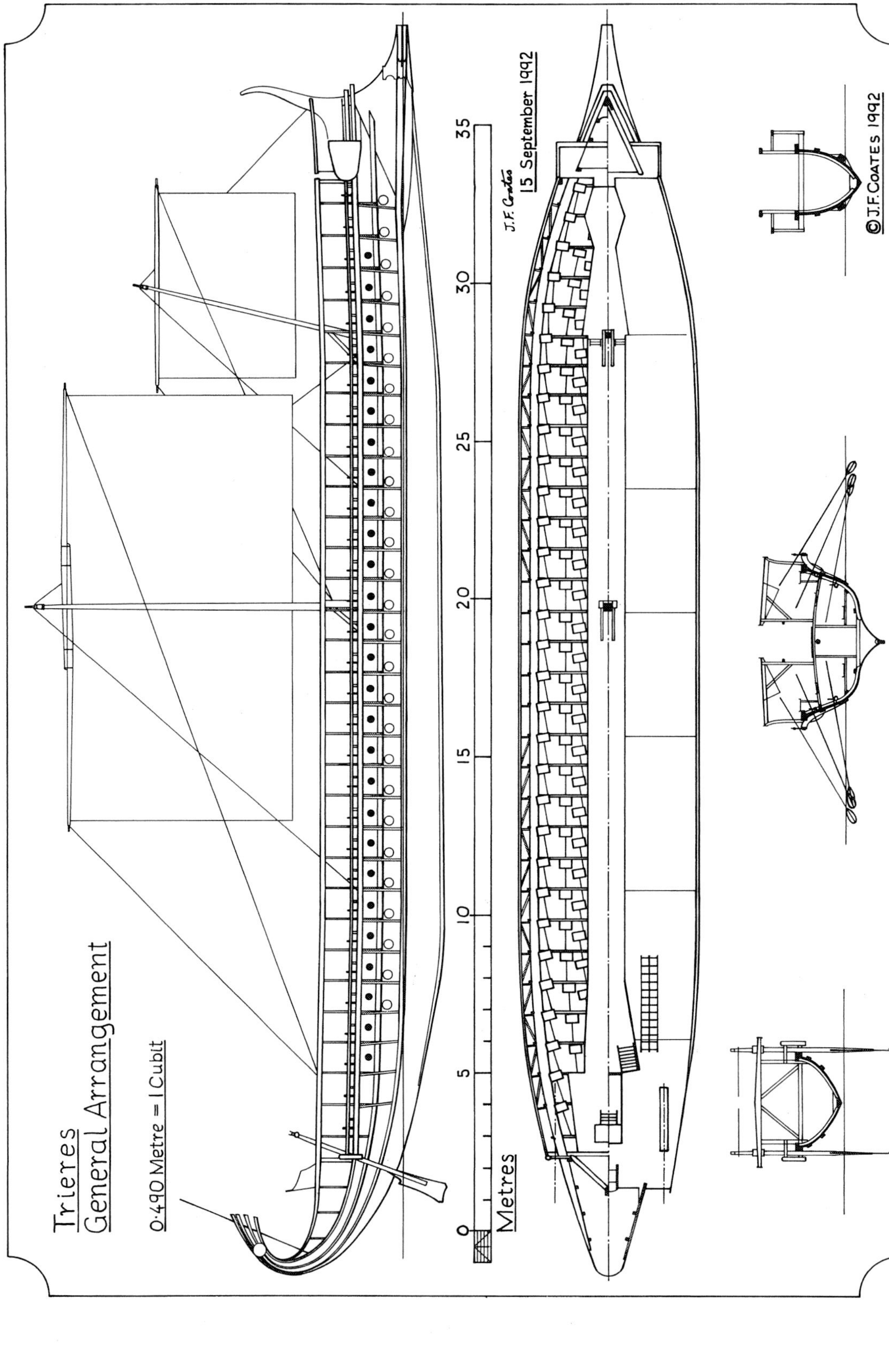

Trieres
General Arrangement
0·490 Metre = 1 Cubit
Metres
0
5
10
15
20
25
30
35
J.F. Coates
15 September 1992
©J.F.Coates 1992

55

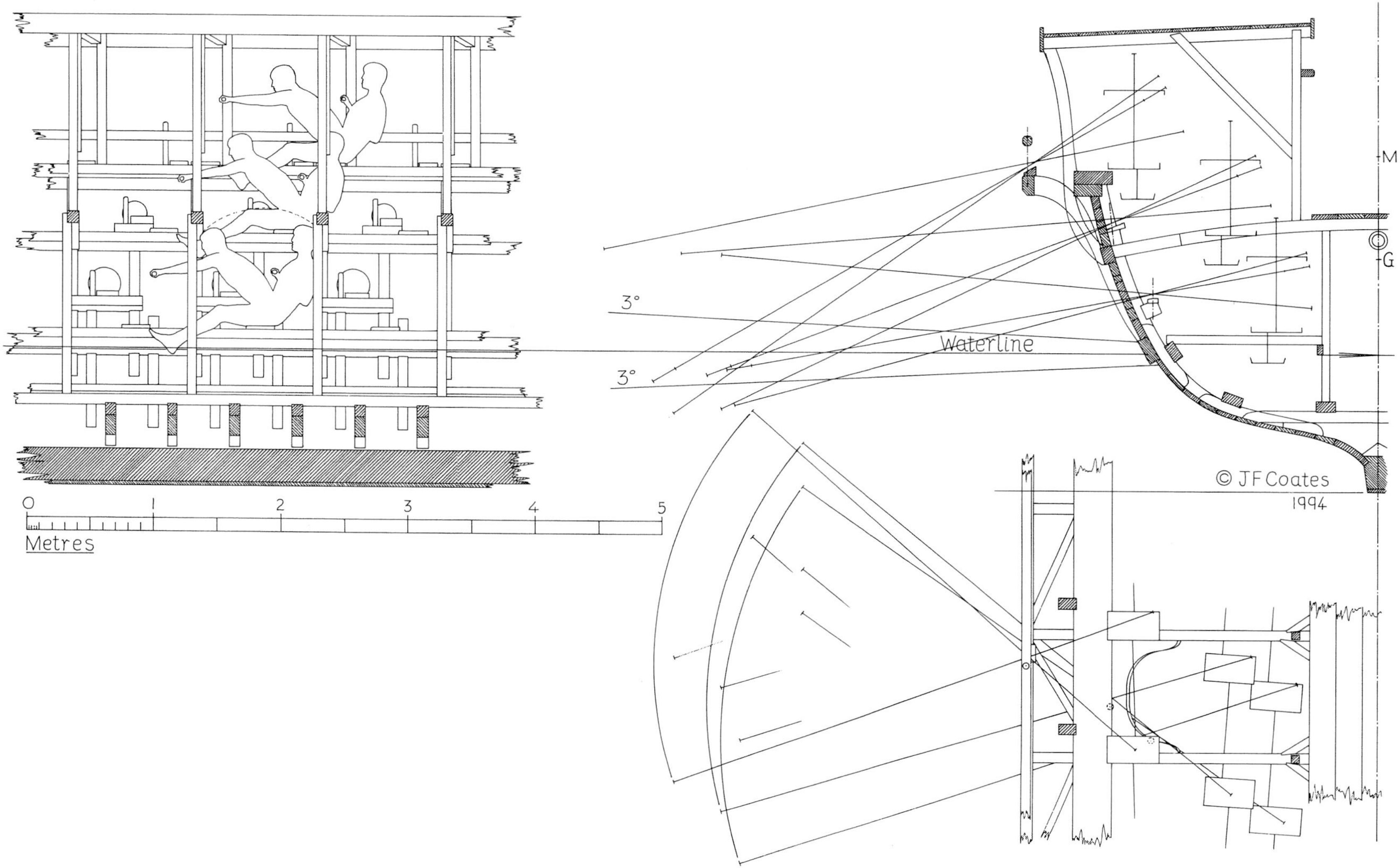

56 *Greek* Trieres c. 400 BC – mid-ship section

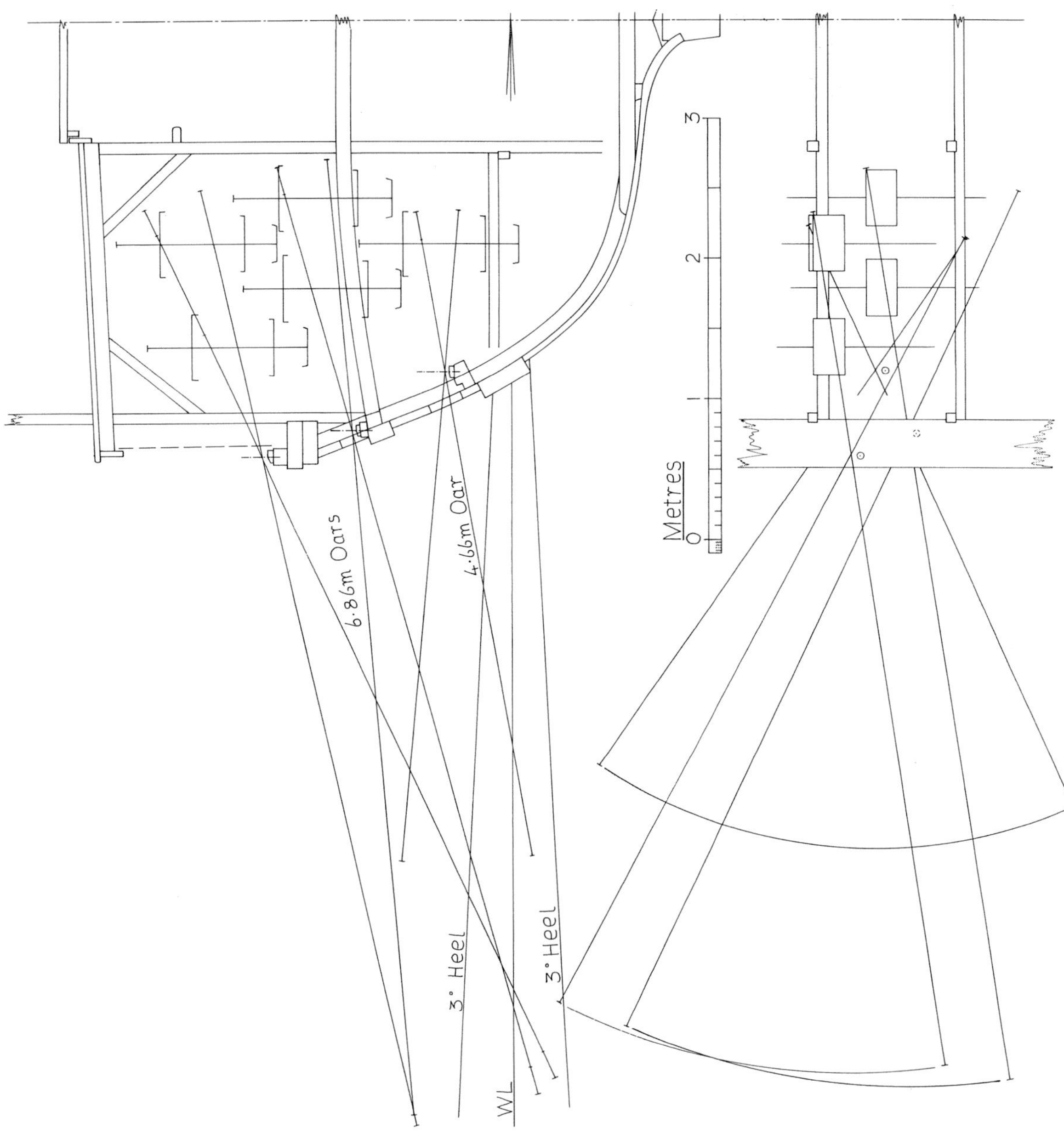

57 *Syracusan five: c.* 400 BC – mid-ship section

period, one must assume successfully, but it is likely that they were not worked faster than about 25 strokes a minute and did not achieve a ship speed of more than about 6 knots.

The five brings with it the very real problem raised in making oars of very different lengths and inertias work in synchronism, which it must be assumed that they did, at least at some point in the stroke if not throughout. Past writers have put forward the view that that was possible only if all the oars had the same gearing (Anderson: 1962), but that neglects the longer time taken by longer oars to start and finish strokes as well as to bring the oar forward for the next stroke, causing the man on the short oar to have to pause, waste time and therefore reduce his power output. It seems more likely (but this needs experimental verification) that the one-man oar should be given an increased gearing to enable its rower to keep the blade usefully in the water longer, finishing after the long oars but catching up with them in the recovery to synchronise at the catch. In (**57**) the thalamian oar has therefore been given a gearing of 3.5, compared with 2.7 in the two-man oars. The long oars follow each other through the water without overtaking but owing to the wider arc of the one-man oar below them that oar has to overtake the zygian blade. However, the two blades are separated by a metre horizontally and there is half a metre vertical clearance between the two oars, so that overtaking should be practical in this case.

It may on the other hand be asked why fives, fours and higher denomination polyremes would have used two-man oars. If however they did not, the fives and fours would have had to have, respectively, one three-man with two one-man oars (or one four-man with one one-man oar) and one three-man with one one-man oar. All such combinations would require oars of a greater disparity in length to work together. In the absence of any surviving knowledge of the working of mixed-length oarsystems in fast vessels, one has to rely on what can be drawn from theoretical dynamics and the nearest related historical information available. The first has indicated the combination of two- and one-man oars in the series of reconstructions shown in this chapter, and that mixing three-man and one-man oars together would not be practical on account of the difficulty in synchronising them when all oarcrew are working fast. The second is provided only by the different lengths of oar in the *alla sensile* medieval galleys, which are dubiously relevant because their oars worked on a single level and were therefore more tightly restricted between each other than would be the case between oars working on different levels. Nevertheless it should be noted that those oars differed in length by 15% at most, whereas the two-man oars proposed in (**57**) and (**61**) are nearly 50% longer than the one-man oars with which they have to be synchronised. The *alla sensile* galley oars were however very long to be worked by one man, about 10 m, and the maximum rate of striking with them would have been strongly determined by their moments of inertia and hence by their length. Until it can be proved that three-man oars can work successfully with one-man oars at the required rate of striking in fives and fours, they should be rejected in reconstructions of these ships in favour of two-man oars.

Interpretations of the Erment Model and Representations of Phoenician Threes

The model, being made of clay formed by hand with a hand-formed deck, pillars, rails and oarstubs pressed into place, needs much interpretation with the limitations of those processes in mind. It has about 20 oars only at three levels on each side and shields extend along each side of the deck. It could therefore be interpreted as a troop-armed ship and, having three levels of oars, as a three, a five or a six.

If it represents a three, then, as that was a fast type, the oars would be of minimum efficient length and the breadth on the waterline no more than necessary for adequate stability, as shown in the three in (**56**). If however the model is taken to be of a troop-armed ship with therefore a higher centre of gravity, it will need a greater breadth on the waterline which would cause the sides of the ship to be more vertical. That would demand that the zygians, and their tholes, be moved inboard so that these men sit on the other side, inboard, of the thalamians, as shown in (**58**). The thranites could then also be moved inboard so that they would no longer need an outrigger to support their tholes.

To have adequate stability with 60 troops on board (i.e. one man for each shield, one being stowed in every 'room' of files of 30 oars), and an appropriately strong deck to support them, the ship must need a breadth on the waterline (BWL) of about 4.5 m and about the same to accommodate the oarcrew in this way with an adequately wide (1 m) gangway fore and aft on the middle line. The breadth overall (BOA) would be about 5.2 m and the deck 2.7 m above the loaded waterline (cf. the three of (**56**) where BWL is 3.7 m, BOA 5.6 m and deck height 2.5 m). The greater breadth of the hull would make it broad and shallow in the water and the hull beams would also be low relative to the breadth of the hull. The first ratio would carry a penalty in resistance and the second in torsional stiffness of the hull. The ship would be heavier by about eight tonnes and about 6% slower in speeds, i.e. capable of 9.2 knots in a ten minute sprint and 7.1 knots maximum continuously all day (cf. 9.8 and 7.5 knots). This ship being heavier would also be slower in turning and manoeuvre. Those would have been the penalties for the addition of the appreciable offensive capability of a sizeable company of troops on board.

Such a reconstruction would represent a three with a balance of capabilities presenting some dangers in a fleet action against lighter threes relying entirely upon superior manoeuvring and rams. It would be more prone to be rammed by the lighter type which however would have had a feeble defence against boarding. Any troop-armed version would probably have had heavier waterline wales and protective structure to resist ramming attacks. and the balance of advantage in action between the two types would have depended very much upon the qualities of the opposing oarcrews.

If the model represents a three without troops as the main armament, the waterline breadth would surely have been no more than that of the Greek type compared with which it is attested as being as fast if not faster. (**58**) therefore shows a reconstruction of a Phoenician type of three with a BWL of 3.6 m. It has two courses of rectangular openings for the upper levels of oars. That smaller breadth combined with the outriggerless oarsystem gives no room for any gangway at hull-beam level. That essential access would therefore have to be provided above the heads of the zygians.

The absence of outriggers would cause the blades of the three levels of oars to be more nearly equidistant from the ship, unless the upper oars were longer than the lowest. As however they are all one-man oars and the ship is fast, any increase in length of oar would have to be minimised if the oarsystem were to work satisfactorily at a fast rate of striking. At the same time, as the blades would tend to sweep similar paths, their arcs must be arranged to prevent any overtaking between them. To avoid that, some variation in oar length from one level to another is necessary. It is also necessary to prevent the upper oars from working between the shafts of the others. In (**58**) the lengths of oars, from top to bottom, are 5.21 m, 5.14 m, and 4.46 m with gearings of 3.0. This three is higher than the Greek type and to prevent the thranite oars from sloping down to the water at more than 30° (about the maximum for efficient rowing with one-man oars) they have been lengthened by just over half a metre. The zygian tholes would have to be about 0.6 m inside the ship and that would explain the need for the large oarports at that level in the model.

If on the other hand the model represents a five or six, it would be of a ship similar to that shown in (**57**). That would not however explain so well the nearly vertical sides of the model or its large zygian oarports. The latter would call for the pairs of oarsmen to be close-coupled as in the arrangement in (**61**), with both pairs then moved inboard to obviate the need for the outrigger shown in that drawing. The result would be a beamy ship, shown in (**58**), with a BWL of about 5.8 m and a displacement of 130 tonnes or so. It would be wide enough to be a six (**67**) but even as a five, because it could carry about 100 or so troops, it would have been a formidable ship in battle if suitably protected against being rammed. As historical evidence indicates that there were no sixes in the eastern Mediterranean at the relevant time, if the model is not of a three it must be a five.

There remains, whichever type of ship the Erment model represents, the major structural question of how, in the presence of the large square oarports at the middle level of oars, the main hull, being on that account so shallow, could have been adequately strong to enable the hull girder to resist bending in waves. The large square oarports would would reduce the effective depth of the hull as a girder by about 30%. To keep maximum hogging bending stresses in waves about 0.8 m high from trough to crest and of the same length as the ship within the limit of 4.5 Nmm^2 (the design criterion applied to *Olympias* and which, following White

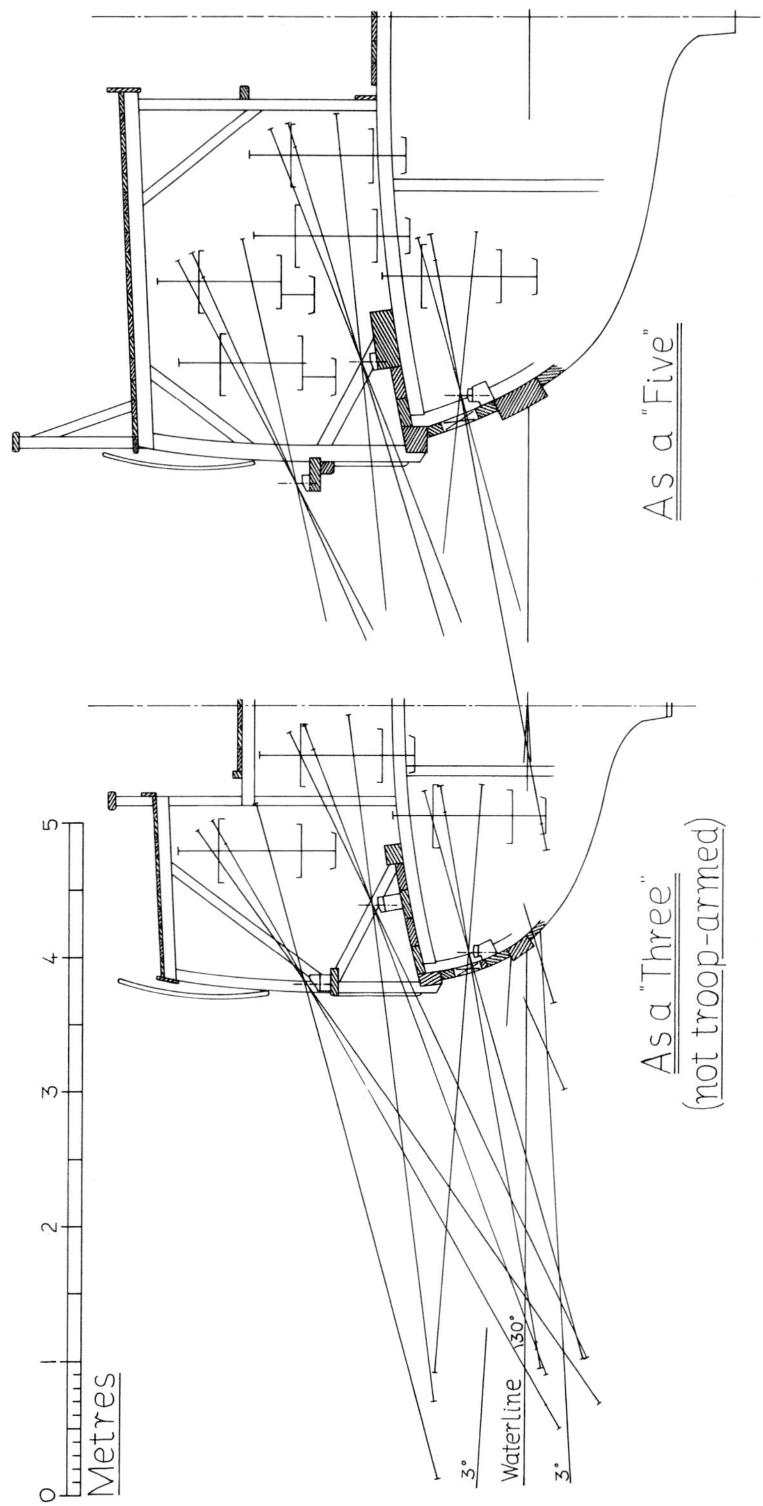

58 *Interpretation of the Erment Model*

(1877) may be taken to be the maximum allowable in a viable wooden ship), longitudinal material with a considerable effective cross-sectional area would have been necessary at the level of the bottom of those openings. Owing to the movement of the zygians inboard, described above as necessary if outriggers are to be dispensed with, there is room for such longitudinal material if laid as planking on the hull beams and made effective as part of the hull girder by being tenoned together. Side decks so formed extending inboard as far as the zygians would suffice to restore hull bending strength to the necessary level. Examples of what would seem to have been required are shown in (**58**). Such a major structural feature, though invisible in the representations, may be considered to have been necessary in any hull more than about 15 depths long on the waterline. It would lead to the proposition that the main hulls of outriggerless Phoenician warships were to some extent decked. Another reason for proposing such a feature lies in the low freeboard of such ships up to the level of openings much larger than the open zygian oarports in other types of ship.

A Reconstructed Four

At Athens in the later 4th cent. BC, fours were housed in the Peiraieus shipsheds. Those ships were therefore approximately 5.6 m BOA. The four was developed, either from the pentecontor with oars of two levels (Ch. 5 **i-vi**) or from the five, with the object of producing an economical troop-armed ship of acceptable performance, capable of fighting in line of battle in the presence of troop-armed fives. That it could be stored in sheds built for threes in various places may have been a not insignificant consideration behind their adoption.

A four, shown in (**59**), can be seen to be a simple modification of a two-level pentecontor (**vi**) and by comparison with the five in (**57**) to be an equally simple modification of it, consisting of the removal of the thranites and the addition of a thalamian below. The hull in both cases would have to be adjusted in its dimensions, e.g. in the case of the modification of the five the BWL reduced by 0.5 m and hull depth by 0.4 m. By also, in the latter case, shortening the hull (indicated by evidence that in fours the length was less (p. 154–55) and the number of oars (p. 269) was about 88) the displacement would have been reduced by no less than a third, without reducing the number of troops carried. If the four was a modified five, the reduction in the size of the hull of the four could have caused stowage for water and stores to be rather cramped.

As attested in literature (p. 68) the deck of the four shown in section here is low compared with other types of warship, it is 2.2 m above the loaded waterline, 0.7 m or more below those of fives and 0.4 to 0.6 m below those of threes. One might wonder if raised foredecks were ever fitted to mitigate this shortcoming: there is however mention of fours carrying towers (p. 155), shown in (**76**).

A further consequence of the low deck would have been the need to cover over the gangway by a casing topped by ventilation louvres and running down the middle of the deck, to provide protected walking headroom. Such a feature would make sense of Appian's reference (5.106) to oarsmen breaking through the deck of a swamped ship. The deck proper would have been too tough for that to be done in a hurry, whereas to break through one side of such a casing with the buttends of oars could have been done much more quickly. It does not follow that all fours would have had casings over their gangways or a raised foredeck; neither is shown in the Alba Fucentia graffito (**38**), a rough sketch, which leaves out many necessary features.

Calculations (see Appendix B) indicate that the length of two-man oars can vary between about 4.7 m and 7 m with little effect on the effective propulsive power able to be delivered per oar. The reason is that with increase in length the power contributed by the man nearest to the thole increases, but the greater inertia of the oar reduces the maximum rate of striking with the net result that the total power being delivered by the two men appears theoretically to be roughly constant. With a relatively minor amount of modification the four in (**59**) could use oars of the same length as those of a three as effectively as the longer oars shown there. The heights of oars and of the deck as well as athwartships dimensions would have to be adjusted however to an extent which would not make it possible for oars of either length to be used interchangeably in the same ship. In a ship built for shorter oars they would be nearer the water, and the advantage of a ships with longer oars would be better performance in waves.

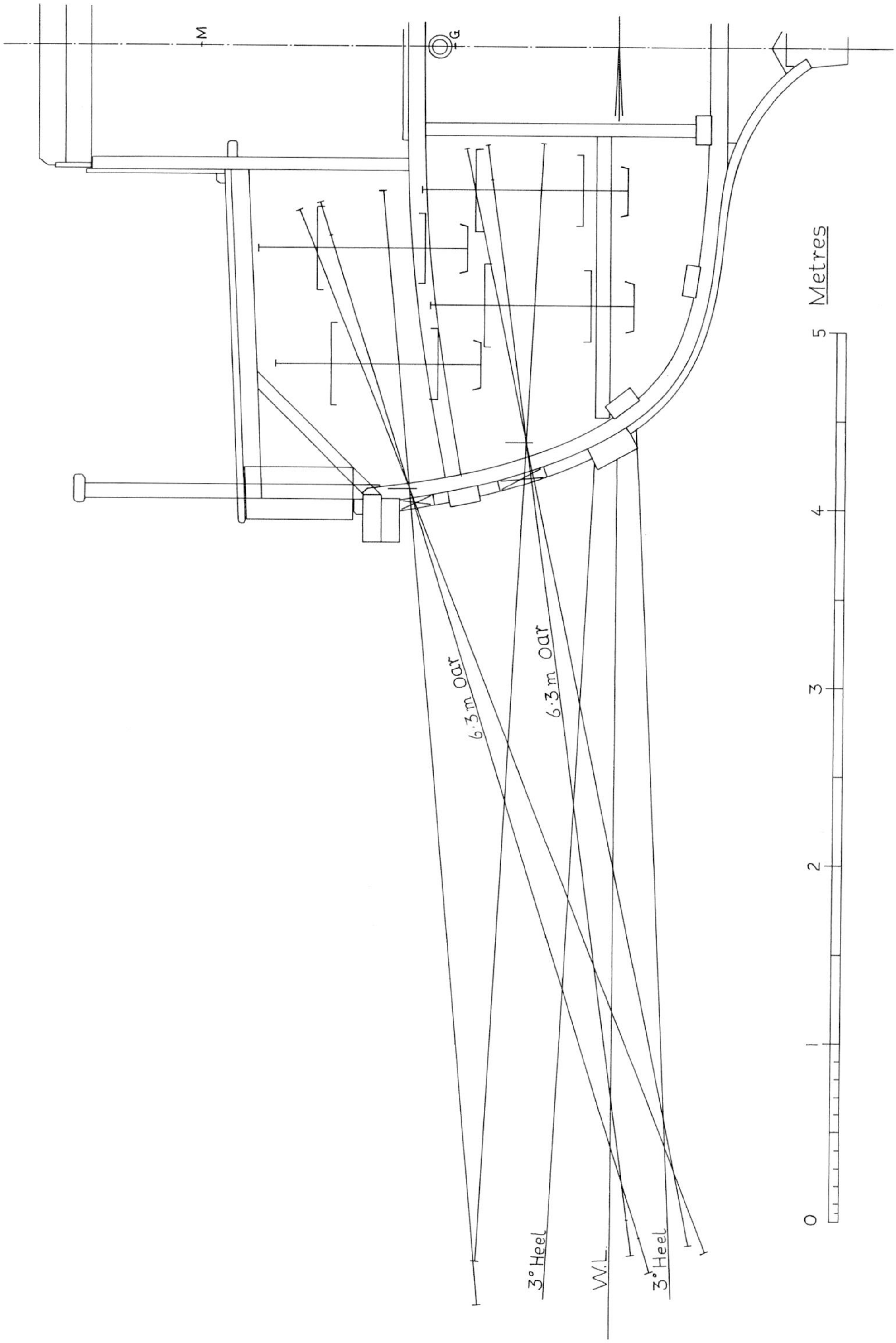

59 *A four to fit Peiraieus shipsheds*

The four would probably have been a little faster under oar in a sprint than a five and at endurance speeds probably as fast, making it a useful and economical ship of the line. It is not surprising that they were built in large numbers (by Antigonos I and Ptolemy I), though against fleets mainly or exclusively of fives and above their lack of height would have been a serious handicap. They were not, probably for that reason, used in the line during the Punic wars, though they saw battle service in many other conflicts stretching over a period of four or five centuries, making it one of the longest-lived types of ships-of-the-line.

Reconstructing the ship of the Isola Tiberina, Rome

1. Assuming that the monument is a full scale representation

Since it has been thought that this monument is on full-scale, in profile at least, possible oarsystems which could work inside such a ship were considered on that basis. First, if, as has also been thought, the deck is at the top edge of the monument (Krauss: 1944), while there would be vertical room for three levels of oar crew, the oar of the top level could not avoid intruding into the *πάροδος* unless the loom was very long, when its gearing would be too low or the oar much too long. The internal height implied by this assumption cannot therefore be used by oarcrew and the ship cannot be a three-level five, though the height of the deck would be correct for a five, taking the loaded waterline to be half-way up the heavy wale.

The ship could not be a four either, on this assumption, because then the deck would be too high to agree with literary evidence. It could be a two-level five, but that would be a slower ship than that shown in (**57**) which makes it a rather improbable hypothesis in which furthermore much of the height of the deck would serve no purpose except to elevate the troops. If however the deck is assumed to be not at the top edge but at the next beading down, about half way to the *πάροδος* (the upper area representing a bulwark), then it would be at the right height for the deck of a four and two two-man oars can be satisfactorily arranged inside the ship, as shown in (**60**). It is not possible for both levels of oars to be worked through the oarbox, so the ship would look rather like the Praeneste relief (**29**). This is the only practical oarsystem that could be found to fit the ship on full scale.

This interpretation is however unsatisfactory because:

a. BWL would have to be too large, 5.1 m or more, nearly as big as that of a five and probably larger than shown in (**60**) because there oarcrew have been crowded laterally to minimise the ship's breadth. To be practicable the ship would have to have been about 0.6 m wider than there shown. It would have been too slow and too shallow relative to breadth;

b. the depth of the hull-structure from topwale to keel is inadequate for hull bending strength;

c. the hull beams are necessarily too low to provide adequate torsional stiffness to the hull, and the *ὑπόζωμα* is also too low to serve its purpose;

d. the oarbox is too cramped for necessary access.

It is concluded that in profile this monument is not on full scale.

2. Assuming that the Scale of the Monument is Three-Quarters Full Size

That scale makes the height of the deck, if interpreted to be at the beading half-way between the top and the *πάροδος*, 2.9 m above the mid-height of the wale, the right height for the deck of a five above the probable loaded waterline of the real ship. (**61**) shows how a practical arrangement of structure and a five-file oarsystem would fit into such a ship. The faults in (**60**) do not arise and it is a realistic arrangement in principle, though here too the BWL at 5.3 m may be too small owing to spacing the pairs of oarsmen 10 cm closer together than the recommended 65 cm, and, in order also to restrain the size of BWL, the gangway is minimal in breadth. In (**61**), BOA is 7 m. (**63**) shows a section with the recommended lateral spacing and a more realistic breadth of gangway. It is 0.8 m wider both overall (7.8 m) and on the waterline (6.1 m) and such a ship would be about ½ knot slower as a result, unless the less confined oarcrew could produce more power. Where the best compromise lies between such a gain in power and the greater hull resistance and hence loss of speed owing to increased beam cannot be found without experimen-

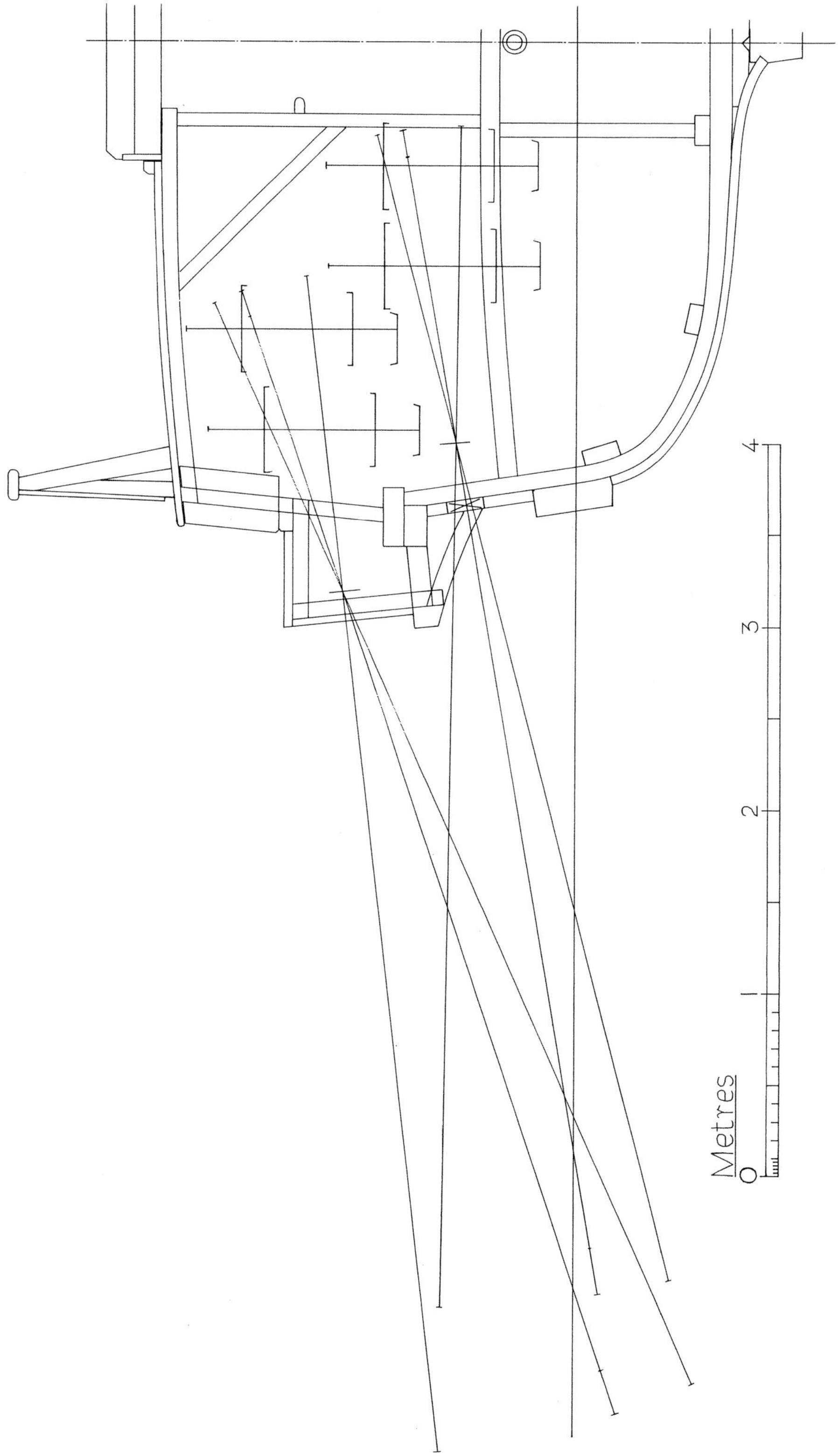

60 *The Isola Tiberina monument as a four, midship section*

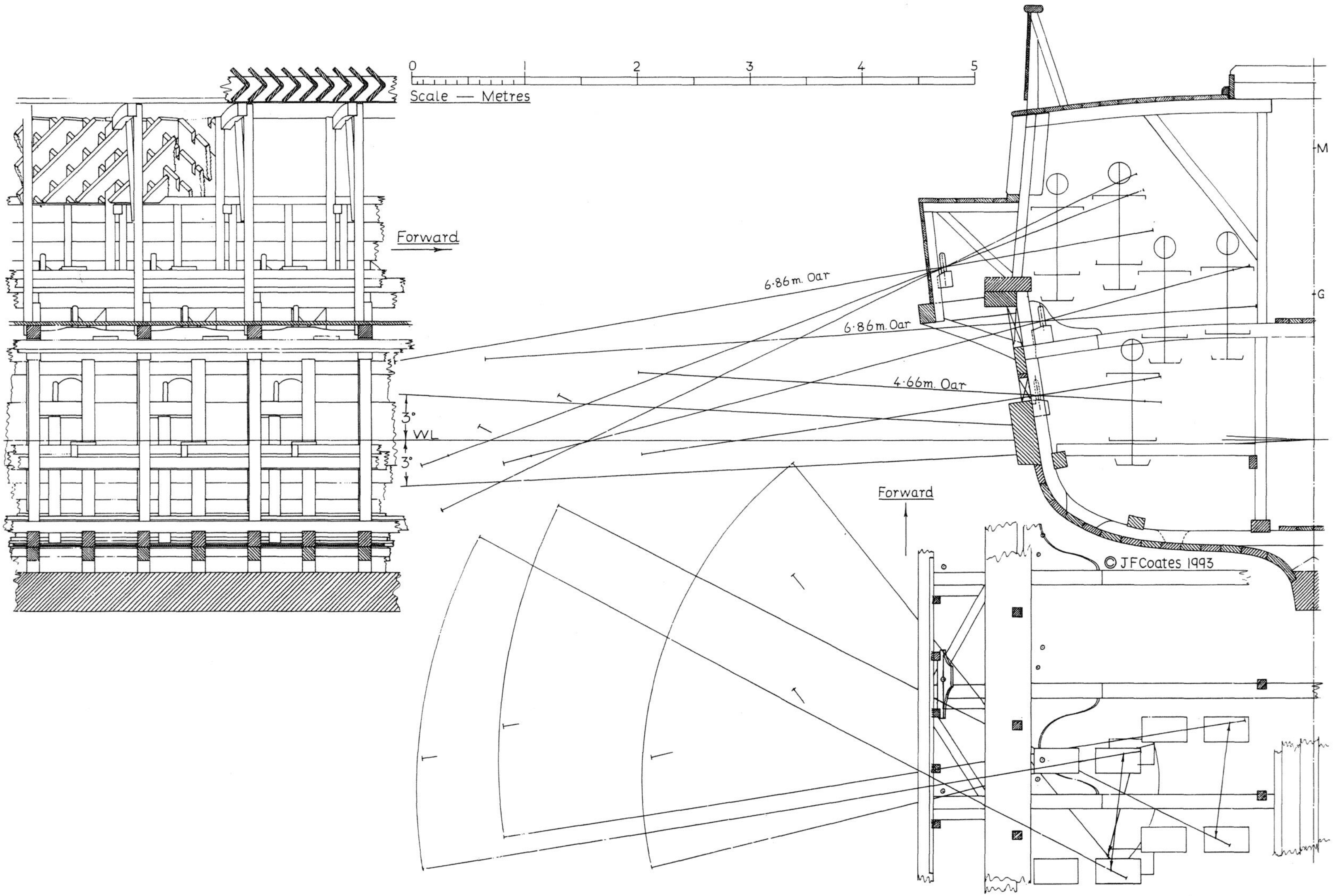

61 *The Isola Tiberina monument as a five – midship section*

tation with a section of five oarsmen and appropriate oars or their dynamic equivalents. In the meantime (**61**) has been kept at the spatial minimum the more graphically to present those factors affecting oar power and speed.

In this oarsystem oars and oarcrew are as low as they can be, and the oars are as short as possible, sweeping out arcs arranged so that the two-man oars do not overtake each other during the stroke. The one-man oar, as in (**57**), has a much wider arc so it has to overtake the middle oar. It is however thought to be sufficiently clear of the middle oar, particularly at the finish, for the arrangement to be practical.

Again, as in (**57**) it is not possible in the cross-section of the Isola Tiberina ship to place a one-man oar at the top level because, to reach the water at a reasonable slope, it would have to be more than 6 m long, and even at that length it would not work clear of the oars below. Further, to accommodate two pairs of oarsmen without the benefit of the outrigger would demand a BWL half a metre bigger, and therefore a penalty in speed, besides being greater than is needed for stability. At the same time the space under the deck would be largely empty. That arrangement, while not being unworkable, should be rejected in favour of putting the one-man oar at the lowest level, as in (**61**), when all oars will keep clear of each other and their working would be much more robust in coping with waves and other disturbances. There can be little doubt that this would have been the normal oarsystem in fives of this type.

Two variants of this scheme have been considered but also rejected. In one both lower oars worked over a lowered topwale; but for that to be possible the topwale had to be too low to give the hull adequate bending strength. In the other both oars worked through oarports at about the same level below a raised topwale, but then too much planking would have to be cut away, to the detriment of the hull.

The two-man oars are 6.86 m (14 cubits) long, which should be amply short enough to allow them to be worked at more than 35 strokes a minute with a gearing for the inboard man of 2.8 which should be suitable for a sprint speed of 8 knots. As in (**57**) the one-man oar is 4.66 m long with a gearing of 3.5. (**62**) by Burlet shows in diagrammatic form the movements of the oarsmen as arranged in (**61**), making the more normal strokes of 0.8 m at mid-handle (at the butt end of the loom in the case of two-man oars). The length of the oar strokes shown in (**61**) are, as in the other reconstructed oar-systems presented, the absolute maximum in length, 1.1 m at the butts, at which stroke-length the butts of oars would be in contact, or worse, with the back of the next man aft, given an *interscalmium* of 0.98 m. The doubtful area of oar-handle movement at the finish, indicated in the case of thranite No. 1, draws attention to the need for oarsmen to bend their arms at the end of the sitting stroke, diminishing handle pull and therefore the value of unduly extending the stroke at the finish. This is a contentious point in sea-rowing where extraction can be made difficult if the blade is buried in a wave. There are various styles practised at sea, some of which involve considerable lie-back of the body and recovery by pulling up on the oar to extract it from the water decisively.

The draft of the ship with a BWL of 5.3 m would be about 1.5 m and the loaded displacement about 110 tonnes. The metacentric height would be about 1.5 m, which should be sufficient to prevent the ship from rolling, owing to movement of troops on deck, by more than 3°. Lateral movements on the deck would in any case be restricted by the middle line vent casing, but there would probably have been disciplinary restrictions on the freedom of troops to move about the deck while on passage under oar.

The underside of the oarbox is open to allow air to be drawn into the ship by convection owing to the temperature inside the ship being higher than the ambient. Protective louvres are shown on a casing over the gangway and in the upper side of the ship also over the *πάροδος* though there is no suggestion of the latter in the side of the monument. Louvres in this position, and above oarports in the sides of oarboxes are however shown in other representations (e.g. **13**, **29**, **36**, **38**, **40**, **45–49**) and, as explained, some arrangements for ventilation would have been necessary. The zygian oarports would contribute to the supply of air, and so too would louvres in the bow, shown in the general arrangement of the ship (**64**). The value of forward- facing openings for ventilation was demonstrated during trials in *Olympias*.

The Isola Tiberina monument and the Praeneste relief both show an oarbox with a horizontal top, a

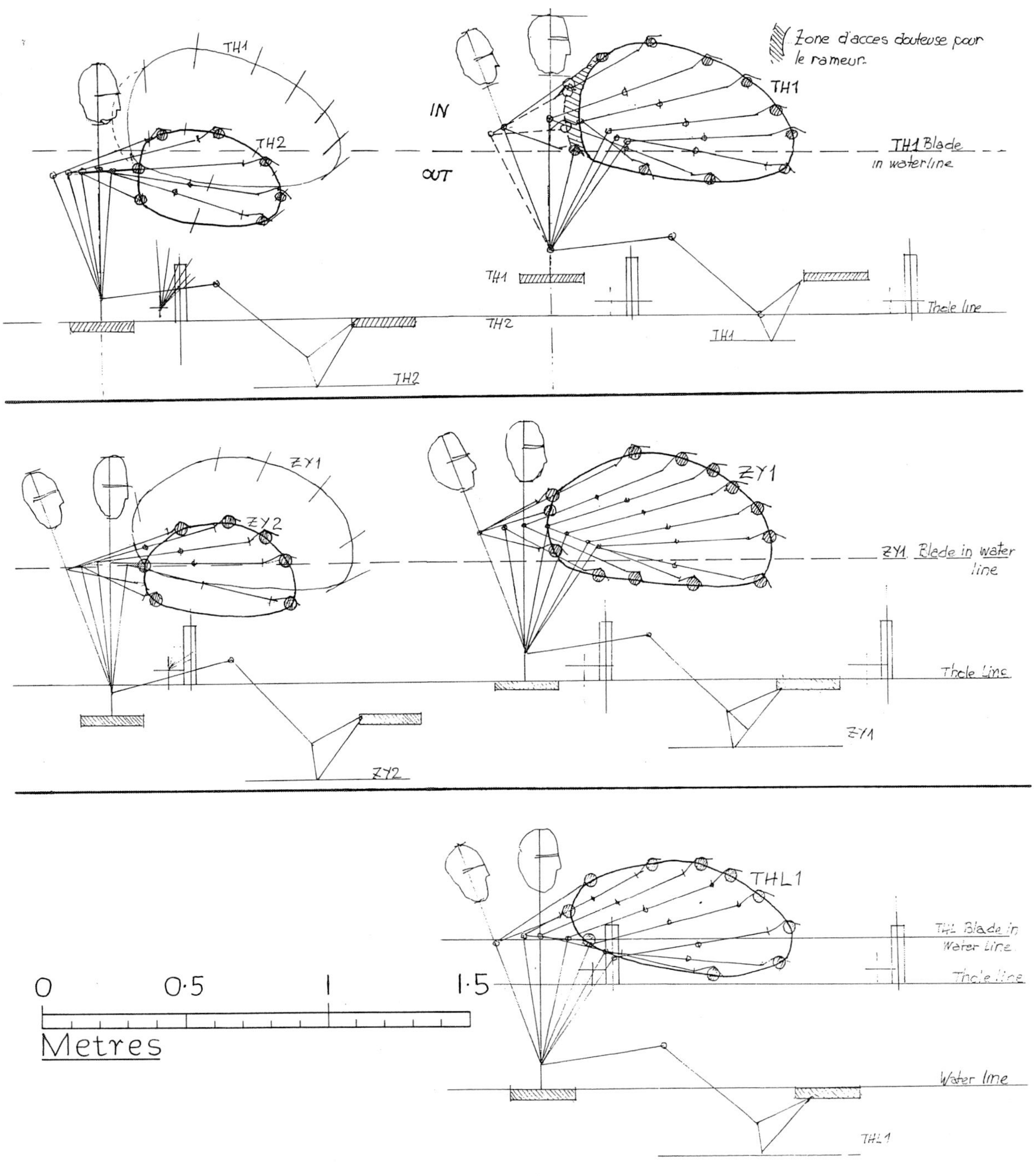

62 *Movements of oarsmen in the ship of* **61**: *Burlet*

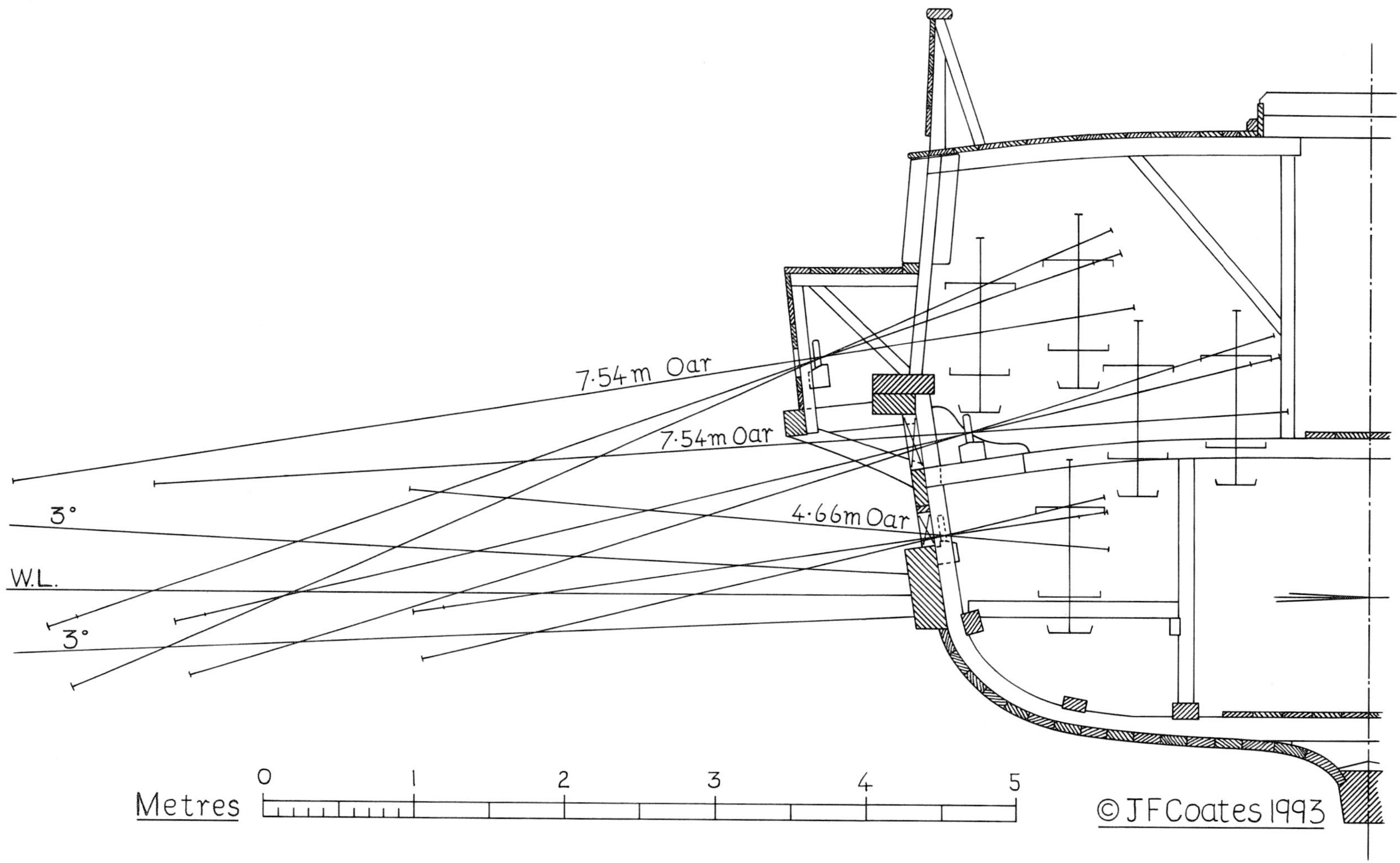

63 *The five of (**61**) broadened to give oarsmen their recommended lateral spacing*

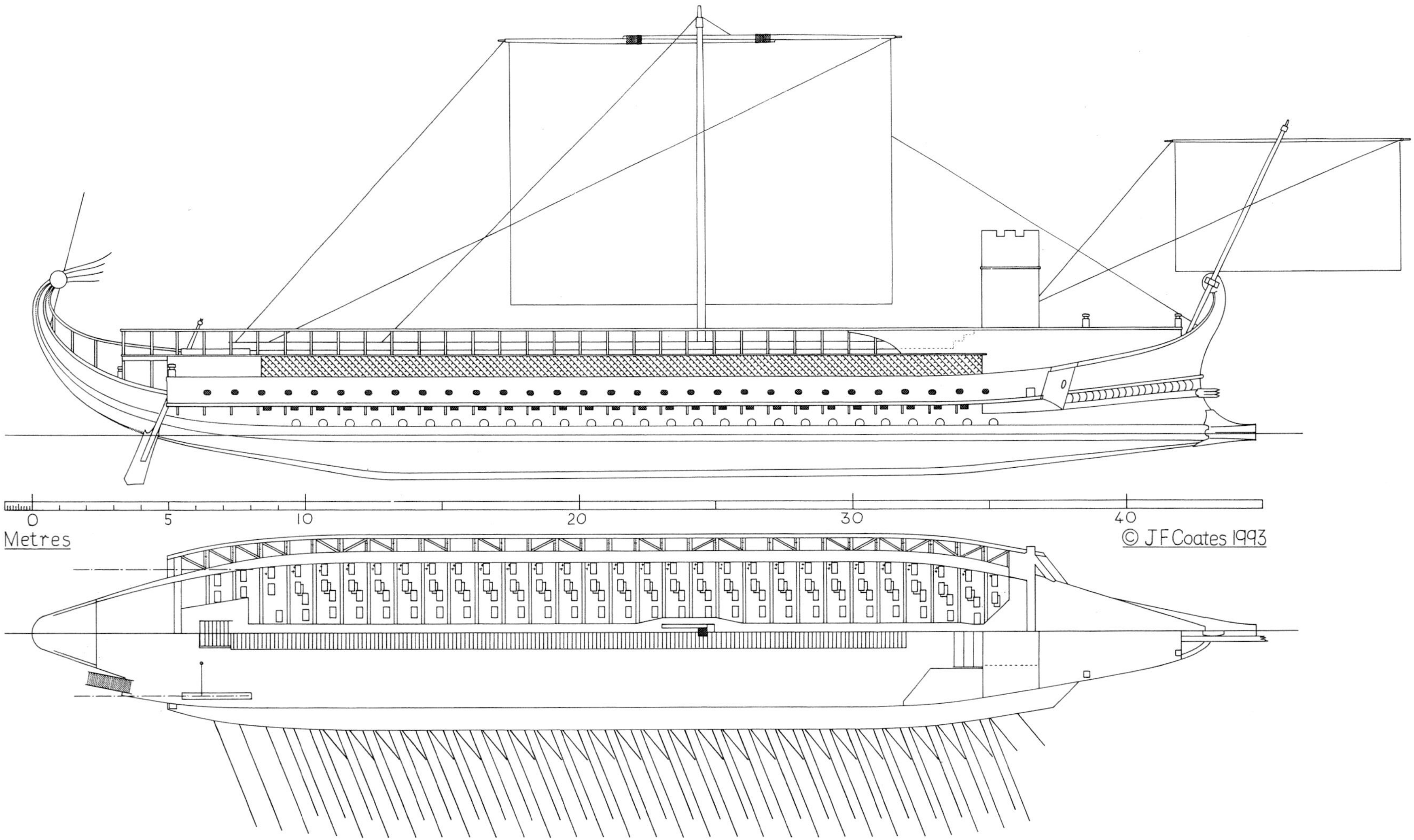

64 *The Isola Tiberina monument as a five – general*

πάροδος (p. 227, 230). While forming a side deck or gangway, which is occupied by armed figures in the relief, through being horizontal it limits the number of levels of oars that could be worked through the oarbox to one and the oarsystem therefore to the Greek type of five. It also limits the use to which the space under the main deck can be put to accommodate oarsmen. Its value presumably lay in attack or defence in boarding battles between ships heavily armed with troops, though being lower than the fighting deck of most warships it could not have made a good springboard from which to board an enemy. The fives of the Pompeii shipshed frescoes, on the other hand, had sloping tops to their oarboxes. They would have acted as *glacis* by preventing troops whether attacking or defending, from standing on them except precariously. The same is true of the curved top given to the oarboxes of the *τριημιολία* in (**74**), but if that light type of ship carried few troops, as has been indicated (p. 266), the need to make the tops of its oarboxes into *glacis* is not difficult to imagine.

Boarding would cause ships to heel as troops went to one side of both attacking and defending ships, but heel would be less when the boarding point was near the bow as it must usually have been to be clear of oars. A *πάροδος* could present boarders with a route by which the defenders could be outflanked and the command of the ship attacked directly, unless there were enough defending troops astern of the main combat to spear any enemy on the *πάροδος*. While there is ignorance of the detailed tactics of boarding between these ships, the purpose of the *πάροδος* in battle must remain obscure.

The general arrangement of a five shown in (**64**) is based largely on the Isola Tiberina monument and its main particulars are listed with those of other reconstructions in Appendix D. It has 282 oarsmen, but it would be quite practicable to add two more 'rooms' to the length and if one of those were near one end of the ship and had two-man oars only, the strength of the oarcrew could be brought up to 300. The perspective drawings, (**65**) and (**66**), also of this reconstruction, show what such a typical ship would look like in reality, first from a boat as she approached under oar with sails rigged but brailed up, as they would be for entering harbour, and secondly inside the ship with the oarcrew in action. The men depicted in these drawings give a visual sense of the scale of a major warship of the Roman Republic, a sense which is destroyed in most ancient representations by the gross exaggeration of the size of any figures present.

The precise details of features and their exact positions shown in this, as in other reconstructions presented here, should be regarded as no more than typical. They must be to varying degrees speculative, but they are derived from evidence. In the absence of a complete specification and physical definition of a particular ship, one cannot, in drawing a typical ship of a particular kind go further without entering upon less defensible speculation about less essential features. Warships of any one kind would in any case have varied from place to place and over the years as they do today.

In (**64**) features normally shown in ships' general arrangement scale drawings are included:

- Profile of ship including underwater part of the hull
- Decks, access and compartments in plan
- Bollards and fairleads for anchoring and mooring
- Main means for propulsion (except oars and oarcrew in internal plan) and for steering the ship

In warships:

- Main and secondary armament (except the troops themselves and their weapons)

Reconstructing a six and a seven on the basis of the Isola Tiberina Monument

The Six

As it has been shown in (**61**) that a five could have oars of equal length in the upper two levels, the possibility that in a similar six all oars could be of the same and equal length, each double-manned, was explored.

Starting with the arrangement in (**61**), and keeping the lowest thole near the planking, it was possible to place the heads of the two thalamians next to, and one of them between, the foot-stretchers of the middle oarsmen (the zygians). They would also then have the correct elbow-room between them.

The middle men and their tholes were moved 0.18 m inboard to allow the thalamian loom to be long enough to give that oar the same gearing as the others, namely 2.8 for the inboard men, to give the arrangement shown in (**67**). The movement inboard of the middle men necessitated an increase in BWL of 0.38 m to preserve the breadth of the gangway.

The height of the thalamian thole was also raised by 0.22 m to prevent the angle of the now longer thalamian oar from being too small and hampered by waves. That caused its oarsmen to rise further by 0.08 m and 0.12 m (and by a further 0.10 m explained below), raising the others in consequence and the height of the ship above water by 0.4 m above that of the five, implying a slight reduction in the scale of the Isola Tiberina monument from 0.75 to 0.725 (5/7), and that the height of the deck of a six was 11.2 Roman feet, 1.4 Roman feet more than that of the five. If in ancient sixes the thalamians were higher than shown in (**62**), then one may infer that sixes were by that much higher still than fives.

The increase in BWL by 0.38 m is sufficient to preserve adequate stability in face of a rise in the ship's centre of gravity (G) of about 0.15 m owing to the greater height of oarcrew, decks and no doubt the larger number of troops on board a flagship or other principal ship of a fleet.

As all the oars are double-manned and of equal length (an advantage in standardisation), it is necessary to arrange their arcs in plan so that there is no overtaking in the course of the stroke. The position of the middle men relative to the hull beams between them is fairly closely determined by the need for their shins and backs to be clear of them at each end of the stroke. To place the thalamian oar forward of the zygian at every part of the stroke, particularly at the catch where they would be closest together, the thalamians must sit immediately under the beams, making it necessary to raise the beams and everything in the ship above that level by the 0.10 m already mentioned.

The longitudinal position of the top men, the thranites, is as usual independent of the beams but determined more by the positions of upper structure, in particular the essential deck-edge pillars, and oarbox beams, brackets and framing, which are all associated together. Oarbox beams have the important function of resisting collision forces on the oarbox and should therefore be in line with the hull beams. Thranite oars have to work between the deck-edge pillars and they do so most conveniently if they work at every point of their stroke aft of the middle oars.

(**67**) shows a practicable oarsystem for a six on three levels in a ship of the type shown on the Isola

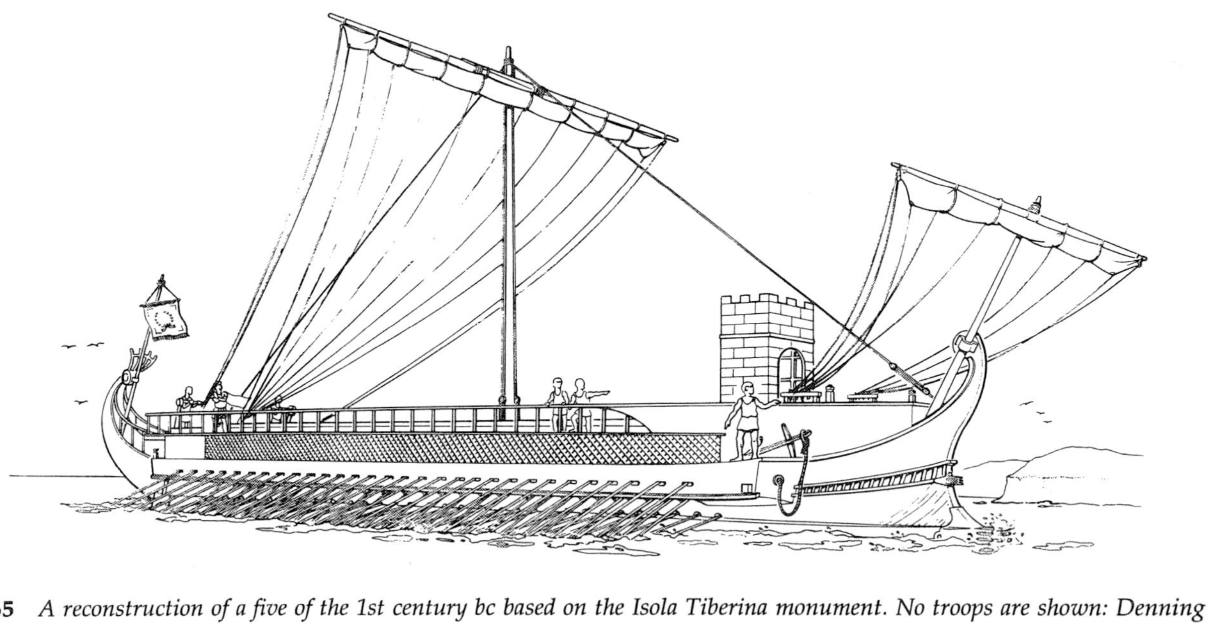

65 *A reconstruction of a five of the 1st century bc based on the Isola Tiberina monument. No troops are shown: Denning*

Tiberina monument. The ship would have a BWL of about 5.6 or 5.7 m, a BOA of about 7.5 m, a draft of about 1.5 m and a likely displacement loaded of about 125 tonnes. It would in other respects, apart from total height, be very similar to the five shown as a whole in (**64**), (**65**) and (**66**). Its position in Rome and the scale of the monument suggests that it represents a flagship such as the sixes which carried the consuls at Eknomos.

The Seven

Continuing from the six, from which the seven was developed and as a fourth level of oars can be dismissed as a possibility, a seven had either to have three-man oars at some level if it had a total of three levels or one level of four-man oars and one of three if it only had two levels. Oars worked by three or more men raise the question of the use of standing men at their butts to increase the possible length of stroke there to restore the angle swept by the oar to that possible with a two-man oar. A man working with the stand-and-sit stroke of the medieval and later galleys needs nearly 0.6 m more height to accommodate him, which was no problem in the galleys but a different matter inside an ancient warship. The space and dimensions required to perform this stroke are shown by Burlet in (**68**). The extension needed is mainly below the heels of the sitting men, though 0.12 m more is also needed for the standing man's head. The standing man has, however, less need of elbow room, and such men can work an oar when only 0.45 m apart, centre-to-centre (Zysberg and Burlet: 1986). On oars worked by four men or more that would be an appreciable advantage in reducing the overall breadth of the oar-system, and hence BWL and so the ship's resistance if its stability allows.

Though the work which it is possible to do in this stroke is rather less than in sitting, its greater length allows the other two, or three, men on the oar to have a longer stroke and so do more work. On balance, however, it would probably have been best to work three-man oars with sitting men only,

66 *Interior of the reconstructed five (see* **65***): Denning*

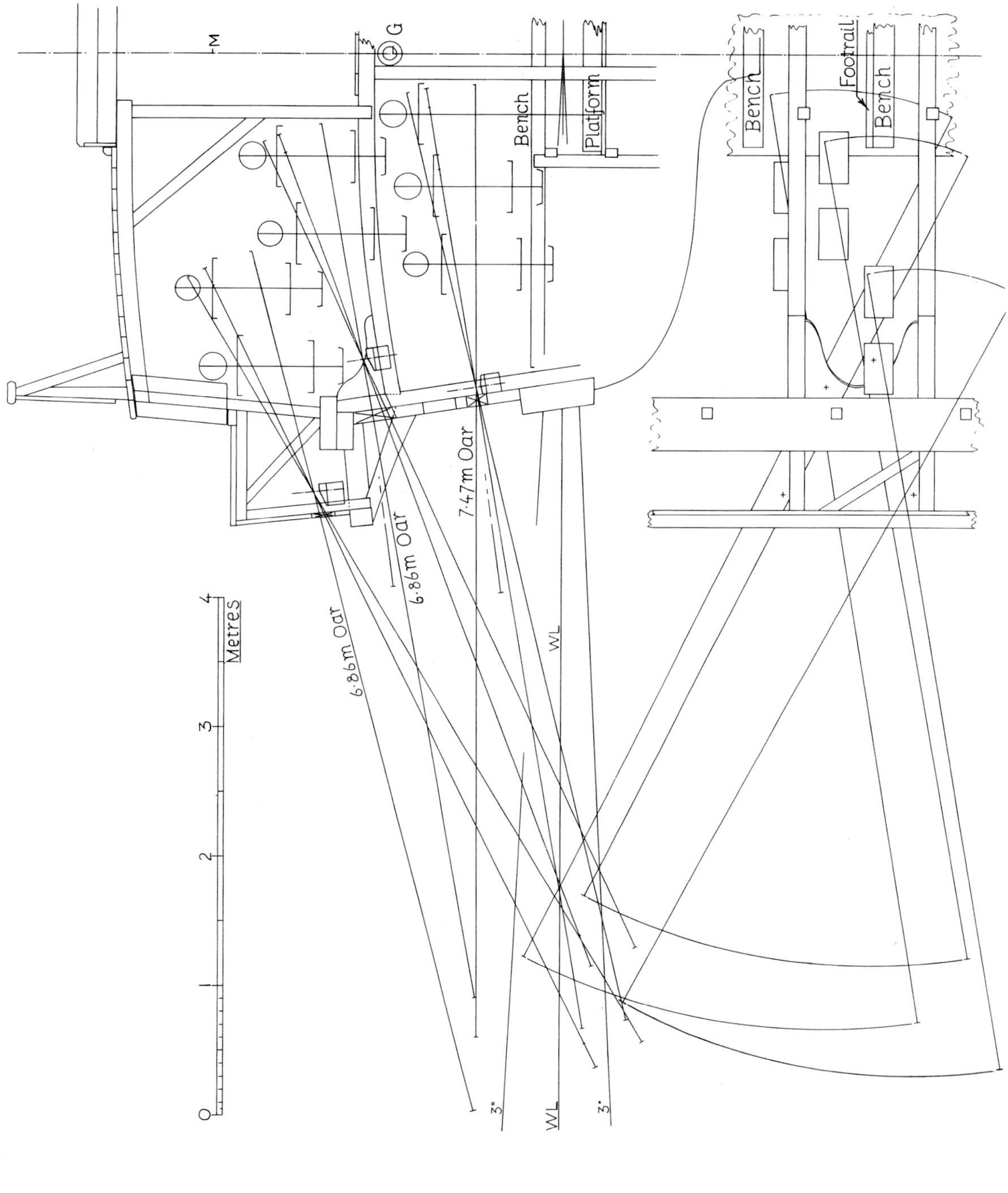

67 *The Isola Tiberina monument interpreted as a six – midship section*

mainly because an *interscalmium* of 0.98 m is less than the ideal for the standing stroke. The most effective arrangement with oars manned by four or more men when enclosed within a ship is more problematical and can be decided only by careful trial. In (**69**) the three-man oar is nevertheless shown with a standing man at the butt to show not only what space would be required to accommodate him, but also to indicate that three-level oarsystems worked by standing men anywhere but in the lowest level could not have been accommodated within three-level ships whose top decks were only about 10 Roman feet or 2.95 m above the water.

The three-man oar in a seven is most easily accommodated at the thalamian level where it is shown in (**69**). The furniture shown for the standing man follows that in French galleys of the 17th cent. (Zysberg and Burlet: 1986) with the omission of the pédagne which would serve no useful function within the shorter *interscalmium* of 0.98 m (1.245 m in the galleys). (**68**), by Burlet, shows in diagrammatic form the movements of the men ar-

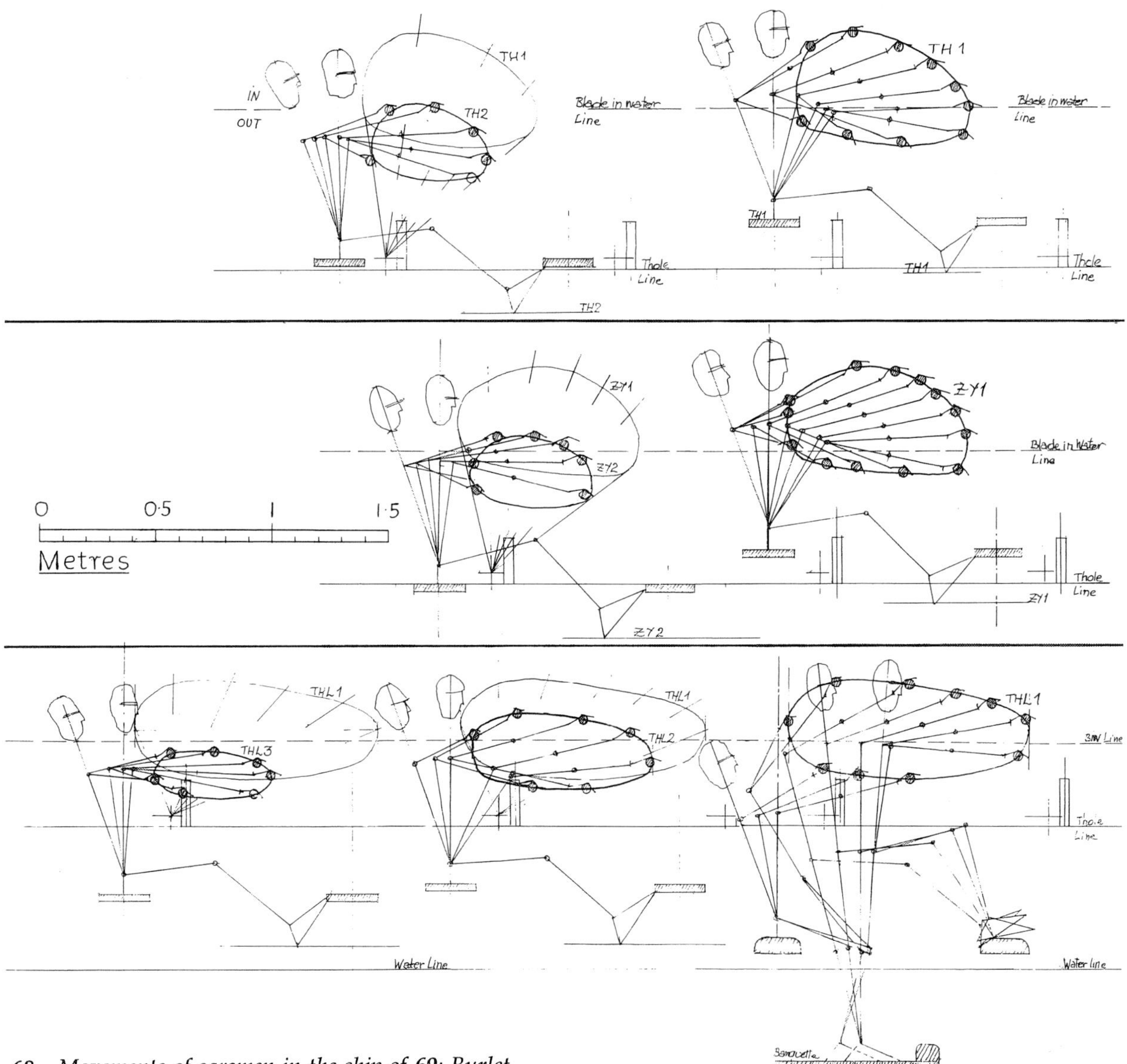

68 *Movements of oarsmen in the ship of* ***69****: Burlet*

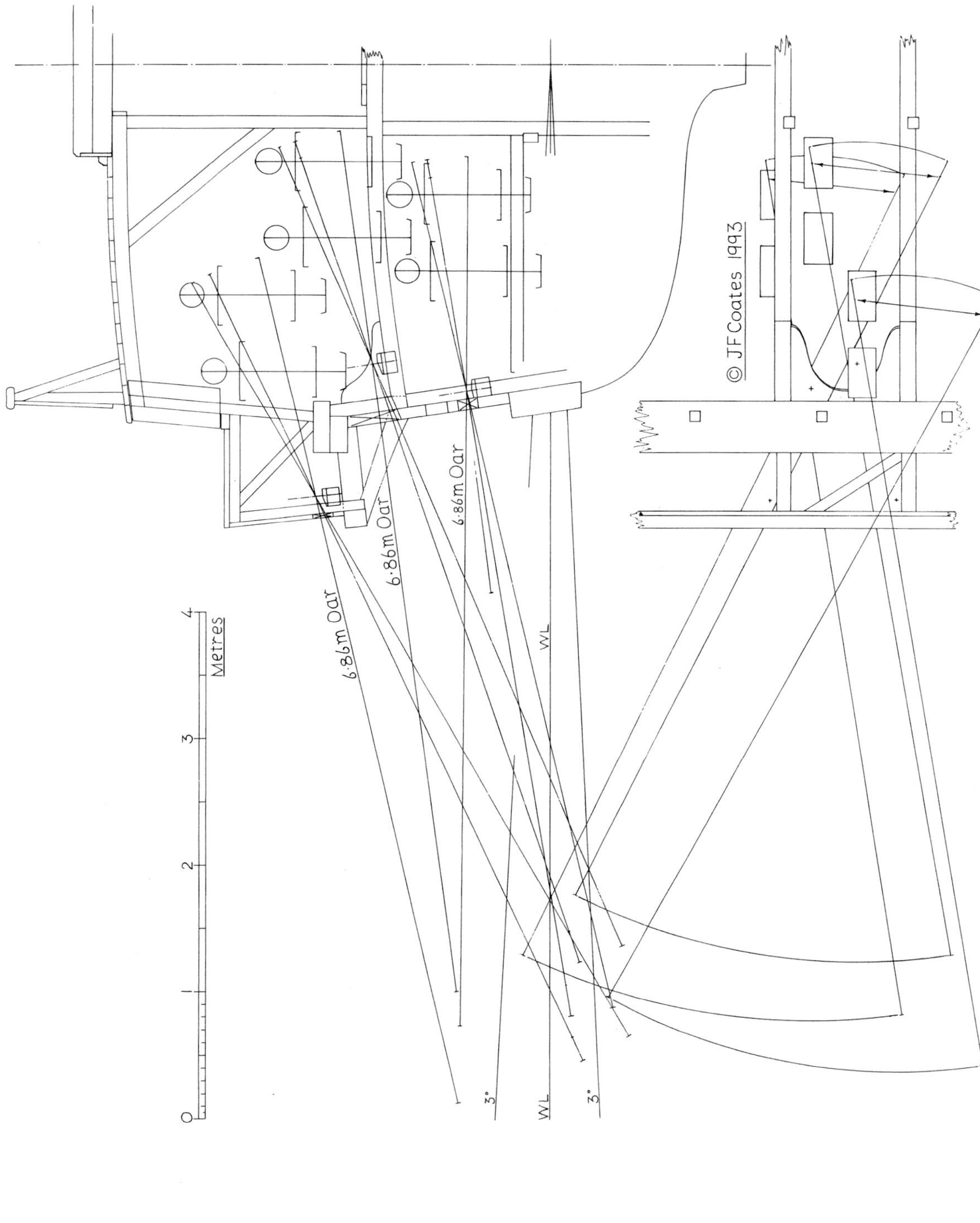

69 *The Isola Tiberina monument as a seven – midship section*

ranged as in (**69**). The presence of the standing man on the three-man oar should make it possible, within the 0.98 m *interscalmium*, to make a maximum length of stroke of 1.3 m so that the maximum arcs of the oars in the seven would be the same as those in the six of (**67**).

The seven of (**68**), if about 15% more power could in this way have been applied on the oar-handles, having little greater breadth on the waterline and only 10 tonnes more displacement, would have been ¼ knot faster than the six. Alternatively the seven could have been developed to carry more troops than the six, and the extra thalamian added to make the best use of the space created in the ship by increasing BWL to maintain stability in face of the additional topweight of troops.

The Larger Polyremes

Surviving accounts suggest that polyremes larger than sevens were built in relatively small numbers, and were probably attempts to create a ship invulnerable to ramming, difficult to capture by boarding, and at the same time carrying a powerful armament of catapults and troops and so able to grapple and overwhelm any lesser type by boarding. A ship with such qualities would have little tactical need for more than an easily attained speed under oar, say 4 or 5 knots continuously for some hours, sufficient for instance to move, in the absence of a fair wind, in a day (or not much longer) from a source of water to a position tactically intolerable to an enemy fleet so as to force action, after which to return to a watering place for the necessary refreshment of her large complement. The balance in the larger polyremes between the weights devoted to armament (split between weapons, missiles and troops), protection from ramming and missiles, and oar power must have exercised the thoughts of many admirals and military leaders. It was the same problem that returned in an acute form with the appearance of the steam-propelled metal battleship two millennia later, when, released from the constraints of timber, gunpowder and sail, that balance which greatly affected a warship's manner of use could again be chosen within wide limits.

While eights and nines did in at least some, probably earlier, cases have three levels of oars, two level systems were probably adopted later in these types: it could well have depended upon the intended use of each ship and so upon the balance of qualities just mentioned. Three levels of oars would have been best if speed was important, but not if armament or protection, or both, was the dominant requirement. It may be assumed that oars worked by four men had at least one standing man on the butt. Three-man oars could also have had one standing (as shown in **69**). If Orosius's description of Antony's heavy ships at Aktion, that they had decks 10 Roman feet above water, is accurate, it implies that their oars were on two levels, not three. A ten on three levels and with the oarcrew arranged within the smallest total height, with 3, 3 and 4 men, from top to bottom, would have been at least 12 Roman feet above water at the deck. Their BWL need not on the other hand have been more than about 7.3 m: they would therefore have been faster but could not have carried so much armament and troops. Internal furniture for the oarsystem would have been complicated and the working of the oarsystem more vulnerable to penetrating missiles (see below). Two-level tens would have met the requirements for heavy ships, to carry a heavy load of armament and troops and be relatively well protected to enable them to act like the floating fortresses which Antony's speech before the battle of Aktion describes. The price would have been paid in cost and speed.

Tens, the largest type recorded as taking part in battle, were almost certainly mostly if not all two-level ships. BWL would have been about 9 m and BOA (including the oarboxes) about 10 m. Loaded displacement would have been in the range of 180 to 200 tonnes, but their length is not likely to have been much, if any, more than that of sixes and sevens because the main structure of their hulls could not have been any deeper than in those smaller types. If therefore they had files of oarcrew averaging 30 men, the oarcrew would have numbered 600 with five men to each oar about 12 m long with a gearing of about 2.2, very much like those in the galleys of the later 17th cent. AD. It is impossible to say whether all the oarcrew also worked standing or whether some were sitting. The total complement would be expected to have weighed about 90 tonnes, allowing 30 tonnes or so for troops and a missile armament. If 200 troops were aboard, about 20 tonnes of other armament could have been carried.

The steadiness of beamy ships (in the absence of swell) would have made them better platforms for missile-throwers, enabling them to be aimed more accurately and thus be more effective. The development of catapults for use at sea is likely to have encouraged a change to two-level oarsystems not only for offensive reasons but also for defence. As explained by Foley and Soedel (1981), some types of missile could not have been prevented from penetrating as far as oarcrews but a two-level system with more men at each oar and on fewer levels would be somewhat less prone to disruption when oarsmen were killed or wounded by a missile.

There is no evidence to indicate that the larger polyremes of any one particular denomination followed any standard design. The larger the number of files of oarsmen the larger the number of ways in which they could have been arranged, and the different balance of qualities called for in different localities and by a variety of threats would in all probability, have given little incentive to try to develop a single optimum design in separate places over so large an area as the Eastern Mediterranean.

The evidence from the memorial for the Battle of Aktion on the waterline breadths of fives to tens

It is strange that of the costly and prestigious larger polyremes so little hard evidence about their design has survived. In literature it amounts to little more than statements that they carried towers, missile-throwers and troops, besides Orosius's remark about the big ships at Aktion. Archaeological evidence about these types is so far confined to the sockets in which the rams from Antony's defeated fleet were mounted in a masonry wall of Augustus's memorial for that battle. These sockets have been measured (Murray and Petsas: 1989) and an estimation is attempted here of the waterline breadths of the types of ships from which the rams so mounted came.

The main ships of Antony's fleet were polyremes up to tens, and Murray has argued that the rams of all the types from fives to tens were represented at the memorial. He has suggested two tentative determinations of the class of ship to which the ram originally in each socket belonged. The breadth of each socket in way of the ram wales is the dimension most likely to indicate the BWL of the corresponding ship. In (**70**) therefore those breadths, numbered by socket according to Murray and Petsas, have been shown in descending order of magnitude; and they can be seen to fall into recognisable groups, as there indicated. Allowing a clearance of 0.02 m the breadths of sockets similar to those at Aktion suitable for mounting the Athlit ram casting and that made and fitted for *Olympias* have been added to (**70**) on the left hand side. While it would be possible to split the breadths of the sockets into similarly-sized groups in a number of ways according to the variation one is prepared to allow within each group, seven groups have been indicated in (**70**), each having a maximum variation from its mean of about 2%.

Though estimation of BWL from breadth of ram casting can only be approximate, to have any validity it must be based on some consideration of the likely proportions of both castings and hulls. If Orosius is to be believed, the heights of the decks of the bigger ships were little different from that of fives, though sixes (and probably some sevens too) were a little higher as attested and already indicated by reconstruction. The height of the main hull above water, whose topwale would have been hidden within the oarbox, could not have been other than a fairly constant proportion of the deck height. Drafts of these types could not have varied very much either, so the total depth of the main hull would not have been much different from one of these types to another. We know that the ratio of hull length to hull depth in the three was at the practical structural limit to resist longitudinal bending in waves for the length of a useful service life; and it is clear that that ratio would have been much the same in the larger types as in the three. Their much greater displacement would have ensured that they too were at the useful limit as regards longitudinal bending strength, if they were of about the same length as a three. It therefore seems unlikely that they were much longer than threes, despite the fact that the earlier and exceptional forty of Ptolemy Philopator (p. 274–277) and the *Leontophoros* of Lysimachus (p. 273) were 2½ or 3 times longer, over 100 m (substantially longer, be it noted, than the longest wooden line-of-battle ship ever built in the 19th century!). Those ships must also have had exceptionally deep main hulls, about 6 m at least if the deck were structurally part

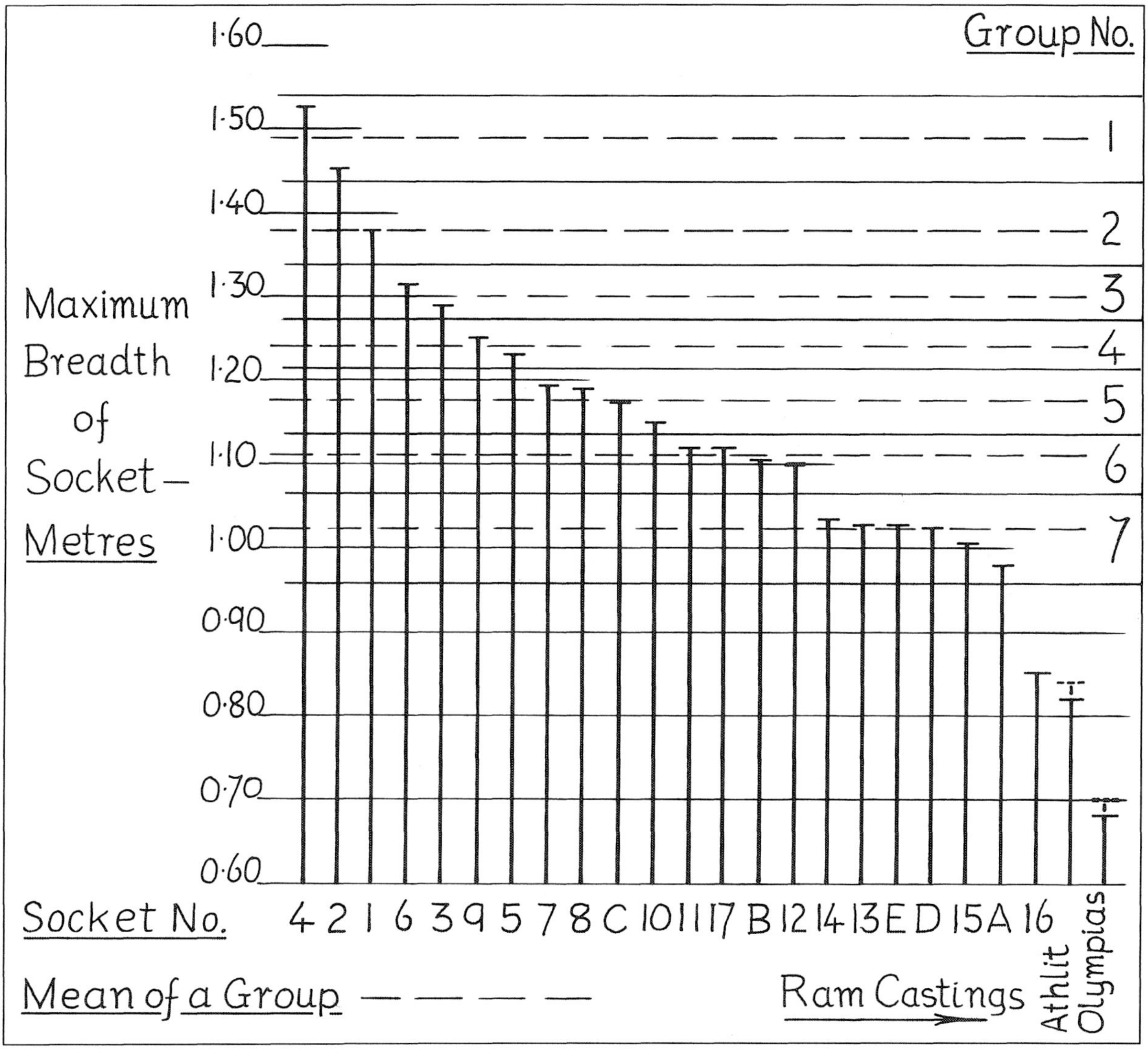

70

of the hull which would have precluded any oarboxes, or otherwise about 8 m deep. They may be expected to have stood 4 to 6 m out of the water, impressive indeed. It would nevertheless be surprising if they did not in fact suffer from severe structural weakness of one kind or another, the most likely reason, apart from cost and difficulties in manning and propulsion, for their uniqueness.

If the lengths of fives and tens were much the same, it seems also likely that their rams would not have been of greatly varying lengths. This is borne out by the relatively small, 20%, variation in the heights of the sockets at Aktion, which bear little relation to their breadths, and by the height of the Athlit ram which is nearly as great as the highest socket at Aktion, but which is most plausibly ascribable to only a four (**22**). A long ram on the bows of a heavy ship might look impressive, but any extension beyond that required for penetration would not only add to cost but weaken the ram in withstanding the considerable lateral forces generated when ramming a target at any large angle from broadside-on, as the square-ended finned design of ram-head was clearly designed to do.

The breadths of polyremes however were very different, as demanded by their oarsystems and probably distinguished their denominations externally more than any other feature. Estimating their BWLs from the breadth of ram sockets here depends on the following assumptions:

a. The breadth of a socket is little greater than that of the ram casting measured across the ears at the after ends of the troughs which fit over the timber ram wales.

b. The ram wales are substantially straight and tangential to the wales on the hull at the waterline, and the angle between them is proportional to the BWL of the ship.

c. The lines of the outer sides of the ram wales intersect near the head of the ram, as in the Athlit ram (Casson and Steffy:1991).

By these assumptions the breadth of a socket, less 0.02 m for a working clearance for inserting the casting, may be taken to be some proportion of the ship's BWL. The proportion is 1/5.44 in the case of *Olympias* and it is found to be 1/5.66 if the Athlit ram is matched to the four of (**59**). These figures suggest that in the larger ships the ratio would be about 1/5.9. Applying that ratio to the mean breadths of the groups 1 to 7 in (**70**), estimates of BWL for fives to tens at Aktion have been obtained. They are tabulated in Appendix E of this Chapter. On the right-hand side of the table, for comparison, are:

a. the BWLs of the reconstructions for which ship sections have been given, together with their minumum lateral spacing of oarcrew (centre-line to centre-line of each man) and breadth of the ship's middle-line gangway, for least hull BWL and resistance, and

b. the BWLs for the same ships with larger spacings and gangways, sufficient to avoid all constriction of movement both between individual oarcrew and in necessarily often repeated embarkations and disembarkations.

The BWLs derived from the ram sockets are nearer to those assuming the larger spacings and wider gangways, and the two sets of estimated BWLs may be regarded as giving likely upper and lower limits for them in ships of the Aktion period from fives to tens. The differences are greatest in the case of tens, 1.3 m, reducing to 0.6 m for fives.

*The ships of the shipshed frescoes from Pompeii (**43**), the frescoes of Aula Isiaca (**40**) and Nymphaion (**13**), of the Ostia Relief (**35**) and of the Calenian Dishes (**18 I** and **II**)*

These frescoes show ships with all three levels of oars emerging through oarports in the sides of their oarboxes. The Shipshed frescoes are nearly unique in showing bow views of ships, and thus exhibiting some dimensions in breadth so significant in oared ships which are normally no wider than they have to be, particularly on the waterline. In these frescoes the proportions of the oarboxes are clearly depicted. (**71**) is an attempt to reconstruct the midship section with a practicable oarsystem for this type of ship.

The oarsystems in which all three levels of oars emerge through the sides of the oarboxes are necessarily very different from those of the foregoing reconstructions, in that the oarcrew is much more nearly on one level.

One simple solution of the reconstruction of this type of ship, which has already been advanced, is that they were threes rowed *alla sensile* with one-man oars just as in the medieval galleys. That however would require the oars to be as long as they were in those galleys, and for the same reason. Such a type of three would certainly not be any faster than the medieval triremi, so far short of the speed of the earlier fast threes that such ships would be slower than the little liburnians, making that solution unlikely.

If they were threes with shorter oars to enable them to have been faster, the overall breadth needed to have accommodated the oarcrew would have been about 5.6 m to 6 m so that, with an oarbox of the proportions shown, the topwale of the hull proper (obscured within the oarbox) would have had to be either inboard of the lowest and outboard oarsman, or alongside and outside his seat. In the first case the BWL could be not more than 3.2 m, insufficient for stability, and in the latter case, while BWL would be big enough, not only would the topwale be too low and the hull open and too shallow to be strong enough in longitudinal bending, but the oarbox, to give the right gearing to the shorter oars would be much narrower than clearly shown in the frescoes. The only way in which all these matters could be corrected would involve adding about a metre to the breadth of the ship, a course which in a fast type of ship must surely be rejected. It can therefore be concluded that these ships were not threes.

If they were fives, with the outboard men working one-man oars and sitting in the oarbox and above the top of the hull, a practical oarsystem can be fitted into a ship about 8 m wide overall and 5.7 m in BWL, about right for a five. Placing a file of oarsmen in the oarbox may seem an improbable proposition but if the height between the bottom and top oarports, vertically above and below each other is considered, the size of the oarbox depicted can be seen to be large enough for such an arrangement, and one may be sure that in these, as in all ships of mature design, no space is left unused without very good reason. Because the top oarports are vertically above the bottom ones, it is necessary for the top oars to clear the tops of the outer oarsmen's heads at the end of their stroke. That determines the height of the sides of the oarbox and therefore its breadth because the ratio of breadth to height is clearly shown in the frescoes.

The lengths of the oars will be largely determined by that of the outer one-man oar which would be as short as efficiency allows in a ship assumed to be capable of about 8 knots maximum. In (**71**) it is shown 4.66 m long, like the one-man oars in previously discussed reconstructions, and it has a gearing of 3.5 like those working with two-man oars in other fives. The two-man oars have been given a gearing, for the in-board men, of about 2.5 instead of 2.8 as before in view of their greater length. To reduce the length of these oars as much as possible (which seems very necessary in this arrangement where the top oars have to be about 10 m long) successive tholes have been set inboard of the one below. That has also enabled the oarports to be of nearly the same size as shown in the representations.

Working inwards from the outer man, the pair of middle men and their oar have to clear the indispensable pillars supporting the deck edge which also have to clear the sweeps of the butts of the outer oars. As in the seven just discussed standing men are shown in (**71**); but with about a 0.6 m increase in ship breadth to give more elbow room they could all work sitting. It is necessary that the faces of the outer men do not collide with the middle oar at any point in the stroke and that has been avoided in the arrangement shown. The arcs of oars are, as before, swung well forward of athwartships, except that of the outer oar which for the reason just described has to be further aft. As in the other fives, the blades of the one-man oars have to overtake those of the middle oars which are 7 m long and, again as before, well clear of them. The middle and top two-man oars have their handles in close proximity at the catch but draw away from each other during the pull, as in the *alla sensile* system. The top oars, though as short as possible, are long, 10 m, as in the medieval *alla sensile* galleys but, being worked by two men, they should be capable of being effective at 8 knots.

Because all three levels of oars must work above the topwale of the main hull, the hull must be relatively shallow if the overall height of the ship to the topdeck is to be about ten Roman feet above water. These ships thus raise the same problem of main hull depth and strength as the Erment model and the Phoenician ships shown with two courses of large rectangular openings (**6**, **1b**, **2b**, **3f** and **g**, **4e** and **5**). There is no geometrical obstacle to placing a structurally effective deck across the main hull of these later ships because, except for the outboard man, the oarsystem is above the highest possible level for the topwale relative to the loom of the outer oar. The hull, 2.3 m deep and thus about 18 depths long assuming an oarcrew of 300, could be strong enough in bending if the deck planking was tenoned and about 80 mm thick, and the bottom about 80 mm thick also. A *ὑπόζωμα* could enable these thicknesses to be reduced by about 10%. If such a shallow hull had been without effective deck, an implausibly heavy topwale would have been necessary instead.

This type of ship has therefore been reconstructed as a five with a decked hull, as shown in section in (**71**) where the top oar is shown worked by standing men. Those men could be sitting, with some adjustments to their oar arcs, but the breadth of the ship, which is determined by that of the oarsystem, would have to be increased by 0.5 m, making the ship slower. The two-man oars would have to be lengthened, the top oar by nearly a metre, also reducing the attainable speed. The sec-

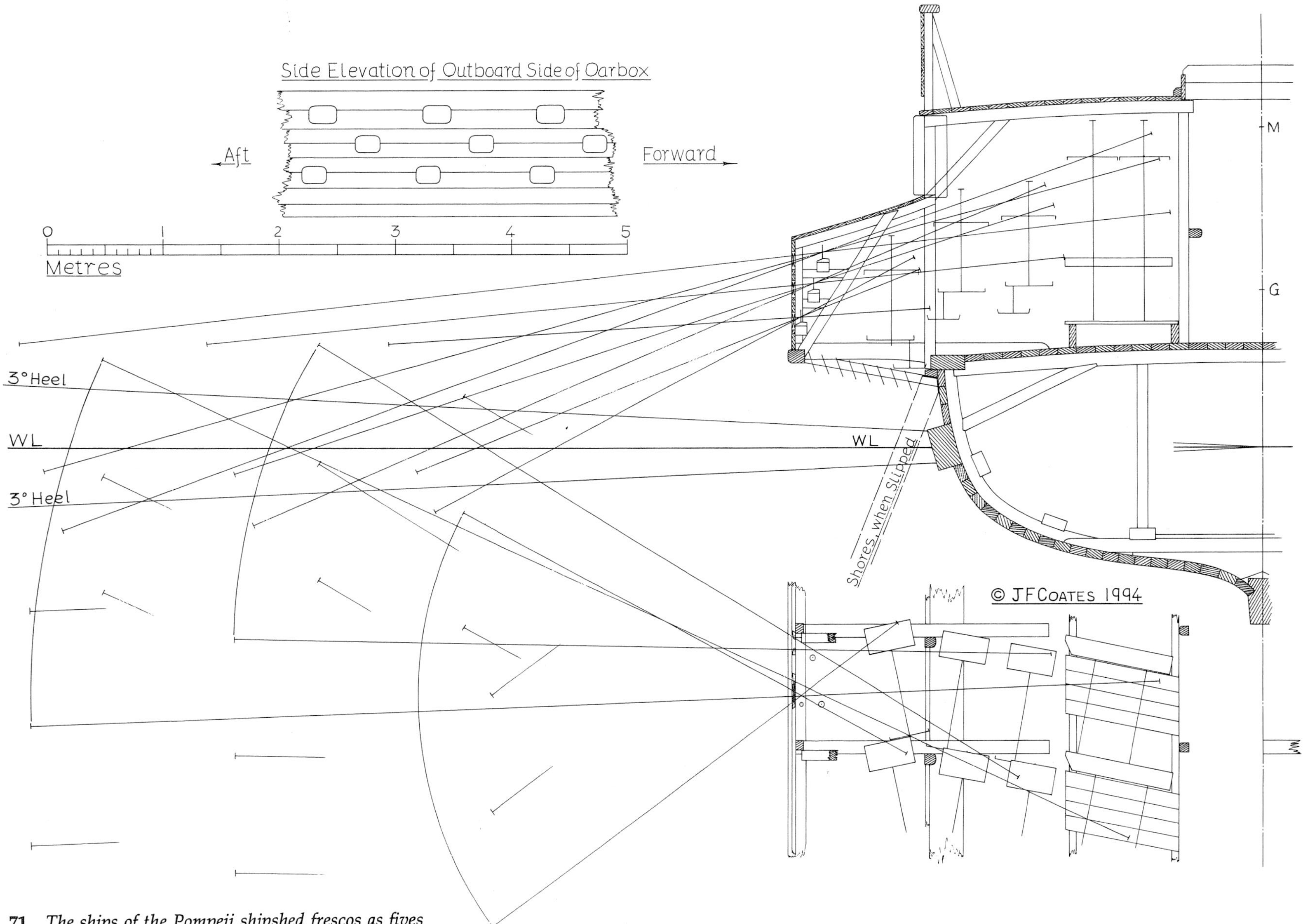

71 *The ships of the Pompeii shipshed frescos as fives*

tion drawn has a BOA of 8.2 m, the breadth of the hull proper is 5.8 m, BWL is 5.7 m and the deck is 2.9 m above the water. In this type of ship the oarcrew are necessarily virtually on the same level, side by side. In view of the additional breadth therefore needed to accommodate any extra pairs of oarsmen, it must be doubted if this type of oarsystem would have been expanded for use in mono-hulled ships of higher denominations, except at the expense of increasing the BWL by a metre or so for every file added. Such files would have been best added to the top oars but the wider resulting ships would have been progressively slower. The arrangement for a six shown in (**67**) would have been superior in speed.

Ventilation for the oarcrew would be improved with this arrangement in which no oarsmen are working low down in the hull, and the air intake through the underside of the oarbox is below all of them. Better ventilation could have been the reason for its adoption, but it might also have been to increase the height of the lowest oars above the waves, or to dispense with the need for oarports cut in the sides of the shallower hull (although these had been in use since the introduction of the two-level pentecontor presumably without having been regarded as creating an unacceptable risk).

A heel under sail of 10° is possible without immersing the bottom of the oarbox. Another advantage might have been the greater defence against ramming attacks afforded by being able to fit struts to the space previously occupied by thalamian oarsmen, as indicated in (**71**). On the other hand, the hull being 2½ times wider than it is deep, would have needed to have its sides supported on the slip to prevent progressive lateral sag and that would explain the shores shown in the Shipshed frescoes from Pompeii. In (**71**) such shores are indicated in dashed lines.

This type has the advantages in building of not needing so many grown knees, never the easiest type of timber to obtain, and also of separating the oarsystem and its furniture, oarboxes and the superstructure of the hull itself, which would simplify the demarcation of trades and organisation and speed of building (for example it would have facilitated the local separation of 'live' and 'dead' work that is recorded in building Octavian's fleet in 37–36 BC (p. 153). It might however have brought with it some penalty in sprint speed, though the better ventilation for all the oarsmen could well have enabled the oarcrew to maintain higher powers on their oar handles for longer periods than in ships with oarsmen situated below the main convective flow of air. This type of ship could also have been attractive to the Romans in the Punic wars because, having no oarsmen within the main hull, there would have been much more room for water and stores, which could have been helpful in waging naval campaigns far from their fleet's main bases.

As there are oarcrew in the oarboxes, protective louvres would have been needed under them, and some would have had to be removable to allow the shores shown in the Shipshed frescoes (and in dotted lines in (**71**)) to be set up under the topwales when the ships were to be laid up for a long period to prevent the ships' sides from dropping as a result of creep in the timbers. Timber ships have always been susceptible to deformation from that cause.

The ship of the Ostia relief is very probably of the same type also (see p.235–237): no practicable arrangement of oars and men has been found with oarports in the side of the oarbox vertically above each other in all three levels, shown uniquely in the Ostia relief. It is also the only representation showing both oarports and oars, all emerging from the oarbox. In all others showing three levels of oarports in the side of the oarbox, the ports are *en échelon*, as in (**71**). The Ostia relief is not very big, so the breadth of the ridges of stone could have been as narrow as could be carved without causing the stone to flake away. The oars seem to be as fine a detail as anywhere in this carving. If in these circumstances all oars were to be shown, the sculptor could do no more than he did by showing the oars lying close together side-by-side. If he also wanted to suggest motion in the oars they would have to be given some inclination from the vertical and the ports, if they were to be shown at all, would have to be put at the tops of their shafts where they intersected the appropriate level in the side of the oarbox. The oarports could not then have been shown *en échelon*.

If the reconstruction of (**71**) is correct in principle, an affinity between the main hull structure of this type of five and those of the proposed reconstructions of Phoenician, and therefore Punic, ships emerges. This may therefore be identified as the type of five which the Romans copied from the

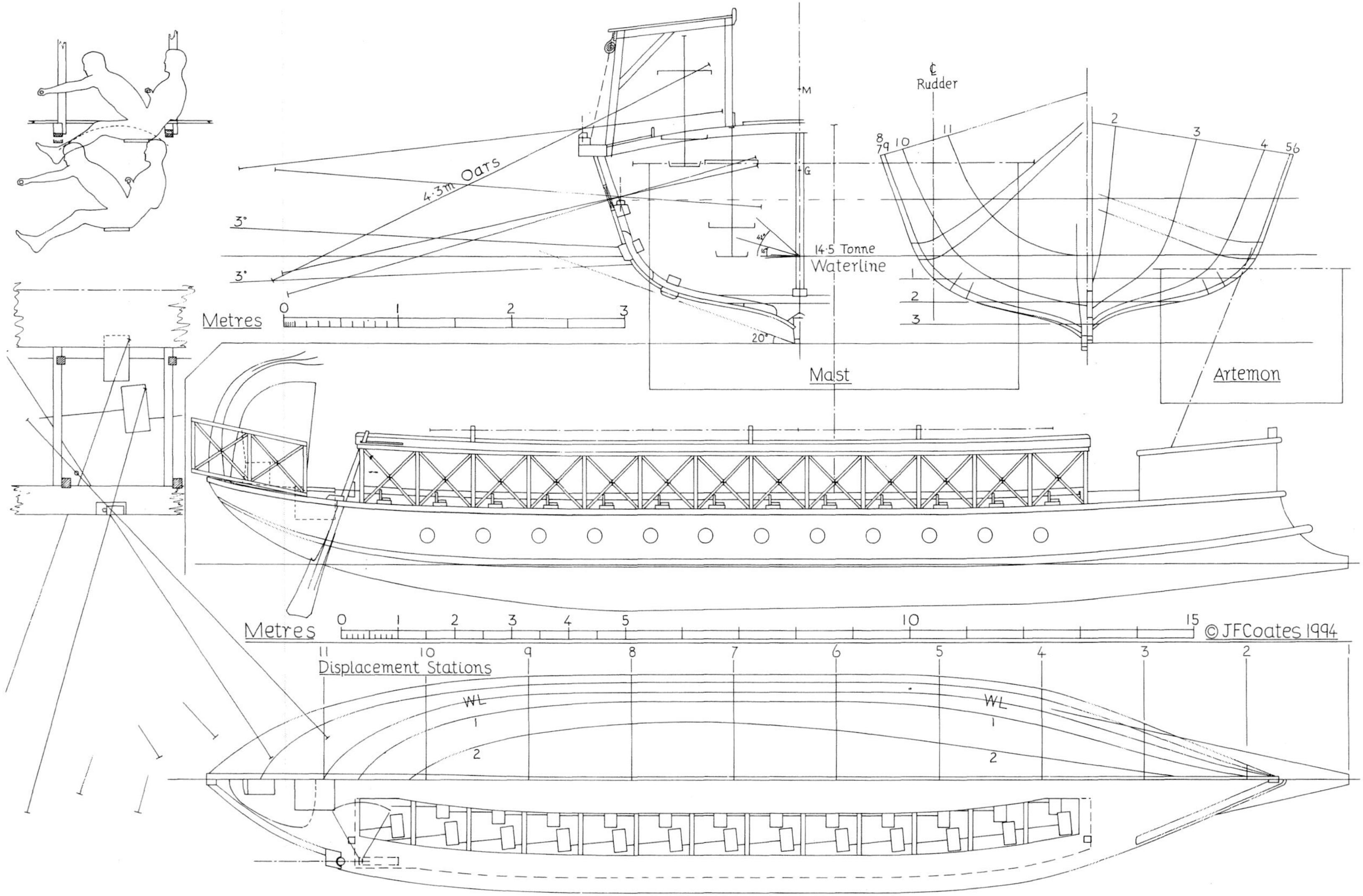

72 *Liburnian of the 1st and 2nd centuries* AD

Carthaginians (p.43). The intricacy of its oarsystem makes its copying by the Romans very understandable, once the suitability of this type of five to their naval requirements had been appreciated. That they copied this type does not prove that they never used the Greek type (**61–65**) too.

The Liburnian

Liburnians, at least in their original form as Illyrian pirate ships, were considered to be fast vessels. Being small, they must therefore have been not only light in displacement but also fine-lined as attested in literature. After having been adopted on account of those qualities by the Roman Republic they were probably developed to suit the needs of the imperial navy in distant provinces of the empire as well as in the Mediterranean. Those modifications probably took some toll of its original speed in, for example, adding a greater protection against missiles. Octavian's liburnians at Aktion were presumably cataphract, for otherwise they could scarcely have been very effective in any role, even if only auxiliary, in face of the missiles of Antony's heavy ships. As with *λέμβοι*, of which they were a type, it is likely that there were liburnians of various sizes. They could have been fitted out for various uses, e.g. fleet auxiliaries, scouts, for anti-piracy patrols or to form light naval forces in the Roman provinces. Their oarsystem is however always referred to as of two levels and it is probable that most had about 50 oars. Cataphract ships armed with troops on a proper deck would have been built broader on the waterline than ships in which speed was mainly required.

(**72**) shows a reconstruction of a light 50–oared liburnian. The oars are on two levels without outriggers, which accords as closely as possible with the available evidence both literary and iconographical, from the first and second centuries AD as interpreted in an earlier chapter (p. 263–264). There is no evidence for outriggers in any representations of two-level oared ships either in general (**i-vi**) or in those identifiable as liburnians (beyond indications of a protruding wale). The ship shown here has light protection for the oarcrew in the form of a wooden canopy supported at its outboard edges by braced pillars set in the topwale. Side protection is by screens let down when required. This protective structure is shown in (**45–49**) and interpreted on p. 251–253, while the side screens are shown rigged in place in (**44**).

This reconstruction displaces about 15 tonnes and is 18 m on the waterline. BWL is 3.0 m, sufficient to give the ship a GM of 0.7 m which would be adequate for effective sailing and to limit rocking by crew movements while under oar. BOA is 3.9 m, and the oars have been made 4.3 m long with a gearing of 2.75 m. They are a little shorter than the 4.66 m of the more ancient three, to help shipping them in a narrower vessel. A sprint speed of just over 7 knots should be attainable.

Ἡμιολία (ναῦς) or Ἡμιόλιος (λέμβος)

A number of arrangements of oarsytem have been proposed for *ἡμιολίαι*. The one offered here (**72**) would best fill the space available in the smallest, lightest and finest-lined hull able to accommodate 50 oarsmen within the topwale of the hull. It would be about 21 m on the waterline and displace about 14 tonnes. As in the case of the liburnian, the other small fast vessel discussed in this chapter, the wetted area of the hull should be minimised in any reconstruction. In the liburnian BWL is 3.0 m while in the *ἡμιολία* it could be reduced to 2.7 m: it may safely be assumed that BWL was as small as stability allowed. With that breadth, and a practical flare of the sides above water of say 25°, the breadth across the topwales of the hull cannot be greater than 3.75 m. If the necessary gangway is to be provided, outriggers are unavoidable in the *ἡμιολία*, owing to the necessary length and gearing of the oars and because the oarcrew are virtually at one level. BOA becomes 4.3 m. In the liburnian, on the other hand, no outriggers are necessary, and so a representation of a single level ship with indications of an outrigger may be suspected to be of a *ἡμιολία*.

In (**73**) all oars are worked by one man, but it is quite possible that the men sitting in the middle body of the hull, where there are two files, rowed two-man oars. Pirates in different places may have preferred one or the other system.

Wetted area would not be much less (5%) than in a liburnian with the same number of oars, so frictional resistance would be that much less too, but wavemaking at a given speed would be reduced also. Wavemaking forms a larger proportion of total resistance at higher speeds, so the finer and

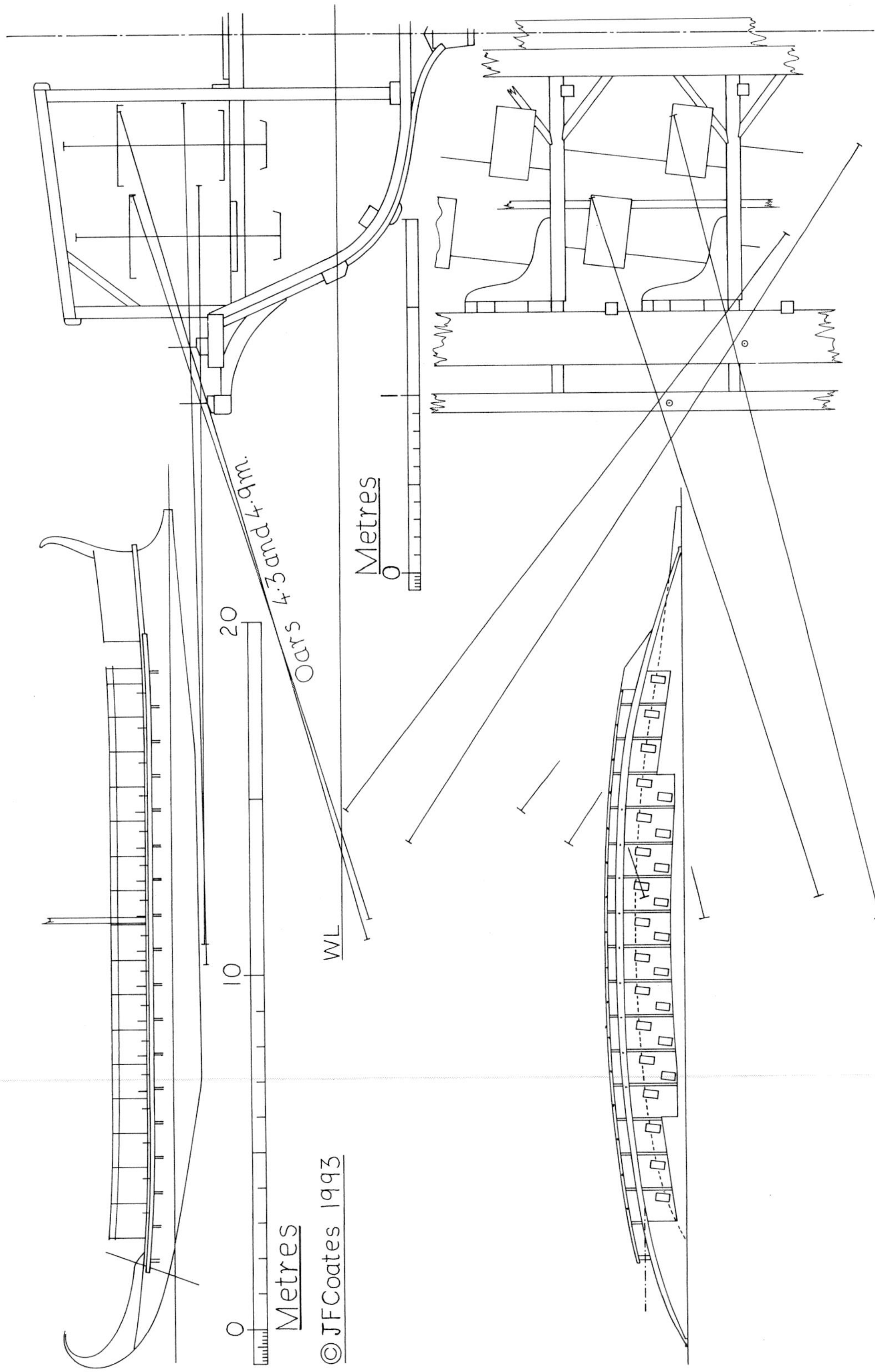

73 *Hemiolia c.* 300 BC

longer hull of the ἡμιολία would give it a speed advantage over the liburnian, and the very similar two-level pentecontor, particularly in a short race. It is not likely that ἡμιολίαι with many more than 50 crew would have been built because if longer, their hulls would have had to be stronger and so deeper and heavier, taking away the advantage of the greater oar power. The earlier single-level pentecontors must for the same reason have had hulls more capacious than was necessary only to accommodate their oarcrews. Alexander appears to have had ἡμιολίαι on the Indus with oarcrews of only 30 (p. 10), and they are stated to have been faster than his two-level ships with the same number of oars.

The Τριημιολία (p. 266)

This type, once more generically called ἡμιολίαι, is mentioned a number of times in the earlier chapters in descriptions of Rhodian naval operations and as belonging to the fleets of Attalus of Pergamum, Egypt and Athens. In the third Punic war (151 BC) Rome's expeditionary force was taken to Utica 'in 50 fives and 100 ἡμιολίαι as well as many aphracts, cercuri and round ships'. Those cataphract ἡμιολίαι were almost certainly τριημιολίαι then taking the place of threes. There are few clues to their design. They were clearly however an important type of warship, which was widely used. The Lindos prow (**11**) and less directly the Lindos relief (**21**) of a ship's stern have been associated epigraphically with the τριημιολία. The Samothrace prow, which has been the subject of many proposed reconstructions ranging from twos to sevens, also has strong associations with Rhodes and might therefore be suspected of being a τριημιολία.

Being in three dimensions, the Samothrace prow has been of particular interest to reconstructors, but it poses the question of its scale and indeed of the extent to which any of its features may have been exaggerated or diminished for sculptural and aesthetic effect. Its scale has been analysed in some depth by Sleeswyk (1982) who concluded that it lies between 0.6 and 0.7 of full scale. He rejects Carlini's reconstruction (1934) of the oarsystem as a two on the ground that the lengths given by him to the one-man oars were too different. He also rightly pays attention to the implications of, and to the practical need for, the manhole in the upper surface of the oarbox just forward of what looks at first sight like a curved bracket at the after end of the surviving part of the monument. Sleeswyk interprets the ship to be a two with the oars through the upper oarports being worked by men standing up and facing forward. That however would not have been easy to do with any appreciable power within an *interscalmium* near to one metre.

Consideration of the likely height of the centre of gravity of the ship as a proportion of her total height, the likely breadth of the ship amidships, her displacement relative to the number of a τριημιολία's oarcrew, and the consequent height of the metacentre, leads to the conclusion that the proportions of the ship are practical as sculpted. Other considerations, including those addressed by Sleeswyk, indicate that the scale may be taken to be $^2/_3$ that of a real ship, whose BWL amidships would then be near to 4.0 m. That is more than that of a three (*Olympias*) and less than that of a four (**59**).

Allowing for an adequate gangway, there is room for no more than two oarsmen to work side-by-side at beam level on each side of the ship. If the ship were a two however it would be too under-oared and slow to be a warship, which it surely must be. It cannot be a boxed-in three because there would be insufficient breadth in the hull of the surviving part for the thalamians, but it could be a τριημιολία with the thalamian files shortened owing to the lack of breadth at the ends of a fine-lined hull, which was probably the essential distinguishing feature of ἡμιολίαι which were fast ships. (JSM notes that in the three for the same reason the thalamian and zygian files are shorter than the thranite files by four oarsmen). Even if shown in the part which has been lost, thalamian oarports would not have appeared in the remaining part of the monument.

The Samothrace prow has therefore been reconstructed as a τριημιολία, a type referred to as fast like ἡμιολίαι and classed with threes, but with an oarcrew of only 120 as compared with the three's 170. (**74**) shows such a reconstruction, and it represents virtually the only practicable way in which the principle of the ἡμιολίαι can be applied to a much larger ship in which the greater depth of the hull, necessary for strength, can be used to accommodate more oarcrew. Photius states that 'the τριημιολία is not three times the ἡμιολίαι but a τριήρης', which indicates quite strongly that there were three files of oarcrew a side in a ship which

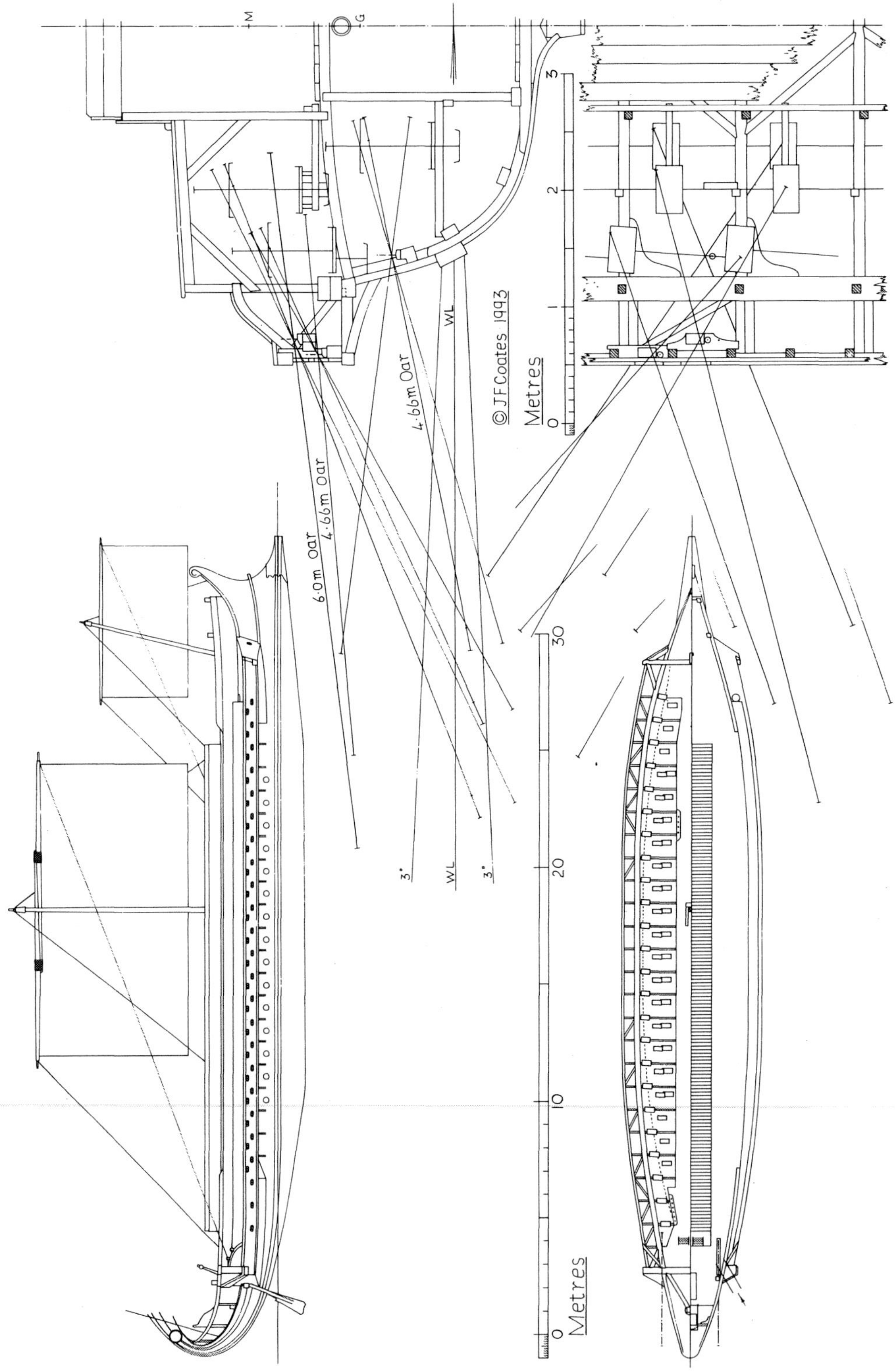

74 *Trihemiolia c.* 300 BC *based on the Samothrace prow* (**20**) *and on the Lindos relief and prow* (**21, 11**)

must have seemed like some variety of a three. The movements of the oarcrew in each of the three files are shown diagrammatically in (**75**) by Burlet.

Features appearing in the Samothrace prow and in the Lindos relief have been incorporated in a ship 35 m in overall length, 5.8 m in breadth overall and displacing about 40 tonnes, 15% less than a three and only 70% of the oarpower (and oarcrew cost). Having finer lines than the three, in which longer files of thalamians have to be accommodated near the ends of the hull, a *τριημιολία* would not have given more than about ½ knot to a three in a sprint if both ships had equally good crews. They would have been good value for money. That three of them could capture a four (p. 34) indicates that they were the faster ships, but that they carried fewer troops. JSM (p. 204) estimates that their *ὑπηρεσία* numbered 24, of whom little more than half would have been troops.

As in the four, protecting the middle line gangway and providing it with walking headroom would have required a raised casing, which may be expected to have been topped by vent louvres. In the Samothrace prow there is however an open sunken gangway which if it is a true representation of that feature seems inconsistent with boxed-in outriggers. The oarbox bracket has in this reconstruction been extended to form a curved and steeply sloping glacis, except forward where, as Sleeswyk has pointed out, access would be required for anchor work and mooring. The *glacis* would deter boarders in a ship carrying relatively few defending troops. A suggested hawse hole has been added in the forward face of each oarbox to complete the anchoring arrangements.

In (**74**) the oarports of each pair do not overlap as they do in the monument. They could do so, however, if the looms of the oars of the outboard (thranite?) file were allowed to cross under those of the inboard (zygian) file at the catch. That would be quite possible, but at what may be judged, necessarily without the benefit of experience, a greater risk of fouling and injury to knuckles owing to variations in heights of oars in short steep waves. The upper thole of each pair has been brought inboard to reduce the extra length required in the zygian oar: in the monument they are represented by lines of equal weight. They could both be just inside the oarport, but then the zygian oar would have been longer, which would appear to have disadvantages in a fast ship. The oarbox is presumed to have been open on its underside for ventilation but boarded over at bow and stern to help keep the ends drier in heavy pitching.

The stern in (**73**) is modelled on the Lindos relief, where there are two features which have not usually appeared in other representations of ships:

a. A vertical extension to deck level of the after end of the oarbox (not as shown in Blinkenberg (1938)'s reconstruction B 782). It is interpreted as the landing for embarkation ladders and also as the post or bumkin for the braces and sheets of the mainsail.

b. A half-arch just forward of a., interpreted as the after edge of the *glacis*, cut away at an angle to give access to the blocks, to support fairleads for the braces and sheets going through blocks on the bumkin and thence inboard for hauling and belaying, and for handling mooring ropes.

The helmsman could stand in a shallow well in the deck, as shown, to reduce the length of the rudder stocks and there could be a cabin, suggested in the relief, into which such a well would be sunk.

Τριημιολίαι would have been equipped with *ὑποζώματα*, for which the ratio of hull length to depth (l/h in Appendix D) of 13.3 would indicate a need. This is suggested (p. 109) for Rhodian ships in general but not specifically for *τριημιολίαι*.The plaited rope shown in the relief passing under the upcurving stern has not been included in (**73**) because its purpose is not clear. It might simply be to provide a hand grip for handling the ship from the beach. Suggestions have been made that it is the after end of the *ὑπόζωμα*, but such a scheme would raise unresolved questions of practical detail within the ship. The rope is also at the wrong angle to be in equilibrium while sustaining fore-and-aft tension and its top ends are above the level of the undersides of the hull beams which is where the *ὑπόζωμα* would have run.

Naval architectural characteristics of the reconstructions

Oared ships in general

Men sitting on fixed seats, or standing, cannot move water past a boat or ship with oars of workable

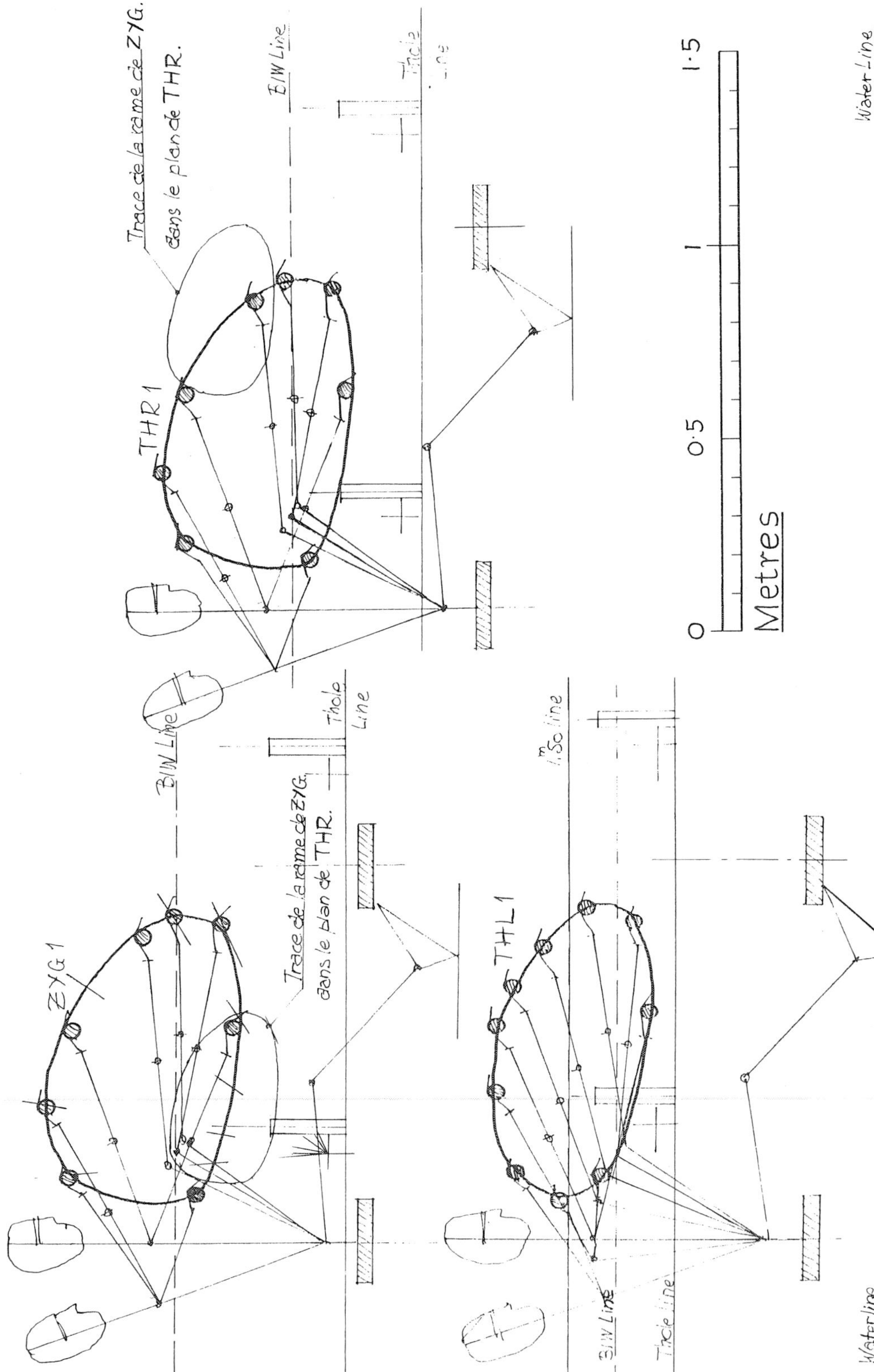

75 movements of oarsmen in the ship of **74**: Burlet

dimensions and proportions much faster than about 10 knots, which is therefore the upper limit of speed at which they can propel a vessel. That limit has only been exceeded in sport rowing of recent times by oarsmen sitting on sliding seats which enable oarstrokes to be longer and bring a larger mass of muscles into play. To be capable of more than about two thirds of the upper limit of speed for fixed seat rowing, oared ships must be proportioned so as to minimise the wetted area of their hulls and avoid as far as possible making waves in the water, while providing room for the largest possible number of oars to be worked effectively at the necessary speed. These requirements become more imperative, to the progressive exclusion of other attributes needing weight or space in the ship, or causing its centre of gravity to rise, as the speed to be achieved under oar rises towards the 10 knot limit.

The whole design of oared ships is dominated by the demands of their oar-systems. Accommodation of oars and avoiding wave-making call for hulls to be long relative to their displacement. Breadth on the waterline should be minimised to reduce wetted area, given the necessity for length to accommodate oars, and the surface of the hull under water should be kept as smooth as possible to reduce frictional resistance with the water. The lateral stability of the vessel in the water and performance under sail both call for much greater beam than performance under oar, so in oared ships, all of which have used sail extensively for making longer passages at sea, a compromise has to be struck between these conflicting requirements. Satisfactory working of oars limits freeboard and so hull depth and these have to be reconciled, one way or another, with the demands of seaworthiness and hull strength.

The average mass density of a fully-manned oar system within a ship is very low, only about 0.045 tonnes/m^3 , or 1/20 of the density of water and its power density over any length of time is, as it happens, about the same number of Watts/m^3, 0.050 w/m^3 at 70w per man. That power density is of the order of 1/5,000th of that of a modestly-sized outboard motor today. It follows that the space required in a 'fast' oared ship by oarsmen has ensured that there has never been much to spare for other things or men unless they were on the top of the ship, making a greater BWL necessary for stability. Even in times when life was dominated by physical toil, whether demanded by the few or given by the many, the physical and psychological fragility of the stamina necessary to sustain oarpower for any length of time must always have provided a strong incentive to dispense with anything on board thought to make the ship harder to pull. In attempting therefore to reconstruct the faster oared ships realistically, it is right to be economical with space.

Hull forms

The hulls of the reconstructions are all of slender form, long and of shallow draft relative to their displacement volumes. The slenderness of hull form is measured by the non-dimensional ratio

$$\text{Ⓜ} = \frac{\text{LWL}}{\text{(Displacement Volume)}1/3}$$

Being the fastest, the three has the most slender hull form whose Ⓜ is 9.0. It is followed closely by the *τριημιολία* then, in descending order, the *ἡμιολία* (8.7), the five (8.5), the four (8.4) and the liburnian at 7.4. For comparison a rowing 'four' has an Ⓜ value of about 15, a modern naval frigate about 8 and the medieval and later wargalleys between 8 and 6.5. Owing first to the bulk and weight of oarcrews, about a third of total displacements, causing their centre of gravity to be high, second to troops whose weight is even higher in the ship, and third to the need for sufficient stiffness adequately to resist rolling under oar and heeling under sail, the breadth of hulls on the waterline (BWL) is critical.

Apart from the heavy, larger polyremes, oared warships, particularly threes and below, were built as lightly as was practicable. For their bulk, they were light in weight, so their BWL was large relative to their drafts, BWL being between 6 and 8 times the depth below water of the main part of the bottom, neglecting the protruding keel and garboards. Such proportions prevent both the wetted area of the hull and so frictional resistance from the water, and wavemaking resistance from being minimised for propulsion alone. There was therefore some penalty in speed incurred as a consequence of their high centres of gravity. Those heights were unavoidable however and in the reconstructions here they have been reduced to the minimum, as surely they would have been by the ancients to minimise loss of speed under oar. On the other hand, the length of an oared ship of about 30 'rooms', about 40 m, kept wavemaking resistance to very low levels except at speeds of 7 knots and more.

Accommodating the largest posssible number of oarcrew caused the ships with full-length files to be relatively full at their ends, though in absolute terms their bows in particular were probably quite fine. Bow waterlines lay at angles of little more than 10° to the middle line of the hull in the smaller types and about 15° in the larger ships. Nevertheless their prismatic coefficients were higher than the optimum for the least wavemaking resistance, though less so in the ἡμιολίαι whose shorter files allowed the ends of their hulls to be finer, with entry waterlines of about 8° to the middle line. At the particular lengths and speeds attainable by those types of ship, their sharper hulls would have reduced wavemaking significantly, thus providing not only a basis for their reputations for speed but conversely the reason for their oarsystems and names.

Oar power

The power with which a given oarsystem can propel a given ship depends upon many factors, the main among which are: the number of the oarcrew and their physical strength, condition and training, the time over which the particular amount of power is produced, ventilation, oar design, gearing and rig, the smoothness of the underwater hull and the state of the sea.

When rowing on fixed seats, oarsmen can produce about 300 watts on their oar handles for about two minutes, as measured by an ergometer, and exceptionally 340w for about 6 minutes (Shaw: 1993). To develop this power, a long handle-stroke is necessary, and achievable power on the handle is little more than directly proportional to the stroke, while being relatively independent of the number of strokes per minute, the rate of striking. That rate, for a given stroke length, is determined by the ship, her speed, oar gearing and blade slip in the water. The maximum pull on the handle by a sitting oarsman is subject to two limits, first the pull force at which the oarsman rises from his seat, and second (which intervenes at higher rates of striking) its diminution at greater handle velocities, reflecting the near constancy of power on the handle with respect to rate of striking. It follows that oar gearing is critical in achieving maximum speed.

The two prime sources of loss in converting handle power into effective propulsive power arise, about equally in the case of one-man oars, from lifting the oar mass once and accelerating and bringing it to rest twice in every stroke, and from slip of the blade in the water. Together they amount to about 40% of handle power at high oar powers and rates of striking. An oar blade cannot, however, exert a force on water except by developing either a drag force by moving perpendicular to its plane in the water, or a lift force by moving in its plane with an angle of attack, like a hydro- or aero-foil, or a combination of the two. Such combinations arise not only in the course of a stroke while the blade rotates about the relatively distant and moving pivot of the thole, but also according to whether the blade is short and wide or long and narrow, and whether the stroke is a long shallow sweep or a deeper and usually shorter stroke in which the blade moves down and up again in the water. They are also affected by whether the arc of the stroke is centred on the athwartships direction or is cast more forward of it.

If the oar gearing is too low for the speed of the ship which corresponds to the maximum effective propulsive power of the oarcrew and oarsystem, both handle pull and blade slip will be too low to enable that power to be developed. If gearing is too high, oars will be unnecessarily long, reducing the force on the blade and raising oar mass rotational inertia losses, or if the looms are too short, oar arcs will be too wide for efficiency, all reducing effective propulsive power. These factors are discussed quantitatively and in more detail by Shaw in Appendix B to this chapter.

A long file of oars, working in a single furrow in the water parallel to the ship, moves the water affected progressively faster aft developing a wake whose speed increases from bow to stern. The effect, which was noticeable in *Olympias*, is to reduce the propulsive power of the after oarsmen. In the reconstructions presented here the arcs of oars have therefore been cast forward of athwartships as far as practicable to reduce that effect by first broadening the affected furrow and second giving the water a lateral component of velocity away from the ship bringing fresh, more stationary water into it. In medieval and renaissance galleys oar arcs were invariably so far forward that they were wholly forward of athwartships: their angular arcs were also restricted by the greater length of the oars in those galleys.

In *Olympias* it was clear that long narrow blades were less effective than short broader blades of the same area. That must be assumed to have been well understood by the ancients. From representations one can draw the general conclusion that one-man oars had broad and short blades, of various shapes and fastened to the shafts (e.g. **vi**, and *AT* Pl.47). In representations of polyremes (e.g. **29**, **36**) where oar blades are visible, they are in contrast, shown narrow, long, straight and plane as if monoxylous like those of the later galleys. This difference indicates the use of different styles of stroke, namely the long shallow sweep with one-man oars and the dipping, down and up stroke with multi-manned oars. If started well forward of athwartships, the shallow stroke gives an advantage to broad blades because the tips become leading edges of hydrofoils in a flow of water in the direction up the shaft. Broader blades are suited to calmer conditions in which the greatest power can be obtained with a long shallow stroke, and that too must be assumed to have been within the experience of the ancients.

The dipping style of stroke, universal latterly at sea in working boats, is necessary in rougher water where the moments of entry into and extraction from the water cannot be so accurately predicted, making the flatter style unworkable. The dipping type of stroke is illustrated in the diagrams by Burlet who has derived them from his studies of rowing the multi-manned *a scaloccio* oars of the later galleys. It has the advantage, which has more weight in the case of heavier oars, of employing a more circular motion which would diminish the magnitudes of the accelerations of the oars necessarily greater at the ends of longer, flatter strokes. A dipping stroke is however necessarily shorter than the other style and therefore less powerful in calmer waters. The two have different virtues and accomplished sea-oarsmen would have adjusted their stroke between them according to wave conditions, though their oars, judging as best one can from the representations, would have been best suited to one or the other but not both styles of rowing.

Longer oars and steeper oars are more limited in the height to which their blades can be raised from the water to clear waves. It becomes necessary, as may be noticed in the reconstructed fives, six and seven, to place the two-man oars rather above the desirable height from the seat of the inboard man so that he should be able to raise the blade 0.6 to 0.7 m above calm water when the handle is pressing on his thighs. There is therefore reason, on this account, to suppose that on oars worked by three or more men the men would have worked standing, with consequences for the number of oar levels already discussed.

As explained by McKee (1983), in working boats of no great oar power and of the very recent past, footstretchers tend to be lower below seat level. This is understandable where oar power is not of paramount importance but out of the question in threes if they could achieve attested speeds and therefore powers. Oarsmen in the working boats also 'stand down' on bottom boards in rough conditions to enable their oars to be lifted higher above waves to clear them. In such conditions high oar powers are impossible anyway and it is essential to be able at all costs to get one's oar forward for the next stroke. To 'stand down' in the same way in an oared ship, where oarsmen are remote from the bottom of the hull, would require a second, lower, footrest, which in a multi-level system would add to the height and reduce stability unless the ship were made broader, and also therefore slower. In view of the importance of footstretchers, and their attitude and position for high powered rowing, it is particularly regrettable that no ancient account gives them any mention.

Other practical questions raised by the longer oars of polyremes, such as shipping them and enabling one level to rest while another carries on working, have not been investigated in this study.

Ventilation

The operational importance, even in the faster type of ship, of high sprint speeds as opposed to speeds sustainable for longer periods is not known. It therefore cannot be known for what speeds oars were optimised in any particular type of ship. Sustainable speeds, as for instance on passage, would have been much the most common and hence probably the most desirable to make most efficient and most comfortable in all respects. They would have been much affected by the physical atmosphere inside the ship, and therefore by its ventilation.

In the earlier fast types of ramming ships, that consideration could have encouraged the continued use of protective screens able normally to be folded away to give the oarcrew in normal circumstances as much ventilation as possible. That amenity could have been judged worth suffering greater risk of injuries in battle owing to the more flimsy protection from hair and leather screens. Battles between ramming ships would however have been generally fought in more open formations and melées than later when boarding became the principal tactic. Such battles also predated exchanges of heavier catapulted missiles between fleets before they clashed in close engagements.

The need to protect oarcrews more heavily and yet to ventilate them must have interacted in determining tactics, battle formations and ship design after the introduction of missile throwers on warships. It could have been the main reason for the disappearance of the three from the line of battle: its speed capability simply could not be combined with protection sufficient to enable it to survive long enough to perform its ramming function in a battle. The emergence of the *τριημιολία* is particularly interesting in this light. How was the balance between protection and ventilation struck in such a way that that type could be effective in ramming heavier ships in battle? The *τριημιολία* is unique in being the only type that was fast, boxed-in and armed principally with the ram at a time when the principal ships in most main fleets were heavy troop-carrying vessels.

The importance of ventilation, first pointed out by Casson (*SSAW* p. 145 n.17) in connection with oared warships, lies in the necessity for the evaporation of sweat to remove waste heat from the body. That necessity is proved by the inability of men working in still air on a cycling ergometer to maintain more than 150 watts for periods of more than half an hour, or 400 watts for more than a few minutes, whereas if working in air moving past them at 12 m/second they can maintain 400 watts for an hour or longer (Whitt and Wilson: 1976). The reason is that in an ordinary room a man can lose heat at the rate of only about 600 watts corresponding to an ability to produce only 150 watts of mechanical work (at a thermal efficiency of 0.20) for any appreciable time, that is of hours rather than minutes. It seems therefore that for protecting its oarcrew the *τριημιολία* must have suffered some penalty, compared with an open three, in the length of time for which it could maintain speeds high in its attainable range. Could only short bursts at high powers have been sufficient for carrying out rammings in battle? Survival and the exploitation of opportunities in battle without incapacitating the oarcrew by heat exhaustion must have tested the skill and judgment of trierarchs of *τριημιολίαι* particularly acutely. The same problem would probably have been less testing for the commanders of heavier ships, fighting more ponderously by boarding, though their oarcrew would have suffered from the same physical limits. Was that type developed mainly with ramming in battle in mind or as anti-piracy ships? The Rhodians seem to have been a sea power based on trade and had a strong interest in controlling piracy.

Fresh Water

The ability of oarsmen to maintain high speeds for long periods or for a succession of periods is also limited by the amount of water made available. The *Daedalus Project* (Nadel and Bussolari: 1988), culminating in the man-powered flight of 4 hours from Crete to Santorini, established that 1 litre of water per hour had to be drunk by a man producing 210 watts for that length of time if he were not to become dehydrated. For that flight the water contained 10% glucose and 0.4 gramme/litre of sodium and the pilot (in this case the engine also) showed no sign of incipient fatigue in the course of the flight and little loss of body weight afterwards. The rate of consuming water was in that case 0.005 litre/watt.hour, which indicates that the allowance of 7 litres/man.day in French galleys would suffice for an average daily expenditure of oarcrew energy of 1000 watt.hours per man, if one allows 2 litres per man per day for the other bodily needs for water. That amount of energy could, for example, allow the crew to be used at the rate of 100 watts for 10 hours, which would drive a five with an effective power of 18 kilowatts from an oarcrew of 300 at a speed of about 6.7 knots, making 80 sea miles in a day under oar only, with a water mileage of 40 sea miles per tonne.

With nearly 400 men on board, the 17th cent. AD scale would have called for an allowed average consumption per day of 2.8 tonnes, so in a five a storage capacity of 10 to 15 tonnes of water may be expected to have been usual, for water would not have been available at every landing. Its replenishment would have been quite a lengthy business. If for example each man carried a 25 kg skinful of water, to embark 10 tonnes would require 400 journeys from the source ashore, say 10 round trips for each member of a watering party of 40, taking 5 hours at ½ hour per trip. The 17th cent. scale might be reduced a little if oarcrews were freemen. While ashore they might be able to drink deeply (about 1 litre) before embarking, but in an hour or so about half that water would be urine, which is not only not wanted on board but cannot be used for sweating. The advantage gained by drinking ashore would be limited because a steadier intake is needed for supplying the sweat glands, rather than the bladder, but where water was available each man could bring some water of his own aboard with him for later consumption after losing water by sweating.

That sweat is salty and that salt lost from the body has to be replaced has been known for centuries, so it is possible that salt was carried by oared ships for that purpose. The amount of water needed to prevent dehydration caused by sustained exertion can be reduced for some hours if it contains a food that can be absorbed quickly, like sodium as in the Daedalus flight. Glucose however has not been known until modern times and the only known reference to food taken during a prolonged passage under oar is by Thukydides (3.49) who wrote: 'they pulled and ate at the same time, barley bread mixed with wine and olive oil'. That food would not have been so quickly absorbed as glucose, to which the bread would have been converted in time by the body. There is no record of ancient routine practices to prevent dehydration, which must always have been a major factor in operating oared ships.

Hygiene

The entirely practical consequences of lack of hygienic discipline by oarcrews working within hulls would have been so severe that it must be assumed until proved otherwise (despite Aristophanes's joke (*Frogs* 1074 ff) about an oarsman excreting from his seat) that in fact excretion and urination inside hulls would have been strictly forbidden (cf. *GOS* pl. 10d: the late 7th cent. ivory plaque, Arch. 31 p. 83, showing a man crouching on the ram of a ship to excrete). It was moreover very likely that bilges would have been periodically swilled down with fresh water and then baled out to wash away dried sweat as is the practice in *Olympias*. Galleys were an altogether different case because their oarsystem was entirely above a heavily cambered watertight deck, freely draining overboard. Nevertheless it was said that the odour of a galley could be perceived a mile or more to leeward (Rodgers: 1940). In those ships much may have depended upon whether the oarcrews were free and paid or chained captives. Ancient ships were rowed with very few exceptions by free men.

Hull Strength and Construction

Long and slender timber hulls, relying on mechanical joints between their components, cannot give satisfactory service if longer than certain limits. The similarity, with very few exceptions, between the lengths of threes to sevens, and probably of the of the larger polyremes also (apart from the apparently efficient eight, *Leontophoros*, p. 273, and the monstrous and apparently useless forty p. 274–277) indicates that they were at the practical structural limit in length when combined with the shallowness of their hulls (which were in most types open) relative to their length. Ratios of LWL/ structural depth of the hull, tabulated in Appendix D to this chapter, were large, between 12 for the four and 14 or so for the three and open-hulled five. In the later decked hulls of galleys it was similar, about 13, if the 0.9 m high heavily timbered *corsia* running down the middle line on deck is included. This ratio affects the strength of timber hulls quite critically, and to show how extreme oared ships were in this respect, Lloyd's Register of Shipping, of London, in the 19th cent. AD demanded that all timber hulls more than only 8 depths long were to have iron diagonal straps, fitted between frames and planking, to resist the mainly vertical shear forces acting upon the hull and tending to cause its ends to drop, i.e. to 'hog'. It follows that hulls 12 to

14 depths long but with no such reinforcement either had short lives or were built most conscientiously and with excellent workmanship, necessary actually to achieve the shell strength and stiffness obtainable by means of the tenoned construction.

That excellent workmanship was indeed available in the ancient world is plentifully attested by the quality of surviving ancient stonework, and there can be little doubt that the shipwrights who built hulls of warships were the cream of their trade, just like those who built the later galleys. In those it was only the best shipwrights who wrought the hulls proper, the 'live work', while the rest, 'the dead work' was left to carpenters of lesser skill and prestige. Much the same could have been the case in the ancient world (p. 153).

A common sign of a strained hull would have been chronic and excessive leakage. There are references in literature to the need for ships to 'dry out' after having become 'heavy in the water', a phrase which must have meant leaky rather than suffering from waterlogged timbers. The weight added to a ship by raising the moisture content to saturation, 100%, of all timbers at and below the waterline is not great, only about a tonne in the case of a 48 tonne three. Bilge water up to the top of the floor timbers, on the other hand, would weigh six times as much, and, by sinkage of the hull in the water owing to that added weight, impede the working and therefore the power of the oarcrew unless other weight on board, e.g. supplies of fresh water or of stores, had been reduced by way of compensation. Even if that were done, bilge water sloshed about by the pulsating motion under oar would have absorbed appreciable energy. The impediment caused by being too deep in the water would be particularly bad in rougher waves for reasons already explained.

Owing to their proportions, oared ships would generally have been prone to leakage with age, and the practical limit to their length is likely to have been set by the acceptable average life of hull at which leakage could be expected from experience to render further useful service impossible. In individual cases that age could have varied very much with severity and intensity of such service, as well as with the level of care given to building and maintenance.

The development of ships capable of 8 knots or more with up to three levels of oars, two of which required fair-sized openings in the sides of their undecked hulls can now be seen to have depended upon the method of shipbuilding practised in the ancient Mediterranean. Demanding and labour-intensive it may have been, but no other technique known in history could have made such ships possible, its essential quality being the stiffness and strength of tenons in resisting shear forces acting in the plane of the hull-shell and which would otherwise cause its planks to slide upon each other. Those forces are most severe in shallow slender hulls and the stresses they generate are made worse by openings in the shell. A note on the action of tenons is at Appendix F to this chapter.

Another quality of the ancient Mediterranean method of shipbuilding which was essential for the development of the lighter warships of less than than 50 tonnes or so, was the thinness of the shell planking, no more than 40 mm and in the smaller ships less. The Northern European method of clench (or clinker) building may have been quite as light, but the strength of the metal rivet fastenings clamping the overlapping planks together in resisting plank slide, compared with that of properly fitted tenons, may be doubted. In frame-first building, shell planking of ships of 50 or 100 tonnes has to be at least about 60 mm thick, to hold fibrous caulking rammed hard into the seams. Framing also had had to be heavier than in the tenoned method of building. It is significant that in the Arsenale of Venice the trade of caulker was second in standing only to that of shipwrights (Lane: 1934). In the galleys of that time it is likely that only the highest quality of caulking withstood the shearing action between the shell planks, forces whose transmission depended upon the caulking alone in the frame-first method of construction (Coates: 1985 p. 437–442, Davis: 1993 p. 70–81).

Ὑποζώματα and hull bending stresses

Longitudinal stresses caused by hull bending are also high in these hulls. White (1877), an eminent naval architect writing when wooden ships were still in general use, gave 4.6 Newtons/mm^2 as the maximum permissible stress in hull members if clear of scarfed joints (but otherwise only 2.9N/mm^2. In *Olympias* the maximum hogging stress in the topwale amidships when the ship was balanced on the top of a wave of length LWL and 1 m high from trough to crest could only be reduced to that figure if the *ὑπόζωμα* was tensioned to 13.5 tonnes. The height of the *ὑπόζωμα*, just under the hull beams, imposed longitudinal compressive stresses on hull cross-sections amidships varying from nearly zero at the keel, (already carrying a compressive stress owing to hull bending) to 1.1 N/mm^2 at the topwale, relieving the hogging stress there by that amount. How *ὑποζώματα* were rigged, tightened and subsequently kept tight as the natural fibres, of which the ropes were made, relaxed as they do under sustained tension, is not known. The problem is the same as in the hemp standing rigging of sailing ships which was stretched before it was made up into mast stays and shrouds and then tightened in place by well greased dead-eyes and lanyards. It is possible that the same method was used in the ancient warships (Shaw: 1993).

Unless a *ὑπόζωμα* is rigged like a hogging truss, as shown for example in the relief of Queen Hatshepsut's ships for the expedition to the Land of Punt, it cannot contribute towards reducing hogging shear forces in a hull. There is no evidence that *ὑποζώματα* were so rigged. Their name (meaning undergirdles) would deny it, and in a warship a tightly-tensioned rope arching high amidships would have been very vulnerable to the enemy as well as to accidental damage. It seems therefore virtually certain that *ὑποζώματα* stretched in a straight line close under the beams and middle gangway between strong points at each end of the ship.

Watertightness

Nothing useful has been recorded about how plank seams were stopped to make them watertight. There are references to a number of materials used for that purpose and for coating the bottom planking (e.g. *ζώπισσα*: *AT* p.189), but no specific details of recipes or methods survive. Plank seams must have been merely stopped as necessary: many may have been made so well and so close as to be watertight without the need for any stopping to be pushed into them during the ship's life. Seams are not likely to have been caulked as in frame-built ships because first the tenons would have got in the way, and could have been damaged by the action of caulking iron and mallet, and second plank thicknesses, except possibly in the heavier ships, would have been too small and in no wreck (admittedly with one exception, the Marsala ship, only of merchant vessels) have seams been found with the gap in the outer edges of the planking, necessary to receive caulking. Material for caulking is however mentioned so it must have been used (p. 355).

There must have been however a direct connection between 'drying out' and stopping seams as well as recoating the bottom planking (*AT* 185–7, 207). No material or composition then available would have adhered to planking unless the bottom of the ship was dry. 'Drying-out' therefore almost certainly had much to do with stopping leaks, if only for a while, and smoothing and recoating the bottoms of ships not only to preserve them but to reduce frictional resistance which would have been of more immediate importance.

Superstructures

It will be seen in the midship sections of the reconstructions presented that superstructures, whether relatively light canopies, oarboxes or heavier fighting decks, are not connected by any shell planking to the hull proper. Taking into account all factors, not the least of which is the necessity for entry of air for ventilation as low as practicable to generate convective air-flow, it is therefore difficult to see how the planking of such superstructures could act as part of the main hull in resisting longitudinal bending of the ship as a whole. Even if it were to have such stresses transmitted to it, it would not have been able to carry them without being tenoned together and being thicker to accommodate them. It must therefore be presumed that superstructures were unstressed 'dead work' as regards longitudinal bending of the ship. They may in consequence have been made in separate sections placed one after the other along the hull.

The ships discussed in this chapter were evidently as impressive and as refined artefacts as any in the ancient Mediterranean world. Given the unavoidable bulk of their oarsystems and the necessity for slenderness and length, they were, like most weapons, near the structural limits set by the materials and techniques of their time. They ranged in size from boats no larger than launches to ships displacing up to two hundred tonnes. The relative sizes of

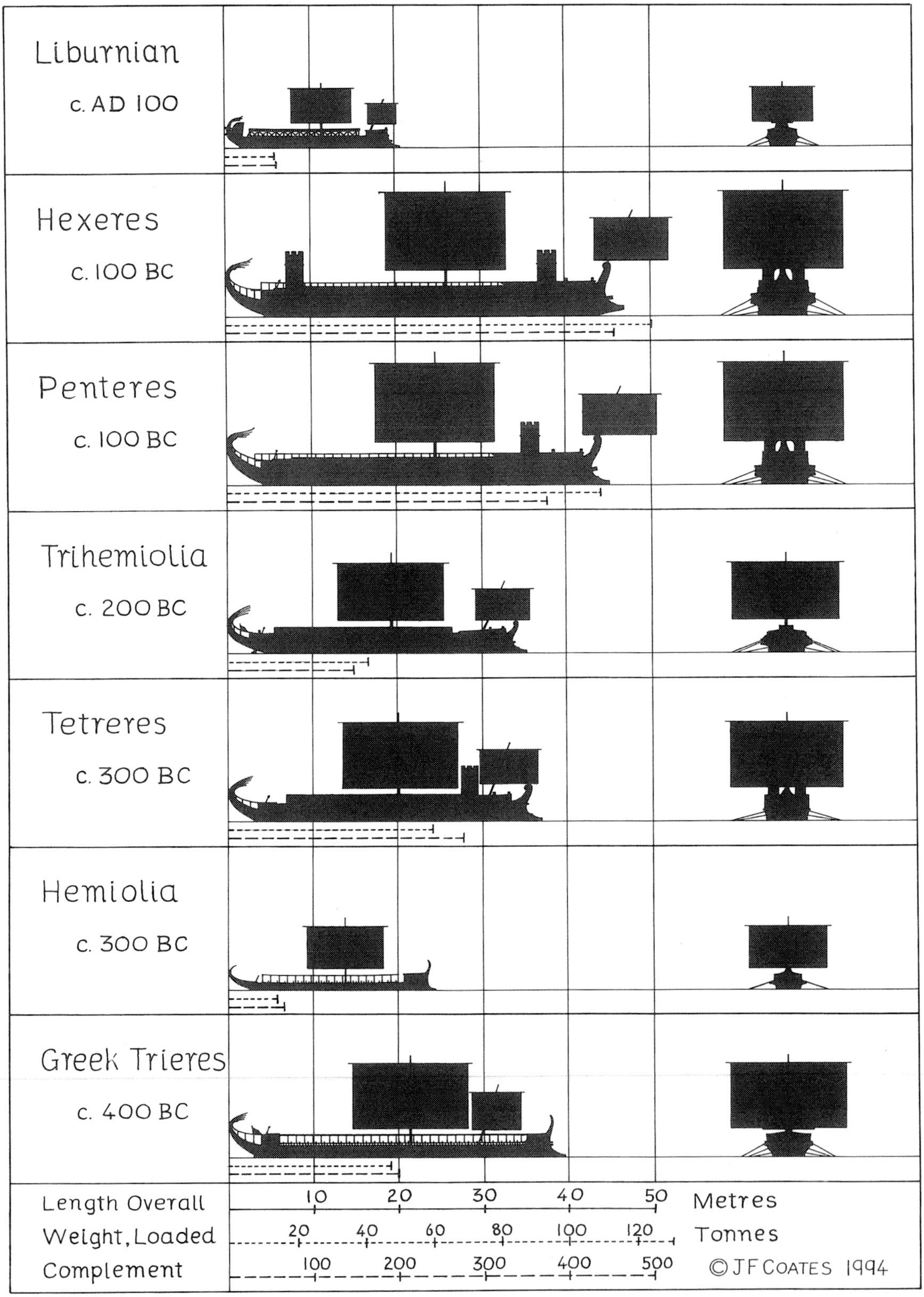
Liburnian
c. AD 100
Hexeres
c. 100 BC
Penteres
c. 100 BC
Trihemiolia
c. 200 BC
Tetreres
c. 300 BC
Hemiolia
c. 300 BC
Greek Trieres
c. 400 BC
Length Overall
Weight, Loaded
Complement
10 20 30 40 50 Metres
20 40 60 80 100 120 Tonnes
100 200 300 400 500
©JF Coates 1994

some of the types that saw the most service over the half millennium covered by this study are illustrated in silhouette in (**76**). The smaller types had light, highly stressed structures for performance under oar and sail. If the larger polyremes were built more massively, it was for the same reason that has applied to heavy warships of the line down the centuries. Massiveness would, as always, have been directed where it would be most effective in resisting battle damage as far as it was likely to contribute to offensive capability. Through the numbers, sizes and refinements of the ships, the fleets of this period of five centuries pose many unanswered questions about shipyard methods, manning and traditions of skills as well as about the organisation, logistics and financing of large navies.

Appendix A

Development of the oarsystem of the Greek Three as shown in (56)

AIMS

Using experience gained in sea trials with *Olympias* (Shaw: 1993), to adjust the oarsystem and the hull:

1. To enable oarcrew at all levels to develop the greatest possible power, and in particular to that end, to enable thalamians to make strokes as long as the *interscalmium* of 0.98 m allows.

2. To reduce risk and incidence of interference between oarblades by:
   a) separating thranite blades when in the water from the others transversely as far as the limitation on overall ship breadth (5.6 m) and the minimum breadth on the waterline necessary for adequate stability allow.
   b) paying particular attention to blade and shaft separation at the finish of the stroke to reduce risk of 'catching crabs'.

3. To reduce oar-race velocity and increase oarblade efficiency by swinging oar area forward so that at the catch oar shafts make angles with the keel line, in plan, of about 45° to 60°.

4. To increase internal clearances to reduce interference between oars and furniture in rough water.

DEVELOPMENT PROCEDURE

FOR SECTIONS AMIDSHIPS

1. Decide length and gearing of oars – all equal in all levels. Decided on 4.66 m and 3.0, from centre of pressure, assumed 0.20 m from blade tip, and from mid-handle, 0.2 m from butt, to pivot.

2. Decide height of pivot of thalamian axis above water. Decided on 0.50 m.

3. Draw thalamian oar immersed in calm water, in its athwartships position and the pivot in the correct position given the chosen gearing.

4. Sketch hull section to WL, decide ship's breadth on WL (BWL) and mark middle line. BWL 3.70 m, reducing height of metacentre above keel from 2.9 m in *Olympias* to 2.6 m and metacentric height from 1.1 m to an estimated 0.8 m.

5. Draw 3° heeled waterlines and draw axis of thalamian oar with blade correctly immersed when ship is upright and when heeled 3° up.

6. Place thalamian seat with its middle line 4 cm outboard of mid-handle and 45 cm below intersection of oar axis (blade immersed and ship upright) and oarsman's middle line.

7. Place beams just to clear thalamian's head equally fore and aft of him, using a template on which is drawn the profiles of a 1.73 m tall man at each end of the stroke, based on photographs, with the locus of the top of his head added, the summit of the locus being 0.90 m above seat.

8. Place zygian seat so that the feet of that oarsman clear both the shoulders and loom (at 3° heel) of the thalamian below, when the middle of the zygian seat is 3 cm above the underside of the beam at that point.

9. Draw the axis of the zygian oar with its blade correctly in the water, athwartships and with the ship upright, its axis intersecting the middle line of the zygian 45 cm above his seat, with his mid-handle 4 cm inboard of his middle line.

10. Mark the pivot of the zygian oar in the position to give the chosen gearing and also draw the position of the oar when the ship has 3° heel. Check maximum possible height of blade clear of water (when loom

axis is 0.2 m above the seat and in contact with thighs). Give the thole chock a high inboard edge if necessary to enable the blade to be lifted high enough.

11. Draw a vertical line at half the allowed overall breadth of the ship from the ship's middle line. Decide that allowed overall breadth is 5.6 m.

12. Draw vertical line of thranite pivot in outrigger having decided sizes of rails.

13. Place the thranite so that his oar has its blade in the water, its pivot at the chosen gearing is on the pivot line, the middle line of the thranite cuts the oar axis 5 cm outboard of mid-handle (measured down shaft) and 45 cm above seat.

14. Check clearance of thranite's heel with zygian oar at 3° heel, the oar being 65 mm diameter. Check the maximum height of this blade above water as previously. Adjust as necessary, by lowering the thranite (but no more than 5 cm). This is one of the factors limiting the slope of oars. Shape the thole chock as mentioned in 10 above if necessary.

15. Place topwale 270 mm wide under thranite seat with its inner edge 18 cm from the thranite's middle line to give room for his foot stretcher.

16. Determine height of the thranite oar pivot.

17. Draw a feasible section of outrigger, topwale and ship shell to suit positions of oar pivots and therefore of tholepins, as well as providing the required BWL. Shell above WL wale 60 mm thick, wale 90 mm thick.

IN THE PLAN

(Drawn vertically below Section on the paper)

18. Draw outrigger, topwale and the lines of the oar pivots in plan.

19. Draw the line of the thalamian oar tip in water, oar athwartships and blade in the water, from the section drawing and choose a position for the thalamian pivot in the plan.

20. Choose an angle in plan for the shaft at the catch. Choose 50° from line of keel forward, which is nearly as far forward as practicable. Draw the arc followed by the tip as the oar is pulled through the water, with its centre at the pivot.

21. Draw the line of the butt of the oar, from the section drawing, as for the tip. Draw the arc of the butt, with its centre at the pivot as before.

22. Decide the length of stroke at the butt, along the chord. Decide upon 1.1 m.

23. Find the position of the butt at the finish, and hence of the shaft at finish and at the catch.

24. Project thalamian seat from section and adjust to suit finish, canting it as necessary to suit the catch, so that the butt is above the forward edge of seat and 16 cm inboard of the middle line of the seat. To decide the cant needed, make the line of the middle of the seat produced aft near or slightly outboard of butt at the catch.

25. Place beam in the plan in accordance with 7 and the template, to ensure clearance of head and beams.

26. Mark intermediate hull top timbers, placing timbers at beams and halfway between.

27. Sketch in the likely position in plan of the thalamian oarport, projecting a horizontal section of shell at oar pivot level from the section drawing. Check that the port clears timbers (at least on the inside of the shell). The hole for the oarport can be chamfered if needed. If the port fouls a timber, adjust port, timber or oar and seat.

28. Draw the zygian seat, projecting down in the same way as for the thalamian seat. Place it in plan between beams so that back, shins and toes clear beams, using template as before.

29. Roughly place the zygian blade at the finish 50 cm from thalamian tip, either forward or aft of it. Decide to place it forward. Draw oar roughly at finish with the butt placed relative to the seat in the same position as the thalamian. Find the arcs of tip and butt, as for the thalamian. Draw oar more accurately, adjusting as necessary, having checked that the position of its oarport is acceptable.

30. Mark the position of the zygian butt at the catch, as for the the thalamian. Check the separation of zygian and thalamian blade tips at the catch. Zygian and thalamian tips must not overtake each other during the stroke, in water or in the air.

31. If the positions of these two oars are acceptable, the zygian pivot has been determined. If the zygian oar at the catch makes less than 45° with keel line forward, adjust both oars, pivots and seat cant angles (but NOT their fore-and-aft positions), until a zygian angle at the catch of 45–50° is obtained.

32. Accept the arrangement provisionally, subject to the satisfactory placing of the thranite oar relative to the other two.

33. Thranites are independent of beams. However, owing to the slope of their oars, the angle swept by them, in plan view, is appreciably greater than that swept by the other two. It is desirable that thranite blades also do not overtake others in the course of the stroke, but if that proves impossible to arrange, within otherwise acceptable arcs and position of seats, it is necessary first to ensure that at the finish the oars are not liable to interfere with each other to hinder extraction and generate 'crabs' particularly by thalamians, and given the mutual separation thus needed at the finish, and that the arrangement of blades at the catch is acceptable. To explore the possible adjustments, make templates on tracing paper or film of all three oars and seats in plan. Explore all possibilities by moving these templates about within the limits affecting seats, tholes and oarports and the constraints of the ship structure.

After general adjustment, an arrangement was drawn in which at the finish the blades of one triad of oarcrew are 45 cm apart from each other in a roughly diagonal row sloping outboard and forward, in the order thalamian, zygian, thranite. However, the blade of the thalamian of the next triad forward is only a few cm. forward of the thranite shaft, but 60 cm nearer the thole and so about 30 cm from it vertically. That horizontal separation could only be increased by closing the other separations: they would be equalised if they were all made 30 cm. If that were done, the pattern of blades at the catch, would, it is believed, be made less satisfactory because the thranite blade would either be on top of the thalamian or be aft of it, causing overtaking.

As drawn, at the catch, the thalamian is just aft of the thranite (but 70 cm short of it), and 35 cm apart from (and aft of)the zygian. The thranite shaft crosses the thalamian's but close to the ship and so they are well clear of each other. Both the thalamian and the zygian blades overtake the thranite. That seems unavoidable without incurring other penalties. However, the two lower oar blades do not overtake each other, which is more important, and, being rowed blind, they are also kept fairly evenly separated throughout the stroke which experience in *Olympias* has been shown to be essential. It is necessary to compromise between separation within and separation between, triads and it is unavoidable that the pattern of blades at the catch is, for each triad, tighter than at the finish, where it is more important for it to be open and evenly spread to reduce the likelihood of blades fouling and causing 'crabs' to be caught when extracting them from the water.

It is believed that the arrangement drawn in (**56**) is near the optimum, all things considered. Separation of the blades of the oars being rowed blind is about as great as it can be, and the onus for avoiding trouble is on the thranite who can see what is going wrong with his and adjacent triads of oarcrew. This drawing provides a suitable basis for adjusting the design of any possible future reconstruction of a Greek three to meet the aims stated above.

APPENDIX B

by J. T. Shaw

Oar mechanics – length, gearing, handle force and efficiency

An oar is a lever enabling an oarsman to thrust his boat forwards by causing water to move in the opposite direction. (**77**) gives a plan view of its action in a racing eight. The loom is not shown. The 'stride' obtained is the distance AB through which the thole is moved. The angle swept, 80° in (**77**), can be as much as 90° in a first class eight. In any ancient galley it would have been much less for several reasons: the

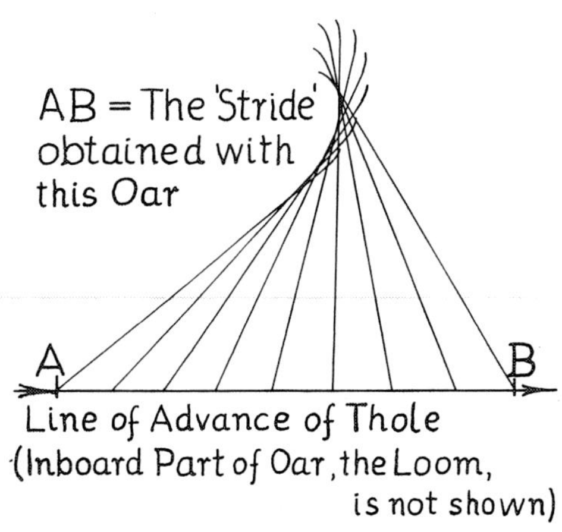

77. Plan view of the action of an oar in a modern rowing eight. After Edwards (1963).

probable short stature of the oarsmen, the near certainty that they rowed on fixed thwarts and the probability that in most cases (perhaps in all) they had longer oarlooms than a modern oarsman does.

As galleys were rowed on the sea they needed a much higher freeboard than an eight and this influenced the outboard length of their oars, as it was and is impossible to row at full power with an oar that is too steeply inclined.

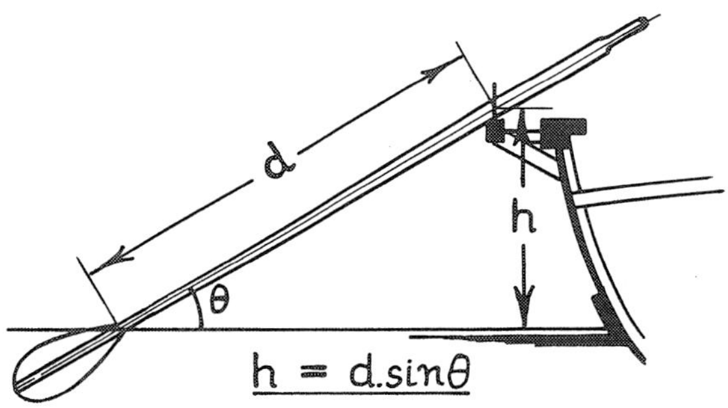

78. Outboard length, height and slope of oar

(**78**), a transverse part-section of a galley, shows that the distance 'd' along the shaft of an oar and the height 'h' of the shaft at the sill of its thole are linked by the relationship h = d sin θ, where θ is the inclination during the pull in calm water. Experiment shows that in the topmost level of a three θ should be about 30°, i.e. d = 2h, since an inclination of thirty degrees does not unduly restrict power; nor does it call for an unduly long and unhandy outboard length of oar. To give enough vertical room for the oarsystem, h in a three must be about 1.4 m and therefore, when the immersed length of the blade, probably about 0.6 m, is taken into account the outboard length of a typical oar of the topmost level of a three is given approximately by 0.6 + 1.4/sin 30°, i.e. 3.4 m. This may have been rounded to 7 cubits (3.43 m).

The total length of such an oar is fairly securely known to have been 4.66 m (9½ cubits) and therefore the inboard length is deduced to have been 2½ cubits (1.23 m) if the outboard length was 7 cubits. This perhaps inverts the reasoning of the ancient designers, who may have argued that "With an outboard length of 7 cubits an inboard length of 2½ cubits is about right and therefore the overall length may as well be made exactly 9½ cubits". Any experienced modern rowing coach can see why an inboard length of 2½ cubits would fit well with an outboard length of 7 cubits: it would have given a well-balanced handy oar with a 'stride' that was long enough to enable fit oarsmen, despite their short stroke, to drive their three at speeds of about 9½ knots in short sprints, and also to cruise economically in calm seas for many hours at about 7½ knots. (There are reasons for thinking that if an oar has been optimised for a speed of 9½ knots at full power it is also optimal for cruising at 7½ knots at half power.)

By multiplying the vertical movement available at the butt by as much as 2.8 (i.e. the outboard:inboard length ratio, often called the gearing) these proportions of the oars could have the further merit of allowing the two upper levels of oars in a three to be rowed in waves of amplitude up to about 0.8 m which would compel the lowest oars to be drawn in. Waves higher than this were dangerous to threes.

A definition of gearing, different from that just given, is sometimes adopted. It acknowledges that the oarsman's pull does not act at the butt nor the blade reaction at the tip, but both act about 0.2 m from those locations. It is therefore the ratio (outboard length m - 0.2 m)/(inboard length m - 0.2 m). In the case of an oar 7 cubits outboard and 2½ cubits inboard the gearing on this definition is 3.15. Neither definition tells the whole story as the first one ignores the dimensions of the blade and the second takes them only partly into account. (**79**) shows these ways of defining the gearing.

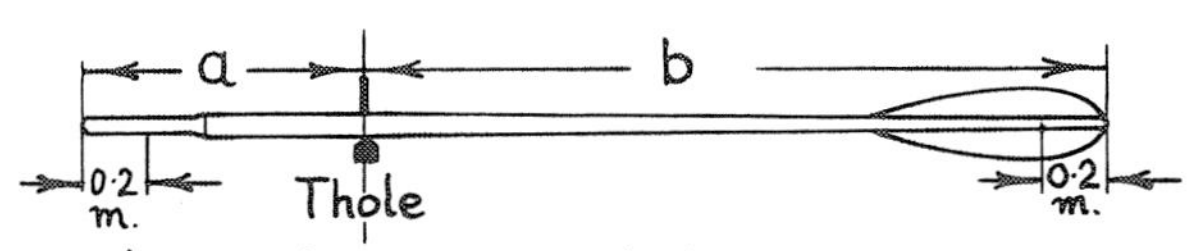

79. Oar gearing

The oars of the ancient Greeks were tied to their tholepins by straps and this suggests that the gearing might not have been a fixed ratio but could be altered to a limited extent by the oarsmen as they were going along. This could have been a useful adjustment as it would have enabled the crew to lower the gearing in a headwind or increase it in a tailwind: the change could be made in a few seconds.

If ancient Greek oarsmen in threes neither rose from their seats nor slid on greased ones, the longest stroke they could row was probably about 1.1 m, measured along the chord of the arc described by the butt. It follows that if the topmost oars were 2½ cubits or 1.23 m long inboard and were inclined at 30 degrees during the pull their swept angle in horizontal plan would have been restricted to about 62½ degrees.

(**80**) illustrates that a seated oarsman's static pull is limited not only by his strength but also by his weight and the way he is rigged. Specifically, his static pull cannot exceed x times his own weight where x is the ratio that the horizontal distance between his heels and his centre of gravity bears to the vertical distance between his heels and the oarhandle. If he tries to pull harder he will merely rise from his seat. In order that his feet can deal with the reaction they must rest against an inclined stretcher of some kind. It is clear that to avoid unnecessarily limiting the pull, the stretcher should be kept high and steep, i.e. the heels not more than 0.3 m below the level of the seat, and the stretcher inclined at up to 60 degrees from the horizon. Whilst conducing to speed in calm water this arrangement is not suitable for rough water because the men's thighs will be roughly horizontal and so will limit the scope for lowering the oarhandle to clear the crests of waves. In practice the pull is not static but is affected by the accelerations of the oarsman's mass with respect to the ship and by fatigue as well as by the considerations already given.

Cornish six-oared racing gigs of the present day are commonly rowed in rough water. They demonstrate a canted rig in which the heels are about 0.4 m below the wooden thwart; the seat is often further raised by a cushion. The cant refers to the fact that the oarsmen do not face the stern but are angled at about 20° from the keel, with their feet near the keel and the cushions on which they sit placed at the end of the thwart that is furthest from the thole. The oarlooms are short enough to pass beside the men's bodies at the finish and recovery and so their thighs are not in the way. A canted rig was applied in medieval galleys but the style of rowing cannot have been the Cornish one.

If a ship has resistance R newtons when her velocity is V m/s the mean power required to propel her is VR watts. The oars however work intermittently. If they work for a fraction F of the total time they must exert a useful mean power U = VR/F watts in a forward direction on the tholepins during that fraction. They also unavoidably push water sideways and sternwards, absorbing power as they do so. A mean ideal mechanical efficiency E (that which the oar would display were it devoid of inertia, hysteresis and air resistance) can be defined by the ratio

$$U/(U + u)$$

where u is the power dissipated in the water surrounding the blade during the fraction of time during which the oars are pulling. (U + u) is therefore equal to VR/EF and to U/E.

E is a decimal usually in the range 0.7 - 0.8.

Real oars do have inertia, exhibit hysteresis and have air resistance, and so their mere reciprocation in the horizontal and vertical senses also absorbs power, mostly during the extraction, run and re-entry. If in particular circumstances this amounts to w watts averaged over the duration of the pull plus return we may define a mean overall efficiency (OE) pertaining to those circumstances such that:

$$(OE) = U/(U/E + w/F) = VR/(VR/E + w) \;\ldots\ldots\; (1)$$

All the power represented by U/E + w/F has to be supplied by the oarsmen.

The quantity (OE) may be described as the ratio of the mean effective power exerted on the ship by the oars to the mean power exerted on the oars by the men.

In the work cited in note (1) the writer has shown that the instantaneous (as opposed to the mean) ideal mechanical efficiency (IE) of an oar is given as

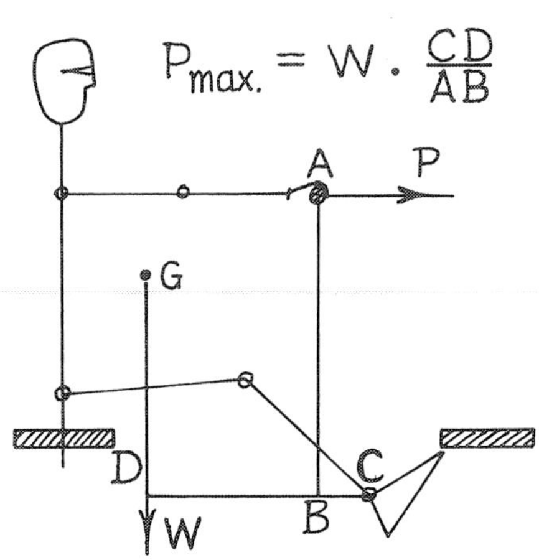

80. The maximum pull on an oar handle.

follows: the symbols are explained in (**81**), except for ds which is the differential distance moved by the thole.

(IE) = (V sin θ)/[b d(θ)/dt] .... (2)

(IE) = ds (sin θ)/[b d(θ)] .... (3)

(IE) = p/(p + q) .... (4)

Equation (4) is perhaps the most useful as it explains why an oar with a shorter wider blade can be more efficient than an oar of the same overall length and outboard:inboard ratio, with a longer narrower blade, even though the blades have the same area. On this basis an oar can have an ideal efficiency as high as 0.8 or possibly even more, but as q cannot vanish unless part of the blade backs water, the efficiency cannot reach unity. After deducting the 'extras' due to the inertia etc. of a real oar the overall efficiency can fall to quite a low value. For example, it has been stated that 116 rowers have driven *Olympias* at 6.8 knots (Note 1). This required about 104 W of effective power per oar, averaged over the whole duration. The dimensions of the oars make it likely that their mean ideal efficiency was about 0.8 and that the power absorbed in overcoming their inertia etc. was given approximately by the formula:

w = 0.96r + 0.016r^2 .... (5)

where r was the stroke rate in spm. This averaged 38.75 and therefore w = about 61 watts per oar. We see that in this case:

VR/(VR/E+w) = 104/(104/0.8 + 61) = 104/191 = about 0.54

(6)

This efficiency is low. It would have been higher if the crew had pulled harder at the same stroke rate, which they could have done if they had had more practice.

Clearly the efficiency of an oar does not depend on the oar alone. Not only is it affected by the skill and power of the oarsman but also by the resistance of the ship (including air resistance) and the number, power and skill of the rest of the oarcrew. A headwind that reduces the ship's forward speed to zero reduces the oar's efficiency to zero also, by definition. These points receive further attention in the reference in Note 1.

Multi-manned oars

The writer knows of no experimental data on multi-manned oars. What follows is therefore supported by no practical testing.

Calculations suggest that an oar very like an oar used in a three-type but a little stronger could have been used in a suitably designed four. At a pinch, oars used in a three-type could have been used in fours. An inboard length of 2½ cubits was just long enough for a second man to be placed between the man at the butt

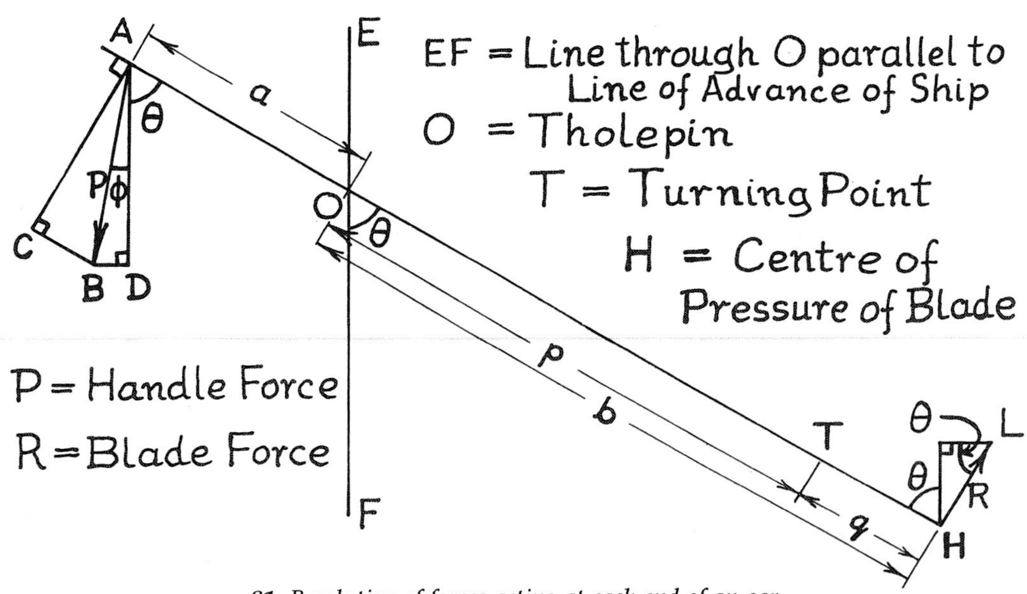

81. Resolution of forces acting at each end of an oar.

and the thole, but it would have been better to have drawn the oar inboard a little further. Then the slightly lower gearing would have matched the (probably) lower top speed of the four and have given the men a little more room. To give the men enough room to work, their centre-lines would have been about 0.65 m apart. As shown by (**82**), the second man would have rowed a much shorter stroke than his colleague and consequently the power transmitted by the oar would have been, not twice that of an oar in a three rowed by one man but only half as much again, if the men pulled equally hard. The smallness of this increase might have made it unnecessary to enlarge the blade although it would have been preferable to have done so. Such an oar could have been worked at high stroke rates, as in a three, and unless other considerations prevented it, could have been used in a suitably designed ship along with single-manned oars designed for threes. If its gearing was about 10% less than that suggested above for a three's oar, the power it would transmit to the ship at its maximum sprinting stroke rate of about 48 spm would be about the same as that of the longer two-man oar described next, given that the latter would have a maximum sprinting rate of about 39 spm.

An alternative two-man oar having longer outboard and inboard measurements is considered below, as an illustration of the pros and cons. It is not suggested that any oar had the exact dimensions here given. Their ratio (the gearing) and the overall length would be governed by the intended speed of the ship in calm water and the maximum height of the waves in which the ship was expected to be rowed. By making the oar longer inboard with the men still 0.65 m apart, the second man's length of stroke comes nearer to that of the first man, which itself increases a little even though the butt moves no further. This is because the swept angle is smaller. However, if the gearing is more or less as before, as it must be if waves are to be cleared and a reasonably high speed maintained, this gain is largely neutralised by the extra weight and inertia of the oar which rule out such high stroke rates as are possible in threes. (The inertia rises faster than the manpower). A consequence is that although the ship could be designed to contain oars of the type used in threes as well as the longer type just mentioned, best use would not be made of her oars of the former type because the stroke rate of all the oars would have to be kept down to that of the heavy long ones.

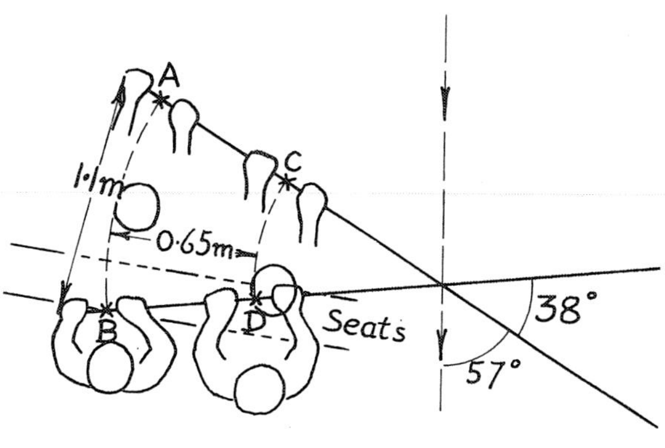

82. *The stroke lengths at a two-man oar.*

As to three-man oars, if all the men remained seated it can be seen that if the inboard length is kept to a minimum a three-man oar can be designed to work with the longer two-man oar discussed above, but if the inboard length is significantly increased the three-man oar's stroke rate is decreased below the best rate of the two-man oar and *a fortiori* below that of an oar of the type used in threes whether that has one man or two. This is one of several arguments making it likely that a four had two-man oars rather than a mixture of one-man and three-man oars. If all the men remained seated a three-man oar would probably have transmitted about 1½ times the power of a one-man oar as used in threes.

With oars that were a good deal longer inboard than three-type oars the restricted length of stroke at the butt by seated men of only about 1.1 m may have caused dissatisfaction. It may be that three-man oars made use of the stand-and-sit stroke which would have increased the length of stroke at the butt by about 0.2 m (in an *interscalmium* of 0.98 m). However it would surely have led to a reduction in stroke rate if not in strength of pull. A stand-and-sit stroke may have been preferable in rough water because by giving more scope for vertical movement of the butt it allowed the blade to be lifted higher to clear waves, gearing being unaltered.

A simplified justification of certain statements made above with reference to one-man, two-man and three-man oars, all men seated, is given in what follows. The butt-end stroke being restricted to 1.1m it is important that the lost motion due to oar flexibility be small in relation to it, even though by skilful rowing much of any lost motion at the catch can be recovered at the finish of the stroke. To retain the same deflection for the longer of the two-man oars as for the one-man three-type oar would make its loom and shaft far too thick and clumsy for a speedy ship. In the absence of relevant experimental data it is uncertain how far the deflection should be allowed to increase. However, when a force of 50 kgf was applied to the handle of one of the experimental spruce oars of *Olympias*, the neck of the blade being fixed, the movement at the butt was 65 mm, or 6% of 1.1 m. A pull of about 25 kgf would suffice to maintain an adequate cruising speed and would result in a proportionately smaller deflection of 3%, small enough that a distinct increase in it could probably be tolerated in the longer two-man oar. This may justify the assumption, in what follows, that it is the radius of curvature of the shafts (at, say, the thole) rather than the deflection at the butt that should remain constant as between the three oars discussed. This entails that the radius of the cross-section of the oarshafts at any given fraction of the total outboard or inboard length should vary as the fourth root of the moment of the oarsman's or oarsmen's pull. (The oarshafts are presumed to have a circular cross-section.) The moment in question is the sum of the moments due to the one, two or three oarsmen; their leverages can be specified on the assumption that they differ by 0.65 m, but it is not easy to specify the pulls. The different men on one oar may all pull with the same force but it is possible that the men with the shorter stroke could pull harder. This remains to be seen. Also it can be shown that the longer oars cannot be worked effectively at such high stroke rates as the shorter ones, but this is partly countered by the stronger pull that should be achievable at the lower stroke rate. The precise trade-off will depend on the fitness, skill and determination of the men and on their orders, but here it will be assumed for convenience that within the usual range of stroke rate the maximum available pull is inversely proportional to the square root of the stroke rate. The effect of this assumption is that if the length remains unchanged the power varies as the square root of the stroke rate (within reasonable limits). Again, the value of the assumption remains to be tested.

The experiments in *Olympias* afford a starting point for the calculations regarding multi-manned oars. Suppose that a high-quality oar of the type used in threes was 4.66 m long of which 1.23 m was inboard, that it weighed 4.4 kgf, its centre of gravity (CG) was 0.5 m outboard of the thole and its moment of inertia about the CG was 6.0 kg-m^2. Then its weight 'in hand' considered to act at the butt was 1.79 kgf (3.9 lbf, which is a suitable quantity); the square of its radius of gyration was 1.364 m^2 and its moment of inertia about the thole was 7.1 kg-m^2. Its centre of percussion (at the blade) was 2.73 m from the CG i.e. it was 0.17 m inboard of the tip which was again about right. (These data are self-consistent.) We may state a characteristic radius of the shaft of this oar as r mm, and a characteristic pull available at 48 spm of P newtons acting 1.03 m from the thole (i.e. at the midpoint between the oarsman's hands). The couple that corresponds to the radius r is therefore 1.03P. The pull at some other stroke rate, e.g. 40 spm, would be P times the square root of 48/40 i.e. 1.095P.

Now consider a two-man oar based on the foregoing three-type oar. If the gearing is unaltered the men have leverages of 1.03 m and 0.38 m and they exert a couple of 1·41P at 48 spm. Accordingly if lost motion is not to increase, r must be increased by a factor of 1.08 (the fourth root of 1.41/1.03) and so the oar's weight, weight in hand, and moment of inertia all increase by a factor of 1.17. This is outweighed by the extra couple the men can exert, so no problem arises. A moderate increase in the size of the blade to absorb the increased thrust without increasing slip velocity can be accommodated. In practice a four with these oars would be a little slower than a three and this would make it desirable to lower the gearing slightly, probably by about 10%, giving both men a little more leverage and more room.

An altogether different two-man oar is now considered in which the outboard and inboard lengths are greater by 50% than those of the three-type oar. The couple exerted is 2.64P if the pull per man is unchanged, but as has been said, the stroke rate will be lowered and therefore the pull can increase. The characteristic radius of the shaft must increase. The weight of the oar increases and the CG moves further out. Unless the loom is counterweighted the weight in hand increases and may become too great. Details of this oar can be found by successive approximation. In order to obtain the stroke rate the magnitude of the horizontal force an oarsman can conveniently apply during the return is needed; it has been obtained by analysing the motion of an oar of a modern eight.

It turns out that the sprinting stroke rate of this oar is about 39 spm, whereas in a three it is about 48 spm. At 39 spm the pull per man is 1.11 times that at 48 spm by our simple rule. The couple is 2.93P and so the square of the characteristic radius is increased by a factor of 1.69 and the weight of the wood in the oar is increased by a factor of 1.5 × 1.69 to 11.15 kgf. The CG is 0.75 m from the thole. These dimensions would make the oar rather heavy outboard. This can be corrected by putting M kg of lead in the loom at a point say 1.5 m from the thole. Recalling that the weight 'in hand' for a one-man oar preferably does not exceed 1.8 kgf measured at the butt we can write down that for the two men now involved:

$$1.5M + 1.8(1.845 + 1.195) = 11.15(0.75)$$

and hence M the mass of lead required is 1.93 kg. The CG is now 0.574 m outboard of the thole.

We can now write down the new moment of inertia about the thole (MIT) which is given by:

$$MIT = (7.1 \times 1.5^2 \times 1.5 \times 1.69 + (1.93 \times 1.5^2) = 40.5 + 4.3$$

$= 44.8$ kg-m^2 (as compared with 7.1 kg-m^2 for the three).

It seems that the centre of percussion of this oar would be in a 'virtual' position beyond the tip of the blade. This would make the oar rather clumsy to handle, as it would tend to move away from the oarsmen's hands momentarily at the inception of the catch. This could be put right by using a considerably smaller mass of lead at the cost of making the oar heavier 'in hand'. If the mass of the lead were reduced to a little less than 0.2 kg without moving its position the centre of percussion would return to a suitable position but the weight 'in hand' would be nearly half as much again as desirable. A compromise may be necessary.

The duration of the return may be thought of as consisting of a period when the oar is being accelerated, a period during which its angular velocity is constant, and a period of deceleration towards the deadpoint just preceding the catch. It appears that in a three the period of constant angular velocity occupies about 92% of the swept angle and it will be assumed that this is the case for the two-man oar also. The total angle is 0.608 radians. Allowing for the slower stroke rate the couple available for the return appears to be about 480 n-m (cf. 170 n-m in a three) and therefore the angular acceleration is 480/44.8 i.e. 10.7 radians per second per second. If the angle swept during acceleration equals that during deceleration it amounts to 0.0243 radians and:

$0.0243 = \frac{1}{2}(10.7)\, t^2$ where t is the duration of acceleration.

It follows that $t = 0.0674$ seconds. The angular velocity reached after time t is therefore 10.7×0.0674 i.e. 0.721 radians/second and we see that if the duration of constant angular velocity is T seconds:

$2 \times 0.0243 + 0.721T = 0.608$ and therefore $T = 0.776$ seconds

The return therefore lasts for $2 \times 0.0674 + 0.776 = 0.911$ seconds. Finally , if the rhythm factor is 2½ (as in the three) the pull + return lasts for 1.52 seconds and therefore the stroke rate is 39.5 spm. As this agrees closely with the figure of 39 spm with which we started, a second approximation is unnecessary.

The power exerted upon this oar and that transmitted to the ship by it at 39.5 spm are now compared with those relating to a one-man, three-type oar at 48 spm. It will be assumed that for a short time a man can exert 300 W during his pull at 48 spm if his stroke length is 1.1 m. All powers quoted are averages over the duration of stroke plus return.

Three: The effective stroke length of a man whose total stroke length at the butt is 1.1 m is about 0.83 m if the midpoint between the man's hands is 0.2 m from the butt, the loom is 1.23 m long and there is a 10% loss in obtaining the catch and the finish. The man exerts $0.83 \times P \times 48/60$ watts during his pull, and this equals 300, therefore $P = 452$ newtons or 102 lbf. The 'ideal' efficiency may be taken as 0.8 and the power absorbed by the oar during the pull as 10 W. The power it absorbs during the extraction, return and descent to the water is about 70 W. We see that the power exerted on the water is $(300 - 10) \times 0.2$ i.e. 58 W. The power left over to drive the ship is $300 - 10 - 58 = 232$ W. The man's total power is 370 W. The overall efficiency is therefore 0.627.

Four: Using a hypothetical two-man oar, 50% longer than a three-type oar, both inboard and outboard. If the butt moves 1.1 m, the midpoint between No.1 man's hands moves 0.98 m and if a further 10% loss occurs in obtaining the catch and finish the effective length is 0.88 m. The No. 2 man has an effective length of 0.53 m.

The men exert a mean pull of:

$$452 \times \sqrt{(48/39.5)} = 498 \text{ newtons.}$$

Power of man at butt during pull:

$$498 \times 0.88 \times 39.5/60 = 289 \text{ W.}$$

Power of second man during pull:

$$498 \times 0.53 \times 39.5/60 = 174 \text{ W.}$$

Total exerted on oar during pull: 463 W. Power absorbed by oar during pull: about 30 W. 'Ideal' efficiency may be taken as 0.8 again. Hence power exerted on ship $= 433 \times 0.8 = 346$ W. This is a little less than half as much again as with the one-man three-type oar, but longer oars permit a higher freeboard and consequently they conduce to a safer ship.

The oar absorbs about 110 W during the extraction, return and descent to the water, i.e. the man at the butt (No. 1) exerts about the same power during this period as his colleague in a three, and the No.2 man exerts about 0.6 as much. No. 1's total power is about 360 W, about the same as in a three, but No. 2's is only about 215 W.

As the No. 2 man exerts much less power than the No.1 he will have greater endurance. It would be sensible to interchange the men from time to time. This reveals the possibility that in a four the power per man available for cruising may be closer to that of the three than the foregoing calculation referring to a sprint may suggest.

If one-man three-type oars were combined with the two-man oars just described they would all be worked at not over 39.5 spm.

Similar calculations may be made for a three-man oar, but need not be given here as the principle has been demonstrated.

It will be realised that a number of more-or-less doubtful assumptions have had to be made. Experimental work is needed to assess their value.

Note

1 The reader is referred to: J. T. Shaw: 1993 *Rowing in Ships and Boats*. Transactions of The Royal Institution of Naval Architects. Part B, Volume 135, pp. 211–224.

Glossary

Centre of Percussion: In the case of a pivoted body such as a solid wooden oar on its thole this is located and defined by the property that a blow received there creates no reaction at the pivot, i.e. the thole. If the pivot is at O, the centre of gravity is at G, the radius of gyration is k and the centre of percussion is at C, then GO.GC = k^2. The position of the centre of percussion depends on how the oar is tapered. In a well balanced oar the centre of percussion is a few centimetres inboard of the tip of the blade.

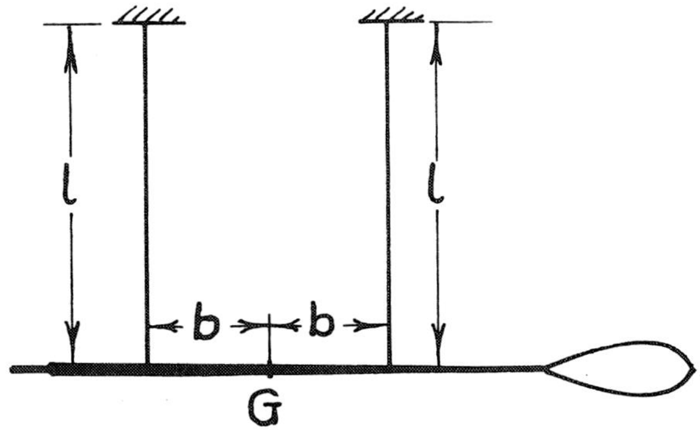

83. Bifilar suspension.

Moment of inertia about the centre of gravity: For an irregular body such as an oar this has to be determined by experiment. One way is to use a bifilar suspension, by which the oar is suspended by two vertical strings of equal length L, each distant b from the centre of gravity, as in (**83**); and measure the time T taken for the oar to make a complete swing about its centre of gravity in the horizontal plane. The moment of inertia about the centre of gravity is then $M(Tb/2\pi)^2$ (g/L) where M is the mass of the oar, T is the periodicity, g is the acceleration due to gravity. See also *Radius of gyration*.

Moment of inertia about the thole: The quantity $M(k^2 + OG^2)$ where M is the mass of the oar, k is its radius of gyration and OG is the distance between the centre of gravity and the thole.

Radius of gyration: k, given by the relation that the moment of inertia of the oar about the centre of gravity equals Mk^2 where M is the mass of the oar.

Appendix C

Ship design evidence from texts and representations

The identification of representations by type may not be certain.

Warships with One and a Half Files of Oarsmen: ἡμιολίαι (νῆες), ἡμιόλιοι (λέμβοι)

Texts

	Date BC	Page
Alexander's Indus flotilla:	326	9
A. puts ἡμιολίαι first in the list of 'fast ships'	326	10
ἡμιολίαι rated with fives as cataphract at Utica may be τριημιολίαι	151	113

Representations

None recognisable.

Warships with Two Levels of Oars

I. With Two Files of Oarsmen a Side: TWOS : named Pentecontors (Aegean) or Λέμβος (Adriatic)

Texts

	Date BC	Page
At the siege of Rhodes the stoutest λέμβος, built aphract, were boxed in and given oarports that could be closed. They carried archers and catapults.	305–3	34, 263
Illyrian pirate craft were undecked, slim and sharply pointed.	400–300	263–264
Mention of a λέμβος as big as a pentecontor	200–100	"
Λέμβος used as fleet scouts	240	"
Λέμβος with and without rams	197	"
Romans call their light, two-level ships *liburnides*	AD 100–200	"
Liburnians 'content to have grown to two levels'	49	"
Λέμβος, fast, light, open, and with up to 25 oars a side		
Liburnians were two-level λέμβος		"
Livy calls λέμβος fitted out to carry troops *biremes*	216	"
Cataphract λέμβος	200	"
A ship, probably a decked liburnian, capsizes when soldiers go to one side.	49	131–2
Similar ship feared to capsize when men grasp topwale to pull themselves aboard	49	"

Representations

	Figure No.	Date	Page
i.	(a) Nineveh relief	after 701	179–181
	(c) Geometric vasepainting	735–710	"
ii.	Tetradrachms of Zankle	490–483	181–182
iii.	Engraved gem	520–480	182
iv.	Attic b/f amphora	c.510	183
v.	Attic b/f cup	c.510	183
vi.	Attic b/f jug	c.510	183
vii.	Ficoroni casket	325–300	184–185
1.	(f) Coin of Sidon	372–361	190–191

44. Tomb relief	AD 100	247
45–9. Trajan's column relief	AD 113	248–253

II. With Four Files of Oarsmen a Side (FOURS: Oars Double-manned)

Texts

	Date	Page
Invented at Carthage	before 368	xii, 267
First historical mention at siege of Tyre	332	6, 267
In Athenian fleet	330/329	267
Alba Fucentia graffito: *navis tetreris longa*	100 BC–AD 100	239, 268
Equipped with turrets	36 BC	268
Housed in Piraeus shipsheds		16
Deck lower than deck of five	202	68, 268–269
Probably faster than a single-level *λέμβος*		269
Built in 45 days of green timber	205	65
Boxed in, two categories of oarsmen, less draft than fives	36	155

Representations

Figure No.	Date	Page
23. Coins of Leukas	3rd-2nd cent.	223
38. Labelled graffito	100 BC–AD 100	239

III. With Eight or more Files of Oarsmen a Side (EIGHTS or ships of higher rating)

Texts

	Date	Page
First mention: Lysimachus's *Leontophoros*	280	273
In Philip V's fleet at Chios: *ἀνάστειρος*	201	272

Representations

Figure No.	Date	Page
25. Relief showing 2 two-level warships	c.100	226
29. Praeneste relief	50–1	230

Warships with three levels of oars

I With Three Files of Oarsmen a Side (One is a Half-File): *τριημιολίαι*

Texts

	Date	Page
Three *τριημιολίαι* captured a four	305–4	34
τριημιολίαι in Egyptian Navy	283–246	37, 266
ἡμιολίαι rated as cataphract may be *τριημιολίαι*	151	113
Crew probably totalled 144		203–205

Representations

Figure No.	Date	Page
11. The Lindos prow (shows oarbox)	285–260	203–205
17. Coins of Hasdrubal	228–221	216
20. The Samothrace prow	200–180	220–221
21. The Lindos relief	190–180	221
26. The Palazzo Barberini mosaic	100–50	226

II With Three Files of Oarsmen a Side (THREES)

Texts

	Date BC	Page
Threes taken across the Isthmus (of Corinth) by the *δίολκος*:		62
428, 412 BC: Thuk. 3.15.1 and 8.8.4. Threes unable to catch up with merchant ships in a strong following wind.	147	114
Warships filled with water by a rising spring tide when drawn up on a beach in Britain	55	123
Threes did not usually carry towers	31	357

Representations

	Figure No.	Date	Page
i.	(b). Nineveh relief	701	180
viii.	Vienna fragment	450	186
ix.	Lenormant relief	c.400	186–187
x.	Ruvo Vase	c.400	188
xi.	Coins of Sidon	5th cent.	188
xii.	Coins of Arados	5th, 4th	190
1.	Coin of Sidon (f)	386/5–332	191
2.	Persian Seals	520/15–331	193
3.	Arados Coin (e)	350–332	194
4.	Coins of Byblos (a)-(d)	399–333	195
6.	Erment Model (or of Five)	350–300	196
7.	Coins of Kios	340–300	199
8.	Octobols of Histiaia	340–338	200
9.	Coins of Phaselis	300–295	201
47.2.	Trajan's column relief	AD 113	253

II With Five Files of Oarsmen a Side: FIVES.

Texts

	Date	Page
Invented at Syracuse	After 399	1
300 oarsmen and 120 decksoldiers(?80) and hyperesia (½40) at Eknomos (an invasion fleet)	256	2, 46
Appearance	in 3rd cent. BC	43
A five higher than a four		269
A five may have been better at keeping off a lee shore than a three	390	3
Fives slower and because of their weight more responsive to the helm in variable currents and so steadier than threes	206	65
A Carthaginian cataphract (?five) was used as a model for the first Roman fleet. Oarsmen trained on shore to row three-level ship	260	43, 353
Fives were too heavy to take over the isthmus of Corinth	217	62
A five made the same speed from Cumae to Rome as a messenger on land	210	63
Roman fives joined in pairs to carry siege engines	203	67
Fives built in 45 days of green timber	203	65
Water taken on board for expedition to Carthage	204	66
Unladen transports had more freeboard than a five		67
Fives were the normal front-line ships.	203	67
75 soldiers carried on board on passage, 50 for battle	202	68
4000 cubits of pine planking needed to build one five and one three	224	355
Fives had more oars than threes or fours	49	131

	Date	Page
Heavy Roman ships withstood broadside ramming by liburnians whose rams 'stuck in'	49	131
A heavy ship sank low in the water without, it seems, turning over. 'She was piled high with carnage and full of blood' and had broken plank fastenings after many ram attacks.	49	131–132
Agrippa added in naval yards boxing-in to hulls of ships built in private yards	37–36	153

Representations

Figure No.		Date	Page
3.	(f), (g) Coins of Arados	350–332	194
4.	(e) Coin of Byblos	399–333	195
5.	Amathus engraved gem	340–330	196
6.	The Erment Model (or of Three)	350–300	196
10.	Coins of Demetrios Poliorketes	300–295	202
13.	The Nymphaion fresco	268–240	209–210
14.	The Cyrene prow	300–100	214
15.	Carthaginian grave stele	3rd cent.	215
16.	Coin of Antigonos Doson	300–200	215
18.	Calenian dishes	250–180	217–218
27.	Isola Tiberina prow (or of six)	100–50	227–228
30.	Coins of the Civil Wars	40–31	231
34.	Orange relief	early 1st cent.	235
35.	The Ostia frieze	soon after 20	236
39.	The Pozzuoli reliefs	100–AD 100	240–241
40.	The Aula Isiaca fresco	1st cent. AD	242
43.	The Pompeian shipshed frescos	1st cent. AD	245

III With Six Files of Oarsmen a Side: SIXES.

Texts

	Date	Page
Invented in Syracuse	before 367/6	3
Agathokles has sixes there	289	3
Six swamped in a storm: 32 survivors out of 500	302	34
Sixes used as flagships by Romans at Eknomos	256	46
Also by Sextus Pompeius	39	149
A six (with towers) said to be higher than fives, threes etc (without towers)	49	129

Representations

Figure No.		Date	Page
27.	Isola Tiberina prow (or of five)	100–50	227–228

IV With Seven Files of Oarsmen a Side: SEVENS

Texts

	Date	Page
Alexander orders construction of 700 sevens	324	12
Seven Phoenician sevens in Demetrios's fleet	304	26
36 sevens in Ptolemy Philadelphos's fleet	283–246	37
Pyrrhus's flagship a seven	280	42
Carthaginian flagship at Mylaie a seven (?Pyrrhus's)	260	45
Three sevens built for Antiochos in Phoenicia	190	102

Appendix D

APPROXIMATE PARTICULARS OF RECONSTRUCTIONS

LWL = Length on waterline BWL = Breadth on waterline LOA = Length overall
K = Underside of keel W = Waterline G = Centre of gravity BOA = Breadth overall
D = Deck at side T = Topwale of hull M = Metacentre

Type of ship	3	Early 5	4	5	6	7	5	Liburnian	Hemiolia	Trihemi.
Figure Number	55, 60	57	59	61, 62	67	68, 69	71	72	73	74, 75
Approximate date	400 BC	400 BC	300 BC	100 BC	100 BC	100 BC	50 AD	100 AD	300 BC	300 BC
LWL (l), m	36	41	33	41	43	43	41	18	21	31
LOA, m	40	45	37	45	47	47	45	20	24	35
BWL, m	3.7	5.2	4.6	5.3	5.7	5,7	5.7	3.0	2.7	4.0
BOA, m	5.6	6.4	5.6	7.0	7.5	7.5	8.2	3.9	4.3	5.8
Mean Draft, m	1.1	1.5	1.3	1.5	1.5	1.5	1.6	0.76	0.78	1.1
Height, K to D, m	3.6	4.4	3.4	4.4	4.8	4.8	4.6	2.8		3.5
W to D, m	2.5	3.0	2.2	2.9	3.3	3.3	3.0	2.0		2.4
K to T, (h), m	2.5	3.1	2.7	2.9	3.3	3.3	2.3	1.75	1.5	2.3
K to G, m	1.8	2.8	2.2	2.8	2.9	2.9	2.9	1.5	1.3	1.9
G to M, m	0.8	1.4	1.4	1.5	1.4	1.4	1.4	0.7	0.7	1.0
Displacement, manned, tonnes	48	100	60	110	125	133	125	14.5	14	41
Light ship, tonnes	26	52	30	58	63	63	65	7	7	23
Crew, tonnes	15	30	20	30	35	40	33	5.5	6	12
Stores, Water, tonnes	7	18	10	22	26	30	27	2.0	1	6
Length/depth (l / h)	14	13.2	12	14	13	13	18 (Decked)	10.3	13.8	13.3
Oarcrew	170	282	176	282	336	390	300	50	50	120
Deckcrew	16	20	16	20	20	20	20	5	5	13
Troops	14	75	75	75	100	100	75	5	10	11
Oars, total	170	168	88	168	168	168	180	50	50	120
1-man oars, No.	170	54		54			60	50	50	120
Length, m	4.7	4.7		4.7			4.7	4.3	4.7 & 4.9	4.7 & 6.0
Gearing	3.0	3.5		3.5			3.5	2.75	2.7 & 2.7	3.2 & 3.0
2-man oars, No.		114	88	114	168	114	120			
Length, m		6.9	6.0	6.9	6.9	6.9	7.4 & 10.0			
Gearing 1		2.7	2.8	2.8	2.8	2.8	2.5 & 2.4			
Gearing 2		4.0	4.2	4.2	4.2	4.2	3.6 & 2.8			
3-man oars, No.						54				
Length, m						7.5				
Gearing 1						2.2				
Gearing 2						2.8				
Gearing 3						4.6				
Estimated speed:-										
for two minutes, knots	9.7	8.0	8.7	8.0	8.0	8.0	7.5	7.1	7.4	9.2
for six hours, knots	7.5	7.0	7.0	7.0	7.1	7.3	6.6	5.0	5.1	7.2

Appendix E

Table of estimated Waterline Breadths derived from the Aktion Memorial & Reconstructions.

Aktion Memorial (From Murray and Petsas)						Class of Ship	Oar System	**Reconstructions** Minimum Breadth			Wider			Oarbox
Socket Number	Group Number (Fig. 70)	Mean Breadth of Sockets in Group (R)	Mean Breadth of Rams in Group (R)	Assumed Ratio BWL / R	BWL of Ship			BWL m	Breadth of Gangway m	Spacing of Oar-crew m	BWL m	Breadth of Gangway m	Spacing of Oar-crew m	Breadth m
2 & 4	1	1.51	1.49	5.9	8.8	10	5 / 5	7.5	1.3	Standing 0.45m apart	8.8	1.7	Standing 0.55m apart	0.7? (Vent only)
1	2	1.38	1.36	5.9	8.0	9	5 / 4				8.1	1.6		1.1?
3 & 6	3	1.30	1.28	5.9	7.6	8	4 / 4			Sitting 0.60m apart	7.7	1.5	Sitting 0.65m apart	0.7? (Vent only)
5 & 9	4	1.24	1.22	5.9	7.2	8	3 / 3 / 2				7.4	1.4		1.1?
7 8 10 & C	5	1.18	1.16	5.9	6.8	7	2 2 3	5.7	1.0	0.60	6.4	1.3	0.65	0.9
11 12 17 & B	6	1.11	1.09	5.9	6.4	6	2 2 2	5.7	1.0	0.60	6.3	1.3	0.65	0.9
13 14 15 & D	7	1.02	1.00	5.9	5.9	5	2 2 1	5.3	0.8	0.55	6.1	1.3	0.65	0.9
Athlit		0.84	0.82	** 5.66	4.6	4	2 2	4.6	1.3	0.65	4.6	1.3	0.65	None
Olympias		* 0.70	0.68	*** 5.44	3.7	3	1 1 1	3.7	1.3	-	3.7	1.3	-	Out-rigger

* An appropriate breadth for a socket for these rams, as at Aktion

** The ratio between the BWL of the reconstruction of a 4 in Fig. 59 & the breadth of the Athlit ram.

*** The actual ratio in *Olympias*.

BWL = Breadth on Waterline

Appendix F

Load on shell plank tenons and their pegs in long hulls

Tenons joining hull shell planks together edge to edge are subjected, with their pegs, first to tensile forces and bending moments across shell seams, in resisting which tenons act in association with transverse timbers, and second to shear forces tending to cause adjacent planks to slide upon each other. The shear forces arise in transmitting the shear stresses generated in the shell, particularly at the mid-height of the sides of the hull, by the shear forces imposed on vertical cross-sections of the whole hull by the buoyancy and mass of the ship, which are differently distributed along its length. In long and relatively shallow hulls such as those of oared ships, the shear forces carried by the numerous tenons are appreciable, and it is their stiffness and strength which have to be relied upon to prevent working of shell seams (by planks sliding on each other) causing leakage and unacceptable hogging of the ship. Plank tenons, and their pegs, are therefore vital components of the hulls of oared ships built in the manner of the ancient Mediterranean.

It may be presumed that it is the shear loading upon shell plank tenons which explains why in the Punic longship excavated by Honor Frost near Marsala (Frost: 1973, 1974) they were twice as thick as the usual thickness of tenons found in the numerous excavated wrecks of shorter round ships. It is also significant that such tenons have been found to be of dense timbers, in particular Turkey Oak (*quercus cerris*) and sometimes olivewood. Turkey oak, while not as useful in most respects as most other oaks, does have a particularly high crushing strength across the grain, which is the property needed in the material of a plank tenon loaded in shear as described.

Some analysis of tenon loading in shear, even if simplified and only approximate, is therefore appropriate in a study of oared ships.

The forces acting on tenons in resisting shearing between planks are shown in (**84**), where P is the bearing force between a tenon and its mortice, and H and V the components of the bearing force between the tenon and its peg parallel and perpendicular to the seam respectively. Let S denote the inter-plank shear force borne by each tenon, here assumed constant in the vicinity considered. In (**84**) the edges of tenons and mortices have been drawn straight and parallel. In many wrecks they have been tapered, which if they had been made with suitable slope and degree of crush-fit, may have helped, by crushing in the direction of the plank grain when the top plank was driven down to make the seam, to obtain a tight fit with a number of tenons simultaneously and so achieve the maximum stiffness against plank-sliding.

The pressure between mortice and edge of tenon, accounting for the force P, is assumed to extend from plank edge to peg-level, as shown in (**84**). It is also assumed that the pressure rises linearly towards plank-edge, being zero at peg-level. Let the coefficient of friction between tenon and mortice be μ.

Equilibrium of the plank requires that

$$V = \mu P \quad \text{and} \quad S = P - H, \qquad (1)$$

neglecting forces required for the rotational equilibrium of the plank.

Rotational equilibrium of a tenon, however, re-

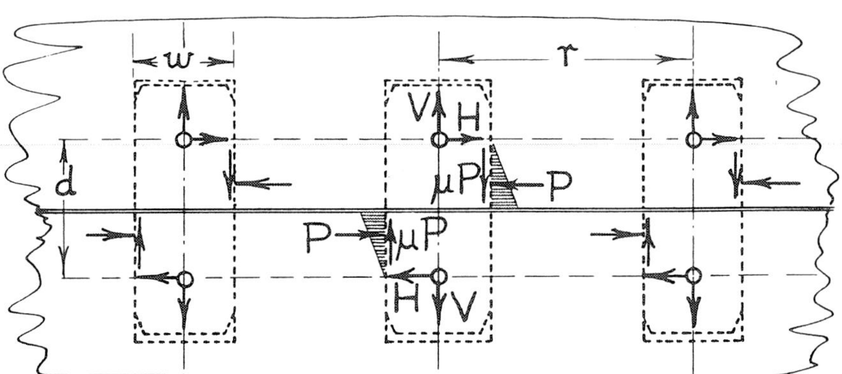

84 *Reconstructed sections of some representations for comparison*

quires that

$$Pd/3 = Hd + \mu Pw, \qquad (2)$$

if each tenon is w wide and its pegs are d apart. From (1) and (2),

$$H = P\,(1/3 - \mu w/d) \qquad (3)$$

and

$$S = P\,(2/3 + \mu w/d) \qquad (4)$$

If the maximum pressure, at plank-edge, is p_{max}, and the tenon has thickness t_t,

then $P = p_{max}\, dt_t/4$

so that $S = p_{max}\, dt_t\,(1/6 + \mu w/4d)$.

S is then the shear force which can be borne by one tenon for a given value of p_{max},which cannot exceed the cross-grain crushing stress, p_c the timber of the tenon.

The shear stress, q_s, in the side shell of the ship's hull, t_s thick, may be estimated approximately by the usual methods of elementary beam theory. The shear force on each tenon, if tenons are distanced r apart, centre-to-centre, in the vicinity where the shear stress in the shell is q_s, is

$$S = q_s\, t_s\, r,$$

so the shell shearing stress, q_s, can be related to the shell plank and tenon dimensions, tenon spacing and maximum cross-grain pressure on the tenon timber, p_{max}, by the equation

$$q_s = p_{max} \times \frac{dt_t\,(1/6 + \mu w/4d)}{t_s r}$$

Shear stress in tenons in the plane of the plank seam will not be uniform but its mean value will be

$$q_t = \frac{S}{t_t w}$$

and it will be evident, if the maximum shear stress that can be borne by the tenon timber is $q_{t.max}$, that in the limit,

S must be not greater than $q_{t.max}\, t_t w$,

i.e. q_s must not be greater than $q_{t.max} \dfrac{t_t w}{t_s r}$

The necessary minimum diameter for pegs may be found by solving for V and H in terms of S or q_s, and given a value for the shear load that a peg made of the appropriate timber (nearly always oak) can carry in double shear without crushing.

8

CREWS, SHIPS AND TACTICS

I. CREWS

An examination (JSM: 1984) of the use in Athenian naval contexts of the words *ναῦται, ὑπηρεσία* and *ἐπιβάται* during the 5th and 4th century BC shows that writers normally distinguished:

1. the oarcrew as *ναῦται*; sometimes as *στρατιῶται* cf. Thuc.2.88.1 and [Demosthenes] *Adv. Polykles* 50.35 and 53;
2. the specialist assistants to the trierarch as the *ὑπηρεσία*;
3. the decksoldiers as *ἐπιβάται*.

This was the strict use of the terms, but *ὑπηρεσία* could sometimes include the decksoldiers and sometimes even the whole crew; and *ἐπιβάται* again had a more general use for anyone carried on deck.

The *ὑπηρεσία* in the strict sense was composed, in threes, of 30 men: the helmsman (*κυβερνήτης*) with an aft deck-gang of 5, the bow officer (*πρῳράτης πρῳρεύς*) with a forward deck gang of 5, the rowing master (*κελευστής*), the purser (*πεντηκόνταρχος*), shipwright (*ναυπηγός*) and the piper (*αὐλητής*). In addition there were ten hoplites and four archers. These, with the 170 oarsmen made up the three's crew of 200 (see *AT* 107–127).

The *ὑπηρεσία* of the Athenian three may be compared with that of a Rhodian ship numbering 45, almost certainly a four, of the 1st century BC. The information is provided by an inscription (see *SSAW* p. 306 Ch. 13 n.28) in which a *πρῳρεύς*, whose last ship was a four, is honoured by his messmates, a helmsman, shipwright, an assistant helmsman (*πηδαλιοῦχος*), 5 men working in the bow and 5 in the stern, two catapultmen (*καταπελταφέται*), 6 archers, a masseur, a doctor, an oar-binder (*κωποδέτας*) and at least 19 (say, 20) decksoldiers. The 28 (2 + 6 + [20]) military personnel, twice the number of those on a three, is in tune with current tactical practice. Otherwise the four's 18 specialists compare fairly closely with the three's 16. The *πεντηκόνταρχος* and *αὐλητής* are missing; instead there is a doctor, an assistant helmsman ('a man holding the tiller') and an oar-binder who may have assisted the shipwright, in matters concerning the oars and their fitting and repair (cf. *naupegus aupiciarius: AE*: 1974 621). The fourth additional man is called 'an applier of olive-oil *ἐλαιοχρίστης*', presumably a masseur or physiotherapist.

Other earlier (3rd-2nd century) fragmentary inscriptions give crew lists including the *πεντηκόνταρχος* and add a secretary of the trierarch (*γραμματεύς τριηράρχου*). A later dedication by a Milesian crew (ibid. p. 307 n. 30) 1st century BC gives *ναύαρχος, τριήραρχος, ἐπίπλους, γραμματεύς*. Casson cites a papyrus (P. Cair. Zen. 59036 = Select Papyri 410 of 257 BC) to show that the *ἐπίπλους* was a deputy or assistant trierarch. Also, Casson cites Cicero (*Divinatio in Caecilium* 17.55: of 70 BC) to show that pipers were taken aboard warships in the Republican period. Cicero says that a prefect of Antony's confiscated from a freedwoman at Lilybaion slave musicians (*symphoniacos servos*) for service in the fleet. A *symphoniacus* also appears in a Roman tomb inscription as a crewmember (*CIL* IX 43).

The function of pipe music in timing the oarstroke in even the largest warships is given very precisely in a passage of Plutarch (*Demetrius* 55). The urn containing the ashes of Demetrios had been sent by Seleukos across the Aegean to his son Antigonos Gonatas. Antigonos met the ship off the islands and transferred the urn to the largest of his flagships. As they arrived at Corinth [presumably Lechaion] 'the most famous of living fluteplayers (*αὐληταί*) Xenophantes, who was seated near the urn, played an accompaniment [to the rowing] with the most solemn music. Furthermore, there was a beat in a certain rhythm as the oars were recovered which kept time with the periods of the flute music, just as there is in a funeral dirge.'

An inscription on the Lindos prow (11 p. 205: 265–60 BC) records the dedication of the firstfruits of spoils by petty officers and men of (two) *τριημιολίαι* serving under the command of a *ναύαρχος* (whose name is not preserved) and two trierarchs (hence two ships). Of the crews (and *ὑπηρεσία*) only seventy names are preserved, but Blinkenberg calculated that there were originally 288, 144 a ship including *ὑπηρεσία*: considerably less than the four with 176 oarsmen and 45 *ὑπηρεσία*).

The ancient historians of the period provide scanty information about the manning of Roman ships. The maritime praetor is fleet commander holding his authority (*imperium*) on an annual basis from the Senate. The ship captains are called *navium magistri* and are presumably appointed to the ship on commission, that is to say when the ship is launched from the shipsheds (*navalia*). When Scipio (p. 66) had all ready for the departure to Africa of his invasion fleet at Lilybaion he sent longboats round the ships with instructions that the captain (*magister*), helmsman (*gubernator*) and two decksoldiers from each ship should assemble in the city square. Celebrating his triumph over Perseus, Gnaeus Octavius (Livy 45.42.2) donated 75 *denarii* to the *socii navales*, twice as much to the helmsmen and four times as much to the captains of his ships. This text suggests that the *socii navales* included, besides the oarsmen, also the seamen who worked the ship other than the helmsman.

Plautus (251–184 BC: *Rudens* 4.3.82) speaks of the *proreta* as the navigational counterpart of the *gubernator* ('You are the *proreta* of that ship and I'll be helmsman). Ovid later uses the words *proreta* and *proreus* in the *Metamorphoses* (3.617 and 634). A *κελευστής* is mentioned by Polybius in connection with the land training of the first Roman crews. He stands in the middle (of both dimensions of the mock ship: see *AT* p. 113. Fig. 31). The Latin name is *hortator* (Plautus *Mercator* 4.2.5). Ovid (*Metamorphoses* 3.618) describes Epopeus in Hades as '*hortator animorum*' one who with his voice gives rest and rhythm (*requiemque modumque*) to the oarsmen-souls. A fragment of Ennius (101) gives his role using the gavel (*portisculus*) at the start of a stroke: 'let (the oarsmen) with oars already in their hands obey, watch out for the moment when the *portisculus* begins to give the signal (to row)' (cf. also Plautus *Asinaria* 3.1.14). Silius Italicus (AD 26–101:6.360) gives a fine description of the officer's duties: 'there stands in the middle of the stern's extremity (towards bow) one who with his voice regulates the alternate (*alternos*) strokes of the oarsmen' (forward and backward), 'who gives to the oars their sound and when the oars have been brought forward to the number (i.e. in unison) he smites the resounding waves'. A later name for the *hortator* is given by Seneca (*Ep.* 56) who speaks of the *pausarius* 'with a very penetrating (*acutissima*) voice giving the time to the oarsmen'. The *pausarius* may, however, be a separate officer.

There are indirect references to the deck-gangs. In the hurried embarkation of the Roman ships before the battle of the Ebro (p. 58) the soldiers on deck hinder the seamen there as they carried out their work in getting the ships away, and Scipio's address (p. 66) to the captains, helmsmen and representatives of the decksoldiers, instructed the last named not to get in the way of the seamen on the voyage. No other members of the non-rowing crew of Roman warships are mentioned in literature.

Polybios (1.26.7) gives the number of oarsmen in the Roman fives at the battle of Eknomos (258 BC) as 300 with 120 *ἐπιβάται*. The six of Kassandros's *ναύαρχος* Pleistarchos in 302 BC was lost in a storm with 500 men on board (Diodoros 20.112.4). Since a six would have had a larger company than a five, it seems likely that the total company of a five would have been 420, and that the *ἐπιβάται* at Eknomos included the *ὑπηρεσία* (of, say, 40 in addition to the normal military contingent). Both the fives at Eknomos and Pleistarchos's six were part of an expeditionary force and would have carried extra soldiers on deck. By this reasoning the six with a total crew of 500 would have had 360 oarsmen and 140 *ἐπιβάται* (again including the *ὑπηρεσία*).

Recruitment

Athenian threes in the fifth and fourth centuries drew their crews at the outset largely from Athens herself. But at the beginning of the Peloponnesian war (432 BC) Perikles speaks, according to Thukydides (1.143.1), of possible attempts by her enemies to lure away 'the foreigners among our *ναῦται* (oarsmen) with promises of higher pay'; but he boasted that Athens 'possesssed citizen helmsmen and the rest of the *ὑπηρεσία* more in number and better in quality than all the rest of Greece'. By the middle of the next century the best *ὑπηρεσίαι* and oarsmen were mercenaries (see *AT* p. 120–27), and Athenians were taking service as *ὑπηρεσία* in Syracuse and the Bosporan kingdoms. But while the skilled seamen were mercenaries, the decksoldiers were an élite posted on board by those who launched the ships, partly to fight when required and partly to ensure the loyalty of the mercenaries.

The fleet of 160 ships which Alexander assembled and employed to take his army across the straits to Asia in 334 was sent by the cities of the Hellenic League, but the decksoldiers were Macedonian. Moving south against Miletos and Ephesos after the battle at the Granikos river, he declined engagement with the 400 strong fleet under Persian orders and composed of Phoenician and Cypriot ships. He disbanded his navy for the most part on the ground that he did not need it since the capture of the cities of the coastal region of Asia would 'break up the Persian fleet since they would no longer have a source for recruitment of *ὑπηρεσίαι* and no naval bases in Asia'. Here *ὑπηρεσίαι* could have the wider meaning of the crew in general.

After the second land defeat of Dareios at Issos, Alexander turned to secure his own rear before pursuing him eastwards. His first move was against Phoenicia. (Arrian 2.17.3) 'With Tyre destroyed the rest of Phoenicia will be in our (i.e. Macedonian) hands and it is to be expected that the Phoenician squadron, which is the most numerous and the most efficient contingent in the Persian fleet, will come over to us. For neither the Phoenician oarsmen nor the *ἐπιβάται* will risk serving under another power at sea while we hold their cities. Cyprus will then come over to us or be easily subdued by a seaborne invasion. And if we deploy a naval force of Macedonian and Phoenician ships, and Cyprus adheres to us, we would securely command the sea, and the Egyptian expedition would at the same time easily be carried out'.

The Phoenician contingent in the Persian fleet seems to have had Phoenician *ἐπιβάται*. The word here may be used of all those aboard who were not oarsmen; but even if it did, it would include the normal military contingent. In Xerxes' invasion fleet Persian soldiers, in addition to the cities' own *ἐπιβάται*, were put on board the ships manned by their subjects; and this must certainly have been the practice here. When Alexander moved his fleet from Sidon to Tyre, considerably reinforced by defections from the Cypriot and Phoenician squadrons of the Persian fleet, he took care to put on deck as many as he thought fit of the *ὑπασπισταί*, the élite of the Macedonian army, 'in case the expected engagement turned out not to be fought by manoeuvre but by hand-to-hand conflict'.

These passages are most revealing: first of the coastal cities as a source of naval recruitment and then of the Macedonian decksoldiers on board the ships of the Hellenic League. They foreshadow the picture, or rather the background to the picture, of the eastern Mediterranean fleets of the future centuries, with the ships provided, sometimes after subsidy, and manned by the cities 'allied' to the great powers. For a sea battle the decksoldiers put on board allied ships would be Macedonian or Roman. Rhodian and Pergamene ships were exceptions as equal allies. The selection of decksoldiers from the Roman armies is often mentioned.

On two occasions a fleet declined battle because of the absence of decksoldiers. One was when Caesar in Alexandria could not spare soldiers from his land defences; the other was at Aktion before the sea battle when for some reason not disclosed Antony had no soldiers to put on board.

Crews for Alexander's Indus fleet are first mentioned (Arrian 6.1.6) when preparation is being made for the voyage to the sea. 'The *ὑπηρεσίαι* for his ships were recruited from the Phoenicians, Cypriots, Carians and Egyptians' who were already accompanying the expedition, apparently by chance, although this is hard to believe. However if it was by chance it only demonstrates that a high proportion of the ordinary inhabitants of the eastern Mediterranean had nautical skills. The author of the *Athenaion politeia* 2.19–20 said this of 5th century Athenians but it may have been widely true. In the *Indica* the mention is rather more detailed (18.1–2): Alexander selected all the Phoenicians, Cypriots and Egyptians who were accompanying the march inland, and manned the ships from them, selecting as *ὑπηρεσίαι* and oarsmen all the men who had experience of the sea. There were also a good many islanders in the army who had experience of this sort, Ionian and Hellespontine Greeks as well. It is to be noted that in the *Indica*, which is strongly influenced by, if it does not actually derive from, Nearchos, ὑπηρεσία is used in its strict sense whereas in the *Anabasis* ὑπηρεσία is shown by the parallel passage in the *Indica* to include also the oarsmen. The list of trierarchs contained 24 Macedonians, six Greeks, one Persian and two Cypriots. As Brunt observes, the Macedonian appointments were honorific, but the two fleet commanders Nearchos and Onesikritos were professional seamen. Later Philip V found that Macedonians of the phalanx made good oarsmen.

On his return to Babylon Alexander put into effect a shipbuilding programme at Thapsakos and recruited widely ναῦται and helmsmen (Plutarch *Alexander* 68), πληρώματα (oarsmen) and ὑπηρεσίαι, 'purple-shell divers and people employed at sea' from Phoenicia and other maritime areas (Arrian 7.19.4).

Concerning Antigonos's sources of recruitment for his grand fleet there is no specific indication, but the Asian coast and Phoenicia, where he built his ships, are the obvious choices. When Demetrios was given the task of capturing Cyprus, he went to the southern coast of Asia, first to Loryma in Karia which had supplied crews for his ships built in Rhodes and then to Kilikia where he obtained soldiers (στρατιῶται including oarcrew)) and ships. The word στρατιῶται is sometimes used to mean oarcrew; and that may be its meaning here. There is no further information about the sources other than south eastern provinces of Asia from which Antigonos and Demetrios drew their naval personnel. What we have is perhaps sufficient. Mithridates preparing a fleet against Rome sent to Egypt as well as Phoenicia to recruit bow officers and helmsmen.

No information is provided as to the source of the crews for Roman fleets in the first Punic war. At the beginning of the second Punic war Scipio in Spain diluted his crews with prisoners of war to man the ships he had captured from the Carthaginians. Faced with the need to defend Italy from possible attack by Philip and Sicily from the Carthaginians, the Senate in 214 (L.24.11) had recourse to private citizens for the first time to man the fleet; and slaves were sent by their masters. Four years later the people had to be taxed for the same purpose and this tax covered the pay of the men serving. Where the men came from is not said; but when in 208 naval forces had to be prepared to meet a large Carthaginian fleet which was expected to attack Italy, Sardinia and Sicily, and to send to Greece, the urban praetor was instructed to build 20 new ships and man them with *socii navales*. These came, one must suppose, like the earlier crews, from the allied cities of the coastal areas of Italy. After the end of the second Punic war and the war with Philip, when Antiochos was threatening to invade Greece, the praetor with the maritime province was ordered to commission and take to Greece the thirty ships (which were already manned), while the urban praetor was to refit the old ships and 'enrol freedmen as *socii navales*'. It is to be inferred that the normal crews were enlisted and paid for service in the Roman fleet according to the terms of the alliance of their cities with Rome. Unlike the slaves sent on board by their masters in 214, these men were technically volunteers and free. The freedmen were enrolled on the same terms.

In the second Punic war when the Roman treasury was empty Scipio undertook to organise, equip and man privately, a fleet of thirty ships. Livy (28.45.13) says that the ships were manned as follows. The peoples of Umbria, of Nursia, Reate and Amiternum and the whole Sabine country promised to send deck-soldiers. Marsi, Paeligni and Marrucini volunteered in large numbers to row in the fleet, and Cameria though of equal status with Rome sent a cohort of armed men. The reference to Cameria sending a cohort in spite of being of equal status suggests that the others were allies not of equal status, and reveals the basis on which the *socii navales* were recruited, an obligation inherent in their lower status.

A different form of treaty obligation with her maritime allies is indicated when in 171 BC the praetor in charge of the fleet, leaving Rome for Greece with 40 ships, sent his brother ahead with a five to collect the ships due under treaty from Rhegion, Lokroi, the district of Uria and Dyrrachion. These ships plainly came completely manned and fitted out, but would carry Roman decksoldiers in any action. The ships of Side in Pamphylia, which followed Scipio in the third Punic war out of friendship for him, constituted at the time a special case, but in the chaotic conditions of the civil war such special cases must have become the norm.

Training

The training and exercising of oarcrew is frequently mentioned. When Alexander had built his fleet on the Hydaspes he trained his oarcrews to row together in time before setting out down the river. Later at the Babylon station he was often employed in conducting trials of his fleet by the time-honoured means of races, following the example of Themistokles, 'between threes and between such fours as were on the river'. There were also contests between oarsmen and between helmsmen.

Polybios gives a detailed description (1.21.1–2) of the training of the crews for the new fives built at Rome when in 261 BC she had decided 'to get on to the sea'. 'Those who recruited the crews for the new ships (fives) began to teach them to pull an oar in the following way: they made them sit at the oars on the dry land in exactly the same arrangement as the seats had on the real ships. Stationing the boatswain (*κελευστής*) in the middle they trained the men to lean back all at once when bringing their hands to their chests, and then to lean forward again as they pushed their hands forward. The men also learned to begin and end their stroke at the command of the *κελευστής*'.

The Attic black-figure hydria (*AT* Fig.31, *GOS* pl.11d) showing the helmsman, *κελευστής* and *πρῴρατης* of a longship with one level of oars has the boatswain in the middle of length and breadth. He would be heard by his small crew in spite of having his back to half of them. But Silius Italicus (above p. 350) speaks of an officer who is plainly the *κελευστής* standing amidships forward of the stern and aft of the rowing area. This is a better position for the *κελευστής* of a big warship. If the five is a three-level ship with five files of thirty oarsmen on each side, it would be no good the *κελευστής* standing half-way towards the bows, as he does on the hydria, since he would not be heard by the majority of the 300 oarsmen. The place for him to stand would be on the edge of the stern where the rowing area begins, facing forward; and even then he would have to shout with a very loud (or high-pitched ?) voice, *acutissima voce* in Seneca's words.

The long stroke of seated oarsmen described implies oar manning no more than double. Lucan's description of the oarstroke at the battle of Massalia is much the same although he starts with the action of leaning forward instead of the action of leaning back with the oars in the water: 'the oarsmen brought their oars forward over the sea's surface (to the catch) and fell back on their seats hitting their chests with the oars' (at the end of the stroke).

After training of the Roman novice crews was completed short sea trials were carried out, and then the fleet moved along the coast southwards and into action. At Drepana 12 years later the Roman ships, in spite of early successes, were still heavier and their crews less experienced and less fit than the Carthaginian. Finally, in 243/2 Rome decided to take naval matters seriously. They again copied a successful Carthaginian hull design, and when 100 new-model ships had been launched they had some success. Their commander Lutatius 'spent every day in trials and practice manoeuvres with his crews, at the same time paying attention to their diet'.

In the autumn of 219 Philip V decided to develop a naval capability at Corinth/Lechaion and rather surprisingly recruited as oarcrews not mercenaries but his own Macedonian phalanx. He trained them by continuous practice. 'They were', Polybios says, 'very ready to undertake sea service in an emergency'.

The programme of cutting timber and building ships in the winter when the sap was down, followed by a bout of rowing practice and ship trials in the spring, was followed by Mithridates in 74 BC. Thus Julius Caesar with a naval war against the Veneti and a crossing of the Channel to Britain in mind ordered Crassus to build ships on the Loire and train local crews during the winter season.

In the Alexandrian war of 47 BC Hirtius describes the Egyptians, faced with a pitched battle against Caesar's front line of practised Rhodian and Pontic ships, exercising their ships in the harbour; and Cassius later with the intention of provoking a battle with the much outnumbered but much respected Rhodian fleet felt the need for rowing practice at Myndos.

In the years 37 and 36 Octavian made a final effort to defeat Sextus Pompeius at sea, building a new fleet and recruiting oarsmen. In the newly made Lucrine harbour Agrippa carried out the boxing-in of the new ships. He also trained the crews on land using a mock-up of the oarsystem (*ἰκρια*) such as had been used when Rome first took to the sea for the conquest of Sicily 225 years before.

For the Aktion campaign against Antony in 31

Octavian had a fast, well- trained fleet, manned by Italian *socii navales*, part operating against Antony's communications under Agrippa and part under his own command at Aktion. Antony's fleet at Aktion is described by Dio (50.12.8) as in poor shape. There was sickness in his camp partly because of the unhealthy situation, bad in winter and worse in summer. 'They were of different races, wintering some way from their ships, and they had not undergone any training'. The logic of these sentences is that the oarsmen went home for the winter to distant places and as a result missed the normal training of commissioned crews they would otherwise have had in the early spring. When Antony who was based elsewhere with his army visited his fleet there early in 31, Orosius says that he found that a third of his oarsmen had died of hunger. As a result Antony's ships were not fully manned and moved badly.

II. SHIPS AND GEAR

In India after the defeat of Poros (p. 9) Alexander carried out a programme of shipbuilding on the Hydaspes. He felled in the forest on the Emodi mountains and brought down to the river 'much silver fir ἐλάτη (*abies Cephalonica*) and cedar κέδρος (*Juniperus makropoda*) and other ship-timber of all kinds' (Strabo 15.1.29). Diodoros (17.89.4) mentions πεύκη (*pinus laricio*) as well. Aristophanes (*Knights* 1300–1310) well illustrates the relative merits of ἐλάτη and πεύκη (*AT* p. 180–181) in ship-building.

After Alexander's return from India (p. 11) he sent a party to the Caspian Sea to fell timber and build ships of the Greek type. At his ship-station at Babylon he built ships of κυπάρισσος (*semper virens*), the only wood available locally, while at Thapsakos he ordered the construction of a large fleet of sevens using κέδρος (*Juniperus excelsa*) from 'the mountain of Lebanon' and copper, caulking and sails from the Cypriot kingdoms.

Antigonos's grand fleet (p. 20) built in Tripolis, Byblos and Sidon relied for timber on Lebanon and the Tauros mountains in Kilikia. The timber which he supplied for the ships built for him at Rhodes presumably came also from the Tauros mountains. Demetrios's conquest of Cyprus (p. 30) gave him access to the long timber necessary for the large longships (Plutarch *Demetrios* 20.1) he proceeded to build.

In an emergency in the 2nd Punic war when the Roman treasury was empty Scipio organised the building of thirty ships to go to Sicily and then invade Africa. Green wood was used and when they reached Sicily they had to be hauled up and their hulls repaired. The contributions made by the Italian allies for the construction, victualling and gear of these ships are interesting:

Caere	grain for the *socii navales*
Populonium	iron
Tarquinia	linen for sails
Volaterrae	internal furnishing (*interamenta* cf. Gk. ἐντερόνεια; see AT p. 182 and n.5), corn
Arretium	3,000 shields, 3,000 helmets, 50,000 javelins, short and long spears, also enough axes, shovels, sickles, baskets, and hand-mills (for corn) for 40 warships, 120,000 measures of wheat and contributions to the victualling allowances (*viaticum*) for decurions and oarsmen
Perusia, Clusium, Rusellae	silver fir (*abies* = ἐλατή) for shipbuilding and a great deal of corn

Scipio also used wood from the state forests, a unique indication of the source of Rome's ship-timber.

He pressed on with the work, Livy says, so hard that on the 45th day after the timber had been brought from the forest the ships were built, rigged and equipped.

Arretium's provision of victualling allowances for decurions and oarsmen is interesting. Such an officer appears in the Greek form δεκάταρχος in an inscription (*SEG* 1.345) of the 1st century AD relating to a Rhodian ship which can be identified as a τριημιολία. Either δεκάταρχος is an indigenous Rhodian officer and such an officer was indigenous also to and closely connected with the oarsmen of the *socii navales* coming from the Greek speaking coastal areas; or, as one of the centurion's subordinates, the decurion is early evidence of the military organisation of the manpower of a warship. In the latter case the δεκάταρχος mirrors that organisation now adopted in a Rhodian ship. A third possibility is that the resemblance of the two names is fortuitous.

Green wood was again used by Julius Caesar in Spain in the civil war against Pompey when he needed ships against the Massaliot fleet. Twelve ships were laid down at Arelate (mod. Arles) and built in thirty days from the cutting of the wood. With these Decimus Brutus, whose flagship, a six, was probably not so built, defeated the Massaliots in battles described by the poet Lucan about a century later. Lucan says: 'Raw timber was joined together in the state in which it fell on the mountain-side to make a stable deck for sea-fighting'. There is no evidence that the ships were unseaworthy, but they were certainly heavy and slow.

After the earthquake which devastated Rhodes in 224 BC (p. 56) the maritime powers, out of respect for her eminence at sea and as a result of astute fund-raising on her part, made substantial donations to aid her recovery. These included much naval equipment and material as follows:

Hiero and Gelo of Sicily
- 30 catapults for 3-cubit missiles

Ptolemy
- ship-building material for ten threes and ten fives
- 40,000 measured cubits of pine planking
- 3,000 talents of coined bronze
- 3,000 talents of tow for caulking
- 3,000 pieces of sailcloth

Antigonos
- 10,000 pieces of (long) timber 8–12 cubits long
- 5,000 cross planks of 7 cubits
- 3,000 talents of iron
- 1,000 talents of (solid) pitch
- 1,000 talents of liquid pitch

Seleukos
- 10 fully equipped fives
- 10,000 cubits of timber
- 1,000 talents of hair (for catapults p. 46) and resin

Other rulers, Mithridates, Prusias etc, gave smaller gifts of a similar kind.

Ship Maintenance

On three occasions (*Indica* 24;33.9 and 38.8–9) during the voyage of Nearchos with his fleet of small ships selected from Alexander's Indus fleet, the ships were hauled right out of water for attention to their hulls. This operation for a fleet possibly of 100 ships required a suitably large beach to be found. Xerxes on his coastal voyage to Greece in 480 BC hauled up his much larger fleet of threes for 'drying out' at Doriskos by the mouth of the river Hebros.

On the first occasion (*Indica* 24) at the mouth of the Tomeros river Nearchos found a lagoon where those ships that had been weakened by rough weather were hauled up for repair, work which took five days. This was plainly an occasion for repairs to ships needing it rather than general maintenance. The second occasion (*Indica* 33.9) was at the mouth of another river at the head of the gulf of Hormuz. A man had been met who spoke Greek and told them that Alexander's army was encamped inland not far off. Nearchos decided to go to it with a few companions. He accordingly hauled the ships up on land for the repair of those that were weak; and for security while he was away, he built a double palisade round them. There is no indication then as on the previous occasion that general maintenance was done, although the opportunity may well have been taken.

On the third occasion (*Indica* 38.8–9) Nearchos found at the mouth of the river Sitakos (Mund) a large cache of corn sent for the fleet by Alexander. The fleet stayed there 21 days. The ships were hauled up and those that had become weak were repaired and maintenance was carried out on the rest (ἐθεράπευον). The long stay of 21 days, and the cache of grain to victual the fleet for a period, suggest a planned stay for maintenance such as the 'drying out' regularly necessary for threes in the 5th century (see *AT* p. 152–3). This operation would have involved removing the bilge-water and carrying out caulking where necessary, also if the materials were on board the application of liquid pitch and wax to the hull below the waterline (p. 132). If ὑποζώματα were fitted in such small ships they may have been replaced by the spares carried on long voyages (*AT* p. 197–9).

The only other occasion when hauling up of a fleet in commission is recorded in this period is on the occasion of Demetrios's Cyprus invasion. After a successful crossing to the NE extremity of the island 'he constructed a camp and hauled the ships ashore'. Nothing is said of maintenance and he may have felt that since he would not need the ships in his military operations against Menelaos on the north coast the ships were better out of water. On the other hand a good part of the fleet must have come with Demetrios from Athens and with a confrontation at sea inevitable, at least with Menelaos's 60 ships and at most with a fleet under Ptolemy from Egypt, the opportunity for maintenance was not to be missed.

Fleets were in general hauled out of the water (*ἀνέλκειν*, *subducere*) during the winter and kept under cover in shipsheds (*νεώσοικοι*, *navalia*) and launched again (*καθέλκειν*, *deducere*) in the spring. General maintenance would have been carried out during the winter. Occasionally, to effect surprise, fleets were used in the winter, as in Julius Caesar's midwinter crossing to Epiros against Pompey and his subsequent invasion of Africa. Pompey maintained his patrols of threes during the winter. The crossing to Africa was a more successful gamble which found the Pompeian fleets hauled up and their armies in winter quarters.

Ὑπόζωμα: AT[2] *(see Index)*

There are only two mentions of the *ὑπόζωμα* in the texts of our period. On the threat of war with Perseus of Macedon Polybios says that the Rhodian president Hagesilochos advised the Rhodians to put forty ships in commission (p. 109). The word used is *ὑποζωνύειν*. In the naval inventories at Athens ships are classed as either *ζωστός* or *ἄζωστος* girded or ungirded, with the *ὑποζωμα* fitted or without. The forty Rhodian ships are likely to have included fives, fours and *τριημιολίαι*. If the Rhodians fitted the *ὑπόζωμα* as part of the regular, and thus, as it was in the case of Athenian threes, essential gear of their warships, it is likely that it was similarly fitted to the warships of the other maritime powers. The second mention confirms the likelihood. Kallixeinos says that Ptolemy Philopator's forty had twelve *ὑποζώματα* [six for each hull] (p. 276).

Bulwarks, guard or deck rail

On the mid-5th century three shown on the Vienna fragment (**viii**) there is a guard-rail at the edge of the deck. At the end of the 5th and the beginning of the 4th century the Phoenician custom of hanging shields at the edge of the decks of their warships may be seen on coins of Arados (**xii**, 3). Shields are hung at the edge of the deck of the somewhat later Erment model (**6**) and of the late 3rd century ships of the Hasdrubal coinage (**17**). The guard-rail reappears on the coins of Histiaea of the last half of the 4th century BC (**8a** and **d**). These show not only a substantial guard-rail but a *πάροδος* between it and the edge of the deck and frequently on coins thereafter. In the Praeneste relief of the 1st century BC (**29**) shields appear as decoration of a planked bulwark which is common thereafter.

Bollards

The coins which Hasdrubal issued in Spain in 228–221 BC (**17**) and the somewhat earlier Roman coins (**12**) show ships' prows with a pair of bollards on the starboard *ἐπωτίς* (and it is likely that there was a pair also on the port side), each pair presumably for making fast mooring ropes. A different system of bollards appears on the ships's prows of a Pompeian painting of the 1st century AD (**43**). The ships are shown laid up in shipsheds. There is the same number, four, but disposed, one each side of the stempost and one on each of the *ἐπωτίδες*.

Towers, turrets (Gk. *πύργοι*, Lat. *turres) (**36**) SSAW p. 122 and 197*

The use of towers erected on board ships for offensive and defensive action is described first in Thukydides's account of the Athenian siege of Syracuse in 415 BC (7.25.6) when a large merchantman (*μυριοφόρος*) equipped with wooden towers and side-protection (*παραφράγματα*) was sent against the Syracusan stockade at the northern end of the Great Harbour. Marcellus (L.24.34.6) made similar use of towers mounted on fives in linked pairs against Syracuse in 217 BC: and Cassius in 43 BC used folding towers (*πύργοι ἐπτυγμένοι*), erected for an attack against Rhodes in 43 BC (Ap. *CW* 4.72). Siege engines and catapults were also put on board ships in sieges involving attacks from the sea (e.g Alexander's siege of Tyre: p. 9 above and Marcellus against Syracuse).

Towers on ships for use against other ships first appear in Moschion's detailed account of the large grain-ship (*σιτηγός*), named *Syracosia*, built by Hiero of Syracuse in the last half of the 3rd century BC (Athenaios 5. 206d–209e). The description of these towers, their mounting and capacity, being unique, is relevant to the towers regularly mounted on the larger warships from fours upwards in the second and first centuries BC and later. (See **24**: c.100 BC, **29**: 2nd half of 1st century BC, **30c** 1st century BC, **32c** 25–19 BC, **36** 1st-2nd century AD copy of Hellenistic original). Silius Italicus (writing in the 1st century AD about the 2nd Punic War) speaks of a large Carthaginian warship possibly a seven (see p. 272) set on fire from a tower mounted on two threes.

(Moschion in Athenaios 207c) 'In rating (*oarsystem*, *κατασκευή*) the ship was an *εἰκόσορος* (twenty-oared ship), but [not a simple one because] it had three side-gangways (*πάροδοι*: giving access at three levels to accommodation for the crew and passengers)'...If the ship was an oared merchantman she was a large and luxurious version of the ships illustrated by Casson (*SSAW* 139 and 140): a ship more 'long' than 'round'.

(208b) 'There was a course of (*ἄτλαντες* of six cubits in height) running round the ship on the outside. They supported the highest *ὄγκοι* and the *τρίγλυφον*, all at regular intervals... There were also in the ship eight towers as big as the ship's *ὄγκοι* allowed, two in the prow, the same number in the stern and the remaining four amidships. Each of these was equipped with two spars to which were rigged containers by means of which stones were dropped on to enemies passing beneath. Each tower was manned by four young armed men and two archers. The whole space inside the towers was full of stones and missiles'. Then a structure to carry a missile-thrower is described, a platform on deck protected by a planked bulwark and parapet.

In Doric architecture *ἄτλαντες* are pillars in the form of statues, the male equivalent of karyatids. Pillars supported the architrave (*ἐπιστύλιον*) above which is the frieze with alternate decorative panels (*μετόπαι* and *τρίγλυφοι*), the latter representing the ends of original roof beams. Above the frieze is a cornice. The equivalents for the *ἄτλαντες* in terms of a ship are, butting on a wale, deck-stanchions which support the highest part, the deck. (There are apparently other supporting timbers for other lower projecting parts). The equivalent of the architrave which the *ἄτλαντες* support is the horizontal beam on which the ends of the crossbeams of the deck (the equivalent of the *τρίγλυφοι*) rest. The phrase used '*τοὺς ὄγκους τούς ἀνωτάτω καὶ τὸ τρίγλυφον*' is a hendiadys indicating the composition of the architrave-like load on the *ἄτλαντες*. This load consisted of the fore-and-aft timbers (*ὄγκοι*) on which rested the ends of the deck beams resembling the triglyph. The horizontal timbers (*ὄγκοι*) on which the triglyph-like ends of the deck beams rest.

The maritime translation and explanation of the word *ὄγκοι* of which the basic meaning is 'swellings' is not easy to see, but a clue is given by the sentence 'there were in the ship eight towers, as big as the ship's *ὄγκοι* permitted' (*σύμμετροι τὸ μέγεθος τοῖς τῆς νεώς ὄγκοις*) taken with the account of the incident in the battle of Chios. The flagship of Attalos's nauarchos Dionysodoros (P.16.3.13) collided accidentally side to side with an enemy ship 'causing her to lose her own starboard oars and to have her *πυργοῦχοι*, tower-supports, carried away as well'. These *πυργοῦχοι* are 'brackets', flat topped projections from the hull, 'shelves with slanting underprops' (OED: *mutatis mutandis*) serving to carry at any rate part, if not all, of a warship's tower, one of whose functions was to drop stones on to enemy ships as they approached. They would clearly be vulnerable in a side to side collision. The use of *ὄγκος* in Homer (*Iliad* 4.151) for the barb of an arrow illustrates this meaning. The size of the towers was governed by the amount of room afforded by the sideways extensions, the 'swellings'.

The tower seems to have been the mark of a flagship in the smaller fleets. Dionysodoros's flagship at the battle of Chios, probably a five, (above p. 81) had towers. Decimus Brutus's flagship, a six, at the battle of Massalia in 49 BC is introduced by Lucan (3.514) as a 'tower-carrying ship'. No other ship is said to have carried them in that (rather minor) battle.

Octavian's final naval campaign against Sextus shows the importance height then had in the missile warfare that had developed at sea. Dio says (49.2) that Octavian's confidence in the new fleet he had built in the years 37–36 BC in Italy and had equipped and trained under Agrippa on the Lucrine Lake, rested on the height of his ships: 'they carried towers as well so that the decksoldiers could fight from a commanding height as from a wall' (of a besieged city). Servius (4th century BC) in his commmentary on Vergil *Aeneid* 8.693 (*turritis puppibus* see p. 166) says that Agrippa first invented this kind of tower so that as soon as battle was joined towers unsuspected by the enemy which had been unseen on passage could be suddenly erected from prefabricated boarding (*de tabulatis*). Appian may have been anachronistic in attributing 'folding towers' to Cassius in his attack on Rhodes in 43 (p. 146–7). But it would seem that seaborne towers which were not collapsible would have much interfered with navigation, so that it may be Servius who is wrong. In any case Servius's attribution is an indication of the importance of the towers in Octavian's new fleet and of their nature.

Appian says (*CW* 5. 106) that for the first engagement (at Mylai) both sides were splendidly (λαμπρῶς) equipped: the ships had towers at bow and stern. He describes how the flagship of the Pompeian commander Papias when rammed by Agrippa's ship 'shook off the men in the towers' suggesting that the towers were not very solid structures, or that the flagship was not very stable (being small). But the Pompeian ships do not seem to have had towers which could match the higher ships of Octavian also equipped with towers. After the battle Sextus promised that he would add height, presumably by increasing the height of the towers, before the next and decisive engagement. At Naulochos Appian gives the total of ships engaged on both sides as 300, carrying missiles of all kinds, towers and as many engines as they could muster. (120–121) The colour of the towers was the only distinguishing mark (within each category) between the two sides. When the Pompeians fled they jettisoned their towers (Ap. *CW* 5.121).

Towers play a big part in the accounts of the battle of Aktion. The references to them are mainly in connection with Antony's ships, but it is difficult to believe, after the emphasis on them in the preparation for the battles at sea against Sextus, that Octavian did not use them there. There, as against Sextus, they gave additional height to ships already higher than the ships of their opponents, and so became memorable in the speech Dio (50.18.6) gives to Antony before the battle. Antony claims the 'additional advantage' his men enjoy of being able in towers to attack the enemy from above.

Later (50.23.2) Dio observes that Antony's ships stood much higher 'and on top of that he had built high towers and put on board a great number of men to fight as from a wall'. Plutarch (*Antony* 66.2) speaks of Antony's men fighting 'with catapults from wooden towers'. It was the big ships, from fives to tens, on which 'high towers' could be built. Horace's mention of Maecenas (*Epodes* 1.1) going amid the lofty fighting towers (*alta propugnacula*) at Aktion refers to the towers in the big ships of both fleets. Vergil again (8.693) speaks of ships with towers (*turritis puppibus*) in connection with Antony's fleet. Antony's men, in flight, to lighten their ships throw overboard their collapsible towers and other gear.

Towers seem to have become by the end of the 2nd century BC part of the regular gear of the bigger warships, fours and upwards. They were light, made of wood, when not in use folded up so as not to interfere with the ships' navigation (and possibly on occasion to surprise an enemy). They were light and could easily be taken down (jettisoned in a hurry). Pictures show a single platform with an arched side (cf. **27**, **36**), but Livy (24.34.7) speaks of towers with several platforms (*contabulatae:* see **32b**) used by Marcellus at Syracuse in the 3rd century BC. For the siege of a maritime city or a pitched battle at sea they were erected to provide additional vantage for missiles, including stones, thrown by hand or mechanically, and for archers. They were placed in the bow, at bow and stern and sometimes amidships also. Their size depended on the space available and thus on the size of the ship, her outboard projections (ὄγκοι) at the required point. Even towers on the deck of the huge *Syracosia* only accommodated six men (four armed men and two archers).

In **28** (1st century BC) a firepot is shown rigged to a tower in the bow of a warship.

The Boarding Bridge

After the success of the boarding bridge (κόραξ) in the opening sea battles of the first Punic War at Mylai and Eknomos (above p. 45, 49) no more is heard of its use in Roman fleets until Octavian's naval campaigns against Sextus Pompeius (p. 151, 155) in which the tactics of manoeuvre were neglected in favour of close combat, locking the ships together with grappling irons and boarding.

In two battles Cumae and Mylai the boarding bridge is again mentioned. Since there were many battles fought by Roman fleets in which close combat was deliberately chosen but the κοραξ is not mentioned, it is difficult to choose between the two possible reasons for the silence. Either the bridge was a regular item in the equipment of the larger warships and its use was too common to be noted, or it became obsolete when tactics became more sophisticated and was only reintroduced in the disastrous period of Octavian's naval command. The former of these alternatives is perhaps the more likely.

III TACTICS

The influence of tactical preference on ship-design

When Alexander sent his fleet in battle order against Tyre he put on deck his élite footsoldiers in case the expected engagement turned out to be fought not by the breakthrough (διέκπλους) but by hand-to - hand combat. The Macedonians and still more the Romans were inclined to trust hand-to-hand fighting in which they excelled. The Romans invented means, the boarding bridge (κόραξ), the catapult-launched grappling iron (ἅρπαξ) and the ordinary grappling hooks to ensure close combat after the initial hail of missiles and head-on clash of battle lines.

Reliance on hand-to-hand combat led to certain developments in ship design. Height of deck became important and the thickness of hull timbers subject to blows from rams was increased in efforts to frustrate such attacks. These in his fives gave Octavian confidence against the lower and lighter ships of Sextus Pompeius which were mostly fours. Before the battle at Aktion Antony expressed a confidence, similar to Octavian's against Pompeius, in his ships as fewer but higher than Octavian's and built of timbers that could, he claimed, withstand ramming. At Aktion it was said that there was no ramming by Antony's ships because they could not achieve the necessary momentum. But there is evidence that Octavian used it nevertheless. At the battle of Cypriot Salamis it was noticed that height played an important part and that Ptolemy's many fours were at a disadvantage in conflict with the larger and higher ships of Demetrios. After that battle as has been seen fours became less popular as first line ships.

The effect of thick timbers was to withstand ramming or at any rate to diminish the damage it did, but they added mass and reduced speed and agility. Octavian's ships had not taken this development to extremes, Antony's, it appears, had. Height was achieved significantly by the five over the four, less significantly by the six up to the ten over the five. But the invention of the tower, on which catapults could be mounted, added a new factor. A four could benefit, but it gave greater advantage to the already higher, heavier, and probably more stable ships, which also had more room for them on deck. Reliance on hand-to-hand fighting led eventually to high, heavy ships against which ramming was less effective, and to static engagements.

The Rhodians on the other hand inherited from the Athenians the practice of mobile sea-fighting with the ram as the principal weapon. They would carry out an encirclement if their ships were faster than the enemy's and there was sea room: if not, they would make a violent breakthrough in which casualties were inevitable. The aim was to obtain tactical advantage for the use of the ram (see below). The outcome of this tactical preference was that the Rhodians chose ships that were light and fast, fours and τριημιολίαι, with only a few fives and nothing bigger.

The Roman preference for the five as the main ship of the line, with sixes as prestigious flagships and threes as fast scouts and auxiliaries, was a safe, sensible, and undoubtedly effective, compromise. On their Danube frontier they used cataphract liburnians with rams and a three as a flagship (p. 248–253)

Preliminaries to fleet engagement

The regular formation of a fleet in transit, or in the first stage of an engagement, was in column under sail or oar. The preliminary, vulnerable, movement off a beach (cf. Aigospotamoi *AT* p. 73 n. 10), was into the defensive formation of line abreast, achieved therefore as quickly as possible. The fleet might form up in as many as four lines deep. The next movement, for transit if the enemy was at a distance, was 'to the wing' (ἐπὶ κέρας) the whole fleet turning together into column ahead with either the right or left wing leading. Normally the right wing led with the commander at its head and the left wing formed the rearguard. The column (Latin: *agmen*) might again be of up to four files. The fleet would proceed under sail if the wind was favourable. The route was usually along a coastline.

When the enemy was sighted or, out of sight, signalled from points of vantage or scouts sent ahead, the first order to a fleet under sail was usually to furl sails and strike masts and yards. The column then moved under oar into lines abreast (Greek: *μετωπηδόν*; Latin: *acies*) with the ships deployed to the left or right of the commander at right angles to the line of advance. In usual circumstances, if the column had been hugging the shore, this operation was not easy to carry out neatly since the commander had to leave the correct amount of room for his ships to occupy in as many ranks deep as the column had files. If he was too far out a gap formed between the left wing and the shore, and if he was too close inshore, there would not be enough room for his ships to form a line abreast without confusion. On one occasion (Korykos) sails were used in this deployment.

It is certain that these manoeuvres were normally carried out under oar. The fleet commander's first order would have been to brail up sails, proceed under oar and stow away masts and sails. With the fleet now under oar it would in most cases be changed from lines ahead into lines abreast by a series of turns in succession followed by turns together in the manner of all fleets down to the time of Jutland.

An indication of these preliminaries is given by Livy's account of the opening stages of the battle of Korykos (p. 95–97). 'When the Roman commander of the column under sail saw what was happening' (the enemy in line abreast) 'he furled his mainsail and lowered his mast and stowing away the tackle awaited the ships that were following. By this time there were about thirty ships of the Roman right wing in line abreast; and to bring the ships of the left wing level with them he gave the order to raise foresails and stood out to sea to cover the enemy's left wing, while ordering the ships behind him (i.e. the left wing) to point their bows to the shore against the enemy right'. He had to stretch his line, as it formed, in both directions to cover the enemy's line which was already formed.

At Side the Syrian line was already drawn up (abreast) when the Rhodians approached along the coast in a long column with Eudamos's flagship leading. 'When Eudamos saw the enemy's line drawn up and ready for engagement he also (as well as the Syrian commander Hannibal who was on the Syrian left, seaward, wing) moved out to sea and ordered those that were following him to move one after the other into line abreast keeping their station'. Eudamos was not far enough out when he started the manoeuvre; and then moving out too fast to correct the error he found himself isolated with five ships and was attacked by Hannibal before the line was properly formed.

At Myonnesos there was a similar situation, except that there both fleets approached each other in column. The Syrian fleet was 89 ships to the Roman and Rhodian fleet of 80. The Syrians approached in a column of two files which when deployed into line abreast (of two ranks) was able to attempt a *περίπλους* of the Roman right wing. But Eudamos with the Rhodian ships was bringing up the rear and saw what was happening. He switched his ships from their proper place on the left wing to the right wing to counter the *περίπλους*.

Ramming: 1. Tactics

In the first recorded confrontation between fleets at sea (Hdt.1.166.1–2) at Alalia in c.535 BC the Phocaeans won a doubtful victory over the Carthaginians and Etruscans, losing forty of their sixty pentecontors and having the rams wrenched off the remaining twenty. Loss of the ram is likely to have been as much the result of faulty tactics as of weak construction, since the effect of a pentecontor of 50 oarsmen ramming a similar ship passing with momentum across her bows would put a great strain on the wooden structure of the forefoot of which the ram was a bronze sheath. In the following fifty years, in which the three was developed as the ship of the line with the ram as her chief offensive weapon, much thought must have been given to the tactics of ramming.

It is perhaps not surprising that it was a Phocaean, Dionysios, who was chosen to command the Ionian fleet in the revolt against Persia of 494 BC and that he trained the ships in the use of the *διέκπλους*, the breakthrough of an enemy's line to achieve the optimum conditions for a successful ramming attack. Herodotos (6.11.2–12.1) describes how he 'took the crews out regularly in column (*ἐπὶ κέρας*) to train the oarsmen by making a *διέκπλους* through each other's line, and to get the decksoldiers under arms'.

This description is highly condensed. It implies that the fleet was divided into squadrons and that each squadron, in column and with decksoldiers under arms, was required to 'break' through another squadron drawn up in line abreast. There is the further implication (from the arming of the decksoldiers) that in a real battle that passage would be contested and was likely to involve hand-to-hand fighting. The tactical objective was to get to the rear of the enemy drawn up in line abreast. The use of the διέκπλους in subsequent battles shows that this objective was to ram the enemy ships in the stern (when they had no momentum or a minus quantity, either stationary or moving forward).

Later at Artemision in 480 the first thing the Greek fleet did when the Persian fleet arrived at the beaches opposite was to put to sea, Herodotos says (8.9), 'to make trial of their fighting tactics and their use of the διέκπλους' (a hendiadys). In fact, the Persians did not need to break through the Greek line when it formed. Being more numerous and faster they were able to move round it in a circle (a περίπλους). The διέκπλους played an important part in the subsequent battle of Salamis (*GOS* p. 139–43, JSM (1991) p. 196–200). The Greek fleet after forming line abreast off their moorings and moving forward to meet the Persian fleet coming up the channel in lines abreast, moved to the right and forward in column, breaking through the Persian line at the Salamis end and coming round behind their ships into a favourable position for ramming, 'Delivering their blows in a circle skilfully' as Aischylos says in poetical language. He does not call the operation a διέκπλους or a περίπλους (which it became), but that is what he describes clearly and accurately.

In the Peloponnesian war there were several battles at sea in which the περίπλους, on one occasion a double περίπλους (i.e. round both wings of an enemy line), played its part. It must be accepted that in trireme battles it was the prime consideration to get to the rear of the enemy fleet and that objective is to be explained as an attempt to secure a favourable position for the use of the ram. Thukydides makes it quite plain that the διέκπλους and the subsequent U-turn (*ἀναστροφή*, later *ἐπάνοδος*), were the preferred tactics of the faster fleet in an engagement of threes; and that bow-to-bow ramming was only adopted of necessity, e.g. in the battle of Erineus in 413 BC (7.34: *AT* p. 1165) and in the following year in the Great Harbour of Syracuse. The careful and detailed description of the battle of Arginousai by Xenophon shows (JSM 1991) the Spartan commander advancing in (several) columns 'intent on the διέκπλους and περίπλους' against the Athenian fleet drawn up in separate divisions supported by divisions in the rear of them so as to thwart such moves.

The effect of the διέκπλους and περίπλους is effectively illustrated by the story in Arrian (*Indica* 30 1–7) of the meeting of Nearchos's fleet with the school of whales. When the whales were sighted they caused consternation among the oarsmen. 'Nearchos ordered the ships to form line abreast as for a sea-battle, and to row at a high rate of striking. When they came near the whales they shouted as loudly as they could, the trumpets gave the signal and the oarsmen made all the noise they could with their oars. The whales dived and appeared astern'. Strabo, who also tells the story (15.12), says the whales appeared to carry out naval manoeuvres, that is to say, the (unusual submarine) περίπλους or διέκπλους.

In the Hellenistic period there were occasions when attempts were made by a fleet entering battle in column to effect a περίπλους. This was the opening move of Mithridates at the battle of Rhodes in 87 BC (p. 115), (probably) of Cassius against the Rhodians at Myndos in 43 (in both cases to prevent them carrying out their traditional tactics)(p. 146–147), and of Papias against Agrippa at Mylai in 36 BC (Sextus Pompeius's light ships having been described as particularly good at encirclement) (p. 154).

Polybios describes the Carthaginians at the battle of Mylai (p. 45) in the first Punic war as underestimating the newly built Roman fleet and not bothering at first to use their normal tactics of the διέκπλους and περίπλους. But when the boarding bridge caused them some casualties 'they began to use the superior speed of their ships to move out and round the enemy ships and to ram some broadside (those presumably that were stationary), and some in the stern'. Later, speaking of the battle of Drepana Polybios says (1.51.9): 'To achieve a διέκπλους of the enemy's line and appear astern of ships engaging others (which is the most effective manoeuvre) was impossible for the Romans because of the heaviness of their ships and their crews' inexperience'.

However, at Myonnesos in 180 BC (p. 107) the Roman squadron in the fleet of Roman and Rhodian ships, facing the Syrian fleet under Polyxenidas by the use of fire pots slung in the bows broke through the Syrian centre, made a U turn and attacked in the stern the ships engaging the Rhodians. This was a *διέκπλους* by a squadron after, not before, the formation of the battle line. A similar kind of *διέκπλους* seems to be envisaged by Livy (37.24.1) when describing the possibilities open to the Rhodian ships at the battle of Side (p. 103–104) after the clash of the two lines.

These possibilities are: to smash an enemy's prow, to carry away his oars, or to ram his stern after a free passage between his line. Exactly how the third possibility was achieved is not explained. It could only happen either if a fortuitous opportunity offered or if there was a carefully planned operation. The latter was the case at Myonnesos as described above.

At Tyre Curtius describes as a fortuitous event an attempt by a five of Alexander's, backed by two threes, to break through the Tyrian line . This may have been the opening gambit of a planned attempt at a breakthrough by a number of ships. The breakthrough, as Dionysios of Phokaia showed, was a manoeuvre likely to result in deck-fighting and hence in at least one ship-casualty. But it would be worth casualties if it was successful and if a number of ships could get behind the enemy line, execute a sharp turn (*ἀναστροφή, ἐπάνοδος*) and take the enemy in the stern.

The most detailed account of the breakthrough is given by Polybios (16.4.14) in his account of Rhodian tactics at the battle of Chios (p. 83). It begins with the penetration of the enemy's line abreast formation. 'In *διέκπλους* they (first) swept away the oarsystems of enemy ships and made them useless. After that (passing through the enemy's line) they moved round and back (*ἀναστροφή, ἐπάνοδος*), and ramming some ships in the stern and others amidships, while their opponents were still turning (to meet them) they would succeed in holing some and damaging occasionally some necessary item of gear in others. Employing this method of fighting the Rhodians accounted for a large number of enemy ships'.

On other occasions when the tactic is described as being used or contemplated, or can be recognised, a column, a leading ship with close support, achieved the breakthrough at one point and as a result moved behind and surrounded the enemy ships. It has been alternatively argued that in the breakthrough all the ships of a fleet in line abreast attempted separately to penetrate the opposing fleet also in line abreast. Since the line-abreast formation is adopted defensively to protect the side of an oared galley, where it is most vulnerable, attempts to penetrate it must have been strongly resisted. As a result single ships attempting it would be in great danger and would only have had a chance of success if closely supported.

In the battle of Chios a squadron in column is indicated; the first ship, her sides covered by ships following closely, succeeded in reaching the position where she and the supporting ships could brush away the oars of the two ships between which the passage was to be made; and then the rest of the column was able to follow through and carry out the manoeuvres described by Polybios above. Polybios's description of these does not rule out the possibility of the first stage of the breakthrough having been made by individual ships operating separately, but seems more naturally to be describing the options in the second stage carried out by a number of ships of a squadron that had together achieved the first stage successfully at one point in the enemy's line.

Rhodian tactics are also described by Appian (*CW*.4.71) in his account of the battle of Myndos. 'The Rhodians with their light ships' (fours or *τριημιολίαι*) 'were accustomed to move through the enemy's line quickly and round them and use sharp turns (*ἐπάνοδοι*). But the Romans in heavier ships whenever they made contact were accustomed to prevail because of the greater momentum as in a land battle'. Appian's two sentences suggest the customary practice of the Rhodians and Romans. The sentence which follows describes what actually happened. Horace White's translation in the Loeb edition of Appian obscures this. The Rhodians' customary practice was to go through (*διέκπλεῖν*) and round (*περίπλεῖν*) the enemy and to make U-turns.

This sentence is illuminated by a passage in Phormio's speech (Thuk. 2.89.8: before the famous second battle in the Gulf of Corinth) in which he explains to his men the disadvantages of a confined space to a fleet of a few ships which are faster than the enemy and have experienced crews...for there can be no breakthroughs (*διεκπλοῖ*) or turns (*ἀναστροφαί*) which are proper manoeuvres of the faster ships. (The sharp turns are the sequel to the breakthrough not to the encirclement after which the ships are facing the right way for ramming the enemy in the stern).

At the battle of Myndos Cassius drove the Rhodian ships into a small space where neither breakthrough nor encirclement was possible. Their ramming attacks and ἀποσιμωσεις against the heavier Roman ships were ineffectual. Ἀποσιμώσις is a 90° turn (cf. Thuk.4.25.5 where ships moving along the shore turn to face an attack from the sea) .

Ramming: 2. Techniques

The technique of ramming depended on the intention of the ramming ship. In some cases the object was to become firmly attached to an opponent and decide the issue by boarding. In others it was to hole, and thereby put out of action by swamping, the enemy vessel, withdraw and attack another in the same way.

The usual effect of ramming was to swamp the ship rammed; but it did not sink. At the battle of Chios (p. 81) Attalos's flagship rammed an eight of Philip's below the waterline. Philip's ship was swamped, but the men on deck went on fighting for some time, in spite of being at a low level and thus at a disadvantage. At the battle of Panormos (p. 98–99) Pausistratos's flagship, probably a five at least, was rammed by three fives and swamped with the result that the decksoldiers were overwhelmed by the missiles thrown from a higher level, the decks of the attacking fives.

In 212 BC a fleet of 20 Roman ships met a hostile Tarentine fleet of equal numbers near Sapriportis and an engagement followed. Livy (26.39.7) says that when the signal was given on each side and the ships went in to ram (presumably prow-to-prow) 'they did not back down after ramming, but cast grappling irons and prevented the ships they had rammed from separating. Both sides were intent on a hand-to-hand fight, like a land battle'. The important words here are: 'they did not back down'. The technique of backing down at the moment of impact was developed for ships built for offensive action with the ram alone. It was therefore important that the ram should make a hole in an enemy ship to let in the water and lower her deck, but not penetrate so deeply or strike in such a way as to make it difficult for the attacker to disengage.

Dio describes Octavian's ships at Aktion (50.32.2): 'Octavian's men, having smaller and swifter ships accelerated noisily and put in the ram being themselves completely protected from missiles. And if they swamped' that is to say holed ' a ship so much the better, but if not they would back down before a hand-to-hand fight developed'. This statement in inconsistent with Antony's, possibly exaggerated, claims that his ships were ram-proof, but it sets out the classical ramming technique (and incidentally illustrates the reason for boxing-in) as well as indicating one of the objects of building ships mainly armed with boarding troops to resist ramming attacks.

Lucan (3.544) gives clearly the normal ramming procedure of which Dio's account is a rather muddled version. '*As soon as* the rams crashed together (in a prow-to-prow impact), the ships went astern (*ut primum crepuerunt obvia rostra, in puppim rediere rates*)'. At the battle of Chios Polybios (16.3.4) relates that Philip's flagship accidentally rammed a τριημιολία which moved across her path; 'and giving her a powerful blow in the middle of the oarbox stuck fast, since the *helmsman* had been unable in time to check '*or reverse*' the ship's *momentum* ('τοῦ κυβερνήτου τὴν ὁρμὴν νεὼς οὐκέτι δυνηθέντος ἀναλαβεῖν'). The Greek word ἀναλαβεῖν can mean equally check or reverse, and in view of Lucan's testimony the latter is likely. It seems at any rate that normally in ramming the momentum of ships is checked at the moment of impact or just before, and that they went astern immediately. Polybios adds that it was the helmsman's responsibility to give the order, (presumably to the κελευστής), so as to prevent the ram from penetrating the enemy ship too far and becoming jammed. Polybios and Lucan are very different kinds of witness but both reliable, and their agreement on a rather surprising procedure is impressive.

In the account (p. 27) of the battle of Cypriot Salamis some of the trierarchs are said to have scored a sideways hit and the rams became hard to disengage so that the men jumped into the sea. JFC suggests that the ram might jam by turning in the hole made; also that boarding a ship somewhere along its length from the bow of one's own ship would give the boarding troops a hard task because the first aboard would be fighting men ahead and to each side of them. This would certainly have been the case if the ramming ship had been lower than the ship struck.

In the Hellenistic period prow-to-prow ramming seems to have been the normal sequel to the confrontation of battle lines. At the opening of the battle of Cypriot Salamis first the trumpets gave the signal, the crews answered with the paean, and then the ships moved in to ram with a great noise of oars. As they closed, first there was a hail of arrows, stones and javelins, then just before impact the men on deck sat down and the oarsmen put in their greatest effort. The result on this occasion is said to have been either carrying away the oars or direct impact of bows (i.e. *ἐπωτίδες* see *AT* p. 165), leading to a second ramming while the men on deck hurled missiles at close range. There is no mention of the third possibility, *διέκπλους*, since no organisation for it had been mentioned. At a later date catapults would have increased the range at which missiles could have been thrown, and owing to their slow rate of action they would have caused the initial closing together of fleets to be carried out slowly, as in the age of cannon.

In Polybios's account (16.3.4 ff) of the individual encounters between Attalos's fleet and the head of Philip's column at the battle of Chios an interesting factor in prow-to-prow ramming is introduced, the height of the rams relative to each other. Attalos's flagship (type unspecified) gave a fatal blow to an eight below the waterline and swamped her. Philip's ten rammed a *τριημιολία*, which chanced to cross her path, below the thranite thole, i.e. in the lower part of the oarbox, well above the waterline. Sticking fast she became unmanageable and fell a prey to two fives who 'destroyed' her by ramming (below the waterline), one on each side.

Next, Deinokrates, a nauarch in Attalos's fleet, in a ship unspecified, ramming an eight (prow-to-prow) was hit above the waterline by the enemy ship, 'since she was *ἀνάστειρος*, with a high prow. At the same time his ship holed the eight 'under the weaponry (*τὰ βίαχα*)'[1] and was unable to get free until Attalos came up and rammed her opponent.

Later Polybios (16.4.11: p. 83) comments on the Rhodian tactics in the battle saying that 'they made technical provision against prow-to-prow ramming (which they avoided as a rule because of the Macedonian courage in deck-fighting). They made their ships low in the bow (*ἔμπρῳρα*) and thus received strikes above the waterline while giving them below it and thus causing damage which could not be repaired'.

This 'technical provision' has been taken (e.g. by Paton's Loeb translation) to be 'dipping the bow' presumably by moving the men on deck forward, which is likely to have had the effect described if it could be carried out in the heat of the battle. Polybios may be referring to a characteristic of the favourite Rhodian types the four and the *τριημιολία*, which like the three would have had their rams half submerged as opposed to the higher position described by the word *ἀνάστειρος*. If 'dipping the prow' involved total submersion then a movement of the crew would have been involved.

It is more difficult to explain the high rams of the eight and the ten both of which struck above the waterline, in the case of the ten much above it. The Ostia relief (**35** p. 235–237) which is likely to represent a five, does in fact show oars entering the water and the hull curving upward and ending in the ram substantially above that water level. She was an *ἀνάστειρος* five like the Isola Tiberina ship (**27**), a six. The only other representations of the bigger ships, fives and upwards are the Pompeian shipshed frescoes (**43**), but the ships are in dock and the waterline is not easy to determine. The Ostia relief is however sufficient to corroborate the conclusion from Polybios's text that some of the fives were built *ἀνάστειροι*, with their rams above the waterline. The object of such a characteristic would be to pierce and hold the ships attacked so that the decksoldiers could board and capture them. Since the bigger ships were built to carry large numbers of decksoldiers, this additional characteristic is not surprising. The Rhodians seem to have perceived the vulnerability, in prow-to-prow ramming, of *ἀνάστειροι* ships to their own equipped with rams at water level.

If a return is made to the individual engagements in the first battle off Chios, it is seen that some fives were not *ἀνάστειρος*. Attalos's ship which hit the eight below the waterline was at most a five; and so was the ship of Attalos's nauarch Deinokrates since she also rammed an eight below the waterline, being herself rammed by her opponent which was *ἀνάστειρος*. These are important conclusions about the structure of the bigger ships, fives and upwards where the wale terminating in the ram does not as in the case of the earlier ships attested e.g. by **7**, **9**, **10** and **12** sink to it level with the keel. Instead in the bigger ships the wale remains level with or in some cases rises to the ram which is above water level.

The damage to prows from such action is described by the words *ἀναρρηγνύναι* 'to break into', *'lacerare'* to tear. At the battle of Mylai II (p. 155) Agrippa with a prow-to-prow encounter 'crashed into Papias's ship (a four) at the ἐπωτίς, shattered the ship and broke into the hull. The result was that the soldiers in the towers were thrown off and the ship let in a surge of water' which drowned the lower oarsmen while the upper oarsmen were saved (by making their escape) through the deck.

This is one of two occasions when the ἐπωτίς, the timber extension on each side of the bow protecting the outrigger or oarbox, is mentioned in the accounts of Hellenistic and Roman battles (see *AT* p. 142, 165–8).

The earlier occasion (p. 154) in which the ἐπωτίς is mentioned is when Dio, comparing Octavian's ships with Sextus Pompeius's, speaks of the former's greater height, their towers and the thickness of their ἐπωτίδες. On another occasion, after a prow-to-prow encounter the ram of one ship was 'shaken off' but the ship was 'held together by its timbers' i.e. remained watertight, evidence that the ram structure was additional to that of the hull proper.

The reference to the thickness of the ἐπωτίδες of Octavian's ships at Mylai may explain how and why Agrippa in a five risked crashing into Papias's ship (a four) at the ἐπωτίς. In 413 BC when the expeditionary fleet of Athens was trapped in the Great Harbour of Syracuse the Corinthians, allies of Syracuse, devised a method, since the Athenian ships were now restricted by lack of space to prow-to-prow ramming, of strengthening the ἐπωτίδες of the Syracusan ships to give them an advantage in such encounters (*AT* p. 165–167); and tried it out with their own ships at the battle of Erineus.

It appears that in the encounter between Agrippa's and Papias's flagships, Agrippa's ship turned sharply and hit Papias's ship 'at the ἐπωτίς' carrying it away with her ἐπωτίς and breaking into the hull with her ram, thus using her strong ἐπωτίς and adjacent ram to inflict the maximum damage. It seems possible that the passage also provides an explanation of the Rhodian ἐμβολαί καὶ ἀποσιμώσεις rammings and (sudden) 90% turns (a hendiadys) (Appian *CW*.4.71: above p. 363).

There are various words in Greek and Latin for the result of successful ramming. Most of them mean that the ship attacked was submerged e.g. unambiguously in the battle of the Adriatic 'many of Octavius's ships were captured; and many after holing were submerged (*rostris perforatae merguntur*)'. Since wrecks are said to be towed away after battle, the words cannot mean 'sunk' as they are frequently translated, but 'flooded', 'swamped' i.e. filled with water and put out of action. Occasionally the ships rammed are 'destroyed', with the meaning 'made useless'. The word *'perforatae'* in the passage just quoted (Hirtius *BA* 46) and the Greek διατετραίνειν in Appian *Pun.* 122 leave no doubt that the effect and purpose of ramming was not as has recently been argued merely to 'spring the timbers' but to make a hole in the enemy ship. Better understanding of ramming must await kinetic and structural analysis.

It may finally be noted (p. 27: Diodoros 20.51.2: the battle of Cypriot Salamis) that 'when the ships came close together and the impact of the ram was imminent [and the hail of missiles particularly intense], the men on deck sat down as one man'. The action recalls the unskilled javelin men who were on board the Athenian ships in the final battle in the Great Harbour of Syracuse and would, the Spartan commander forecast, be unable to throw their javelins sitting down (Thukydides 7.67.2).

JFC suggests another, and less specific reason for their sitting down. 'The men on deck would have sat down at the moment of impact in order to avoid being thrown off their feet and sent sprawling on the deck, from which they would not have been able to recover and be useful for 10 seconds or so, or much longer if hurt in the process. If they sat down they would be in a much better position to resist the shock of impact which would be akin to that experienced by standing passengers in a bus when the brakes are applied fiercely to avoid a collision.

It could well have been the practice to throw javelins at the ship as soon as possible after impact when the relative speed of the ships was small, and the target close. That would have had to be done quickly while sitting down.

Another deduction is that there must have been room for the troops on board all to sit down. A man sitting on a deck in a braced position would occupy a space of about 2ft × 3ft (60 cm × 90 cm) or say 5 ft^2 (5400 cm^2). The two halves of deck (on each side of a 1m gangway at a lower level) would have been no more than 5 m wide. 4 men could sit side by side on each side of the ship i.e 8 men in 0.9 m of the ship's length or 175 men in 20 metres of ship.

Ramming: 3. Structural Mechanics (JFC)

A preliminary study by John Haywood (Shaw: 1993) of the structural mechanics by which a ram of the type found near Haifa (Casson and Steffy: 1991) could penetrate a hull has shown that, in the case of a three like *Olympias* attacking an identical ship, the speed of the attacking ship need be only 3 to 4 knots at angles of attack (i.e. the angle between the middle lines of the two ships in plan view) between 20° and 70° if the target is either stationary or moving towards the attacker. As might be expected, somewhat smaller speeds, 2 to 3 knots, are sufficient when the target ship is struck amidships. In attacks on the quarter of a pursued ship, on the other hand, greater attacking speeds are necessary and these increase rapidly at finer angles of attack, as indicated below:

Angle of attack degrees	Factor increasing required speed	Approximate upper limit of speed required, knts
40	1.2	4
45	1.6	5
50	2.4	8

As mentioned above, the right-hand column gives the speed of the attacking ship only. The speed of the target ship is not given. It could be even higher than that of the attacker, if the target were unfortunate enough to cross the bows of the attacker at the critical moment. Nevertheless it appears that attacks on the quarter (following for example a *διέκπλους* or *περίπλους*) were tactics for fast ships only. If that point were to be firmly established, it would have a great bearing on our understanding of tactics.

These results suggest that resistance to penetration could be appreciably increased by thickening the waterline wale and increasing the flexural stiffness or the numbers of the side frame timbers supporting the wale in resisting the ram force. Roman representations of the heavier ships developed from the three during the Hellenistic period show much heavier wales; and there are literary references pointing to the ability of later, heavy, ships to resist ramming attacks on the waterline, at least by lighter ships.

Steering a three to ram another has also been considered by Shaw (1993), particularly one pursuing the other to ram on the quarter. He shows, based on Haywood's findings, that the difference in speed between pursuer and pursued need not be very great, on account of the closing speed with which the pursuer could collide after turning towards his victim to ram.

Were this not so, the attested tactic of ramming from the stern (cf. GOS p. 292) would have been successful only against grossly inferior crews, and against ships that for some other reason were stationary or nearly so.

Heavy waterline wales are shown in (**61**), (**67**) and (**69**).

Heavy Roman ships were sometimes if not always built *ἀνάστειρος*, it is said, to lock them to their victim for boarding, not to cause them to swamp. It may be thought that so raising the ram could have reflected the success of heavy protective belts at the waterline. The alternative use for rams implied acceptance of the longer time required for boarding compared with ramming to cause swamping, a time during which the attacker was a stationary target for attack by another enemy ship.

The recorded tactic by Rhodian *τριημιολίαι* of ramming heavier ships under water, below the waterline belt, presumably by trimming down by the bow, also indicates the effectiveness of heavy protection at the waterline in defeating ramming at that level. The necessary bow trim in a *τριημιολία* could have been obtained by moving, for example, about thirty men 30 m forward in the ship. It was a good tactic in that a hole of a given size below waterlevel would cause quicker flooding than one of the same size at the waterline.

After being holed by a ram, a ship would not necessarily be immobilised immediately (unless also locked to its attacker). Flooding would take some time. The amount of water entering the ship through an idealised rectangular hole b metre wide and h metre deep below the waterline would be about

$$100\ b\ (h^{3/2})\ \text{tonnes per minute.}$$

For example, if the hole were 0.33 m both wide and in depth below the waterline, water would flow into the ship at the rate of about 5 tonnes per minute. In the case of a three that would cause the ship to settle by about 6cm after one minute, and after 3 minutes about 18 tonnes would have been taken on board and the ship would be 0.2 m lower in the water, making the oars much less effective, and the ship less manoeuvrable and more crank, heeling over noticeably if people moved athwartships. Eventually, when completely bilged and lying waterlogged in the water, she may be expected to have floated with the hull beams awash inside the ship and have little lateral stability. In such a state ships are likely to have lolled on to one παρεξειρεσία or the other, quite immobilised and so *hors de combat*. Movement of men on board would cause exaggerated changes of trim and heel and if many men were to climb on to the canopy or deck the ship might roll over far enough to tip them into the water and then she might recover or capsize.

A waterlogged hull would be exposed to extreme straining if in any appreciable swell, owing to its much increased weight which would include that of the water inside the hull. That hazard would have had to be avoided by victors towing hulks away from the scene of battle. A warship of the types presented in this chapter would sink to the bottom of the sea after being holed only if she had on board sufficient dense stores, cargo or other material to weigh *in water* enough to overcome the buoyancy of the hull structure and its furniture, roughly 40% of the weight of the complete hull *in air*, assuming that its density is 0.6 tonnes per cubic metre. The weight of a man in water is negligible. A bilged ship on the verge of sinking would in practice usually sink by the bow or the stern owing to lack of longitudinal balance between weight and buoyancy. The Punic ship excavated by Honor Frost would seem to have been a case in point.

In penetrating their targets ram castings were analogous in action to the heads of arrows or spears, but on a larger scale and with much lower velocities. The timber structure behind the cutting edges of the casting was quite as important as the casting itself and to refer to the casting alone as the ram is misleading. Upon impact, the structure had not only to sustain a large compressive force, of the order of the ship's mass, between the casting and the main mass of the ship, but also lateral and vertical forces, both of which could be appreciable.

Finned rams were designed to cut into planking and longitudinal timbers along their grain, and to do so at large angles from the athwartships direction so that penetration could be achieved over a wide range of angles of attack. The more glancing impacts however would generate large lateral forces and so call the ram wale timbers into play in resisting them. To be effective in supporting the whole ram sideways, the wale timbers must be assumed to have been scarfed tangentially on to the waterline wales of the hull, which, next to the keel and topwales, were the most substantial longitudinal timbers of the ship. It must be expected that, in view of the real risk of the ram being wrenched off sideways in battle, the ram was a structure wholly external to the hull proper of the ship, so that in the event of the ram being torn off (by, for instance, attacking a moving target), the attacker would not necessarily be holed forward and flooded.

Rams would *also* have been subjected to appreciable vertical forces after impact with a target. As the target ship would have been struck well below its centre of gravity, it would immediately start to roll towards the attacker and press down on the ram with the structure just above the breach in its hull. The target would also be accelerated bodily sideways by the main ramming force and as its velocity increased so would the water resistance. The resistance force would act at a level below the waterline so the target would soon be subjected to a moment rolling it the other way, away from the attacker and reversing the direction of the vertical force imposed on the ram. Those vertical forces would have had to be carried by the heavy bracing timber, found in the Athlit ram and also to be seen in (**85**). The vertical forces can be expected to have been large enough, if fracture of the ram timbers were to be avoided, to prevent the ram extending very far forward of this brace.

The ram of *Olympias* (**85**), while following the design of the Athlit ram, was external to the hull (which ended in a stem, vertical in that case but not necessarily so) for the above reason and also because the upper strake (No. 3) of the Athlit ram (Casson and Steffy: 1991) was at a steep angle sloping up and forward, an angle too steep to be part of a hull strake. It must therefore have been part of some other planking, to fair over the space above the ram wales: that planking would have formed a triangle with its base on the wale, its forward side on the nosing of the ram and the after side on the line where its plane met the side of the hull along a line from the stem sloping aft down to the wale.

Contrary to the reconstruction of the Athlit ram

85 *The ram structure of* Olympias

structure as an integral part of the bow of the ship, made soon after its discovery, it is proposed for the above reasons that rams were generally external to ships and built on to the bows of the hulls themselves. It is not unlikely that at the larger naval building centres rams were built by specialist tradesmen who might have made the castings too. The moulds for making such castings would have had to be made individually, probably by means of the 'lost wax' process used for casting bronze statues, a very similar operation. It would in that case have been easiest to form the wax 'positive' on the ram structure itself because in that way the necessarily slow process of fitting those timbers to the inside shape of the casting would be much reduced. The evident lack of conformity in the height of castings from ships of the same class in the same (Antony's) fleet at Aktion suggests the individual moulding of each one.

The weights of ram castings would not have been excessive relative to that of their ships. The Athlit casting weighs 0.465 tonnes. If geometrically similar, the weights of other rams would vary from that weight in proportion to their main dimensions divided by those of the Athlit ram casting. Thus the mean size of casting for the tens at Aktion, 1.84 times the breadth and 1.53 times the height of the Athlit casting, would have weighed about

$$0.465 \times 1.84 \times 1.53 = 1.3 \text{ tonnes}$$

if it had been no longer than Athlit. If its length was in the same proportion to its height as Athlit, then it would have weighed about 1.3 x 1.53 = 2.0 tonnes. These are probably upper and lower limits for the weights of ram castings for tens. They are 0.7% and 1% of the manned weight of a ten. In a four the ratio would have been rather less, about 0.7%, but only 0.4% in a three, on the basis of the weight of the weights in *Olympias* (0.20 and 48 tonnes).

Breaking the oars of an enemy ship (JFC)

It may be estimated that in a combat between threes, one ship, initially going at 5 knots, would have enough kinetic energy to break about 50 oars by sweeping close alongside the other before coming to rest having stopped rowing and having also shipped oars on the engaged side before breaking the first oar. However, a more likely method of carrying out this disabling manoeuvre would have relied less on initial speed and the ship's kinetic energy but have been to approach the victim at about 20° to 40° off his bow or stern, ship the oars on the engaged side and drive ahead hard with the others when the ἐπωτίς is nearly in contact with the victim's παρεξειρεσία. The oar thrust generated would be more than sufficient successively to break, by bending, the victim's oars not shipped in time on the stem of the attacker. Before being broken, oars would have been pushed aft, or forward as the case may be, 50° to 60° from athwartships before jamming in oarports or against stanchions. The attacker therefore needed to keep his ἐπωτίς against the victim's outrigger. The unbalanced oar thrust from the oars on one side of the ship only would provide a turning moment which would just about balance that from the oar-breaking force acting on the stem. In the manoeuvre described, the ἐπωτίς performs the important function of keeping the stem about a metre away from the tholes and oarports to give it enough leverage to bend and break the victim's oars easily.

This manoeuvre would seem to be more difficult with ships without ἐπωτίδες and παρεξειρεσίαι because oars would be harder to break if the stem pushes on them near their tholes and oarports: they would then have to be sheared, not bent, and larger forces would be needed to break them.

Boarding (JFC)

Troops assembled towards one side of the bows for boarding another ship would cause the attacking ship to heel by as much as 3° and thus risk hindering the oarcrew at a crucial time. The practice may therefore have been for troops to stay centred on the middle line of the ship before boarding and springing towards the victim at the last moment just before contact was made. Making fast by grappling irons on short lengths of chain (to prevent grappling ropes from being cut immediately) must have called for much skill not only to grapple successfully but also to prevent those doing it (obvious targets in trying to defeat the action) from being shot by archers defending the other ship. Downward missiles from towers would have added to the casualties on the other side and given shelter to troops as ships approached bow to bow. The manner of the approach, however, details of weapons, protection, numbers of troops, how formed up for boarding, timing, and tactics used in capturing the other ship are all unknown. This could be a rich field for research by operational analysts likely to cast light upon the lay-out of the forward decks of warships.

Missiles (JFC)

The use of missiles in naval warfare during our period has not been much studied and, except insofar as it would have influenced ship design, it lies beyond its scope. The main response to the use of missiles at sea has already been discussed under the various ship types, namely to require the oarcrew to be protected first by screens and with the advent of heavier missiles by boxing-in and fitting ventilation louvres. The accuracy and therefore the lethal capacity of missiles shot from one moving (and possibly rolling or listing) ship at another is easily overestimated. There are references to the first exchanges between approaching fleets being a hail of missiles and arrows. It was presumably worthwhile in spite of the difficulty of achieving accuracy from moving platforms. Speeds may have been deliberately kept low, but without losing steerage, to minimise the surging motion of an oared ship at higher speeds. In threes, earlier, troops were trained to throw javelins from the sitting position, probably for the same reason.

The accuracy of shooting would have been greater in training than in range, so a target ship which is head-on to thrower or archer is more likely to be hit somewhere along its length than a target lying at an angle to the line of flight. Ships approaching in line abreast would be good targets. On the other hand, missiles and arrows would be coming mainly from one direction only which would make use of shields or other protective devices more effective, except against the heavier ones such as those thrown by catapults. An arrow with a pyramidal head of a type developed about 500 BC and thrown by the smallest sinew-powered catapult could penetrate 50 mm of limewood (Foley and Soedel: 1981).

Missiles from more powerful catapults could penetrate timber of a greater thickness than could easily be provided in decks, except in the heavier ships which could carry the additional topweight without undue further loss from their already modest performance under oar. The need for what amounted to armoured decks could have been a significant factor in encouraging the development of heavier ships. Equally, the effectiveness of heavier missiles in penetrating ships' decks must have been a spur to their use at sea. The disruption caused to the working of an oarcrew by an intruding missile needs no explanation.

The effective range of catapults and bows operated on board ships was probably 200 to 300 m; and it would have been much affected by sea conditions and the consequent motion of ships. The time taken to rewind and reload would have been short enough to allow several shots to be made at the likely approach speed of fleets. Judging range however must have been a matter of great skill. Ranging shots by catapults of known performance would presumably have been used to ascertain when a more general release of missiles would be effective. The range of catapults may be surmised to have been continually tested relatively to each other with missiles of various weights, the heavier ones for use as the range closed. Practice would have made for such greater effectiveness in the opening phase of a battle that it must be presumed to have been a frequent part of fleet exercises, though no record of such, or of other details about shipborne artillery, has survived. Any means of causing smoke within a ship would have been particularly effective in incapacitating its oarcrew (e.g. the fire pots (**28**), used in the 1st century BC; and missiles aimed at doing so were probably in use before the advent of Greek Fire during the late Roman Empire.

Endnote

1. *Τὰ βίαχα* seems to be seaman's slang for the system of rams, 'the business end' of the big warships: cf. similarly formed seaman's slang *θάλαμαξ, στύππαξ, οἰάξ, ἅρπαξ, θρῆνυξ* (but not *κόραξ*).

GAZETTEER

Letters refer to Maps, Arabic numbers to Plans

C.	=	Cape
Is.	=	Island(s)
Mt(s)	=	mountain(s)
Pr.	=	Promontory
Pen.	=	Peninsula
P.	=	Port
R.	=	River

Abdera	AE
Abydos	AE, B, H
Achaia	G
Adriaticum mare	AW, E
Aegates Is.	E, F(i)
Aegimurus Is.	L (i)
Aenaria Is.	M (i)
Aetna Mt.	M (i)
Africa	AW
Aigina	B, G
Aigion	G
Aigousa Is.	F(i)
Ainos	H
Aiolis	I
Aithalia Is.(mod. Samiopoula)	I, J (iii)
Aitolia	G
Akarnania	G
Akragas, Agrigentum	E
Aktion	G, N
Alalia	AW
Alexandria (Egypt)	AE, 6
Alexandreia (Troas)	H
Amantia	K
Amastris	AE
Amathus	AE, C
Ambracian Gulf	N
Ambrakia	K
Amisos	AE
Ammochostos (Famagusta)	(ii)
Amorgos	B
Amphipolis	K
Ancona	AW
Andros	B
Antigoneia (see Nikaia)	
Antikyra	G
Antiocheia	C
Aous R.	K
Apameia	H
Aphetai	K
Apollonia	K
Apollonos Pr.	L (i)
Apsos R.	K
Aquae Calidae	L (i)
Arabia	AW
Arados	C
Arelate (Arles)	AW
Argennon Pr.	I, J (i), 5
Arginousai Is.	I
Argolic Gulf	B
Argos	G
Arsinoe (Famagusta)	(ii)
Asparagion	K
Aspendos	D
Aspis (Clupea)	E, L (i), L (ii)
Aspis Is.	J (iv)
Athamania	K
Athens	AE, B, G
Atrax	K
Attika	B, G
Axios R.	K
Bagradas R.	AW, E, L (i)
Balaros	M (i), M (ii)
Balearic Is.	AW
Bargylia	I
Belgae	AW

Hiera Is. (Lipari)	M (i)
Histiaia (Oreos)	G
Ialysos	D
Iapygian Pr.	E
Iasos	I
Iberus R. (Ebro)	AW, 4
Igilium Is.	AW
Ikaria	B, I
Ikos Is.	K
Ilion	H
Illyricum	AW, K
Imbros	B, H
Iolkos	K
Ionia	AE
Ipsos	AE
Iris R.	AE
Issa Is.	AW
Issos	C
Ister R. (Danube)	AE
Italy	AW
Ithaka	N
Itium, Pr.	AW
Kaikos R.	I
Kalchedon	AE, H
Kalydna	I
Kamarina	E
Kamiros	D
Kanai	I
Karia	AE
Karpasia	C
Karystos	G
Kasion	AE
Kasistes	J (i)
Kassandreias	K
Katana	E
Kaunos	D
Kaystros R.	I, J (iii)
Kenchreai	G
Keos	G
Kephallenia	G, N
Keraunian Mts	K
Kerkyra	K, N
Kilikia	AE, C
Kios	H
Kissus (mod. Kavaki)	J (i), J (ii), J (iii)
Kition	AE, C, (ii)
Klaros	J (iii)
Klazomenai	1, J (ii)
Kleides Pr.	C
Knidos	D
Koile Syria	C
Kolchis	AE
Kolophon (Notion)	I, J (iii)
Komaros Bay	N, 7
Korykeion Pr.	I, J (ii), J (iii)
Korykos Mt.	I, J (i), J (ii), 5
Korykos P.	J (i), J (ii), 5
Kourieus, Kurion	C
Kreusa	G
Kroton	E, M (i)
Kydnos R.	C
Kyklades	B
Kyllené	G, N
Kyme	I
Kynos	G
Kynoskephalai	K
Kynossema Pr.	D
Kyrene	AW
Kythnos	G
Kyzikos	H
Lakinion Pr.	M (i)
Lakonika	G
Lamia	B, G
Lampsakos	H
Laodikeia	C
Larissa	K
Lebedos	I, J (i), J (iii), J (iv)
Lechaion	G
Lekton Pr.	H
Lemnos	B
Leptis	L (ii)
Leros	I
Lesbos	B, I
Leukas	G, N, 7
Leukate Pr.	G
Leukolla	2
Leukopetra Pr.	M (i)
Liburnia	AW
Libya	AE
Liger R. (Loire)	AW
Lilybaion	AW, E, F (i), F (ii)
Limnaia	G
Lindos	D
Lipara Is.	E
Lipari Is.	E, M (i)
Lissos	K
Lochias Pr.	6
Lokris	G
Lokroi	E
Loryma	D
Lykia	AE, D
Lysimacheia	AE, H

GLOSSARY

OF GREEK AND LATIN WORDS

Names of ship types will be found in the General Index; page numbers, and figure numbers (in bold type) relating to the iconography in Chapter 5, refer to some of the occasions when the terms occur. Numbers in italics indicate the pages in which the main treatment of an item is given.

Aes grave: early Roman bronze coinage weighing 1 lb 205

ἀκρόπολις: citadel of a Greek city 1

ἀκροστόλιον, ἀκρωτήριον: culmination of hull timbers in the stern of a longship 115, 203

ἀμφορεύς, amphora: jar with two handles used to contain a cargo in a ship's hold

ἀνάστειρος: epithet of longship the ram of which is above the waterline **23**, **30**, **35**, 81, 364, 366

ἀναστροφή, ἐπανόδος: U-turn 83, 361, 362

antesignani: front-line Roman soldiers

ἀποσίμωσις: 90°turn 147, 363, 365

ἁρμονίαι: plank fastenings *121*

ἅρπαξ: mechanically launched grappling iron *156*

As: Roman bronze coin nominally worth 1 lb of bronze 205

ἄσκωμα, ἀσκώματα: leather sleeves for keeping water from entering through the thalamian oarports x, **29**, 188, 229

αὐλητής, symphoniacus: piper, a regular member of an oared warship's *ὑπηρεσία* 349, 350

aureus: Roman gold coin 231

ἄφλαστον, aplustre: sternpost and/or the ornament thereon 202, 211, 237, 239

ἄφρακτος, apertus, aphract: open, undecked ship 255, 258 and *passim*

γραμματεὺς τριηράρχου: captain's secretary 349

denarius: Roman silver coin worth first ten as and later twelve

διέκπλους: the manoeuvre by which oared warships usually in column break though an enemy fleet in line-abreast 53, 83, 103, 108, 154, *360–363*

δίκροτος, δίκροτον: an oared ship rowed by two files of oarsmen a side 10, 115, 130, 261, 262

δίολκος: haulage way for ships across the isthmus of Corinth 62, cf. 159

διπηχυαῖα, interscalmium: the two-cubit (*πῆχυς*) space between one tholepin (*σκαλμός*) and the next in a file of oarsmen 281, 284, 289, 299, 307, 319, 331

doliolum: cask **24.1**, **46.3**, **48**, 224, 249, 250

δόλων: foresail 85, 125

δορυδρέπανον: a spear terminating in a scythe wielded from the deck of an oared warship to cut the rigging of an enemy ship 120, 121

duumvir: one of the two chief magistrate of an Italian municipality 236

ἐγχειρίδια: oar handles 274

ἐλαιοχρίστης: oil masseur: on Rhodian warships 349

ἔμβολος or *ἔμβολον*, *rostrum*: the forefoot of a longship armed as a ram

ἔμπρῳρος (*ναῦς*): a ship with ram below the waterline 83, 364

ἐπιβάται: men, principally soldiers, carried on the deck of an oared warship 2, 6 n., 5, 46, 48

ἐπίπλοι: ships of the line 48; deputy ship's captain 349

ἐπίσημον: the panel of the prow of an oared warship containing a symbol or figure to indicate the ship's name (cf. *παράσημον*)

ἐπωτίς: the ear-like projection on each side of the bow of an oared warship formed by a beam lying athwartships at the forward end of the outriggers or oarboxes protecting them from damage in bow-to-bow collision **12a**, **17**; strengthening 155, 365 *passim*

ζύγιος: epithet describing the file of oarsmen who sat on the beams (zyga) of a two or three level oared warship, also the oars they worked 155, 181, 185, 287, 292, 294, 299, 303, 361–362

ἡγεμόνες: officers 147

θαλαμιός, thalamian: the file of oarsmen working in the hold (*θαλάμη*) of an oared ship, also the oars and the oarports through which these oars were worked 155, 181, 185, 188, 303–304, 319

θρανίτης, thranite: the oarsmen rowing at the highest level in a three-level ship, and their oars 180, 181, 276

θρῆνυς: cross plank in the stern of an oared ship (*Iliad* 15.729) 221

ἴκρια: mock up of an oarsystem for training purposes 153

interscalmium (see *διπηχυαῖα*)

καταπελταφέται: catapult artillerymen: mentioned in an inscription as members of a Rhodian warship crew (*SSAW* p. 306) 349

καταπέλτης, *catapulta*, catapult: invented as a siege engine by Dionysios I of Syracuse and employed as such by Alexander at Tyre and Demetrios at Rhodes, using levers of rope and hair it became an important offensive weapon on the ships of Hellenistic navies throwing missiles of all kinds including arrows from the towers then common on board the bigger ships 2, 3, 24, 32, 34, 56, 286, 309–10, 326

κατάφρακτος (*ναυς*), *tecta*, *constrata* (*navis*), cataphract (angl.): an oared warship with a protective (nonstructural) deck supported by stanchions; boxed in *λέμβος* 34, 43, 153, 255–257, 317 *passim*

κελευστής, *hortator*: a regular officer of the *ὑπηρεσία* of an oared ship, rowing master or boatswain who controlled the oarcrew 10, *353*, 363

κυβερνήτης, *gubernator*: helmsman, first officer (in the *ὑπηρεσία*) under the trierarch, in control of the after deck-gang in an oared warship

κωποδέτας, oarbinder (possibly a man responsible for fitting to the tholes and maintaining the *τροποί*, or *τροπωτῆρες*, leather thongs against which the oar was worked 349

μέτοικος, metic: foreigner resident in a Greek city 19

μετόπη: in Doric architecture the panel between triglyphs which had originally been the ends of roof beams 187, cf. 357

μετωπηδὸν μεταστρέφειν: of ships, to form line abreast 55

μέτωπον, *frons*, *acies*: line abreast 95, 101, 103, 107, 161; danger in abandoning in face of an enemy 115–116

μονήρης, *μονόκροτος*: a ship in which one file of oars is worked on each side 261

μυοπάρωνες: ships with a single file of oars on each side 114

ναύαρχος: fleet commander

ναυμαχία: formal sea-battle 18

ναυπηγός: shipwright 349

ὄγκοι: 357

ὀκτώβολος, *octobol*: a coin worth eight obols of which there were six to the drachma

ὁλκάς (*ναῦς*), pl. *ὁλκάδες*, cf. *στρογγύλοι*: a merchant ship without an oarsystem and hence moving under tow when not under sail 114, 148, 153, 255

oneraria, *-iae*: cf. *ὁλκαδες*, *στρογγύλοι*: merchant ships without an oarsystem and hence moving under tow when not under sail 24, 123, 143–144, 145

ὁπλίτης, *ὁπλῖται*, hoplite(-s): foot soldier in armour 8

ordo, ordines see *στοῖχοι*

παράρρυμα, *παράρρυσις*: side-screen to protect oarsmen 256, 286, 326

παράσημον: the panel on each side of the bow of an oared warship facing half-front containing a symbol or figure illustrating the ship's name **13**, **18 IB**, **27**, **29**, **31**, **35**, **39a**, **43**

παρεξειρεσία: outrigger of a three through which the thranite oarsmen worked their oars 287, 317 *passim*

πάροδος: gangway on each side of an oared ship, sometimes on the flat upper surface of the oarbox **13**, **29**, **36**, **37**, 269, 299

πηδαλιοῦχος: assistant helmsman 349

πεντηκόνταρχος: purser, one of the regular officers of the three's *ὑπηρεσία* 349

περίνεῳ: of men, passengers; of oars, spares

περίπλους: manoeuvre of ships in column to move round the wing of a fleet in line abreast 108, 115, 131, 154, 167, 360–363

πεύκη: see timber for shipbuilding in General Index

πίθος: large (earthenware) jar 283

piscatoriae: fihsing ships 128

πλήρωμα: general word for a warship's crew 54

pontones: barges 136

πολυήρεις, polyremes: epithet of ships of higher rating than the three

πόρια στρατιωτικά: troop transports 22, 24, 30

praetores, *ἄρχοντες*, praetors. Under the early Roman Republic the highest officials after the consuls at Rome were the *praetores urbanus* and *peregrinus*. Later there was a *praetor maritimus 102, 110,* and territorial provinces were allocated to praetors as governors.

προεμβόλιον: upper ram **12a**, **16**, **23**; crocodile head **24 Ia**, crocodile **29**; **30 b**, **d**; ram's head **33a**; lion's head **34**, **35**

πρωράτης, *πρῳρεύς*, *proreta*: bow officer: second after

the helmsman in an oared warship, with the forward deck-gang under his command **ixb, 30c, 39a**, 115, 349

quaestor, pro-quaestor: financial officers of the Roman government who were attached to and accompanied abroad consuls, pro-consuls and praetors

ῥήτωρ: speaker in the the Assembly at Athens 14
rostrum: see *ἔμβολος above*

σάμαινα: Samian two-level oared ship **ii**, 181–182
sestertius, sesterce: a Roman, originally silver, coin of which there were 4 to the denarius 233
sextans: a Roman coin of which there were 6 to the *as*
σκαλμός: thole, tholepin 261, 313, 321, 334
σκηνή: the stern shelter shown in the representations of Roman warships **42, 45–49**, 50
socii navales: the cities and peoples of Italy among the terms of whose alliance with Rome was the obligation to provide crews and in some cases ships and supplies for the Roman navy 43, 110–111, 349–353
στρατιῶται: soldiers, also naval crew 22
στρατιώτιδες: troop-carriers see *AT* p. 154 n. 53; heavier 3, 22, 25, 26, 257
στοῖχοι, ordines, versus remorum xiv, 90, 261, 277 n.8
στυλίς: The description in *SSAW* p.346 is complete: 'The *stylis* was a pole, generally fitted with a short crosspiece, which was set up [in Greek oared warships] alongside the *aphlaston* and which bore either a device symbolizing the guardian deity of the ship or his name written out' **xi, 9, 21, 36**, 190
συγκροτεῖν: to harmonise the stroke of an oared ship 54, 261
symphoniacus: see *αὐλητής*
συνεκδοχή: LSJ 'a mode of expression by which the whole is put for the part or vice versa'. The use in Latin of 'puppis' (prow) when 'navis' (ship) is meant is an example 129

τετράδραχμον, tetradrachm: a Greek silver coin of four drachmas
triarii: an élite category of veterans occupying the third rank in the Roman battle line 46, 48, 49

ναύαρχος, navis magister: captain of a warship (not restricted to triremes) 55, 66, 131, 171, 205, 262

ὁπλίτης: footsoldier in armour 8
uncia: a Roman coin of which there were twelve to the *as*
ὑπαίθριοι: ships not accommodated in shipsheds when ashore 16
ὑπασπισταί: Macedonian armoured soldiers 8
ὑπερκέρασις: outflanking tactic 48
ὑπηρεσία: a term used generally for any assistant personnel or gear on board an oared warship and specifically for the regular officers subordinate to the trierarch 2, 5, 48, *349*; auxiliary weapons 46
ὑπηρετικά (πλοῖα): auxiliary vessels in a warship fleet 25
ὑπόζωμα: an assembly of tightened ropes pulling two points of a hull together to reduce tensile bending stresses 109, 276, 281, 283–284, 296, 313, 321, 328–329, 356

φάρεα: pieces of linen cloth which composed a sail 182

WORDS OTHER THAN GREEK AND LATIN

a scaloccio: the Renaissance oarsystem in which more than one man worked an oar 325
alla sensile: the medieval oarsystem in which up to three men on the same bench each worked his own oar 291, 312, 313

belaying pin: wooden pin round which a rope is coiled and secured
bollard: a stout post on which to secure mooring ropes **17, 43**, 216, 230, 246, *356*
boxing-in: enclosing the hull of an oared ship with a canopy-deck and permanent sidescreening to protect the oarcrew from missiles xii, 2, 255, 257
brace: a rope attached to the end of a yard for swinging the yard so that the sail catches the wind
bracket: angular wooden support
brail: a rope attached to the bottom edge of a square sail, led up its forward surface, over the yard through a fairlead and then to a point aft where it can be secured and manipulated. By pulling on the brails

of a sail its area exposed to the wind can be reduced, or it can be pulled up completely to the yard
brow: inclined landing gangway
bulwark: 'raised woodwork running along the sides of a vessel above the level of the deck' OED
bumkin : a short boom or post to which a block is secured to give a rope reeved through it a desired lead 321
butt: a joint joining two timbers end to end
butt, butt-end: of an oar, the inboard end

cant: angle from the normal direction of the item in question
catch: entry of oarblades into the water at the start of the pulling part of the stroke
caulking: fibrous material rammed hard between the planks of a hull to make the shell watertight and prevent the planks from sliding upon each other when the hull is subjected to longitudinal bending actions 121 (with seaweed), 329, 355 (with tow)

deck gangs: in oared warships there were two parties of deck-hands one (aft) under the helmsman, the other forward under the bow officer 349

effective power: of a ship, at any given steady speed, the product of her speed and her resistance to motion in the water, e.g. (speed in metres/second) × (resistance in newtons) = effective power in watts
en échelon: formation of units in two parallel lines, each unit behind the middle point of the space between the pair in front
ergometer: lit. work measurer. If combined with some form of clock it can measure the gross mechanical power of a rower. In the ship, not all of this power can be employed effectively to propel her, as some of it is unavoidably wasted in setting water in motion, in overcoming the mass-inertia of the oar, and in other ways.
etesian (or melteme) winds: in the Mediterranean these blow regularly from mid-July to September from the NW.
'eye': an eye was regularly represented either realistically or symbolically on each side of the bow of an ancient longship *passim*

fairlead see brail
file: of ships; of oarsmen, a fore-and-aft row, whether sitting or standing 103, 261
finish: exit of oarblades at the end of the pulling part of the oar stroke
flagship: the ship which carried the commander of a fleet is here called the flagship although the *σημεῖον* or *vexillum insigne* which enabled it to be recognised may not always be a flag (see SSAW p.247 n.88)
flare: outward slope from the vertical of the sides of a ship
foot: Roman: 0.295 metre 163, 309
foot stretcher: support for an oarsman's feet to allow him to pull effectively on his oar 284, 303, 325, 335
foredeck: of an oared ship, the deck forward of the *ἐπωτίς* and aft of the stempost **iv**, **v**, **vi**, 9, 23, 30; absence of **29**, **34**, 294
forefoot: an unarmed projection forward of the stempost of a longship 178, 225; with the development of ramming as the longship's main weapon the forefoot was armed with a metal (usually bronze) sheath detectable on representations by the fastening band as in **ib**

galea, galley: strictly the term galley used of Greek or Roman oared warships or merchantships is an anachronism, but that usage is now common.
gearing: of oars, the ratio between the distances of the centre of pressure of the oarblade in the water and of the middle of the handle of the tholepin from the pivot
glacis: part of a fortification designed to be untenable by attacking troops; on a warship the sloping surface of the oarbox 303, 321
graffito: writing or drawing scratched roughly on a wall

heel: of a ship, an angle of inclination from the upright
hog, hogging: bending or shearing of a ship's hull so that its ends drop relative to the middle 281, 327, 329

joule: the unit of work: in mechanical terms 1 joule = 1 newton metre

knees: in a hull, angular timber brackets supporting the cross-beams

loom: of an oar, the inboard part between the tholepin and the handle
louvre: in an oared ship, the protected ventilation course replacing the open side of the three **13**, 212, **29**, **30b**, **d**, **e**, 229, 230, 231, 256, 264, 286, 294, 299, 315, 321; lattice **34**, **36**, **38**, **40**, **45–49**
metacentre: the point, usually designated M, in the middle plane of a ship through which the buoyan-

cy force passes when the ship is inclined from the upright by a small angle
metacentric height: the height of the metacentre above the ship's centre of gravity (usually designated G): it is usually designated GM
mile, sea or nautical: the international sea mile = one minute of latitude = 1852 metres
monoxylous: made from one piece of timber, see General Index under 'oars'
mortice: recess cut to receive a tenon

Newton: the unit of force: 1 Newton is the force needed to accelerate a mass of 1 kilogram by 1 metre/second/second

oarbox: the projection on each side of a *τριημιολία* or polyreme which is required by the oarsystem *passim*
outrigger: see *παρεξειρεσία* in Glossary I

pédagne: the lower foot-rail in a medieval and later galley
prismatic coefficient: a non-dimensional measure of the fullness of the ends of a hull-form. It is the ratio of the displacement volume to that of a prism of length equal to the waterline and in cross-section identical with the immersed mid-section of the ship

quarter: a side of the ship near the stern
quincunx, quincunx-fashion: arrangement of units equidistant from each other in each of three parallel lines so that in depth each triad of proximate units, one in each line, forms a diagonal

room: see *διπηχυαῖα*, interscalmium. A room in an oared ship is the space in the rowing area across the ship marked out by the distance between one tholepin and another on each side. A half-room is such an area on one side only

satrap: the governor of a province (satrapy) of the ancient Persian empire 5
scarf: butt joint in which the end of each member is shaped to overlap and fit the other to increase its strength
sheet: of a sail, a rope holding down the aftermost bottom corner
slip: of an oarblade, the movement aft relative to the water, from the instant of the catch to that of the finish
stay: of a mast, a rope preventing fore-and-aft movement
stempost: of an oared warship, the curved timber rising from the keel in the bow and culminating in an ornament or figurehead
stopping: a setting composition brushed or trowelled into the seams of planks to make them watertight
strake: a row of planks end-to-end. The shell of a hull is built up of a succession of strakes
striking, rate of: spm, the number of oarstrokes performed in one minute
stringer: longitudinal timber laid across and secured to transverse hull timbers

tenon: rectangular block of hard wood, typically proportioned 2:1:$^1/4$ or $^1/3$, each half-length being fitted into opposing mortices to join two timbers side-by-side. Tenons were usually locked into place by being drilled through and pegged.
topwale: longitudinal timber forming the top edge of a hull, in more recent times known as the 'gun'wale
triad: of oarcrew, three rowers sitting roughly in the same vertical plane on one side of the ship and whose oars must synchronise with one another

wale: an assemblage, end-to-end of thick and broad planks along a ship's side and worked into the hull planking. Wales appear as external supports for the ram and *προεμβόλιον* **ii, ixb, 7, 9, 10, 12–18, 23, 35, 43**
watt: the unit of power: 1 Watt = 1 Joule/second = 1 Newton.metre/second

yard: spar supporting the top edge of a square sail

BIBLIOGRAPHY

Alertz, U. (1991) *Vom Schiffbauhandwerk zu Schiffbautechnik* Hamburg.

Amy, R. (1962) 'L'Arc d'Orange' *Gallia* Suppl. XV Paris.

Anderson, R.C. (1962) *Oared Fighting Ships* London.

Ashton, N.G. (1977) 'The *naumachia* near Amorgos in 322 BC' *BSA* lxxii.

Assmann, E. (1889) 'Zur Kenntnis der antiken Schiffe' *JdI* iv pp. 91–104.

Babelon, E. (1901–1932) *Traité des monnaies grecques et romaines* Paris.

Badian, E. (1952) 'Philip's Naval Plans' *BSA* p. 59.

Badian, E. (1968) 'The King's Notebook' *HSCP 72.*

Barron, J.P. (1966) *The Silver Coinage of Samos* London.

Bartolini, P. *Rivista di Studi Fenici* 7. 1979A p. 21.

Basch, L. (1969) 'Phoenician Oared Ships' *MM 55* 2 and 3.

Basch, L. (1979) 'Roman Triremes and the outriggerless Phoenician trireme *MM* 65.4.

Basch, L. (1987) Review Article of *AT* and Coates and McGrail 1983: *MM* 73.1:; 93–105.

Basch, L. (1987) *Le Musée imaginaire de la marine antique [MIMA]* Athens.

Beazley, J.D. (1947) *Etruscan Vase Painting* Oxford Monographs on Classical Archaeology 1.

Beckh (1895) *Geoponica: Cassiani Bassi scholastici de re rustica Eclogae* Leipsig.

Bellinger, A.R. and Berlincourt, M.A. (1962) 'Victory as a coin type' *Numismatic Notes and Monographs* New York.

Beloch, K.J. (1925–7) *Griechische Geschichte IV ed.2. [Beloch].*

Berthold, R.M. (1975) 'Lade, Pergamon and Chios: operation of Philip V in the Aegean': *Historia* 24, pp. 150–163.

Berthold, R.M. (1984) *Rhodes in the Hellenistic World* London.

Betlyon, J.W. (1982, c.1980) *The Coinage and Mints of Phoenicia: the pre-Alexandrian period'* Chico California.

Blackman, D.J. (1995) 'Naval Installations' in *The Age of the Galley* 224–33.

Blinkenberg C. (1938) 'Lindiaka 7: Triemiolia': *Det KGL. Danske Videnskabernes Selskab Archaeologisk-kunsthistoriske Meddelelser II.3* Copenhagen.

Blinkenberg C. (1941) *Lindos: Fouilles et Recherches: 1902–14: Inscriptions,* 2 vols: Copenhagen.

Boisacq, E. (1916) *Dictionnaire Étymologique de la Langue Grecque* Heidelberg, Paris.

Bosworth, A.B. (1971) 'The Death of Alexander the Great: Rumour and Propaganda' *CQ* ns.21 112–136.

Bosworth, A.B. (1980) *A Historical Commentary on Arrrian's History of Alexander* Vol.1 Books 1–3, Oxford.

Breitenstein, N. (1941) *Catalogue of Terracottas in the Danish Maritime Museum* Copenhagen.

Briscoe, J.A. (1973) *A Commentary on Livy 32–33* Oxford.

Briscoe, J.A. (1981) *A Commentary on Livy 34–37* Oxford.

Briscoe, J.A. (1989) *CAH*^{2} p. 65–67.

Brunt, P.A. (1976–1983) *Arrian: History of Alexander and Indica* 2 Vols. Loeb Classical Library.

Büttner-Wöbst, Th. (1901) 'Beiträge zu Polybios': *JKD.*

Burlet, R., Carriere, J. and Zysberg, A. (1986) 'Mais comment pouvait-on ramer sur les galères du Roi Soleil?' *Histoire et Mesure* 1–3/4 187–208.

Callot, O. (forthcoming) 'Les hangars du port de Kition (Ve–Vie siècles av. J.-C.) *Res Maritimae* Nicosia.

Calvet, Y. (1993) 'Kition Mission française' in *Kinyras, l'archéologie française à Chipre* Lyon.

Carlini, D. (1934) 'Les galères antiques' *Bulletin de l'association technique maritime et aeronautique* 38 49–89.

Cary, E. (1917) *Dio's Roman History* Loeb Classical Library.

Cary, M. (1951: 2nd Ed. 1963) *History of the Greek World: 323–146 BC; Appendix 4: The strengths of the Fleets at Salamis* London.

Casson, Lionel (1959: 2nd Ed. 1991) *The Ancient Mariners* Princeton.

Casson, Lionel (1971: paperback Ed. 1986) *Ships and Seamanship in the Ancient World: SSAW:* Princeton.

Casson, Lionel (1983) *AJA 87* p. 418: review of Ermeti.

Casson, Lionel (1994) *Ships and Seafaring in ancient times* London.

Casson, Lionel and Steffy, J. Richard (1991) *The Athlit Ram* Texas A & M University Press.

Cichorius, Konrad (1896) *Die Reliefs der Traiansäule* Berlin.

Coates, J.F. (1984) 'The Greek Trireme of the 5th Century BC' *Sailing into the Past: 60–67.* Roskilde, Denmark.

Coates, J.F. (1985) 'Hogging or 'Breaking' of Framebuilt Wooden Ships' *MM 71* pp. 437–442.

Coates, J.F. (1987) 'Three of What' *Wooden Boat. No. 75*
Coates, J.F. (1990) 'Research and Engineering Aspects of Reconstructing the Ancient Greek Trireme Warship' *Trans. Soc. Naval Architects and Marine Engineers*. Jersey City, USA.
Coates, J.F. (1991) 'The Ancient Greek Trireme – An early pre-stressed shell' *Advances in Marine Structures 2*. London and New York.
Coates, J.F. (1994) 'The Naval Architecture of European Oared Ships' *Trans. Royal Institute of Naval Architects*.
Coates, J.F. (1994) 'Power and Speed of Oared Ships' *Proc. ISBSA-6* Roskilde 1991. Oxford.
Coates, J.F. and Morrison, J. (1987) Authenticity in the replica Athenian trieres *Antiquity 61:* 87–90.
Coates, J.F. and Morrison, J.S. (1993) 'Sea Trials of the Reconstructed Athenian Trireme *Olympias' MM 79.2* pp. 131–141.
Coates, J.F., Platis, S.K. and Shaw, J.T. (1990) *The Trireme Trials 1988* Oxford.
Cook, R.M. (1979) 'The diolkos': *JHS 99.*
Crawford, M.H. (1974) *Roman Republican Coinage* 2 Vols Cambridge.
'Croniques des fouilles à Chypre' *BCH* Annual Reports since vol. 112.
Daremberg, Saglio et Pottier (1877–1919) *Dictionaire des antiquités grecques et romaines* Paris.
Davis, Andy (1993) 'Hog, Understanding the longitudinal deformation of wooden ships' *Wooden Boat 113* July-August pp. 70–81.
De Montfaucon, B (1717) *L'Antiquité expliquée IV 2* Paris.
De Sanctis, G. (1916) *Storia dei Romani III* Turin-Florence.
Delts, M.R. (1974) *Aelians* Teubner.
Duff, J.D. (1928) *Lucan* Loeb Classical Library.
Dunand, F. (1973) *Le culte d'Isis dans le basin oriental de la mediterranée* Leiden.
Dunand, M. (1937–9) *Fouilles de Byblos Vol.I* Paris.
Dunand, M. (1975–6) *Les Rois de Sidon* Mélanges de l'université de St Joseph XLIX.
Ermeti, Anna Lia (1983) 'L'Agora di Cirene: 3.1.: Il monumento Navale' *Monographie di Archeologia Libica 16.*
Errington, R.M. (1977) 'Diodorus Siculus and the Chronology of the Early Diadochoi: 320–311 BC': *Hermes 105* pp. 478–504.
Ferrabino, A. (1924) 'La battaglia d'Azio' *Riv. Fil. 111* p. 433ff.
Fischer (1906) *Diodoros*.
Foley, V. and Soedel, W. (1981) 'Ancient Oared Warships' *Scientific American.*
Forster, E. M. (1971) *Alexandria,* New York.
Foucher, L. (1957) 'Navires et Barques' *Notes et Documents xv: Institut National d'Archéologie et Arts:* Tunis.
Fraser, P.M. (1972) *Ptolemaic Alexandria* Oxford.
Frost, H. (1973) First Season of the Excavation of the Punic Wreck in Sicily' *IJNA 2.1.* 33–49.
Frost, H. (1974) 'The Punic Wreck in Sicily' *IJNA 3.1.* 35–54.
Geer, R.M. (1962) *Diodore de Sicile: Livre xviii. Texte établit et traduit par P. G.:* Paris.
Goukowsky (1978) *Diodoros* Budé.
Grach, N.L. (1984) 'A New Monument of the Hellenistic Age from Nymphaeum' *Vestnik Dreveistorie 1* 81–88.
Gransden, K.W. (1976) *Aeneid Book 8* Cambridge
Grant, Michael (1946) *From Imperium to Auctoritas* Cambridge.
Green, Peter (1990) *Alexander to Actium* London.
Griffith, G.T. (1966) *Alexander the Great: the Main Problems* Cambridge.
Guilmartin, J.F. (1974) *Gunpowder and Galleys* Cambridge.
Hammond, N.G.L. (1938) 'The sources of Diodorus XVI' *CQ 32* pp. 137–145.
Hammond, N.G.L. (1945) 'Naval operations in the south channel of Corcyra 435–433 BC': *JHS 65*. pp. 32–54.
Hammond, N.G.L. (1956) 'The Battle of Salamis': *JHS 76* pp. 32–54.
Hammond, N.G.L. (1982) 'The narrative of Herodotus VII and the Decree of Themistocles at Troezen' *JHS 102* pp. 75–93.
Hammond, N.G.L. (1988) *History of Macedonia III* Oxford.
Hampl, F. (1953) 'Alexanders des Grossen Hypomnemata und letzte Pläne': *Studies presented to D.M. Robinson 2*. pp. 816–829 St Louis = Griffith (1966) 308 ff. Cambridge.
Hauben, H. (1970) *Callicrates of Samos: A Contribution to the Study of the Ptolemaic Admiralty* Louvain.
Hauben, H. (1975/6) 'Antigonus's Invasion Plan for his attack on Egypt in 306 BC': *OLP 6/7* pp. 267–271.
Hauben, H. (1976) 'The Expansion of Macedonian Sea Power under Alexander the Great' *Ancient Society 7.* pp. 80–105.
Hauben, H. (1977) 'Rhodes, Alexander and the diadochi: 333/332–304 BC' *Historia 26* p.37.
Haywood, J.H.: see Shaw, J.T. Ed.
Heinen, H. (1984) *CAH*² p. 415.
Heitland, W.E. (1909) *The Roman Republic* 3 Vols: Cambridge.
Helbig-Speier (1963) *Führer durch die offentlichen Sammlungen im Vatican und Lateran in Rom: 1. Die papstlichen Sammlungen im Vatican und Lateran* Rom.
Höckmann, O. (1985) *Antike Seefahrt* Munich.
Hornblower, Jane (1981) *Hieronymus of Cardia* Oxford.
Hurst and Stager (1978) 'Punic Harbours' *World Archaeology ix* pp. 334–346.
Hurst, Henry (1979) 'Excavations at Carthage 1977–8: 4th Interim Report' *The Antiquaries Journal LIX Pt. 1* pp. 19–49.
Jenkins, G.K. (1972) *Ancient Greek Coins* London.
Jenkins, G.K. and Lewis R.B. (1963) *Gold and Electrum Coins of Carthage* London.
Kirk, G.S. (1949) 'Ships on Geometric Vases' *BSA 33*.
Köster, A. (1923) *Das Antike Seewesen* Berlin.
Kraay, C.M. and Hirmer, M. (1966) *Greek Coins* London.

Krauss, F. (1944) 'Die Prora an der Tiberinsel in Rom' JDI: *Römische Mitteilungen 59* pp. 159–172.
Kromayer, J. (1931) 'Nachtrag zur Schlacht von Actium' *Antike Schlachtfelder iv* pp. 662–671.
Kromayer, J. and Veith, G. (1928) *Heerwesen und Kriegführung der Griechen und Römer* Munich.
Lane, F.C. (1934) *Venetian Ships and Shipbuilders of the Renaissance* Baltimore.
Layard, A.H. (1849) *Monuments of Nineveh* London.
Lepper, Frank and Frere, S. (1988) *Trajan's Column* London.
Lipke, Paul. (1988) 'Trials of the Trireme' *Archaeology 41.2*: 22–29.
Lockett Collection (1938–1949) *Sylloge Nummorum Graecorum III.*
McDonald, A.H. and Walbank F.W. (1969) 'The Treaty of Apamea (188 BC): The Naval Clauses' *JRS 59 11* 30–39.
McKee, J.E.G. (1983) *Working Boats of Britain* London.
Mattingly, H. (1923) *Coins of the Roman Empire in the British Museum 1.*
Meiggs, R. (1973: 2nd Ed.) *Roman Ostia* Oxford.
Meiggs, R. (1983) *Trees and Timber in the Ancient World* Oxford.
Meijer, Fik (1986) *A History of Seafaring in the Classical World:* London.
Mevker, I.L. (1960) 'The Silver Coinage of Antigonus Gonatas and Antigonus Doson': *ANS: Museum Notes. 9* pp.39–52.
Miltner, F. (1931) 'Seewesen': *RE* Supplementband V pp. 906–962.
Morrison, J.S. (1980) *Long Ships and Round Ships* London [LSRS].
Morrison, J.S. (1984) 'Hyperesia in Naval Contexts in the 5th and 4th centuries BC' *JHS 104* pp.48–59.
Morrison, J.S. (1987) 'Athenian Sea Power in 323–2 BC: Dream and Reality' *JHS 107* pp. 88–97.
Morrison, J.S. (1990) 'Tetrereis in the fleets of Dionysios I of Syracuse' *Classica et Mediaevalia 41* pp. 33–41.
Morrison, J.S. (1991.i) 'Ancient Greek Measures of Length in Nautical Contexts' *Antiquity* Vol. 65 No. 247 pp. 298–305.
Morrison, J.S. (1991.ii) 'The Greek Ships at Salamis and the *Diekplous*': *JHS 111* pp. 196–200.
Morrison, J.S. and R.T. Williams (1968 Cambridge: reprinted Oxford 1995) *Greek Oared Ships: 900–322 BC. [GOS].*
Morrison, J.S. and Coates, J.F. (1986) *The Athenian Trireme,* Cambridge; (1989) editors: *The Athenian Trireme Reconstructed: The British sea trials of Olympias, 1987: BAR International Series 486; (1992) CR NS 42* pp. 476–7 J Review of Casson and Steffy (1991).
Murray, William and Petsas, Photios M. (1989) 'Octavian's Campsite Memorial for the Actian War' *TAPS Vol. 79 Pt. 4* .
Nadel, E.R. and Bussolari, S.R. (1988) 'The Daedalus Project' *American Scientist 76* July-August: pp. 351–360.
Newell, E.T. (1927) *The Coinage of Demetrius Poliorcetes:* Oxford (1941) *The Coinage of the Western Seleucid Mints NS 4* New York.
Nietzold, W. (1905) *Die Uberlieferung der Diadochengeschichte bis zur Schlacht von Ipsos* Diss. Dresden.
Ormerod, H.A. (1924: 2nd Ed. 1979) *Piracy in the Ancient World* Liverpool.
Pagenstecher, (1909) 'Die calenische Reliefkeramik' *JdI: Suppl. VIII.*
Panciera, Silvio (1956) 'Liburna', *Epigraphica: Rivista Italiana di Epigraphia: 18,* pp. 130–158.
Paton, W.R. (1922) *Polybius: Histories Bks 1–39; text with English translation in six volumes:* Loeb Classical Library.
Peskett, A.G. (1908) *Gai Iuli Caesaris commentarium liber primus* Cambridge.
Picard, G. (1968) *Roman Painting* London.
Pijoan, Soteras L. (1949) *L'Arte Romano* Madrid.
Rankov, Boris (1994) 'Reconstructing the Past: the Operation of the Trireme. Reconstruction in the Light of Historical Sources' *MM 80.2:* 131–146.
Rawson, K.J. and Tupper, E.C. (1976) *Basic Ship Theory* London and New York.
Reinach, S. (1922) *Répertoire des peintures Grecques et Romaines:* Paris.
Reiske, J.J. (1763) *Animadversionum ad Graecos auctores* Vol.4 (Polybius) Lipsiae p.518.
Rice, E.E. (1983) *The Grand Procession of Ptolemy Philadelphus* Oxford.
Rice, E.E. (1983) 'The Carthaginian Navy in the First Punic War' *Naval History: The Sixth Symposium of the U.S. Naval Academy.*
Rice, E.E. (1991) 'The Rhodian Navy in the Hellenistic Age': *New Interpretations of Naval History: Papers from the Ninth Symposium at the U.S. Naval Academy* October 1989.
Robertson, Martin (1975) *A History of Greek Art* 2 vols. Cambridge.
Rodgers, W.L. (1940) *Naval Warfare under Oars: 4th-16th Centuries* Annapolis.
Rostovtzev, M. (1930) *CAH* VIII pp. 569–581.
Ruesch, A. (1909) *Guida Illustrata del Museo Nationale di Napoli.*
Schachermeyr, F. (1954) *Jahrb.der oesterreich.-arch. Instituts 1954,* pp.118ff = Griffith (1966) pp. 322ff.
Scheffer, J. (1642) *Aelianus.*
Schiff, A. (1905) *Alexandrische Dipinti 1:* Leipsig.
Schmitt, J.M. (1974) 'Les premières Tetrères à Athenes' *REG 87* pp. 80–90.
Scullard, H.H. (1989) *CAH*[2] pp.537–566.
Seibert, J. (1969) 'Untersuchungen zur Geschichte Ptolemaios': *MB*: 56 pp. 190–206.
Shaw, J.T. ed. (1993) *The Trireme Project: Operational Experience 1987–90: Lessons Learnt.* Oxbow Monograph 31: Oxford.
Shaw, J.T. (1994) 'Rowing in Ships and Boats' *Trans. Royal Institute of Naval Architects* London.
Skeat, T.C. ed. (1974) *Greek Papyri in the British Museum*

(now in the British Library) Vol. VII The Zenon Archive, London.
Sleeswyk, A.W. (1982) 'The prow of the Nike of Samothrace reconsidered' *IJNA 11.3:* 233–243.
Squarciapino, M.F. (1955) *Scavi di Ostia III Le Necropole Pt. I* Rome.
Starr, Chester G. Jnr. (1941) *The Roman Imperial Navy,* Cornell University Press.
Stroheker, K.F. (1958) *Dionysius I: Gestalt und Geschichte der Tyrannen von Syrakus* Wiesbaden.
[Suidas] Ed. Ada Adler 1928–38 Leipzig.
Sydenham, E. (1952) *The Coinage of the Roman Republic* London.
Tarn, W.W. (1905) 'The Greek Warship' *JHS* 25.
Tarn, W.W. (1910) 'The dedicated ship of Antigonus Gonatas' *JHS* 30.
Tarn, W.W. (1913) *Antigonus Gonatas* Oxford.
Tarn, W.W. (1930: reprinted Chicago 1984) *Hellenistic Military and Naval Developments* Cambridge.
Tarn, W.W. (1931) 'The Battle of Actium' *JRS* xxi pp. 173–199.
Tarn, W.W. (1948) *Alexander the Great* 2 volumes.
Thiel, J.H. (1946) *Studies in the History of Roman Sea Power in Republican Times* Amsterdam.
Thiel, J.H. (1954) *A History of Roman Sea Power before the second Punic War* Amsterdam.
Tibbs, G.H. (1985) 'The Battle of Ecnomus' *Historia 34* pp. 432–468.
Tillyard, H.J.W. (1908) *Agathocles* Cambridge.
Tod, M.N. (1948) *Greek Historical Inscriptions II 403–323* Oxford.
Torr, Cecil (1894: reprinted Chicago 1964) *Ancient Ships* Cambridge.
Ucelli, G. (1940: 2nd ed. 1950) *Le Navi de Nemi* Rome.
Viereck, H.D. (1975) *Die römische Flotte: Classis Romana* Herford.
Walbank, F.W. (1940) *Philip V of Macedon* Cambridge.
Walbank, F.W. (I 1957, II 1967, III 1979) *A Historical Commentary on Polybius* 3 Vols. Oxford.
Walbank, F.W. (1982) 'Sea Power and the Antigonids': in *Philip II, Alexander the Great and the Macedonian Heritage ed. W.L. Adams and E.N. Borza*: pp. 213–236: Washington D.C.
Wallinga, H.T. (1956) *The Boarding-Bridge of the Romans* Groningen.
Wallinga, H.T. (1993) *The Ancestry of the Trireme* Leiden.
Warmington, E. (1935–40) *Remains of Old Latin* Loeb Classical Library.
Werner, W. (1993–94) 'Der Diolkos' *NBA* Heft 10 pp. 103–118.
White, W.H. (1877) *A Manual of Naval Architecture.*
Whitt, F.R. and Wilson, D.G. *Bicycling Science – Ergonomics and Mechanics* M.I.T. 1976.
Wilcken, U. (1922–37) *Urkunden der Ptolemaerzeit 1–11*: Berlin.
Will, Edouard (1984) *CAH*[2] VI Pt. 1 Chapters 2 and 4.
Willers, H. (1902) *Geschichte der Römischen Kupferprägung* Leipsig *NZ* p. 86.
Williams, R.T. (1958) 'Early Greek ships of two levels' *JHS 78:* pp. 121–130.
Williams, R.T. (1959) 'Addenda to ships of two levels' *JHS 79:* pp. 159–160.
Williams, Hector (1981) *IJNA 10. 1* pp. 23–27.
Yon, M. (1989) 'Kition et la mer', *Symposium européen 'Flotte et commerce dans la Méditerranée'*: Ravello.
Yon, M. (1993) 'Kition et la mer à l'époque classique et héllenistique' *Colloquium 'Cyprus and the Sea'*: Nicosia.
Yon, M. (1993) 'Le port de guerre de Kition' *Dossiers d'Archéologie* 183, 40–41.
Yon, M., O. Callot & J.-F. Salles (1991) 'Neosoikoi at Kition' *Tropis* 4.
Zysberg,A. and Burlet, R. (12/1986) 'Le Travail de la Rame sur les Galeres de France vers le Fin du XVII Siècle *Neptunia* No. 164, 16–35.

INDEX OF CLASSICAL AUTHORS

GENERAL INDEX

Small Roman numbers refer to pages of the preface, Arabic numbers to pages in the text. Small Roman and Arabic numbers from (i–xii) and from (1–50) in bold type refer to items of the iconography in Chapter 5. Small Roman and Arabic numbers above 50 in brackets refer to illustrations in Chapter 7. Large Roman numbers differentiate persons similarly named. Numbers in italics indicate the pages in which the main treatment of an item is given. For place-names mentioned in the text and appearing in the maps the reader is referred to the Gazetteer. Greek words are in Greek script, other non-English words are in italics.